1095

THE SOCIOLOGY

OF RELIGION

An Anthology

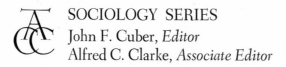

SOCIOLOGY SERIES
John F. Cuber, *Editor*
Alfred C. Clarke, *Associate Editor*

EDITED BY

Richard D. Knudten

VALPARAISO UNIVERSITY

THE SOCIOLOGY

OF RELIGION

An Anthology

New York

Appleton-Century-Crofts

DIVISION OF MEREDITH PUBLISHING COMPANY

TO MY PARENTS

DR. AND MRS. ARTHUR C. KNUDTEN

whose faith led them to spend their lives
as missionaries to Japan

PREFACE

The Sociology of Religion has been written with both the college and seminary student in mind. While it takes religion as its subject matter, it treats religion primarily from a sociological perspective and accents the research base of this tradition. Most sociological writers allude to social research but slight the precise description of the investigative procedures followed in the research cited or used. Thus although students learn about the conclusions of research, they are too often unacquainted with the investigative methods used. Interested students are forced to search for original studies in journals that are often buried in inconvenient locations in the library. To this point, no single book of readings has been published that assembles contemporary research on religion in a form which is compact and convenient to the student. Although many of the articles have been edited, the essential content of the article has remained intact. The unabridged text may be found in the original journal.

Introductions to each article have been provided in order to place each article in perspective. The authors represented in this volume cover wide areas of concern including anthropology, sociology, Christian ethics, social philosophy, Jewish studies, political science, economics, church planning, church history, and religious education. Some are social scientists, others are religionists. Some attempt to be objective, others make no pretense of objectivity. But each offers insight into the problems and conditions of religion in contemporary society.

More than sixty journals and periodicals integral to the field of religion have been systematically examined. In the original investigation over 400 articles of merit were marked for potential inclusion. Fewer than fifty now remain. Final selection was based upon the following criteria: (1) the intrinsic value of the research; (2) the potential of the article as an analytical teaching aid; (3) the readability of the writing; and (4) the degree to which the article either illustrates a research procedure or presents a concept. Selections were confined to contemporary American journals and periodicals. Many of these articles have been used previously in the classroom and have proved provocative for class discussion and analysis.

This volume of essays and commentary is divided into eight parts, each part including from four to nine articles. Although every article is related to the others in the section as shown in the interlacing introductory comments, each is individually important. The utility of this volume lies in its flexible nature, which makes it adaptable to a wide variety of professorial techniques and approaches. Although functional analysis tends to be implicit in the theoretical approach, the editor has purposely refrained from creating a formal functional theoretical framework. The articles have been gathered together because of their broad inherent value rather than because they fit a theoretical structure. They are presented as stimulants for discussion or as fundamental insights, not as explanations of some theoretical posture.

This book is the result of an earlier unpublished collaboration with Judith F. Kerr, a former student and now friend, who gave tirelessly to the search for meaningful materials on the sociology of religion. Although she has not been present at the final stages of this writing, her contribution cannot go unnoticed. She served as both investigator and critic when this volume was still only an idea in the editor's mind. Others, too have left their mark. Students and colleagues at the College of Wooster and Newberry College have contributed ideas which they may or may not recognize. In several instances their criticisms have led to the exclusion of materials originally slated for this volume. Without the special grant from the Lutheran Church in America Research and Creativity Fund the costs of manuscript preparation would have been prohibitive. Mary Knudten, my wife, has served with great patience and understanding as personal secretary, confidant, evaluator, and proofreader whenever the occasion has required. My children—Stephen, David, Thomas, and Susan—have been both causes for forgotten ideas and exponents of joy, and have made the writing of this volume both a drudgery and a delight. John F. Cuber, editor of the Appleton-Century-Crofts Sociology Series, has done all in his power to encourage a new author to reveal himself in his writing. Special recognition, however, must be made of the authors who gave immediate and gracious permission to reproduce their writings in this new form. Without their cooperation there would be no book. To them I give my thanks and offer this volume as another hopeful step in the growth of a Sociology of Religion.

R.D.K.

CONTENTS

PREFACE   vii

PART I   THE CURRENT STATE OF RELIGION AND
          THE SOCIOLOGY OF RELIGION

Introduction   3

1   SYDNEY E. AHLSTROM
    Theology and the Present-Day Revival   5

2   LISTON POPE
    The Negro and Religion in America   17

3   J. MILTON YINGER
    The Present Status of the Sociology of Religion   26

4   GLENN M. VERNON
    Measuring Religion: Two Methods Compared   39

5   GIBSON WINTER
    Methodological Reflections on "The Religious Factor"   46

6   WILLIAM PETERSEN
    Religious Statistics in the United States   57

PART II   THE CULTURAL CONTEXT OF RELIGION

Introduction   71

7   CHARLES Y. GLOCK
    Religion and the Integration of Society   72

8   ALEXANDER ALLAND, JR.
    "Possession" in a Revivalistic Negro Church   83

9   PHILLIP E. HAMMOND
    Religion and the "Informing" of Culture   93

10 THOMAS R. FORD
    Religious Thought and Beliefs in the Southern Appalachians
    as Revealed by an Attitude Survey   103

PART III   VARIETIES OF RELIGIOUS ORGANIZATION

    Introduction   121

11 BENTON JOHNSON
    On Church and Sect   123

12 FRANK W. YOUNG
    Adaptation and Pattern Integration of a California Sect   136

13 TRUMAN B. DOUGLASS
    Ecological Changes and the Church   147

14 FREDERICK A. SHIPPEY
    The Variety of City Churches   157

15 MANFRED STANLEY
    Church Adaptation To Urban Social Change: A Typology
    of Protestant City Congregations   167

PART IV   SOCIALIZATION AND RELIGIOUS ROLES

    Introduction   179

A. PROCESSES OF SOCIALIZATION

16 DAVID ELKIND
    Age Changes in the Meaning of Religious Identity   182

17 JOHN L. THOMAS, S.J.
    Religious Training in the Roman Catholic Family   188

18 MURRAY B. SEIDLER and MEL JEROME RAVITZ
    A Jewish Peer Group   196

19 RICHARD MC CANN
    Developmental Factors in the Growth of a Mature Faith   204

B. THE MINISTRY

20 SAMUEL W. BLIZZARD
    Role Conflicts of the Urban Protestant Parish Minister   212

21 WALDO W. BURCHARD
    Role Conflicts of Military Chaplains   218

22 ERNEST Q. CAMPBELL and THOMAS F. PETTIGREW
    Racial and Moral Crisis: The Role of Little Rock Ministers   228

23 SAMUEL W. BLIZZARD
    The Roles of the Rural Parish Minister, The Protestant
    Seminaries, and the Sciences of Social Behavior   240

C. THE LAITY

24 PAUL M. HARRISON
    Church and the Laity Among Protestants   250

25 JOHN J. KANE
    Church and the Laity Among Catholics   261

26 MARSHALL SKLARE
    Church and the Laity Among Jews   270

PART V   RELIGION AS A SOCIAL PROCESS

    Introduction   283

27 THOMAS F. O'DEA
    Five Dilemmas in the Institutionalization of Religion   285

28 ALLEN SPITZER and MARY L. SPITZER
    Religious Reorganization Among the Montana Blackfeet   295

29 JAMES S. COLEMAN
    Social Cleavage and Religious Conflict   305

30 OLIVER E. GRAEBNER
    Pastor and People at Kennedy's Casket   315

PART VI   RELIGION, STRATIFICATION, AND
           MINORITY LIFE

    Introduction   329

31 ALBERT J. MAYER and HARRY SHARP
    Religious Preference and Worldly Success   332

32 WILLIAM M. KEPHART
    Status After Death   346

33 J. OSCAR LEE
    Religion Among Ethnic and Racial Minorities   357

34 HENRY CLARK
    Churchmen and Residential Desegregation   368

35 HAROLD L. SHEPPARD
    The Negro Merchant: A Study of Negro Anti-Semitism   378

PART VII   RELIGION AND OTHER INSTITUTIONAL
           CONTEXTS

Introduction   387

36 GERHARD LENSKI
    Religion's Impact on Secular Institutions   389

37 LAWRENCE H. FUCHS
    American Jews and the Presidential Vote   402

38 EDUARD HEIMANN
    Christian Foundations of the Social Sciences   418

39 REGINALD STACKHOUSE
    Darwin and a Century of Conflict   430

40 R. B. DIERENFIELD
    The Extent of Religious Influence in American Public Schools 436

41 GERHARD LENSKI
    Social Correlates of Religious Interest   446

42 GLENN VERNON
    Interfaith Marriages   459

PART VIII   RELIGION IN THE MIDST OF
            MODERN CHANGE

Introduction   467

43 WILL HERBERG
    Religion in a Secularized Society: The New Shape of
    Religion in America   470

44 J. MILTON YINGER
    Religion and Social Change: Functions and Dysfunctions
    of Sects and Cults Among the Disprivileged   482

45 J. MILTON YINGER
    Religion and Society: Problems of Integration and Pluralism
    Among the Privileged   496

46 WILL HERBERG
    Religion in a Secularized Society: Some Aspects of
    America's Three-Religion Pluralism   513

47 BENSON Y. LANDIS
    Trends in Church Membership in the United States   523

48   RICHARD D. LAMBERT
     Current Trends in Religion: A Summary   531

49   CHARLES Y. GLOCK and RODNEY STARK
     Is There An American Protestantism?   542

AUTHOR INDEX   557

PART I

THE CURRENT STATE OF RELIGION
AND THE SOCIOLOGY OF RELIGION

INTRODUCTION

THE ATTEMPT to analyze religion from the disciplined approach of the scientific method is of recent origin. Although men have studied religion from the beginning of time, the major impetus towards the sociological study of religion has taken place within the last fifty years. The field has remained largely undeveloped, although there has been increasing evidence of scholarly interest. It is refreshing to know that the Durkheims, Webers, Troeltschs, Wachs and Simmels of the past have their counterparts in the Lenskis, Yingers, Popes, Glocks, Winters, and Herbergs of the present.

The sociologist of religion is a student of religious behavior. Theoretically free of doctrinal or dogmatic position, he undertakes an objective, unbiased study of human behavior in order to ascertain human religious processes. His study is a study of the interaction and functions of society, culture, and personality in religion. Whereas the social scientist remains objective in his approach to religion, the man of faith follows subjective procedures. The religious man gives more attention to internal feelings and reactions than he does to evidence which is empirical. He tends to think in terms of dualities: right and wrong, good and evil. His proofs depend upon speculations about the life to come, something which he has not yet experienced but which he fears or welcomes on other bases. Whereas faith is central to the religious man and method, evidence is central to the scientific man and method. Whereas religion depends in large part upon appeals to authority, science depends upon facts. Religion supports values openly; science attempts to remain value-free. Religion seeks to explain the unseen; science testifies only to that which can be experienced.

Sociological analysis of religion in America poses problems not present in other societies. Religious forms are diversified. Multiple value systems are often in conflict. Variables of class, education, income, race, and interest compound investigation. The severe fragmentation of religious groups and the rise of diverse sects has made a monolithic analysis of religion impossible. The field is too vast, variables too many, and social change too sweeping to allow easy definition and generalization.

Six inclusive articles basic to an understanding of religion in America are presented in Part I, The Current State of Religion and the Sociology of Religion. Although they are largely descriptive and analytical, they identify some of the problems, aims, and approaches of the sociologist of religion. Sydney Ahlstrom presents an analysis of the major themes common in present-day religion. He identifies the changes that have occurred in religion since the turn of the century and the relationship of these changes to current religious practice. Liston Pope traces the history of the Negro American and the rise of the Negro church. In doing so, he discusses the religious basis of Negro leadership in the immediate Civil Rights struggle. J. Milton Yinger analyzes the status and content of the sociology of religion. He defines the basic processes of scientific research and notes the central problems of the social scientist. Although such a study offers major theoretical and methodological problems, Yinger suggests areas of investigation and hypotheses for future research, setting forth the scope of modern sociological investigation. Glenn Vernon offers an analysis of the strengths and weaknesses of the direct and indirect approaches to religious investigation. He makes clear that the value of any research depends upon adequate research design and methodology. Gibson Winter discusses two current major sociological volumes on religion and contrasts their findings in an attempt to ascertain tenable interpretations of seemingly contradictory research and analysis. Winter notes that diversity of findings may lead to a unity of understanding if findings are interpreted with the necessary precision and within the context of a research design. William Petersen identifies the data-gathering problems that hinder research in American religion. Although the focus of his article centers upon the need for a national census, his writing gives insight into the diversity and some of the problems of religion at the present time.

1 THEOLOGY AND THE PRESENT-DAY REVIVAL

Sydney E. Ahlstrom

INTRODUCTION   Fundamentalism and modernism represent two opposing poles of American religious expression. Because fundamentalism is a form of doctrinal conservativism that
seeks the return of society to absolute religious values, the fundamentalist is at odds with the world and seeks to remain free from
personal contamination and irreligious materialism. The fundamentalist argues that correct belief will result in correct action. Because
he supports the *status quo* in the attempt to forestall social change
which would cause further erosion of absolute religious ideals, the
fundamentalist expresses only limited concern for social reform.
Christian fundamentalists focus their beliefs within five core propositions that they hold central to religious faith and purity: (1)
The infallibility of the Bible; (2) The Virgin Birth and the total
Diety of Jesus the Christ; (3) The physical resurrection of Jesus'
body; (4) The substitutionary atonement of Jesus for the world's
sin; and (5) The second coming of Jesus in bodily form.

The modernist, on the other hand, argues that all religious
doctrines must be interpreted in the context of their origin and in
the light of current conditions. Only the extreme modernist, however, tends to reject all traditional doctrine, believing that revelation comes differently in different times. To the modernist the
action of the individual becomes the test and proof of faith. Correct
action results in correct belief. Therefore, the modernist places
greater emphasis upon the primacy of reason, the desire for personal freedom, the need for a contemporary religious expression,
and the continuity of revelation. Although these groups represent

Abridged and reprinted from *The Annals*, Volume 332, (November, 1960), pp. 20-36,
with the permission of the author and editors.

SYDNEY AHLSTROM is Professor of American Church History at Yale University.

two dissimilar attitudes, *each viewpoint exists in varying degree within most established denominations and churches.* Much of the politico-religious argument taking place in America today centers around one or the other of these two religious perspectives.

Sydney Ahlstrom, a church historian, suggests that the contemporary period of Christianity in America began with the Depression. Only then did the changes brought about by the challenges of the Civil War, increased immigration and urban growth, and World War I, stabilize in a new approach in American theology and religious practice. The writings of Washington Gladden, Walter Rauschenbusch, and Horace Bushnell, proponents of the social gospel, dealt theologically with man in a social setting. Although they lived primarily at the turn of the century, these men generated a gradual recognition of the need for social salvation in order to hinder the rise of social systems that would imprison man within his own society. They argued that the changing nature of industrial and social life demanded a new religious approach. Fragmentation of religious power, based so long upon cultural variations and ensuing social suspicions, became a luxury that religious groups could no longer afford in a rapidly changing society. The rejection of the evolutionary theories of Herbert Spencer and William Graham Sumner and the development of practical steps toward interdenominational cooperation issued in a new spirit within American religion.

The Christian neo-orthodox movement owes its existence in large part to the successful effort to blend together a social liberalism and progressive biblicism in the attempt to offer an alternative to atheism and to the extremes of fundamentalistic and modernistic Christianity. Although most national denominations have long since rejected the fundamentalist position, the tensions generated by basic human needs, persistent social change, scientific discovery, and the rise of neo-orthodoxy have continued to influence the thought and action patterns of religious people. The rejection of absolute religious values and the rise of relativistic attitudes have marked, and masked, religion in America. Although religious pluralism has served to weaken religious solidarity it has also strengthened it by appealing to wider varieties of religious thought and action. Modern religion has often become a pseudoform of religious nationalism, paradoxically identified both by increased membership participation and financial commitment, and by decreased recognition of the essentials of belief and weakened personal dedication.

THE FAILURE of the peace [after 1918] became chiefly an excuse for both political and theological isolationism. The influence of the churches fell to its lowest ebb. The liberals took new and more daring theological and biblical positions, to which the fundamentalists responded with horror and righteous wrath; the "Monkey Trial"[1] in Dayton, Tennessee, provided the most spectacular religious news of the postwar decade. Walter Rauschenbusch and Washington Gladden died in 1918; the temperance movement and pacifism became surrogates for the social gospel. For most churches it was the heyday of the lawn social. Fleeing a fictional Elmer Gantry and a very much alive Bruce Barton, the intellectuals abandoned the Church in droves, with H. L. Mencken piping the tune. By almost every legitimate canon of measurement the great depression came upon religion during the booming but troubled Twenties.

NEO-ORTHODOXY.   Yet, in a certain sense, even this era had its "underground men" quietly developing a revulsion for the culture-protestantism in which both liberals and conservatives seemed to be conspiring to rob the Christian message of relevance and prophetic content. H. Richard Niebuhr brought his thought to focus in 1929 with trenchant reflections on *The Social Sources of Denominationalism*.[2] Before Niebuhr's work appeared in print, Douglas Horton had already found Karl Barth's *Das Wort Gottes und Die Theologie* on the Harvard Divinity School's new book shelf, and Horton immediately undertook the translation of Barth into English—which in a literary sense marks a turning point in American theology.[3]

EVENTS AND CRISES.   After 1928 and 1929 both literary and personal theological events occur with increasing rapidity, with the harsh noise of the Crash hastening the process. The year 1932 marked the passing of the old order in more ways than one. The acute realism of Reinhold Niebuhr's *Moral Man and Immoral Society* and H. R. Niebuhr's translation of Paul Tillich's *The Religious Situation* ruffled the placid waters of liberal social Christianity. Because both works were conceived on the borderlands of secular and religious concern, they reached a new kind of American audience. Speaking more directly to the Church in that year was Walter Lowrie's long-gestated demand that we give heed to the "theology of crisis." A close acquaintance with Albert Schweitzer's *Quest of the Historical Jesus* (1906) and cognate works was readily apparent in his impassioned analysis; and his emphasis clearly fore-

---

[1] [The trial of John T. Scopes, indicted in 1925 for teaching the theory of evolution in a public school.—*Editor*.]

[2] [In this work Niebuhr argued that American religious differences were based on other "social sources" than those stemming from the old world.—*Editor*.]

[3] [Blending a conservative-biblical theology with a progressive social policy, neo-orthodoxy offered a third alternative to emphases upon personal religion or nonbiblical social concern. It sought to assimilate the discoveries of science, yet offer a theological foundation for belief which was lacking in the social gospel movement.—*Editor*.]

shadowed a lifetime's preoccupation with making Kierkegaard known to the English-speaking world.

THEOLOGICAL RENEWAL.   Books and men that had been ignored during the Twenties took on new significance; other new thinkers were found for the first time; and still others arrived in person. Paul Tillich's American career began at Union Theological Seminary in 1933-34. Many diverse trends of thought came to a focus: Russian, Berdjaev; Spanish, Unamuno; Swedish, Nygren and Aulen; English, Forsythe and Temple; French, Marcel, Maury, and Maritain; German, Heim and Gogarten; and preeminently two Swiss thinkers, Emil Brunner and Karl Barth. The two books which best clarify to even the most unprepared mind the nature of these exciting new theological currents are Barth's commentary on *The Epistle to the Romans* and the work translated by Dr. Horton which was mentioned above. It was the intense, existential message of the young Barth that put its indelible imprint on American neo-orthodoxy. Other "discoveries" followed: Kierkegaard, Pascal, Luther, Calvin, and Augustine; and beneath all came a reentry into the "strange world of the Bible." The biblical world was reentered not just to seek the religion or social teachings of Jesus or the prophet Amos, but to apprehend the evangel, the kerygma, the proclamation of the gospel, the good news of God to his covenant people.

NEW BIBLICAL EMPHASIS.   Quite aside from various superficial readings "from Luther to Hitler," the "Luther renaissance" and later a "Calvin renaissance" began to change the academic approach to the Scriptures even in the old liberal bastions where biblical research had become merely an ancillary aspect of Near-Eastern and Hellenistic studies. Genesis gradually ceased to be a hornets' nest of the Fundamentalist Controversy[4] and—without the slightest abandonment of historical research and scientific textual criticism—became a foundation stone for a Christian's theological understanding of the world. Thanks to Kierkegaard, the account of Abraham and Isaac on Mount Moriah, far from being an immoral vestige of primitivism, came to reveal a whole dimension of the religious life. The Gospels were untangled from the Synoptic and Johannine problems[5] to allow a concern for the gospel, and St. Paul was restored to the canon as something more than the villain who twisted the pure religion of Jesus into an Hellenistic mystery cult. Yet, again, there was no inclination in either case to repudiate historical methods or findings. Indeed, it must be emphasized at this point that one major feature of neo-orthodox thinking was its complete willingness to join contemporary philosophical discussion, to share the liberal respect for scientific endeavor, and to accept and extend the nineteenth century's massive tradition of religious scholarship.

---

[4] [A prolonged doctrinal dispute between the liberal and more conservative branches of Protestantism over concepts of creation and evolution.—*Editor*.]

[5] [Synoptic, referring to the first three Gospels, is distinguished from Johannine, which refers to the fourth. The problem mentioned is one of dating these two groups.—*Editor*.]

Never lapsing into pessimism, however, the movement promoted a veritable revival of the social gospel.

THEOLOGICAL ETHOS CHANGED. By 1945 neo-orthodoxy had effected a significant alteration in the country's theological ethos. Most obviously it had reduced to a small remnant the tradition of liberalism which had been expanding so vigorously and so constantly ever since the days of Emerson's Divinity School Address in 1838 and Horace Bushnell's manifesto on *Christian Nurture* in 1847.

The final and perhaps the most decisive way in which neo-orthodoxy affected the total American religious scene depended on the way it transcended the old controversies, animosities and suspicions while at the same time laying the foundations for a whole new set of ecumenical approaches. To no small degree it voiced the central fundamentalist complaint that modernism was not the Christian religion but a religion of another type entirely.

THE REVIVAL. For more than a century after 1800 revivalism was a continuous factor in American religious life, and its techniques and theological assumptions were the most important single factor molding the church-life and intellectual attitudes of American evangelical Protestantism. Through this channel they worked an immense formative effect on American democratic attitudes, practices, and ideals.

The importance of big-name, high-jinx revivalism, on the other hand, must not be exaggerated. Especially in the post-Civil War period it probably achieved little more than surface effects on the basic pattern of American religious growth. Even after World War I when professional mass-manipulation of the Billy Sunday variety suffered a decline, revivalism of a less pretentious sort continued unabated in the small towns, in the urban rescue missions, among countless sects, and in individual congregations of the revivalistic denominations.

RECENT POPULAR TRENDS. Having duly emphasized this point, one may cautiously concede that during the Twenties American Protestantism suffered a decline which continued after 1929. Contributions for missions and benevolences were declining despite the prosperity. Church-going and membership declined as well. During the later 1930's, however, the membership losses sustained by American churches during the darkest days of the Depression were gradually recouped and the rate of expansion prevailing since the Civil War was resumed. Then after the Second World War there did, undeniably, occur a surge of piety, an upswing in religion or a revival of interest in religion as it has been variously termed. The material principle of this new reformation seems to consist of positive thinking, or justification by faith in faith. Its leading apostle is Norman Vincent Peale, with the wise and perceptive Rabbi Joshua Loth Liebman as its best-selling forerunner, and Dwight D. Eisenhower as its most distinguished exponent.

CURIOSITY ABOUT RELIGION.   Closely related to these forms of utilitarian piety has been another which is characterized chiefly by an interest in religion, frequently at a very high intellectual level and often in the university. It may or may not be accompanied by great confidence in religiosity-as-such or the assumption that religious curiosity is certainly good and possibly redemptive. A genuine or even intense curiosity about or fascination with religion is its hallmark, and it may lead a person merely to taste some popular book, to take up the study of some religious topic or course, to become a disciple or fan of some religious poet, or to dedicate himself to a lifetime vocation of religious research.

All of the foregoing manifestations of revival have been essentially indi-vidualistic, even self-centered in their appeal. Christianity, however, has been persistently corporate in its emphasis and expression—from the Feeding of the Five Thousand and the Last Supper on through its permutations in every age. Of Judaism the same must be said. As could be expected, the American per-mutations of the present day are no exception. Just as Luther's justification by faith in no sense reduced the significance of "the Holy Catholic Church, the communion of saints," the contemporary justification by faith in faith simi-larly leans heavily on the lonely crowd's need for community and its prefer-ence for a community which, in Milton J. Rosenberg's phrase, offers "the pleasures of sacred gregariousness."

MASS REVIVALISM.   In this context a brief consideration of Billy Graham is in order for almost solely on his broad and manly shoulders has rested the burden of reviving mass revivalism and preventing it from becoming only a cheap and emotional accommodation of vague American yearnings or a senti-mental reversion to a not-so-old "old-time religion." Not sufficiently realized, however, is the significance of his solitariness in the field and the drastic con-trast of this situation to that in the days of Moody and Sunday from 1870 to 1917 when the country was criss-crossed by roving teams of competing re-vivalists. Now Graham is ecumenical in a sense, though nondenominational is a better description of his stance. His city-wide campaigns depend on the cooperation of an extremely wide range of churches; in many cases he works through local councils of churches which some of his most fervent admirers refuse to join. . . . Like all men who have to depend on an organization and who have to sell a standardized product to a mass audience, he nevertheless becomes a victim of the very forces he would oppose. Madison Avenue has put its unmistakable mark on the crusader's tactics and even on his message, which becomes increasingly slick and rounded off. His shortcomings thus illuminate the spirit of the times as much as do his successes.

REVIVAL IN JUDAISM.   The present state of American Judaism allows many similar observations, though the qualifications entered in the final sec-tion of this paper would also apply to a degree. A Jewish revival and a highly visible return to the synagogues is taking place; and as Nathan Glazer and others have pointed out it has taken place to a large degree in the new social setting created by the current migration to the suburbs and by the corresponding occupational shift. To these forces must be added the powerful stimuli provided by Nazi persecutions, the rapid growth of Zionism and, still later, the actuality of an Israeli republic. As a result the American Jewish community has become not only remarkably homogeneous in its social composition but more determined to root its Jewishness in some form of its religious tradition. Living in this new situation amidst Christian neighbors who, whether Protestant or Catholic, are on the average much more regular in their religious participation, Jews are returning to increased observance and to providing a Jewish education for their children.

ROMAN CATHOLICISM.   The prominence of the Irish among American Roman Catholics and their dominance in the clergy and hierarchy has had much to do with the Church's easy and persistent fusion of religion and nationalism. Nor is it enough to say, merely, that Catholics are in general patriotic; both in neighborly conversation and through national spokesmen they proclaim the great usefulness of the Church in the advancement of national aims in a hostile world, and they often do so in accents that blend indistinguishably with the maturing national religion that Dr. Marty has described in *The New Shape of American Religion.* Arthur Mann goes too far in saying that "the idea that religion is handmaiden to democracy has made such headway that American Catholicism, American Protestantism, and American Judaism appear like parallel shoots on a common stock." But the general point is worth making.

A second aspect, not unrelated to the foregoing, is the now general Roman Catholic acceptance of its tradition as one of three great faiths of this country —or, in John Courtney Murray's phrase, as one of the four conspiracies, for he righly sees secularism as an active ingredient in the melting pot. In other words, the Church in a practical way accepts the basic—and, for the foreseeable future, unchangeable—pluralism of American life and the statistical fact that since the ending of immigration, and despite the influx of nearly a million refugees since 1935, the Roman Catholic Church has grown somewhat more slowly than Protestantism. Though with less force than in established state-churches, this acceptance of pluralism conduces in its own way to nominal, superficial religion. If Bishop Fulton J. Sheen were cited as the Roman corollary of Dr. Peale or Rabbi Liebman, it must be insisted that he stands in radical contradistinction to them. He is in command of nearly all the persuasive arts, but with far more success than Billy Graham he seeks to transcend the advocacy of belief in belief with a more substantial, prophetic message. He preaches no minimized Catholicism however popular his apologetics may be. His theology rests on the Thomistic foundations outlined in his *God and Intelligence in Modern Philosophy,* published in 1925, and he develops the mystical and existential emphases latent in that tradition.

PRESENT THEOLOGICAL TRENDS. Neo-orthodoxy and the revival of religious interest are unquestionably major aspects of the contemporary situation. The surge of popular piety, however, was to a large degree a response to peculiarly American needs in the postwar world and therefore so singularly tame and conformist that important creative achievements could hardly be expected from it. True to these expectations, the revival has been unaccompanied by the emergence of new institutions or the bursting of traditional structures and practices such as came with the other great revivals in the medieval, reformation, and modern periods or in the long, unbroken series of American Protestant revivals of the nineteenth century. The chief contemporary exceptions may be certain trends toward denominational federation or consolidation and the growth of community churches.

In contrast to this state of affairs, the movement of vigorous theological protest and revision which waxed in the 1930's led almost necessarily in the post-war years to new and more constructive movements in Christian thought.

NO FACILE GENERALIZATIONS. American theology since the neo-orthodox period defies neat and unified characterization. The most important fact is that it has been renewed. Twentieth-century Christendom has seen a theological renaissance unparalleled since the age of the Reformation. Americans, moreover, have avidly participated in it, and with a catholicity of interest noticeable in few other countries. As a consequence theologians have come to occupy the place in American life that during the half-century after James and Royce was occupied by secular philosophers or almost secular liberal theologians. American philosophy has been preoccupied chiefly with formal questions and has nearly abandoned the large issues of human existence. Since the deaths of Dewey and Whitehead, it would be difficult to find any American philosophers of public eminence who have addressed themselves to the problems of men. The major fact about the American theological enterprise is its broad concern with the whole gamut of human problems.

BIBLICAL SCHOLARSHIP AND THEOLOGY. As one attempts a more detailed characterization of this enterprise, the new locus and importance of biblical scholarship and exegesis are the inescapable points of departure. The Dead Sea Scrolls, the gnostic materials found in Egypt, and archaeological evidence have been brought into the field of inquiry, put under analysis, and consecrated to the single purpose of better understanding the Holy Scriptures. Any thing or any auxiliary discipline that can shed light is welcomed. As it happens, the findings of recent decades have tended to vindicate or approach many traditional interpretations.

Biblical scholarship, however, is increasingly understood not only as a department of scientific historical studies but also as contributory to biblical theology; scholarship and exegesis are thus inextricably joined in a task involving matters far larger than the dates, authorship, and texts of documents. Exegesis of both the Old and New Testaments is, in turn, closely linked with the task of Christian preaching. The resurgence of interest in biblical study is thus related to the restoration of the preaching office in the Church; and much of the renewed interest of theological students in the Greek and Hebrew languages stems from their theological and homiletical responsibilities.

EFFECTS ON PRACTICE. The impulse has at least three points of origin: in the Lutheran revival of the nineteenth century and cognate movements among the German Reformed, in the English Oxford[6] movement, and in Roman Catholicism, especially in France, Belgium, and Germany, and notably among the Benedictines. The movement seeks most directly to reinvigorate the worship and devotional life of the Church, but only after broadening and deepening the idea of worship, *leiturgia*. The royal priesthood of all believers, therefore, is of vital importance—with large consequences for traditional notions of the laity. In its desire for genuinely liturgical preaching it responded to many contemporary theological emphases. Among Roman Catholics it awakened interest in the vernacular mass and lay use of the Bible, thereby underlining the liturgical significance of reformers like Luther and Cranmer. Yet this movement was not restricted to those communions which preserved traditional worship forms. In Presbyterian and other Reformed churches there were efforts to forego the excesses of Puritanism and reclaim the less radical attitudes of Calvin and the German Reformed leaders. Pervading this entire movement of renewal, as must be apparent in even this brief account, is a more serious concern for the meaning of church membership and a desire to realize a deeper understanding of the church as a fellowship, a *laos*—a people or laity—of God, an *ekklesia*—assembly—of God.

SYSTEM IN THEOLOGY. The Church's assumption of a teaching role is but the practical corollary of the intensely intellectual task of the systematic theologian, namely, the rigorously reasoned formulation of dogmatics. By 1930 dogmatics had almost become a swear word in most American religious circles. Successive waves of rationalism, revivalism, romanticism and liberalism had almost entirely eroded the idea of a scientific discipline for studying the faith of the Church. During the last two decades, however, some of its ancient dignities and perquisites have been restored both in realms where fundamentalism once ruled with anti-intellectual absolutism and where liberalism more indulgently sought to evoke a message from the religious consciousness itself. At the present time the chief fact of interest is that theology as a rigorous and more or less systematic pursuit is becoming an increasingly lively enterprise. It continues to work, as it must if it is to flourish, in close union with philosophical, historical, and, above all, biblical disciplines.

CONFLUENCE OF MAINSTREAMS. American theologians reflect their country's varied background. At the same time they manifest the integrative effects of both a more widely opened door to the great tradition and the social forces of church unity operative in the United States. Within this common approach

6 [First known as the Tractarian movement.—*Editor*.]

to common problems one may discern at least six diverse trends, none of which can be justly treated in the brief statements possible here. The *first* of these trends is deeply indebted to Paul Tillich and reflects his existential idealism. Committed to the ontological concerns of the post-Kantian tradition, above all, Hegel and Schelling, its broad and catholic correlation of human problems and Christian answers is expressed in philosophical rather than exegetical argument. Closely related is a *second* trend in which is continued the long enterprise of turning Plato, Aristotle and classic Stoicism to Christian purposes, as did Augustine and Aquinas and Richard Hooker in their characteristic ways. This is, of course, the dominant trend in Roman Catholicism, especially in America, and also a persistent feature of Anglican thought. The widely varying uses of Whitehead should also be noted in this connection. A *third* trend, related to the above two, may be noted, I think, in the renewed interest being shown in Friedrich Schleiermacher, F. D. Maurice, Horace Bushnell, and other great nineteenth-century liberals, though it is by no means always being turned to the development of a new liberalism. Thinkers in this group obviously share much with H. Richard Niebuhr and Tillich, most of all in their determination to keep theology free from what they might call dogmatism and open to creative dialogue with the world, society, and culture. They do not emphasize a radical disjunction between the church and the world; and they inherit a measure of the liberal's optimism about Christendom and the formation of a Christian society. A *fourth* trend owes much to Rudolf Bultmann and through him to the existential philosophy of Martin Heidegger, but always with the biblical orientation indicated by Bultmann's two greatest works, a commentary on *St. John's Gospel* and a *Theology of the New Testament*. During recent decades Bultmann has done more to invigorate biblical theology than any other thinker, and it is appropriate to designate a trend with his name even though many whom he has influenced do not share either the radicalism of his demythologizing or his confidence in Heidegger as the lamplighter of Christian theology. In his emphasis on making the scandal of the gospel relevant to the present era, Bultmann shares a concern with each of the three foregoing trends.

Less accommodating to the ways and wisdom of the world and possibly—perhaps as a result—less influential among American theologians is a *fifth* trend which is best designated by the massive, Christocentric effort of Karl Barth to disengage dogmatics from all kinds of crippling alliances. [In Barth and his supporters] dogmatics flourishes in its purest form, being rooted in the Scriptures and guided by the church's creeds and confessions.

The *sixth* trend here delineated owes much to an initial impulse given it by Reinhold Niebuhr and is specially marked by its strong ethical interests. Its thought is marked by an insistence that a Christian ethic—or the life of the Christian in this world—can make sense only when it is Christocentric, theologically oriented, and biblically grounded. It is suspicious of abstract or autonomous principles, often including natural law philosophies insofar as they ignore the situation of the individual person. Yet it affirms the goodness of the creation, the significance of law, and the meaningfulness of the Christian's vocation in the institutional life or orders of the creation. Luther is frequently a great resource to such thinkers, and also Dietrich Bonhoeffer, who was put to death by the Nazis in 1945.

PROSPECTS. A comprehensive survey of American theology, if undertaken, would show, I believe, that the country's legendary pluralism is an enriching fact though also a disappearing one. Diversity, however, leads to catholicity as well as homogeneity; and in this fact there is reason for believing that the impressive uniqueness of the American religious experience will in time bear some distinctive fruit. In the United States voluntaryism, freedom, church-state separation, and positive, constructive "laicism" have long and abundantly flourished. In almost every faith and communion, whether its roots are in old state-church traditions of Europe, in strong movements of tolerated dissent, or in circumstances of positive persecution—or in all three, as is the case with Roman Catholicism—this situation has conduced to new and exciting developments that will probably be reflected sooner or later not only in practical achievements but on a theological plane. Ironically, though understandably, the most significant manifestation of this possibility was Roman Catholic Americanism. In Protestantism, so far, the American contribution has consisted chiefly of a disposition to activism, the social gospel, and more recently a sociologically and theologically rooted social ethics. But from the theological ferment of the present day we can perhaps expect still other developments. In the meantime, this same ferment can be expected to do much toward sublimating the traditional anti-intellectualism of American Christianity. It may further reduce the alienation of the intelligentsia which was so prominent during the past century or more when so many churches seemed to have set themselves athwart the entire movement of modern science, scholarship, and literature. Finally, it may extend that deeper revival of the church which goes on at the level of faithful commitment rather than religious interest.

POSTSCRIPT, 1966. Not often in American history has a half-decade witnessed so large a transformation of our social, religious, and moral ethos as that which has elapsed since this essay was written. I am struck by the number of contemporary movements and trends which could be ignored or merely mentioned in 1960. Simply to mention Dr. Martin Luther King, President John F. Kennedy and Pope John XXIII brings to mind three massive signs of change. Vietnam, the "New Morality," eruptions in the universities, Supreme Court decisions on reapportionment and on religious exercises in public school, and the creation of a cabinet post on urban affairs betoken other vital dimensions of recent experience. Midst these troubles and challenges there has, of course, been religious adjustment and theological ferment, popular responses and serious thinking. References to American civilization as post-Puritan, post-Protestant and even post-Christian, coupled as they have been with reference to the "end of the Counter-Reformation," have won widespread acceptance as salutary reminders of a drastically altered social and ecclesiastical situation. Interracial demonstrations, Protestant-Catholic conversations, and interfaith dialogues are another aspect of this response. The Vatican Council and the civil rights movement have given new urgency to ecumenical issues, with a consequent deepening of interchurch discussions. Theologians, pastors, and laity, meanwhile, have been showing unprecedented concern for being "Honest to God" in doctrinal matters. Conventional patterns of parish life have been subjected to searching criticism. In theology, ethics, and social action, the entire realm of the "secular" has been appreciatively reappraised—often in a manner that owes much to Bonhoeffer and Bultmann. In these diverse contexts a new chapter in our theological development is taking shape even now. The religious situation has rarely seemed so open or so unpredictable.

Prognostication, fortunately, is not part of the historian's task, and I am not required to speculate on the portent of our present unrest. But five years' additional perspective on the recent past, covered in the foregoing essay, has impressed upon me that I did on that occasion deal with a meaningful unit of historical experience. What has happened and transpired during the intervening time has emphasized the concrete and discrete place in our country's spiritual history of the "period" extending from the Great Depression to the Great Society.

2 THE NEGRO AND RELIGION IN AMERICA

Liston Pope

INTRODUCTION   Any examination of the American religious situation must include a consideration of the Negro church.
Negro slaves, transported from Africa to America, were forced to
accept a new environment, culture, and religious practice upon
arrival. As they became acculturated, they shared in the local
church dominated by the white society. However in time the separate Negro church, according to E. Franklin Frazier, grew from
two roots: (1) The efforts of the free Negroes in the North to escape from their inferior position, and (2) The development of the
"invisible institution" on the plantations during the slavery period.
Free northern Negroes organized the African Methodist Episcopal
Church and the African Methodist Episcopal Zion Church near
the beginning of the nineteenth century. The "invisible institution" in the South developed in areas where slaves were permitted
to conduct their religious services with a Negro preacher. After
emancipation, it emerged in the form of the independent Baptist
and Methodist Negro institutions. Although the joint worship of
Negroes and whites was common before the Civil War, it was not
a sign of equality. Instead, it was an attempt of planters and own-
ers to control their slaves. The appearance of the segregated
churches after the war reflects the tensions of the period and the
cultural need of the recently emancipated minority group.
    Although modern Negroes participate in a wide variety of re-
ligious groups ranging from ecstatic sects to more formal and deliberative institutions (see Alland, Article 8, and Johnson, Article
11) most Negroes attend segregated churches. Because the Negro

Abridged and reprinted from *The Review of Religious Research*, Volume 5, Number 3,
Copyrighted 1964 by the Religious Research Association, Inc.

LISTON POPE is currently Professor of Social Ethics at Yale University.

church has served as one of the centers of Negro social life, it has assumed considerable importance. Offering members an opportunity for self-expression, leadership, and acceptance in a hostile white world, the Negro church has served as a focal point of minority group unity. Although it is no longer the only Negro institution in the United States, it provides the theological and moral foundation for the Negro movement toward equal rights. Where the Negro has had the right to vote, the Negro church has possessed a strong political influence. Current Negro religious leadership has been instrumental in the progress made to date in the civil rights struggle.

The Negro clergyman holds a high status within the Negro community, even though his position is being increasingly challenged by Negroes in other occupations. White clergymen occupied a similar position in past generations. Once viewed as the intellectual leader of his community, his status fell when increased educational opportunities developed for persons desiring other occupations. The Negro clergyman, however, remains to a greater degree the educated leader in proportion to the other minority members surrounding him. His leadership in the civil rights controversy is a natural outgrowth of his position and status. However, the non-Negro clergyman has only been a late arrival in the civil rights movement. He has been reluctant to seek salvation in terms of society rather than the individual.

The perceived roles of the Negro and non-Negro minister differ sharply. The cultural results of majority and minority status permeate their interpretations of Scripture, activity in the ministry, contacts with church membership, and attitudes toward society. While the Negro minister represents those facing real or imagined injustice, the non-Negro ministry generally represents the more conservative and established community leadership. Because denominations in America tend to represent middle and upper class interests, non-Negro leadership toward resolution of the questions of civil rights has remained vague and ill-defined.

Although religion generally serves as an agent of social unity (see Glock, Article 7), it may also be dysfunctional. Most men, whether white Klansmen or Negro laymen, interpret religious teaching to reinforce their own presuppositions and to reject potential social challenges to their position. Therefore, in the same situation religion may be both functional and cohesive, and yet dysfunctional and disintegrative. The religiously motivated Klansman, who rejects integration because his interpretation of biblical teaching has led him to take overt action to suppress minority rights, illustrates this potential.

T HE TOPIC CHOSEN for discussion here is a very challenging but difficult one. The religion of Negroes in America is even more variegated
than that of whites, and any generalization about it is dangerous and is
certain to apply to some Negroes but not to others.

NEGRO ESPOUSES CHRISTIANITY.   From the standpoint of sheer
logic it is rather remarkable that Africans brought to America should have so
largely accepted the Christian religion. Transported to this country against
their will, by perilous and wanton voyages that frequently decimated their
numbers, they found themselves in an utterly strange environment, subject to
masters who were often harsh and cruel. It would have been only natural for
them to attempt to maintain their precious adherence to Animism, Fetishism,
and magic—and some did and still do, especially in the West Indies. Further,
the first Africans, or Negroes, as they came to be called, were usually not considered proper candidates for conversion, especially by the slavemasters, lest
their Christianization might seem to require their emancipation. Servitude and
slavery thus created a religious barrier at the outset, and their justification on
grounds of race became prevalent only when *evangelistic zeal replaced the
earlier religious attitudes,* seeking to make the Negro nominally a Christian
though keeping him a slave as a member of an allegedly inferior race.

Actually, however, acceptance of the Bible and the traditions and practices of Christianity proved to be perhaps the most significant bridge by which
the Africans crossed over into the emerging American culture. By being gathered up into the Christian heritage the Negro gained a new but ancient tradition, a new set of values, and elements of a new community, to replace all
the traditions, values and bonds he had lost.

The Negro was assisted in this religious transition after the middle of the
seventeenth century by admonitions or even instructions from the governors
of many of the American colonies and from the King of England himself that
slaves should be given instructions in the Christian religion. These public officials were supported by the efforts of a number of religious leaders and denominational bodies, notably the Church of England, the Methodists, and the
Baptists, to establish missionary work among the slaves. Though most of the
Protestant denominations were skeptical about the institution of slavery, only
the Quakers were strongly opposed to it before the Revolutionary War.

Then came the Declaration of Independence and the War for Independence, with their emphasis on freedom and equality among men and the form
of the great American dilemma began to emerge. Before the century was
ended, most of the religious bodies in America, outside the South, had joined
the opposition to slavery, and Abolition societies had begun to appear in a
number of northern cities.

In general, the early response of Negroes to the efforts toward their conversion was that of going into the churches composed predominantly of white members and having white preachers. But there soon were a few all-black congregations, and there were also a great many Negro preachers, some of them reported to be of great eloquence and power. A few served as pastors of white congregations. It was not until the 19th century that the all-Negro denominations, a prototype of the pattern that was later to prevail, began to appear. Meanwhile, the comparatively free-wheeling, wide-ranging, Methodists and Baptists quickly outstripped the more liturgical and intellectual Episcopalians and Presbyterians and the geographically remote Congregationalists in gaining the adherence of Negro converts, and they have maintained their numerical advantage overwhelmingly to this day. As Booker T. Washington once put it, "If you find a Negro who is not a Methodist or Baptist, it is a sure sign that some white man has been tampering with his religion."

Growth of the Negro population, combined with intensification of discrimination and segregation in the white churches, led to the emergence of separate Negro denominations, generally founded in Northern cities, from 1816 on. The mounting spirit of revolt among Negroes, often robed in Biblical teachings on release from bondage, revealed most especially in insurrections and revolts in the period between 1800 and 1831, was also related to the creation of separate Negro denominations.

In the Southern states, however, slaves continued to be members of congregations controlled by whites, though now the colored members frequently outnumbered the white. As a matter of fact, separate religious meetings of Negroes without white supervision were discouraged or even prohibited, lest they become a source of insurrection.

Despite all precautions by whites, insurrections did occur, led by Gabriel Prosser in 1800, Denmark Vesey in 1822, Nat Turner in 1831, all of them preachers. In each of these cases, Biblical teaching was important or even central in the inspiration of the leader, and support from Negro churchmen was often available. In religion, Negro leaders had begun to find sanction and support for their movements of protest more than 150 years ago.

THE SEPARATE NEGRO CHURCH.   In general, the Southern churches declared the question of slavery to be a civil and political one in which the church had no right to interfere, though some ecclesiastical bodies went so far as to attempt to sanction slavery by appeal to scripture. The reaction of the churches outside the South was varied, at first they tended to support gradual emancipation or colonization in Africa, but most denominations moved swiftly to a demand for immediate emancipation: crusading abolitionists like William Lloyd Garrison drew much of their sustenance from the churches. At last the Methodist, Baptist, and Presbyterian denominations were split regionally over the issue, and organic division continues in all these bodies to the present day.

After the gruesome conflict of the Civil War both Southern whites and Negroes had to pick up the pieces of their lives, and to redefine especially their religious relationships to each other.

It is not true that "Negroes preferred their own churches" in the sense in which white people generally use that statement; there is overwhelming evidence that most Negroes opposed segregation as enforced discrimination. But nearly all *preferred their own churches to inferior status in white congregation.*

The separate Negro church quickly came to occupy a unique and central place in its community, north and south. It was the first, and for decades almost the only, organization entirely under the control of Negroes, and expressive of their own self-identification.

The Negro church came to be more closely related to the daily life of its members than the white church could hope to be—to their politics, economic problems, recreation, and aspirations. In relations with the white community it was for its first ninety years, for the most part, a defensive and accommodating institution, but it often modified the harshness of caste and was the birthplace of schools, social organizations, and other facilities that have improved the condition of the Negro community as a whole.

It should not be assumed that the Negro Church has been a segregating institution, any more than it should be assumed that every white church without Negro members has deliberately practiced segregation. Although the very existence of the Negro church reinforces the caste system and establishes certain vested interests in the maintenance of the *status quo,* that is not its intention.

The conditions that produced the separate Negro church are not yet outmoded. But its future is being called seriously into question, as is that of Negro schools and colleges, at a time when desegregation is proceeding rapidly in other areas of society. It is no longer the only significant institution in the Negro community. For a time, such agencies as the Negro press and the NAACP largely took over the leadership once exercised, often rather haltingly, by the church.

A DEMANDING NEW ROLE.   Since 1955, however, the role of the Negro church in its community has changed enormously; at least, its image in the minds of both whites and Negroes has shifted focus. From being a fellowship of comfort to its members and of accommodation to white society, the Negro church has now emerged as a prime training ground and staging area for protest and the fight for opportunity and freedom. Nowhere is this change more apparent than in the image of the Negro minister. Long the acknowledged leader of the colored community, the Negro minister began to lose prestige and authority rather rapidly as his own education was comparatively neglected while an educated Negro leadership of lawyers, doctors, and civil rights leaders began to appear. These new leaders often used the churches as channels through which to reach their constituency.

But the general picture of the Negro minister as of twenty years ago has drastically altered. Under the leadership especially of Martin Luther King, Jr. (Ph.D., Boston University) and other well-educated, fearless, clerical champions of the rights of their people, *the Negro ministry is on the ascendancy,* in the eyes of most Americans, though there are still those who deplore that fact, for various reasons.

There can be no doubt of the leadership given by Negro ministers and churches to the fight for civil rights in the last eight years—as evidenced in the Montgomery bus strike, the desegregation of schools, inspiration and training for the sit-ins, and demonstrations in the streets in the summer and fall of 1963. Most of these marches began in churches, though it would not be fair to say that the churches began them all or that all churches approved. Other protest organizations have played their respective and important parts. But Negro preachers and churches are building new edifices on Freedom Road, sometimes at the cost of dynamite for the old ones.

ALL-NEGRO CHURCH PROBLEMS.   At the same time, *the all-Negro* church continues to have its problems. Innumerable divisions in the church create confusion to rival that of the white churches; there are about twenty-five denominations and uncounted smaller sects and coteries, organized in many instances around a single leader and often meeting in store fronts or residences. The average congregation is much smaller than in white churches and much less capable of supporting an adequate program or ministry; most urban centers have two or three times as many churches as are needed. Most serious of all, Negro churches are reported to be losing their young people faster than white churches though this may now be less true than a dozen years ago; and they are likely to lose them faster still as these young people find themselves more largely integrated in other aspects of American life but still segregated in the churches. Add to all these difficulties the problem the church has faced in trying to follow the vast migration of Negroes in recent years and to adapt to impersonal, overcrowded urban conditions of life, and the prospects for the Negro church are seen to be rather uncertain.

The pattern of segregation in the churches continues to be reinforced, however, by other factors. The most important of these is *residential segregation.*

Through one device or another most minority groups are still concentrated in particular areas of a city, especially in the inner city area surrounding the central business section. This area was formerly inhabited for the most part in many cities by immigrant groups, who were largely Roman Catholic in affiliation and who have moved in large numbers to the suburbs as their economic situation improved. The inner city has now been taken over in a number of places by Negroes, whose Southern religious background makes them overwhelmingly Protestant in religious preferences. Wherever it may be located, there is generally a "Negro section," North or South.

Residential concentration of minority groups helps to explain the continuation of segregated churches. Churches located in so-called "transitional zones," where a new group (often Negro) is moving in and the old settlers are moving out, have special opportunities to transcend race in their composition. For many years, the usual procedure was that of selling a church building formerly occupied by the retreating whites to a Negro congregation. The situation has changed markedly in the last decade: a great many white churches have refused to follow their members to the suburbs, choosing instead to remain where they were and attempt to minister to their new type of community. A large percentage of the mixed churches is to be found in situations of that kind. The old "downtown churches" may find a new source of constituents among the newcomers. The influence of boards of home missions has often been decisive in helping a church in an inner city or transitional zone to stand its ground and to minister effectively to the new residents of its area, instead of yielding to the temptation to sell the church building to Negroes and relocate. Many churches still follow the old pattern, but in a rapidly increasing number of instances mission grants and advice from home mission boards have encouraged declining churches to adapt their programs and replenish their constituencies from the new occupants of their changing neighborhoods. A great many mixed churches have resulted, especially in the larger cities.

INDIGENOUS DEFICIENCIES. Economic factors also influence racial segregation in the churches. As Myrdal and other observers have pointed out, many Negro churches are very much like certain white churches of lower income groups in important respects, such as equipment, type of service, tendencies to emotionalism, a less-educated ministry, and the like. The official boards of Negro churches are often made up of minor supervisors, janitors, clerks, cooks, and other persons of low income and limited opportunity. On the other hand, the corresponding white churches have frequently been more jealous of their racial purity than have more affluent congregations. The churches have had little success in bridging the gulf between social classes, especially in the cities; most congregations are composed predominantly of people from the same general level. When this problem is added to that of racial stratification, the difficulties of integration are compounded. It may be that the churches will not be able to overcome racial segregation significantly in their lives until they learn also to break down class lines.

Congeniality appears to be valued more in a congregation than common fidelity to a single Lord. In many Protestant parishes the semisocial functions require more time from members than the worship services. Under these circumstances there is a great temptation to use such social criteria as race or class as standards of acceptability for membership.

What about the integration of the churches at this present time? It has been said that "eleven o'clock on Sunday morning is the most segregated hour in the week." One could qualify that conclusion: eleven o'clock on *Saturday night is even more segregated* for the country club set, and other purely social clubs, white or Negro, are in general more completely uniracial than are the churches.

Its record indicates clearly, however, that the church is the most segregated major institution in American society. It has lagged behind the Supreme Court as the conscience of the nation on questions of race; it has fallen far behind trade unions, factories, schools, department stores, athletic gatherings, and most other major areas of human association as far as the achievement of integration in its own life is concerned.

Statistics indicate that less than two percent of the white congregations had Negro members at the end of World War II and that probably considerably less than one percent of the Negroes in American Protestantism were included in white congregations. The mixture of racial groups in a congregation, where it occurred, hardly deserved that description in most instances; typically it involved the membership of three or four Negroes in an overwhelmingly "white" church, generally in a rural area or small town with a Negro community too small to be of public importance or to form, or be segregated into, a church of its own.

The overall statistical picture of segregation in the churches has not changed very much in the last twenty years. The size of the entire Negro community in America had grown to about nineteen million by 1960. Figures pertaining usually to the year 1960 show a total membership in Negro denominations of 10,000,000 with at least 59 percent of this total accounted for by the five largest bodies. A reasonably reliable estimate would put the number of Negro members of predominantly white denominations at slightly more than 600,000 with about 375,000 in the Methodist Church alone. It is still true, as in 1954, that 94 percent of the Negro Protestants are in Negro denominations, having few religious relationships with other Protestants.

Though the Roman Catholic Church played a comparatively small part in the enlistment of the Negro American until recent decades, except in the Gulf states, this analysis might also be expanded to include the role of that church. Negroes comprise a very small fraction of its membership—about 620,000 or approximately one-and-a-half percent—and the church is reported to be making a very special effort to win Negro converts. There has been a very large increase in the number of Negro priests in recent years; only twenty-six were in active service in the United States in 1949, but by 1957 there were at least forty-two.

The official position of the Roman Catholic Church has supported integration from the beginning. This position derives in part from the church's conception of itself as the Universal church—or, as Father John LaFarge put it, "the church of the human race."

NON-CHRISTIAN ORIGIN OF SEGREGATION.   The fact remains that segregation is still overwhelmingly the pattern that prevails in local churches, Protestant and Catholic. Very few, if any, churches have a legal or formal policy to require it; Negroes generally assume that they would not be welcome in most white churches, and whites generally take it for granted that Negroes will stay away.

Now, in conclusion, some theological considerations. Can the church, white or Negro, really be the church and be true to its Lord so long as it is split asunder on racial grounds? The central message of the Gospel, later made even more specific by the eloquence of St. Paul, is that Jesus Christ, through his life on earth, his death for all men, and his resurrection as the hope of all men, has brought reconciliation between man and God and man and man. Those who accept him as their Lord live in a new dimension in which love and unity are regnant, though still tainted by sin. This unity is not only spiritual; it pervades life in all its relationships, and it seeks ever to remake society.

Out of faith in the life, death, and resurrection of Jesus Christ came a new community composed of many peoples. Men "from every nation under heaven" (fifteen are named in the second chapter of Acts) were present at Pentecost, generally considered to have been the beginning of the larger Christian community, the birthday of the Church. Each was speaking his own tongue, but in a common bond of unity in Christ.

Through many vicissitudes this community swept out across the world, gathering up Greek and Jew, slave and free man, barbarian, scythian, Roman, Egyptian, Asian, African, European, American. For nearly eighteen centuries, the church knew little discrimination within its life; not until white men began to overrun the world did this new division among men by races come to pass; not until the nineteenth century did elaborate justifications of it begin to appear, and these originated for the most part outside the churches. In our time in certain churches—still a small minority, to be found for the most part in the United States, and the Union of South Africa—these pagan theories have largely supplanted the ancient Christian doctrines of brotherhood and have perverted the life of the churches themselves, so that they use these theories even to interpret the Bible.

For the most of its history the Christian church has followed within its own life the Biblical implications for the question of race. Racial discrimination in the church, as in the world, is largely a phenomenon of the last two centuries. In this matter the church has adapted its practices in several regions, to those of the surrounding society. But it should also be remembered that *most of the Christian churches in the world still refuse to practice discrimination or segregation.* If the church as a whole had capitulated it would have lost its integrity and denied its Lord. Whatever the regional defections may be, it is the very nature of the Church to be an inclusive and integrated community of the faithful and most major religious bodies have been saying so for the last twenty years.

3 THE PRESENT STATUS OF THE SOCIOLOGY
OF RELIGION

J. Milton Yinger

INTRODUCTION   The two previous articles have been
primarily descriptive. The sociological student of religion, however,
passes beyond these descriptive levels. Basically, he participates in
an empirical study of religious phenomena within the framework
of the scientific method (*see* Introduction, Part I; also Articles 4,
5). As a result Sociology of Religion—or at least certain aspects of
the field—may rightly be classed as a branch of scientific sociology.
A sociologist of religion studies the processes by which religion enters into human interaction and how the interaction of men influences religion.

Religious research is difficult because most persons are not
objective by nature. Even the scientist possesses values which may
influence the formation of hypotheses and the interpretation of
evidence. In the area of religion each person is his own expert.
Each individual generally possesses some commitment, is either for
or against a religious group, which position he defends with vigor.
And yet the basic assumption present in the scientific method is
that the scientist is able to operate outside and above personal bias.
While each person, including the sociologist, may hold to certain
values, the scientific investigator is expected to set aside his values
in order to bring about a sound empirical investigation of the object of study. Although perfect objectivity remains the goal of
science, it generally fails to become the reality. For this reason,
Milton Yinger notes that a competent religious researcher needs a
rare combination of theoretical and empirical skills and interests
which allow him to be both scientific and knowledgeable regard-

Abridged and reprinted from the *Journal of Religion*, Volume 31 (July, 1951), pp.
194-210, by permission of the University of Chicago Press.

J. MILTON YINGER is Professor of Sociology at Oberlin College.

ing religious groups and practices. Science may involve a study of values, but it is not a method for creating values. Because so much of religion is personal, unconscious, and dependent upon faith, the task of measurement and investigation of religion is exceedingly complex.

A further problem is the difficulty of gaining accurate and meaningful statistics concerning religious groups (see Petersen, Article 6). Few groups desire to undergo the scrutiny assumed in the scientific approach to religion. Most compile data which is analytically superficial and inaccurate. Therefore, answers to problems of relationships between religious differentiation and social differentiation, religious processes and processes of social change, the church and state, religion and morals, religion and personality needs, and religious commitment and doctrinal belief, are not readily available or completely accurate when given. The sociological study of religion, as of other institutions, requires hypotheses which are testable by social experience and knowledge.

Although there are those who continue the fifty-year-old argument of the incompatibility of science and religion, the seeming chasm between dogma and research is not as large as some scientific researchers and theological dogmaticians make it out to be. Sociology does not seek to be dogmatic; to do so would be to deny the basic assumption: scientific empiricism. Religion does not attempt to be scientific although religion and religious groups may learn much from objective research. Neither may indefinitely remain indifferent or antagonistic to the other. The dialogue between representatives of religion and science will continue in an increasingly cooperative spirit in the coming decades. In the next twenty years significant studies, probably not as theoretical as Weber's study of Protestantism and capitalism, but more substantive than the ad hoc formulations published in current journals, will appear in the field. Tensions, however, may be expected to continue between the dogmatic religionist and the social scientist, for one holds rigid values which the other attempts to be value-free.

———

THE SOCIOLOGY OF RELIGION is a field of great importance in which many people have shown an active interest, an area of study in which many of the ingredients for sound scientific work are available, and yet a discipline in which relatively little of scientific sociological importance is being produced. After highly auspicious beginnings in the work of such men as Robertson Smith, Max Weber, Émile Durkheim, Georg Simmel, Ernst Troeltsch, and many others, it has, in the judgment of the present writer, failed to move very far in the direction of greater theoretical adequacy. It is the purpose of this paper to assess some of the resources available to the sociology of religion, to indicate a few of the advances that have been made in recent years, to try to explain some of the weaknesses, and to indicate some of the lines of development that seem to offer promise for future research.

Unfortunately, there are still important disagreements concerning the definition of the sociology of religion. This may be inevitable in a field which attracts the attention of students from many different disciplines—theology, history, philosophy, sociology—and which involves significant value perspectives. I shall offer my definition to indicate the subject matter of this paper: The sociology of religion is a branch of scientific sociology. It is not a marginal field between theology and sociology: religion is the datum and sociology the method of approach. It is nonvaluative, objective, and abstract. It studies empirical phenomena to try to isolate generalizations concerning the interconnections of religious behavior with other social behavior. If one defines sociology as the scientific study of those influences on behavior which flow from human interaction (not using the narrower "cultural" definition but including data that some writers prefer to assign to another science, social psychology), then the sociology of religion is the scientific study of all the ways in which the interaction of men influences religion—influences its origin, its doctrines, its practices, the types of groups which embody it, the kinds of leadership, etc. On the other hand, it is also the study of the ways in which religion enters into human interaction—how it influences the ways in which individuals and groups behave toward each other.

THE REQUISITES FOR A SOUND SOCIOLOGY OF RELIGION. The sociology of religion requires a group of integrated and testable propositions, harmonious with the larger theoretical schemes of general sociology. This demands that hypotheses be made entirely explicit and be posed in such a way that they can be tested by a constant flow of reliable and valid empirical work. Some of the ingredients for this kind of study are at hand; but the systematic interrelation of all the component parts is manifest in only a small minority of the studies with which I am familiar. In an analysis of the sociology of knowledge (a discipline which overlaps more or less—depending on how one defines "knowledge"—with the sociology of religion) Robert Merton calls attention to the contrast between the European and the American studies in the field. It is a contrast well deserving study, because it indicates clearly the need for bringing theoretical and empirical work together. European sociology of knowledge, Merton says, "belongs for the most part to the camp of global theorists, in which the breadth and significance of the problem justifies one's dedication to it, sometimes quite apart from the present possibility of materially advancing beyond ingenious speculations and impressionistic conclusions. By and large, the sociologists of knowledge have been among those raising high the banner which reads: 'We don't know that what we say is true, but it is at least significant.'" American students have been more interested in canvassing mass opinions. They have been concerned with getting representative samples of opinion, recorded on objectified scales. Their motto might be: "We don't know that what we say is particularly significant, but it is at least true."

This difference in approach influences the judgments of what are facts and data that can be useful for scientific study—with the European scholar, in most instances, ready to accept a wider range of material. If an author has high intellectual status, his impressions, Merton points out, are often taken for facts. If this is true in Mannheim's sociology of knowledge, it is certainly no less true in Joachim Wach's sociology of religion, where generalizations are frequently supported by reference to the writings of "the outstanding scholar" in the field. The same "tolerance" for somewhat questionable "facts" is also found in the work of Max Weber, despite his brilliant mastery of the logic of science. He built his theories of the relationship between religious ethics and economic behavior, for example, partly on his judgment that the nonreligious factors in China of the sixteenth and seventeenth centuries were as favorable to the rise of capitalism as were the nonreligious factors in western Europe. This judgment of an enormously complex theoretical problem was based on examination of the few score written records—with very little possibility for checking them for reliability and completeness. The present writer must confess—and thereby apply a little of sociology of knowledge to himself—that such research is insufficiently empirical for his American taste. The need, of course, in both fields, is to bring the theoretical and empirical emphases into close and fruitful interaction. That has happened all too rarely in the sociology of religion, and it may be helpful to try to discover the reasons. These two factors seem to be involved.

1. Competent research in the sociology of religion demands a combination of skills and interests that is not very common. The researcher must, in the first place, have a thoroughly adequate grasp of contemporary sociological theory and research methods. He must be entirely objective in his handling of the data of religion; yet he must be strongly interested in the material and deeply acquainted with it.

2. Despite the almost inexhaustible supply of data on primitive and civilized religions, on church history, on sectarian movements, and the vast supply of religious materials in written form—sermons, official publications of church bodies, etc.—there is really a scarcity of empirical material out of which to fashion adequate generalizations. It is very difficult to judge the reliability of much of the data.

Many of the data available for use by the sociologist of religion, moreover, are lacking in comparability. This greatly hinders a study that is trying to discover generalizations. A related problem is that data which were gathered without the guidance of explicit scientific concepts are often of limited usefulness for scientific purposes. Ideally, empirical materials are gathered in direct reference to testable hypotheses. Very few of the data with which sociologists of religion have been working satisfy this requirement.

SOME RESEARCH AREAS IN THE SOCIOLOGY OF RELIGION.
Without attempting to be exhaustive, we can perhaps approach our topic
most successfully by indicating some of the major theoretical problems faced
by the sociology of religion, noting some of the hypotheses that have been
suggested and some of the data relating to those hypotheses.

I. PROBLEM: In what way is religious differentiation related, as cause
and/or effect, to social differentiation? It is well known that in socially differentiated societies, the various secular groups tend to exhibit differences in doctrine, worship, and religious group structure. The membership of many religious groups is drawn largely from individuals of a particular social class or
race or of a given educational status.

> HYPOTHESIS: Religious beliefs as well as practices are profoundly
> affected by the special problems inhering in the social and economic
> status of mill workers. Their religion is intimately related to the everyday
> struggles and vicissitudes of an insecure life, and proves useful for in-
> terpretation and for succor. It "works" and "changes things." . . .
> Attempt at summary of the satisfactions he [the millworker] finds in his
> church points to economic influences even more clearly. In general terms,
> he derives two benefits: the organization of life, and the transvaluation
> of life. . . . Less exclusively than in rural areas, but more largely than
> in uptown districts, the church in the mill village is a community center;
> in the comparative absence of other social institutions, it is the focal
> point around which noneconomic life in the village largely revolves.
> Natural leaders among the workers find in it almost their only vehicle
> for expression of leadership. . . . But the worker also looks to his church
> to find transvaluation of life, which may take the form of reassurance or
> of escape, or both. By affirmation of values denied in the economic world,
> the church provides comfort and ultimate assurance; in its religious serv-
> ices it often affords escape temporarily from the economic and social situ-
> ation in which workaday life must be spent. The difficulties of life for the
> mill worker in this world help to explain the noteworthy emphasis on
> otherworldliness in his churches.[1]

A central thesis of this study is that social differentiation finds its counter-
part (not without complicating factors) in religious differentiation. A long
series of studies gives indication of the fruitfulness of this approach in the
sociology of religion. Pre-Reformation sects, the Reformation itself, the rise
of Quakerism and Methodism, the denomination-forming process in the United
States and Canada, and the religious groupings of minority groups have been
interpreted as, in part, religious expressions of secular conflicts and social distinctions. This can be understood partly in terms of different personality needs
and tendencies (see Problem 5 below), but in part it reflects the way in which

[1] Liston Pope, *Millhands and Preachers* (New Haven: Yale University Press, 1942),
pp. 86-88.

secular differences invade the religious sphere to get support for secular battles.

Religious institutions also reflect, of course, the place of those who are low in status and power. Sectarian groups probably develop an escapist doctrine more often than a doctrine which directly challenges the secular powers. One of the largest gaps in this area of the sociology of religion is the determination of the conditions under which a religious group will (a) accept the secular order, (b) "withdraw" from society by devaluating it, and (c) challenge and attack the secular power structure. Such variables as the nature of the religious tradition out of which the sectarian movement grows, the chance of success in the secular world, the presence or absence of more strictly secular institutions trying to change the *status quo,* the tendencies of the leadership, the availability of governmental channels for registering protests, etc., would have to be considered.

The opposite side of the hypothesis we have been discussing has been examined much less often. How does religious differentiation, once established affect social differentiation? Does it tend to fix social divisions, or does it only reflect them? We know that, when some of the social factors for the religious division have disappeared, there tends to be a reunion (e.g., the Methodist movement, 1840-1940). But what consequences grow out of the lag? Does the experience of being brought up in close touch with a "lower-class" church tend to give one values, levels of aspiration, and motives that fix one in lower-class status? It was once thought that the sect-to-church transition disproved this; that, as John Wesley declared, the virtues that went along with religious fervor helped one to climb the class ladder. Now some evidence casts doubt on this idea; the transition from sect to church may be characteristic of the institution only and not be indicative of what is happening to the status of individual members. If churches become middle class in values, doctrine, and ritual, lower-class members tend to drop out and to look for some other religious (or secular) expression more in keeping with their desires.

Finally, it should be observed, with regard to the hypothesis under discussion, that the role of religion in *reducing* social differentiation—in unifying a society—has often been discussed. This is central in the work of Durkheim and receives an interesting formulation in Wach's study, where he distinguishes between situations where religion and natural groups are coterminous and situations where specifically religious groups have developed. Again, the need is for careful specification of the *conditions under which* the unifying influences of religion are operative and those under which the differentiating influences are operative.

2. PROBLEM: How is religion related as cause and/or effect to the processes of social change? Propositions in the field range from vast generalizations—"religion is the opiate of the people," inhibiting social change, and its opposite, religion is "the clue to history," a force of central significance in the directing

of social change—to modest monographs, seeking to establish the role of religion in one specific setting.

HYPOTHESIS: The rise of Holiness and Pentecostal churches in the southeastern United States "is largely the natural product of the social disorganization and cultural conflict which have attended the over-rapid urbanward migration and concomitant urbanization of an intensely rural, and among other things, religiously fundamentalist population."[2] To put this in terms of a more general theoretical proposition, one might say: When a religiously fundamentalist group living in a society of free religious choice and activity migrate from a fairly isolated, stable, communal social structure into a mobile, associational situation, they will tend to join or create religious groups that help to re-establish a communal feeling, that declare unambiguous standards of behavior, that bolster the feeling of importance—very often by an otherworldly emphasis. Variables to control: Differing individual personality tendencies, the degree of communal and associational character of the two settings (this is a continuum, not a dichotomy), the proportion of the population of a community made up of migrants, the availability of alternative modes of adjustment (e.g. trade-unions), etc.

> HYPOTHESIS: In 1876 Protestantism presented a massive, almost unbroken front in its defense of the social *status quo*. Two decades later social criticism had penetrated deeply into each major church. Some of the most prominent Protestant leaders were calling for social reform; Christian radicals, not unheard, were demanding complete reorganization of society. The immediate cause of this important change lay neither in theological innovation nor in the world "climate of opinion" but in the resistless intrusion of social crisis, and particularly in a series of large-scale, violent labor conflicts.[3]

May's fine study is primarily historical in character and should not be criticized for not being sociological when that was not his intention. His hypotheses are partially "unself-conscious" and are not related to larger theoretical problems. His material, nevertheless, is of value to the sociologist of religion who is interested in social change. These methodological difficulties would need study: Is his sampling of religious views adequate, both in coverage of written records and in distinguishing between religious opinions that were written and the far larger number that were only spoken, or perhaps silently held? His generalizations seem to me to be highly probably but, granted the methodology, far from proved.

HYPOTHESIS: "The religious valuation of restless, continuous, systematic work in a worldly calling, as the highest means to asceticism, and at the same

[2] John B. Holt, "Holiness Religion: Cultural Shock and Social Reorganization," *American Sociological Review*, V (October, 1940), 740.
[3] Henry F. May, *Protestant Churches and Industrial America* (New York: Harper & Row, 1949), p. 91.

time the surest and most evident proof of rebirth and genuine faith, must have been the most powerful conceivable lever for the expansion of that attitude toward life which we have here called the spirit of capitalism."[4] This is perhaps the best-known hypothesis in the sociology of religion. It expresses Weber's belief that Protestant asceticism, particularly Calvinism, was highly influential in the appearance of the capitalist spirit. His data are not only the writings and activities of churchmen but the high correlation between Calvinism and the particular kind of capitalism he is talking about. His essay, as an emphasis on the *interaction* between ideas and "material conditions," is in harmony with what most sociologists today would consider adequate theory. It is not, however, without serious errors of which the sociologist of religion needs to be fully aware. It shares, as we have seen, the difficulties of large-scale historical sociology—the problems of selectivity of material, the difficulty of checking reliability. Weber, in seeking to supplement one-sided materialistic theories, skipped over too lightly the way in which Calvin himself, trying to be effective in semicommercial Geneva, was partially shaped by emerging capitalism. A central problem in the sociology of knowledge and religion is that of the "audience": the group to whom one addresses himself, in speaking or writing, influences, by its values and needs, the problems one sets for himself, the emphases, even the criteria of validity. In other words, spoken and written ideas that survive are not so "immanent" (a very slippery concept in Weber's work) as he indicated, for they go through a process of winnowing strongly influenced by the "audience" involved. Weber also failed to take sufficient theoretical account of the importance of the great changes in Calvinism over a period of two or three centuries. His own concept of "selective affinity" puts a different light on the causal relationship of Calvinism to the spirit of capitalism. This is not to deny, however, that religious ideas have a measure of independent development (their own inner dialectic, as Troeltsch would say), and that, once established, they influence the activities of those who hold them. Wherever Calvinism's emphasis on "this-worldly asceticism" came from, it seems highly likely that a child brought up believing in it, socialized to its values, would, if he as an adult became involved in capitalist economic activities, approach them in a different spirit from one whose value orientations were of a different order, toward, for example, sharp denial of the importance of success in this world, or away from asceticism. Weber's theory gets, therefore, when properly qualified, if not empirical proof, at least a measure of support from its harmony with other theoretical work that is capable of empirical testing. Perhaps the major contribution of Weber's hypothesis, however, is the stimulation it gave to further work. Controversy has surrounded it from the beginning—both because of value questions involved and because of the great difficulties of empirical tests.

It is very difficult to isolate a purely religious influence in social change,

---

[4] Max Weber, *The Protestant Ethic and the Spirit of Capitalism*, trans. Talcott Parsons (London: G. Allen, 1930), p. 172.

because religious institutions and movements contain many nonreligious elements (*see* Problem 1), and secular institutions and movements are often led by persons with religiously derived interests and supported by persons with religiously influenced values.

3. PROBLEM: What are the causes and/or effects of various kinds of relationship between religious institutions and the state? There is a vast literature on the question of "church and state," most of it historical in approach, and much of it polemical. It may be that the problem is too large for adequate scientific work. Certainly full attention must be paid to the many different kinds of religious groups and kinds of states involved—one cannot talk about *the* relationship between church and state. The consequences of connection between church and state in England (Established church), Spain (Catholic church), Russia (Re-established church), and Japan (pre-war Shinto) are clearly of very different orders.

HYPOTHESIS: In a society with a highly centralized state power structure, the religious groups tend to be subservient to the state whether or not there exists a formal institutional connection; or, in *times* when the state becomes the central locus of power (e.g., during a war), church and state become highly interrelated. Whether or not a church is "established" is less significant—in terms of its place in society—than the structure of power of the society within which it works. In societies where, from a democratic point of view, it is most desirable to separate church and state, it is least possible to do so. In scientific and in value terms, the significant relationships between church and state are not only the formal ones, the ones easily described by institutional structure, but also the pervasive, informal interaction.

4. PROBLEM: What are the kinds of relationship to be found between religion and morals? This is an area where it is peculiarly difficult to state hypotheses in a way that permits testing. One group of writers holds that in its earlier stages, and in its origins, religion had no connection with morals. The common element in several different theories, among which I shall not take time to draw distinctions, is that religion (in the first instance) is a product of insecurity and fear. Buffeted by natural forces, plagued by illness, dismayed by the fact of death, the human mind created a "compensation ideology" to reduce the insecurity. Only later, this theory goes on to state, do moral elements become associated with religion. The development of the Hebrew conception of God from a tribal deity of vengeance and wrath to a universal God of love is perhaps the classic illustration of this idea. The precise ways in which the experiences of the Jews affected this development are questions of great interest—but of even greater difficulty. The hypothesis that defeat, bondage, and culture contact were important factors is plausible. At any rate, by the eighth century we see an ethical God who cared not for gifts but for repentance.

Another theory holds that religion and morals must be seen as emerging together—that beliefs and cultic practices are, in essence, the reflection of community solidarity and moral unity. Religion is a kind of projection, on a cosmic screen, of the tribal organization and the moral order.

Whatever theory may, ultimately, seem most adequate to describe the origin of the relationship between religion and morals, the effects of their relationship deserve careful study.

HYPOTHESIS: In a highly dynamic society, the belief that morality is a fixed pattern of behavior "revealed" to man as one aspect of his religion, and in an important sense, therefore, subservient to his religion, is a belief that makes moral behavior *less* likely.

My reasoning, if such it be, in suggesting such a heretical hypothesis and in believing that it might have some research value is somewhat as follows: The idea that morality is a fixed item of religious belief attaches a static quality to morality and religion that weakens them both, in a rapidly changing society. One dare not challenge outmoded religious beliefs for fear of weakening the moral code which those beliefs supposedly bolster; and, on the other hand, one dare not question an inadequate moral code because it seems to be an attack upon religious absolutes. In the modern world, where the need for continually revising some aspects of both morality and religion is great, this rigidity weakens both. In the field of morals there has been a great lag in developing a code of behavior that is appropriate to the urban, mobile, secondary world in which so many of us live. To a significant degree we literally do not know how to behave. We are equipped with standards of morality which help us to adjust to the face-to-face contacts of a communal relationship (the kind of setting in which our moral code developed) but which leave us much less well instructed about the moral problems that arise from the fact that we deal with strangers more than with friends, that we affect hundreds whom we do not know for every one that we do know. A man may support the church, love his wife, befriend his neighbors, and then manufacture a patent drug which cheats millions and perhaps injures thousands. And our society does not know whether to call him a smart businessman or a scoundrel. An effective moral code for modern urban life would tell a man, not how he ought to act toward neighbors alone, but also how he ought to act toward strangers, toward people whom he will never see or know about, but whom he will affect in this highly interdependent and specialized society. It would indicate the important role of social institutions and other social mechanisms in affecting social interaction, instead of emphasizing that a "right heart" alone is necessary to moral behavior.

The hypothesis also suggests that the assumption that moral standards are simply one phase of revealed religion also has important consequences for religion, for such an assumption helps to prevent the continuing development of religious thought which is necessary if religion is to remain vital. There is a constant need for the shuffling-off of accidental and outworn religious beliefs and practices—the traditional elements—in order that the intrinsic elements may flourish.

Another aspect of my reasoning in posing the hypothesis stated above is concerned with the way in which religious sanctions have been used by powerful people to hold or increase their power. The ruling classes of all societies have discovered that, when correctly used, religion can be a very effective weapon for them. Not only could supernatural sanctions be used to enforce the moral code, but the same halo of sanctity could serve to give protection to any power structure, provided only that it had the power to control the definitions of "the moral" and "the good."

5. PROBLEM: What are the personality functions of religion; in what various ways does religion become connected with, express, and influence the tensions, fears, anxieties, hopes, and aspirations of individuals?

Social psychology is furnishing us with more and more valid material, both empirical studies and theoretical formulations, on which to build analyses of religious behavior. In addition, there is a noticeable trend toward integration of research and theory in cultural anthropology, sociology, and social psychology that promises a much more adequate theoretical framework for religious studies.

HYPOTHESIS: The origins of religion and changes in religion can partly be understood as efforts to adjust to fear and insecurity. A corollary: When a satisfactory "definition" of critical life-events is disturbed or destroyed, many religious movements will arise to try to reestablish a sense of security (and, one might add, many nonreligious movements, sharing elements in common with religion, will also arise to try to solve the same problems). This hypothesis, expressed in many ways, has been stated over and over again. It is probably the explanation most frequently used by anthropologists to account for the phenomena of primitive religions and is scarcely less frequently applied to contemporary religious movements.

Malinowski found that two closely related tribes among the Trobriand Islanders had very different approaches to their common task of fishing. One tribe fished largely in inland waters and lagoons; they were seldom unsuccessful and rarely endangered. They pursued their work with a matter-of-factness that had little room for precautionary ritual. The other tribe fished in the open sea. Their catch was much less certain and the hazards far greater. Around their work they had woven an elaborate web of rite and ceremony whose function it was to rid them of insecurity, to placate the unknown forces that constantly threatened their success. It seems a plausible explanation that their institutionalized religious forms were related to their economic and personal fears and anxieties.

When Europeans overran and destroyed much of the culture of the

American Indians, enormous problems of social disorganization and personal confusion inevitably arose. The average Indian with his culture discredited, his leader made helpless, his old mode of life made impossible, became thoroughly disorganized. Efforts to "Christianize" him often produced a strange blend of pseudo-Christianity which reflected his personal needs as well as the group struggle. In some accounts, Hiawatha, the famous Iroquois sachem, and Jesus, become blurred and blended into an Indian savior who will drive the white man from the continent. The Ghost Dance among the Plains Indians can be read almost as a running psychoanalysis of their fears and hatreds, clothed in religious terms. Before this simple comparison could be held to be a proof of the hypothesis, many other variables would have to be controlled—for example, degree of contact with the shamans or others who were teaching the new religious ideas, response of native leadership, congeniality of different cultures for this kind of religious expression, etc. Tentatively, however, the material at hand seems to support the hypothesis.

CONCLUSION. There is not time to discuss other equally significant problems in the sociology of religion. An adequate sociology of religion must study types of religious leadership—the processes of recruitment and training, relationship to the institutional structures, strategies of social action, etc. It might study the way in which specific religious doctrines (e.g., the concept of God) developed under varying social conditions. It would be interested in the phenomenon of religious toleration: under what kinds of conditions does it occur, or fail to occur—and with what results? Among these, as among the questions we have discussed, there is a wide range in the degree to which hypotheses can be framed in a manner capable of testing.

This brief review of some of the problems and some of the hypotheses that have grown from study of those problems in the sociology of religion may give us a general picture of the present status of the field. It also indicates the steps necessary for continued improvement in our understanding of religious phenomena: Most studies demand a far more explicit awareness of the problems of scientific methodology; the integration of the work of those who have been primarily concerned with theoretical formulations and those largely interested in gathering data must be much more thorough; and the sociology of religion must be related more closely to larger theoretical schemes, for example, personality theory, the sociology of knowledge, theories of culture and culture change, and the sociology of conflict.

If one were to assess the resources available to the sociology of religion today, they might be listed somewhat as follows:

1. Some ambitious and often useful large-scale theoretical propositions. These have perhaps been too ambitious, based on too few data. We would be better served by "theories of the middle range."

2. A great deal of church and other religious history, often containing

interpretative insights which, if rephrased, could serve as hypotheses. We have noted above the difficulties involved in building an empirical science on historical materials.

3. A rather large accumulation of facts in addition to church history—data on church membership, groups from which membership is drawn, denominational differences, recent social movements. Since much of this was gathered without reference to specific theoretical problems, it is often less useful than it might be.

4. Extensive anthropological material, often accompanied by theoretical propositions and interpretations. These have seldom been posed in testable hypotheses but are rich in guiding insights.

5. A few specifically sociological concepts and typologies that have proved useful in interpreting limited ranges of data.

6. An emerging general theory of personality, society, and culture that, when applied to the sociology of religion, sharpens its hypotheses and assists in organizing the data.

7. And, finally, one must add, we have some studies that make rather full use of the above—and other—resources to indicate the possibility, and indeed, the great importance, of a thoroughly adequate sociology of religion.

4 MEASURING RELIGION: TWO METHODS COMPARED

Glenn M. Vernon

INTRODUCTION   Is it possible to distinguish between
the superficially and deeply committed religious person by using
sociological techniques? The present social tendency to be *for religion* but to remain *above* (i.e. outside of) *religion*, as Gerhard
Lenski and Will Herberg suggest (*see* Winter, Article 5), com-
pounds the question. The author observed during a visit to Denmark in 1953 that fewer than forty persons from a congregation of
3,000 were present at the Sunday morning service. When asked
about the lack of attendance, a prominent member replied: "Do
not be taken back by the Sunday attendance; people do not worship very often, but they are deeply religious and apply religious
principle to daily life. . . ." Here is the issue: How *does* one
measure personal religiousness? Does church attendance indicate
religiosity? Do contributions? Do actions in daily life? Does personal faith?

Variations in perception may exist among (a) what the person
himself believes, (b) what the person believes others believe, and
(c) what the person believes others want him to believe. Each of
these dimensions confuse and frustrate the attempts of social science researchers to measure personal religiosity and religious practice. Because standards of religious expectation are no longer absolute, what seems to be a high degree of dedication to one person
may be a minimal standard to another. Data collected from persons
who perceive their religiousness differentially reduce data reliability.

Abridged and reprinted from *The Review of Religious Research*, Volume 3, Number 4,
Copyright 1962 by the Religious Research Association, Inc.

GLENN VERNON is Head of the Department and Professor of Sociology and Anthropology
at the University of Maine.

The measurement of religious beliefs and group tendencies may take several forms. Common devices and techniques used in the scientific approach to religion include simple or systematic participation, written questionnaires, personal interviews, scaling techniques, psychological measurements and testing, population analysis, psychoanalysis and introspection. Each of these approaches lends itself in greater or lesser degree to the indirect or direct procedure as described by Vernon in the following article.

But the issue still remains. How objective can social science really be? We know that the methodology put into play will clearly affect the observations made by the researcher. The theoretical and hypothetical assumptions formed at the outset of the investigation exert a profound effect upon the final conclusions. Winter's analysis in the next article makes this clear. Is it possible for the observer to be free of personal bias or individual error? Even the scientific method involves a certain bias in its own right, an assumption that the scientific approach will yield the most valid understanding.

Meanwhile religion does not presume a scientific basis. The religious person generally makes only a limited pretense of rationally understanding his own religious faith. Therefore, the full implications and generalizations about current religious practice remain dubious, even though often predictable, to the social scientist.

ANYONE WHO attempts to do any extensive research in the area of religion sooner or later runs up against the problem of measuring religion and the many difficulties involved therein. Even such an apparently simple project as counting the members of different religious groups poses difficult problems, centered in part around the question as to just what is a "member." Efforts to measure religious *behavior* of one type or another run into complex problems. Paying attention to church attendance figures, for instance, raises questions as to whether church attendance of different individuals and/or groups means the same thing.

If one attempts to measure some of the "deeper" aspects of what has been called religiosity, the problems multiply tremendously. Not much effort has been made along this line. The majority of research attempting to relate religious factors to other social factors has concentrated on such measures as membership, preference, and attendance.

There is also the problem of techniques to be used in any measuring efforts. Some feel that making distinctions of a religious nature should primarily involve such procedures as "insight," "inspiration," "vision," and "supernatural guidance." Certainly religious leaders of one type or another are frequently called upon to differentiate between different types of members, such as those to whom baptism should be given and those to whom it should be refused;

those who should teach a Sunday school class and those not "worthy" to teach such a class; and members in good standing and those to be disfellowshipped. Exactly what is involved in the process of coming to such decisions would seem to be essentially an unanswered question at the moment. Many of those who make such distinctions would most likely indicate a belief that religious phenomena are essentially incapable of empirical, scientific measurement.

The limited research which will be discussed in this article has permitted the comparison of two different measures of religiosity, which we might call the direct and indirect. In the direct method the researcher follows the standardized procedure of directly asking the respondent to indicate degree of religiousness. In the research here considered, the following direct questions were utilized:

1. How important is religion in your day-to-day living?
2. How would you rate your feelings toward religion?

In such questions the researcher sensitizes the respondent to the religious area and asks for a direct answer pertaining thereto.

Another more indirect method of getting at religiosity is to utilize a research instrument which permits the respondent to voluntarily produce his own measure. One such instrument is the Twenty Statements Test (TST), which asks the respondents: "In the space provided below please give twenty different statements in answer to the question, 'Who Am I?' Give these answers as if you were giving them to yourself, not somebody else. Write fairly rapidly, for the time is limited." Following these instructions are twenty numbered blank lines. The test is administered in an eight-minute period. The instructions given include no clues as to what sort of content should be included in the answers. The respondents are told only to follow the instructions on the sheet of paper, without asking questions or communicating with anyone else about it.

The responses to the TST can be analyzed in several different ways. One type of content analysis is to pay attention to the answers which serve to identify particular types of self-identification, such as occupational, familial, educational, or religious identifications. Identifications of a religious nature, thus, are one of the types of self-identifications to which one can pay attention. Religious identifications include such statements as:

I am a Christian
I am a Sunday School teacher
I attend church regularly
I am a Presbyterian
I am religiously inclined
I don't live up to the teachings of my church
I go to church regularly
I am an immortal soul

I am a child of God

I work in the church

Since the attention of the respondents is in no way specifically directed to the religious dimension of his self-conceptions it would be logical to assume that what the respondents write on the TST is an expression of identifications important to the *respondent*, not the *investigator*. It is logical to assume that respondents for whom religious identifications are important, would voluntarily provide such identifications somewhere among the twenty statements.

Content analysis of the answers provided by the respondents then permits one to divide respondents into two broad categories:

1. Those who make one or more religious identifications.
2. Those who make no religious identifications.

More precise measures can be obtained for group one, by paying attention to the order in which these religious responses occur among the twenty statements. Presumably, religion is more salient or important for those who provide such identifications among the first five answers, than those who do so among the last five answers.

Further refinement can also be provided by distinguishing between those who make evaluative and nonevaluative identifications. Within the nonevaluative identifications would fall role identifications, such as, "I am a Baptist," and "I attend church regularly." Under the evaluative heading would fall statements which identify the individual or his behavior patterns in terms of goodness or badness. The evaluative category then can be further subdivided into favorable or unfavorable items. From the nature of the research instrument, it is clear that the respondent provides his own definitions as to what is good and what is bad.

Here then we have identified two different methods of getting at the religious component of behavior—the direct and the indirect. It is logical to hypothesize that those who identify themselves religiously on the TST would also provide high measures of religiousness on the direct questions, and conversely, those who do not identify themselves religiously on TST would indicate low religiosity on direct type questions.

Data collected in a study of college students permit a comparison of these two methods. The following analysis stems from data collected from 178 students enrolled in sociology classes at a Michigan university. Of these 178 students, 137 were on-campus students, at levels from freshman through graduate. Twenty-nine were from an off-campus center, with about half of these being older, more mature students than the on-campus group, many of them being teachers who were acquiring additional college credits. The sample also included twelve respondents who made up a noncredit course in an industrial center. Questionnaires were administered during regular class periods. The TST was administered first, so that other questions about religion would not sensitize the students to the religious area.

It is obvious, then, that this universe of study is not representative of any larger group, and any generalizations from this data with reference to specific groups would be highly tenuous. However, the study does permit us to compare different types of measures of religiosity, and it is with this aspect that we are most concerned here. Future studies might relate these findings to specific groups.

Let us turn our attention now to a comparison of the results obtained by these two methods, as shown in Table 4-1 and Table 4-2.

TABLE 4-1   Number and percent of respondents providing predetermined responses.

How important is religion in your day-to-day living?	Number	Percent	Cumulative Percent
Of great importance	70	39.3	39.3
Of moderate importance	82	46.0	85.3
Of slight importance	15	8.5	93.8
Of very slight importance	7	3.9	97.7
Of no importance	4	2.2	99.9
	178		
How would you rate your feelings toward religion?			
Strongly favorable to religion	106	59.9	59.9
Moderately favorable to religion	53	29.9	89.8
Slightly favorable to religion	7	3.9	93.7
Not religious but not opposed to religion	9	5.1	98.8
Slightly opposed to religion	1	0.6	99.4
Moderately opposed to religion	1	0.6	100
Strongly opposed to religion	0		
	177		

TABLE 4-2   Number and percent of respondents providing religious identifications on TST.

	Number	Percent
Providing Religious Identification	128	72
Providing No Religious Identification	50	28

With reference to the direct questions it is obvious that a high percentage of respondents fall in the religiously favorable categories. For instance, 85 percent indicate that religion is of moderate or great importance in their day-to-day living. Only four of the 178 respondents (.02 percent) indicate that religion is of no importance to them, whereas 22 or 12 percent indicate slight or very slight importance.

Sixty percent indicate that they are strongly favorable to religion and a

full 90 percent of the group are moderately or strongly favorable toward religion. None was strongly opposed and only two individuals were slightly or
moderately opposed.

On the TST of the 178 respondents 128, or 72 percent, made some sort
of religious identification.

In comparing these results it is clear that more people express favorable
attitudes toward religion than identify themselves in terms of religion on the
TST. Thirteen percent more individuals say that religion is of great or moderate importance to them in their day-to-day living than identify themselves
religiously on the TST. And 19 percent more individuals express strongly or
moderately favorable feelings toward religion than identify themselves religiously on the TST.

In general, then, it is clear that more of the respondents are willing to
provide positive answers on religion in response to direct questioning than will
voluntarily or spontaneously produce religious identifications when asked to describe themselves.

It was further found that there is a lack of association between responses
to the direct-question type and the self-identification material. In no case was
there a statistically significant association between mention of religion on the
TST and responses made to the check-list items. This was due to the fact that
regardless of whether or not individuals identified themselves religiously on
the TST, they displayed highly favorable "public" attitudes toward religion.
For example there were fifty respondents, or 28 percent of the total sample of
respondents, who failed to mention religion in the course of their twenty self-
identifying statements. However, 78 percent of these same individuals indicated on the check-list item dealing with the importance of religion, that religion was either of great or of moderate importance in their day-to-day living.
It is easy to understand why persons who define themselves in religious terms
would feel that religion is of considerable importance in their day-to-day living. What is difficult to understand is why three-fourths of the sample who
failed to make religious self-identifications also indicate religion is of considerable importance in their day-to-day living.

The explanation of such findings is not easy, especially at the empirical
level. One thing is clear. That is, that the TST and the check-list items with
respect to religion produce quite different answers.

This finding might be explained by hypothesizing that there is a widespread practice in our society to define religion as being necessary, good, and
desirable. If this is so, it might then follow that in order to maintain one's
standing in society it would be important to indicate when necessary, favor-
ability toward religion, or at least no opposition to it. In other words, favorabil-
ity toward religion might be one requisite of being a good American, even
though those making such definitions are not particularly religious themselves.

An almost certain way of making oneself suspect of everything ranging
from incompetence to Communism is to declare himself against religion. This

is tantamount to saying, "I am for sin, degradation, and the decline of our society." Yet it appears that it is enough to be for religion without being religious.

Even though the Bible continues to be a best seller, 53 percent of our population when asked to name the first four Gospels could not even name one of them. We seem to be buying, but not reading the Bible. When thirty outstanding Americans were asked not long ago to rate the hundred most significant events in history, Christ's birth and crucifixion was listed in 14th place, in a tie with the discovery of the X-ray and the Wright brothers' first plane flight. And even though Billy Graham feels he has accomplished a great deal for the crowds who publicly thronged to hear him, a follow-up study found little if any change in the individuals attending his services.

Maybe appearing to be religious is the thing which is important to many Americans. Regardless of whether or not those findings and hypotheses stand up under more systematic and extensive research, there is an important methodological point emphasized by these results. The point is that the nature of the instruments of observation have a great deal to do with the results which are obtained. Considerably different findings resulted from the two instruments used herein. Careless interpretation could have resulted in quite erroneous and contradictory "findings."

It should be emphasized that neither of these two techniques for eliciting information is "naturally" and absolutely superior to the other. The specific kind of information sought is the determinant of which is more usable.

This research has at least provided enough evidence to indicate the desirability of further research of the association between "public" and "private" religiosity, or between direct and indirect methods of measuring religiosity.

5 METHODOLOGICAL REFLECTIONS ON "THE RELIGIOUS FACTOR"

Gibson Winter

INTRODUCTION   As we have already pointed out, social scientists attempt to study religion within the framework of the scientific method. Although procedures vary, five tasks are agreed upon. First, the scientist stipulates the problem for investigation and refines concepts regarding the phenomena to be studied. Second, he formulates hypotheses concerning the problem which he intends to illumine, based upon previous research and information. Third, he gathers the data concerning the problem, using the appropriate tools (e.g. interview, questionnaire). Fourth, he objectifies his data and evaluates his concepts and hypotheses, reaching conclusions on the basis of the evidence. Finally, the scientist verifies these results by retracing the steps involved in the original research design or by some other means.

One approach to religious analysis is typified in the following article by Gibson Winter in which he evaluates two of the most provocative books of our day: Will Herberg's *Protestant-Catholic-Jew* and Gerhard Lenski's *The Religious Factor*. Winter illustrates how different theoretical and methodological approaches may result in diverse conclusions (*see* Vernon, Article 4). Will Herberg based his writing upon a synthesis of scientific and nonscientific works published in the field, caring little for specific experimentation. Gerhard Lenski, on the other hand, conducted an empirical (experimental) test in Detroit of Weber's ideas expressed earlier in *The Protestant Ethic and the Spirit of Capitalism*, a classic study in sociology of religion. Notice how Winter proceeds to redefine

Abridged and reprinted from the *Journal for the Scientific Study of Religion*, Vol. 2, No. 1 (Fall, 1962), pp. 53-63, by permission of the author and editors.

GIBSON WINTER is Professor of Ethics and Society at the Divinity School, University of Chicago.

the nature of the problem, review data and concepts, identify differences, and reconcile, where possible, two seemingly contradictory viewpoints. Using a form of comparative analysis, Gibson Winter contrasts the theoretical and empirical contributions of the two men.

Scholarly criticism is basic to the advance of any science. The findings of each experiment must be open to further investigation if the scientific study of religion is to grow. The verification of research is possible only when each scientist identifies the procedure and order of steps undertaken in a study for reinvestigation by his peers. Verification implies the thorough review and reconsideration of the original problem, data, and concepts in order to determine the accuracy and meaning of the original research.

GERHARD LENSKI raised some serious questions about the role of religious pluralism in America in his study of religion in metropolitan Detroit.[1] This research added a new element to the understanding of religion in the United States. It also introduced some confusion into several dimensions of the question. Some clarification is needed on this study both in order to lift out an unremarked dimension and also in order to indicate the effects of interest and method in the organization of the data.

The unremarked factor in American religiousness emerges in reflection on Lenski's differences with Will Herberg's thesis about the overarching unity of American Religion.[2] Herberg claims that there are three legitimate ways of being American—Protestant, Catholic and Jew; thus, one's identity and sense of belonging within the larger American community takes specific form in religious communities. This tri-faith structure does not undermine American unity, for each of these faiths is estranged from its basic heritage and supports the religion of democracy. The Religion of Americans is, as Herberg puts it, Americanism; hence, religiousness may increase year by year without becoming a divisive factor. Herberg concludes that America enjoys secular unity in religious guise.

In contrast to Herberg's position, Lenski suggests that religious pluralism may well bring rigid compartmentalization and a radical shift in values to American life. He raises this question particularly with respect to the growing dominance of Catholicism and the divergence of Catholics from the norms of an industrial society. Where Herberg sees a consensus on the values of the American Way of Life, Lenski finds a deepening disunity which is rooted in religious diversity. This opposition to Herberg's interpretation arises in part from a difference of method which can now be explored.

[1] Gerhard Lenski, The Religious Factor: A Sociological Study of Religion's Impact on Politics, Economics, and Family Life (Garden City, N.Y.: Doubleday, 1961).
[2] Will Herberg, Protestant-Catholic-Jew: An Essay in American Religious Sociology (Garden City, N.Y.: Doubleday, 1955), especially chapter V.

INTEREST AND METHOD.   The antithesis between Lenski and Herberg arises, in part, from a basic difference of interest in the two studies. Social scientists would like to think that their findings reflect an organization of "objective" facts, but *facts* are made (as the term suggests) by selection and organization. Herberg focuses upon the common elements in American religiousness. He is conscious of differences among the religious communities, of course, but he is not sufficiently concerned even to disengage the Negro Protestant subculture for special consideration. Religion has, at least, three meanings in Herberg's study: meanings (a) and (b) are the religious attitudes and practices of people—what they say and do in the name of religion; meaning (c) is authentic religion, as a relationship to a transcendent reality disclosed in the Judeo-Christian events and perpetuated in this heritage. Since Herberg's final goal is to delineate the dialectical relationship between the Judeo-Christian heritage of transcendence and the common elements of American religiousness, he assimilates differences within American religion (a) to the common element of Americanism—religion (b); in the final chapter, he sets this in opposition to religion (c).

Lenski is primarily interested in differences between the religious communities; moreover, the survey and research technique lends itself to this type of interest, for it collects samples of responses to a series of stimuli which have been designed to categorize respondents and their orientations; it, then, tests these observations (the data created by the instrument) for noticeable differences. Lenski carries through a series of statistical controls on his associated elements (types of religiousness and norms) in order to reduce the causal force to the "religious factor"; thus, when educational level, region of birth, generation in America, occupational position and other relevant forces have been eliminated as causes of variance by holding them constant, the "religious factor" emerges as accounting for such and such differences in the orientations of the groups. The isolation of the "religious factor," in other words, depends precisely upon the discrimination of differences at the phenomenal level. The argument is *retrospective* from manifest norms to causal forces and depends upon discriminable differences.

The contrast in these perspectives on American religion is very striking. Herberg begins with contraries and synthesizes them in higher unities, as, for example, the religious communities which are unified under the rubric of the American Way of Life. Lenski begins with a common set of stimuli—the constructed items of the survey; he, then, isolates the contrasts in the groups according to differences in response; from this point, he establishes his controls to isolate the differentiating factor—"the religious factor." Thus, Herberg reconciles the differences in the religious communities to find the religious factor, while Lenski focuses on these very differences in order to isolate this factor. Herberg only gets to religions (b) and (c) when he gets to the transcendant unities. Lenski only gets to the religious factor when he gets to the underlying source of difference in religion (a).

If the opposition between Herberg's interpretation and Lenski's arises from differences of interest and method, one should be able to pool their results and obtain a more adequate perspective on the religious phenomenon. In order to combine the studies and their conclusions, one would only need a common element; for example, the studies might be considering the same object (religion) or examining manifestations of a common principle. Unfortunately, agreement on a common object will not resolve the difficulty, since Herberg considers the religious communities to be communities of identity, religion (a), whereas Lenski treats the religious communities as *bona fide* expressions of religiousness, religion (c). These studies purport to deal with rather different objects; consequently, one cannot treat them as perspectives on a single object.

There is also the possibility that both studies are examining manifestations of a common principle or cause; in this case, Lenski's analysis of differences among the religious subcultures could be combined with Herberg's consideration of common elements in order to provide a more comprehensive picture of the enduring forms of religion in America; hence, both studies would be perspectives on manifestations of one force. Unfortunately, Herberg interprets the religious communities as products of a search for belonging, whereas Lenski understands the religious associations as products of "the religious factor." To be sure, Lenski separates these religious associations from the subcommunities which cluster around religious identities, but the differences in normative perspectives which he isolates are more closely associated with activity in the formal, religious associations than with the subcommunities. The only possibility is that the formal religious associations are manifestations of a search for identity, religion (a), and Lenski's assumption that he is examining manifestations of religious commitment—"the religious factor," religion (c) will prove on closer inspection to be an unwarranted inference. If this were, indeed, the case, Herberg and Lenski would be looking at a common object, founded in a common principle and seen from different perspectives out of disparate interests and methods. Herberg's insight into the unity of American religion (b) could then be balanced with Lenski's data on diversities in religion (a).

THE UNIFYING PRINCIPLE. On closer inspection, these studies can be reconciled as analyses of religion (a)—communities of identity. A reconsideration of Lenski's discrimination of differences among the religious subcultures gives good grounds for rejecting his inference of purely "religious" causation. He has isolated several normative perspectives on the basis of which he differentiates these groups. These normative perspectives can be summarized in four clusters. Catholics are distinguished from white Protestants through attachments to an extended family. Strong bonds with extended kin, beyond the range of the nuclear family, are viewed as dysfunctional in adaptation to industrial society. The Jewish group manifests this kinship bond, and yet they have made a successful adaptation to American capitalism; however, Lenski treats this subculture as a special case. The kinship bond, thus, becomes an important point of difference between white Protestants and Catholics, for the Catholics show themselves to be maladapted to industrial society on this norm.

A second normative perspective focuses on the birth control question. Lenski interprets Catholic opposition to birth control as evidence of anchorage in agrarian, nonindustrial values. In general, this is a sign of Catholic rejection of technology in favor of traditional practices. Catholics, active in the religious association, members of the middle class and of the third generation are more opposed than other Catholics to birth control; this fact leads Lenski to conclude that these agrarian values arise from the religious factor, for they are intensified in the urban American setting. The Negro Protestants also reject birth control, but Lenski treats this as a special case.

A third, normative perspective centers on attitudes toward the education of children. Lenski makes a great deal of this item, for it involves an evaluation of what is most important for a child's development—"learning to think for himself" or "learning to obey." There were other possibilities which could be ranked, but these two discriminated most sharply between Catholics and white Protestants. Here again, Jews and white Protestants fell together, whereas Catholics and Negro Protestants held roughly the same position. Lenski interprets these data to mean that Protestants, out of their tradition of religious protest, give preference to intellectual autonomy, while Catholics hold a heteronomic position of submission to authority. According to this interpretation, Catholics inculcate a spirit of obedience out of their religious commitment and Protestants stimulate their children to thoughtful creativity.

A fourth broad cluster produces a normative perspective on civil rights and the role of government intervention on behalf of human needs. The first aspect of this cluster, including sentiments such as support for those who speak against religion, in favor of communism, in favor of fascism, etc. splits much like the third cluster, for white Protestants and Jews tend to support civil rights, while Catholics and Negro Protestants would limit such rights as free speech. The big differences between Catholics and white Protestants emerge, however, on the general question of the welfare state, for Catholics, Negroes and Jews all tend to favor governmental intervention much more than white Protestants. Lenski interprets this Catholic position as indicative of support for welfare capitalism, and again treats the peculiar inclination of Jews and Negroes as special cases.

The main question arises with respect to Lenski's inference that these normative perspectives are rooted in "the religious factor." Even this crude summary, which does justice to the basic findings though not the details, suggests that there are too many special cases for an adequate interpretation. If Protestant attitudes were really grounded in a religious factor, the positions of white and Negro Protestants would not be diametrically opposed on all issues. If one takes the line that advance of the Negroes to middle class status will bring their orientation closer to the Protestants, which is the point that Lenski makes, it is evident that the inference of a "religious factor" as presently operative is unwarranted. If Negroes have to become middle class for the religious factor to operate, one is at a loss to comprehend this "factor." Furthermore, the Catholic group can hardly be treated as inimical to capitalistic and industrial development without including the Jewish group in this category, for the latter favor a welfare state even more strongly and also maintain an extended family. If one wished to make a special case of the Jews, it might simply be on the point of birth control rather than on the other two clusters; thus, they are liberal on birth control, perhaps, because they reject crowded housing. Even more decisive, however, is the ambiguity of Lenski's stress on intellectual autonomy, especially when Catholics approach white Protestants rather closely on this item. As for the Catholic view of birth control, it is well known that the Catholic Church has made a *cause célèbre* of this issue. The fact that Catholics support the Church's position on this issue, after they can afford a large family, raises very serious questions about the use of such a response to categorize Catholics as holders of agrarian values. Lenski's findings on these norms are interesting and important, but the "religious factor" is most ambiguous. In general, the inference that a religious factor accounts for these differences in normative perspectives seems unwarranted.

Lenski himself makes reference to the real factor underlying these differences in the final section of his conclusions, where he notes that "socioreligious groups are rapidly replacing ethnic groups as the basic units in the system of status groups in American society."[3] He continues: "Of the four major socioreligious groups, the white Protestants enjoy the greatest social honor, Catholics rank second, Jews third, and Negro Protestants fourth. As the position of the Jewish group indicates, status-group rank by no means parallels class position." The amazing thing is that Lenski did not take this point of departure in making his final analysis, for most, if not all, of the differences between the socioreligious groupings can be more adequately understood from the struggle for status among these groups. All four religious subcultures are committed to the material values of American life; Lenski is perfectly clear on this and only obscures this common element when he hypothesizes that the Catholics may be too spiritual for American life.[4] He has no evidence for this latter statement, and, indeed, has found a consensus among religious subcultures on material values. The principal differences among the subcultures arise over *means* to achieving these material values. If one follows the ranks in honor which differentiate these groups, bearing in mind their social heritages, since heritage is an aspect of status, it becomes quite evident that social position is decisive to the normative perspective.

The white Protestants support industrial values on all four perspectives, since they are the top prestige group and have everything to gain by a main-

[3] Gerhard Lenski, *op. cit.*, p. 327 f.
[4] *Ibid.*, pp. 311 and 315 f.

tenance of the *status quo* in American life. The Catholic group ranks next in
prestige, but they have fought a long battle against their minority status; in
fact, Catholic social critics have noted that their own people hold nineteenth
century feelings about their status. The historic affiliation of these groups with
the Democratic party and their experience of the use of free speech against
them readily account for their divergence from Protestant bourgeois values.
The minority attitude of Catholics, based on their American experience, shows
up in these normative perspectives.

The deepest elements of a heritage are sustained by political affiliation
and familistic rituals. Unless there is considerable pressure to switch affiliations, as happens with richer Catholics and certainly is common when Negroes
come to Northern cities, these elements of the heritage persist. There is no
reason to assume that they should lessen with advancing Americanization; indeed, these elements become more significant, for the third generation grasps
for symbols of their identity. Familistic values, political affiliations and increased activity in religious associations come together in this search for a sense
of continuity. If one asks why the Jewish groups show less inclination to associational activity in the synagogue on this principle of explanation, it can be
answered that they too are conforming in the suburbs on this point; however,
the synagogue has less significance in Jewish tradition than the Mass within
the Catholic heritage. Similarly, the ambivalent attitudes of Negroes toward
religious associations, manifest as they move into the middle classes, have been
much discussed. Americanization deepens attachments to elements of the heritage. This is Herberg's basic thesis. Lenski has confirmed the thesis, and yet
he has denoted much more precisely the specific aspects of the social heritages
which have been selected by the common principle of search for social identity.

Social heritage and status position differentiate the groups. Religion (a)
—search for identity—is the common principle. For example, the Jewish group
strongly supports civil rights, and yet they approve of a welfare state more
than other groups. One need only reflect on the Jewish heritage of persecution
at the hands of religious agencies in the Western world to appreciate their
strong support of civil rights. On the other hand, the strong tradition of social
justice and communal intervention for the common good inclines the Jewish
subculture to favor a corporate resolution of many problems. Having seen this
helping hand become an oppressive boot, they retain the safegard of civil
rights.

A similar analysis accounts very well for the position of Negro Protestants
at the opposite pole from white Protestants. The impulse behind the differences is not a "religious factor" but the social and economic handicaps of their
community. Lenski has noted this in treating them as a special case. Their
conservatism on birth control and intellectual autonomy can readily be accounted for by heritage and social position, as Lenski himself has noted. Their
inclination to seek help from governmental agencies to meet their needs is
understandable in the light of their social position; indeed, they have no other

resource to advance their aspiration for the materialistic values of American life.

In brief, the differences in normative perspectives do not stem from differences in religious commitment but are understandable in terms of the relative social prestige and power held by the religious communities. There is a common impulse underlying the formation of these communities—the search for a community of social identity. Herberg had focussed attention on this principle, even as Oscar Handlin had earlier referred to this principle in the formation of ethnic churches. Lenski has confirmed the notion that this impulse continues to be a strong force in the formation of religious subcultures.

On the other hand, Lenski has brought into focus another aspect of these religious communities—their role as factions struggling for social power. The differences between these groups on social norms, and the differences are very real even though they are overshadowed by the common elements, pertain to the different strategies of the groups to advance their own claims to social power. What Lenski interpreted as differences on fundamental American values turn out, on closer inspection, to be conflicts over *means* of climbing the economic and social ladder.

A major difficulty in Lenski's interpretation arises from his notion of the religious factor. This is the element which Herberg treats as religion (c), the transcendent reality represented in the Judeo-Christian heritage. Lenski infers this authentic factor (Catholicism, Protestantism, Judaism) from the normative perspectives which are peculiar to the religious associations; hence, the religious factor is the commitment or force which is left when other factors have been controlled. It is this disjunction which has been rejected by suggesting that the normative perspectives are largely understandable from the status positions of the religious subcultures; thus, the religious factor is the commitment or force which is left when other factors have been controlled. This is really an argument by disjunction, for it assumes a positive factor by eliminating other factors. It is this disjunction which has been rejected by suggesting that the normative perspectives are largely understandable from the status positions of the religious subcultures; thus, the religious factor is not religion (c) but religion (a). Several methodological points surround Lenski's procedure, though only one of them need be pursued in detail.

First, the research and survey technique can be useful in formulating hypotheses about factors such as Lenski's religious factors; however, this is only an hypothesis and research is required to test it. The preceding reinterpretation really drew on available data to test the hypothesis of a religious factor; Lenski's postulate was rejected in favor of a broadening of Herberg's hypothesis.

Secondly, Lenski's study lends much support to Herberg's thesis on the secularism of America's religious subcultures; that is, his data can be understood in this way if the preceding reinterpretation is acceptable. Lenski hints as much in the concluding section of his study, where he refers to "mature

Protestantism."[5] This kind of judgment presumes some understanding of authentic religion as a criterion. Herberg seeks this criterion in the authentic, Judeo-Christian heritage. Lenski refers to "basic spiritual goals" and Biblical tradition, but he has no real criterion; in fact, this problem of the nature of the religious appears as a decisive difficulty in the study.

This general problem of the religious comes to focus in the difficulty of discriminating "the religious factor." Herberg has assimilated various elements of the religious subcultures to the search for identity to the religious impulse. Why should this search for identity come to focus in the religious associations?

On this point, Lenski is a better guide than Herberg, for he is, at least, searching for manifestations of the religious impulse in the sphere of human events and decisions. This is not to say that Herberg's focus upon transcendence is irrelevant but only that it dichotomizes reality somewhat too neatly. The human sciences need an understanding of religion which is more historical than Herberg's pure transcendence and less reductionistic than Lenski's residual factor. When the search for identity is so evidently embedded in the religious milieu, it becomes essential to identify the authentically religious dimension of this search. We need to discriminate religion (c) within religion (a), but this calls for a criterion.

A CRITERION OF THE "RELIGIOUS."   Lenski attempted to formulate a relatively neutral definition of religion—one that would be broad enough to include all of the phenomena which anyone might affirm to be religious; at least, so it seems when one considers his definition. He considers religion to be "a system of beliefs about the nature of the force(s) ultimately shaping man's destiny, and the practices associated therewith, shared by the members of a group."[6] He, then, goes on to broaden this definition to the notion that everyone is religious for everyone speaks and acts from "unproven and unprovable assumptions," even though most people could not articulate the assumptions underlying their speech and actions.[7] By this very inclusive notion, Lenski has brought Bertrand Russell into his community of the religious, for everyone is religious except small children and persons of subnormal intelligence. The basic notion is one of original cause, premise or beginning point.

Lenski is concerned to isolate one dimension of the intentional structure of the religious—*the subjective ground of commitment.* However, the subjective ground in the religious is commitment to a principle or source of being which is other than the subject himself. It is precisely on this point that Bertrand Russell rejects the manner of being as faith and absolutizes his manner of being as rational. Ultimate causation is much too general a notion to delineate the religious, since it obliterates distinctions between metaphysics and

[5] *Ibid.*, p. 317 f.
[6] *Ibid.*, p. 298 f.
[7] *Ibid.*, fn. 5, p. 299.

religion, leaving research without guidelines in the field of subjective orientations.

However, Lenski's interpretation is also deficient in attempting to reduce religion to a subjective state; thus, he stresses commitment without content. Commitment is commitment to something. There is no such thing as commitment in general, any more than there is consciousness as such but only consciousness of something. Lenski's failure to reckon with faith as loyalty to a realm of value, as well as confidence in a source of being, leads him into several misinterpretations of the religious subcultures. He accepts the religious associations as expressions of "the religious factor" without asking what such a religious commitment would mean, because he is defining the religious as commitment in general. The problem of religious sociology is to understand the objects of the commitments which are expressed in religious associations, for these objects are the sources of ambiguity.

The fundamental issue is that human reality can only be understood from the inside, from the structures of meaning within which it is constituted. A structural-functional analysis *purports* to do this, but it ultimately assimilates the meaning to an alien structure. Whether or not a particular religious structure contributes to the maintenance of a value system in any culture cannot be predetermined by some systematic concepts which define its function in systems as such. The very idea of *system* is an affirmation of value which is built into social scientific theory—the values of harmony and order. The claim that human action can be grasped under the rubrics of a social system is an hypothesis grounded in the principle of harmony; such an hypothesis cannot be the explanatory principle of a religious phenomenon, for religious realities among others are the test of the hypothesis itself.

Herberg avoids this common mistake of subsuming religion under the notion of a social system, and yet his utterly transcendent interpretation of the Judeo-Christian heritage over against American religion obliterates all distinctions and overlooks the Judeo-Christian understanding that the God who disclosed Himself, now discloses Himself in and through the events of human life and history. Herberg is fully aware of this understanding of God in the Judeo-Christian tradition, but he is subjecting all of American religion to a blanket condemnation. In this way, he fails to take seriously the religious dimensions of the search for identity in the United States. Faith, if present, is commitment in the form of the search for identity and the need to belong. Faith is not a relationship to a transcendent reality outside of any historical context but rather the apprehension of a source and realm of value in and through the historical realities of experience. So far as Herberg is inclined to ignore the immanent character of the divine-human encounter for the sake of the divine transcendance, he fails to turn attention to the complexity and richness of the struggle for authentic religion in the United States. To this extent, Lenski's study is more attentive to the historical actualities.

Herberg is unquestionably right in his appraisal of the secularism of much of American religiousness. One does not speak of the Holy One of Israel as a "Livin' Doll." Nevertheless, a reflective study of the range of American religious experience is not furthered by a blanket assimilation of all of these phenomena to a single rubric—Americanism. Religion is no more an utter transcendence than it is the psychological state which Lenski postulates; indeed, a dialectical relationship does clarify the meanings of the religious in a significant way, but here research begins. Religion, at least so long as we speak within the Judeo-Christian tradition, is wrestling with the source of being who is also source of value, never means to our ends and yet ever redeeming and transforming our means. This suggests that the principal categories for understanding man's being as faithful are those of *meaning* and *temporality*—the categories of history. Sociological research may build its *types* at a much lower level, but any attempt to reduce the constitutive meaning of religion to this level will only obscure the phenomenon in question. It was precisely this kind of reduction which caused Lenski to fuse the search for identity with the religious factor.

Religion can no more be understood as a function of a system contrived by social science than social science can be reduced to a function of its social context. Both fields and all other human activities need to be grasped within their intentional structures before attempts can be made to delineate their interrelations with other structures and contexts. This means asking what the religious structure really is today both as confidence in a source of being and as loyalty to a center of value.

6 RELIGIOUS STATISTICS IN THE UNITED STATES

William Petersen

INTRODUCTION   Many Americans hold to the myth that America was founded as a Christian nation. Moreover, they fail to recognize that the general religious basis of the country has changed. Five general periods mark the development of American religious history. During the Pre-Colonial and Colonial Period, the church and state were intimately related in the persons of the original settlers who formed separate colonies in order to guarantee the religious and personal freedom denied them in Europe. In the second phase of the first period, however, the arrival of dissimilar religious groups necessarily led to religious accommodation. The desire to gain revolutionary support from Roman Catholic France in the war against Anglican England led to growing interest in the concept of separation of church and state. In the Period of Independence the disestablishment of the church occurred with the adoption of the Constitution and First Amendment: "Congress shall make no law respecting an establishment of religion or prohibiting the free exercise thereof. . . ." At the time only an estimated 3½ million persons (including 20,000 Roman Catholics and 6,000 Jews) populated this nation.

The Post-Civil War Period was marked by loose church discipline and increased immigration of culturally distinct Protestants, Roman Catholics, and Jews. In the Early Twentieth Century the continuing heavy immigration of Jews and Roman Catholics, coupled with the rise of urbanism, resulted in a strong nativist reaction which culminated in the adoption of a restricted quota system fa-

Abridged and reprinted from the *Journal for the Scientific Study of Religion*, Vol. 1, No. 2 (Spring, 1962), pp. 165-178, and from William Petersen, *The Politics of Population* (Garden City, N.Y.: Doubleday, 1964).

WILLIAM PETERSEN is Professor of Sociology at the University of California (Berkeley).

voring the white, Anglo-Saxon Protestant (WASP) at the expense of the southern and eastern European. This period was also marked by the rise of the social gospel and Neo-orthodox movements (*see* Ahlstrom, Article 1), alternative responses to the liberal and fundamentalist tensions of the period.

We live in the Period of New Definitions. Since World War II both religious and antireligious minorities have been seeking their "rights." Under the protective and expansive decisions of the U.S. Supreme Court, religious pluralism has become a social and legal reality. The United States has entered into the post-Protestant or the Neo-Pluralistic period in spite of the continued growth of church membership from an estimated low of five percent in 1776, to fifteen and one-half percent in 1850, thirty-five percent in 1900, and sixty to sixty-five percent in 1960. Against this background the issues raised by William Petersen, a sociologist, appear in sharp focus.

Any reliable research is dependent upon adequate information. Statistical data on religion, however, are typically *in*adequate because they are gathered in a voluntary and incomplete manner, in sharp contrast, for example, to the population census. The absence of reliable data explains in part the minimal analytical efforts in sociology of religion to date (*see* Yinger, Article 3). Because American mass society places a high premium upon quantitative data, the facts are often knowingly (and unknowingly) falsified in order to gain prestige. Variable membership definitions cloud the issue of church membership. The best that can be said for current data concerning religious membership is that they represent a general distribution pattern rather than actual fact. Attempts to gain access to more accurate data through a national census have been hindered by public and private interest and pressure groups in the name of separation of church and state.

Are the assumptions of those opposed to a national religious census valid? Does the concept of religious freedom also mean freedom from religious identification? This argument seems to stretch the concept of religious freedom. Why should a free society fear accurate data concerning religious life, especially since religion is generally regarded as a major influence in the formation of an individual's personal and social identity (*see* Winter, Article 5)? The tendency to invoke the principle of separation of church and state in all issues pertaining to *any* religious group and *any* governmental agency ignores the deep relationship between religion and the rest of social life and compartmentalizes the religious dimension of life even further.

E VERY SOCIETY," I remarked to a Dutch sociologist, "has its sacred subjects, protected from empirical research and analysis by a high wall of
magical taboos." I was commenting on his statement that a Kinsey report
would have been impossible in the Netherlands.

"Indeed," he replied; "in Holland the sacred area is sexuality, and in the
United States it is religion."

The contrast is apt. In the Netherlands, where the church is recognized
as a significant social institution and religion as an important ideological force,
the time and effort that sociologists devote to studying them are correspondingly large. In the United States, on the contrary, research in this area engages few social scientists and is generally of indifferent quality, in part because even the most elementary data are faulty or absent.

I. The weakness is apparent with respect to the most fundamental sociological issue—what are the social effects of religious faith? The usual answers
to this question in theoretical works, derived from either Karl Marx or Emile
Durkheim, consist in paraphrases of these men's dicta that religion is the
opium of the people, or that it functions to unite those who adhere to it into
a single moral community. Such characterizations, wholly negative or wholly
positive, are no prelude to analysis, which must start with an attempt to distinguish, to differentiate, to compare.

This contrast in social philosophy is matched, moreover, by a parallel one
in national mythology. One official doctrine in the United States is that religious faith has no social consequences of any importance. Immigrants urged
to acculturate in every other sense were guaranteed the right to religious freedom by the Constitution itself. No religious test may be put to a candidate
for public office, even the highest and most important.

On the other hand, it would not be accurate to describe the separation of
church and state in the United States as absolute. In most of the recent cases
specifying this relation, the courts have applied the constitutional prohibition
of religious establishment, or the correlative prescription of religious freedom,
with respect to particular practices that allegedly discriminated against one
denomination or illegitimately favored another. Thus, members of Jehovah's
Witnesses need not salute the flag, children may ride to parochial schools in
buses paid for out of general taxes, and so on. But the fact that all Americans
now pledge allegiance to one nation "under God" has not been successfully
challenged. It is taken for granted that churches are partly supported out of
public funds: The institutions themselves pay no taxes, and individuals may
deduct donations from their taxable income.

It cannot be both that religion generally has no effect on social attitudes
and behavior, and that it typically has an effect. Most people apparently hold
to both positions, and sociologists have done remarkably little to resolve the

contradiction. If we were to try to specify each of the variables, the first thing we would require is accurate statistics relating religion to other social facts, information such as would be available in a census. But the census in this country has no information on religion. The local data gathered in community surveys or similar studies, however valuable they may be in other respects, cannot be accepted as an accurate description of religious behavior over the whole nation. And the information from national public-opinion polls on the social correlates of religious faith, contrary to what some persons have alleged, is not an adequate substitute for official statistics.

A timely illustration of this last point is the consensus among all pollsters and commentators that Kennedy's religion was an important factor in the 1960 presidential election. According to Roper's estimate (which is more or less in line with that of the other polling firms), between 75 and 80 percent of the Catholic voters, but only about 35 percent of the Protestant, supported Kennedy. The contrast is striking and one would think decisive.

It is undoubtedly true that proportionately more Catholics voted for Kennedy than non-Catholics, but it does not follow automatically that the two factors can be described as cause and effect. For we know from even our poor statistics that Catholics are concentrated in social groups with a normally high proportion of Democratic voters—in northern cities, in trade unions, in some ethnic minorities (such as Puerto Ricans and Mexicans), among young voters (who, according to Gallup, supported Kennedy by a 3-to-2 margin). And Protestants, on the contrary, are concentrated in social groups that are normally Republican—businessmen, Mid-Western farmers, and so on. Whether religion actually influenced the vote or was merely an accidental characteristic can be determined only by analyzing several factors at once. Among trade-union members, for instance, or among farmers, was the vote for and against Kennedy split along religious lines? This the polling firms do not tell us; nor can they, for their samples are too small to permit the simultaneous analysis of several variables.

From this example one can reasonably draw three conclusions. (1) Whether or not religious faiths are differentially associated with social attitudes, the national myth denying that this may be so really convinces no one. Indeed, the very fact that the relation contradicts the myth makes it "news," so that journalists often seize on it and pass over other, better established, and therefore duller, explanations. (2) We cannot depend on polling firms to correct this tendency. They are business enterprises catering to mass journalism, and this market hardly induces them to analyze a complex social pattern with adequate care. (3) On the other hand, the fact that a question on religion has been asked in several dozen polls during the past decades proves that by and large Americans have no objection to it.

Census data on religion would not enable us, of course, to analyze the 1960 election precisely, since the vote is secret. Even so, a comparison of religious affiliations and votes by precincts would probably be an improvement over the polls, or at worst a valuable supplement to them.

II. National statistics on religion in the United States are available from three sources: the membership figures of various churches, as reported in the *Yearbook* of the National Council of Churches; the one nationwide sample survey made by the Census Bureau, in 1957; and the aforementioned data of public-opinion firms and institutes. Representative breakdowns from each of these three sources are given in Table 6-1. Later membership figures and poll data are now available, but these have been chosen because they are most directly comparable with the 1957 survey.

The compilation of membership figures, as shown in the first two columns, is deficient in a number of respects:

1. The data depend on the voluntary cooperation of the denominational leaders. Some sects, in particular Christian Scientists, prohibit the publication of their membership figures. Many others are certainly not equipped to maintain an accurate register, and the *Yearbook* lists annually the latest available figures for each denomination, even though in some cases these are quite out of date.

2. "Membership" is defined differently by various denominations. Most Protestant groups include only those who have been confirmed and are currently enrolled with a specific congregation. As defined by the Catholic Church, the Protestant Episcopal Church, and several Lutheran groups, however, "members" are all who have been baptized, and thus include infants and children up to the age of confirmation, as well as some who have drifted away from the church but not specified their alienation. The definition of a "Jew" is particularly difficult, and apparently synagogue officials typically include totally irreligious persons who could be designated as Jewish by their family background and culture.

3. The statistics of the older, well-established denominations are probably more accurate than those of the fluid world of the sects, but it does not follow that the latter are in their aggregate overrepresented in the published statistics. *A priori* one would suppose, on the contrary, that many of the groups meeting in store-front churches, which lack the ecclesiastical apparatus necessary for the collection and transmission of accurate rolls, might be passed over entirely in such a compilation as that by the National Council of Churches.

4. The classification of denominations is inadequate. In the traditional trichotomy into Protestants, Catholics, Jews, "Protestant" is little more than a residual class, which includes groups (like the Unitarians) who are not even Christian as this term is ordinarily used. Most of the major denominations, moreover, cannot be interpreted as altogether meaningful units. The divisions are based on differences in doctrine, in language, and in social class or region

TABLE 6-1   Distribution of the population by claimed church membership and stated religious preference: United States, 1956 and 1957.

Religious Group	Claimed Church Membership[a]		U. S. Census Bureau Sample Survey[b]		Gallup Poll Sample Survey[c]	
	Thousands	Percent	Thousands	Percent	Total[d]	Actively Religious[e]
Protestant	60,149	58.6	78,952	66.2	58.1	59.8
Baptist	19,934	19.4	23,525	19.7	11.3	12.6
Methodist	11,946	11.6	16,676	14.0	13.1	12.7
Lutheran	7,401	7.2	8,417	7.1	8.2	9.4
Presbyterian	3,963	3.9	6,656	5.6	5.2	5.4
Prot. Episcopal	2,853	2.8			3.5	2.8
United Church of Christ[f]	2,179	2.1	23,678	19.8	2.1	2.2
Other Protestant	11,873	11.6			14.7	14.7
Roman Catholic	34,564	33.7	30,669	25.7	21.9	28.3
Jewish	5,200	5.1	3,868	3.2	2.5	0.2
Other Religion	2,791	2.7	1,545	1.3	16.4	11.2
No Religion			3,195	2.7		
Religion not reported			1,104	0.9	1.1	0.5
TOTALS	102,704	100.0	119,333	100.0	100.0	100.0

a *World Almanac and Book of Facts for 1958* (N.Y.: World-Telegraph, 1958, pp. 711-712; based on National Council of Churches of Christ in the USA, *Yearbook of American Churches*, 1958, supplemented by a private questionnaire.
b U.S. Bureau of the Census, *Current Population Reports*, series P-20, no. 79 (February 2, 1958). Civilian population 14 years and over.
c The data from this poll, taken during the 1956 campaign, were furnished to me by Charles Y. Glock.
d Sample of the voting population weighted regionally according to the proportion of the electorate that votes, N = 1,484.
e That is, all who said they attended church or its equivalent at least once a month. N = 951.
f Formed in 1957 by the union of the Congregational Christian Churches and the Evangelical and Reformed Church. The Gallup poll figure pertains only to the Congregationalists.

(particularly the splits between North and South and between Negro and white). Undoubtedly both theological doctrine and social attitudes differ more between the fundamentalist and modernist wings of any one denomination than among the variegated Protestants (or even Americans, apart from religion) in the same social class and region.

5. Membership rolls tell us nothing, of course, of those who are not members of any church. In 1957 these apparently totaled more than 67 million, or not quite 40 percent of the population—a rather substantial proportion in view of the much discussed postwar revival of religion.

The next two columns of the table give the results of a sample survey made by the Census Bureau in March, 1957. While this survey was subject to the usual sampling variability, its results were undoubtedly more accurate than the compilation of membership rolls. Enumerators queried only persons aged 14 and over, thus eliminating the infants and children listed as members of some churches. The principal difference between the two sets of data, however, is that the second pertains to the self-identification of respondents rather than to the number of adherents claimed by church officials.

In accordance with the best usage of public-opinion polling, the Census Bureau should have asked the question, "Have you a religion?" and then, if the reply was in the affirmative, followed it with, "What is it?" The question as it was actually put, "What is your religion?" exerted a certain pressure to name some denomination, and it is likely that merely nominal adherents to any faith in general replied by citing it. The sum of these personal preferences for any denomination, then, would certainly be greater than the number of formal members, as indeed it is for the larger Protestant denominations. That the number of persons who reported themselves as Roman Catholics or as Jews was less by a considerable margin than the claimed membership of these churches suggests that the latter figures are very much inflated, even apart from the fact that they include (or may include) children under the age of 14.

The data from the Gallup poll given in the last two columns of the table permit a comparison between the proportion who identify themselves with the various denominations and those designated as "actively religious," who attend church or its equivalent at least once a month.

Let us first compare the total with that from the Census Bureau survey. The Gallup poll question was asked only of voters, and since its main purpose was to forecast the election correctly, major regions were represented according to the estimated proportion of the electorate that had actually voted in the previous election. Thus, the South, which by the usual indices is the most religious region, is underrepresented in the sample; and this bias may be the reason for the finding, certainly erroneous, that the country has fewer Baptists than Methodists. Note that the combined class "Other religion" and "No religion," which made up only 4 percent in the Census Bureau survey, constituted 16.4 percent of the respondents to the Gallup poll.

About two-thirds of those who identified themselves with one or another denomination said that they attended church or its equivalent as often as once a month. This index is not an equally meaningful measure of active participation for all faiths: for example, Catholics are under greater pressure to attend church regularly than Protestants, and indeed a larger proportion do so. Note that by this index Jews almost disappear from the religious population; this finding supports our supposition that many persons of Jewish family background who are more or less secular in their beliefs and behavior are included in membership statistics, and some, though a considerably smaller number, also designate themselves as Jewish in a "religious" census.

As the figures in this table suggest, we have no accurate basis for classifying the American population by religion. The percentage of Baptists, according to the three sources cited, ranged from 11.3 to 19.7, that of Presbyterians from 3.9 to 5.6, that of Catholics from 21.9 to 33.7, that of Jews from 2.5 to 5.1, and so on. These are not the widest ranges to be found. Other estimates of the number of Catholics, for instance, have been as high as 50 million, rather than the 30 to 35 million shown here. And the figures needed for social analysis—the proportion of each denomination living in cities and in the countryside; with large, medium, and small incomes; and so on—are even less precise than these totals, approximate as they are.

Indeed, the question whether membership in churches is growing as fast as the population cannot be answered with any assurance.

III. For a time it seemed as though a question on religion would be added to the schedule of the 1960 census, but this tentative plan was abandoned in response to the objection of a small number of persons and a few organizations. Opposed were the American Civil Liberties Union; various Jewish organizations, including the American Jewish Congress, the American Jewish Committee, and the Anti-Defamation League; the liberal Catholic weekly *Commonweal*; the Protestant magazine *Christian Century*; some Christian Science groups; and James A. Pike, then Dean of the Cathedral of St. John the Divine. Public stands in favor of the question were taken by two professional societies of social scientists, the Population Association of America and the American Sociological Association; a large number of Catholic organizations, including the Jesuit weekly *America*, the editorial staff of the *Catholic Digest*, the Catholic Press Association, the National Catholic Welfare Conference, the National Council of Catholic Men, and the editor of the *Official Catholic Directory*; and Paul Blanshard. Protestant groups were divided, with more for the question (or indifferent) than opposed. The National Council of Churches took no position at this time, presumably continuing the positive stand toward a census question on religion that its executive committee had taken in 1935; its committee concerned with religious statistics continued to be in favor also in the 1950's.

Nevertheless, the Census Bureau announced at the end of 1957 that it would not include the question, primarily because "a considerable number of persons would be reluctant to answer such a question in the Census, where a reply is mandatory. . . . An alternative approach which would avoid the difficulty about the mandatory character of answers would be to rely on the analysis of results obtained on a voluntary basis, such as through the current Population Survey. Such a survey was taken in March 1957 and the results are now being analyzed and, according to present plans, will be published before very long."[1] "Present plans," however, underwent a change. As we have seen, the breakdown by religious preference was published, and it constitutes the best information we have on the subject. But the additional data collected on the social economic characteristics associated with the various religions were not.

Why is accurate information concerning religion considered to be reprehensible or dangerous? What were the arguments against including a question on religion in the census schedule? They can be reduced to two main points —that religion is so intensely and exclusively a personal affair that no intrusion of society can be permitted, and that in any case this intrusion should not be by the state. Let us look, then, at the more specific arguments. Do they hold up any better?

1. A question on religion in the census, it was alleged, would be unconstitutional. This point was made, for example, by the American Civil Liberties Union, reversing a prior stand of that organization. According to its revised opinion, "it would be contrary to the First Amendment to ask anyone questions about religion or membership in a religious body," and this would be so even if the response was voluntary.

Comment. Even the ACLU is not firm in its opinion on constitutionality; its church-state committee intends to review once again the arguments that led the organization to reverse itself four years ago, and the present position may also be rescinded. As a professor of political science at Brandeis University put it, "It seems a pity that the important principle of separation of church and state should be invoked so frequently against such a simple and unthreatening proposal as this one."[2]

2. Sometimes the constitutional issue, though not raised directly, was implicit in references to legal tradition. In 1957, Leo Pfeffer, director of the Commission on Law and Social Action of the American Jewish Congress, for example, quoted James Madison on why the question should not have been asked in the first census: "As to those who are employed in teaching and inculcating the duties of religion, there may be some indelicacy in singling them out, as the General Government is proscribed from interfering in any manner whatever, in matters respecting religion."[3]

[1] U.S. Bureau of the Census, release, December 12, 1957, and supplementary, "Statement of Reasons."
[2] Letter from Lawrence H. Fuchs, *The New York Times*, August 19, 1957.
[3] Leo Pfeffer, "Is It the Government's Business?" *Christian Century*, October 30, 1957.

Comment. The sentence that Dr. Pfeffer quotes could be used to support either side of the issue: If James Madison believed that including the question might involve no more than "some indelicacy," is it stretching his language considerably to interpret this as an opinion on constitutionality. A law exists expressly permitting the Bureau to take a "census" of religious bodies, based on the existent records, and in the 19th century—especially in 1870—this law was interpreted rather broadly. In this century, there were four special censuses of religious bodies—in 1906, 1916, 1926, and 1936. In 1946 Congress refused to allocate the funds needed to continue the service, and ten years later no one in Congress was enough interested in the question even to propose that the series be renewed. The compilation is now made by the National Council of Churches, with what results we have seen. In spite of the fact that the government collected statistics on religious affiliation for many decades. Dr. Pfeffer had not thought the issue important enough even to mention it in *Church, State, and Freedom* (1953), his excellent and exhaustive analysis of state-church relations in the United States.

3. Asking a question on religion, it was alleged, would constitute an invasion of personal privacy.

Comment. Religious affiliation (rather than religious belief, which no one proposes should be included in the census) is a social fact. Whether it is more "personal" than one's occupation, education, income, age, national origin, marital status, and so on, is a matter of opinion. In both the 1957 sample survey and an earlier test (in Milwaukee, November, 1956), the Census Bureau attempted to evaluate opposition to the question. Only 0.5 percent declined to answer it, as compared with 0.6 percent on the number of their children, 1.3 percent on the respondents' education, and 7.0 percent on their income.

Under the law every adult is required to answer every legitimate question put by an authorized representative of the Census Bureau, but as a matter of fact not all questions are answered by everyone: Many census tables include a residual category of persons of whom the characteristic is unknown. However, according to standard legal compilations, only two persons have been prosecuted under this law.

It is not at all accidental that so few prosecutions have been initiated. The Census Bureau is well aware that accurate statistics depend ultimately on the willing cooperation of the population, so that the general reluctance of a democratic state to apply force is in this case strongly reinforced by a particular technical requirement.

4. One important reason for opposition to the question on religion was often an intense—though usually also vague—concern about the uses to which the information might be put. Israel Goldstein, then president of the American Jewish Congress, went farther: "If Americans can be compelled to disclose to government officers their religious beliefs, they can equally be compelled to disclose their political, economic, social, and all other beliefs." One can suppose that this fear of the government, even when not specified as such, may

have been one reason why so many Jewish organizations opposed the question.

Comment. It must be stressed that census information is completely private, carefully guarded even against other government bureaus and never published in a form that would make the identification of individuals possible. This protection has been upheld in the courts a number of times. On one occasion a life-insurance company claimed that a client had lied about his age and thus forfeited the beneficiary's right to the payment. It petitioned the Census Bureau for Information from its records, and the court upheld the Bureau's refusal to give it out, adding the following comment: The legal defense protecting a person against the use of census data to his detriment "is akin to the protection afforded by the prohibitions against the evidential use of communications between attorney and client, priest and penitent, and physician and paient."[4] In 1960 the Supreme Court declined to review a decision by a Circuit Court of Appeals which upheld the Census Bureau in its refusal to release to the U. S. Trade Commission information from the Census of Manufactures about one specified manufacturer.

But suppose these legal protections break down, we may ask; Jewish leaders are not likely to have forgotten the Nazi holocaust that overwhelmed the legal structure of Weimar Germany. This kind of argument is difficult to answer, for logic is overwhelmed by the tragedy of European Jewry. If Jewish leaders practice an exaggerated caution, trusting nothing and no one, can one blame them? Can we absolutely be certain; dare we believe that it can't happen here? The lists that the Nazis used to guide their anti-Jewish campaigns, it should be recalled, were usually the rolls of the Jewish community, not the census lists or even the population registers in countries where the latter existed.

5. The data collected would be of limited usefulness or, in the opinion of some, of none at all. Stated affiliation by itself, Dean Pike suggested, would not be meaningful, and it would be necessary to add questions about church attendance during the past year, the performance or not of Easter duties, and so on.

On the other hand, a number of persons, including Patrick Murphy Malin of the American Civil Liberties Union, condemned the question in part because it would be useful, specifically to the churches. In Mr. Goldstein words, "It would make out of the Federal government an agent of religious groups and would employ Government instrumentalities for church purposes."

Comment. Dean Pike's *reductio ad absurdum* applies almost equally well to every question in the census schedule. For some purposes the information on occupation and income, for instance, is usable as such, but as indices of social class—the typical use to which sociologists put it—it could be usefully supplemented by questions on style of life, on membership in organizations, on social attitudes.

The government furnishes valuable information to corset manufacturers,

[4] *Brauner v. Mutual Life Insurance Company of New York*, 4 D & C 2d 106 (1929).

orange growers, air lines, advertising agencies, schools and colleges, municipal and state bureaus and so on through the entire body of American commercial and institutional life. It is a strange notion that if a proposed procedure can be shown to be of some benefit to the churches, that fact in itself condemns it.

IV. The social concomitants of religion, whatever they may be, cannot be wished out of existence by repeating "separation of church and state" like an incantation. Prejudice feeds on ignorance, and those who would combat prejudice should not fight for maintaining ignorance in any area. The know-nothing liberalism of the American Civil Liberties Union and the Jewish agencies is a contradiction of their own basic principles. Whenever liberals have fought discrimination against Jews, against Catholics, against any religious or ethnic minorities, they have been able to make good use of whatever statistics there were, for if discrimination exists, how can it be indicated more effectively than by the correlation between group membership and various social indices? If the designation of race were to be deleted from the census schedule, as various persons have suggested, such a work as Myrdal's *American Dilemma* would become impossible. One could still write philosophical essays on the virtues of equality, but it would no longer be feasible to show, as he did, that Negroes get less schooling and worse jobs, that their health is poorer and their lives are shorter, that in general the discrimination has social effects.

Members of a faith constitute a meaningful subgroup within a broader society, and religious differentiation is thus a part of many research problems. We know from case studies, for example, that relatively few Jews are alcoholics, and that this seems to be so irrespective of their occupation, income, or other social characteristics. But analysts have not yet been able to specify the relation exactly, and better data on religion would probably help. There is also a marked difference by religion in the incidence of cancers and heart diseases, and with better data it would be possible to eliminate extraneous factors (such as that Episcopalians, who are wealthier on the average, therefore see a doctor more often) and establish whether these diseases are actually related to differential patterns of living, as some analysts now believe. As we have already noted, the variation in family size by religion is a complex phenomenon, the analysis of which is seriously hindered by lack of data. Attempts to understand better the relation between ethical values and fertility are not the consequence of idle curiosity; the welfare of the large sector of the world presently undergoing modernization depends on whether national income can be increased faster than the population.

The principal argument for including a question on religion in the census, in short, is the humanist one that knowledge is good, and more complete and accurate knowledge is better. Religion is not only a personal experience and a sacred theology; it is also a social institution. As such, it should not be protected from empirical research and analysis by a high wall of magical taboos.

PART II

THE CULTURAL CONTEXT
OF RELIGION

INTRODUCTION

ACH OF THE ARTICLES in Part II deals with one aspect or another of
the cultural impact of religion. Charles Glock discusses the influences
modifying the impact of religious culture upon the total culture.
Alexander Alland, Jr., analyzes the meaning of the religious trance as a means
of maintaining group solidarity and of freeing the member from the frustrations of social life. Phillip Hammond discusses several of the cultural variables
which have undermined the social impact of religion and given rise to a form
of civic religion. Thomas Ford concludes this discussion with a survey of attitudes which reflect the influence of secular culture upon fundamentalist religious culture.

The potential relationships between religion and the rest of culture are
unlimited. Religion serves many possible functions in various societies. Each
culture, and for that matter subculture, both encourages and limits the influence of religion upon the total culture. Whereas early American colonists
reflected the prominence of religious cultural influence, the twentieth century
American citizen acknowledges the separation of church and state. The elimination of religious influence from organized secular processes in local, regional,
national and international affairs has become a major concern of those who
decry the weakening of American moral fibre. However, to equate the decline
of religious dogmatism with moral decline is to overlook the parallel development of a new ethical humanism which has arisen within the context of scientific rationalism.

If the student is to understand religion, he must understand the inter-
active relationships taking place between religion and the rest of society. The
simple study of religious doctrines does not give a picture of the value of these
doctrines to social life. Human history is filled with aborted religious and
philosophical systems which were theoretically sound but socially unaccept-
able. The written word has little meaning until it is used as a basis for behavior. A study of religion cannot be meaningfully undertaken apart from the
analysis of the total culture and the society in which it exists.

7 RELIGION AND THE INTEGRATION
OF SOCIETY

Charles Y. Glock

INTRODUCTION   Americans have traditionally viewed
religion as the moral adhesive maintaining "our way of life." Although any lasting group must have a series of unifying cultural
patterns, the tendency to ascribe the total function of maintaining
social unity in a complex society to religion alone ignores both the
role of religion in social *disorder* and the function of other institutions in society in the promotion of social cohesion. To be sure, the
mores of many groups, when broadly accepted within the culture,
may be reinforced by religion. In such instances behavior possesses
the dual sanction of society and religion. Religion, however, may
have one unique sanction: while religion is only one of many potential sanctioning agencies existing within a society, it alone
claims the right to determine supernatural and eternal validity. In
recent years, however, there has been a growing tendency to rely
upon reason rather than upon supernatural authority as the source
of values. The authority of religion has been challenged at least
partly because pluralistic religion does not possess a unity of values
and thus opens the door to alternative ideology. Modern society
has increasingly turned to economic or political systems as integrating forces.

The religious sanction in the long run is, however, generally
stronger than the economic or political sanction, although a consistent political or economic sanction may in time also be defined

CHARLES Y. GLOCK is Professor of Sociology and Director of the Survey Research Center
at the University of California (Berkeley).

Abridged and reprinted from *The Review of Religious Research*, Volume 2, Number 2,
Copyright 1960, by the Religious Research Association, Inc. Also published as Chapter
9, *Religion and Society in Tension*, by Charles Y. Glock and Rodney Stark (Chicago:
Rand McNally, 1965).

religiously. The long-run social integration of any type of group, whether a small social group or a broad mass society, is thus reinforced by a value system which gives convincing evidence of both supernatural authority and social stability. However, no single sanctioning system any longer possesses the potential of maintaining social cohesion.

Religion may not integrate at all. It is possible, for example, that religion will integrate an individual into a small but deviant group which is antagonistic to the values of the broader culture. In such instances religion may lead to social disorder and dysfunction because of its immense influence upon the members of the smaller group. Where religion has sanctioned an ideal which has been challenged by social change, religious groups often find themselves unable to accept the change being brought about and, therefore, offer a reactionary posture to the society at large. A clear example of the tendency both to integrate and yet be dysfunctional can be seen in the Amish community. Because the Amish reject many electrical and mechanical devices, preferring the simple necessities of the horse-drawn buggy and candlelight, progress as symbolized by automobiles and electricity is resisted on the basis of supernatural authority. In this instance the individual is integrated to the group, but the group religious expression causes the Amish member to reject highway safety (horses on the highway) and health standards (milking cows by hand).

Many religious norms tend to remain ultimate, even when violated with impunity, because they serve as *ideals* for future group behavior. Because religion demands individual perfection, an unattainable state for the common man, the ideal remains as a goal of personal behavior in spite of man's failure to reach this goal. Religious ideals have meaning even when violated because men are finite in a universe which seems to them to be infinite. And yet, paradoxically, men today remain humanistically centered, rejecting the concepts of absolute truth in favor of relative and flexible interpretations of cultural norms.

ONE OF THE ABIDING general propositions of sociology is that religion serves the central and crucial function in society of supporting what has been variously called social integration, social solidarity, and social cohesion. Underlying this proposition is the still more general one, namely, that in order to maintain itself, every society must achieve some consensus around a set of basic values, an agreement that they are meaningful and afford an appropriate basis for social organization and common action.

The concept of social integration is an ideal-typical one. It does not imply that every society achieves universal consensus or that every one of a society's members shares precisely the same set of values. It is argued, however, that considerable consensus must exist if a society is to withstand diversity and cleavage without breaking down. Where consensus is at a minimum, collective social action becomes more and more difficult to achieve and eventually a state of disintegration or social disorganization sets in.

The term integration has a favorable connotation in our language, disintegration an unfavorable one. However, as the term is being used here, to say that a group or a society is highly integrated is not necessarily to express approval of it. Religion has been especially singled out as the prime force in the creation and maintenance of social integration. A number of scholars, Durkheim among them, have expressed the belief that religion is so important to social integration that, without it, social disintegration would inevitably follow. Its integrating role is seen as manifold. One, through its belief system, it gives basic support to social and individual values. Two, through its ritual, it repeatedly reinforces identification with and commitment to these values. Three, through its system of eternal rewards and punishments, it helps to insure the embodiment and acting out of values in behavior.

We have lived with these notions for a considerable time now. Developed at the turn of the century, they have continued to be salient, with little modification, ever since. As we attempt, however, to apply them to contemporary American society—or for that matter to any existing society, whether primitive or modern—we are confronted with a number of difficulties.

For one thing, we find it difficult to reconcile the general theory with the considerable evidence of religious conflict. On every side, it would seem that religion threatens social integration as readily as it contributes to it. The history of Christianity, with its many schisms, manifests the great power of religion not only to bind but to divide.

It is also difficult to find evidence that, with increasing secularization, there is a general decay of social and personal values. To be sure, the values of Western society have changed during the past centuries and are still changing. Some observers have lamented that the changes in America reflect a gradual departure from the values of the Judaeo-Christian heritage and attribute many of our social ills to this fact. At the same time, however, our society appears to be maintaining itself with a reasonable degree of success. Moreover, many of the pathologies of contemporary society are paralleled by significant advances in social responsibility and individual ethical conduct. Though only the future can decide the question, there seems to be no immediate danger of the disintegration of our society or the wholesale retrogression of our moral life.

What seems evident, certainly in modern complex societies and probably in most primitive ones as well, is that religion is not the only source and support of social values. It is highly unlikely that religion has ever been the sole source of social cohesion. It becomes relevant to ask, therefore: what are the ways in which religion enters into and influences human values and human action and more parochially, what contribution is religion making currently to the value structure of American society?

SOME DEFINING CONCEPTS

NORMS, VALUES, AND BELIEFS. Social integration requires and presupposes consensus on three distinct levels. First of all, there must be agreement on norms. Norms are prescriptions for action; they formulate the accepted ways of doing things. Second, there must be agreement on the values which the norms embody or further. Values underlie norms in the sense that they sum up what makes the norm worthwhile and a proper and good way of behaving. Third, there must be considerable agreement in belief concerning the nature of man and the world, that is, there must be agreement that the nature of reality makes a particular set of values both viable and rational.

In a stable society, most action follows directly from the norms. The norms prescribe what is to be done in given situations and action follows almost automatically without any question being raised explicitly as to the meaning of the action. The ability of norms to function in and of themselves as effective guides to behavior is a consequence, of course, of the socialization process. From earliest childhood we are indoctrinated in the norms so that acting in conformity to them becomes almost instinctive. Indoctrination in the norms also involves, however, indoctrination in values and beliefs, subtly as this may be done. We come to learn what is expected of us, but we also develop a sense, however vague, of the meaning and value-import of these expectations.

If norms are described as prescribed ways of behaving then a value can be defined as a preference for some state of being. Americans value democracy insofar as they prefer democracy over other forms of political organization. Beliefs, often confused with values, are to be distinguished from them in that they are not preferences but constitute statements about the true nature of things.

The three concepts may also be distinguished in the following way: norms deal with means, values with ends, and beliefs with their rationale.

NORMS IN CONFLICT. Theoretically, all action would automatically follow the norms in a fully integrated society. There, occasion would never arise for questioning the norms since complete consensus would exist at all three levels: norms, values, and beliefs. In reality, of course, such complete integration probably never exists. Almost inevitably, circumstances arise in which the norms are not sufficient to govern action in and of themselves. This will be the case when contradictory norms exist, when traditional norms are challenged by new ones, when for one reason or another norms do not further the ends for which they were designed, and when norms have been inadequately internalized.

Norms are often contradictory even in simple and homogeneous societies, but in complex and pluralistic societies some contradiction almost always exists. A society may be homogeneous and consistent in its norms and yet have its traditional norms challenged by a new set of norms coming in from outside.

Norms can also lose their self-warranting character when they turn out to frustrate rather than to further some basic value of a society. This can happen because underlying values are changing and are rendering traditional ways of doing things obsolete and irrational. However, it can also happen that a devised norm turns out to have been ill-advised for one reason or another. This is especially the case with legal norms.

Finally, norms are not always so thoroughly internalized that they are automatic. Though the power of society is great, it is not absolute. Norms are always more or less internalized, and therefore always more or less open to doubt and challenge.

THE NATURE OF COMMITMENT. The concept of commitment has a central bearing on social integration. In our theoretical model of the wholly integrated society, there would be total consensus as to where primary commitment lies just as there would be consensus on norms, values, and beliefs. In actual societies, the locus of commitment becomes a problem wherever action does not directly follow from a norm. When conflicting norms imply distinct values and beliefs, then resolution of conflict can be achieved only through a decision as to where primary commitment lies: on the level of the norm itself or on other and deeper levels.

Locating one's primary commitment may be entirely relative to a particular conflict situation. Commitments to given norms, values, or beliefs may all be relative and insisted upon only in some contexts and not in others. At the same time, we can nevertheless conceive of ultimate commitments, i.e., commitments which are inexorably held under all circumstances and conditions. Commitments of such kinds may be said to be "sacred" in two senses: one, they are held to be unalterable and two, any sacrifice will be endured in order to withstand a threat to the commitment.

The locus of a commitment, whether "sacred" or otherwise, may be a belief, a value, or a norm. Where, for example, the commitment is to a value, beliefs and norms as well as other values become subject to change whenever they undermine that value. Thus, in time of war, the norm—thou shalt not kill—and the belief in the sanctity of the individual is sacrificed in order to sustain the commitment to what is more ultimately valued: the nation. The ability of a nation to wage war, and presumably therefore to maintain itself, is dependent upon a high degree of consensus that in fact the nation represents an ultimate commitment. Were ultimate commitment to be attached to the belief that human life is more sacred than national identity, war would not be possible.

But, as we have suggested, ultimate commitment may not always be at the level of beliefs or values. It may exist at the level of the norm. In such cases, values and beliefs are subject to change in the service of maintaining the norm. The norm of segregation is a case in point. The members of the White Citizens' Councils in the South have their primary commitment to the "norm" of segregation. The values and beliefs which are conceived to give meaning to this norm are relatively unimportant. In fact, the way in which the norm is rationalized may shift and change. Thus, the White Citizens' Council member may argue that his adherence to segregation is a consequence of his belief that God ordained segregation as is shown in the Biblical story of Ham. Yet, his commitment to this belief is weaker than his commitment to the norm. Faced with a different interpretation of the Biblical story, he will find another belief to support what to his mind is an unquestionable norm. Where norms are ultimate, beliefs are their servants.

Ultimate commitment is likely to be at the level of the norm wherever the norm is deeply imbedded in the traditions of a society or group. Norms have become so much a part of a way of life that they come to be perceived as "sacred." In such instances, the values and beliefs which originally gave meaning to the norms may no longer be applicable; they may indeed be irrelevant to contemporary adherence to them. The meaning of the norms, insofar as it exists, and is rooted in other than bare self-interest, is supplied by the high value placed on tradition or custom itself.

AUTHORITY AND SANCTIONS. In sum, it is important to social integration that the members of a society share commitments to certain norms, values, and beliefs and that some of these commitments be ultimate in character. Essential to producing commitment is some form of authority with the power of constraint over the members of a society. Societies depend not on one but on a number of sources of authority to produce the kinds of commitments necessary to assure that norms are acted out in practice. Four kinds of authority may be identified, each of which includes its own sanctioning or reward-and-punishment system.

First, there is legal authority and its sanctioning system. In every society, implicit and sometimes explicit judgments are made that certain norms, and sometimes certain beliefs and values, are so crucial to the social order that disconformity in these respects cannot be tolerated. It is these crucial elements of a social order that are ordinarily covered by its laws, which specify illegal actions and their punishments. Punishment for breaking a legally established norm frequently takes the form of depriving the law breaker of the rights and privileges which the society values most highly.

Akin to the legal authority of the state manifested in its laws is the authority of private bodies to formulate and enforce their rules and regulations. Thus, in any society, legal authority will be lodged within some government to which everyone is subject, but it will also be lodged in private associations—business firms, labor unions, universities—to whose authority employees or members are subject and which constitute in effect private governments.

Not all norms, even basic ones, are incorporated into formal laws and regulations. Societies also depend upon the force of social authority and its sanctioning system to sustain commitment. Societies differ, of course, in the relative degree to which legal and social authority are relied upon to secure adherence to the norms. The more traditional the society, probably the greater the reliance on social authority.

Social authority is no more or less than the authority of the group to exercise a degree of control over the behavior of its members. Like legal authority, social authority includes a sanctioning system—a much more informal one to be sure—through which "good" conduct and beliefs may be rewarded and "bad" conduct and beliefs punished.

A third type of authority is the suprasocial one, which too has its accompanying sanctioning system. Here, beliefs, values, and norms derive their authority from a transcendental referent. Suprasocial authority operates most clearly through institutionalized religion. Like legal and social authority, it also has the power, theoretically at least, to reward and punish. The rewards and punishments, however, are not immediately imposed but are promised for the future.

There is still a fourth authority: the authority of the self as manifested in the individual conscience. It does not seem to be arbitrary to say that the individual conscience can exercise authority and is capable of rewarding and punishing. The authority it exercises is not entirely independent of legal, social, or suprasocial authority, but neither are the other three entirely independent of each other. To point to self-authority is to point to the obvious fact that societies differ greatly in the extent to which they produce individuals more or less free to choose their commitments for themselves.

In any society, the relative saliency and influence for these various authorities and their sanctioning systems will vary. Furthermore, they will not all be relevant to every situation. Social integration is maximized, however, where different sanctioning authorities reinforce rather than contradict each other in the values, beliefs, and norms they support.

RELIGION AND SOCIAL INTEGRATION

With these defining concepts in mind, we now wish to return to the first of our two original questions, namely, the place of religion in social integration. From what we have learned, it is evident that if we define religion as a "sacred" or ultimate commitment to some set of norms, values, and beliefs, then religion is indeed essential to social integration. Though society is not capable of maintaining itself when it lacks a high degree of consensus as to what it is ultimately committed to, what is essential is not the kind of authority from which the commitment's "sacred" quality is derived but the simple fact that the commitment exists.

Seen in this perspective, traditional sociological theory concerning religion's contribution to social integration, though highly general, does not appear to be general enough. What contributes to social integration is not institutionalized religion but what society defines as the "sacred." The reinforcement is not necessarily provided by religious ritual; it may be provided by entirely secular forms of social support. And, though the acting out of the "sacred" in behavior requires a sanctioning system, it does not demand that it be a suprasocial one.

It follows from what has been said that institutionalized religion is not essential to social integration; theoretically, a high degree of social integration may exist without it. Where it exists, institutionalized religion may or may not contribute in large or in small measure to social integration. Where it is in conflict with other moral authorities, it may indeed contribute to social disorganization.

How much of a contribution it makes to social integration, and the direction of that contribution, depends upon a number of factors. First of all, there is the degree to which suprasocial authority is granted precedence over other forms of authority as the source and support of norms, values, and beliefs.

Secondly, there is the degree to which suprasocial, social, and legal authority support the same values. Where they do, the contribution of institutionalized religion to social integration is dependent on whether it informs and influences other sources of authority or is influenced and molded by them.

Thirdly, the role of transcendental authority is dependent upon the degree to which a society is ruled by tradition. Where custom and habit form the primary basis of social organization, the belief system of organized religion is likely to play an important role in rationalizing tradition. However, it must be pointed out that, insofar as institutionalized religion is tied too closely to one set of secular norms and customs, it can quickly lose its moral authority when new norms gain acceptance. When this happens, there is a propensity either to abandon traditional religious belief or to empty it of all practical application.

Fourth, organized religion's integrating role depends upon the degree of consensus which exists in the religious community itself. Where internal dissent pervades organized religion, it is not likely to contribute to the integration of the society at large though it may heighten the cohesion of particular groups. At the same time, however, unless there is dissent, the commitment to organized religion may well be so slight as to have little influence on the value structure of the society.

In the very nature of things, religion can never serve as the exclusive basis for social integration. It can only be more or less important; there have been societies in which religious authority was dominant; we know of many today in which its role is negligible. There is good reason to believe that where religious authority is accepted, its power to generate and sustain commitment in the face of opposition, and even of persecution, is very great. Historically, revolutionary movements have often been closely associated with religious movements. In contemporary society, this is not the case. Yet, because they also require commitments that are difficult to carry out in practice, present-day revolutionary movements construct secular ideologies that have much of the flavor and many of the characteristics of transcendent religious belief.

Little is known as to the empirical circumstances under which religious authority gains dominance and under which its influence decays. Perhaps a crucial factor in the acceptance of religious authority is the capacity of religious institutions and their personnel to organize society, that is, to provide the institutional framework in which the ongoing everyday life of a society is carried on. This happened in medieval Europe but the history of Western society is the history of the gradual spread of wholly secular institutions.

ORGANIZED RELIGION AND VALUES IN AMERICAN SOCIETY

The basic normative structure of American society derives in large measure from the high value placed on democracy as a basis for political and social organization. At the present time, this commitment to democracy rests primarily on secular beliefs and values. It is nevertheless fair to say that the respect for human individuality which underlies democratic conviction is rooted in and has been informed by the Judaeo-Christian heritage as it has been interpreted in the light of history.

This capacity of religion to inform the secular normative structure seems to be largely a thing of the past. In a complex society, and particularly in a democratic one, contributions to the normative structure come from many sources: the body politic, the economic order, the mass media, labor unions, private citizens, as well as the church. These sources at once inform the norms and values of our society and are informed by them. The process is a dialectical one but it is not necessarily a matter of even exchange. Any particular institution may at times be influenced by the surrounding value structure considerably more than it is able to exercise influence over it.

Organized religion in the United States, we would assert, is currently much more on the receiving than on the contributing side of the value process. This is not because of lack of opportunity to make explicit what secular values should be, to elaborate on the implications of religious faith, to question the existing normative structure. The avenues open to the church for making a contribution are many: sermons, church periodicals and educational materials, official pronouncements, church programs, discussion groups. The available audience is large; the majority of the population is regularly exposed to the church's influence through Sunday worship as well as in other ways. Yet, the evidence indicates that the church is not availing itself of its manifold opportunities.

This is not to say that norms and values are ignored in what the church seeks to communicate. On the contrary, they are the major themes of much that is talked and written about. But the level of abstraction at which the topic is pursued has the consequence of leaving to other sources the final say in determining everyday norms and values. The church's emphasis is over-whelmingly on man's relationship to God. The implications of the faith for man's relation to man are left largely to the individual to work out for him-self, with God's help but without the help of the churches. Man is exhorted to be a "steward of God," "to exercise choice and initiative in his use of leisure time in keeping with the new life of Christ," "to manage economic wealth in terms of Christian responsibility and leadership," "to accept the political re-sponsibilities of Christian citizenship on the basis of his citizenship in the Kingdom of God."

How man behaves, and what he values, is not informed by his faith but by the norms and values of the larger society of which he is a part. Con-fronted on the one hand by the abstract prescriptions of his faith and on the other by the concrete norms and values made explicit by law, by the context in which he labors, and by secular groups, man is almost inexorably led to follow the latter—partly because their sanctioning systems are more salient but also because the nature of a religiously inspired choice is not clear.

There are good and perhaps sufficient reasons, aside from theological ones, to account for the church's failure to contribute significantly to informing present-day values. The implications of the faith are simply not clear enough to be expounded authoritatively and unequivocally. Also relevant, most no-ticeably on the contemporary scene, is the high value which the church ap-pears to place on harmony and the avoidance of conflict. Wherever choice is between maintaining harmony and taking a stand on an issue which would produce conflict, the church most often chooses harmony. What is being here spoken of is perhaps no more than another facet of the frequently commented upon "dilemma of the churches." Were the church to insist upon strict obedi-ence to a set of norms, values, and beliefs, it would probably lose whatever power it now exercises in the larger society.

Because of this dilemma, it is unlikely that the church could succeed in generating a general commitment to its standards even were it to make ex-plicit the behavioral and attitudinal implications of the faith. Insofar as it has made its position explicit on given issues, its constituency has not widely adopted its values, at least not in situations where there are conflicting secu-lar norms. Witness, for example, the relative failure of the churches to foster racially integrated congregations though this is an issue on which most major denominations have spoken out in unequivocal terms.

That the church is being informed by, more than it is informing, the values of the larger society is an indicator that our society no longer appeals to suprasocial authority and its sanctioning system to validate its norms. It is also a sign that organized religion is committed, implicitly at least, to maintaining the society as it is rather than to fostering its regeneration along lines formulated by the church. In this latter sense, religion is indeed making a contribution to social integration though perhaps on terms which compromise its distinctly religious character.

It is not being suggested that the contemporary church cannot inform the lives of individuals and exercise an influence on society through them. Nor can it be said that, within particular minority religious movements, suprasocial authority may not still have precedence over other forms of authority. Looking at American society as a whole, however, organized religion at present is neither a prominent witness to its own value system nor a major focal point around which ultimate commitments to norms, values, and beliefs are formed.

8 "POSSESSION" IN A REVIVALISTIC
NEGRO CHURCH

Alexander Alland, Jr.

INTRODUCTION   Although a religious value system, as
we have shown, may not necessarily serve as the basis for the integration of the total society, it may work to integrate the person
into a particular religious group (*see* Glock, Article 7). Offering
strong support for persons of like inclination, most religious groups
tend to attract persons of similar interest, social class, and education. Anthropologist Alexander Alland describes the effects of the
group upon the individual in a study of the trance as an integrating
mechanism.

   Negro religious expressions in the United States follow four
basic lines, as generalized from a study of the relationship of social
class membership and preference for various types of ritual made in
Chicago by V. E. Daniels. The ecstatic sects or cults appeal primarily to the solid lower class and tend to be of the dancing-crowd
type similar to the group represented in this article. The semi-
demonstrative groups, however, appeal primarily to the lower middle class and are characterized by a tendency toward vocal assent
in shouts of "amen" and "hallelujah." Deliberative churches appeal to the upper middle class and center their worship around
sermons. The fourth grouping, the liturgical or formal denomination, tends to be ritualistic and appeals more to the upper class
Negro membership which prefers Episcopal, Presbyterian, or Congregational churches.

   Although the dancing or demonstrative sect is only one of

Abridged and reprinted from the *Journal for the Scientific Study of Religion*, Volume 1,
Number 2 (Spring, 1962), pp. 204-213, with the permission of the author and editors.

ALEXANDER ALLAND is Professor of Anthropology at Columbia Univerity.

many alternatives open for Negro religious expression, it is designed in large part for those who seek to avoid the implications of modern life and who possess limited success potential. Group participation frees the seeker from his inhibitions and allows him to reach and "possess the spirit." The ecstatic sect is in one sense a denial of the world (see Johnson, Article 11). Its origin lies in the attempt of man to overcome his present inadequacy and inferiority in the hope that the freedom of the trance will transcend the limitations of present reality and injustice.

The social class of an individual affects the type of religious group he will join. The lower class, for example, shows a tendency to join a sect, whereas the middle to upper class tends toward an established denomination. The attitudes of the sect to the world differ from those of the established church or denomination (see Johnson, Article 11). Although the Roman Catholic Church contradicts this assumption because of its inclusive character, Protestant religion is a combination of sects and denominations which reflect existing social stratification.

Religious behavior may follow many potential cultural forms. The trance is only one of these forms, and yet it illustrates the effect which culture may have upon the individual and the process by which he is integrated into the group. Those who join the movement of "Sweet Daddy" Grace are a preselected susceptible group, inclined in this direction because of personal needs. But then, this is generally the story of the rise of religious groups. They usually develop to serve some persons facing a special need at a particular time in history. However, their future depends upon their success in adapting the sect to the changing needs of their changing membership.

———

TRANCE HAS an almost worldwide distribution, particularly if we include as equivalent phenomena the ecstatic states of the shaman and priest, possession induced by the physiological action of various drugs, and multiple possession at religious and semireligious ceremonies.

If we exclude chemically induced trance, the other forms may be distinguished on two possible grounds: (1) a suggested, but not proved, physiological and psychological difference between the two states, and (2) the valid sociological distinction that in one case only people occupying particular and limited statuses within a wider group experience trance, and in the other case, the experience is open to all members of a defined group, regardless of status.

The type of trance referred to in this paper is of this latter category and is associated with participation in a religious ceremony during which one or several of the lay or ecclesiastical participants may manifest the behavior patterns to be described below.

This does not mean that we assume an inherent difference between "types" of trance, but rather that we are primarily involved in the analysis of our own field data and feel that the sociological distinction drawn above will be useful in the following discussion in which we shall attempt to show a connection between group participation and possessive states.

Our analysis centers upon the external (physical and sociocultural) circumstances and the internal (individual psychological and physiological) states which elicit trance. Our major assumptions are: (1) that individuals acting in social situations are affected by the behavior and attitudes of other individuals with whom they interact, and (2) that social responses can be learned and internalized in sets which may become more or less automatic when triggered by the proper cues.

Trance state shall be defined descriptively for the moment as: a configuration of behavior patterns involving (1) mild body convulsions (snapping of the neck, bending of the trunk and/or legs in which the person regains control almost instantly); (2) prolonged dancing, usually to music, in what appears to be a semistuporous state, and (3) falling to the floor either with body contractions or remaining still as in a faint. The latter two forms of trance may last from less than a minute to (rarely) several hours. This behavior is described by participants as a prolonged or momentary loss of voluntary control over body movements. "You have no power over yourself when the Holy Ghost enters."

DATA.   The United House of Prayer for All People was founded by C. E. (Sweet Daddy) Grace, a Portuguese-Negro immigrant from the Cape Verde Islands. Early in the present century Grace settled in New Bedford, Mass., a city with a large Portuguese population.

In 1921 he constructed his first House of Prayer in Wareham, a suburb of New Bedford. Members were attracted to the new sect by the story that Grace had raised his sister from the dead. The sect was relatively ineffective in New England and Grace moved south where he rapidly obtained a substantial following. As Grace's reputation as a curer and miracle worker grew, the church gradually spread northward. This growth was probably facilitated by the great lower-class Negro migrations during the depression and the Second World War and the impetus created by the successful southern crusade.

Grace opened a church in Brooklyn in 1930 and in New York city in 1938. The first church in Connecticut was built in 1956 in New Haven. Since that time, branches have been organized in Stamford, Bridgeport and Hartford— other cities with substantial Negro populations.

While the national organization is large, the local chapters in New England are quite small. Middle-class Negroes do not join this kind of church, and the religious lower-class Negro divides his allegiance among several churches of this type. What make this group stand out in the local community is its substantial building, paid for out of Grace's accumulated fortune.

The theology of the United House of Prayer is similar to that of other eschatological churches with the emphasis on imminent doom and salvation. Salvation, however, can only be achieved through the intercession of Daddy Grace who is accepted as God's last earthly prophet. The church grants the unique gift of salvation to those members who live according to church doctrine (a strict code: no smoking, drinking, dancing, or adultery) and who experience the Holy Ghost. The latter is manifested in a trance state, the achievement of which is uppermost in the minds of the membership. Members are enjoined to come and enjoy themselves, to "have a good time"; to shout and sing. The emotions of the community are poured into services which are attended by the faithful several times a week and on Sundays. Part of the service on special nights consists of a program in which members perform for one another, singing hymns, reciting prayers or testifying to the power of the church. Sermons follow the free-flowing hell and damnation extemporaneous tradition of the store-front church.

If members "live clean," i.e. follow church rules, they have few, if any, social outlets beyond the church. This isolation is increased by their status within the local community, which is low. Their church is considered an oddity, and on special occasions, such as visits from Daddy Grace or the newly elected Bishop, many local people, white and colored, attend service to watch the spectacle. Unsurprisingly, members are not unaware of this attitude of the community at large and they make frequent mention in testimonials to the attitudes of outsiders which are taken as tests of faith.

The yearly cycle culminates with a traveling convocation and baptism which tours the cities in which there are member churches. Those who can afford it attend the convocation in several cities to enjoy the drama of the church and to be near the leaders whom it is believed project spiritual powers.

In addition to these activities members are enjoined to purchase a range of Grace products which include soaps, perfumes, pomades and other toilet articles, including bleaching cream. At the height of his entrepreneural career Grace even offered coffee from his plantation in Brazil and eggs from the Grace farm, all of these products believed to be endowed with curative powers.

The members' lives literally overflow with "Grace." The double meaning of this expression has not gone unnoticed within the group and is used as a main theme in sermons.

THE TRANCE.   In this section we shall present a more detailed description of trance behavior and "seeking," i.e., the attempt to achieve the first possessive state.

Trance usually occurs during musical interludes. These are under the control of the pastor who may start or stop the band on signal, but band playing is usually structured into specific parts of the service. Women are generally the first to go into trance states, and under most conditions more women than men have trance in any one evening. There are definite parts of the service in which trance is inappropriate. It may occur at these times, however, if there is some extra cause of excitement such as a visit from the Bishop or some other charismatic leader in the church. When the trance occurs at an odd time, and it is a full dance trance, the band is likely to commence playing and continue to do so as more people go into trance. Mild or momentary trances occur when people are seated in the pews during less exciting parts of the service or testifying before the congregation. These are usually accompanied by a flinging of the arms and possibly some "speaking in tongues."

THE DANCE TRANCE. *Body:* Usually almost erect with little movement although there is some bending forward and, in some people, varying degrees of pelvic movement. When a person falls to the floor he or she may writhe for a few minutes and then lie still, usually on the side but sometimes on the back. *Feet and legs:* Some variation on the Lindy step is the most common movement. This may be done in half time, time, or double time, to the music. *Head:* The head may be rocked back and forth or held steady. One or two people snap their necks rather vigorously. *Face:* Facial expressions vary from what is best described as painful to euphoric. *Arms:* May fling freely or be held up, bent at the elbow. The hands may wave or may be rubbed over the body, especially over the hips and stomach in what appear to be erotic movements. *Duration:* The trance usually lasts from 10 to 15 minutes per person, but many have shorter or longer trances. One female was timed at one and one-half hours. People may have from zero to five trances in any one evening. Frequency, duration and number of trances are higher when the church is crowded and attended by special personalities.

SEX DIFFERENCES. Men have fewer trances than women. We have observed no instances of males in trance during normal services except during the music periods. Some women appear to have trances much more easily than others. Fewer men fall to the floor than women. There is less "speaking in tongues" by the men. The overt intensity of the men's trance may be as strong as the women's, if not stronger.

SEEKING. Seeking involves the active attempt of a person who has never experienced the Holy Ghost to achieve first trance. In this process the person is aided by the congregation, the band, and the pastor. Special "Flood Gate" weeks are set aside for those seeking the Holy Ghost, and traveling evangelists make the church circuit working with initiates.

Seekers fast all day before coming to the "mountain," a raised platform at the front of the church. There they kneel down and repeat rapidly Daddy Daddy Daddy, etc. . . . The band plays loudly with a highly repetitive, simple melody and strong beat while the pastor preaches directly to the person or persons attempting to gain trance.

Elder B. operates differently. A few direct quotes from the field notes collected during his visit to the local church will best illustrate his technique.

"Toward the end of the evening Elder H. got up to deliver the sermon. He then told the congregation that Elder B. was with them for the week. He explained that Elder B. was the greatest evangelist. B. is an old but vigorous man of 78 or 79. He has rather long, white hair, is of medium build, and is quite short. B. began his sermon by telling a joke about his daughter, a well-known Negro entertainer. He then began the usual stomping and shouting sermon. . . . Occasionally he would stop without warning and shriek 'Yeh' at the top of his voice.

"After several minutes B. asked the congregation if there were any there who were seeking. Four women eventually went to the 'mountain.' B. told the congregation that they 'were going to see something.' He then asked the women to hold up their right hands and to look at the floor. They did so. B. told them that the Devil was down there and that no good came from that direction. Then he told them to look up at the ceiling. After they did this he told them that Jesus was up there and that He would come to them. He lowered his hand in a swift movement and three of the four women fell to the floor in trance. This was the signal for several of the other women to go into trance and with this the band began to play. The trances were more violent than usual and several women fell to the floor."

It is important to note that the four women who came forward in response to Elder B. were not seekers in the strict sense, that is, they had already had the Holy Ghost and were highly susceptible to trance.

Working with real seekers B. developed the following pattern: "First B. invited the band to come down off the podium. He asked them to join hands in a circle, that is, to form a star with their left hands, and to raise their right hands. He instructed all the men to close their eyes, to hold their lips tight and to think hard of Daddy. Deacon T. was the first man to go off. He was followed by the rest of the band except the two youngest boys (about 10 and 11).

"After his success with the band, B. asked for young girls who were seeking. He said he did not want anyone to come up who had had the Holy Ghost. A group of young girls came up and formed a star. The band began to play but only one girl went into trance. She went into violent trance and fell on the floor, remaining on the floor emitting cries of gibberish for over one hour. Toward the end of the evening the women gathered around her and began to sing and clap their hands. They kept this up until she came to, but the excitement of the clapping seemed to put her back in trance for a short time. Finally a chair was put under her and she calmed down. After this B., working on various individuals, tried with limited success to put her back in trance. He told her that the Holy Ghost was in her mouth, and also had her hold up her right arm. Finally he told her that the Holy Ghost was in her right arm. Her arm began to shake and then as she walked across the floor she stopped shaking in one arm and picked it up in the other. B. had little success with the other young girls, possibly because one of them, who was a seeker, laughed during the session. (B. tried very hard to get this girl and another into trance states.)

At the side of the mountain we noticed a man tarrying, i.e. repeating Daddy, Daddy, over and over again. He was obviously seeking the Holy Ghost. The pastor took the microphone and began to sing over him. Finally after the pastor had worked himself into a state of shouting, the man went into trance."

It is clear that when working with seekers who are actual novitiates it is difficult to induce first trance. B. always has his greatest success with experienced people. These, however, are used by him to infect seekers with the spirit and there is no doubt they add to the general excitement and drama generated by seeking sessions.

No interviews were obtained with members who had recently experienced their first trance. For this data we must borrow from field data collected in another church in New Haven which has a similar belief in the Holy Ghost and possession.

". . . It's a matter of faith, and once your mind is made up, there shouldn't be a lot of tarrying. Once your mind is made up that you want the Holy Ghost, it will come. But you can't doubt it, you can't doubt the Lord you know. . . . Now I'm talking about the day on which I really got it. Oh, I had my experiences before . . . but I was really determined in my heart I was going to get it. I got down on my knees and some people came around me and started tarrying with me. . . . There I was with my eyes closed and I was trying to picture Him on the cross or on the throne or something, just to get my mind only on Him and to forget all about everything all around me, and just keep my mind directly on heavenly things you know. . . . Before you know it I was speaking tongues. . . . I forgot about myself, I forgot about everything, I forgot about my feet feeling tired, I forgot about my legs, I forgot about people saying Hallelujah, tarrying, I forgot everybody around me and I kept my mind on one thing, that was Jesus and getting the Holy Ghost, and I was telling the Lord in my mind, 'Lord, you know my heart, you know, please give me the Holy Ghost.' . . . And I was light and nobody was around me, and it was a good feeling inside, I mean you just feel clean . . . you feel peace and joy right deep in your heart. . . ."[1]

ANALYSIS. Old-line psychoanalysts and psychologists writing on trance can generally be divided into two schools: those who favor hysteria on the etiology of trance and those who favor schizophrenia. Neither of these theories is acceptable in the light of the sociocultural data. In fact it is a general blindness to the social environment associated with trance which leads to these gross oversimplifications.

A culture or subculture composed of either hysterics or schizeophrenics would be difficult to imagine. Schizophrenia is a serious illness in which the affected individual has a great deal of difficulty communicating, much less adjusting to the outside world. Members of the United House of Prayer are not only adjusted to their social environment but are unlikely to commit antisocial

[1] Sparky Ravenscroft: Personal communication.

acts either against the community at large or within their own group. Hysteria fits the picture only slightly better than schizophrenia. To grant that this extreme form of neurosis were operational we should have to assume that trance was an automatic result of personality disorder rather than a technique learned with a certain amount of difficulty by participation in a special group.

Some of the more recent workers in ego psychology have suggested that trance is a form of hypnosis and that hypnosis itself is a form of regression in the service of the ego in which a transference-dependency relationship is set up between the hypnotist and his subject. It is this sort of analysis which seems most reasonable. While we accept the data of Hilgard and Gill and Brenman that susceptibility to hypnosis depends largely upon specific types of socialization, our data show there is actually a wide range of susceptibility among members of the church. The significant variables in what we might call trance culture are both sociocultural and psychological, with child training perhaps turning out to be rather insignificant in the overall etiology of possessive states.

Hilgard[2] cites several studies which show that normal subjects are more susceptible to hypnosis than schizophrenics and suggests that this may also apply to hysterics, although there is some contradictory evidence in regard to this latter point.

There is no doubt that some people find it easier than others to have trance. This confirms the suggestion that the susceptibility to trance may be, and probably is, related to personality traits. These may be based on neurotic patterns emerging from the guilt and anxiety which is known to be high in the lower class Negro church community. It seems reasonable, however, to regard the overall phenomenon of religious trance primarily as a sublimation of a range of frustrated drives which is patterned as a specific aspect of a given cultural vocabulary. Trance is in one sense a highly distilled essence of all activities in the United House of Prayer which are directed toward joy, ecstacy and final salvation, and away from the deprivation and misery of the Negro community. Attention to the sociological situation highlights the additional fact that trance fulfills a member's status rights in the eyes of the congregation. Repetition of trance acts to reinforce the belief of performers and spectators alike, proving that the people involved have not wandered from a state of grace.

The extreme deprivation of members of this sect which is economic and psychological is not in itself a sufficient cause of trance. There are other deprived groups which do not experience this kind of release. Possession has been borrowed from other groups. First cause may possibly be explained by the existence at one time of one or a few truly psychotic personalities who acted as models for behavior within the context of some ceremony in the presence of psychologically receptive normals. Nonpsychotic skills may then have taken

[2] E. R. Hilgard,"Lawfulness Within Hypnotic Phenomena." Paper presented at Colgate Symposium on Hypnosis, April, 1960.

their places in the ranks of teachers so that the process could continue and be transferred to other exposed groups.

Who joins this particular kind of sect may ultimately be a combination of chance circumstances in which a receptive person is accidentally exposed to the available cultural pattern. Lower-class urban Negroes are more likely to be both receptive (due to their social status and personality problems flowing from it) and exposed (due to the proliferation of this kind of church in the urban Negro ghetto). For recruitment to occur, a particular personality type must intersect with the proper sociocultural conditions.

Observation in the church suggests that the occurrence of the all-important first trance experience is maximized by the following conditions and pressures upon the seeking individual which tend to lower ego defences and prepare the subject for the hypnotic transference:

1. Physical conditions.
   (a) *Heat.* A hot, stuffy room seems to be the pattern for all seeking sessions.
   (b) *High percentage of CO_2.* Windows in the House of Prayer are rarely opened and most seeking sessions are attended by enough people to create a situation which, in combination with the hot air heating system, is probably high in CO_2.

2. Physiological-psychological conditions.
   (a) *Loud, rhythmic music with a simple, repetitive beat.* This type of sensory stimulus tends to create ideal hypnotic conditions.
   (b) *Fasting.* Fasting contributes to a general weakening.
   (c) *Motivation.* The motivation for trance is high. It represents salvation for the individual and demonstrates to the group that a particular individual is worthy not only of God's affection but of their respect.

3. Sociocultural conditions.
   (a) *The presence of strong models for trance in significant others who set the pattern for behavior in the church.* Children coming to services night after night with their parents see them and others in trance.
   (b) *Lack of information.* For the phenomenon of trance to impress initiates they must be ignorant of its possible explanations. It must fit into what becomes a mystical experience.
   (c) *Isolation.* The activities of the United House of Prayer tend, as we have pointed out, to isolate the faithful from the community at large and cut them off from outside relationships. Members are expected to give most of their reading time to the Bible which, they are reminded, must be interpreted to them by the pastors of the church. At work they are thought of as members

of a peculiar sect, which further isolates them from their fellow
workers. Late converts to the church often come laden with
guilt feelings which can be unburdened through the obviously
cathartic experience of trance.

One informant made an interesting comment in this respect when he told
us that people come to "tarry" before the mountain to get the Holy Ghost
when they are feeling "heavy." "Tarrying lightens the soul."

Even when all these conditions are optimum and operating together,
many people find it difficult to have their first trance experience. Seekers continue their quest until they have received the Holy Ghost. Receptivity to the
trance is most certainly influenced by personal differences such as: range of
experience, needs of the individual, and tolerance for various physiological
stresses. Once the trance is learned, however, its repetition is assured. Hypnosis becomes autohypnosis and after the first experience it becomes less difficult
for members to enter into the trance state. We suggest that certain internal
cues (internal sensory states) become hooked into a system of developed external cues (associated with appropriate time for trance) which trigger the behavior pattern. If this is true, then the gradient hypothesized above for receptivity
to trance should occur. Unfortunately we have no evidence as yet for the existence of such a gradient. Further research is necessary before this hypothesis
can be tested.

From our field data it is clear that the response is learned. It is probably
facilitated by the learning of internal cues which act as secondary reinforcers
for the behavior pattern. If these internal cues do function in terms of secondary reinforcement, we would expect that their occurrence outside the initial
learning environment should trigger trance states. Informants tell us that it is
indeed possible for members to have trance on the outside *once* they have had
the experience in church.

Trance, then, within the context of religious ceremony, may be defined as
a cultural response to a series of internal and external cues which operate in a
particular kind of motivational state. The behavior which we have called
trance is most likely a form of hypnosis which later becomes autohypnosis
through a continuation of the learning process.

9 RELIGION AND THE "INFORMING"
OF CULTURE

Phillip E. Hammond

INTRODUCTION   To what extent can religion bring about social change? Is it possible to re-establish the primacy of religious values in a secular society? Is religion an independent or dependent variable in the process of social change? Answers to questions such as these are not easy, for the nature and structure of society has changed greatly since the medieval period when the religious ideal tended to control the European state. Luther's Reformation emphasis upon individual conscience shattered the dependence of man upon the church and freed him from "dogmatic" religion. The French Revolution continued this secularizing tendency in which reason was elevated above faith and speculation was replaced by science.

Although Auguste Comte, the father of Sociology, was unsuccessful in establishing a positive (scientific) form of religion devoid of theological (fictitious) or metaphysical (abstract) emphases and beliefs in the 1830's, the present worldwide scientific and ideological inclination has led to the development of nontheological and rational forms of civic and national religion. In this setting the primacy of religious values has been lost. The former cooperation existing between the church and the state has been replaced with modern forms of totalitarianism which have developed competing and parallel semireligious organizations to insure commitment of all age groups to prescribed forms of ideology.

Even in America the dual concepts of democracy and separation of church and state have led to the elimination of overt cooperation. Denominations no longer possess access to the legitimizing

Abridged and reprinted from the *Journal for the Scientific Study of Religion,* Volume 3, Number 1 (Fall, 1963), pp. 97-106, with the permission of the author and editors.

PHILLIP E. HAMMOND is Professor of Sociology at the University of Wisconsin.

power of the State for the enactment of singular group goals. Being powerless to enact denominational policy nationally, religious groups remain powerless to resolve issues of social conflict. The gradual tendency of government to take over the ethical decision-making functions of the Church has produced in part a sterile religious commitment.

The rationalistic outlook of American society and the predominant scientific ethos has led to the decline of eschatological (future life) concern. The use of political lobbyists by religious groups is the result of the recognition that religious values and goals must find legitimacy within political structures, if they are to have any meaning to the general society. Because religion no longer possesses the dominant power to integrate society (see Glock, Article 7), it can not bring about major social change without cooperation with other social institutions. Although religious leadership has been prominent in the civil rights movement in recent years, few concrete results would have been effected if political and economic institutions and leadership had not cooperated to bring about this social change. Without the power and prestige of local leadership and the federal government the movement would not have succeeded in gaining legitimacy through Congressional sanction.

Experience indicates that social change in America affects beliefs, rites, ceremonies, and religious group structure in greater degree than religion influences the nature and direction of social and cultural change. However, the history of religion testifies that the fundamental elements of the religious group tend to remain fixed and absolute, having been judged by its members to be the very essence of existence and the basis for group survival. Therefore, sociologically, we must assume that religion possesses the power to change and to be changed. Religion may be both the independent and dependent variable, although its dependency seems more pronounced in the modern setting.

THE PASSING PHRASE is no respecter of the abiding truth; religion too has its share of slogans. "Culture religion," "Post-Christian era," "syncretistic religiosity," "religion no longer informs culture"—these are a few currently heard. Like many slogans, taken literally they can obscure as well as illumine. The clergyman seeing his community, even his parish, headed for ruin despite his warning may rescue some comfort from believing that in the nation at large "Christianity has lost is hegemony," that "the relationship of religion and culture has been subverted," that "God is dead."

But what do the phrases mean? To religionists as to social scientists, religion has always been a cultural phenomenon (though of course some of the latter and most of the former have disagreed on what else religion is). Does the term "culture religion" connote therefore that religion is only a cultural thing?

Much history, including contempory, can be and is written with religion as a force in events. Does the phrase "religion no longer informs culture," mean, then, that history might better be written by ignoring religion since its impact is illusory?

In the United States, it is said,

> The traditional relation between religion and culture is for culture to stand under the judgment of the God to whom religion points. But in this newer American religiosity, the relation is inverted, subverted. Conventional religion is now validated in terms of the American Way.[1]

For most people presumably "the judgment of God" and "the American Way" are distinguishable. But what is the difference between them?

The significant referent of the phrases revolves around a change in the social structural location of ethical decision-making.

THE MEANING OF THE PHRASE. Some possible meanings of "religion does (not) inform culture" can be dispensed with immediately:

(1) It is quite clear that in America in these times of almost universal self-designation as member of some religious tradition, affiliation with church, synagogue, mosque, temple, etc., is *not* understood as indicative of "informing." By the same reasoning neither is attendance in these religious organizations taken as a sign of potency. If it were, claims that religion had lost its edge would decrease, not increase. Indeed some of the phrase-users, like their analogues in the fine arts, take popularity as proof of impurity.

(2) It is equally clear that theological sophistication or awareness is not acceptable as a measure of religion's informing culture. Again, despite some nostalgia for the era of Bible-toting and quoting, the fact must be that, absolutely and proportionately, more people today know more theology. Simply the relative number of persons attending college and the number of theological-type paperback books purchased support the contention.

(3) A third meaning of the phrase might be the philosophical or artistic excellence—the high quality—of theology. Religion fails to inform when the quality of its theology declines. One of those who claims that "God is dead," however, claims that such excellence is here.[2]

(4) Certainly a reasonable meaning of the phrase "culture is (not) informed by religion" suggests the possible *general* influence religion has had, and is having, on the affairs of man. But what person is prepared to argue that the Judaic-Christian tradition generally, and the Protestant tradition specifically, are *not* observable today in American economic goals, political proce-

---

[1] Will Herberg, "Protestantism in a Post-Protestant America," *Christianity and Crisis,* 22 (February 5, 1962), pp. 5-6. The general theme we are to discuss is found many places. Martin Marty, *The New Shape of American Religion* (New York: Harper & Row, 1959), and G. Vahanian, *The Death of God* (New York: George Braziller, 1961), are two good examples.

[2] Vahanian, *ibid.*

dures, judicial systems, and humanitarian welfare measures? Surely the values
of contemporary American society are religiously rooted.[3] And if the response
is that this "informing" is only indirect and "in the long run," then evidence is
also available that even now, today, Americans behave differently according to
which segment of that tradition they belong to, and how involved they are
in it.[4]

(5) If, then, by "religion no longer informs the culture" is not meant any
of the above, what does it mean? An answer is suggested in Vahanian's observation that "The Christian vocabulary has very little meaning for modern
man . . . [Religion] fulfills civic ends."[5] That is, persons no longer behave *because* of religious motives; rather their motives are secular, civic, "American."
"You will note the complete subversion of the relation of religion and culture
implied here. The American Way becomes the ultimate value; religion is recommended by its terms."[6]

THE PROBLEM OF THE MEANING OF THE PHRASE.   But to
assess religious motivation in this sense is an exceedingly difficult task. The
Protestant clergyman who journeys South to "sit-in" and the indigenous clergyman who heads the White Citizens Council to defend against meddling
Northerners are, to the observer, both "informed" by religion, or else neither
is informed.[7]

When two or more of these "powers" (be they persons or groups) are in
conflict, a decision must be reached regarding which is "right." If the contending factions are to remain in the same society after the decision is rendered,
they must grant "legitimating power" to whatever procedure (king, priest, leg-
islature, court, etc.) it is that decides the "right."

In this context, then, it is suggested that the phrase "religion no longer
informs society" has reference to this legitimating power—the power to make
decisions at times of conflict. This power is no longer "religious." The social
structures that do determine ultimate legitimacy *for the society* do so in "nonreligious" language, and have replaced organizations commonly thought to be
religious. Churches, in other words, no longer make some decisions they once
did. What kinds of decisions are these?

Not for a long time has the church claimed to decide conflicts of a cognitive and empirical nature. The "right" way of building bridges and plotting
planets has long since been institutionalized elsewhere. There is and has been,
so to speak, a "culture-science." Religion no longer "informs" science.

Conversely, the church's claim has not been questioned in matters of a

[3] Talcott Parsons, *Structure and Process in Modern Society* (New York: Free Press, 1960), p. 311.
[4] E.g., Gerhard Lenski, *The Religious Factor* (New York: Doubleday, 1961).
[5] Vahanian, *op. cit.*, p. 59.
[6] Herberg, *op. cit.*, p. 5.
[7] The poignant illustration comes from Peter Berger, *The Noise of Solemn Assemblies* (New York: Doubleday, 1961).

cognitive and nonempirical nature. Few if any other segments of society have challenged (and none denies) the religious organizations' leadership in developing, modifying and transmitting nonempirical beliefs. Though doubtlessly theology changes shape as other features of society change, the religious organization is free to espouse any belief, and free even to require assent to any belief on the part of members. Not the term "culture-religion" but "religious-culture" can apply here. Religion can and does inform culture in matters of a cognitive and nonempirical nature.

The one area where contention has existed, where the church once exercised authority but does no longer, is the area of ethics. Deciding the "higher good," a continuing problem for society, can be institutionalized in the church only as long as society is religiously homogeneous, only as long as society and church are coterminous. Under these conditions the church can be authoritative in ethical affairs, and the result is a "religious-culture." Under conditions of religious pluralism, however, the churches must relinquish that authority, and the result is a "culture-religion." Religion no longer informs society in the sense that religious organizations no longer resolve ethical conflicts.[8]

If spokesmen for one church claim divine sanction for demanding that the races be segregated, and spokesmen for another church by the same reasoning claim the opposite, then most assuredly it cannot be the church that decides the policy. And if it is the state (with its legislative and judicial procedures) that decides, then note that both sets of spokesmen, if they are to remain in the same society, *must* give higher allegiance to those decision procedures than to their own substantive positions.

In their "political patterns" religious organizations have had to relinquish their legitimating rights. But it is only their *legitimating* of ethics or behavior and not their *influence* that religious organizations have had to give up. There is a failure to see that (1) the change does not mean that organized religion no longer *influences* culture, (2) the change is in the sphere of ethics and not necessarily beliefs, and especially (3) the change is in the *social structural location for resolving conflicts* between contending ethical positions and not necessarily in the *source* or *motivation* for those ethical positions.

The third point, generally obscured in discussions of "culture-religion," deserves further comment.

THE ARGUMENT. The contention here—that the change revolves about the social structural location for deciding the higher good—has five parts: (1) The change connoted by the phrase "religion no longer informs culture" is not a recent change but began more nearly at the time of the Reformation and developed concurrently with religious pluralism, (2) the significance of the change is to be found in the changing social structural relations between churches and government. (3) One accompanying change has been

[8] A single, Established Church was involved in each of Troeltsch's instances of a "Christian Society."

the tendency of a "civic religion" to develop around the government. (4) Another accompanying change is found in the language used by persons to describe the motives for their behavior. (5) The churches' belated recognition of the change can be seen not only in proliferating alarms about the death of God, but also in the theological and political stances being taken by contemporary churches.

THE CHANGE IS NOT RECENT. Once theology removed the church as a necessary means of grace, once a religious leader articulated for followers their mutual belief that "the Lord hath more truth and light yet to break forth," then the way was open for religious heterogeneity. Whereas dissenters once were banished, now they are permitted. Immediately the problem then becomes: Suppose persons all claim transcendental direction but interpret it differently. Who decides? Luther's answer, his ambivalence toward the state, has led to the suggestions that he "divided life into compartments, or taught that the Christian right hand should not know what a man's worldly left hand was doing."[9]

Another common answer was to substitute one Established Church for another. Certainly the three centuries following the Reformation saw no decrease in the number of migrating sects, i.e., people escaping from situations where their interpretations of God's will were not given equal status. But the fact remains that Protestantism facilitated in the Western World a large measure of theological liberty and thus heterogeneity.

And where there develops theological heterogeneity, it clearly is the case that authority relinquished by the church is assumed by the government. The struggle toward religious pluralism is too well known to elaborate in this essay. Of significance here, however, is the fact that in that struggle the government takes on the ethical decision-making that once was the church's.

THE CHANGE IS IN THE RELATIONSHIP BETWEEN CHURCHES AND STATE. The move away from religious homogeneity occurred over several centuries. It was the American experience, however, where a "liberty-infused culture" became most fully translated into a "liberty-providing social structure." It was the sustained interaction of persons with disparate beliefs, which beliefs potentially could lead to opposing behaviors, that required the government to assume decision-making power that once was the church's, or was shared with the church.

The government assumed decision-making power over behavior, however, and not beliefs. Only the essentially ethical aspects of religion, and not the essentially cognitive aspects, needed to be relinquished to the state. And only the power to resolve conflicts in behavior, not the creation and transmission of ethical guides for behavior, was to be the state's alone. The case of conscientious objection provides an illustration. A church may hold beliefs about

[9] As discussed by H. Richard Niebuhr, *Christ and Culture* (New York: Harper & Row, 1951), p. 171.

the sanctity of life, the effect on others of passive resistance, etc. It may preach these beliefs to others. It may derive an ethical position which denounces violence. And its members may share this ethical position. But the members may not refuse to bear arms. Rather, the government exercises the right to decide the higher good and may grant them special status *if they register for it.* Failure to register, i.e., failure to acknowledge the government's right, is considered deviant and leads to imprisonment.

A "CIVIC RELIGION" HAS EMERGED AROUND THE GOVERNMENT. When ultimate power to make ethical decisions is concentrated in the social structure, and when the exercise of this power is both visible and long-term, conditions exist for the emergence of a set of accompanying beliefs about that process of decision-making. When, therefore, the locus shifts from church (or person, in the charismatic leader case) to secular government, the beliefs shift accordingly. Something like this seems to have happened in the United States. Members of society, having granted that maintenance of democratic procedure has higher legitimacy than their own substantive positions, raise to hagiologic stature the persons thought to have conceived and instituted the procedure: the Washingtons, Jeffersons, and Lincolns. And the emerging beliefs make sacred the strategic locus of the decision process, chiefly the judicial system.[10] Like the doctrine of the divine right of kings, the new doctrine maintains the divine right of the majority and, ideally, the divine protection of the minority.

An analogue to this "civic religion," this "religion of democracy," is necessarily found in any integrated society. *It is only when churches and government are structurally differentiated, however, that the "civic religion" is seen as competing with "church religion."* When the essentially ethical aspects of religion are institutionalized apart from the essentially cognitive aspects, any set of "religious beliefs" developing around the ethical institution may appear to be a threat to the cognitive institution. To the latter it will seem that "religion no longer speaks to modern man," that "religion no longer informs the culture."

THE LANGUAGE USED TO DESCRIBE MOTIVES HAS CHANGED. One factor that makes the churches' burden more difficult is a linguistic change. People no longer justify their actions in the same words. Not simply have expressions with transcendent referents tended to disappear; the growth of scientific knowledge has undoubtedly led to changes in what persons seek for and accept as explanations of behavior. The replacement of notions of devil and sin by notions of mental illness may be more dramatic but is only one example of this change. The general "rationalization" of society, the increasingly utilitarian outlook of its members, has had the effect of diminishing the use of "religious" language.

---

[10] It is of some interest in this regard that the American public ranks Supreme Court Justices highest of some 90 occupations. Of more significance is the continuing debate over the "proper" role of the judiciary—whether it is to "decide values."

No assertion is being made of course about the death of religion. Non-empirical meaning is still sought for the empirically unanswerable issues, and, as was shown above, decisions about the higher good are always "religious" in character. But this is the point; these latter decisions are no longer made by churches. Consequently, discussions of them are carried out not in "church language" but in secular language. The choice of words, however, ought not to obscure the fundamental change in the locus of decision-making or, if you please, the locus of interpreting God's will.

To quote again, then, the "shift from biblical authority and religious sanctions to scientific and factual authority and sanctions" is a misleading characterization. The relatively insignificant recent linguistic change should not dim the older, significant redefinition of the churches' place in the legitimating process.

THE RECENT CHANGE IS THE RECOGNITION OF THE OLDER CHANGE.   This lag in the language may have delayed recognition of the social structural change. Actually, the religious organizations' loss of authority in the realm of ethical decision-making is centuries old. Churches, it would appear, were slow to acknowledge their redefined place in society, and their belated recognition is manifested in part by slogans: "religion no longer informs culture," "God is dead," etc.

The slogans may be accurate as judgments on how well the churches carry their burden of relevance; they are not accurate as statements that the social structural role of churches in America is *recently* changed. For how early in the nation's life there came about the separate institutionalization of religious beliefs and ethics, even with the ensuing "sacredness" of the government, can be seen in Tocqueville's commentary. In 1831 that astute observer, had he been of the bent, could have written "Culture-Religion in America" or even "God Is Dead in America." He is quoted variously here[11] to illustrate that

(a) democracy and religious pluralism are joined:

It may be asserted that in the United States no religious doctrine displays the slightest hostility to democratic and republican institutions. (I, 330) In France I had almost always seen the spirit of religion and the spirit of freedom pursuing courses diametrically opposed to each other; but in America I found that they were intimately united, and that they reigned in common over the same country. (I, 337)

(b) beliefs become separated from ethics:

In America religion is a distinct sphere in which the priest is sovereign, but out of which he takes care never to go. . . . Although the Christians of America are divided into a multitude of sects, they all look upon their religion in the same light . . . [the clergy] endeavor to

11 All quotations from Alexis de Tocqueville, *Democracy in America,* edited by Henry Steele Commager, translated by Henry Reeve (New York: Oxford, 1947).

amend their contemporaries, but they do not quit fellowship with them.
(II, 27-28)

(c) Americans may be heterogeneous in beliefs, but not in ethics:

[Americans] differ in respect to the worship which is due from man to
his Creator, but they all agree in respect to the duties which are due from
man to man. Each sect adores the Deity in its own peculiar manner, but
all the sects preach the same moral law in the name of God. (I, 331)

(d) The government, with its procedures for resolving conflicts, takes on
    a sacred quality:

The men who live at a period of social equality . . . commonly seek
for the sources of truth in themselves . . . at such periods no new religion could be established . . . for such a purpose would be not only
impious but absurd and irrational. . . . It may be foreseen that faith in
public opinion will become a species of religion there, and the majority
its ministering prophet. (II, 8-10)

(e) Finally, although churches cannot arbitrate disputes over ethics, they
    do exert influence, even in the ethical sphere:

There is no country in the whole world in which the Christian religion
retains a greater influence over the souls of men than in America . . .
religion exercises but little influence upon the laws, and upon the details of public opinion; but it directs the manners of the community, and
by regulating domestic life, it regulates the state. (I, 331-332)

Taken together, Tocqueville's observations indicate that at least by early
in the 19th Century this society had a recognizable "culture-religion," that
Americans worshipped a "religion-in-general," that in the legitimating of ethics
there was an "erosion of particularity." And if the United States was to be one
nation, one integrated society, this situation had to be.

The required change, however, let it be said again, was only in the structural location where decisions on competing ethical claims are made. The
churches could still exert influence on its parishioners and the public at large,
as could any other individual or organized collection of them. Furthermore,
the churches still could claim authority in the realm of beliefs, even if some
chose not to. The telling event is that Roman Catholics in America, though
the church's ideology does not acknowledge it, have shifted their allegiance in
the ethical sphere away from the church, as Fichter's data clearly indicate.[12]

As with the Roman Catholic Church only less so, Protestant Churches
have retained a language that makes recognition of this change difficult and
an orientation that makes it distasteful. The devout, motivated by religious
ideals, cannot but feel frustrated when confronted with others who may be
similarly devout but whose religious ideals indicate different behavior. The in-

[12] Joseph Fichter, *Southern Parish* (Chicago: University of Chicago Press, 1951), pp.
259-271.

clination has been to doubt the devoutness, the *religiousness* of the motivation. But precisely because such techniques do not remove the conflict, there develops the alternative of the persuasion game *of necessity* demands a greater commitment to the rules, the game, and the judge than to the message of which the player is persuaded.

To some observers of this situation the religious ideals appear to have not only no control but also no possible influence. But what Tocqueville noted in 1831 the churches have not yet grasped as well.

These pages have tried to show, however, that only in a special sense are these slogans accurate. Religion necessarily fails to inform only in the sense that churches have had to give up the authority to resolve conflicts in the ethical sphere. They still may exercise ethical influence, and they remain the developers and transmitters of nonempirical beliefs. In these ways, God is not dead, and religion does inform culture.

This situation being the case, it is tempting to interpret the churches' renewed interest in biblical theology and their "search for political realism"[13] as indicating a growing awareness of their structural location in a society. Doubtlessly this is exaggerated. Many forces have contributed to these events. Yet recognition that (as Summer put it) "the pulpit no longer speaks with authority" has probably had a role in the establishing of lobbies, the coordination of information campaigns, and the interdenominational efforts to concentrate influence. So, too, the awareness that religious beliefs in the religiously pluralistic society are not automatically reflected in predictable behavior has probably had a role in the re-examination of those beliefs. American churches' renewed concern for "truth," that is, may well reflect recognition of their changed location with respect to the "good."

[13] Donald B. Meyer, *The Protestant Search for Political Realism,* 1919-1941 (Berkeley: University of California Press, 1960), traces the churches' enormous though short-range change from their optimistic position in the first part of the century to a more "realistic" position at mid-century.

10 RELIGIOUS THOUGHT AND BELIEFS IN THE SOUTHERN APPALACHIANS AS REVEALED BY AN ATTITUDE SURVEY

Thomas R. Ford

INTRODUCTION   The effects of social change upon a specific religious cultural area are illustrated by Thomas Ford. Using an exploratory attitude survey of inhabitants in the Appalachian region, Ford offers insight into the nature and strength of religious traditionalism and also into the particular processes and effects of change. Note the changes in attitude apparent within the second and subsequent generations. Strict fundamentalism (*see* Article 1) has given way to a modified fundamentalism which incorporates the current social welfare practices and attitudes of the secular world. Already the seeds of religious change are planted. Preliminary evidence indicates that sectarian attitudes have declined in an area where they would be expected to remain strong.

The changing nature of both religion and general culture is apparent. Although religious literalists and absolutists attempt to define the essence of religion in definitive terms, modification of religious attitudes and doctrines continues. When doctrines become incompatible with the dominant directions of social life, the religious group may die. On the other hand, if the religious group adjusts its procedures and doctrines sharply to coincide with secular demands, it may lose its purpose for existence. A third and more meaningful alternative lies in the willingness of religious groups to remain flexible and yet adhere to the basic elements of faith. The neo-orthodox movement, discussed in Article 1 has sought to offer this alternative to Protestant Christianity in America. A flexible religious group is more likely to remain both a participant and a critic in the process of change, thereby presenting a system of

Abridged and reprinted from *The Review of Religious Research,* Volume 3, Number 1, Copyright 1961, by the Religious Research Association, Inc.

THOMAS R. FORD is Professor of Sociology at the University of Kentucky.

values which may contribute to the general cultural values of a mass society. This recognition has led the National Council of Churches to play a more active role in the promotion of social change, an action decried by the fundamentalist American Council of Churches (commonly known as the Carl McIntire group).

Note the process by which this survey was developed. Although the study is based upon data gathered from a larger survey, the findings suggest further areas of investigation. The methodology of the study is simple and uncluttered, indicating in itself that sociological research does not have to be complex to be effective.

R ELIGIOUS VALUES so permeate the culture of the Southern Appalachian region that it is virtually impossible to treat meaningfully any aspect of regional life without taking them into account. Consequently, in the planning of a broad study of social and economic change in the region, it was decided that a major portion of the effort should be devoted to the determination of religious values, beliefs, and practices. The approach used was a sample survey of the population, using a formal schedule that included an extensive section on religious attitudes and beliefs.

The overall objectives of the survey questions pertaining to religion were to provide some indication of the nature and strength of religious traditionalism and to gain some insight into the complex relationship between religious outlook and secular change. In this brief essay primary attention will be focused on the relationship of selected respondent characteristics to: (1) the expression of sectarian beliefs and attitudes, (2) the expression of fundamentalist beliefs and attitudes that transcend contemporary sectarianism but are probably vestiges of the sectarianism of an earlier day, and (3) attitudes concerning the participation of the church and minister in secular activities that have as their end the promotion or influencing of social change.

SAMPLING DESIGN AND CHARACTERISTICS OF SURVEY RESPONDENTS.   The universe of the sample was defined as all the households in the Southern Appalachian region, which had been earlier delineated to include 100 counties in a seven-state area. A stratified, two-stage area sample was used in the selection of specific households from which interviews were secured. The strata employed were three types of residential areas: (1) *metropolitan*, which included all counties designated as portions of standard metropolitan areas in the 1950 U.S. census of population; (2) towns and cities in the population range of 2,500 to 49,999, designated for purposes of simplicity as *urban* places; and (3) *rural* areas, which embraced the remainder of the region and contained both village and open-country population. It was assumed that these three strata formed a rough continuum with respect to the degree of exposure to the influences of urban industrial society, an assumption which later analysis of the data proved to be essentially correct.

The selection of households and the interviewing of respondents took place during the summer months of 1958. Some 1,466 interview schedules were obtained. Of these, 31.5 percent were from metropolitan, 19.1 percent from other urban, and 49.4 percent from rural households. After the interviews were collected, other subcategories of the population were established on the basis of respondent characteristics. Sex and residence categories were maintained in all tabulations and, in addition, separate tabulations were made by age, educational level, and socioeconomic status of the respondent.

Socioeconomic status categories were based on a composite index that included household income, occupation and schooling of the household head, possession of various items of household equipment, and the respondent's identification of himself as a member of the upper, middle, or working class. Four status categories were established using deviation from the mean index score as the classification criterion. *Upper* status respondents were defined as those with scores one standard deviation or more above the mean, *upper middle* as those with scores ranging from the mean to one unit above it, *lower middle* as those with scores from (and including) the mean to one unit below, and *lower* as those with scores one unit or more below the mean. About a fourth of the respondents could not be classified according to socioeconomic status; they were mostly older persons, many of them widowed and retired, for whom no valid occupational data were secured.

Some of the more important characteristics of the survey households and respondents are shown in Table 10-1. Because the sampling unit for the survey was the household rather than the individual, the respondents do not constitute a representative sample of the adult population of the region. For that reason the observed distributions of responses to the attitude questions are not necessarily generalizable to the entire adult population of the region.

SECTARIAN BELIEFS AND ATTITUDES. Sectarianism is a useful connotative concept but, like so many other sociological concepts, there is no general agreement on a precise definition of it. This difficulty stems in part from the fact that sectarianism is generally conceived of as a complex of religious traits, not all of which are found in all sects and some of which are found in religious groups not generally considered to be sects. There are several ways in which the problem of definition may be handled in actual research. One way is by dealing individually or collectively with specific traits that are common to most recognized sects but are rarely found in more highly organized religious groups. Another method is to employ one of the church-sect scales, such as that devised by Dynes, in which case sectarianism becomes operationally defined in terms of scale score. In this discussion we shall employ the former method.

It is generally conceded that most churches serving the Southern Appalachian region today are direct descendants of sects that flourished on the American frontier of the late eighteenth and early nineteenth centuries. The basic religious tone of the region was established during the latter century, which was marked by a series of religious revivals that began with the Great

TABLE 10-1   Selected Characteristics of survey households and respondents, by residence, Southern Appalachian Attitude Survey,
1958.

	Rural	Urban	Metropolitan	Total
Household characteristics				
Number of households	724	280	462	1,466
Percent white	98.5	95.7	93.3	96.3
Average (mean) number persons per household	3.9	3.0	3.3	3.5
Median total household income reported (1957)	$2,830	$4,478	$5,475	$3,951
Respondent characteristics				
Percent male	40.3	34.3	24.8	34.2
Percent distribution by age (years)				
Under 30	13.8	14.3	12.3	13.4
30 to 44	30.9	28.9	38.9	33.0
45 to 64	37.7	42.2	34.6	37.6
65 and over	17.4	12.5	11.7	14.7
Unknown	0.2	2.0	2.5	1.3
Percent distribution by years of schooling completed				
Under 7	27.3	16.4	9.5	19.6
7 and 8	31.8	13.2	13.4	22.4
9 to 11	15.2	19.3	18.0	16.8
12	13.4	21.8	28.6	19.8
13 or more	11.0	28.6	30.3	20.5
Unknown	1.3	0.7	0.2	0.9
Percent distribution by socioeconomic status categories				
Upper	5.0	12.5	22.1	11.8
Upper middle	14.4	25.4	33.5	22.5
Lower middle	30.2	23.6	21.4	26.2
Lower	20.7	7.5	5.2	13.3
Unknown	29.7	31.1	17.7	26.2

Revival of 1800–1802 and continued almost without interruption throughout most of the century. Although the Presbyterian Church was the most important religious body on the early frontier in the eighteenth century, it failed to retain its strength or popularity as the line of frontier moved westward into the Appalachian mountains. Baptist and Methodist bodies were the chief beneficiaries of revivalism in the region and by the end of the nineteenth century accounted for about 70 percent of the reported church membership. They continue to predominate in the region, with about 40 percent of the respondents expressing preference for churches in the former group and 20 percent for churches in the latter.

Among the specific traits that presumably distinguish sects from organized churches are three for which the survey provided pertinent data: (1) sectarian emphasis on evangelism and conversion versus church emphasis on religious education; (2) sectarian preference for unspecialized, part-time ministry versus church preference for specialized, professional, full-time ministry; and (3) sectarian stress on "otherworldliness" to the virtual exclusion of secular interests versus the more balanced consideration of sacred and secular affairs by church groups.

Relating to the first of these was the survey question: *Which is more important in leading a religious life, conversion or religious training?* The distribution of responses within different residential groups was as follows:

	Rural	Urban	Metropolitan
Conversion	47.1%	38.6%	43.5%
Religious training	41.8	47.8	48.3
Equally important	5.1	4.3	2.8
Don't know	5.9	9.3	5.4

Considering that in highland religion conversion was generally regarded as "the climax of human experience," to use Hooker's words (*Religion in the Highlands,* p. 153), the response pattern seems to indicate a clear decline in sectarian outlook in the mountain region. Although conversion was regarded as more important by relatively more rural than urban or metropolitan respondents, the residential differences were not consistent when other respondent characteristics were held constant. In all areas the proportion of respondents who attached greater importance to conversion declined appreciably with rises in educational level and socioeconomic status. A majority (53 percent) of the respondents with less than 9 years of schooling but only 31 percent of those with schooling beyond high school considered conversion more important. Similarly, the proportion of all lower-status respondents who chose conversion as the more important factor (52 percent) was twice as great as the proportion of upper-status respondents (26 percent).

With respect to a second trait differentiating sects from churches—type of minister preferred—a series of four questions was asked. Responses in the three residential areas are summarized in Table 10-2.

Considering the sectarian background of Southern Appalachian religion, the evidence presented in Table 10-2 reveals a surprisingly strong preference for a professional ministry. An overwhelming majority of respondents in all areas expressed the belief that the minister should be paid, and even in rural areas two out of three respondents who thought he should be paid also thought he should be employed full time in church work. Nearly half of the rural respondents and close to three fourths of the urban and metropolitan respondents said the minister should have a college education or seminary training, but relatively few considered such training more important than "a call" to the ministry.

TABLE 10-2   Beliefs concerning the employment and training of Ministers: percentage distribution of responses to specified questions by Southern Appalachian Survey respondents in rural, urban, and metropolitan areas.

Question	Response	Rural	Urban	Metropolitan
Should the minister be paid for preaching?	Yes	82.9	93.5	92.8
	No	14.9	5.4	5.7
	Unsure	2.2	1.1	1.5
		100.0	100.0	100.0
If paid, should a minister give full time to church work or work at a non-church job as well?[a]	Full time	66.4	89.2	88.8
	Part time	26.6	4.2	5.6
	Unsure	7.0	6.6	5.6
		100.0	100.0	100.0
How much education should the minister have?	Seminary	29.1	51.8	50.6
	College	19.6	22.5	23.8
	High school	10.1	6.1	5.6
	Makes no difference	39.6	18.2	18.2
	Unsure	1.6	1.4	1.8
		100.0	100.0	100.0
Which do you think is more important for a minister — training for the ministry or a call to preach?	Training	13.3	21.8	17.3
	Call to preach	72.5	54.3	53.7
	Equal importance	12.6	21.8	26.6
	Unsure	1.6	2.1	2.4
		100.0	100.0	100.0

a Asked only of respondents who thought the minister should be paid for preaching.

The strongest support for lay ministers, as would be expected, came from the least educated and lowest-status rural residents. The strongest support for professional, full-time ministers came from upper-status urban residents. In all areas the proportion of respondents who claimed that the schooling received by the minister was not important to his mission was strongly and negatively associated with educational level and socioeconomic status.

Several questions were directed toward the exploration of the other-worldly orientation of the respondent population, one of which was concerned with millenarian beliefs. The specific survey question was framed as follows:

Some religious groups teach that the world is soon coming to an end. Do you believe this is true? The percentages of respondents, by residence and socioeconomic status, who replied affirmatively to this question are shown in Table 10-3.

TABLE 10-3   Percentage of Southern Appalachian residents expressing belief that *the world is soon coming to an end,* by residence, socioeconomic status, and schooling level.

Socioeconomic status and schooling level	Rural		Urban		Metropolitan		Total	
	%	Base[a]	%	Base	%	Base	%	Base
All respondents	30.5	724	14.6	280	15.2	462	22.6	1,466
Socioeconomic status								
Lower	37.3	150	14.3	21	45.8	24	35.9	195
Lower middle	31.5	219	16.7	66	18.2	99	25.5	384
Upper middle	17.3	104	7.0	71	11.6	155	12.4	330
Upper	0.0	36	0.0	35	3.9	102	2.3	173
Unknown	36.3	215	33.8	87	23.2	82	31.0	384
Years of schooling completed[b]								
6 or less	33.8	198	26.1	46	20.5	44	30.6	288
7 and 8	40.0	230	13.5	37	37.1	62	36.5	329
9 to 11	29.1	110	27.9	54	24.1	83	27.9	247
12	21.6	97	6.6	61	7.6	132	12.1	290
13 or more	7.5	80	3.8	80	5.7	140	5.7	300

a Base is number of individuals in category used in computing percentage.
b Percentages not computed for 12 respondents whose educational level was unknown.

In none of the tabulated categories did a majority of respondents claim to accept the premillenarian belief implicit in the question. Most, although not all, of the greater prevalence of premillenarians in rural areas is associated with differences in the social and economic composition of the population. The high proportion of premillenarians in the lower socioeconomic status group in metropolitan areas may be partly attributable to an influx of rural migrants, but in any case the base is too small to attach great importance to the percentage. The data clearly indicate the close relationship between socioeconomic status and acceptance of the premillenarian dogma.

Another survey question, which was selected primarily as a measure of the value ascribed to individual striving and achievement but which by implication may be indicative of an otherworldly orientation, was *Do you think God is more pleased when people try to get ahead or when they are satisfied with what they have?* The percentage distribution of responses by different residential groups was as follows:

	Rural	Urban	Metropolitan
When people try to get ahead	36.5	52.1	55.2
When people are satisfied	57.5	39.3	37.7
God is not concerned	1.4	2.1	1.3
Don't know and no response	4.6	6.5	5.8

Again, the associations of response with socioeconomic status and level of schooling were much greater than the associations with residence, as seen in Table 10-4, which shows the percentage of respondents in each socioeconomic status category and educational group who expressed a passive view.

TABLE 10-4   Percentage of Southern Appalachian Survey respondents expressing the belief that *God is more pleased when people are satisfied with what they have than when they try to get ahead,* by residence, socioeconomic status, and schooling level.

Socioeconomic status and schooling level	Rural		Urban		Metropolitan		Total	
	%	Base[a]	%	Base	%	Base	%	Base
All respondents	57.5	724	39.3	280	37.7	462	47.7	1,466
Socioeconomic status								
Lower	77.3	150	52.4	21	91.7	24	76.4	195
Lower middle	53.0	219	59.1	66	56.6	99	54.9	384
Upper middle	34.6	104	19.7	71	25.8	155	27.3	330
Upper	19.4	36	17.1	35	15.7	102	16.8	173
Unknown	65.6	215	46.0	87	48.8	82	57.6	384
Years of schooling completed[b]								
6 or less	72.7	198	58.7	46	63.6	44	69.1	288
7 and 8	67.0	230	59.5	37	56.5	62	64.1	329
9 to 11	58.2	110	48.1	54	53.0	83	54.3	247
12	29.9	97	32.8	61	32.6	132	31.7	290
13 or more	23.8	80	18.8	80	17.1	140	19.3	300

a Number of respondents in category used in computing percentage.
b Percentages not computed for 12 respondents whose educational level was unknown.

The extremely high proportion of "passivists" in the total population suggests that more is behind their response than simply an otherworldly orientation, however. Quite possibly it is nothing more than the very human tendency to attribute divine sanction to one's own actions, a tendency which in this instance would seem to be as true of those who were achievement oriented as of those who were not.

RELIGIOUS CONSERVATISM.   If the main body of religious belief and practice has discarded many of its sectarian attributes, it still adheres strongly to a variety of fundamentalist principles. What is commonly meant by fundamentalism as applied to Southern Protestantism is a system of beliefs that are frequently but not always closely associated, the core element being Biblicism, or acceptance of the literally interpreted Scriptures. Built around this core are various other religious tenets which usually stress some particular Biblical accounts or precepts to be accepted or practiced as evidences of Christian faith. There is also an ethical aspect to fundamentalist Protestantism commonly referred to as "Puritan morality" that finds expression in strong condemnation of such practices as drinking, dancing, gambling, swearing, card playing, and using tobacco.

Although most sects in the Southern Appalachians are fundamentalist in their religious doctrine, it is not true that most fundamentalists are sectarian. Fundamentalism is quite prevalent in urban and metropolitan parts of the region where the sectarian traits and beliefs discussed in the preceding section are relatively uncommon. Evidence of this is provided in the responses to a survey question in which respondents were given four statements concerning the Bible and asked to indicate which was closest to their own view.

	Rural	Urban	Metropolitan
The Bible is God's Word and all it says is true	74.3%	59.6%	62.1%
The Bible was written by men inspired by God, and its basic moral and religious teachings are true, but because the writers were men, it contains some human errors	21.8	35.7	36.1
The Bible is a valuable book because it was written by wise and good men but God had nothing to do with it	1.0	2.5	0.2
The Bible was written by men who lived so long ago that it is of little value today	0.8	0.7	0.2

About 2 percent of the respondents were unable or unwilling to select one of the four statements as representative of their view, so the totals of the figures shown do not add up to 100 percent.

The only groups in which Biblicists did not predominate were those of upper socioeconomic status and those with more than 12 years of schooling, as shown in Table 10-5. Particularly interesting is the fact that nearly two thirds of both the upper-middle status respondents and those who had graduated from high school but had not gone beyond subscribed to the fundamentalist interpretation. The great majority of these respondents are manifestly not members of sects, as evidenced by their responses to other survey questions as well as by their denominational affiliations, but they are still extremely conservative in this particular regard.

The persistence of a fundamentalist philosophy is indicated by the fact that 64.5 percent of the youngest group of respondents (under 30 years of age) chose the Biblicist interpretation of the Bible while only 32.5 percent chose the Modernist interpretation as being closer to their own view. In comparison, 68.5 percent of the respondents aged 65 and over selected the Biblicist view and 26.5 the Modernist interpretation. Among metropolitan respondents the proportion of Biblicists was actually greater in the youngest age group (63 percent) than in the oldest (52 percent). This may represent a resurgence of fundamentalism, but more probably it reflects the heavy migration of young adults from rural to metropolitan areas.

TABLE 10-5   Percentage of Southern Appalachian Survey respondents endorsing the statement *the Bible is God's word and all it says is true,* by residence, socioeconomic status, and schooling level.

Socioeconomic status and schooling level	Rural		Urban		Metropolitan		Total	
	%	Base[a]	%	Base	%	Base	%	Base
All respondents	74.3	724	59.6	280	62.1	462	67.7	1,466
Socioeconomic status								
Lower	75.3	150	96.2	21	91.7	24	79.5	195
Lower middle	76.3	219	66.7	66	65.7	99	71.9	384
Upper middle	66.3	104	53.5	71	67.1	155	63.9	330
Upper	36.1	36	20.0	35	35.3	102	32.4	173
Unknown	81.9	215	89.2	87	73.2	82	76.6	384
Years of schooling completed[b]								
6 or less	78.3	198	78.3	46	88.6	44	79.9	288
7 and 8	80.0	230	78.4	37	77.4	62	79.3	329
9 to 11	76.4	110	61.1	54	66.3	83	69.6	247
12	64.9	97	65.6	61	62.1	132	63.8	290
13 or more	53.8	80	33.8	80	34.3	140	44.0	300

a Number of respondents in category used in computing percentage.
b Percentages not computed for 12 respondents whose educational level was unknown.

To measure the prevalence of Puritan morality associated with fundamentalism, respondents were asked to rate each of a list of frequently condemned practices and activities as being always wrong, sometimes wrong, or never wrong. The categorical rating of a practice as *always wrong* was assumed to be a manifestation of the fundamentalist ethic. One of the more significant findings from the ratings was the tremendous variation in the disapproval accorded different practices as shown in Table 10-6. Quite possibly the variation indicates that this aspect of fundamentalism is undergoing rapid change, but it is not readily apparent why some previously condemned practices, such as dancing, have become so much more widely accepted than others, such as keeping a store open on Sunday or drinking.

The proportion of respondents professing Puritanical views varied inversely with socioeconomic status and educational level, as was true in the case of other fundamentalist traits, but appreciable differences still obtained between residential groups even when these factors were controlled. This suggests the greater exercise of community influences on the ethical aspect of fundamentalism than is found in the case of belief aspects of a more personal nature. Because of the symbolic significance of certain "personal" beliefs, though, it is not easy to draw generalizations as to which are considered of public concern and which are not. A further complication in seeking to interpret expressed ethical views is the frequent existence of a double standard of morality, as in the case of individuals who themselves drink but support local prohibition because they genuinely feel that the easy availability of alcoholic beverages poses a threat to community welfare.

TABLE 10-6   Percentage of Southern Appalachian Survey respondents, by residence, rating specified activities and practices as *always wrong*.

Activity or practice	Rural	Urban	Metropolitan
Swearing and cursing	96.8	88.6	92.4
Gambling	91.7	80.3	76.8
Drinking	87.8	71.1	61.3
Keeping a store open on Sunday	55.1	49.3	40.0
Divorce	42.5	28.6	24.4
Card playing	44.5	24.3	17.1
Using tobacco	28.6	22.1	18.2
Dancing	32.2	13.6	10.2

Unlike some other aspects of fundamentalism, Puritanism was clearly related to age of respondents in all areas. To illustrate, the percentages of respondents in various age groups who rated dancing, card playing, and keeping a store open on Sunday as *always wrong* were as follows:

Age group	Card playing	Dancing	Keeping a store open on Sunday
Under 30	18.3%	9.1%	31.5%
30–44	25.2	16.3	42.4
45–64	36.8	25.2	55.0
65 and over	50.2	38.1	65.1

It is especially interesting that the decline of Puritanism with decreasing age was consistent in metropolitan areas as well as in rural and urban, for it will be recalled that the youngest group of metropolitan residents contained a higher proportion of Biblicists than the oldest age group. It seems obvious that the ethical aspect of fundamentalism is changing more rapidly than the creedal aspect, with which it is linked implicitly rather than explicitly, but the reasons for the varying rates of change pose an interesting problem for further research.

RELIGION AND SOCIAL CHANGE.   Despite the pervasive influence of religion in mountain life, there has traditionally been a sharp cleavage between religious and secular activities. Sectarian religion, of course, provided a psychological escape from the harsh realities of worldly life, and this strategy of retreat is still followed to a considerable extent at the present time. Even when they are not otherworldly oriented, many mountain people feel strongly that religion should be concerned solely with the preaching of the Gospel and the salvation of souls, keeping aloof from secular affairs. But in the past as in the present, some churches have directly administered programs that have had as an objective the improvement of social and economic conditions; however, the underlying rationale has been evangelistic, and it is significant that most such programs have not only received their major support from institutions outside the region but have also been largely staffed by outsiders.

Respondents were asked to tell in which of eighteen activities or practices listed they thought churches should engage. Included in the list was the item *community improvement programs,* endorsement of which implied a belief that the church should engage directly in social action that was not of a specifically religious nature. Approximately 84 percent of the respondents endorsed the item, 12 percent indicated they did not think churches should engage in community action, and 4 percent said they weren't sure. There was very little variation by type of residential area, but the strongest opposition (about 15 percent) came from metropolitan residents.

In comparison with the other specified activities *community improvement programs* ranked well down the list in popular endorsement—eleventh out of the eighteen. It was clearly not considered as vital an activity as missionary work, revival meetings, Sunday schools, and prayer meetings, all of which were supported by more than 90 percent of the respondents. On the other hand, it ranked well ahead of such activities as church bazaars (49 percent endorsement), square dances (20 percent), and raising money for the preacher (66 percent). Acceptance of an activity cannot be interpreted as a demand for or even support of it. Nevertheless, the surprisingly small proportion of respondents who were positively opposed to this type of church program indicates that social action is no longer considered outside the legitimate sphere of religious activity.

A second approach used in the determination of attitudes toward participation of the church in social action programs was the evaluation of ministerial functions. Respondents were asked to indicate which one of six functions commonly performed by ministers they considered most important and which one least important. The functions and percentage distribution of ratings are shown in Table 10-7. The item which received the fewest number of *most-important* ratings was *speak at community functions and work in community activities.* It also received the next highest number of *least-important* ratings, being exceeded in this regard by the function *look after the finances and activities of the church.* Apparently the juxtaposition of money and religion is still distasteful to many Appalachian residents.

TABLE 10-7   Percentage of Southern Appalachian respondents, by residence, rating specified ministerial activities as *most important* and *least important.*

Ministerial Activity	Rural		Urban		Metropolitan	
	Most important	Least important	Most important	Least important	Most important	Least important
Visit in homes of members and talk with sick and troubled	55.0	1.2	47.1	0.7	41.0	0.2
Preach in regular services and on other occasions	30.2	0.3	32.4	0.4	36.9	0.2
Bury the dead, perform marriages, hold Lord's Supper, perform Baptisms	2.5	0.6	7.6	0.4	9.8	1.3
Teach church membership classes and the Bible	4.0	3.6	2.5	5.0	3.1	0.4
Look after the finances and activities of the church	0.2	47.3	0.7	47.5	2.6	49.0
Speak at community functions and work in community activities	0.2	32.3	0.0	36.7	0.7	43.6

These rankings do not indicate that participation in community affairs by the minister is considered to be of no importance, but they do indicate a clear preference for his serving primarily as pastor and prophet, secondarily as priest and teacher. Presumably after he has given priority attention to the performance of these functions, he may, and perhaps should, serve as church administrator and social reformer.

A final survey item, which dealt with the "social gospel" issue, was the question *Do you think ministers ought to take a public stand on public issues facing the community?* The distribution of responses to this question by residence of the respondent was as follows:

	Rural	Urban	Metropolitan
Minister should take a stand	51.8%	64.6%	65.6%
Minister should not take a stand	29.8	23.9	22.7
Don't know if he should or not	18.4	11.5	11.7

In all areas the majority opinion was that the minister should "stand up and be counted" on important social issues, but one may infer that there is still strong sentiment, particularly in rural areas, for him to confine his preaching to the Scriptures.

Unlike many other aspects of religious belief, attitudes toward social action were not consistently related to socioeconomic status, educational level, or age of respondents. The strongest opposition to church participation in community improvement came from upper-status women in all areas, about a fourth of whom indicated that the church should not participate in such activities. Less than ten percent of the upper-status men and from seven to ten percent of the women in other status categories expressed opposition. Female opposition was particularly strong in metropolitan areas but was concentrated in the upper-status, college-educated, and oldest groups. The responses of men in these categories did not differ appreciably from those of other men.

So far as the community role of the minister was concerned, the attitudes of the upper-status and college-trained men and women did not differ consistently from those of other respondents. All rated it of little importance compared with the other roles except that of church administrator and financial overseer, and lower-status respondents and elderly women rated the community service function of the minister even less important than his administrative function. On the question of whether the minister should take a public stand on community issues, upper-status respondents expressed the greatest opposition (37 percent) followed closely by lower-status respondents (32 percent). A fourth of the lower-middle and a fifth of the upper-middle groups were opposed, and respondents over 65 years of age were slightly more against such ministerial influence than were younger respondents. But with few exceptions (notably, lower-status rural men and elderly metropolitan women) more respondents favored than opposed the minister's speaking out on important public issues.

The data on attitudes toward church and ministerial involvement in social-action programs indicate a shift in belief in this area of religious thought, resulting in some obvious inconsistencies in the overall religious philosophy of different groups. Many Southern Appalachian residents of lower social and economic status who implicitly endorse the view that there is no earthly escape from the hardships and evils of secular life explicitly endorse church participation in programs aimed at improving social and economic conditions. On the other hand, some of the strongest opposition to such secular activities of churches and ministers comes from groups who strongly subscribe to a philosophy of social progress but apparently do not feel that the promotion of this progress is a proper function of religion. Although it certainly will not come as news to social-minded ministers that they are likely to receive their strongest resistance to social-action proposals from the ranks of the best educated and financially secure, the fact that such members are also likely to exercise considerable influence in congregational decisions would seem to justify further investigation of the underlying reasons for this resistance.

SUMMARY. The religious questions included in the Southern Appalachian attitude survey were of an exploratory nature rather than designed to test rigorously any specific theory or hypotheses. Nevertheless, the data do seem to support several general conclusions. First, sectarian religious beliefs and behavior do not seem to be as prevalent in the Southern Appalachian region at the present time as has been popularly supposed. They are probably more common there than in other parts of the nation, but they do not represent the dominant mode of religion even in rural parts of the region. The survey data support the thesis that sectarianism is a product of social and economic deprivation, but this is only a partial explanation, for large proportions of the lower-status and poorly-educated respondents were not ardent sectarians by any means. This is particularly significant in view of the religious heritage of the region and suggests the need for further research in the isolation of factors associated with the acceptance or rejection of a sectarian philosophy.

Second, the religion of the region is still highly conservative even though it has lost many of its sectarian attributes. The firm rock upon which it stands is the staunch belief in the Holy Scriptures as the revealed word of God, unadulterated and infallible, and this belief shows remarkably few signs of disintegrating. The reasons for the persistence of this aspect of fundamentalist religion, even among the relatively well educated and economically secure who have discarded most sectarian attributes, poses another challenging research problem. The Puritan ethic shows somewhat greater signs of erosion, but not as a general body of belief. That is, some activities such as drinking and gambling were regarded as unconditionally evil by most respondents, while other activities such as dancing and playing cards were considered categorically wrong by relatively small minorities.

Finally, the idea that the church should play an active role in the promotion of social improvements seems to be generally accepted, but the social-action function is not accorded high priority. Furthermore, there was no simple relationship of beliefs in this regard with respondent characteristics. Although religion still operates as a restraint on individual initiative for those who continue to use it as an escape from unpleasant reality, not even the otherworldly oriented are inclined to reject summarily church participation in social improvement programs. On the other hand, there is little evidence that a social gospel is more fully accepted by the better educated and more prosperous. If this is the case, there is little reason to suppose that the churches of the region will play a direct, major role in the social and economic development of the Southern Appalachian area in the near future. But whether or not this proves true, there still remain, in a virtually unexplored area in the sociology of religion, the questions of what gives rise to social-action movements in a church, who supports such movements, and why.

PART III

VARIETIES OF RELIGIOUS

ORGANIZATION

INTRODUCTION

A s RELIGIOUS GROUPS pass from the cult and sect to the denomination, the need for elaborating and formalizing organization becomes more pronounced. The intended permanence of the group requires admission standards, places for worship, a ministry (informal or formal), training of children in the faith, and formalization of belief. The eventual result is an organization designed to carry out these imperatives efficiently. The exact form of the religious organization, however, may follow several ideal types, each of which may be modified to support the particular needs of the group. Whether sect, denomination or ecclesia (see Johnson, Article 11), three forms of religious organization predominate: (1) Episcopal; (2) Presbyterian; and (3) Congregational. The Episcopal form of policy (church government) is marked by a belief in the authoritarian succession of the priesthood which is believed to have originated from God. In Christianity this succession has been interpreted as either Apostolic or Historic. The Apostolic Succession, a cardinal dogma of the Roman Catholic Church, is centered in the belief that the power of the Pope, the Bishop of Rome, is directly derived from Jesus Christ through St. Peter and is dispensed to those cardinals, archbishops, bishops, and priests who constitute the true church. The leaders of the church remain in the direct succession of the Apostles. Although the Anglican form of Historic Succession also involves the "laying on of hands," the emphasis is upon the historic continuity of the faith rather than the flow of supernatural power to the newly consecrated priest or minister. In the episcopal type of religious organization authority for temporal and spiritual matters is vested with the hierarchy and its supporting priesthood. Although clergy may seek the advice of the laity, they are in no way obligated to observe lay suggestions. Essentially an authoritarian form of religious organization, episcopal polity has possessed the organizational strength necessary to counter forces which have attempted to corrupt or deny it.

Under the Presbyterian form of religious organization the geographical unit, called the presbytery, supervises the churches within its jurisdiction. Each local church, governed by the minister and a small group of elders, sends its minister and one delegate to constitute the presbytery in the territorial district. The presbytery possesses the power to replace or approve the appointment of a minister of a constituent church, or to organize and divide local congregations. A series of presbyteries comprises the general assembly, which makes decisions on matters of denominational concern. In the Congregational system of polity the congregation is supreme unto itself. Each congregation remains autonomous and manages its own affairs, only loosely and voluntarily cooperating with its denominational association. Officers of the larger association serve in advisory rather than authoritarian capacities. Power within the congregation rests with the assembly of church members. They may delegate some authority to committees but in the final analysis hold the power.

Two conflicting trends have long been apparent within urban and rural religious groups (*see* Part V). As religious movements grow in complexity in a complex society, they tend to break down into smaller units, whether orders, sects, brotherhoods, or even denominations. And yet, small informal groups tend also to grow into larger units. In each instance the religious group is changed from what it was. In each instance the group is forced to select some form of church government (polity) in order to function efficiently. Although these three types of religious organization are apparent in the diverse forms of American religious expression, they are not necessarily found in pure types. Offshoots from established congregations may follow a congregational form of polity, and yet the tendency to relate to other groups of like mind may lead eventually to the adoption of a presbyterian or episcopal system. In each of the three types the core issue is the degree to which hierarchical or congregational power will dominate. The centrality of the hierarchy is paramount in the Roman Catholic Church. The balance between hierarchy and congregational control is most apparent in the Presbyterian Church. In Judaism, as in the Congregational Church, the power of the congregation is unquestioned.

A basic problem in the study of religious organization is the classification of group types. In the opening article of Part III, "Varieties of Religious Organization," Benton Johnson discusses the weaknesses of the typologies which have been previously suggested and offers an environmental definition of sect and church as an alternate classification system. Frank Young describes a situation in which a sect has developed to the stage of an "established sect," illustrating the problem which Johnson has attempted to solve. Truman Douglass approaches the problem of religious organization from an ecological standpoint. Noting that changes in America are outstripping changes in the church, he urges religious groups to seek qualitative excellence and adjustment to the changing social environment. Frederick Shippey describes the wide variety of church types in relation to criteria of parish geography and population served, offering a typology of urban churches. Manfred Stanley, however, recommends an alternative approach to the description of urban churches, seeking to evaluate them in relation to their environment as suggested by Benton Johnson in Article 11.

11   ON CHURCH AND SECT

Benton Johnson

INTRODUCTION   The wide diversity of religious group
types has long posed a problem to sociological inquiry. The earliest
attempt to classify religious group differences was made by Ernest
Troeltsch who proposed the simple dichotomy of church and sect.
The inadequacy of the typology, however, led to the formulation of
alternative variations, including the typology of Howard Becker.
Becker suggested that four religious group types were common to
society: the cult, the sect, the denomination and the ecclesia. The
cult is not a stable group inasmuch as one simply believes as others
do and this commonality of belief is almost the sole organizing feature. Formal membership is unnecessary. The *sect*, on the other
hand, is at best a somewhat informal grouping which generally is
at odds with the "world," and which seeks to maintain the purity
of its membership by urging separation from worldly evil and sin.
The *denomination*, larger and and more formal than the sect, is a
religious group which has lost its separatist attitudes and has made
at least some peace with the world. The *ecclesia* represents an established religious body which has developed a vested interest in
the social situation, causing it to remain conservative, although
expressing universalizing attitudes. Becker further subdivides the
ecclesia into two types: (1) national, and (2) international. A national ecclesia can be seen in the state churches such as the Lutheran in Scandinavia; an international ecclesia is, of course, the
Roman Catholic Church.

The study of religious group typology takes on an added dimension, however. The attempt to classify religious groups may be

Abridged and reprinted from the *American Sociological Review*, Volume 28, Number 4
(August, 1963), pp. 539-49, with the permission of the author and editors.

BENTON JOHNSON is Professor of Sociology at the University of Oregon.

at the same time an attempt to understand the *process* which a group undergoes. In general, most religious groups pass from the sect to the denomination stage. Some sects, however, never do emerge as denominations, but instead remain in an intermediate category of what J. Milton Yinger calls an "established sect." Similarly, some denominations never become national or international churches either. With the exception of the Roman Catholic Church in the United States, most of the well-known religious groups are best categorized as denominations. The problem of classification, however, becomes more complex when we realize that some denominations express sectarian-type attitudes.

Sociologist Benton Johnson proposes an alternative approach to the problem of classification. Following the lead of Max Weber, he writes that a sect is a religious group which rejects its existing social environment, while the church is a religious group which accepts the same social environment. Although this differentiation is rather simple and is fraught with difficulties, it shifts the focus of classification from the form of organization to the group's reaction to its environment. It may be, however, that form of organization may be related to a group's relationship to its environment. Johnson suggests that the dominant value system, the "American way of life," must serve as the basic environmental reference point in the study of American religious groups.

SINCE ERNST TROELTSCH formulated the church-sect typology more than half a century ago it has come to be regarded by most sociologists of religion as a singularly useful device for the analysis of the characteristics of organized Christian groups in relation to their environment.

Yet the typology as developed by Troeltsch has been subjected to a great deal of criticism. During the past generation many students have reworked it in various ways to make it more serviceable in sociological research. These attempts have been largely of two kinds. The first kind is best represented by Richard Niebuhr, who criticized Troeltsch's formulation for its classificatory or static character and sought to incorporate it into a propositional scheme resting on the assumption that the sect type is inherently unstable and tends over time to develop into a church.[1] The second kind of attempt at reformulation has focused on the definition of the types themselves. Many students, among them Howard Becker, Milton Yinger, Peter Berger, and D. A. Martin have refined and expanded the typology to embody distinctions they deemed important.

If, as we believe, it can be shown that the definition of the typology remains ambiguous, then this ambiguity must be cleared up before the typology

[1] H. Richard Neibuhr, *The Social Sources of Denominationalism* (New York: Holt, Rinehart and Winston, 1929), pp. 16-24.

can be fruitfully used at the propositional level. In this essay we propose to show that a serious definitional problem does remain, to redefine the terms sect and church, to suggest guidelines for their proper use, and to illustrate the manner in which the distinction can be applied by using it to classify the major religious groups in American society.

Troeltsch's formulation of the typology is too well known to require extensive recapitulation. He conceived of church and sect as independent sociological expressions of two variant interpretations of Christian tradition. The sect, interpreting the teachings of Jesus in a literal and radical manner, is a small, voluntary fellowship of converts who seek to realize the divine law in their own behavior. It is a community apart from and in opposition to the world around it. It emphasizes the eschatological features of Christian doctrine, espouses ideals of frugality and poverty, prohibits participation in legal or political affairs, and shuns any exercise of dominion over others. Religious equality of believers is stressed and a sharp distinction between clergy and laity is not drawn. It appeals principally to the lower classes. The church, on the other hand, stresses the redemptive and forgiving aspects of Christian tradition. It compromises the more radical teachings of Jesus and accepts many features of the secular world as at least relatively good. It seeks to dominate all elements within society, to teach and guide them, and to dispense saving grace to them by means of sacraments administered by ecclesiastical office holders. Although it contains organized expressions of the radical spirit of Christianity in its monastic system, it does not require its members to realize the divine law in their own behavior. It is conservative and allied with the upper classes.[2]

Although this formulation has been criticized, almost no one has called attention to two of its most serious problems. First, Troeltsch arrived at his definitions of church and sect on the basis of an examination of the history of Christian Europe prior to about 1800. He therefore tended to assume that a Christian society would have a legally established, politically protected religious monopoly. He had before him primarily the cases of Catholicism, Lutheranism and Anglicanism, and he framed his definition of the church with these cases clearly in mind. Troeltsch had groups like the Hussites and the Anabaptists in mind when he defined the sect type.

Even the most cursory review of the modern European or American religious scenes should suggest the artificiality of a church-sect distinction phrased in the above terms. In Europe, for example, there are few nations whose traditional churches can be said in any realistic sense to enjoy the regular support of most of the population.

Since the United States has no official religion, it cannot be said to have a church in Troeltsch's sense. There are a few withdrawn communities like the Amish and the Hutterites, and there are a few ambiguously radical active

2 Ernst Troeltsch, *The Social Teaching of the Christian Churches,* translated by Olive Wyon (New York: Macmillan, 1932), Volume I, pp. 328-49.

protest movements such as the Black Muslims or the Jehovah's Witnesses, but these sects make up only a tiny fraction of the religious bodies of the nation. The United States, unlike Europe, contains a large number of prosperous and popular religious organizations, but the vast majority of them cannot be validly classified as either churches or sects in terms of Troeltsch's typology.

Nevertheless, many have tried to apply the typology to the contemporary religious situation. But attempts to do this have revealed a second problem inherent in the typology. Troeltsch's definitions of sect and church each contain a large number of characteristics, or elements. Even when allowance is made for the fact that the United States has no official religion, or that modern European churches no longer command the allegiance of most of the population, it is clear that many of the remaining elements vary independently of each other. Two examples are sufficient to document this. First, membership in the sect is supposed to be based on voluntary adherence. Yet several groups that researchers have not hesitated to call sects, e.g., the Amish, have in effect instituted ascribed membership. Second, the sacramental system of the Roman, Orthodox, Lutheran and Anglican communions is supposed to be characteristic of churches. But many modern Protestant groups often called churches completely lack this kind of sacramental system.

If elements vary independently, the classification of mixed cases becomes an almost impossible task. So far the major response to this difficulty has been to coin new types or subtypes on an *ad hoc* basis as important new mixed cases present themselves. As we have pointed out elsewhere, this is what Troeltsch himself did when he coined the term free church to describe latter-day ascetic Protestantism.[3] The trouble with most of these newer typologies is that they have never really stipulated all the elements under consideration and they have never succeeded in transcending the particular considerations that led to their development. In other words, they are as limited in their own way as Troeltsch's typology.

Where we begin in the reformulation of the church-sect typology is an arbitrary matter provided the characteristics selected for incorporation within it are relevant to Christian groups. Since there is some merit in striving for as much continuity with customary usage as possible, we will try to embody one basic distinction which has figured prominently in most previous formulations of the typology.

To do this with clarity, however, it is useful to rely not on Troeltsch himself but on his close associate Max Weber. According to Weber,[4] the world religions have been molded in large part by what he calls prophets, or charismatically legitimated bearers of distinctive religious teachings. Prophets regularly present a relatively systematized or cognitively rationalized cosmic

---

[3] Benton Johnson, "A Critical Appraisal of the Church-Sect Typology," *American Sociological Review*, 22 (February, 1957), pp. 88-92.
[4] Max Weber, *The Sociology of Religion*, translated by Ephraim Fischoff (Boston: Beacon Press, 1963).

image which in principle permits all events in heaven and earth, but particularly those affecting joy and suffering, to be interpreted in terms of a single framework of causal principles. Prophets often succeed in changing the cosmic image of the masses from one in which various deities and demons affect human destiny without regard to any overall plan to one in which the cosmos is seen as a meaningful whole.

Weber distinguishes between prophets who promulgate the idea of a personal supramundane god who makes specific demands on men, and prophets who promulgate the idea of an impersonal cosmic law which can be appropriated by men. The first kind of prophet is called the *emissary* prophet and the second kind is called the *exemplary* prophet. Mohammed and the ancient Hebrew prophets are of the emissary type, whereas Buddha is of the exemplary type. Emissary prophecy conveys the idea that man's ultimate fate depends on how well he is a servant of the Lord's will. It has a strong ethical orientation, by which Weber means a disposition to regulate everyday conduct in terms of divinely given norms. Exemplary prophecy, on the other hand, tends to foster a relative lack of concern with ordinary mundane matters because its guiding idea is that individuals, through ascetic exercises, orgies, contemplation, or absorption of esoteric lore, can obtain power or other benefits which may be used for a variety of purely private ends. Emissary prophecy requires man to forget his own worldly interests and to join with others in promoting the ethical interests of the Lord.

The cosmic image promoted by emissary prophecy is of special interest to us because it constrains man to concern himself very seriously with questions of social policy, i.e., with the arrangements by which men live in society. Since the world is the Lord's principal theater of operations, how things are done there is likely to be a matter of the most intense concern to Him and therefore to His followers as well. They may be pleased with the way things are going or they may be displeased, but they are not likely to be indifferent. We would like to base the church-sect distinction on this consideration. *A church is a religious group that accepts the social environment in which it exists. A sect is a religious group that rejects the social environment in which it exists.* Since Weber emphasized that the world religions of the West were for the most part molded by emissary prophecy, whereas the religions of the Orient were molded by exemplary prophecy, we are safe in assuming that the church-sect distinction may be applied to most groups in the Jewish, Christian and Islamic traditions.

We have deliberately defined church and sect at a very high level of generality. Its application is in principle limited only by the criteria contained in the foregoing discussion. But unless the distinction can be validly and reliably operationalized and applied by investigators, it will have no merit at all. It will therefore be helpful to suggest some guidelines for its proper use.

First, it is necessary to specify the group to be classified and the environment to which it is to be related. It would seem perfectly acceptable to use a congregation, a monastic order, or an entire religious body as one's basic unit. It must be stressed that the classification of a group will not necessarily depend on qualities intrinsic to the group but on the nature of its relationship to its environment. For example, the Catholic Church in Portugal is far more acclimatized to its environment than it is in Hungary.

Second, the distinction between church and sect involves a single variable the values of which range along a continuum from complete rejection to complete acceptance of the environment. Therefore, where one draws the cutting point between sect and church or how many additional distinctions one wishes to make are to some extent arbitrary matters.

Third, the distinction is well adapted to comparative analyses. One may compare a number of religious groups within a given environment in terms of where they fall on the continuum.[5] One may compare two environments in terms of the proportion of religious bodies within each that fall at certain points along the continuum. Or one may compare a given religious group with itself in another environment or with itself at a different point in time.

Fourth, the redefinition of church and sect in terms of a single variable of broad applicability means that no assumption is made about the manner in which other characteristics are related to any state of the defining variable. This strategy should alert investigators to the importance of specifying other variables to be included in their analyses. In the past the typology has tended to be applied very loosely, in part because of the formal deficiencies which we have already discussed. Consequently, generalizations about churches and sects have probably been made which may in fact be true only under special circumstances. The existing empirical generalizations in this area need to be reexamined.

Finally, although hard and fast criteria cannot be given for determining toward which end of the continuum given groups stand in any environment, a few rules of thumb appear consistently in the literature that fit our conception of church and sect very well. We shall make use of these indicators in applying the typology to contemporary American society. First, since a sect tends to be in a state of tension with its surroundings, we are safe in supposing that religions that have totally withdrawn from participation in a society or that are engaged in open attack on it are likely to fall close to the sect end. By the same token, we may assume that religions enforcing norms on their adherents that are sharply distinct from norms common in secular quarters should be classed as relatively sectarian. Churches, on the other hand, are comparatively at ease with the established values and practices of a society. Therefore we will probably be justified in classifying as churches those religions that comprehend the entire society or at least its dominant classes. Similarly, bodies permitting their members to participate freely in all phases of secular life should probably also be classified as churches.

[5] *See* Russell R. Dynes, "Church-Sect Typology and Socio-Economic Status," *American Sociological Review*, 20 (October, 1955), pp. 555-60.

Since many of the drawbacks of Troeltsch's typology only became apparent when it was applied to the United States, one criterion of the usefulness of the revised typology will be the ease with which it can be applied to the American scene.

The first step is to specify the environment to be used as the basic point of reference in classifying our religious groups. Although all societies contain a variety of subcultures, and the United States is no exception, most sociologists believe that this country does have a dominant value system.[6]

The most striking fact about the American religious situation is that the vast majority of religious bodies seem to accept the dominant value system. Herberg and others have argued this point quite convincingly.[7] Most groups, therefore, should be placed toward the church end of the church-sect continuum. To be sure, some religious groups are strongly at odds with the dominant value system. But these groups are few and small and most of them are not actively struggling against the very foundations of the social system. Many of them are groups that have historically elected to retreat from the world into communities of their own making.

There are several telling bits of evidence for the assertion that religion in the United States supports the dominant values. First, most religious bodies, though with varying degrees of enthusiasm, accept the basic norm of mutual toleration, which is essential if they are to coexist peacefully. Second, almost all of them allow their members to move about freely and to engage in most kinds of legal activity. Third, the United States lacks any serious, sustained social cleavages associated with religion. Although we will argue later that significant cleavages of a limited kind are associated with religion, differences in outlook among the religious bodies of this country are not nearly so great as those which have occurred from time to time in Europe. One need only recall the prolonged and bitter struggles between Huguenot and Catholic or between Anglican and Puritan to appreciate this fact.

Religion not only supports the dominant values, it is enormously popular in comparison to religion in most other industrial nations. In Europe, for example, the old state churches tended to identify themselves strongly with reactionary values and interests during the stressful period of the transition to industrialism and democracy. Partly for this reason and partly because of the historic weakness of popular sectarianism on the continent, reform movements tended to attack not only the old order but the Christian religion as well. Although many Christian leaders have made significant adjustments in their social outlook, religion has continued to remain controversial in the largest sense of the term in Europe and is still regarded with profound suspicion by a

---

[6] Examples are: Robin Williams, Jr., *American Society* (New York: Knopf, 1960), chapter 11; Cora Du Bois, "The Dominant Value Profile of American Culture," *American Anthropologist*, 57 (December, 1955), pp. 1232-9; Gunnar Myrdal, *An American Dilemma* (New York: Harper & Row, 1944).

[7] Will Herberg, *Protestant-Catholic-Jew* (Garden City, N.Y.: Doubleday, 1960); Peter L. Berger, *The Noise of Solemn Assemblies* (Garden City, N.Y.: Doubleday, 1961).

significant segment of the population, in particular the urban working class.[8] The United States is one of the few industrial nations of the world that has not undergone a marked decline in popular religious interest since the beginning of industrial development.[9]

These considerations make it plausible to suggest that we should regard the United States as the second major historical example since the beginning of the Christian era of a culture that has an essentially comprehensive and integrative religious system.[10] The first of these historical examples—represented by medieval Catholicism and perhaps by early Reformation Lutheranism—has long since been superseded in much of Europe by religiously based conflict and by popular alienation from religion.

The foregoing analysis, which classifies most American religious bodies as basically churchly, is a fruitful one for many purposes of crosscultural comparison. But it conceals a number of more subtle distinctions that may prove important for purposes of internal comparison. These distinctions concern the extent to which there appear to be reservations in the support given to the dominant values. Since the church-sect typology as conventionally applied to the American scene, tends to obscure this phenomenon, it will be useful to suggest where several of the prominent religious traditions should be placed in relation to each other on the church-sect continuum. All of them are, of course, basically churchly.

Few would dispute that old-line Protestant denominations, such as the Methodists, the Presbyterians, the Congregationalists, and the Episcopalians stand very near the church end. Closely allied with these bodies are groups like the Baptists, the Disciples of Christ, the Evangelical-United Brethren and the Lutherans. These bodies, together with certain other smaller denominations, are to be regarded as the most churchly of all American religious groups. As Protestants they tend wholeheartedly to accept mutual toleration and the separation of church and state, two basic features of the American system. They are, in addition, bodies which are strongly identified with the relatively privileged segments of the population. Finally, with minor exceptions, they impose few if any distinctive expectations on their members. It is, for example, very easy to become and remain a Methodist or a Presbyterian. By the criteria we have suggested for determining where a religion should fall on the continuum, these groups seem clearly to belong very near the church end.

The same cannot be said, however, for the Roman Catholic Church in the United States. Although some observers have noted that American Cathol-

---

[8] See Irenaeus Rosier, "El catolicismo en Europe en la aurora de 'una epoca nueva" in Rosier (ed.), *Essays on the Pastoral Problems of the Catholic Church in the World Today* (Rome: Institutum Carmelitanum, 1960), pp. 10-72.

[9] See F. Boulard, *An Introduction to Religious Sociology, Pioneer Work in France*, translated by M. J. Jackson (London: Darton, Longman and Todd, 1960).

[10] See Talcott Parsons, "Some Comments on the Pattern of Religious Organization in the United States," in *Structure and Process in Modern Societies* (New York: Free Press, 1960), pp. 298, 310-11, 320.

icism has been obliged to take on characteristics which sharply distinguish it from European Catholicism, it has rarely been suggested that it should not be regarded as the sociological equivalent of, say, Congregationalism. There is a natural hesitancy to think of the lineal descendant of medieval Catholicism as anything but a sociological church. But a strict application of our criteria reveals that Catholicism cannot be regarded as among the most churchly bodies on the American scene. Although there are indications of a movement within Catholicism toward approval in principle of political democracy, religious pluralism and the separation of church and state, the Church in the United States has not apotheosized these landmarks of the American system to the extent that most Protestant groups have. There is, moreover, a sect-like quality in the official Catholic development of distinctively religious structures paralleling those of the secular society. We have in mind chiefly the educational system of the Church, as well as the numerous separate professional societies which it has fostered, especially among those vocations that are closely related to ideological concerns. For these reasons it is wise to classify Catholicism as somewhat more sectarian than most of the major Protestant bodies.

Judaism has usually not been classified as either sect or church because of the custom of applying the typology only within the Christian tradition. But Judaism was historically molded by a series of almost ideal-typical emissary prophets. We have, therefore, excellent reason to include it in our classification of American religions. Until recent times Judaism existed as an officially restricted sect that had been forced to withdraw from full participation in the larger society. Although the Jewish tradition always nurtured hopes for emancipation, it was not well prepared for the kind of emancipation that might require the close mingling of Jews with members of other religions on a basis of equality. In part this was due to the elaborate system of ritual segregation that served for centuries to draw the Jewish community closer together. Where traditional Orthodoxy persists it must be classified as a relatively sectarian form of religion. It is significant, however, that Orthodoxy has tended to decline rapidly wherever full emancipation has been readily available to the Jews.[11] This decline has been paralleled by the rise of Reform and Conservative Judaism, both of which have relaxed most of the religious restrictions against the full participation of Jews in secular society. These branches of Judaism tend also to be enthusiastic supporters of American values. They should probably be classified as more churchly than the Catholics.

Sociologists have devoted a great deal of attention to the study of religious groups which they have identified as sects. They have shown special interest in those modern revivalist groups which nowadays consist chiefly but not exclusively of the holiness and pentecostal movements. These are bodies that Wilson would call conversionist sects.

Even by our criteria these groups have certain sectarian characteristics. They disdain "worldly" things, they insist on the total commitment of their

[11] Herberg, *op. cit.*, pp. 193-4.

membership and they enforce a moral code more stringent than any code usually observed by nonmembers. But it is also clear that the opposition of these groups to the secular environment is partial and highly selective. They neither attack the society nor withdraw from it. Moreover, in many respects their members are less insulated from secular influences than good Catholics tend to be. They may forbid their members to patronize bathing beaches where the sexes swim together, but they usually allow them to attend the public schools. These groups, then, are sectarian only in the limited sense of being less churchly than bodies such as the Methodists. The same appears to be true of the Mormons, the Seventh Day Adventists, or more militant nonrevivalist fundamentalist groups such as the Orthodox Presbyterians or the Christian Reformed.

We have elsewhere presented evidence for the view that many of these groups actively convey value orientations which Weber and Troeltsch would identify as ascetic Protestant.[12] Since most observers would agree that the ascetic Protestant tradition has been influential in setting the religious and even the institutional tone of the entire nation, we may be justified in considering almost all bodies within this tradition as belonging closer to the church end of the continuum than either Roman Catholicism or Orthodox Judaism. It may well be that one of the most important functions of the conversionist bodies in the United States, both now and historically, has been to socialize potentially dissident elements—particularly the lower classes—in the dominant values which are our basic point of reference. The differences sociologists have seen between the Protestant "churches" and the Protestant "sects" may be matters of taste, rhetoric and expressive symbolism in general far more than they are matters of basic value orientation. The fact that the ascetic Protestant tradition has been so well able to adapt itself to the peculiarities of the various subcultures, including races and classes, with which its numerous branches have always been closely associated, may be one of the reasons underlying the popularity of religion in the United States.

The foregoing analysis has illustrated that with varying degrees of enthusiasm the great majority of American religious bodies support the dominant values. But one can easily make the mistake of supposing that this is the only relevant conclusion a sociologist can reach regarding the manner in which American religion is related to the environment as defined in terms of value orientations. Controversy over matters of social value and public policy is a regularized part of a democratic nation. To be sure, in this country these controversies seldom concern the dominant values themselves, which is perhaps one reason why American society has been politically more stable than many other industrial societies. But within the limits set by these values, important and deep-seated conflicts do exist in America. Moreover, for many purposes it is more important to know of the existence and bases of these conflicts than

[12] Benton Johnson, "Do Holiness Sects Socialize in Dominant Values?" *Social Forces,* 39 (May, 1961), pp. 309-16.

it is to know that most parties to them share a higher order of value commitments which serve to confine and restrain their disagreements. Like most groups in American society, religious bodies tend to share similar commitments at one level of generality. But if we shift our environmental point of reference down to the level of the major value-relevant cleavages in American society, a very different picture emerges.

It is a striking fact of American history since about the turn of the century that the ideological controversies between left and right, which have been waged on a variety of fronts and which are roughly reflected in the division between Republicans and Democrats, have also broken out in religious circles, particularly within Protestantism. To be sure, in the seminaries and pulpits these controversies were sparked by theological issues, but it has turned out that the resulting theological factions have tended to line up on opposite sides of the fence in terms of political ideology as well.

Theologically, the dispute has centered around the validity of traditional supernaturalist doctrines. Liberalism, and to some extent neo-orthodoxy, has made important doctrinal modifications in response to recent developments in natural science, philosophy and historical research. These modifications have evoked strong negative reactions from groups that initially called themselves fundamentalists but presently seem to prefer the term conservative. They have dogmatically reasserted and even embellished the supernaturalist aspects of Protestant theology.[13]

There has been a marked elective affinity between theological and political liberalism on the one hand and theological and political conservatism on the other. These alignments have been brought to public attention most vividly in the social gospel movement that arose shortly after the turn of the century and in the strong fundamentalist backing presently being given to the various movements making up the "radical right."[14] But underlying these more visible and dramatic examples of recent political polarization is the fact that during the past half century most of the major Protestant groups have come to be associated with inter-denominational alliances that have grown up on the right and on the left. The National Council of Churches represents the relatively liberal viewpoint, and the National Association of Evangelicals and the American Council of Christian Churches represent the relatively conservative viewpoint. There is evidence, moreover, that political philosophy and to some extent party preference as well are closely related to theological position even among the ordinary parish clergy. There is also evidence that the same relationships exist, though in attenuated form, among the more active laity.[15]

---

[13] See Donald B. Meyer, The Protestant Search for Social Realism, 1919-1941 (Berkeley and Los Angeles: University of California Press, 1960) and N. F. Furniss, The Fundamentalist Controversy, 1918-1931 (New Haven: Yale University Press, 1954).

[14] See Ralph Roy, Apostles of Discord (Boston: Beacon Press, 1953) and Ralph Roy, Communism and the Churches (New York: Harcourt, Brace & World, 1960).

[15] Benton Johnson, "Ascetic Protestantism and Political Preference," Public Opinion Quarterly, 26 (Spring, 1962), pp. 35-46.

These facts strongly suggest that the liberal-conservative split within Protestantism cannot be overlooked by any researcher who wishes to investigate the actual manner in which religious bodies are related to the value climate of the contemporary United States. For many research purposes it will yield far more positive and meaningful results than will breakdowns based on denomination or on distinctions in the extent to which groups enthusiastically endorse the dominant values.

The church-sect distinction can be usefully applied in this context if we shift the environmental reference point to the generalized controversy between left and right over matters of value and social policy. The leadership of most religious bodies can be roughly classified as predominantly conservative or liberal in a theological and ideological sense. Such a classification should not be attempted, however, in the case of withdrawn or hostile sects that have no use for *any* viable contemporary ideational system.

We can safely assume that the more extreme forms of liberalism or conservatism reflect a higher degree of dissatisfaction with the values and institutional *status quo* than do the milder forms. We can therefore distinguish between a churchly center group of relatively satisfied and therefore ambiguously liberal or conservative bodies and a more sectarian fringe group of relatively dissatisfied and therefore markedly liberal or conservative bodies. The former tend to be the groups we have previously labeled the most churchly bodies in America. Although there are important variations from region to region and even from parish to parish, in general the Congregationalists and the Methodists stand somewhat to the left of center, followed perhaps a notch or two to the right by the Episcopalians and the Presbyterians. The Baptists, the Lutherans, and the Disciples of Christ stand somewhat to the right of center.

At the extremes we may distinguish between the relatively sectarian bodies of the left and right. On the left are the Unitarians, many Quakers and certain Jewish bodies, especially those of Reform or Conservative persuasion. On the right are groups such as the Bible Presbyterian Church and several other small, aggressive fundamentalist bodies. While in recent years dissatisfaction has subsided on the left, it has risen markedly on the right. We may therefore speak of an increasingly sectarian trend within many Protestant groups. The denominations involved are in most cases those that were never prominently identified with theological liberalism, the social gospel or the National Council of Churches. The leadership of this large and growing sector of Protestantism did not therefore make the transition to a liberal or reform capitalist position. In the years following World War II, when it began to appear that recent shifts in the value and institutional climate of the nation might become permanent, criticism of the status quo became progressively bitter in these circles. The strong mixture of religion and rightist politics coming from protest movements, such as Billy James Hargis' Christian Crusade, the spread of premillennial eschatology, and the new interest shown in the Christian school movement among groups previously supporting the public schools, are evidence of a sectarian intransigence in the face of social change. A stiffening posture toward everything that has become identified with the left may be found among many Baptists, Disciples of Christ, Mormons, and others.

Almost all the facts mentioned in the preceding discussion of American religion are well known to sociologists. But they have seldom been comprehended in a systematic manner within a single conceptual framework. It is hoped that our redefinition of the church-sect distinction with the suggested rules for its use and their illustrative application to the American situation will lead to the kind of ordering of our perspectives on religion that will stimulate the asking of questions of theoretical relevance.

12 ADAPTATION AND PATTERN INTEGRATION OF A CALIFORNIA SECT

Frank W. Young

INTRODUCTION   How do fundamentalist sects arise?
What is their function within society? One interpretation suggests
that fundamentalist sects develop as responses to inadequate social
environments. Persons with low incomes, meager cultural resources,
and low status tend to form small insulated groups marked by distinctive and unconventional religious beliefs. Attempting to grasp
security in a time of extensive social change, these persons find desired stability by holding to a set of beliefs and absolute ideals.

Bryan Wilson, an English sociologist, has identified four sect
subtypes, based upon the kind of mission the sect undertakes. The
conversionist sects attempt to alter men, and through them, the
world. Placing their major emphasis upon evangelism, they focus
upon the Bible as the only guide to truth. Primarily a Protestant
phenomena, the conversionist sects stress acceptance of Jesus Christ
as the means of salvation. Their strong emphasis upon guilt and
personal sin has resulted in an antimodernist posture, expressed as
opposition to scientific endeavor. The *adventist sects* predict drastic
alteration of the world and seek to prepare for the new dispensa-
tion. The Second Coming of Christ, the divine commander, will
usher in a new kingdom open only to the morally upright. Although antirevivalistic, the adventist sect views the established
church as part of the world of the Antichrist. The *introversionist
sects* reject the world's values and replace them with higher inner
values which are openly cultivated in daily living. Being somewhat
pietistic, members seek possession of the Spirit through the activities in which they engage. The Bible is the source of inspiration

Abridged and reprinted from *The Review of Religious Research*, Volume 1, Number 4,
Copyright 1960, by the Religious Research Association, Inc.

FRANK YOUNG is Associate Professor of Rural Sociology at Cornell University.

and insight. Doctrine holds lesser value than the cultivated spirit. Members serve as unofficial ministers of the group which tends to withdraw from the world. The *gnostic sects* largely accept world goals but seek a new and esoteric means to achieve their ends. They offer a new and revived interpretation of Christian teaching in which the Bible is viewed as supplemental to the group's own gnosis (positive knowledge). Identified by a sense of mysticism, their members argue an optimistic eschatology (last things, life after death).

Frank Young, a rural sociologist, describes the changes which took place in the Highlands Church as its constituency, values, and leadership changed (*see* also Alland, Article 8, and Ford, Article 10). Although the sect moved toward the denominational religious type, it did not become a denomination in its own right. Instead the group became a modified sect, reminiscent of the "established sect" of J. Milton Yinger (*see* Johnson, Article 11). The philosophy and values of the congregation changed in such a manner that inconsistent views are rationalized to form a unity of viewpoint.

The role of the minister has changed. He has been forced to become an administrator, forsaking the earlier emotion of the preacher role. The new church, the tendency toward lessened emotionalism, the paid ministry, the increased influence of rationalism have tended to attract new types of persons to group membership. The earlier introversionist sect tendency of the Highlands Church, affiliated with the Pentecostal Church of God in America, has given way to an established sect emphasis, identified as the membership has become more prosperous by a partial acceptance of the social environment and a decreased antagonism towards the world.

———————

O NE INTERPRETATION of beliefs and practices of fundamentalist sects is that they are reactions to the defenses against nonsupportive social environments. Under such conditions, persons with low incomes and meager cultural resources—in short, those with no other ready means of survival—tend to form small, insulated groups marked by distinctive and unconventional religious beliefs. These value-orientations have survival value such that as the precipitating social conditions abate, the sect gains organizational stability and achieves an institutionalized relation with the community. In so doing, it approximates the organizational pattern of the denominations and is then considered a "church."

The results of the present field study (vide *Sociocultural Analysis of a California Pentecostal Church*, Cornell, M.A. thesis, 1954) seem to accord with this view and add a small increment to the existing evidence. However, analysis of the data of one case suggests that the basis of survival under anomic and supportive conditions is different and that the change from sect to church involves an extensive reformulation of the group's dominant value-orientations. Such reworking of belief is associated with internal reorganizations and personal conflict among the members. Despite the goal of stability inherent in the trend toward denominational status, the value-orientations show decreased pattern consistency (vide Parsons and Shils, *Toward a General Theory of Action*, pp. 172 ff.) during the transition.

A STUDY OF URBAN PENTECOSTALS.   The sect in question (here called the "Highland Church") is affiliated with the national group called the Pentecostal Church of God in America. It is one of some three dozen such organizations that have similar features and make up what can be termed the "Pentecostal type." According to Clark (*The Small Sects in America*, pp. 85 ff.) this classification includes the Assemblies of God, the Pentecostal Holiness Church, the Church of God (several varieties), the International Pentecostal Assemblies, the Pentecostal Fire-Baptized Holiness Church, and various others, including ethnic groups. Their salient characteristic is the practice of "speaking in tongues," but a few have indulged in bizarre practices such as handling snakes or exaggerated exaltation of the cult leader.

The Highland Church is one of ten Pentecostal-type groups in an urban strip extending for perhaps 12 miles along the California coast. The area includes the three towns of "Walford," "Segura," and "North Segura," with populations in 1951 of about 9,600, 16,100, and 10,200, respectively. Walford is a high-income residential district; Segura, a middle-income business district; and North Segura, where Highland Church is located, a low-income residential zone. Together, they form a loosely integrated urban area.

In 1921 the first Pentecostal group established itself in Walford, and thereafter ten more sects located in the general area (one Walford group died out, leaving the present ten), so that in 1951 they comprised 24 percent of the 41 churches.

In 1951 seven of the ten Pentecostal congregations met in North Segura, the low-income residential zone. The two in Segura were barely surviving, due mainly to the competition of the dominant Catholic groups, and the remaining church in Walford was so like the denominations as to be Pentecostal in name only. In short, the Pentecostal groups have developed principally in the low-income area, which, relative to the other two districts, is less organized. Cursory observation is sufficient to make the judgment that North Segura has fewer social centers, lacks economic structure and that the households have less material and social resources than is true in the other two zones.

Within North Segura, the proportion of Pentecostal groups has declined steadily since 1930. In that decade three of the four churches were Pentecostal, but in the decade ending in 1951 only seven of some 18 churches were of this type.

A third variable of sect activity is the intensity of expression during the meetings. By this is meant the tendency for the congregation to speak in tongues, make "interpretations," and to engage frequently in overt emotional demonstrations like "dancing" and shouting that depart from the formal pattern of the meetings. In addition, other practices, like "cottage prayer meetings" (i.e., in the homes of members), fasting, foot-washing, and high frequency of conversions are associated with such religious fervor. Considering all of these as one intensity variable, it appears that there has been a decline during the 20 years under consideration. Informants were unanimous in thinking that the sects were becoming "cold" and "worldly."

In 1932 the population of North Segura was about 500 (compared to several thousands in the other two zones), but shortly thereafter an influx of migrant workers, who had left their homes in Arkansas, Texas, Oklahoma, and Missouri as a result of the depression, arrived in the hope of obtaining work in the nearby fish canneries. The district was unincorporated and consisted of little more than sand and sagebrush. There was no gas or electricity, and water had to be carried in some cases for several blocks.

Compared to such early conditions, there is little doubt that North Segura attained greater organization and stability during the postwar period. Although the district still voted Democratic in the 1952 election (in contrast to the Republican majorities in Walford and Segura), and many of the roads were no more than sandy lanes, it was clearly more prosperous than before. The high wages during the war and the expanding industry of the area promoted a general rise in the standard of living.

Another relevant factor is the difference in the characteristics of the migrants between the early period and the later period. During the depression it is probable that the journey across the country was more arduous than during and after World War II. The later immigrants came as members of the military or as tradesmen. They were better off when they arrived and had more prospects afterwards. It is probable that their presence strengthened the social structure of North Segura.

Intensive study of the Highland Church corroborates the foregoing picture of declining sect activity in relation to gradually increasing support from the social environment. But close scrutiny reveals that the sect's capacity to survive as a group—its adaptation—increased as the anomic social conditions of the neighborhood abated, while the consistency of its belief system—its integration—tended to decrease. The sect was poorly adapted during the early period, despite its birth under such conditions. Its first meeting place was a tent. When a storm blew this down, the group barely stayed intact until it found another meeting place, a rented building that was formerly a gambling hall. Both of these locations, as well as the first actual church building, were in poor neighborhoods, and this early level contrasts markedly with the present $30,000 structure in the heart of an expanding middle-class neighborhood.

A second measure of adaptation is the occupational level of members. In the 1930's eight of the nine household heads held relief jobs (for which the pay was a grocery order) but in 1951 only 22 percent fell into this unskilled or unsteady category, while 46 percent were semiskilled and 32 percent white-collar or skilled. Finally, it is not insignificant that the Highland Church is the result of a schism which took place during the early years and which involved, among other reasons, the ownership of the church building.

In addition to these internal changes in survival capacity, there have been changes in the sect's relation to the community. The minister and the congregation show less hostility toward other churches, the schools, and the government than retrospective accounts indicate they once did, and they have discontinued the "street meetings" which formerly generated friction with the Segura authorities. On the side of the community, there is increasing awareness that the sect members—particularly the school children—are a special problem, rather than a group that was either not considered at all, or else consciously ignored.

INGROUP SUPERIORITY AND OUTGROUP DAMNATION.   Did such adaptive changes lead to increased pattern integration? Just the contrary. At least during the period of transition, the Highland Pentecostals experienced discord and uncertainty. For the later purpose of assessing (in the next section) this decreasing consistency in the value-orientations, they have been cast into a series of statements specifying, first, a cognitive proposition, and, secondly, a practical guide to behavior that is thought to be derived from it. Although the statements are based only on evidence secured by participant observations and the analysis of documents, they have been grouped into dominant axes of belief, and these are thought to have a high degree of reliability.

The first group of value-orientations seems to reduce to what Parsons has called the dimension of affectivity—affective neutrality:

1. There is a powerful religious force, the Holy Ghost, which, when an individual has secured a proper relation with it, will allow him to manifest marvelous powers.

2. There is a divine mediator between God and man, who, by virtue of the fact that he submitted to death at the hand of man, is able to respond to man's prayers for succor and support.

3. There is an all-powerful Being who created the world and who directs the major events taking place in it. A Pentecostal should accept this divine plan but can be encouraged that there is a place for him and all other converted persons in the millennium which will eventually come.

4. There are many ways and many occasions to give praise to divine powers, but all of these should be overt, fervent, and ecstatic demonstrations. Religious expression should not be stiff and formal.

5. Man is helpless and in constant need of aid and support from divine powers. Prayer and praise are the means by which such aid can be secured.

6. Even though one is saved, he is still subject to the temptations and dangers of worldly things that once beset him as an unsaved person. Consequently, he should continue to repudiate such worldly interests and fortify himself by striving for emotional spirituality.

The connecting thread in all these separate orientations is the emphasis on emotionality. The Holy Ghost is the force that determines psychological changes and special powers. Almost anything that is mysterious is attributed to this deity. When a person is converted, the Holy Ghost is said to have been at work, and, when a person first speaks in tongues, he has "got the Holy Ghost." Similarly, succeeding instances of ecstatic behavior, like speaking and interpreting tongues, "dancing in the Spirit," as well as the special powers of ministers (the change in their voices as they preach, or their healing ability), are all due to the Holy Ghost. The attitude toward Jesus, although more personal and intimate, is nevertheless charged with what may be called emotional dependency. The group prayers resound with the repetition of this name, and, indeed, such repetition may constitute for some the complete prayer. Usually it is uttered as if to say: "Jesus, won't you help me!" Finally, the concept of God as a creator and administrator of the world, although vague in Pentecostal belief, is often expressed in the context of catastrophe or threat. If a national calamity arose, God would be looked to for relief.

Other aspects of this underlying theme deal with the proper expression of religiosity. In Pentecostal meetings, there is an initial round of syncopated singing accompanied by hand-clapping, after which follows a group prayer in which everyone (independently) prays aloud. During this prayer, people pound the benches with their fists, weep, and call out. Later, when there are testimonies, they are supposed to be public "witnessing for Christ." When the preacher gives a sermon, he should exhort and "preach it." He usually takes off his coat during the course of the sermon, and perspiration is a sign of real force. One of the strongest justifications of sect emotionality is that "the big churches are like ice boxes."

However, aside from these public demonstrations, adherents are encouraged to cultivate a submissive attitude in their daily life. There is much weeping among Pentecostals, and much prayer for support in bearing sickness or simply of "one's burdens." During conversion, the specified attitude is one of abject humility: the convert kneels and sometimes writhes as he implores divine aid, trying his best to "let the Lord have his way." After conversion, it is thought that an adherent is still subject to temptations, against which his main defense is a continuing emotional uplift. Instead of the inward seeking after moral perfection that characterizes some other sects, Pentecostals require overt signs of religious excitement.

A second axis of belief specifies the ingroup-outgroup relations:

7. The locus of a distinctive, intimate, and sufficient life is within the

religious group. This way of life must be upheld and extended against a hostile world.

8. There are two general conditions in which a man may exist while on earth. He may remain unsaved and suffer the immediate spiritual deprivations and long-term damnation of such a state, or he may seek contact with the divine mediator, have his sins expunged, and enter into the second condition, that of the saved or reborn state.

9. A person's decision regarding his condition in the world determines his state in the future order: if he chooses to be worldly, he will be damned and consigned to a fiery hell; if he chooses the religious way, he will reap the rewards awaiting him in the millennium.

10. Everyone has potential religious impulses and needs which the Pentecostal way can satisfy, and Pentecostals should work to bring people to this way of life.

11. "Things of this world," material goods, pleasures, even secular knowledge, are inconsistent with strong faith, and they are unnecessary if a person is living a really religious life.

In these ways Pentecostals might verbalize their fundamental sociological position. The sect reacts to felt exclusion with a conception of the ingroup superiority which theoretically puts everyone in the position of choosing between Pentecostal salvation and outgroup damnation. The way of life is distinctive by virtue of its charismatic qualities, its possession of the true Christian gospel and the correct mode of its expression. There is consequently no need for a person to seek achievement in other groups. No matter how a person may fare in business or other situations outside the church, what really counts is his spirituality. There is no need to join organizations, to participate in school or community activities, or to become interested in politics. To go further and attend movies or frequent bars is outright sinful; interestingly enough, carnivals and circuses are tacitly approved.

Pentecostals believe that every man must make a weighty decision: whether to "come to Christ" or whether to "reject Him." Impending catastrophe is seen as the consequence of remaining unsaved. During the altar call, a minister will become quite emotional over the possibility that someone in the crowd may still be living a life of sin. His attitude is one of pity and deep concern. Similarly, during testimonies, a frequent pattern is to tell how one changed from a worldly to a spiritual life. A common prayer request is for all those "unsaved ones." "Are you saved?" is one of the first questions that comes to a Pentecostal's mind when he meets a stranger.

If a man dies without repenting his sins, he is condemned to a literal and eternal lake of fire. Nevertheless, it is generally thought that Christ will eventually descend to earth and reign a thousand years. When this time comes, "the dead in Christ shall rise first," meaning that all those who were Christians when they died will receive preferential treatment. "The fellows who have fallen into the concrete in the Golden Gate bridge will rise, breaking the concrete when they do." Then those Christians who are still alive will be caught up in the clouds with them, to meet the Lord in the air, and later they will be "priests and kings."

One of the immediate consequences of this sharp differentiation between the sect and the community is to categorize all outsiders as potential converts and all members of the group as potential "soulwinners for Christ." In practice, missionary efforts are led by "personal workers" and evangelists, and the most usual targets are the poor and down-and-out, soldiers, and people in foreign lands, especially native populations. But the missionary impulse is also reflected in the unrelenting approaches that Pentecostals make toward strangers in their church, toward acquaintances who chance to be unsaved, and even toward the people with whom they work during the day.

Finally, Pentecostals express a general antipathy toward the dominant pursuits of the rest of the community. Dancing, smoking, movies, drinking, and other secular activities, whether business, politics, or sometimes even food, are tainted. When a Pentecostal testifies that he once led a life of sin, he may mean only that he smoked and took an occasional drink. Professors and evolutionists are criticized, and doctors and science are open to censure, although in fact they rarely are. The term "worldly" is for Pentecostals a strange mélange of the secular, sinful, tempting, and the conventional. But basically, it is something to be avoided.

TRANSITION FROM SECT TO CHURCH. Something of the early consistency of this sect's value-orientations is reflected in the fact that so many of the statements formulated in the field could later be organized in a minimum way by two major axes. The only such statement that does not fit at all is the well-known literal interpretation of the Bible. With this exception the specific value-orientations seem to interweave and elaborate each other. Given the basic dichotomy between the ingroup and the outgroup, much of the rest of Pentecostal belief aligns itself. The members of the ingroup are the select while the others must suffer—unless they finally make the right decision with the help of a missionary who is especially gifted in reaching the outgroup. The material possessions and general attitudes of non-members are criticized and barred as immoral. They are judged by the criteria of the second theme when their "coldness" is condemned. Similarly, the emotionality theme colors the conception of the Holy Ghost, Jesus, and God, and proper ritual behavior is defined in terms of it.

But inconsistencies are beginning to develop and give rise to compromise formulations. Some of these may be stated as follows:

12. Acquisition of material goods and participation in certain voluntary activities can be consistent with the spiritual life, but one's main contribution should go to the church.

13. Science, although fundamentally antithetical and subordinate to divine forces, is nevertheless of considerable utility.

14. As a religious group becomes established and acquires a larger and more respected church, and as the group matures in its beliefs, the religious expressions of its members have to change.

15. Women are more receptive to the emotional types of spirituality but men are more qualified for higher types of leadership and special expression.

Through hard work and self-discipline, the present leaders of the church have acquired their own houses, automobiles, and especially, television sets. Already a few have protested against television by quoting Paul to the effect that if it offends my brothers to eat meat, I'll eat no more flesh. Since television is offensive to some in the church, the others should give it up. But the rejoinder is made that in the Bible school they were taught that one must have three scriptures to prove a point, and besides, if that scripture were interpreted in such a manner, many other things like clothes and personal habits would have to be given up, and that would be going too far. The emerging compromise formulation has already been put into words: "Surely God expects us to have enough for our needs."

There is practically no one in the church who would not agree that one should go to a doctor in case of serious illness. However, some are reluctant to go and have to be urged, and the more conservative members say that if people had enough faith they would not need the help of doctors. At the other extreme there are a few who recognize that the faith healers who sometimes visit the church "pick" their cases pretty good.

With the recent acquisition of the new church, the problems of religious expression have become verbalized. The conservatives see the problem as a "falling away" and as a sign of the "last days." One of the most widely accepted explanations of the "loss of spirituality" is simply that the church is getting rich. Interestingly enough, a few proponents of the moderation philosophy have come to the point of explaining the former intensity of religious expression in terms of the poverty and hardships of the people during those years.

Apart from the verbalized pattern inconsistencies, certain behavioral conflicts reflect confusion and differentiation of belief. These are focused in three areas: leadership, youth, and—curiously for such a group—the attraction and maintenance of deviants.

Until 1947 the sect had been led by a series of ministers who stayed for a year or two and then went elsewhere. But in that year a man appeared whose outlook and actions were fundamentally different from those of his predecessors. Previous to his conversion he had been a marine engineer—a high status occupation compared to the general level—and had attended Bible School in preparation for the ministry. He felt that the sect should have better relations with the community, and under his leadership the congregation built the new church and moved to a better location. Consequently, his resignation about six months after the inauguration of the new building brought on a crisis. The congregation had to decide whether to seek an "organizer-administrator" type of minister or whether to choose an evangelistic type who would stimulate the fading emotionality.

They first chose the latter. They elected one of their own members, a man who had previously led the street meetings and who had been a stormy assistant pastor. But within several months the congregation began to criticize his lack of leadership and his constant exhortations in favor of the "old-time religion." It became evident that his bare grammar school education, his tendency to revert to carpentry when his duties overwhelmed him, and his ignorance of church affairs were handicaps. Very shortly the situation resolved itself, because the new minister had a nervous breakdown and had to resign. The congregation then chose an opposite type, a man who had been in the ministry for many years but not as an evangelist, who had pastored two rather rich churches and who appeared to be the administrative type.

Another area of strain concerned the support of the young people. Formerly, when the Pentecostal young people mixed only with their own friends in the church and at school, and when the recreation facilities of the neighborhood were so meager as not to merit their attention, there was little conflict between their religious beliefs and their slight contact with the social environment. But in 1951 the adjustment problems of the adolescents broke out into the open. More and more frequently the young people who gave "sermons" or testimonies complained of "persecution" at school, even though they struck back by branding their schoolmates as "worldly" and "un-Christian." The adults exhorted the children not to be ashamed of their religion, and during one meeting the minister called upon the young people to join in and not be embarrassed even if they had brought their friends to church with them. Various compromises and adjustments had already developed. Several adolescents complained of frequent headaches or fainting spells, and it was generally acknowledged even by the members that the adolescent girls were very emotional in church with their frequent weeping and screaming and their tendency to "dance" at the least stimulus. Another reaction was the wearing of either very drab clothes or very conspicuous clothes—such as taffeta party dresses, sheer stockings, and high heels by girls of fourteen years. And finally there were the young people who saw no recourse but to reject the church. One girl who was learning to dance and who wore lipstick at school said that, although she still went to church, she considered herself to be "pretty much backslid."

Even the fringe members of the sect were confused and disquieted. Those whose husbands drank or who had serious illnesses—physical or otherwise—and those who had committed some social transgression—all these had formerly gained a measure of acceptance and support from the very emotional meetings in which even the most lurid public confessions were approved. They could also count on the sect members to pray for a beserk husband even in the middle of the night. But the atmosphere of the new high-ceilinged church seemed to inhibit such public support, and the fringe members began to feel that the majority of the congregation was uncomfortable around them and did not welcome them as before. They felt that they were now considered "not quite respectable." As a consequence, these fringe members were beginning to shop around to other churches, and in these (usually smaller) congregations they complained about how even some of the Pentecostal churches were getting "too good for people with real burdens."

Thus, the data of this case can be interpreted according to the general hypothesis that anomic social conditions are associated with sect activity, and additionally, that the adaptive and pattern integrative aspects of sect activity are inversely related under differing conditions of anomie. When the social environment is anomic, the group barely survives but shows great consistency in its value-orientations; the reverse is true when conditions are supportive. The present data do not allow the more refined formulation of the relations of integration and adaptation that is probably possible, but they do suggest that the complexity of the transition from sect to church is not exhausted by a polar-type formulation.

13 ECOLOGICAL CHANGES AND THE CHURCH

Truman B. Douglass

INTRODUCTION   Ecological changes exert a profound influence upon the church environment. Age characteristics of the community, migratory patterns such as suburbanization and succession in neighborhood occupancy, freeway development and similar changes have clear effects upon the church's relationship to the community. If the religious group is to survive in a specific area, it must respond to such changes in community characteristics. The religious institution, however, is dominated by an inherent conservative bent, although recent actions suggest that some denominational leaders are making greater attempts to interrelate the church and community. An awkward location, a ramshackle building in a high income area, and a program out of touch with community needs have negative effects upon the strength of the local religious institution. All religious groups have been forced to some degree to modernize their programs, especially in the urban setting, and to alter the rural traditions of religious goals. Probably the greatest limitation to urban adjustment is the rural-born minister who fails to grasp the context of the urban situation. Even more disturbing, however, is the fact that the greater number of men recruited for positions of religious leadership have been students of average or below-average capabilities.

Truman B. Douglass criticizes the church for its failure to be inclusive and to adjust to the changing scene. However, is it possible for any church or religious institution to serve *all* people? Can they appeal at once to the liberal and the fundamentalist, the sec-

Abridged and reprinted from *The Annals*, Volume 332 (November, 1960), pp. 80-89, with the permission of the author and editors.

TRUMAN DOUGLASS is Executive Vice-President of the United Church Board for Homeland Ministries.

tarian and denominationalist, the emotionalist and the rationalist, the lower class and the upper class? Does not the social attitudinal diversity of these groups cause necessary differentiation of religion into smaller and more varied groupings (see Johnson, Article 11, and Young, Article 12)? Although urban change has made denominational labels somewhat irrelevant, many denominations are finding that certain denominational practices and views are still relevant. Denominations which have accepted only those persons who have undergone intensive membership preparation have evidenced greater strength than those which have received members by simple request. However, the evidence is inconclusive. A large proportion of Americans do not pay much attention to denominational labels, making "shopping around" for a church a common American phenomenon. The high mobility rate (some 20% of the population moves each year) may account for this tendency. Increasing sophistication, too, leads the potential member to seek out more intelligent and capable religious leaders and more progressive congregations. Religious groups have been forced to an understanding that the church is clearly susceptible to the same evaluations which affect other human institutions. Failure to keep pace with the changing contexts of personality and milieu result in the atrophy if not the total failure of the religious institution itself.

The response of the religious group to changing conditions varies considerably. In general, the sect stands in opposition to society and seeks change, although a change which tends to be other-worldly (see Introduction to Article 12). The denomination or ecclesia, on the other hand, being prominent in the society, finds social criticism and adjustment difficult. The essential personal and conservative nature of American religion has led the religious man to a sense of self-satisfaction and contentment rather than leading him to consider institutional re-evaluation. Where ministerial success is dependent upon the cooperation of a satisfied membership, adjustments to changing ecological and social situations may take a long time to accomplish. Because religion functions in a context which already meets the needs of those living within that setting, members are generally unwilling to follow leadership which challenges the adequacy of the existing situation. Where community leaders look to the church to sanction their activities, any disruption may be viewed as a potential challenge to their power. Although the lay leadership of most religious groups tends to be dominated by economically progressive businessmen, managers, or proprietors, the same leadership tends to be religiously conservative. Since these leaders generally live some distance from the churches they attend, they often lack sensitivity to the perspective of the propinquitous and more numerous membership.

AN ADEQUATE REVIEW of ecological changes as they affect the church would include consideration of nearly all the major sociological changes that have occurred in American life in recent years. These changes constitute important aspects of the environment with which the church interacts. There is scarcely any feature of human society which does not influence the estate of the churches. Economic conditions, population shifts, family life, class structure, race relations, education, leisure, changes in the distribution of age groups, the condition of the general culture, the definition and redefinition of social goals—all have their consequences for the church.

Because the church is in many respects a conservative institution, these ecological changes frequently present themselves to the church in the form of problems and dilemmas for those who shape its policies, plans, and program.

There are, of course, churchmen who adopt what is essentially a transcendentalist view of the church. They would claim that in its essential characteristics the church is untouched by outward change. If, however, one believes, as does this writer, that in addition to its divinely given attributes the church bears the marks of a human institution, then every change occurring in society and its culture has implications for and effects upon the church.

QUANTITATIVE CHANGES. A quarter of a century ago the Protestant churches were persuaded that the period of church extension—of establishing new churches—was virtually ended in the United States. This conviction was articulated at a congress of home mission boards held in Washington, D.C. under the sponsorship of the Home Missions Council of North America. At this meeting the conviction was expressed that the settlement of the country had been completed, that the population had reached a point of stability, that the nation was adequately provided with churches, and that, therefore, the home mission boards could turn their energies and resources to other tasks.

These prognostications were completely negated by subsequent events —primarily by the population explosion, the wartime and postwar migrations of the American people, the continuing suburban trend, and the creation of multitudes of new communities. For a number of years the churches have been organizing new congregations at the rate of approximately 10,000 per year. The value of new construction of religious buildings rose from $117,000,- 000 in 1923, to $863,000,000 in 1958 and will closely approach a billion dollars in 1960.

Thoughtful church leaders are beginning to realize that these expansionist phenomena have their dangers. There is danger that the denominations will be more interested in reaping a statistical harvest than in making certain that the religious needs of communities are well served. Churches are likely to give more attention to quantitative growth than to the improvement of the qualitative excellence of their programs. There is danger that in the vast reshuffling of our population, and in the attendant concentration of the churches upon numerical increase, individuals will be lost to view. A mobile population requires more mobile forms of pastoral care than the Protestant churches have yet devised. There is danger that with all the building and rebuilding of church edifices, churches will be known for the comfort and modernity of their structures rather than for the Gospel they preach and for the quality of Christian life exhibited by the congregation.

THE RELIGIOUS REVIVAL.   Church members now constitute 63 percent of the population of the United States. This compares with 16 percent in 1850 and 22 percent in 1900. There is much debate about the accuracy of these figures. One variable which is not taken adequately into account in comparing the statistics reported by the churches is the changing conception of a church "member." For example, in the case of the Episcopal Church, in 1916 only 1 percent of its members were children under 13, as compared with 26 percent in 1926. Efforts have been made to standardize the statistics by calculating the percentage of people aged 13 and over who are recorded as church members, since denominations vary greatly in their practice of enrolling children. When this correction is made the figures do not show, as is frequently assumed, a steady rise in the proportion of church members in the total population since the beginning of the century. They show, rather, a decline from 1916 to 1940—55 percent in 1916 and 50.7 percent in 1940—and a notable rise thereafter. "In other words the American revival dates not from 1900 or before, but from 1940 or shortly after."[1] The growth since 1940 has been impressive—from 50.7 percent to 63 percent of the population in 1958. Today the membership of religious bodies in the United States exceeds 110,000,000.

There is a question whether this increased popularity represents a success or an embarrassment for the churches.

CLASS AND RACE.   The effects upon the churches of changes in the class structure of American society are largely indeterminate.

Evidence is abundant that a revolution is occurring in the racial and class composition of our nation. One relevant set of facts pertains to the composition of the labor force. The number of farmers, for example, declined from 16.5 percent of the labor force in 1910 to 7.3 percent in 1950. The proportion of farm laborers declined from 14.5 percent in 1910 to 4.3 percent in 1950. During the same forty-year span, professional persons increased from 4.4 percent of the labor force to 8.5 percent, and the proportion of clerks, salespeople, and those in similar occupations increased from 10.2 percent to 18.9 percent.[2] White-collar workers increased in number from 5,115,000 in 1900 to 21,600,-000 in 1950. They now constitute 36.6 percent of the labor force as compared with 17.6 percent in 1900.[3] There has been a parallel change in the distribution

[1] Michael Argyle, *Religious Behavior* (New York: Free Press, 1958), pp. 28-9.
[2] Joseph A. Kahl, *The American Class Structure* (New York: Holt, Rinehart and Winston, 1957), p. 57.
[3] United States Census Bureau, News Release, August 31, 1958.

of income. In 1929, 65 percent of the population had incomes under $3,000 per year. In 1951 this portion was reduced to 46 percent. The proportion receiving incomes between $3,000 and $7,500 rose from 29 percent in 1929 to 47 percent in 1951.[4]

Little is known of the effects of these changes upon the Church. No significant amount of research has been done in this field. It seems evident, however, that some of the widely held presuppositions regarding the relationship between social class and the churches have not been substantiated. For example, it might have been expected that with the virtual disappearance of an American proletariat, the so-called pentecostal sects—churches which allegedly drew their membership primarily from the economically disadvantaged groups —would have ceased to flourish. This has not been the case. The Assemblies of God increased their membership from 6,700 in 1916 to 148,000 in 1936; they continued this growth and reached a membership of more than 505,000 in 1958. The Pilgrim Holiness Church had 5,300 members in 1916, 20,100 in 1936, and 32,600 in 1958. The Pentecostal Holiness Church had 5,600 members in 1916, 20,100 in 1936, and 49,600 in 1958.[5]

Conversely, the churches which might have been expected to benefit from the number of what Vance Packard calls "the strivers for upward mobility"— namely, such denominations as the Episcopal, Congregational, and Presbyterian Churches—have exhibited no gains which are disproportionate to those made by other denominations which presumably offer fewer social advantages.

At least three factors seem to have contributed to the failure of church members to behave according to anticipated formulas. First, church affiliations seem to be more stable than other social affiliations and do not seem to be affected—at least not immediately—by a change of status. Second, some of the Pentecostal sects have steadily grown more respectable, have changed their character to conform to the changed class status of their membership, and have taken on more of the ways of the conventional "old-line" churches. Third, the evangelizing zeal of the Pentecostal groups has not waned as their members have acquired economic advantage and social status—nor has the zeal of such denominations as the Episcopal, Congregational, and Presbyterian notably increased, it would seem, as changes in the class structure of the nation have presented them with the sociological bases of larger opportunity.

One of the anomalies in this area of class-race relationships is the fact that the denominations which have been known as churches of the proletariat have made slower progress toward the integration of Negroes into their membership than have some of the longer established and presumably more socially conservative bodies. In 1950 a survey of Presbyterian, United States of America churches disclosed that out of 2,706 reporting congregations, 832 were integrated. A 1958 study of Congregational Christian churches in metropolitan

---

[4] Figures from *Business Week*, October 1952, with income in terms of dollars.
[5] Figures from *Census of Religious Bodies* 1906-36 and *Yearbook of American Churches* 1960 (New York: National Council of the Churches of Christ in the U.S.A., 1960).

areas found that 12 percent included Negro members and that 49 percent were willing to accept Negroes as members. The Protestant Council of New York City asserts on the basis of a recent study that half the churches in that city have an interracial membership. Liston Pope estimates that about 10 percent of the total number of Protestant churches in the nation are interracial.[6] This figure is five times as large as the corresponding figure for ten years ago. There is no evidence that the Pentecostal sects have shown any similar disposition toward integration. This is probably due, in the first place, to their tendency to make a radical separation between faith and social ethics and, in the second place, to the fact that many of these sects have their greatest strength in the South.

The most intensive study yet made of the attitudes and practices of a single denomination respecting racial integration covered the Congregational Christian churches in standard metropolitan areas. Questionnaires were sent to all the churches of that denomination in such areas. When Congregations showed themselves willing to participate in the study, interviews were held with the minister and at least one lay official. Of the 1,500 churches of the denomination located in standard metropolitan areas, 1,054 took part in the study.

Two significant and encouraging facts were disclosed. First, some modest gains in racial inclusiveness were revealed. The survey showed that 26.6 percent of the churches in metropolitan communities included in their membership representatives of at least one minority group. A less thorough study made twelve years previously revealed that only 17 percent of these churches could be classified as inclusive.

Second, in the opinion of ministers and lay leaders, well over half the congregations studied—63.4 percent of them—would support their pastors in implementing a policy of racial inclusiveness.

There were some disheartening findings. Nearly half the local churches that were studied had no definite policy for receiving members of racial minorities. Approximately 70 percent said they had never confronted a situation that required decision in that area of policy. Since the study was limited to highly urbanized communities where the size of racial minorities has rapidly increased in recent years, it is evident that the churches are not aggressively pressing toward a policy of racial inclusiveness.

In the opinion of a large number of lay officers of churches, the pastors would have more support for programs of desegregation in the community than in their own churches. Dr. Herman Long, the director of the study, considered this the most negative finding.

A majority—51.4 percent—of the lay respondents from the Midwest believed that there are exceptions to the denomination's announced policy of unconditional hospitality to members of all racial groups. It is alarming that

[6] Liston Pope, The Kingdom Beyond Caste (New York: Friendship Press, 1957).

what has been considered the southern pattern may also be the midwestern pattern.

A general result of the study was to indicate that in a period of history when events in the realm of human relations move with lethal swiftness the churches proceed with glacial slowness. The extent of integration in the churches compares unfavorably with accomplishments in other areas such as employment in federal and state governments, the armed services, professional sports, labor unions, institutions of higher education, and so on[7]

CITY AND SUBURB.   The city and the suburb are obverse sides of a primary problem-area for the work of the churches. Nearly every denomination has acknowledged publicly that from the standpoint of institutional strength it is losing ground in the inner city. Most denominations also acknowledge that with the whole nation coming under the influence of a predominantly urban culture, the failure of the Church to find its place in the city raises questions concerning the relevance of its message and program to modern society.

Meanwhile, the "exploding metropolis" continues to explode. The 168 standard metropolitan areas have steadily increased their share of the country's population. In July 1958 these areas included 59 percent of the total population of the United States. Within these areas, the suburbs continue to grow at a faster rate than the central cities. Between April 1950 and July 1958, about 12.4 million people were added to the population of communities adjacent to our larger cities, giving an average annual increase of 3.7 percent annually. This is almost three times the rate of growth within these cities and more than double the rate for the country as a whole. While, for example, there has been no appreciable population change in New York City, Jersey City, and Newark, the adjacent communities have increased at the rate of 3.9 percent a year. A gain of 1.6 million persons has occurred in the New York-Northeastern New Jersey standard metropolitan area. This gain is exceeded only by the increase in the Los Angeles area.[8]

The Church does not minimize its responsibility for providing religious ministries to the millions of people who have moved to the burgeoning suburbs, nor does it ignore the fact that many of these people occupy positions of strategic influence in American society. The Church is ill at ease over its success because of the relative simplicity of its adaptation to a suburban environment. Church leaders are beginning to recognize that the task of establishing a successful church in a new, rapidly growing suburb is scarcely more difficult than the problem of establishing a filling station on a new superhighway. The Church is disturbed at finding itself too readily at home in a one-

[7] Herman H. Long, Fellowship For Whom? (New York: Department of Race Relations, The Board of Home Missions, 1958).
[8] Metropolitan Life Insurance Company, Statistical Bulletin (New York: Metropolitan Life Insurance Co., October 1959).

class community. It is haunted by the consciousness of its essential nature as an inclusive fellowship in which distinctions of "Greek and barbarian, wise and simple, bond and free" are transcended.

On the other hand, the problems of the Protestant churches in the central city are not simply functions of population increase or decrease. There appears to be something in the urban community and its culture which is alien, if not hostile, to the Church. For example, during a period when 200,000 people were moving into New York City in the area below Fourteenth Street, seventeen Protestant churches moved out.[9]

One probable cause of the Church's alienation from the city is the fact that a large proportion of ministers come from rural and small-town communities. A recent study of the sources of the Protestant ministry revealed that in a sampling of 1,709 ministerial students only 36 percent came from cities of more than 25,000 population. Because of their rural and small-town origins, many ministers bring to their work in a city church a distaste for city ways. The minister is likely to be disabled from dealing with city people by his moralistic approach to their problems. He looks with disapproval upon an institution of such importance as the neighborhood tavern. He is appalled by the extravagance, late hours, and alcoholic excesses of city people and judges these "sins" far more harshly than small-town snooping, gossip, philistinism, and cruelty toward the nonconformist.[10]

OTHER CULTURAL CHANGES.   Other changes in the culture are presenting the Church with problems and with opportunities only partially realized.

There is, for example, the growth of leisure. More and more the attention of the individual American and the family is centered on the use of the hours and days away from productive work. Approximately 15 percent of total consumer expenditures are annually spent on leisure-time activities. With the arrival of the five-day week, and with the prospect of the four-day or even three-day week, the Church must reconsider its program in the light of a three-day or four-day "sabbath." The inviolability of the hour of eleven o'clock on Sunday morning and the universally observed time for corporate worship is brought into question. One church in New York City has had some success in its experiment with holding its weekly service of congregational worship on Friday evening in the summer time. Many churches are developing programs of adult education—often in the form of small groups engaged in the study of theology and biblical subjects—as ways of providing constructive leisure-time activities.

Another major cultural change is what Peter Drucker calls the educa-

[9] Ross W. Sanderson, *The Church Serves the Changing City* (New York: Harper & Row, 1955), p. 238.
[10] Truman B. Douglass, "The Job the Protestants Shirk," *Harper's Magazine* (November, 1958).

tional revolution. Education today, instead of removing people from the productive enterprise into a leisure class as it often did in the past, has become almost a prerequisite to effective participation in the productive process. This fact constitutes an authentic revolution.

What does it mean for churches whose outlook has been essentially anti-intellectual? The presence in their congregations of large numbers of persons who have been trained in the principles of critical thought constitutes a new situation which the churches have only begun to face.

DENOMINATIONAL IRRELEVANCE.   Finally, a general observation that must be made about the changed situation of the churches is that the denominational system which characterizes religious affairs in America is becoming increasingly irrelevant to the actualities of our society and culture. While this irrelevance is becoming more clearly visible, the denominations, with their enlarged memberships and increased financial prosperity, become more self-assertive and tend to dominate the religious scene.

All churches in the United States, including the Roman Catholic Church and the "undenominational" association of Community Churches, are also sects. As the sectarian system becomes stronger and its constituent denominations become increasingly powerful, it also becomes less and less pertinent to the realities of American life. The so-called religious revival of the last decade has to be appraised in the light of the increasing irrelevancy of the fundamental structure of the church in this nation.

No church, not even the largest, is ubiquitous. When people are moving to the extent that the American people have been moving since 1945, many of them settle in places where no church of their traditional denominational affiliation is present. In consequence, many of them change their denominational associations. They discover that this can be done without impairing—often, indeed, enriching—their religious experience. It is evident that for many persons denominational loyalty ranks low among the considerations which influence their choice of a local church. Convenience of access, good Sunday School facilities for the children, the general excellence of the church's reputation and program, even availability of parking space may be more important factors than the continuance of an existing denominational affiliation.

A recent survey which included interviews with 4,100 members of Congregational Christian churches in all parts of the country revealed that only one member out of three was originally a Congregationalist.[11] The churches studied derived over one half of their present membership from four other denominations: Methodist, 18 percent; Presbyterian, 15 percent; Baptist, 11 percent; and Lutheran, 8 percent. Two percent of the members included in this study originally were Roman Catholics.

On the point of the historic theological and ecclesiological controversies which produced the separated denominations, the indifference of the laity is

[11] Yoshio Fukuyama (Research for doctoral dissertation, University of Chicago).

monumental. It has increasingly come to be recognized by both clergy and laity that many of the persons who avoid the Church do so not because of the "offense of the Cross," but because they are repelled by the offense of competing denominations.

DENOMINATIONAL DILEMMA.   Can anyone seriously believe that these separated clans and tribes of the Christian family have any relevance to the real problems that humanity confronts in our time, or that their prosperity or lack of it provides any standard for judging the advance of the Christian movement? The statistical records of the denominations are not only notorious examples of the do-it-yourself craft of "how to lie with statistics," but are virtually meaningless as measurements of Christian accomplishment. One reads the recruiting literature of almost any denomination and tries vainly to find some resemblance to the criteria of the New Testament. The motivations to which appeal is made are not essentially different from the apologetic for the Junior Chamber of Commerce or the Neighborhood Improvement Association.

Thus the movement toward the overcoming of denominational disunity is generated not only by religious considerations but also by sociological factors. At the present moment it is being somewhat retarded by the economic prosperity of the denominations and by the illusions of omnicompetence which this prosperity produces. While there are some four hundred state and local councils of churches representing the cooperative tendencies of Protestantism, the denominations are reluctant to assign to them any real responsibilities except statistically unproductive functions such as work with agricultural migrants, share-croppers, and American Indians.

The dilemma of denominationalism gives a significance far greater than their quantitative dimensions to the movements toward actual unions of denominations—particularly those movements which aim at a reconciliation of fundamental differences of polity such as the differences between the episcopal, presbyterian, and congregational systems. Such unions are far more important than the reunion of separated branches of the same denominational family. One such union—the union between the Evangelical and Reformed and the Congregational Christian Churches—has already been accomplished in this country. Others are under consideration.

14 THE VARIETY OF CITY CHURCHES

Frederick A. Shippey

INTRODUCTION   Rural and urban religious organizations follow separate lines of development. In rural areas the
churches tend to be organized on the basis of primary values and
primary relations (*Gemeinschaft*). Members feel and express a
broadly based loyalty to one another, exerting thereby effective
social control upon each other. The rural religious group is often
similar to an extended family. Theologically, rural religion tends
toward a fundamentalist expression. It stresses emotional release
and emphasizes the good (ethico-moral) life. In recent years the
flight from the farm has caused the closing of hundreds of rural
churches.

The urban church, meanwhile, has both prospered and declined. In urban areas secondary group relations and values
(*Gesellschaft*) tend to dominate religious expression. Church business is carried out by committees charged with special administrative tasks. Sunday worship centers around institutional ritual and
a thought-provoking, generally unemotional, sermon. Theologically, most urban churches tend toward a liberal position, although
many urban sects and some denominations as well maintain a
strained form of fundamentalism. Emphasis is placed upon the
need for success and personal adjustment to the wonders of impersonal group living. The former centrality of religion as found
in rural America is not found in the same sense in urban religion
—nor is it ever likely to be again. Where rural religious expression
tends to be more exclusive, other-worldly, and theologically traditional, urban religion is more inclusive, this-worldly, and liberal.

Abridged and reprinted from *The Review of Religious Research,* Volume 2, Number 1,
Copyright 1960, by the Religious Research Association, Inc.

FREDERICK SHIPPEY is Professor of Sociology of Religion at Drew University.

To the average religious person in America an urban church is simply a church in the city. However, to the student of religion, the church takes on many crucial variations and special characteristics. The types of activities carried out by the congregation, the location of the church, the language used for services, the nature of congregational theological assumptions, the class of persons served or the type of ministry rendered all flavor the organization of the congregation and the subjective experiencing of religion. These institutional variables exist in addition to the previously mentioned dichotomies of emotional and rational, fundamental and liberal, worldly and other-worldly, and sectarian and denominational. Frederick Shippey, sociologist, has focused in this article upon the variety of churches appearing in the urban environment. Noting the ecological, theological, and sociological criteria which have served as the basis of the past typologies developed by Sanderson, Douglass, Leiffer, and others, Shippey has attempted to present a classification of church types based upon criteria of parish geography and population. In his typology he distinguishes between two basic church types: Type I, which involves the dispersed parish and selective clientele, and Type II, which is identified by the compact neighborhood parish reaching significant numbers within its boundaries. Those churches which do not fit either of these two types are "transitional" churches. Although the typology is not without its weaknesses (see Stanley, Article 15), the article does point out the great variety of urban religious organizations commonly included in the concept of "the church."

A CROSS THE YEARS numerous scholars have manifested an avid interest in local church life. Hundreds of books attest to the breadth and depth of this continuing academic interest. Within this body of literature treatments range the continuum from the most theoretical to the most practical discussions. The particular force of this article, however, is quite narrow and specialized, bringing into critical review a segment of the literature. The paper concerns itself mainly with the variety of churches appearing in the urban environment.

SELECTED URBAN CHURCH TYPOLOGIES.   Ross W. Sanderson, in *The Strategy of City Church Planning*, undertakes the task through a survey of one thousand churches located in sixteen U.S. cities. In this older study the basic factor utilized is the linear distance a member resides from the church with which he is affiliated. After discovering *two* primary types of churches—city-wide and neighborhood—he elaborates the typology into a system of submodal and supermodal classifications.

Joseph Van Vleck, Jr., regards the general approach espoused by Sanderson, Douglass, and others as misleading and unfruitful. Hence, he proposes in *Our Changing Churches* a unique approach based upon the dominant conduct pattern of a church group in terms of its conception and formulation of ultimate reality. How people define God and the ways in which such an understanding influences conduct describe Van Vleck's approach. His analysis yielded *three* types of city churches. The "priestly" church is liturgical and formal. The "individualistic" church is dominantly evangelical and informal. Located on a continuum between these two extreme types appears the "democratic" church. This last unites its members in the pursuit of a common purpose through the educational processes.

In *One Thousand City Churches* and *The Protestant Church As A Social Institution,* H. Paul Douglass insists that a bona fide city church does not exist; it is only an evolved rural church. In earlier writings this thesis was a ventured guess. But later the rural church prototype hardened into a dogma. In support of this contention, he drew up a list of thirty-three functions and activities of a local congregation, ranging from conventional religious services to highly specialized ministries. With this empirical measuring stick, it was easy to compare and to contrast the church of the countryside with the church of the city. The latter is more complicated because of the environmental demands. Douglass, in summarizing his extensive studies in the field, suggests *five* types of city churches: (1) the slightly adapted, (2) the unadapted, (3) the internally adapted, (4) the socially adapted, and (5) a general category called variant types. Douglass does not believe that the church is indigenous to the urban environment and hence he elaborated the rural prototype into varying stages of adaptation to an alien milieu.

Murray H. Leiffer, in *The Effective City Church,* bases his typology upon the familiar Burgess zonal pattern of urban community structure and growth. The Burgess analysis consists of five concentric zones centered upon the principal business district of the city. The ecological zones are designated as follows: downtown, area in transition, working-men's homes, better residential, and suburban. Theoretically the pattern is as symmetrical as a target, but in reality the urban configuration is quite irregular. Due to the research of Hoyt and others, the Burgess pattern was modified by sectors and culture islands. Since many cities are characterized by such ecological areas, standard church types are possible. Following this scheme, Leiffer describes *five* corresponding types of churches as determined by the geographical location of the edifice. The downtown area produced the downtown church. The area in transition produced the inner city church. And so on. The ability of each type of church to penetrate its own geographical territory is stressed.

Charles H. Sears, in *The Crowded Ways* and *City Man,* proposed *six* types of city churches. Because of extensive pragmatic experience in church life, Sears classified churches according to the varieties of problems which confront an administrator. Sears recognizes that religious opportunity varies from one section of a city to another, and therefore he suggests the following church types: (1) downtown, (2) older residential, (3) new residential, (4) foreign language, (5) Negro, and (6) economic groups. Despite evident weakness respecting sociological sophistication, this analysis of ecclesiastical situations emphasizes that Sears espouses pre-eminently the practical viewpoint. This orientation can be both a weakness and a strength.

Arthur L. Swift, Jr. (*Religion Today* and *New Frontiers of Religion*), indicates that he accepts the Douglass thesis respecting the rural church proto-type, but prefers to elaborate this concept against the background of his own survey findings in a major metropolitan area, New York City. His consid-erable experience with eleemosynary institutions provides significantly fresh perspectives. The external aspects of the local church situation commend themselves to Swift as he drafts a classification comprised of *six* types. One may note some correspondence with the variety of city churches already men-tioned: (1) "platform" or downtown, (2) foreign language, (3) institution-alized, (4) church settlement, (5) suburban, and (6) newer family. A variety of criteria become explicit guides in setting up this scheme. But Swift's main emphasis is upon necessary specialization, paralleling modern business, which feels impelled to serve various urban publics. This is an interesting modifica-tion of the Douglass viewpoint. The church adapts itself to the city's demands.

Finally, Samuel C. Kincheloe (*The American City and Its Church*), like Swift, Leiffer, and others, accepts the basic Douglass thesis of the rural church prototype. However, due to his sociological training, Kincheloe attaches much more importance to the impact of the city upon churches and how this pres-sure in turn compels religious specialization and adjustment. But the church also has a modifying effect upon the urban environment. It interacts dynami-cally with the milieu and out of such interaction arises the Kincheloe classifi-cation of city churches. Urban tension and pressure are explicit. He finds *seven* different types: (1) downtown, (2) inner city, (3) "moving," (4) "fed-erated," (5) interdenominational, (6) "dying," and (7) institutional. One may note some striking resemblances between this scheme and the analyses of Sears and Swift.

Several impressions arise from this brief survey of literature on urban church typology. Most scholars acknowledge the ethnic heterogeneity of the city environment and the difficulties inherent for religious work. Indeed some writers actually utilize the ethnic factor as a basis for church types. Moreover, there is a general recognition of urban heterogeneity in economic and/or cul-tural characteristics. However, opinion is divergent respecting the practical implications for typology. Several authors utilize economic levels as a basis for church differentiation. The experts agree that different types of church work actually do exist in the city. Hence, undoubtedly a typology of some kind is necessary and inevitable.

A NEW CLASSIFICATION OF CITY CHURCHES.   The purpose here is to present a typology which achieves at least three objectives: (a) the specification of local churches which can be recognized reliably as belonging to a given category, (b) the utilization of sociological insights without injury or hindrance to the attainment of religious objectives, and (c) the effective isolation of churches in trouble. If these reasonable goals can be attained, an urgently needed service will be rendered to busy pastors and harassed church leaders. No classification is more important than the churches. Yet, properly conceived and adequately validated, the typology can aid congregations in reaching a new level of self-understanding and program relevance.

This proposed classification is based upon two primary factors: parish geography and the population served. Parish geography refers to the linear distance a member resides from the church with which he is affiliated. The analysis takes account of the dominant congregational pattern in this sphere. The population served refers to the principle utilized in the recruitment of a congregation. Some churches attract people from the immediate neighborhood; others reach out across the city in order to gather a clientele. This new typology is diagrammatically shown below in chart form. One observes that there are three vertical columns. The two outside columns represent the two basic types of urban churches which are designated as Type I and Type II. The middle column does *not* reveal an additional type but rather a group of congregations which belong in an intermediate status. They are *churches in transition*, and eventually will go into the Type II category. At the present time, however, these churches in transition *cannot qualify as true types*. The category is useful here as a device to isolate the city churches in trouble from the remaining congregations and to guarantee proper administrative direction during the transitional period.

FIRST MAJOR TYPE. Type I is a church which has a widely dispersed parish and a selected clientele. An objective survey in urban communities would disclose four kinds of churches which satisfy the descriptive terms listed above. First, the *downtown* church is located literally in the central business district of a city. It is situated on the green, on the central square, across from the main post office, or close by some other important public building characteristic of the downtown area. To qualify, this church must be actually situated geographically in the central business district. No exceptions can be made here.

A second subtype is the *"prestige"* or *"voice"* church. This ecclesiastical organization is situated in that portion of the community where people of wealth or of exceptional cultural or educational advantage reside. In some cities, the territory is known as the "country club" area or the area where superior housing abounds. With its edifice situated in one of the finest residential areas, this church attracts to its religious services the leading business and professional people of the community and other persons who like to fellowship with them. It has a widely dispersed parish. However, the pattern of dispersion is not as broad as that of the downtown church. People are drawn chiefly from the better residential areas. A selected clientele is gathered, showing a dominance of business and professional interests. Prestige factors loom **important** here.

A CLASSIFICATION OF CITY CHURCHES

TYPE I	TYPE II
A widely-dispersed parish	A compact parish
A selected clientele	A dominant neighborhood penetration

Downtown church	Traditional church
Prestige church	Institutional church
One-of-a-kind	"Store front"
Church-for-the	Sect church
handicapped	Foreign-language church
	Suburban church

CHURCHES IN TRANSITION*

———————→

A semidispersed parish
An unstable constituency

Local church merger
Bilingual background
Merged denominations
Theological eccentricity
Stranded church
Relocated church
Federated church

* Churches in Transition occupy an intermediate status, are currently in transition and cannot be considered as types at all. Eventually the seven situations will yield Type II churches. However, this eventuality can be realized only at the end of a process of settling down and emergence from the intermediate status.

The third subtype of church is the sole representative of the denomination in the city. It is called *one-of-a-kind*. A Christian Science church often finds itself alone in a Southern city. A Methodist church in a New England city provides another illustration of this phenomenon. Similarly, in various parts of the United States, numerically weaker denominations possess but a single local church in the community. Under such conditions, people must be attracted from throughout the city if they desire the ministry of this particular denomination. Minority religious bodies usually find themselves in this category. A scattered parish and a selected clientele have a different meaning in this situation.

A fourth subtype is the *church-for-the-handicapped*. Reference here is made to churches which serve people with physical handicaps. Indeed the congregation is made up almost exclusively of persons who have sustained a common physical defect. Usually the clergyman is similarly handicapped. Such religious ministries are available for the deaf and dumb and possibly the blind but do not include serious psychological disabilities. People are drawn to the edifice from distances up to a twenty-five-mile radius. This, indeed, is a widely dispersed parish with a highly selected clientele. But it has a unique and authentic meaning.

SECOND MAJOR TYPE. Type II is characterized by a compact neighborhood parish and a dominant neighborhood penetration. It draws its members from a relatively short radius around the church and hence is able to penetrate the life of the community in a remarkable way. There are at least six authentic subtypes which can be identified here. The first can be called the *traditional* church. The traditional church conforms, maintaining all the required organizations and program elements demanded by the practice or polity of the denomination. It is the conventional neighborhood congregation found in most cities. And as the usual church, it displays neither conspicuous imagination nor exceptional resourcefulness in discovering or meeting the unique needs of its territory. Apparently such is not required in order to show conventional results. What is good enough for the denomination is good enough for this church also.

The second subtype is the *institutional* church. Here the term "institutional church" is used in the technical religious sense, describing the urban religious organization which since the 1870's has combined social service with a regular religious ministry. Further, this combination often involves a referral relationship with social service agencies of the community and occasional finances from community chest funds. Institutional church work appears most frequently in the inner city or slum territory. It compels a proliferation of program offerings quite beyond the customary pattern of the local church.

A third subtype is designated as the *store front*. Here reference is made to the small religious program which is conducted in a rented store or kindred type of facility. The neighborhood comprises residents in modest economic circumstances. It represents a protest against the abandonment of the territory by the old-line denominations. Usually a self-appointed, independent religious leader (or more rarely a denominational pastor) conducts a work aimed primarily at the urban poor. This ministry stresses informality and a minimum of organization. Religious services which stress group singing, individual witnessing, Bible readings, and short evangelical talks are preferred.

The *sect* church constitutes a fourth subtype. This religious unit functions as a protest against what is being done or not being done by the old-line denominations. It is a protest against the alleged worldliness of the denominations. This attempt to purify and to simplify religion at the neighborhood level attracts urban attention. Leaders here unmodestly regard themselves as the only exponents of "true religion." These independent organizations vary from tiny to gigantic enterprises. Utilizing a Bible-centered motif, they stress many of the personal and revivalistic emphases which characterized the work of denominations during the frontier period.

A fifth subtype is the *foreign-language* church. In numerous cities there persists still the limited need for a ministry in languages other than English. Currently, Puerto Ricans and other Spanish-speaking Americans of the Southwest require religious services in their native tongue. However, most of the older language churches (German, Italian, Polish, etc.) have disappeared from the American city.

The sixth subtype is the *suburban* church. This neighborhood congregation has its parish on the periphery of the city. Because there are suburbs of varying economic conditions, the churches may be expected to display various levels of economic consumption and cultural attainment. With the enormous development of territory around American cities, it is not surprising to discover an enormous increase in the number of suburban churches.

CHURCHES IN TRANSITION. But what of the remaining urban churches which thus far remain unclassified? What can be done with them? It is the present writer's judgment that they should be placed in a category representing an intermediate status and under the appropriate rubric—"churches in transition." Empirical studies and practical analysis lead one to the important conclusion that they are *not true types.* These churches gravitate toward Type II, being in movement somewhere between the two ends of the practical continuum. Special urban and religious conditions involving adjustment have set them in motion, and it is unwise and probably fruitless to finalize classification until the churches have become more fully stabilized. At least seven kinds of churches emerge from the analysis. Manifold situations produce them.

The first is the product of *a local church merger.* Churches which previously have had separate existence up to a particular point in time (perhaps five, ten, or twenty years ago) now are combined into a church merger. If the original edifices were widely separated geographically, the parish configuration will show wide dispersion. An inexperienced observer, lacking knowledge of the genesis of this local congregation, would draw the erroneous conclusion that it belonged in the Type I category. Obviously a false impression is gained by noting merely the widely scattered membership. When the facts are known, one must regard the congregation as being in transition.

A second kind arises from *a bilingual background.* During the period when the foreign-born immigrant filled our teeming cities, the church specialized in Danish, German, Italian, Polish, Swedish, and many other tongues. Now times have changed. A foreign language is barely necessary any longer. Hence the local congregation in polyglot areas is making a transition from the past into an English-speaking church. This change is to be expected. However, due to the antecedent bilingual ministry, and the proneness of some ethnic groups to scatter geographically as they become amalgamated in American culture, it is common for this church to possess a widely dispersed parish. Extensive research supports this observation, and the facts warrant placing the church in an intermediate status.

A third situation derives from *merged denominations*. Heretofore, single churches went their separate ways in the neighborhood because allegiance belonged to disparate denominations. Meanwhile, on the national level, parent bodies recently have combined. Thus now, in a particular community, there arises the necessity to combine neighboring churches across newly-merged denominational lines. If a local merger is thus consummated, one finds an abnormally dispersed parish as described in the first part of this section. A merger conveys the misleading impression of a somewhat widely dispersed parish and/or a selected clientele.

A fourth kind develops from *theological eccentricity*. Who does not know that the city is a haven for the bizarre? Esoteric beliefs or emphases are observed when a particular Biblical idea or theological concept is elevated in an unwarranted fashion above all others and belabored continuously. By this means, the minister gradually surrounds himself with a group of people who are more or less equally eccentric in a narrow Biblicism or distorted theological outlook. Cranks and misfits from other churches across the city are attracted and assembled into a single congregation. Thus this church achieves a wide dispersion of members and an unstable constituency. Unfortunately this congregation usually disappears or shrinks sharply to numerical feebleness when there is a change of ministers.

The *stranded* church becomes a fifth kind. This congregation is situated in the inner city where considerable shuffling of population occurs. Changes in racial, ethnic, and economic status affect the fortunes of many local congregations. Drastic alterations often seriously jeopardize the work of organized religion. Whenever a neighborhood where Caucasians once lived predominantly changes through the influx of Negro, Puerto Rican, Jewish, or Roman Catholic population, religious work enters a pattern of transition. Protestant institutions are usually affected. Often the erstwhile indigenous Caucasian church spurns the opportunity to change over into a new and more inclusive ministry. An inevitable result is the ministry to an ever-scattering people and a specialized clientele. Changing neighborhoods produce changing church situations.

A sixth kind is noted in the case of a church which has *relocated recently*. The congregation has shifted from one geographical location to another. Obviously some members continue to reside near the original church site, while others who have more recently affiliated cluster near the new location. This process produces a widely dispersed and a dumbbell-shaped parish configuration. It is a bifocal parish which conveys a false impression to the inexperienced observer. A relocation usually places the congregation in a state of transition for a period of years.

A seventh kind emerges from *federation*. The federated church comprises several congregations drawn together from across denominational lines. The maintenance of respective identities and the use of common physical facilities over a period of years is characteristic here. Usually the church of multiple congregations displays a widely dispersed parish and an unstable constituency.

VALUES OF CITY CHURCH CLASSIFICATION.   Stated briefly, there appear to be at least two major considerations which arise in connection with an adequate empirical classification of city churches within Protestantism. *First,* the environment demands a typology which satisfies the multifarious socioeconomic conditions of the modern urban community. Indeed it must be relevant to cities of varying population size, to different kinds of urban places, to the range of social classes, to the various ethnic groupings, and to the manifold denominations and sects within Protestantism. In view of this formidable set of requirements, a typology must achieve a remarkable social applicability.

Second, religious leaders demand that the classification of city churches accomplish a battery of practical miracles: i.e., furnish insights for congregational self-understanding, point directions in program planning, inform local churches contemplating a relocation, give guidance in the establishment of new congregations, instruct discussions of city-wide denominational strategy, and, finally, provide an undergirding philosophy for the comity process in local ecumenical relations.

15 CHURCH ADAPTATION TO URBAN SOCIAL CHANGE: A TYPOLOGY OF PROTESTANT CITY CONGREGATIONS

Manfred Stanley

INTRODUCTION   In the preceding article Shippey presented a characterization and classification of various church types found in urban areas. Manfred Stanley, another sociologist, now discusses the processes which cause a congregation to become a specific church type. The Involuted Church is one which has turned in upon itself, interacting with its environment only to a minimal degree. The Involved Church, on the other hand, has come to grips with its surroundings. The middle church type, the Transition Church, is in the process of adaptation from the involuted to the involved church type. The close relationship between Stanley and Johnson (Article 11) is obvious. The involuted church is similar in attitude to the sect which is generally antagonistic to its environment. The involved church is closely similar to the denomination, which operates peacefully within its environment.

E MPIRICAL RESEARCH in the sociology of religion has varied widely in terms of units of analysis. Three general foci have tended to underlie most of the empirical work done in this field: the individual (e.g. the social psychology of religion); religion as a social movement (e.g. the sect-church typology); and individual churches of a deviant or unusual nature. With certain exceptions there has been relatively little attention paid to the more "normal" type of urban congregation.

This paper seeks to remedy the deficiency in this area of research by

Abridged and reprinted from *The Journal for the Scientific Study of Religion,* Volume 2, Number 1 (Fall, 1962), pp. 64-73, with the permission of the author and editors.

MANFRED STANLEY is Assistant Professor of Sociology at Wagner College.

presenting an analysis of urban congregations in one city based upon research carried out on a sample of 37 local congregations representing two denominations. First we will present a brief discussion of the research on which the typology is based. Then we will proceed with a detailed discussion of the typology itself, ending with a brief summary of what the paper has attempted to accomplish.

THE EMPIRICAL BASIS.   A typology of urban congregations can proceed from any number of theoretical vantage points. This analysis is constructed around the concept of adaptation for the following reasons: First, cities are obviously undergoing rapid social, demographic and cultural change which challenge the adaptability of any social institutions which had their origins in a more stable social environment. This is especially relevant to Protestant churches, most of which have had a rural social history in America. Second, until quite recently the adaptation problem was solved by withdrawal of Protestant congregations into the suburbs or into more stable parts of the city itself. Finally, many denominations now officially discourage the withdrawal solution and an ideology of adaptation to change and service to the "inner city" is now being actively promulgated. This has elevated the problem of adaptation of local congregations to their environment to a religio-moral level, and presents an interesting opportunity for research in religion and in social change.

The studies upon which the present analysis is based were commissioned by the Baptist (A.B.C.) and Lutheran (U.L.C.A.) denominations to help them gain a better understanding of the life of their local congregations as a basis for future coordination of effort and planning. Each study lasted on average one and a half years, although they were carried out more or less concurrently. The research process was organized as follows:

(A) Each local congregation was first located in a specific community, the boundaries of which were determined according to a variety of criteria. The community was studied both through existing municipal and agency records, and through independent interviewing and observations carried out by the research team. Information concerning demography, local institutions, social problems, and local history was gathered.

(B) Worship services and lay society meetings were attended in each individual church by one or more members of the research team in order to acquire some impression of the "feel" of the church in its daily activities. Literature and brochures about the church were collected and filed, membership records analyzed, and researchers introduced themselves to members of the congregation and explained the study.

(C) Interviews were held with the minister and assistant minister (if any), the head of the church council, and when possible with two or three leading laymen of the congregation. Each interview was scheduled for three hours, but in some cases lasted for four and sometimes five hours. Information gathered in these interviews included the history of the church, the social structure of the congregation as seen by the respondent, the church program and its purposes, the respondent's knowledge of the surrounding community and its problems, impressions about the relationship between religious attitudes and church programs, finance, relations between the local congregation and the larger denomination, and church government.

(D) Short questionnaires were sent to all leaders and members of every lay society in the church. Information gathered included degree of involvement in activities, length of membership in society and congregation, length of residence in community, knowledge about the community, socioeconomic information about the individual, and general attitudes toward program and other aspects of church life. Aside from the aforementioned information, from these questionnaires we were able to ascertain what the informal leadership structure of the church was as against the formally listed leaders and what the significant social groupings in the congregation really were.

(E) A group interview was held in each congregation by a member of the research team. The group was usually restricted to six members (excluding the interviewer) but an attempt was made to include at least one representative of each of the following groupings: "old faithful" members, irregular members, an official of the church council, a teenager, and an elderly member. The minister was not invited to this interview. The discussion was held in an informal style around a table and, subject to the permission of the group, was recorded on tape.

(F) After the foregoing information had been collected, the research team met together in a series of conferences to compare notes and combine the various data concerning each congregation and its community into a coherent relationship.

THE TYPOLOGY.[1]   The typology now to be discussed was evolved by the writer out of the empirical material gathered in the manner just described. Since this analysis involves the use of some common terms which have diverse meanings, some preliminary definitions will be presented to facilitate more precise discussion.

(1) A church: For purposes of the present formulation, a church is defined as a local congregation which meets these three criteria:
    (a) a fellowship gathered for religious worship and instruction
    (b) a fellowship characterized by continuous association
    (c) a fellowship characterized by consensus of self-definition as a local church.

---

[1] This typology is based upon extensive research done on 37 churches by the research staff of the Protestant Council of New York. See Manfred Stanley and Carolyn Odell, *Fifteen Baptist Churches* (for the New York Baptist Society), 1958; Leland Cartrell, *Five Baptist Churches*, 1960; and Carolyn Odell, Manfred Stanley, *Lutherans in Manhattan*, 1960, for the U.L.C.A.

(2) A church "decision": For present purposes only those decisions made by the legally constituted decision-making authority within the local church will be recognized as representative for the church as a totality. (In the case of the Protestant churches this is usually some form of church council). This is a proper operational definition because, no matter what divisions of opinion may exist, local Protestant congregations are united in the recognition of the legitimacy of authority of their church councils.

(3) Environment: This refers to the geographical surrounding of the local church. It is used in three senses in the present analysis. First, local environment or "neighborhood." The neighborhood is the immediate geographic area around the church, usually not exceeding one-half a mile in radius. Second, nonlocal environment or "region." The region refers to a large geographical area, often a borough or even the city itself, which the church conceives itself as serving. Finally, the term environment refers also to the various social groupings and strata within the particular geographical limits. This forms the basis for the concept "inclusiveness-exclusiveness of environment" which is one of the two criterion variables of the adaptation concept used in this typology. (The other one being "degree of involvement in the environment").

TABLE 15-1   Church-environmental interaction.

1. No Church-Environment Interaction	2. Transition Process		
Involuted Church	Value Stage	Planning Stage	Crisis Stage

3. Church-Environment Interaction			
Local		Nonlocal	
Exclusive	*Inclusive*	*Exclusive*	*Inclusive*
Linguistic	Neighborhood	Linguistic	"Regional"
Racial	Church	Racial	Church
Theological		Theological	
Class	"Neigh. Center"	Class	
Other Special	"Supplementary"	Other Special	
	"Coordinating"		

Table 15-1 introduces the typology in terms of a continuum of church-environment interaction ranging from no interaction in the case of the "Involuted" church to the nonlocal and fully inclusive or "Regional" church. Also Table 15-1 suggests a basic adaptation dynamic. At one end is a church concerned exclusively with its own inner life and problems. Then a transition process takes place involving various sub-processes which culminate either in a frozen stage of conflict, or else in a commitment of some sort. Commitment is followed by various social forms or types of adapted churches which are listed in the typology and will be explored in the ensuing discussion.

Table 15-2 presents the typology of adaptation in terms of the criteria involved. We shall briefly discuss each church type with the help of these criteria.

TABLE 15-2   Degree of inclusiveness of environment.

Degree of Involvement in Environment	Inclusive		Exclusive	
	Nonlocal	Local	Nonlocal	Local
Involved	"Regional Church"	Neighborhood Church	Linguistic Racial Class Theological Other Special	Linguistic Racial Class Theological Other Special
(A) Program (officially sanctioned)		"Neighborhood Center" "Supplementary" "Coordinating"		
Transition				
(B) Stated plans on part of legal authority	Commitment Stage			
(C) Conflict within Church	Crisis Stage			
(D) Formal suggestions for program tendered	Planning Stage			
(E) Informal consensus of value orientation	Value Stage			
Not Involved				
(F) No involvement criterion present	Involuted Church			

THE INVOLUTED CHURCH.   A church is termed involuted (or not involved in the environment) if research indicates that all the following conditions are present:

(1) Within the last ten years no program relative to a specified environment has been undertaken in any department of the church, officially sanctioned or otherwise. The criterion of program in this analysis is based upon empirical evidence concerning the kind of activities which churches wishing to adapt to their environment generally undertake. A church in this typology is considered to have a program relating it to its environment if it has undertaken any of the three following activities:

(a) An evangelism program consciously geared toward residents of a defined sociogeographical environment.

(b) A service and or education activity, financed and staffed by the church, designed for the benefit of the environment and not necessarily for the existing members or just to gain new members.

(c) Involvement of clerical and or lay church leadership, *representing the church,* in the institutional life of the environment, i.e. civic councils, social agencies, economic boards, informal planning groups, etc.

(2) Within the last ten-year period no record exists of formal commitment on the part of the legitimate decision-making authority of the church to such a program.

(3) There are no conflicts between any factions of the church on the issue of such a program.

(4) Within the last ten years there is no record of concrete suggestions having been made with reference to such a program on any formal level.

(5) Research fails to uncover any wide spread degree of voluntary expression on the part of church members as to the desirability or necessity for a program of outreach to the environment. There may even be a consensus of opinion against such a policy.

Involuted churches are churches which are 'turned in on themselves'; that is, they are concerned only with the standing membership. No one exclusive set of factors leads to this kind of situation. However, it is often found that churches with a long and sometimes aristocratic tradition which find themselves in a rapidly changing environment in which their traditions are growing irrelevant, often become involuted through a kind of psychological "closing of ranks." The membership may have moved out of the vicinity, but still comes to church for "old time's sake." The desperation with which some of these churches maintain their sense of tradition suggests that, while as churches they are not adapting to change, they may be fulfilling the function for their members of providing a small subculture of stability and familiarity in a "sea of change" and "sea of strangers."

THE TRANSITION CHURCH. Research evidence suggests that churches which do not remain involuted undergo a transition phase of adaptation characterized by four general stages:

(1) *Value Stage:* The criterion for placing a church in this category is research evidence of widespread voluntary expression of interest in the environment and a growing consensus that the church "should do something about relating to the community." (In terms of Table 15-2, factor "e" is present). There is usually little conflict generated at this stage, because the implications of the consensus have not been worked out.

(2) *Planning Stage:* The criterion for this stage is evidence of the appearance of formal suggestions for concrete programs presented in some public manner (e.g. in Council, open congregational meetings, department confer-

ences, etc.). These formal suggestions place the congregation face to face with some potential concrete implications of what was formerly only a general value expression of the desire for adaptation.

(3) *The Crisis Stage:* Sometimes a church may move from the planning stage to the commitment stage. But more often than not, suggestions for concrete planning bring forth latent divisions within the congregation. During the conflict stage, concrete implications and the various divisions of congregational opinion toward them are examined and reconciled. Sometimes the adaptive process at this stage involves a change in the power structure and even a partial loss of membership. It is not uncommon to find a situation in which conflict resolution does not occur. In this event the church freezes at the crisis stage and due to a deadlock in the power structure, no official policy of commitment can be formed.

(4) *The Commitment Stage:* If the crisis stage is resolved, official commitment to a concrete program occurs which is designed to reflect the church's understanding of adaptation to its environment. Committees are set up, funds are allocated, and congregational support and assistance is mobilized.

These four transition stages may be viewed as a generic process of institutional adaptation to an environment. First, there is an initial awareness of the environment and a general desire to relate the institution to it (the Value Stage). Next comes the delineation and examination of concrete implications of this general desire for adaptation (The Planning Stage). Then the institution must readjust internally to these projected changes. Differences of perspective and opinion must be worked out and this often involves structural realignments (the Crisis Stage). Conflict either ends in resolution and preparations for commitment to a policy, or else the institution as a unit becomes immobilized and fragmented at this point. It is also possible that the conflict stage is bypassed altogether, which can occur if other events bring about a high homogeneity of opinion and orientation, or if potential dissidents are too unorganized or apathetic to intrude their opinions into the planning process. Finally, there is a process of commitment to a particular policy, and program plans are undertaken (the Commitment Stage).

One of the more difficult research questions in this area concerns the origin of the transition phase. Available evidence suggests that while general value consensus seems to evolve spontaneously, it remains latent unless concrete suggestions are initiated by, or receive support from individuals who are on a high level of the power structure of the local church. A church can remain on a latent value stage for a considerable length of time but once the concrete planning stage is reached, the issues are in the open and the internal dynamic of examination and debate quickens the transition process.

THE INVOLVED CHURCH. The Involved Church is one which has consciously as a unit come to terms with its surroundings. The criterion of involvement here is a program relating the church to its environment and which is sanctioned by the legitimate authority of the church. The following are subtypes of the involved church:

(1). *The Inclusive Nonlocal ("Regional") Church*: This church has chosen to define its environment in inclusive terms (e.g. it attempts to attract most if not all strata and cultural groupings within the geographic limits of its outreach); secondly, it defines the environment in nonlocal terms. This church's outreach is directed beyond its immediate neighborhood toward a larger region, which can be the borough or even the city. Such a church often attempts to maintain a high level of prestige through mechanisms such as a "name" pastor, high level "cultural" activities, a wealthy and influential stratum in its congregation, etc. But at the same time, it will make an attempt at greater inclusiveness through the use of a foreign language-speaking assistant pastor or parish worker, and activities directed toward the needs of special minority groups (usually minority group children). It is this element of inclusiveness of outreach which differentiates the "Regional" church from a nonlocal exclusive "Class" church.

(2) *The Inclusive Local ("Neighborhood") Church*: This is a church which defines its environment in inclusive terms, but which restricts the geographical limits to the local neighborhood. Evidence indicates the existence of three general subtypes of this category.

(a) Supplementary Service Church: This is a neighborhood church, often located in a nonresidential area, which seeks to make itself relevant to people associated with the area (workers and business people for instance), through activities which supplement those of the churches with which these people are affiliated in their areas of residence. Thus it attempts in a sense to be a "second church" to them. Special activities of these churches may include weekly worship services and Bible lessons during noon hours, pastoral counselling, education programs and discussion groups, etc.

(b) Neighborhood Center Church: This is a church related to its immediate environment by virtue of a program which ranges from worship activities through specialized social service work. Such a church, through the planned use of its facilities and finances, makes itself the focal point of services to the local environment and its residents. It may develop initially as an interdenominational church in a heterogeneous neighborhood or as a denominational church in a homogeneous neighborhood in which it shares the sociocultural identity of the majority of local residents.

(c) The Coordinating Church: This is a church which attempts to coordinate already existing neighborhood facilities and power groups through its own initiative and leadership for the sake of more effective community organization. Such a church occasionally is found to act as a political force as well, if it represents political and social interests of a societal minority group which happens to be the dominant group in the particular neighborhood in which the church is located (e.g. a Negro church in a Negro neighborhood which has a politically active pastor and staff).

(3) *The Exclusive Church (Local and Nonlocal)*: The exclusive church is one which, whether it defines its environmental geography as local or nonlocal, makes a distinction among the people it attempts to reach. An exclusive church attempts to serve a portion of the environment it feels is neglected and whose interests it sees itself as representing. There are various subtypes which are identical for local and nonlocal oriented churches alike:

(a) The Language Church: This church is usually culturally homogeneous and faces the choice of being a traditionally conservative or an assimilating influence. Internal structure and decision-making processes often but not always reflect the cultural traditions of the particular congregation rather than the larger American community. The congregation tends to become composed of older people, since the young often move away or join American churches. Immigration is the major source of recruitment of new members and the church is often engaged in refugee relief work.

(b) The Racial Church: The most common situation leading to this type of exclusiveness is when a "white" church is located in a community which is gradually receiving a heavy immigration of nonwhites. If the consensus of opinion in the church agrees to the exclusion of racial groups other than its own, the church may gradually evolve into a kind of "outpost" ministering to the white community in the area. Eventually, it will become a racial church totally unrelated to the immediate environment and accepting only a white congregation no matter how dispersed it may become. This process can operate in the opposite racial direction as well.

(c) The Theologically Exclusive Church: This church is exclusive on the basis of theological criteria of membership which act as barriers to church involvement in community affairs except on their own terms. Examples of this range from the existence of strict personal standards such as no smoking, drinking, dancing, movies, etc., which preclude many forms of community involvement and cooperation, to an explicit definition of the environment as evil and only to be converted.

(d) The Class Church: Exclusiveness here is based upon social class barriers.

(e) The Specialized Ministeries: These are churches which minister to special groups such as the blind, the artists, the crippled, the college student.

SUMMARY.   We have tried in this paper to focus attention upon the rather neglected area of the ordinary range of Protestant urban congregations in New York City. An attempt has been made to analyze them with regard to their position in a typology of adaptation to social change. It was found that churches range from noninvolvement in their environment through a fairly complex transition process to a state of active involvement in which various subtypes or "adaptive specializations" become discernible among them. The apparent multiplicity of urban Protestant church types suggests that simple distinctions between rural, suburban and urban churches are quite untenable. Future research should seek to determine:

(1) what accounts for differential tendencies toward church adaptation to the environment;

(2) what functions are served both by the involuted and the adapted churches;

(3) if the various church types are significantly related to patterns of religious ideology, sociocultural traditions, personality profiles of membership, structure or denominational administration or to none of these?

PART IV

SOCIALIZATION AND RELIGIOUS ROLES

INTRODUCTION

OCIALIZATION IS THE PROCESS through which the individual comes to internalize group values as his own. The continuity of any religious group is dependent upon socialization of its members, their children, and others who are converted from without the faith. As the individual learns the religious values, attitudes, and sentiments, he makes them a part of his own personality pattern. Socialization begins in infancy and ends only in death. Although the early agency of socialization is the family, it loses primacy as the child grows to maturity. Each group, whether religious or irreligious, exerts an influence upon the general and religious personality of the individual. As the person acquires an identity, he either accepts, rejects or remains neutral to religious ideals.

The socialization of man is possible because man is a rational being capable of acquiring and sustaining culture. Man acts in some measure by reason, not solely by instincts and impulse. Although he has drives, each man is capable in some degree of controlling or satisfying their fulfillment. His drives may push him toward a type of activity, but they do not determine the exact activity which he undertakes because his actions are always susceptible to social and individual controls. Religious value systems attempt to channel personal responses to religious ends. But these responses must be learned and internalized. As the child grows, parents transmit values to him. The lengthy period of childhood dependence serves as a time of crucial socialization of the child to his parental ideals. These may or may not be retained in adulthood, but their stamp is nevertheless significant.

In the long run socialization is dependent upon the willingness and the ability of the person to learn what is taught. The willingness of the person to be socialized to specific ends varies with the individual. Generally, religious socialization attempts to develop a basic sense of discipline within the individual. In this process one learns to postpone, modify, or even forego immediate gratification in order to reach some religiously-sanctioned short or long-range future goal. The inner-directed man (*see* Seidler and Ravitz, Article 18) is an example of this disciplined person. However, the postponement of gratification is usually dependent upon the predominance of some goal or aspiration which the person desires to reach. If the end aspiration is life eternal, the sacrifices required in tithing, e.g., remain inconsequential. Fulfillment of aspirations usually involves self-denial and a sense of dedication.

Religious socialization results in the teaching of religious roles and their supporting sentiments. Any religious group depends upon a certain division of labor and role-playing for institutional stability. Worshippers and worship leaders, musicians and singers, teachers and students, clergy and laity are all expressions of specialized roles necessary to maintain the religious institution. As the individual learns to synchronize and coordinate his behavior with other group members, the religious institution becomes a lasting social reality.

As the person continues within the institution, he learns specific skills of particular value to the religious group, such as the memorization of the Torah, singing of the service, or recitation of the catechism. The clergyman who leads the worship service, administers the sacraments, or preaches the sermon expresses skills central to his role. The skills which are learned in early socialization prepare the individual to participate in the religious institution. If institutional socialization is strong, a trend toward membership conformity results. However, many other factors, discussed in the subsequent articles, affect the nature and direction of individual socialization and the kinds of religious roles he assumes.

The *process of socialization* within religion is first examined in a series of four articles. David Elkind notes that a child goes through a process of cognition of religious identity as he grows in age. He finds that religious growth parallels the general development of the child through a series of three stages. Religious identity finally develops in the 10-12 year age range. In discussing religious training within the Roman Catholic family, John L. Thomas, S.J., identifies a marked gap between traditional and modern expectations of family responsibility. The decline of home religious training poses a threat to the continuance of traditional religious ideals. If the religious groups are not to lose their younger members a revitalized program of religious education is necessary. Murray Seidler and Mel Jerome Ravitz focus upon the processes inherent in the Jewish peer group and identify its basic contribution to the socialization process. Although the peer group under study is not a religious unit, the very nature of the group illustrates the degree of control which peers may possess over the individual member. Richard McCann traces the process by which mature faith comes to fruition. Although faith may decline, the person may still practice the morality taught by this faith. New environments may cause new responses to religion.

Ministerial roles are examined in the second section of Part IV in a series of four articles. Samuel Blizzard probes the problem of nervous breakdowns among ministers and suggests that role conflicts are responsible. The conflicting expectations of the minister, the congregation, and the community take their toll in the mental health of the clergy. Waldo Burchard probes the specialized role of the military chaplain and notes that role conflicts among chaplains are modified by abandoning one role, rationalizing its meaning, or compartmentalizing role behaviors. He examines in detail the authoritative setting in which the chaplain expresses permissive role behavior. Ernest Campbell and Thomas Pettigrew present a study of ministerial responses to the integration crisis in Little Rock, Arkansas. Noting that the clergy remained essentially silent during the crisis, they suggest that the reference systems of the self, membership (congregation), and profession (denomination) account for their behavior in a time of moral dilemma. Samuel Blizzard examines the differential roles played by the urban and rural minister. Noting that rural roles, too, are becoming more specialized, he urges a new approach to training of rural parish ministers.

The *roles of the laity* within the Protestant, Roman Catholic, and Jewish churches are examined in the concluding section of three articles. Paul Harrison describes the Protestant attitude toward lay participation, noting that the very nature of Protestantism assumes the priesthood of all believers. The future of religion in America relies on the extent to which laymen will assume leadership in religious growth. John J. Kane analyzes the nature and character of the Roman Catholic church. Although lay participation has been growing within the church in recent years, the episcopal nature of the church limits lay decision-making in religious activities. Marshall Sklare discusses the nature of Judaism, a form of ethnic religion. Although Judaism is expressed in three major forms within America—Orthodox, Conservative, and Reformed—Sklare argues that it is essentially a religion of the layman. The close relationship between the family and religious activity has served as a strength in maintaining Jewish values and practices.

A.   PROCESSES OF SOCIALIZATION

16   AGE CHANGES IN THE MEANING OF RELIGIOUS IDENTITY

David Elkind

INTRODUCTION   The basic aim of religious socialization is to teach the child his religious identity. Because children
represent an immediate membership reservoir, all religious groups
strive to socialize their youth in the faith of their fathers. The
growth process of the child, however, limits the potential understanding of the faith which he may gain. This study by David
Elkind, Director of the Child Study Center at the University of
Denver, identifies three specific stages in the growth of the religious
identity of children. In the first stage, five to seven years of age,
children possess an undifferentiated impression of their religious
denominations. In the second stage, the seventh to ninth years,
concrete conceptions of religious identity begin to develop. The
third stage is attained in the period between ten and twelve years
when the child begins to comprehend his own religious identity,
beyond the denominational ideas of faith, teaching, and belief.
Only in this pre-adolescent period does the child's conception of
religious identity begin to correspond to the adult's. As Elkind
notes, this fact alone possesses many practical implications for religious policy regarding children and youth.

———

FROM THE AGE of about five or six and frequently earlier, most children
are aware of their religious identity. When asked, children of this age
will readily admit that they are Protestant, Catholic or Jewish. The problem arises, however, as to just what children at this age mean when they make
such a pronouncement. It is quite likely, for example, that the five-year-old

Abridged and reprinted from *The Review of Religious Research*, Volume 6, Number 1,
Copyrighted 1964, by the Religious Research Association, Inc.

DAVID ELKIND is Associate Professor and Director of the Child Study Center, University
of Denver.

who says, "I am a Catholic" is thinking of something quite different than the adult who makes a similar statement.

METHODOLOGY.   It is not an easy task to get at the true meaning behind children's remarks. If we merely ask a youngster, "Are you a Protestant?" an affirmative answer tells us little if anything about what the child means by such an admission. To ferret out the real ideas embedded in the child's verbalizations, we need to employ a more indirect method.

One such method involves asking questions that require the child to apply his conceptions to new or novel situations. Experience has shown that when the child is forced to cope with a new problem he is much more likely to reveal the true content of his thought than if he is faced with a familiar or routine task.

In my own investigations, therefore, I devised six novel questions that I hoped would lead the child to reveal the meaning behind his remark, "I am a Protestant (Catholic or Jew)." The questions were as follows: (a) Are you a ——? Is your family ——? Are all boys and girls in the world ——? (b) Can a dog or cat be a ——? (c) How can you tell a person is a ——? (d) What is a ——? (e) How do you become a ——? and (f) Can you be an American and a —— at the same time? These questions were the starting point for an interview in which I tried to encourage the child to amplify and clarify his answers.

Almost eight hundred children participated in the investigations, and with the exception of some of the Protestant children all the subjects were individually interviewed by the writer. Of the 790 children tested 300 were Congregational Protestant, 280 were Catholic and 210 were Jewish. The Protestant children ranged in age from 5-14, the Catholic children from 6-12 and the Jewish children from 5-11. With the exception of the 5-6 year old Protestant children there were at least thirty children at each age level within the age ranges indicated.

RESULTS.   The results obtained from the three denominational groups were essentially the same with a few exceptions that will be mentioned later. For all denominational groups the replies to the various questions fell into three stages that were related to age.

The evidence that these were truly developmental stages was of three kinds. First of all, the replies of children at the same age level or adjacent age levels were similar. Secondly, the responses tended towards a more abstract conceptualization with increasing age. Finally, among the replies of the youngest children there were hints of the replies found at later ages while among the more advanced replies of older children there were still faint residues of the more immature conceptions held at an earlier age.

These findings are characteristic of developmental sequences generally and indicate that religious identity does grow in a regular sequence of stages that is related to age.

STAGES OF RELIGIOUS IDENTITY FORMATION. At the *first stage* (usually ages 5-7) most children had a *global*, undifferentiated impression of their religious denomination as a kind of family name. When, however, they were forced to break down this impression and state what the name meant, it was immediately clear that they had only a vague, confused notion of religious denomination.

A couple of examples will help to illustrate the types of confusion prevalent at this developmental level:

Lin (5-10) Are you Jewish? "Yes." And is your family Jewish? "Yes, well, all except my dog; he's a French poodle."

Bob (6-5) Are all boys and girls in the world Catholic? "No." Why not? "Cause some are Irish and some are Russian."

Beth (6-4) Can you be a Protestant and an American at the same time? "No." Why not? "Cause you can't have two (names)." Never? "Well, you could if you moved."

As these replies suggest, children at the first stage confused their religious denomination with national and racial designations. Furthermore, they thought of such designations as mutually exclusive and that being an American precluded being a Protestant, Catholic or Jew. This was no juvenile attempt at separation of church and state but rather represented the child's confusion between family and other designations. It was because the child knew he had only one family name that he thought he could not possess two general designations at the same time. One could then speak of the child at the first stage as having a *nominal* conception of his religious denomination.

Children at the *second stage* (usually ages 7-9) had what might be called a concrete conception of their religious identity. These children clearly differentiated between religious and nonreligious designations and related religious denominations to specific practices. But at this stage all the discriminations were rooted in descriptions of personal observation and had no abstract formulation or rationale.

The examples below will illustrate the replies given by second stage children:

Hal (8-7) Are all boys and girls in the world Protestant? "No." Why not? "Because some are Catholic and some are Jewish."

Will (8-2) How can you tell a person is Catholic? "If you see him go into a Catholic church."

Shirl (9-0) Can you be an American and a Jew at the same time? "Sure." How is that? "You live in that country and you go that synagogue."

In contrast to the children at the first stage these second stage youngsters had a clear cut notion as to the meaning of religious denomination. Their conception of religious denomination was, however, rooted in behavioral manifestations. For these youngsters religious denomination was determined by what a person *did*, and in this sense the children at this stage had a *functional* conception of religious identity. It should be noted, however, that the second stage child's view of religious denomination as a form of behavior existed without awareness of *why* these behaviors were engaged in. Only at the third stage did a rationale for religious behavior emerge.

By the age of 10 and more frequently at ages 11 and 12 children displayed what might be called an *abstract* conception of their religious identity. Their conception was abstract in the sense that they thought of their denomination as involving nonobservable qualities such as *belief, faith* and *intelligence*. The appearance of these concepts at the *third stage* indicated that the children had gone beyond immediate observation and had reflected upon and conceptualized their own thought processes.

A few examples will help to illustrate the responses given by third-stage children:

Tom (11-7) Can a dog or a cat be a Catholic? "No." Why not? "Because they don't have a brain or an intellect."

Sid (10-4) What is a Jew? "A person who believes in one God and does not believe in the New Testament."

Lee (12-0) Can you be a Protestant and an American at the same time? "Of course." How is that? "Well, Protestant is a religion and American is a nationality. They are two different things."

These replies are comparable to the adult's in the sense that religious identity is no longer conceived as an objective, outward form but rather as an inner, subjective reality. This transition from the conception of denomination as an outward form to an inner conviction was revealed most strikingly in the replies to the question of "How can you tell a person is a ——?"

Whereas the youngest children said one could tell by hair, skin color etc. and the middle-aged children said denomination could be detected by such things as Christmas trees, medallions, and skullcaps, the oldest children said either that there was no way to tell or that you would have to ask the person in question. At the third stage, then, the child's thoughts regarding his religious identity are as abstract as those of the adult.

DENOMINATIONAL GROUP DIFFERENCES. At the outset of this summary of developmental findings, I mentioned that there were denominational group differences and this seems an appropriate place to present them. In general, the differences were not great and tended to vary with the developmental stage under consideration.

At the *first stage,* for example, the most notable difference was between the Catholic and Jewish children and the Protestant youngsters. The difference was in the age at which a majority of children were aware of their religious identity. For the Catholic and Jewish children this awareness was clearly present by the age of five or six, while this was not true for the majority of Protestant young people.

A possible reason for this difference is the fact that the term Protestant may be used less frequently by Protestant parents than the terms Catholic and Jew are used by Catholic and Jewish parents. It may well be that the profusion of independently named Protestant sects is a major reason for the Protestant child's retarded awareness of his religious identity.

Among *second-stage* children denominational group differences appeared between the Catholic and Protestant children and the Jewish youngsters. Whereas the majority of Protestant and Catholic children traced the origin of their religious identity to church activities, the majority of Jewish children traced the origin of their identity to the family.

A possible reason for this is that Judaism is more of a defined subculture than is either Protestantism or Catholicism. That is to say, there are things like "Jewish cooking" that are not necessarily religious in nature and that are associated with the family rather than with the synagogue. Furthermore, a great many religious observances are carried on in the Jewish home so that it would be as natural for the child to trace his religious origins to the home as it would be for him to trace them to the synagogue.

At the *third stage* denominational differences emerged between the Catholic children and the Jewish and Protestant children. When the Catholic young people defined their religion they did so positively, with respect to their beliefs and without reference to other religious creeds. Both the Protestant and the Jewish children, however, tended to define their religion negatively, in contradistinction to other creeds. Protestant children, for example, often said they believed in Christ but not "in the Pope." Likewise, Jewish youngsters frequently said that they believed in "one God and not in the New Testament."

This last finding may reflect a greater religious self-consciousness on the part of Jewish and Protestant children than is true for Catholic young people. While such a greater self-consciousness is to be expected among the minority group of Jewish children, it was rather unexpected among Protestant youth. Perhaps some of the current controversy regarding dogma in the Protestant Church is filtering down to our young people and is making them more defensive about their religious beliefs. The possibility cannot be ignored and requires further exploration.

SUMMARY AND CONCLUSIONS.   The results of the investigations reported in the present paper have revealed that the meaning of religious identity changes regularly with age and that it is not until preadolescence that the child's conception corresponds to that of adults. To the young child, religious identity is no more than a name that the child confuses with the names for race and nationality. During middle childhood religious identity comes to mean a form or behavior or a characteristic way of acting including the wearing of particular symbols. It is only at the third stage, when the young person is preadolescent, that religious identity comes to be thought of as something emanating from within rather than from without the individual.

From these findings we can conclude that until adolescence the child *knows much more than he understands about his religious identity*. This fact should caution us to be careful in interpreting the child's verbalizations about religion. For while it may be true that the child can go through the motions and verbalize a religious service, such activity is not coupled with faith and conviction until the child is reaching pubescence. It is, therefore, no accident that religious conversion occurs most frequently in adolescence and that the Rabbis placed the barmitzvah, or ritual acceptance of religious responsibility, at the age of thirteen.

17 RELIGIOUS TRAINING IN THE ROMAN CATHOLIC FAMILY

John L. Thomas, S.J.

INTRODUCTION   Religious socialization occurs
through personal interaction. For the preschool child it takes place
almost completely within the family, and, to a lesser extent, the
church. The religious faith and practice of the parent generally
forms that of the child. A small child simply imitates those who
interact most often with him. Identifying with his parents, he begins to emulate their values and behavior. Using their actions as
models for his own behavior, the child illustrates their religious
commitment in his own action.

As has long been expected, American children are not being
fully trained in traditional denominational attitudes and expectations. Although the attitudes developed as a child are generally
recognized as the foundation for the future conduct of the man,
most Americans in recent times have been trained to an ethical
rather than doctrinal end. In fact, most Americans can now be
characterized as biblical and doctrinal illiterates. Where the church
fails to impress its children with the procedures and symbols of its
faith, the future allegiance of the child to the church may be
threatened. Do the symbols of the past have meaning in the present? The continuing problem within religion is the need to rein-
terpret past symbols for present understanding. If there is a vague-
ness concerning the symbol's meaning, the symbol itself will have
little religious value (see Introduction, Part II).

John L. Thomas, S.J., investigates the nature of religious
home training of preschool children in the Roman Catholic family.
Although the dogmatic character of Roman Catholicism suggests

Abridged and reprinted from *The American Journal of Sociology*, Volume 57 (September, 1951), pp. 178-183, by permission of the University of Chicago Press.

JOHN L. THOMAS, S.J., is Professor of Sociology at St. Louis University.

that preschool children should be well educated in the essentials of the faith by their parents, Thomas finds this not to occur in fact. The changing nature of family instruction suggests several questions which remain unanswered. Has the educational function of the Roman Catholic family been taken over by other institutions? Has the importance of dogma and doctrine declined? Have parents left their children without explicit training in the basic essentials of the faith? The failure of the family to fulfill its religious task suggests the continued need of a strong parochial school system to compensate for the decline of religious home training. Roman Catholics have long argued that parochial schools are necessary to guarantee the religious socialization of the young in a predominantly Protestant culture. Because children only come to a gradual differentiation of the essentials of religious faith (see Elkind, Article 16), the need to maintain continuous access to the child becomes more important to a minority church. Since now fewer than fifty percent of all Roman Catholic students attend parochial schools, the risk of erosion of the ranks of the faithful poses a serious threat.

The decreased emphasis upon religious education in the Roman Catholic family is a consequence of American religious pluralism (see Winter, Article 5). The attempt to develop a positive religious relationship between religious groups which have experienced different histories and confessions has resulted in an emphasis upon points of religious similarity rather than dissimilarity. Although American religion is marked by Protestant, Roman Catholic and Jewish divisions, a type of religious accommodation and consensus has begun to appear which obliterates the clear dogmatism of the past. The decline of family religious responsibility is only a reflection of the changing cultural situation in which the Roman Catholic family now lives.

———————

PERSONS PROFESSIONALLY CONCERNED in the promotion of organized religion agree that one of the most important functions of the family is the inculcation of Christian ideals and practices in the rising generation. On the other hand, it is generally assumed that the contemporary family is declining as a religious institution.[1] Since the religious functioning of the family is affected by trends in religion as well as by trends in the family, this decline is considered an urban, rather than a rural, phenomenon and one which affects the various religious sects differently.

The factual basis for these hypotheses is somewhat meager. The source most frequently cited is an investigation of the declining religious function of the family conducted in 1930 under the auspices of the White House Con-

[1] William Ogburn and Clark Tibbitts, "The Family and Its Functions," *Recent Social Trends in the United States* (New York: McGraw-Hill, 1933), p. 674.

ference on Child Health and Protection. Family participation in four religious practices was studied. Samples were taken of school children in rural areas, in villages, and in cities of various sizes. It was found that about one in eight white American-born school children of the seventh, eighth, and ninth grades participated in family prayers. Little difference in the practice of this custom was noted between the city and the country. Church attendance was the only activity participated in by more than half the families (85 percent of the rural and 40 percent of the urban). The percentage of rural and urban families reading the Bible together was 22 and 10, respectively; the percentage saying grace before meals was 38 and 30 respectively. Acting on the assumption that decreases in a function can be measured by comparing the prevalence of an activity in the city with its prevalence in the country, since the country preceded the city in point of time, some writers, on the basis of the White House study, advanced the hypothesis that there has been a decided decline in at least three religious practices.[2] These data are for families rather than for individuals.

It is not an easy task to ascertain the nature or the extent of the religious training which American families now give their children.[3] Religious training implies a knowledge of a set of dogmas and practices. It is the basic orientation of life toward the supernatural. In practice, it is the interpretation and ordering of actions in terms of an absolute set of moral values. Obviously, it is difficult to measure child training in such a subject. However, it seems that some valid conclusions can be drawn from a study of the dogmas and practices which the child is taught at home. Granting that knowledge of dogma and prayer is not the whole of religious training, nevertheless, in a highly institutionalized religion such as the Roman Catholic, understanding of dogma and practice in prayer generally constitute a considerable part of this training.

The present study is an investigation of some aspects of the religious training which Roman Catholic children receive at home. Since the Roman Catholic church in the United States has established an extensive system of parochial schools, where children are formally instructed and trained in religion, it is difficult to distinguish the role of the family in the religious training from that of the school. The writer attempted to avoid this difficulty by confining his study to an investigation of the religious training which the child receives *before* he enters the parochial school. This, however, reveals much more than the role which the family plays in the religious training of the preschool child; it throws considerable light on the religious function of the family throughout the child's entire life.

Full investigation of this highly important problem involves the following questions: (1) What formal religious instruction and training do parents give

[2] Ernest W. Burgess and Harvey J. Locke, *The Family* (New York: American Book, 1945), pp. 509-10.
[3] Robert Weaver, "Youth and Religion," *Annals of the American Academy of Political and Social Sciences*, CCXXXVI (November, 1944), p. 156.

their preschool children? Judged on the basis of traditional expectation, what items are stressed or neglected in this training? (2) Are there regional differences in the preschool religious training of children? (3) Do rural and urban families differ in the amount of religious instruction and training given the child in the home?

Taking the first set of questions, our problem was to formulate a list of items which would enable us to measure the religious training of the preschool child. After considerable discussion, experienced and competent first-grade teachers, representing six different religious teaching congregations, chose ten items. Their selection was based on the following considerations: (1) the items were such that the child could learn them rather easily if given some assistance by the parent; (2) this knowledge was in conformity with traditional expectations, that is, it was generally assumed that the child was so instructed by parents. Ten items were selected and were grouped under two headings: knowledge of prayers and knowledge of dogmas.

Under the first heading information was sought on the child's knowledge of the following prayers: (1) the Sign of the Cross, (2) the Lord's Prayer, (3) the "Hail Mary"—the traditional prayer of the Roman Catholic church to the Blessed Mother, (4) the prayer for grace at meals, (5) the prayer to the Guardian Angel—this is a traditional childhood devotion in the church. Under the heading of dogma, the child's knowledge of the following items was tested: (1) the story of the Creation, (2) the story of Adam and Eve, (3) the story of Christmas—the birthday of Christ as distinguished from Santa Claus and the giving of gifts, (4) the presence of Christ in the church—the belief of the real presence of Christ in the Host preserved on the altar, (5) the story of the Crucifix. No profound theological explanation of these dogmas was expected of the child, but he was supposed to be generally acquainted with them.

Over five hundred sisters, teaching the first grade and representing a large number of religious teaching congregations, agreed to cooperate in the study. The majority was contacted by a letter in which the purpose of the study was explained, and they were asked to secure the information on the ten items in the questionnaire at the opening of the fall term of 1950.

The present study is based on the returns from 446 schools located in 33 different states. The number of children examined was a little over sixteen thousand. Actually, we received returns on several thousand more, but these were either in kindergartens or in mixed classes, that is, classes in which part of the children had attended some type of kindergarten and, consequently, had been subjected to a certain amount of religious training away from home.

Table 17-1 gives the results for the group as a whole. The data found in this table will be most meaningful if considered as presenting a pattern. With the exception of the item dealing with the Sign of the Cross, one-third or less of the children showed the expected amount of home training. Unfortunately, we do not possess adequate information on the religious home training of children in the past: very possibly, a considerable gap has always existed between

TABLE 17-1   Percentage of preschool children receiving religious instruction at home.

Item	Percentage	Item	Percentage
Knows prayers		*Understands dogma*	
(1) The Sign of the Cross	52.9	(1) Story of Creation	24.9
(2) The Lord's Prayer	23.2	(2) Story of Adam and Eve	13.1
(3) The "Hail Mary"	33.0	(3) Meaning of Christmas	34.2
(4) Grace at Meals	14.1	(4) Presence of Christ in church	33.0
(5) Prayer to Guardian Angel	15.5	(5) Story of the Crucifix	30.6

TABLE 17-2   Percentage of preschool children receiving religious training at home, by region.

Region	Knows Prayers (5 Items)	Understands Dogma (5 Items)
Northwest (2,490 children)	34.9	33.0
Southwest (751 children)	27.2	38.8
Middle states (6,641 children)	27.6	27.8
Northeast (2,201 children)	26.4	27.1
Far West (2,644 children)	25.2	20.1
Southeast (1,374 children)	23.1	20.1
General Average	27.7	27.2

TABLE 17-3   Percentage of preschool children from rural and urban families receiving religious training in the home.

Item	Rural (2,816)	Urban (13,285)	Item	Rural (2,816)	Urban (13,285)
Knows prayers			*Understands dogma*		
(1) The Sign of the Cross	61.8	51.3	(1) Story of Creation	29.1	24.1
(2) The Lord's Prayer	27.7	22.4	(2) Story of Adam and Eve	12.9	12.2
(3) The "Hail Mary"	39.2	31.9	(3) The Meaning of Christmas	32.8	34.7
(4) Grace at Meals	17.5	13.5	(4) Presence of Christ in Church	36.7	32.3
(5) Prayer to Guardian Angel	18.0	15.1	(5) Story of the Crucifix	34.6	29.8

traditional expectations and actual practice. However, it is of some interest to indicate a few of the more surprising deviations from the expected, as revealed by our data. For example, the customary childhood prayer to the Guardian Angel is evidently not taught in most of the homes. The small percentage of those who knew the prayer for grace at meals indicates that this traditional practice is most honored in the breach, although an alternate explanation may be that grace is recited by one of the parents while the child remains at attention. The lack of knowledge displayed by two-thirds of the children in regard to items 3, 4, and 5, listed under dogma, was also unexpected. The story of Christmas is one which children grasp very readily, and the ritual of the church on this feast is so elaborate that it is difficult to understand how they could forget the story, provided that the parents had made some effort to explain it. However, as one teacher remarked, "No matter how I put the question, the same answer came back: Christmas meant only Santa and gifts!" The realization of the real presence of Christ on the altar seems rather easy for the child: the reason he is expected to be on his good behavior in church is because it is the "house of God," and the reverent behavior of the faithful during Mass could hardly escape his attention. But it seems that parents do not take their young children to church, or, if they do, they do not explain their actions. The Crucifix is the most universal of Roman Catholic symbols. The failure of over two-thirds of the children to know its meaning suggests that it is not a prominent symbol in the modern Catholic home.

Obviously, one cannot conclude on the basis of our data that two-thirds of the Catholic families in this country are giving their children no religious training. One may conclude, however, that they are not training and instructing them according to traditional expectations. Further, given the nature of Catholic belief and practice, it is difficult to understand how parents can give their children very extensive religious training if they neglect the basic items specified in our questionnaire. As one first-grade teacher remarked, "In regard to religious training, we have to start right from the beginning. It seems that modern parents are too busy to instruct their little ones!"

Our second problem was to investigate regional differences. In a country as large and religiously diversified as our own, sectional differences were to be expected. The country was divided into regions according to the sixfold division advocated by Odum.[4] Since we are not interested in comparing knowledge of individual items, we have used a twofold classification, combining the five items dealing with knowledge of prayers under one heading and the five dealing with understanding of dogma under a second. Table 17-2 gives the percentage by region. The Northwest and the Southeast differ significantly from the general average for the five items combined under the heading "Knows Prayers." Considering our present scant knowledge of the Roman Catholic populations of these regions, it would be hazardous to venture an

---

[4] Howard W. Odum, *Southern Regions of the United States* (Chapel Hill: University of North Carolina Press, 1936), pp. 5-7.

explanation. However, we might point out that a relatively high percentage of the Roman Catholic population in the Northwest is rural, and, as we shall see, rural families tend to give their children more religious instruction than do urban. This probably accounts for the difference. A tentative explanation for the relatively poor showing of the Southeast is that the Roman Catholic population there is only a small percentage of the total—a circumstance leading to a very high rate of mixed marriage. Studies of mixed marriage lead us to expect less religious training of offspring.[5] For the five items combined under the

TABLE 17-4   Percentage of urban and rural preschool children receiving religious training at home, by region.

Region	Knows Prayers (5 Items)	Understands Dogma (5 Items)
Northwest		
Urban (1,954)	32.4	32.0
Rural (536)	44.3	36.3
Southwest		
Urban (494)	29.3	40.5
Rural (257)	22.9	36.6
Middle states		
Urban (5,530)	26.1	27.2
Rural (1,111)	35.2	30.5
Northeast		
Urban (1,963)	27.3	28.1
Rural (238)	19.6	20.2
Far West		
Urban (2,237)	23.9	19.4
Rural (407)	32.1	23.8
Southeast		
Urban (1,107)	23.2	19.5
Rural (267)	22.6	22.0

heading, "Understands Dogma," the Southwest and Far West also differed significantly from the general average. We do know something about the Roman Catholic population in the Southwest: a good percentage of the schools studied had a considerable number of Spanish or Mexican children. Their teachers pointed out that these bilingual children are retarded to some extent in their knowledge of prayers but show better than average understanding of fundamental religious dogmas.

The third problem was whether urban and rural families differ in the

[5] Judson T. Landis, "Marriages of Mixed and Non-Mixed Religious Faith," *American Sociological Review*, XIV (June, 1949), pp. 401-6; Murray H. Leiffer, "Interfaith Marriages in the U.S.A.," *Lumen Vitae*, IV (July-September, 1949), pp. 447-51.

amount of religious training given the child at home. The children in our sample were fairly representative of the Roman Catholic population as a whole, since 17.5 percent were rural and 82.5 percent were urban. According to the best available data, the Roman Catholic population in this country is 19.4 percent rural and 80.6 percent urban.[6] Table 17-3 gives the percentages for the rural and urban children for the country as a whole. Considered as a group, the rural children differ significantly from the urban in their knowledge of prayers. In their understanding of dogma the rural children also display superior home training, with the exception of items 2 and 3, where the differences are not significant. However, this overall picture of urban and rural differences is deceptive. If we break down the data into regions, it becomes apparent at once that the urban-rural relation is not uniform throughout the country. Table 17-4 gives the percentages for urban and rural children by region. It appears that the religious training received at home by urban children in the Southwest, Northeast, and Southeast is equal to, or superior to, that received by rural children in these same areas. It would be interesting to speculate on the reasons for these regional differences, but our present inadequate knowledge of their religious characteristics would render any explanation dubious. However, Table 17-4 does show that generalizations about urban-rural differences in the religious training of children cannot be made without taking regional differences into consideration.

Returning to the questions posed earlier in the paper, we may summarize our findings as follows:

1. The religious training of the preschool child at home as measured by the ten items employed in the present study falls far short of traditional expectations.

2. Regional differences in religious home training are apparent. It is probable that diverse ethnic backgrounds and the relative scarcity of the Roman Catholic population account for a considerable amount of the deviation from the general average.

3. There is evidence that urban and rural families differ in the amount of religious training given the preschool child. Nevertheless, the pattern is not uniform throughout the country: regional differences must be considered if any meaningful comparisons are to be made.

Our study is open to the criticism that we have stressed formal knowledge at the expense of motivation and religious "outlook." On the other hand, given the organized character of Roman Catholic belief and practice, it seems legitimate to conclude that where there is no formal knowledge there is little religious training.

[6] *A Survey of Catholic Weakness* (Des Moines: National Catholic Rural Life Conference, 1948), pp. 10-11.

18   A JEWISH PEER GROUP

Murray B. Seidler and Mel Jerome Ravitz

INTRODUCTION   Although we have focused upon the
role of the family in the socialization process (see Elkind, Article
16, and Thomas, Article 17), the socializing of the child by his
peers cannot go unnoticed. Murray Seidler and Mel Jerome Ravitz
take note of the importance of the Jewish peer group. Significantly,
the Jewish peer group in this study does not support Judaistic religious belief. Only the ethnic characteristic of the group remains.

A peer group is composed of persons of similar age who learn
from each other and share common interests and activities. Usually, the peer group participants share a corresponding status. In
childhood the peer group may take the form of a play group. In
later life it may be found in the form of a clique, club, or some
other grouping. Whatever its form, the peer group provides the
necessary environment in which the individual relates to his contemporaries. The peer group introduces the child to impersonal
authority, and in the process identifies for him what is right and
wrong. It also supports peer members who attempt to test the limits
of parental and adult tolerance.

An analysis of this Jewish peer group illustrates how sociabil-
ity, the central attraction of the peer relationship, can in time come
to dominate the person through its self-sustaining tendencies toward conformity. Through its system of rewards and punishments,
the peer group indicates its approval or disapproval of the actions
which members take. Harmony of the group tends to be emphasized at the expense of individual self-expression and creativity. In

Abridged and reprinted from *The American Journal of Sociology*, Volume 61 (July,
1955), pp. 11-15, by permission of the University of Chicago Press.

MURRAY SEIDLER and MEL JEROME RAVITZ are, respectively, members of the Departments of Political Science and Sociology at Wayne State University.

most instances strong differences in belief are suppressed and group tendencies reinforced.

The socialization potential of the peer group has not been fully utilized by religious institutions. Although a Sunday school or catechetical class may be a form of peer group, the peer relationship can hardly grow in a weekly one-hour session carried on under outside direction. Other potentially stronger peer groups are often overlooked. Church youth, men's, and women's auxiliaries often fail because the dynamic of the peer relationship has not been understood by the clergy or laity.

David Reisman suggests that *in the long run the peer group is the most important socializing agency in the lives of most people.* Historically, he says, men have received cues concerning pertinent values and beliefs from one of three sources: Tradition, oneself, or one's peers. The *tradition-directed* man, characteristic of folk societies, depends upon traditional patterns of behavior as models for his own action. The *inner-directed* man, found in the last century, bases his decisions upon ideals internalized within his person through contact and participation with family authority. The *other-directed* man of the present day depends upon cues from his environment and his peers for indications of meaningful values and beliefs. Religious teaching, however, is based upon tradition. The end goal of religious conversion is the development of the inner-directed man who is sustained by his religious peers. The future of religion in an other-directed society rests with its success in securing peer groups which will nourish its concepts and perpetuate it. Apartment house ministries, coffee house drop-in points in urban areas, and worker priests are modern attempts to relate peers and faith.

THE AUTHORS ARE original and continuing members of a peer group of Jewish boys formed during adolescence. This fact, perhaps, impairs the objectivity of their analysis. On the other hand, it may provide a certain insight which an outsider cannot achieve.

The group began seventeen years ago, when the members were in junior high school. They were ten boys all but one pupils in the same junior and senior high schools. In fact, half of them attended the same elementary school. The number ten is arbitrary, as some boys have belonged peripherally and some others who consider themselves group members are in reality only friends of members. For geographical reasons, some others seem to be sometimes in, sometimes out, but ten comprise the group's core.

The three schools are all large city schools in Detroit. The elementary school had a population of approximately two thousand, while the junior high school and high school each had approximately three thousand students. All are located on a single plot of land in a neighborhood predominantly middle-class and Jewish. The friendships among the group members generally began in school.

The members were all born in the United States. Both parents of all but two group members were born in Europe, for the most part, in Russia or Poland. Most of the fathers are small businessmen. One is a lawyer. In general, the families have enjoyed a comfortable but not lavish standard of living. None can, by any stretch of the imagination, be considered among the elite Jewish families of Detroit; not even the wealthiest belongs to either of the two exclusive local Jewish country clubs. Several of the parents belong to synagogues, but only very few are religious, and some are definitely not interested in religion and religious activities. The commonest of Jewish traits in their homes were Jewish food and an occasional Jewish phrase, often used because the children would not understand.

During adolescence the members' behavior was typical in many ways of American teenage behavior. Almost all the boys, for example, "dated" extensively. It was more often than not double or multiple dating. There were also innumerable parties, dances, wiener roasts, athletic contests, etc. Most of the boys were very active in organizations in the high school.

In one important respect, however, this group may be considered not typical of American teenagers: the very deep and live interest they manifested in public affairs. Though the fascinating topics of sex and athletics were not excluded from their conversations, social and economic issues interested them profoundly. One problem, of course, loomed above all others: whether or not the United States should become involved in World War II. All but two were interventionists. These—one a socialist, the other a self-styled anarchist—eventually registered as conscientious objectors.

Grist for their discussions also included race relations, socialism, freedom, and religion—despite the fact that not a single member, not even those whose parents were the most devout, exhibited any real interest in religious worship, then or since. A few attended the synagogue during the Jewish high holidays, but that was because of parental pressure.

As at once a social club, an athletic club, a discussion club, and a friendship club, the group differed little from a variety of similar age groups in the same area and probably elsewhere as well. On the manifest level this particular group was not extraordinary. But latently it functioned as a strong surrogate for the family. It was clearly a primary group, and as such it was a crucial agent of socialization.[1]

Not all adolescent groups may be truly said to be primary groups. Not all of them are sufficiently integrated to have so strong a hold over their members. Indeed, the following hypothesis is offered here for subsequent testing: The greater the integration and cohesion of the peer group, the greater the extent to which it will usurp the role of the family in socialization.

[1] See Charles H. Cooley, Social Organization (New York: Scribner, 1911).

In general, during the high-school years the "we feeling" was very strong. As it was the current ruling student group of the school, holding virtually all the important class offices, membership in it was highly prized and jealously guarded.

Beginning with a high-school "revolt," the group came generally to be spoken of as "the boys" both by themselves and by others. Whether it was the outsiders (parents) perhaps who first gave them the name or whether the members themselves, becoming aware of their unity, began to use the name, no one can say. It is not unlikely, however, that the second possibility followed after the first.

Further proof of extremely high integration, even in the face of a basic crisis, may be seen in the following behavior. "The boys," with two exceptions, were members of the first high-school class to graduate after Pearl Harbor. All but the two who had earlier declared themselves pacifists were inducted into the armed services about a year after graduation. This meant an interruption of college. The boys in service, however, all gave moral support to their two pacifist friends and, furthermore, offered written testimony to the Selective Service authorities as to the sincerity of the latters' convictions.

At the time of writing, the average age of "the boys" is thirty-one. Nine of the ten are married, yet the unity persists: the group has been expanded to include the wives. Of course, this is not to suggest that the group has not been affected by the marriages; it has. But the basic feeling of togetherness still exists. Most of the social activities of the married members, for example, continue to be among "the boys." Moreover, an annual New Year's Eve party at one of the homes has become a tradition.

Thus, this clique seems to have survived at least three threats: graduation from high school, World War II and its ensuing dispersion, and, finally, marriage. Scrutiny of the behavior of "the boys" and their parents should reveal how the group controlled its members' behavior in three main areas of life: courtship and marriage, social and political beliefs and behavior, and occupational selection.

To be sure, the clique did not do all the socializing of "the boys" while they were members. Each family certainly contributed much to the son's personality, enabling him to become and remain a member. Though the families must be held primarily accountable for the characteristics of their sons, paradoxically, once the group originated and developed, it reduced family influence. "The boys" were in one another's company constantly. Sometimes they resented staying at home to greet their family's guests or rebelled at going out with the family, because it prevented them from being together. The families recognized the effect of the group on the lives of their sons. Several parents occasionally blamed the group for their sons' objectionable behavior, the immediate effect of which, of course, was that "the boys" defended their friends. Sometimes they denied the rather obvious fact that the group had any hold on them at all. In any event, the group's hold on "the boys" probably was noticed earlier by the parents than by the "independent and individualistic" young adolescents.

So strongly integrated a primary group curtailed its members' contacts with outsiders. Each member was involved in a most satisfying network of relationships and therefore did not seek more than marginal contact with others. Only one new member joined after "the boys" graduated. In short, their outlook was markedly ethnocentric. Symptomatic of their ethnocentricism was the defensiveness of "the boys." They would argue that other groups and other people offered very little of interest; that others were interested in dances, football, parties, and the like, to the exclusion of the important matters of the mind that occupied *their* group.

Limiting contacts with outsiders proved not to be a permanent or serious problem. When a member had to leave for school or the army, he was apparently not at all socially handicapped. The members seemed to make friends with more than average ease, and, though usually these new relationships were not so deep and intimate, some close attachments were established with outsiders—a tendency that appears increasingly prominent. In a way, this moving-out into the world and making outside contacts may be likened to the moving-out of the family by the adolescent and his growing sense of independence and security beyond the confines of family life.

During their high-school days "the boys" dated Jewish girls (they were the great majority at the school) almost exclusively. After graduation, however, they made almost as many social arrangements with non-Jewish as with Jewish girls, which is unusual behavior in young Jewish Americans. Not that other Jewish boys did not date non-Jewish girls; they did, but, as other in-group males with out-group females, it was to exploit them sexually. What was unusual was that the non-Jewish girls they dated were treated as they treated their Jewish girls. These were not clandestine relationships; non-Jewish girls were openly escorted to group parties and were received with cordiality and warmth. They were even introduced to parents. In later years eight of the ten members were to have at least one intense emotional relationship with a non-Jewish girl, in which marriage was a real possibility.

Even more startling is the incidence of outmarriage among "the boys." Of the nine already married, three are married to non-Jews. And, when peripheral group members are counted, there are two more.

The statistics concerning the intermarriage of Jews in the United States are neither clear nor definite. But there is no evidence to indicate that the rate of intermarriage is greater than 5 percent. Of the larger groups in the American community, only Negroes exceed Jews in endogamy.[2] It should be noted, however, that more Jewish men than women intermarry.[3] Even so, the rate of

---

[2] Ruby Jo Reeves Kennedy, "Single or Triple Melting Pot?" *American Journal of Sociology*, XLIX (1944), pp. 331-39.
[3] M. C. Elmer, *The Sociology of the Family* (Boston: Ginn, 1945), p. 195.

intermarriage for this Jewish clique is extraordinarily high. None of their parents intermarried or even contemplated doing so, and in each family the prospect of intermarriage was met with objections. But the integration of "the boys" was strong enough to enable them to defy the mores of their ethnic group.

While hard to substantiate conclusively, it seems clear that certain individuals altered their social outlook, consciously or unconsciously, toward more nonconformity (from the community viewpoint) in order to gain greater acceptance from the clique. One member, for instance, upon first joining the group, argued that Negroes were inferior to whites. It was not long before he became a champion of racial equality, even though his parents still think as he did earlier.

When the second World War ended, "the boys" returned to college. Their social, political, and economic philosophies had become more markedly nonconformist. Several had seen very difficult military service; one had been killed. Another vowed he would never fight in a war again. All had deeply resented every aspect of military life, especially its authoritarianism. Most were considerably disillusioned by the disparity between the declared aims of the war and its results, as they interpreted them. Five voted Socialist in 1948, when they had their first opportunity to vote in a presidential election. One refrained from voting on anarchist principles. All became much more interested in social reform in general. They were especially concerned with bettering the lot of minorities in the United States. Emphatically they rejected every form of racism, including Jewish prejudice toward non-Jews. As a group, with one exception, they were either hostile or indifferent to Zionism.

In contrast, several of the parents were decidedly friendly toward the Zionist movement, nine of the ten parents were staunch Roosevelt Democrats, and several harbored at least a perpetual suspicion of Negroes. Moreover, the siblings of the members, on the whole, followed their parents, with, of course, some "next-generation" modification and liberalization.

The wives of "the boys," in general, adopted their husband's friends and eased away from their former friends. The clique was so strong that in effect it pulled in all intimate associates of its members and left them little time for other relationships. Moreover, of course, "the boys" were more committed to their clique than were their wives, who were involved in the groups in which they had previously participated.

For some members the group may have been influential in reinforcing at least the choice of occupation. In moving all the group members into the professions, it may have been significantly influential. Six of the ten are now physicians, of whom four have decided upon psychiatry as a specialty and at least one other had considered it seriously at one time. Of the others, two are universitity social science teachers, one is a lawyer, and, finally, one is totally committed to the idea of becoming a writer. Only one ever gave any thought to the idea of going into business, yet that is an occupation very common among boys of their particular background. But their clique generally condemned business ethics. Further, the physicians among them are highly critical of the *status quo* in medicine and favor either compulsory health insurance or the outright socialization of medicine. Both the university instructors are members of the American Federation of Teachers.

Inasmuch as medicine ranked very high among Jewish parents as a suitable occupation for their sons, the clique can hardly claim exclusive credit for turning the latter's attention to a medical career. Each of "the boys" would doubtless have been encouraged by his family at least to consider medicine seriously. Three, for example, had brothers who were doctors. The clique reinforced the interest in that profession. Also, their preponderant interest in psychiatry—a branch of medicine viewed with some suspicion even by many doctors—is, very probably, another manifestation of the group's patterned nonconformity: that the four physicians decided to become psychiatrists is surely more than a chance happening. One of the other two decided *not* to specialize in psychiatry only after he had been away from the group for a year while studying in another city. It is likely, too, that the common professional background of "the boys" has helped the group to endure.

To turn to the main hypothesis of this paper, that the clique was so strongly integrated that it became a primary group for its members and took over that role from the respective families—how else can we explain for the group the high incidence of outmarriage, of nonconformist ideas, of professionals—physicians, psychiatrists, and social scientists? There is nothing unusual about the values and beliefs of the parents of these young men which would account for the direction of their ideas and behavior, with one exception. One boy's parents were lifelong socialists, and his attitudes were derived at least in part from his family. However, they were probably strongly supported by the group values. Some seeds of interest in social issues probably stemmed from this source, especially as the group frequently met at this boy's home. The attitudes of the parents were for the most part commonplace, ranging from hearty opposition to reluctant acceptance of intermarriage, from agreement to the more usual disagreement in matters political, social, and economic. There was little parental opposition to the occupational selections; in fact, virtually all the parents were pleased. In keeping with the American promise, the children had surpassed their parents in professional achievement.

James Bossard says: "Each peer group has a culture which is distinctly its own." He goes on to say that peer groups may be considered as primary groups which have a fundamental impact upon the personalities of their members. Moreover, he maintains, as did Cooley, that they can exert, exceeding that of their families, a degree of control over their members.[4] More recently, David Riesman theorized about the influence of the peer group, particularly upon

[4] James Bossard, *The Sociology of Child Development* (New York: Harper & Row, 1948), pp. 504, 508, 516, 519.

what he calls "other-directed" children.[5] Many of the data from the study of "the boys" support Riesman's propositions.

The intense solidarity of the group and its long duration fostered a situation which was extremely favorable to the members' internalization of its culture. Even granting differentials in internalization, it can be safely assumed that all the personalities of "the boys" were fundamentally affected by the group culture.

[5] David Riesman, *The Lonely Crowd* (New Haven: Yale University Press, 1950).

19 DEVELOPMENTAL FACTORS IN THE GROWTH OF A MATURE FAITH

Richard McCann

INTRODUCTION   Richard McCann, psychologist at
Harvard Divinity School, notes in this article that a high percent-
various role requirements daily impinge upon the adult, his religiously. He suggests that religious socialization is a continuing
process which is never fully achieved. Therefore, disparity between
daily behavior and expectations of faith are to be expected. As
various role requirements daily impinge upon the adult, his responses to faith will normally be modified in the process. This may
explain why religion, in spite of its extensive membership, is not
fully able to translate religious ideals into social practice (*see*
Glock, Article 7, and Hammond, Article 9).

The central problem in religious socialization is the need to
teach children and youth through concrete examples which may
later be broadened to the form of abstract concepts usable to adults
(*see* Elkind, Article 17). As the adult grows in maturity and seeks
social and intellectual integration, he may become aware of his immaturity of belief and faith. As the need for religious integration
becomes recognized, the individual generally develops his religious
life in one of two directions. Either he intellectualizes his belief
from the former emotional-concrete level, or he throws off his old
belief, accepting some other belief system in its place. The childhood concept of God, in either instance, is replaced by a new abstraction of Creation and Creator. In the latter instance a person
may lose his faith but still remain an ethical and moral person re-
sponsive to the values of the faith which he has seemingly rejected.

Abridged and reprinted from the May-June 1955 issue of *Religious Education* by permission of the publisher, The Religious Education Association, 545 West 111th Street,
New York, New York 10025.

RICHARD MCCANN is Lecturer in Psychology of Religion at Harvard Divinity School and
Member of the Massachusetts Rehabilitation Commission.

EXAMINATION OF many of the empirical studies of religion carried out during the last half-century disclosed that none attempted a broad description or analysis of the religious beliefs and experiences of individuals. Has supernaturalism been stripped of all but vague ideas of God and Immortality? How many different conceptions are included in the word "God"? How much is left of the original "Articles of Faith" in the thinking of the individual communicant rather than in the pronouncements of the religious institution? How intense and stable are the attachments to the beliefs which people currently avow? To what extent do existing religious sentiments influence and interpenetrate with other values? To what extent do they motivate or modify behavior?

Such questions as the foregoing led to a structure of hypotheses to guide the research; the essential points are as follows: There has been a change in the character of the religion of contemporary North Americans, reflected primarily in the presence of fewer supernatural components. The changes—the loss or decline of supernatural and traditional factors and their replacement by others—may be functionally and meaningfully connected with changing concepts of the self and of society. Far from happening in isolation, religious changes may prove to be interrelated in two dimensions: horizontally, in that they are intimately associated with changes in personal and cultural values; and vertically, in that a change in one religious belief will involve changes in other beliefs, sentiments, and experiences in the religious area.

After a pilot study had been made with fifty research subjects and after noting the considerable shortcomings of the most frequently used methods in empirical religious research—tests, scales, and questionnaires—an interview-guide was constructed to serve as framework for a series of intensive interviews conducted on a person-to-person basis.

Two hundred persons were interviewed for from six to twelve hours each —some of the interview series running over 20 hours per person. The interview series was designed in such a way that the first one or two sessions are devoted to an exploration of the subject's personal and social philosophy—concepts of the self, of relationships, of society, of moral structure.

No subject knew in advance that the main theme of the interview series was to be religion. The panel of 200 research subjects represents varied backgrounds. There are fifteen Protestant denominations represented, in addition to Roman Catholic, Orthodox and Reform Judaism, and Eastern Orthodoxy. There are theists, humanists, agnostics, atheists. They represent a variety and range not only in religious background and experience but also in age, education, sex, marital status, occupation. Percentiles have been worked out in order to describe the panel effectively. For example, 33 percent believe in the divinity of Jesus; 33 percent in personal immortality. Eight-two percent formerly believed in a personal God, and 18 percent had some other concept. Now these figures are exactly reversed: only 18 percent believe in a personal God; 82 percent have some other Deity concept, or are agnostic, or atheistic. More sophisticated statistical procedures, such as the correlation matrix and the cluster analysis, are used to explore the interrelations between religious values and personality variables.

The interview experience has for many subjects an integrating, holistic effect. One expressed it this way: "Going through the interview sessions had a strongly integrative effect on me. It was remarkably like prayer. By helping me sort out my values and look deeply within myself, you were helping me to pray."

CONCEPTS OF DEITY.   Almost all of our subjects are "in process" religiously. Their religious change has been sometimes concentrated, sometimes diffuse; sometimes in the past as well as continuing in the present; and often indicated for the future, for in many cases we can predict the direction and intensity of change. Even those few subjects (18 percent) who seem to show no change in their major belief object, the Deity, have gone through or are going through a process of change—variations in the more subtle spheres of intensity and valuation and of degree of relevance of such belief objects to the centers of the individual life.

Eighteen percent of our subjects continue to hold anthropomorphic, personal, almost pictorial concepts of God. Though they represent the "learned" or "inherited" or creedal ideas of Deity, we find considerable variation among them. Some believe in a glorified, seeable, knowable man with a tangible body, the literal father of the spirits of men. Others conceive of God as the father who knows best, who can be approached in prayer, and who proves his personal interest in us by having become Jesus Christ. Yet for most of these 18 percent who have preserved more or less intact their early beliefs, though the content may still be influenced by some traditional denominational position, the verbalized form at least has been fashioned and refashioned by their personal thought and experience.

Forty-five percent of our subjects have depersonalized and "deconcretized" their ideas of God learned and accepted in childhood, reformulating them in terms more meaningful to their needs and experiences. Some of these think of God as one, omnipotent, and eternal, though never in the image of a person. Other concepts range from "a vague kind of God, connected with being good, within yourself," to "a power that works through conscience" and "a superior force that governs men's lives."

Some are able to attribute the changes in their Deity imagery to specific events or others factors in their past life. One, a Christian Scientist, thought that the type and quality of her belief had been affected by her increasing independence of her family, particularly of her mother. For a former Roman Catholic, the beginnings of doubt were associated with the felt inadequacy of the confessional experience. Almost everything—creed and worship—declined along with his loss of belief in the function of the priesthood. Yet his deep-rooted need for order in the universe prevented loss of belief in God, making of God, for him, the Creator and Bestower and Maintainer of order in the universe. A physicist, who is an Episcopalian, lost all faith in a personal God largely through the influence of science, even to the extent of becoming atheistic for a number of years. Finally seeing that even experimental science seemed aimed ultimately as destruction, he felt a need for God as Judge, for God as the Universe itself. These and the remainder of the 45 percent who derived some spiritualized concept of God, stopped short of rejection or loss of belief, and instead made some kind of reformulation in terms which satisfied their changing outlook on life.

AGNOSTIC OR ATHEISTIC CONCEPTS. Some of our subjects, however, became agnostic or atheistic. Thirty-seven per cent disclaim all belief, or simply do not know, or attempt to work out either some kind of intellectualized ultimate entity or reasonings and justifications for not-knowing. A young Russian Orthodox housewife tells us that even as a child she sensed that religion never really meant much to her parents, though they observed the expected custom of seeing to it that she received some religious education. For a more complete explanation, we would have to explore further the nature of her relationship with her father. "I used to be terrified to walk into my father's study to confess my sins to him," she tells us. It is possible that gradually, after he took on the role of priest as her confessor, she experienced a growing need to reject him. Though she is not conscious of the possibility of having identified father, priest, and God, she may have needed to reject the ideas of God and priest in order to become free of her father.

CONFLICTING CONCEPTS. For another young housewife, of Methodist background, the idea of a benevolent God, held since early childhood, came into insoluble conflict with the fearful teachings about hellfire and damnation which she encountered in her early teens. A twenty-nine year old teacher lost all belief after a loving, protecting Father Almighty permitted indiscriminate loss and survival in a naval bombing attack.

Some of these people had a concept of God that would not tolerate changes in experience. God was all-loving, all-protecting; and a catastrophic experience that seemed to deny his protection or his loving kindness, that took place outside it, shook the belief. The benevolent God who permitted senseless holocausts in this life seemed just as contradictory as the benevolent God who foreordained the holocaust—the fires of hell—in the life to come. Neither God concept could survive, nor could the God who was too harsh, too frighteningly immediate.

Jung holds that personality maturity includes a satisfactory adjustment to a cosmic setting which is conceived of in spiritual terms. Even a neurotic episode, according to Jung, may be a crisis of development advancing toward a more adequate stage of the personality than any it has previously reached. As we examine the responses of our subjects, we can see some of the factors that have been instrumental in their changes in belief, and some of the ways by which they have sought adjustment and integration, sometimes with, sometimes without the "cosmic setting," and often advancing toward "a more adequate stage of the personality." When they reach a level of broadening interests, a level higher and wider on which the personality reaches more closely toward integration, some of them discover that their religious beliefs have been all along at a simple, sometimes immature level, while other values in their personality—interpersonal and cultural experiences and the whole subjective life—have been at a higher intellectual level. When this awareness comes about, there are two directions in which the religious life may develop.

1. The individual can attempt to intellectualize the old belief, to bring it from an emotional to a rational, intellectual level—though he may discover that in the sphere of religion, the emotional aspect is the more important. Frequently this process can be facilitated by a movement, which may go on quite subconsciously, away from the literal, concrete meaning of symbols, to an increasingly more abstract interpretation. But the longer the symbol and its meaning are kept in conceptive contact, the more rigid becomes the identification. The meaning must be relaxed, loosened, so that with the passage of time and the acquisition of maturity, the symbols may become less concrete, less literal, more abstract.

2. In an alternative reaction, the individual may throw away his old belief as being no longer suited to the "new man," no longer satisfying his more mature needs. The learned or transmitted conception of God acquired in childhood—the heavenly, loving, protecting though punishing Father—becomes untenable, with no possibility for a modified concept to take its place.

One fact emerges clearly from study of the responses of many subjects: the traumatic or disintegrating or thwarting factors, when present, were not concentrated in a single flash, but were present in the environment, in the background, in the long-range experience and relationships. It is frequently such factors as these, working unobtrusively upon the personality, that are later responsible for change or loss of belief—and for the acquisition of belief as well.

Although such subjects may have lost their faith in God, they seem to have preserved the moral standards and ethical ideals that had become part of their mental and emotional equipment and part of their behavioral set, in conjunction with the simple level of religion during their childhood.

CHANGES IN BELIEF.   In many cases, as we have noted, the motivations for change in belief may be unconscious. Years, sometimes decades pass following the major change, such as modification or loss of the belief in God. Meanwhile, other changes take place, for the religious life and experience is a process, a constantly moving line of advance and retreat, progress and re-

lapse, interest and indifference, stagnation and growth. Then quite unexpectedly, an individual may find himself in some circumstance, such as our interview series, in which he has the opportunity—and the challenge—to put into
words something that may have gone on in the innermost places of his heart
and personality without ever having come to the threshold of his awareness.
Others deliberately embark upon a conscious process of religious search, which
inevitably results in some degree of change, whether in content or in valuation.
One may seek a tightly organized perfectionist system; another may strike out
on an intellectual journey which may bring him out of a positivistic fundamentalistic background to a relativistic or humanistic resting-place—or mile-
stone—along the road.

In contrast to those who come to a new orientation through forces actively
but often subconsciously at work and those who deliberately, consciously seek,
we come upon some persons whose "religious doubts are not the result of any
intellectual activity on his part, but rather the effect of a climate of skeptical
opinion on a passive and receptive personality." A "climate of skeptical opinion" seems to have been the habitat of many of our subjects at some period in
their lives.

CONCLUSIONS.   1.   Eighty-two percent of our subjects had at the beginning of their religious life a pictorial, personal, anthropomorphic Deity concept. The deconcretized, spiritualized concepts at which many of them have
arrived tempt us to believe that some more spiritualized concept of God should
be the concept taught in our churches and schools and homes. But the original
concept of a personal, visualizable, interested, loving, protecting God may be
just as natural for the early life of the individual as for the earliest phases of
religion itself. Children seem to need concretization. Ideas which are to be part
of their value system for life must, if presented to them at a very early stage of
development, be presented in objective, concrete form. But as their thinking
becomes more capable of abstraction, the pictorialism and personalization of
the early concepts should become more abstract. The anthropomorphic belief
seems to be the early, preliminary, structural stage through which they must
progress to a more inclusive, less strictly defined concept. Emerging out of the
early "concrete" religious imagery rather than starting beyond it, may be a
desirable and necessary experience in the development of the individual.

In view of the large number of our subjects who do not stop at a spiritualized concept but go all the way to rejection or indifference, the question
arises as to how the idea of the Divine can be abstracted, spiritualized, deconcretized without being weakened or lost. It seems that most persons we have
encountered intend to repeat the experience they underwent themselves. That
is, they will not teach their children the beliefs they now hold at this stage of
their religious process, but will let the next generation acquire the traditional
religious content, at the simplest level, of our characteristically or at least

nominally Judeo-Christian culture, and then seek their own level of religious beliefs, behavior, and experience as they mature—with perhaps some anticipation that the children will eventually settle at their parents' present level.

Perhaps it is inevitable that each generation will be exposed to the pictorial idea of God, which they will later have difficulty in deconcretizing. Yet the importance of the pictorial is felt in other areas of learning than those of religious imagery. We cannot ignore the evidence of the growing dependence on pictorial methods in education.

Yet there is hope. The concrete, the pictorial, may be interpreted as the vessel which will convey meaning according to the receptive level of the child —in this instance, the meaning of God. The rigidity, the inelastic and unyielding nature of such imagery is often due to the nature of the relationships with those who present it or who represent it—parents, teachers, and clergy. As we realize more and more clearly the importance of the qualities of the *relationship* in the process of education and socialization, we may be in a better position, as the individual pushes on towards maturity and consistency, to help him change the idea of God without weakening or destroying it, to refashion the container without losing the contents.

2.   The nature of the relationship can be so crucial that we examined with particular care the history of all our agnostic subjects. For convenience we selected a subgroup of those who came from Protestant fundamentalist backgrounds. Ninety percent of them experienced environments or relationships—particularly with parents—which lacked supportive, integrating values for development, or which were rigid and absolutist. Among persons from fundamentalist Protestant backgrounds, we can observe indications of a direct relationship between the nature of early family atmosphere and characteristics —deprived or nondeprived, happy or unhappy, rigid or permissive—and the direction, amount, and kind of change in theistic belief. In fundamentalist Protestant homes, if the early environment is basically unhappy or otherwise traumatic—where there is deprivation of love, of support; or rigid relationships and hence rigid transmission of inelastic, externalized values—the seed for future agnosticism may have been sown. Under such circumstances, future religious development may be blocked and the transmitted values may at some time have to be rejected when they cannot be transformed and reinterpreted, in order to make way for consistency.

While the implications of this finding for religious change in persons of other backgrounds than fundamentalist Protestant suggests a fruitful line of investigation, there is special value in our closer look at this subgroup of ex-fundamentalistic agnostics. For in a fundamentalist church or community, the content of religion transmitted from generation to generation consists almost exclusively of supernatural and creedal concepts. The transmission of religious values through such a closed community may cause one whole area of transmitted sentiments to be out of synchronization with other sentiments "caught" or transmitted from the wider community. The individual is caught in the disequilibrium caused by this cultural lag, and tries to restore balance and consistency. The very imbalance can in itself be a spiritually dynamic force urging the individual on to reformulation, revision, and sometimes fresh creativity in the closely related spheres of religious and social values. Often, however, as the individual works his way out of a position which may be intolerable both logically and psychically, he overcompensates; he passes beyond the line separating reinterpretation and revision from rejection and loss. For some, this is a point of no return. For others, the result is not so much a loss of faith as a suspension of faith.

John Weller is one of those who traveled from fundamentalism to a "suspension of faith." After breaking away from the fundamentalist community, both geographically and psychically, he began to gain a new comprehension of what the individual can be, what the world is really like, and how the individual most effectively relates to his world. When man had become, for Weller, an autonomous, unified organism relating himself consistently with his context, and God had become the "gods" of "respect for the rights of others, trust for the life that is ours," he had to modify his old conceptions of the religious community, its God, and its values. Although intellectual emancipation could take place, Weller's emotional attachment to the church which still insisted on its authority and on its barriers against the "world," and to the God who damned or saved arbitrarily, had been too rigid. The absolutist God, the absolutist religious community—and the absolutist father—could not be spiritualized or reinterpreted in his thinking. Yet Weller had to push on towards inner consistency. Since modification of the inconsistent elements, while necessary and possible intellectually, was impossible emotionally, they had to be swept away to clear the path to that consistency and integration, unity and maturity which are the natural goals of the developing Self.

B. THE MINISTRY

20 ROLE CONFLICTS OF THE URBAN PROTESTANT PARISH MINISTER

Samuel W. Blizzard

INTRODUCTION   The complexity of modern society has caused changes in the religious roles of American clergymen. While ministerial roles in the past centered largely around preaching and sacramental activity, in recent years counseling and "social actions" have taken on increased importance. Scholarship has given way to parish administration and membership recruitment. The tendency toward economic and technological specialization has led also to ecclesiastical specialization. And yet, the parish clergyman, the ministerial general practitioner, remains as the key component of the American religious institution. Each rabbi, priest, or minister assumes one or more religious roles which are suitable to his talents, interests, and position. Although only a small percentage of the clergy currently serve in the specialized and multiple ministries of music, youth, visitation, teaching, inner missions, and chaplaincy, they are forerunners of a growing specialization within American religious groups.

Samuel Blizzard, professor at Princeton Theological Seminary, takes note of the increasing number of nervous breakdowns occurring among young ministers due to the discrepancy between personal abilities and congregational expectations. The flexibility of urban life has caused traditional ministerial roles to become ambiguous. Ten different roles illustrate the diffuse character of the modern ministry. The *ritualist* conducts religious rites and ceremonies as defined by the faith. Expressing the coherence and tradition of his group in the act of worship, he stresses the con-

Abridged and reprinted from the *City Church*, Volume 7 (September, 1956), pp. 13-15, by permission of the author and the editors.

SAMUEL BLIZZARD is Professor of Christianity and Society at Princeton Theological Seminary.

tinuity of the member with the faith of the saints. As a *preacher* he is charged with the presentation of a specific sermon or address which usually focuses upon the definitive writings of the faith, whether the Bible, Torah, or Mary Baker Eddy's *Science and Health*. The role of the *cleric* is assumed when the minister performs services as a recognized official of the state; he performs marriages, invokes prayers, and supervises oaths. In each instance the act possesses a legal significance. The *rector* administers the church plan and local parish. As the director of the local institution, he works with laymen where authorized. The *administrator* differs from the *rector* in that he supervises and administers larger units of the religious institution. Usually this role is confined to larger, centralized church bodies organized along episcopal or presbyterian forms of church government (*see* Introduction, Part III).

The role of the *parson* is most clearly expressed as the religious leader assumes responsiblity and leadership within some welfare setting or agency of the community. Although outside the specific responsibility of his call to a local congregation, he assumes this role as part of his general concern for people and their needs. The *pastor* serves as the shepherd of the flock. Calling on the sick, counseling the disturbed, and comforting the bereaved, the pastor helps those in need. The role of *healer* is a more specialized role. Ranging from medical missionaries to faith healers like Oral Roberts, the healer attempts to free man from the afflictions of body and spirit. The *teacher* role is most fully assumed by the rabbi. Responsible for the propagation of the spiritual heritage of the faith, the teacher socializes the child, youth or adult to the essentials of belief through confirmation and instructional classes, Sunday schools, small group discussions, open meetings, and parochial schools. The role of the *scholar,* although often allied to that of the teacher and preacher, is also a distinct and specialized role. As a scholar the religious functionary probes the scholarship of the past and present in a thorough way. Largely neglected by the modern clergyman, the current scholar tends to be isolated within the college, university, or seminary faculty.

R OLE CONFLICTS ARE a basic, root problem of the ministerial profession. Parish ministers who desire to be effective in these times are aware that there is much ambivalence about the many roles they are expected to perform. Clergymen are also aware that ambiguity characterizes their personal, family and community lives as well as those duties that are professional. The understandings about the role conflicts of the Protestant minister that are presented in this article have been secured with the cooperation of 345 urban parish clergy. The Department of the Urban Church,

National Council of Churches and denominational urban church executives have sponsored this phase of the research by selecting the parish clergymen who have cooperated in the project. Each minister furnished information for the research by granting a mail interview. They are one group of clergymen who are participating in a comprehensive study of the functions of the Protestant parish minister in the United States. This research is being conducted under the joint auspices of Union Theological Seminary, New York, and the Russell Sage Foundation.

A thumbnail sketch of the cooperating urban ministers shows that their average age is 46.8 years. Ninety-seven percent are married and there are on the average 2.4 children in the family. The typical year of their ordination was 1935. They have been in their present parish an average of 7.9 years and ninety-seven percent have the status of minister in charge of the parish rather than that of associate or assistant minister.

All of these ministers serve urban churches. However, four out of five of the churches are located in the metropolitan areas, rather than in the non-metropolitan areas. They are located in all the regions of the United States. Twenty-one Protestant denominations are represented among the ministers in the panel. The average church staff in man years is 4.73 persons. The average number of ministers in each parish is 1.47. Nearly one-half of the churches (47 per cent) have a part-time lay professional worker (religious educator, choir director, church visitor), who receives remuneration. Four-fifths have some secretarial help, and eighteen percent have no paid janitor. The average church served by one of the informants has 960 members and 465 in the church school. The average local budget is $37,646, and the average benevolence budget is $12,820.

The roles of the urban minister are characterized by diffuseness rather than specificity. Role ambiguity, therefore, is inherent in the profession. In the context of conflicting role expectations the urban clergyman faces the problem of emotional maturity and the desire for self-understanding. He is expected to be a man of belief, a saint, but his right to completely express ethical judgments based on his personal understanding of and commitment to the Christian faith are often challenged and jeopardized. He is expected to be a man of action, a practitioner, but he is also expected to be a scholar of religion, a contemplative role. The practitioner roles are both privately and publicly focused (pastor role vs. preacher role). They are oriented to a message or ideology as well as to helping people (teacher vs. organizer). He is expected to perform in his profession as a general practitioner but the success image emphasizes specialization in one role. The definition of an effective urban parish minister is often in conflict with the image of success in the denomination. Contrasting and sometimes contradictory goals are urged on him. A clergyman is expected to be a professional man but his family life may be crowded because his job demands long hours of duty. His professional responsibilities are primarily to one institution in the community (the church),

but many extraprofessional demands are made on him as a community organizer and a leader.

Urban clergymen are seeking self-understanding. This theme occurs in
response to several questions in the survey as ministers examine their present
parish situation or recall previous parishes and nonclergy occupational experiences. More than one-fourth of the ministers mentioned that their experiences
in nonclergy occupations had influenced their way of being a minister by
giving them a greater understanding of people and human nature. One-fifth
found that this occupational experience had also given them a greater understanding of self. Almost as many considered personal emotional inadequacies
as a problem in parishes previous to their present assignment. One minister
expressed it: "myself is the greatest problem." The same proportion gained
personal emotional growth as they functioned in ministerial roles in previous
parishes. More than one-fourth were able to gain a better understanding of
interpersonal relations and to learn to identify themselves with people in parishes prior to their present location. More than one-fifth are critical of other
ministers because of their emotional immaturity.

The role conflicts of urban Protestant parish ministers are reflected in
several themes. The first role conflict is that of the believer or the saint vs. the
prophet. The minister feels that he is expected to be a man of belief, but that
ethical judgments that he derives from his understanding of the Christian
faith are at times challenged. The saint cannot always play the role of the
social prophet. More than one-third feel that time for self-maintenance of the
spiritual life is a problem in their professional life. Ministers in the urban
panel devote one hour and eleven minutes a day to spiritual growth (meditation, prayer, Bible reading). One in twenty recalled that this was a problem
in previous parishes. Twelve percent are critical of other ministers because
they feel that their spiritual life as a believer is inadequate. In the pastor and
counselor role, the minister-believer becomes aware of social questions and
ethical issues. More than one-fourth of these questions deal with ethical issues
involving individual parishioners. Fewer issues involved the local church.
Seventeen percent reported counseling situations involving the application of
Christian beliefs to community problems. In the matter of taking a stand on
controversial issues, only one percent felt free to speak on local church issues
and 28 percent on community issues. However, 78 percent felt free to speak
on general controversial issues. Some suggested that they "preach the Bible
and do not engage in issues." There is a general feeling among the informants
that the minister is expected to be a model to other believers but that he is not
expected to take stands on specific issues involving religious ethical judgments.
The saint and the prophet roles are in conflict.

A second theme in the conflicting role images of the Protestant urban
minister is that of the practitioner, and the scholar. The urban parish ministers
in this panel work an average of ten hours and 32 minutes each day performing the practitioner roles (administrator, organizer, pastor, preacher, priest

and teacher). They devote 27 minutes a day to general intellectual activity. An additional 38 minutes each day is spent in sermon preparation. Time for self-maintenance is seen as a major professional problem by these ministers. When they were asked to name any persons whom they admire or who has greatly influenced the way they think and act as a minister, one-half mentioned seminary professors and a somewhat greater proportion mentioned well known religious authors. They have the scholar image of their mentors. However, they spent the major portion of their time as practitioners, men of action, rather than as scholars of religion, a contemplative role.

The practitioner roles performed by parish ministers have built-in expectancies which foster role discrepancies and conflict. In the pastor-counselor role, the minister is expected to respect confidences. The relationship with the counselor is a private affair, but nearly one-fifth of the informants were critical of the way in which ministerial colleagues practice in this role. In the counseling situations the minister is expected to have a permissive attitude toward the parishioner. The preacher role requires the clergyman to perform in an altogether different mode. Preaching is a public role. It is easy for parishioners to pick up a reference to a counseling relationship if it is alluded to in the sermon. The preacher role tends to call for an authoritarian approach. It is directive rather than nondirective. Hence, the foci of these two practitioner roles basically conflict. Furthermore, three of the practitioner roles place the minister in the position of an actor before an audience. This is the case in preaching, teaching, and liturgical duties as commonly performed by the clergy. The administrator, organizer, and pastor roles involve the minister in interpersonal relations and intra- and intergroup relations. This calls for a different orientation on the part of the minister. It may also be noted that the same grouping of practitioner roles may be viewed as being ideological or message oriented as contrasted to ministering to the needs of people. Hence, as the minister shifts from role to role he must reorient himself to avoid conflicting role expectancies.

The typical urban parish minister is a general practitioner rather than a specialist. Very few (six percent) urban churches are served by three or more ministers. Hence, as the principal professional leader in the parish the minister must be prepared to perform the whole gamut of practitioner roles. The image that he has of success in his denomination places a high value on having a special proficiency in one of the roles. This is cited by more informants in their image of success than any other factor (43 percent). They feel that they may be a success in their denomination if they are a "good preacher," or a "good pastor," or a "good administrator." The single role approach of the specialist is a part of their success image, rather than the multiple role approach of the general practitioner.

The image of an effective minister is oriented to the parish. The image of the successful minister is oriented to the denomination. These images are in some respects in conflict. Character or integrity, an outgoing personality, spiritual maturity, and abilities in the practitioner roles are characteristics of both the effective and the success image. The ranking these characteristics receive differs sharply. Character is rated first for effectiveness, but it is fifth in the success picture. Ability in performing ministerial roles is first for success, but these roles are last in the effectiveness scale. Spiritual maturity is third in the effectiveness image, but it is last in the success ratings. Self-understanding is reported to be important by informants in their effectiveness image, but cooperation in denominational programs is given a higher rating in the success picture. The dilemma that this conflict in role expectancies creates for the minister is often a choice between doing a job in the local parish and doing those things that will result in his professional advancement in the denomination.

The urban parish minister plays a role as a member of a family. In a waking day of 16 hours and 17 minutes he spends one hour and 46 minutes in family activities. This includes spiritual life (five minutes), family fellowship and recreation (59 minutes), family care (24 minutes), and maintenance (18 minutes). Urban panel informants spend 33 minutes a day less with their family than do rural ministers. These facts focus on the conflict the minister faces between his professional roles and his role as a family man.

A final theme that reflects the role conflicts of the urban Protestant parish minister focuses on his professional and extraprofessional roles. As a professional leader in the community, the minister's primary responsibility is to the church as an institution. Certain services are expected of the urban minister that may be a part of his technical training and experience but are not strictly a part of his professional duties. Urban ministers devote an average 29 minutes each day to community organizations. It is expected that he will devote time to educational groups, health and welfare agencies and youth and character organizations. He is expected to be a "chaplain" to many of these organizations. For others he will function as a member of the board of directors, and for other groups he will sanction fund raising campaigns. Ministers feel pressures are placed on them in the community to perform these and other extraprofessional roles. A few resent the time that this requires, and others asked themselves questions about how these roles further their basic religious functions in the community.

The ministry is a free profession with diffuse role definitions in a voluntary institution. Diversity of role performance and lack of clarity in role expectancies is to be expected. In the case of the urban minister the situation is magnified by the number of people each minister serves and the long hours they work. It is also exaggerated by the heterogeneous features of urban life and the mobility of the population. Hence urban ministers must minister to people on the basis of relatively short acquaintances and secondary groups, rather than face-to-face relations. The resulting wear and tear on the professional leader is apparent. This seems to indicate a need for a more probing understanding of the stresses, tensions, and conflicts in the ministry than clergy and laymen in the church have yet displayed. The future of the church may stand or fall on the mental health of the clergy.

21 ROLE CONFLICTS OF MILITARY CHAPLAINS

Waldo W. Burchard

INTRODUCTION   Militarily and religiously, the armed forces chaplain is a marginal man. Although selected as a representative of a denomination, he is usually not accepted as a full-fledged clergyman by his former colleagues who serve parishes. Although serving in the armed forces under an authoritarian system, he possesses a more permissive and flexible religious situation than would generally be found in the normal congregation. Yet he may face greater role conflict because of the need to express a clear allegiance to military superiors. To those in the armed forces, he is neither an enlisted man nor a normal officer. Operating under a commanding officer, he generally becomes a recognized partner of an officer team, depending upon his own capabilities and the willingness of the officer group to accept him.

Chaplains face role conflicts which are especially difficult to resolve. As an ordained clergyman, the chaplain preaches peace, justice, mercy and brotherhood. As the religious sanction for military action, however, he may have to justify war and death. Waldo Burchard states that chaplains resolve role conflicts either by abandoning one of the conflicting roles, rationalizing its implications, or compartmentalizing alternative role behaviors. The rationalization of role conflict tends to strengthen the chaplain's role as a military officer at the expense of his role as a preacher and pastor (see Blizzard, Article 20).

Those entering the chaplaincy face many limitations. As a representative of the state, the chaplain must minimize denominational and sectarian interests. Denominational evangelistic activ-

Abridged and reprinted from the *American Sociological Review*, Volume 19 (October, 1954), pp. 528-535, by permission of the author and the editors.

WALDO W. BURCHARD is Professor of Sociology at Northern Illinois University.

ities tend, therefore, to decline. The need of the chaplain to serve as a functionary of the state is maximized, in spite of the principle of separation of church and state. Although limited in the pursuit of denominational goals, the chaplain is free to reach more general social goals. The development of a moral character guidance program becomes an acceptable alternative to the promulgation of doctrines and symbols of the chaplain's denomination.

The recent attempts to clarify the exact relationship of church and state present a challenge to the whole concept of the military chaplaincy. Already steps have been taken to challenge the payment of chaplains' salaries from public funds. However, the rise of the chaplaincy has been based upon the concept of freedom of worship. Because the Constitution guarantees the right of all men to the worship of their choice, the state, with the cooperation of representative denominations, has provided chaplains for armed forces personnel. Without the chaplaincy the individual serviceman would be deprived of his right to freedom of worship by the state. In this sense the chaplaincy has developed as a compromise between the principle of separation of church and state and the right of the individual to worship in the manner of his choice.

IN A COMPLEX SOCIETY many institutions are required to satisfy the manifold needs and wants of man. This means that any given individual will play many social roles in the course of his lifetime, and at any given time will be playing a number of roles simultaneously. His roles may not necessarily be in harmony with each other, and in some instances, where two or more institutions demand the first loyalty of a person, they may be directly antithetical.

Assuming a "drive toward consistency of self" on the part of human actors in social situations, the person who finds himself playing two such divergent roles will seek some means of resolving the conflict between them. In the writer's estimation, the types of solutions available can be reduced to three: (1) abandonment of one of the conflicting roles, (2) rationalization, which may assume many different forms, or (3) compartmentalization of role behaviors.[1] If and when these techniques fail, the individual will invent new patterns of behavior which are usually thought of as neurotic, aberrant or psychotic, depending upon the severity of the conflict and the social definition of the given situation.

In the summer of 1952 a small-scale study was undertaken in the San Francisco Bay area in an attempt to determine the applicability of the theory in a concrete situation. A population was chosen in which the conflict in roles

[1] C.f. Jackson Toby, "Some Variables in Role Conflict Analysis," *Social Forces*, 30 (March, 1952) and J. W. Getzels and E. G. Guba, "Role, Role Conflict, and Effectiveness," *American Sociological Review*, 19 (April 1954), pp. 164-75.

is extremely severe, since the ends specified by the two major institutions which define their social roles are in some respects mutually exclusive. These were military chaplains. Chaplains not only share the dilemma of the Christian in war time; they also function as officers in both ecclesiastical and military organizations. As officers, they are responsible, in part, for the achievement of the ends specified. It was assumed that chaplains being highly educated and much concerned with consistency of behavior, would have been acutely aware of the conflicts between military and religious ideology, and would have sought some equitable solution.

METHODOLOGY.   The sample was small, consisting of thirty-six chaplains and thirty-five ex-chaplains (who had seen service in World War II)—seventy-one in all. In order to avoid bias in the selection of the sample, an effort was made to include every chaplain and ex-chaplain in the San Francisco Bay Area.

TABLE 21-1   Religious affiliations of chaplains and ex-chaplains in the sample.

Denomination	Chaplains	Ex-Chaplains
Catholic	7	6
Jewish	2	1
Protestant		
African Methodist Episcopal		1
Assembly of God	2	
Baptist (American)	4	1
Baptist (Southern)	4	
Christian Scientist	1	2
Congregational	2	1
Disciples of Christ (Christian)		1
Episcopalian	1	4
Latter Day Saints (Mormon)	2	1
Lutheran (Missouri Synod)	1	3
Lutheran (United)		2
Methodist	6	5
Mission Covenant	1	
Presbyterian[a]		3
Presbyterian (USA)	3	2
Reformed Church in America		1
Salvation Army		1
Total	36	35

a Not otherwise identified.

Rank is more equitably distributed in the sample of ex-chaplains, with three-fifths of them in the two lower ranks. Moreover, it was not actually possible to interview every chaplain and ex-chaplain in the area. Although only one person refused outright to be interviewed, many of them found reasons to postpone the interview until the time limit for the research had expired.

In spite of the difficulties encountered, the coverage appears to be quite broad. All the gradations of rank from first lieutenant to brigadier general are covered; members of nineteen religious denominations, including thirteen Catholics, three Jews and fifty-five Protestants, were included in the sample (Table 21-1); and by coincidence the sample of chaplains includes twelve members each of the Army, the Air Force and the Navy.

The schedule consisted of fifty-seven questions, twenty-nine of which were "open-end." The remainder called for categorical replies. Questions were designed to bring the respondent face to face with the proposition that the role of military officer conflicts with that of minister of the gospel, and to elicit his self-concept with reference to various situations which chaplains regularly face or might conceivably be called upon to face.

Hypotheses to be tested included the following: (1) that the position of the chaplain does lead to a conflict in roles for the incumbent of that office; (2) that the chaplain seeks to reconcile this conflict either through rationalization or through compartmentalization of role behaviors; (3) that rationalization of conflict in roles tends to strengthen the chaplain's role of military officer at the expense of his role of minister of the gospel; (4) that the chaplain serves as interperter of the values of the military organization, helps resolve value-dilemmas of individual service men, and helps promote smooth operation of the military organization.

ROLE CONCEPTS RELATING TO MILITARY DUTY

CHAPLAINS' CONCEPTIONS OF SELF WITH RELATION TO MILITARY DUTY. An attempt was made to discover the factors which motivated the individual respondent in joining the military service. Most of the replies (75 percent) indicated that motives were mixed, but assuming that the first motive mentioned is the primary one, 25 percent were influenced primarily by patriotic motives, while only 10 percent were influenced primarily by religious motives. Another 25 percent had not analyzed their motives beyond a "desire to be of service." The remainder gave replies that were in general noncommittal.

Over 85 percent of the respondents said that they had enjoyed military service. The aspect most frequently mentioned as being enjoyable was, for ex-chaplains, fellowship with men in the service, mentioned 17 times, and for chaplains, freedom, mentioned 9 times. "Freedom" included freedom from the cares and difficulties of a civilian parish, freedom from financial cares, and from the controls exercised by a congregation with its boards of deacons, Ladies' Aid groups, and the like, and freedom to act, preach and live as one chooses.

This fact suggests an interesting possibility for research in personality. It raises the question whether or not the desire to escape from the relatively circumscribed area, dogmatically speaking, of the local congregation into the relatively free atmosphere, dogmatically speaking, of the armed forces plays a large part in the decision of a clergyman to make a career of military service. The foregoing may be stated in the form of a hypothesis. Exactly half of the chaplains said that they intended to remain permanently in the military service. None of them, however, gave freedom as a reason for making such a decision. Instead, the reasons mentioned were security, the opportunity to render a service, the challenge offered by the military situation, personal satisfaction, the existence of a need, and a missionary call. When ex-chaplains were asked to give their reasons for not remaining in the military service nearly 40 percent of them expressed skepticism as to the necessity or propriety of a military chaplaincy in times of peace.

CHAPLAINS' CONCEPTIONS OF SELF WITH REFERENCE TO OTHER OFFICERS. Over 90 percent of the respondents reported that they had not felt out of place as military officers, and a like percentage believed they had been accepted as equals by their fellow officers. Only a few expressed reservations concerning their acceptance, although there appeared to be a good deal of uncertainty on the part of chaplains as to what was expected of them by their fellow officers. For instance, some felt that having a few drinks "with the boys" helped to establish rapport; others felt that they would lose esteem if they indulged. The drinking party presents a good test of the loyalties of a clergyman belonging to an antiliquor denomination. Three chaplains who were members of anti-liquor denominations reported that they did drink at parties. All three, incidentally, avowed their intention to make a career of the chaplaincy.

CHAPLAINS' CONCEPTIONS OF SELF WITH REFERENCE TO MILITARY AUTHORITIES. With respect to military authorities, personal and impersonal, 72 percent of the respondents reported at the outset that they had the full cooperation of their commanding officers. A closer analysis of the replies reveals, however, that at least 50 percent of the chaplains and 40 percent of the ex-chaplains had had experience with a noncooperative commanding officer. There was considerable hesitancy and some attempts at evasion occurred when questions were asked concerning relations with commanding officers.

The practice of "going over the head" of a commanding officer is reserved for extreme cases, although the possibility (and sometimes the threat) of doing so serves as an effective weapon in the hands of chaplains for securing cooperation. Nineteen percent of the chaplains interviewed reported that they had actually gone over the heads of a commanding officer at some time or other.

Reactions to regulations, channels, and red tape, were mixed. Eighty-six percent of the respondents said that they had been successful in circumventing red tape on some occasions, and 72 percent said that they regarded it as their duty to accomplish things in the most expedient manner, yet 31 percent of the chaplains and 66 percent of the ex-chaplains said that red tape had not interfered with their ministry. Over half of the respondents denied that any conflict exists between military regulations and religious ideology, and three of them denied that military regulations involved any moral values. The technique of compartmentalization is involved in these situations. It appears that the chaplain regards himself as operating in a moral context while he is conducting religious services or performing other tasks which are associated in his mind with the work of a clergyman, and which are not covered by military regulations, but not while dealing with commanding officers, fellow officers, channels of communication, and in other nonreligious situations which are covered by the regulations. In religious situations he is guided by religious values; in other situations by other values.

There was evidence of ambivalence concerning the question of military discipline. Eighty-three percent of the respondents said that at some time or other they had tried to intercede for the defendant in disciplinary cases. Fourteen respondents specifically stated that they had interceded only rarely and in cases of extreme injustice, and the majority indicated that in general they identified themselves with the military hierarchy on the question of discipline. Only two respondents appeared to fit the popular stereotype of the chaplain as the champion of enlisted men.

On the other hand, when the question of enforcing the regulation concerning saluting arose, most of the respondents sided with enlisted men. When asked what they would do if an enlisted man failed to show deference to their rank, only 10 percent replied that they would remind him of his status. The explanation for this is not far to seek. The salute is regarded by chaplains as extraneous—an area of indifference—and the failure of an enlisted man to salute is not perceived as a threat to his status as an officer. The court-martial, on the other hand, has traditionally been a sort of battle ground of enlisted men versus officers.

CHAPLAINS' CONCEPTIONS OF SELF WITH REFERENCE TO ENLISTED PERSONNEL. Relations with enlisted men are of great concern to chaplains, since enlisted men form the largest single audience toward which chaplains direct their behavior. All chaplains are aware that the fact that they are officers poses a barrier to primary relations with enlisted men. The chaplain, being both a military officer and a clergyman, must somehow come to grips with the problem of carrying on an effective religious ministry for enlisted personnel and at the same time of retaining his status as an officer.

In an effort to minimize the difference between chaplains and enlisted men, numerous devices have been officially adopted, chief of which are: (1) the practice of addressing all chaplains by the title "Chaplain" rather than by rank, thus de-emphasizing the military status and emphasizing the clerical status of the chaplain; (2) waiving the rule against fraternization between officers and enlisted personnel in the case of chaplains, thus de-emphasizing the social distance between them; and (3) specifically stating that chaplains do not have command of troops, thus making it possible to argue that the chaplain is not really an officer after all, although the command of troops is not the usual function of any staff officer.

Nearly all of the respondents felt that if the individual chaplain were adequate he could overcome the barrier posed by rank. Only 21 percent felt that they could have done an effective job as chaplains if they had not had military rank, and no respondent believed that an enlisted chaplain could perform effectively. Three major reasons were advanced for such skepticism: (1) that without military rank it would be impossible to demand concessions for enlisted men from the military hierarchy, (2) that it would be impossible to minister to officers unless the chaplain were one of them, and (3) that if the chaplain were not an officer he could not command the respect of either enlisted men or officers.

ROLE CONFLICTS RELATING TO RELIGIOUS BELIEFS AND PRACTICES

CHAPLAINS' CONCEPTIONS OF SELF WITH REFERENCE TO RELIGIOUS LIFE IN THE ARMED FORCES.   Most chaplains curtail certain of their religious activities when they enter the military service. The prescribed duties of a chaplain do not include evangelism, and by a sort of gentlemen's agreement he is expected not to proselytize.

Seventy-nine percent of the respondents believed that a man with good religious training would make a better soldier than one who lacked such training, although only 30 percent thought that an appeal to the religious motives of men was more effective in securing military efficiency than an appeal to patriotic motives. All recognize the function of religion in the maintenance of morale, but they prefer to regard morale as a by-product of their spiritual ministrations rather than its major object.

CHAPLAINS' CONCEPTIONS OF SELF WITH REFERENCE TO THE RELATIONS BETWEEN CHURCH AND STATE.   In spite of the traditional American ideology of the strict separation of church and state, military chaplaincy is a state supported religious institution—not actually an official religion, but a form of state established church. It represents an odd situation, since the government specifically disclaims any interest in controlling religious beliefs, and permits individual chaplains or denominations to prescribe rituals, dogmas, and other religious matters. The only religious qualification demanded of an applicant for the chaplaincy is the recommendation of his denomination (or of an officially recognized ecclesiastical agency which reviews applications for the chaplaincy). When asked for their reactions to the statement that the chaplaincy is a form of state established church, 68 percent of the respondents disagreed, more or less violently. A greater proportion of chaplains than of ex-chaplains disagreed (81 percent as opposed to 54 percent), and with greater vehemence, arguing that the presence of many denominations and the failure of the state to recognize any denomination as official preclude a state establishment of religion.

CHAPLAINS' CONCEPTIONS OF SELF WITH REFERENCE TO THE QUESTION OF RELIGION AND WAR. The question of religion and war offers to chaplains even greater difficulty than the question of rank. Various passages in the Bible appear to forbid the use of violence in the pursuit of ends. However, 45 percent of the respondents believed that the killing of an enemy soldier was a righteous act and the remainder called it a justifiable act. None felt that the individual soldier had any moral responsibility in the matter except to serve his country—a duty which in time of war takes precedence over all others. Only 7 percent ascribed any moral content to the act of killing in war time, and these would distribute the guilt over the entire nation. The assumption of a "just" war (or even of a "holy" war) was the argument most frequently used in defense of wartime killing, followed closely by the plea of self-defense.

When asked to reconcile the "turn the other cheek" philosophy with war, one-fifth of the respondents felt that the conflict was so great that it could not be reconciled; with a few exceptions the remainder felt that there was no conflict since: (1) the individual and nation are different, (2) the necessity for self-defense obviates any antiviolence teachings of Jesus, (3) "turn the other cheek" needs interpretation, and (4) this philosophy does not apply in this day and age. There were three respondents who said that they had never faced the question and who refused to face it during the interview.

The practice of giving theoretical adherence to a doctrine while violating it in practice is as old as religion itself, and it poses a major problem for moralists in every age. It accounts, in part, for the Christian's continuing sense of guilt or unworthiness. For the Christian to deny the relevance of the admonition to turn the other cheek is to question the value of the ethical teachings of Jesus; to admit it makes the Christian in military service a violator of his own moral precepts. The position actually taken on this question by most of the respondents was that of moral relativism.

None of the respondents would of his own volition raise questions concerning the morality of killing, or of war in general, or of turning the other cheek, or any question concerning the relationship between religion and war. If such questions came up in the course of a discussion, the majority would attempt to reason them out on a common sense basis rather than on a religious basis. It appears that the greater the dilemma, the greater the tendency to withdraw from it—to compartmentalize role behaviors and to refuse to recognize conflicting elements.

CONCLUSIONS

These data tend to support the hypotheses advanced, in some respects strongly, in other respects less strongly. The first hypothesis, that the position of the chaplain does lead to a conflict in roles for the incumbent of that position is supported in two ways: (1) by a philosophical analysis of the two social roles of clergyman and military officer and (2) by the responses to questions in the interview schedule, particularly those questions dealing with rank and those dealing with the relationship between religion and war.

The second hypothesis, that the chaplain seeks to reconcile his role conflict either through rationalization or through compartmentalization of role behaviors, appears to be well substantiated. The sample chosen did not include any member who had sought to escape the conflict by abandoning one of the roles (although one ex-chaplain had abandoned the ministry after he had returned to civilian life). Therefore, only two escapes were open. Compartmentalization appeared to be the more successful of the two techniques, and more frequently used. Rationalization requires facing the dilemma and arguing away the conflicting elements. Compartmentalization involved refusing to recognize the conflict.

Concerning the third hypothesis, that rationalization of conflict in roles tends to strengthen the chaplain's role of military officer at the expense of his role of minister of the gospel, it needs only to be pointed out that every argument cited tends to assert the military claim and deemphasize the religious claim.

The fourth hypothesis, that the chaplain serves as interpreter of the values of the military organization, helps resolve value-dilemmas of individual service men, and helps promote smooth operation of the military organization, is less strongly supported than the others, partly, perhaps, because of a lack of data bearing on the subject. However, such data as are available indicate that the hypothesis is tenable. If a service man were in doubt about the morality of military activity, a majority of the respondents would endeavor to assure him that his relationship with God would not suffer thereby.

It would be overhasty to generalize on the basis of the data in this study. However, two hypotheses may be suggested: (1) that the role which provides for the individual his primary identification takes first place in his hierarchy of role obligations and (2) that for the chaplain the role of military officer provides his primary identification. Further study along this line would no doubt reveal much concerning techniques of resolving role conflicts.

The role of the military chaplain offers an interesting subject for the student of role conflict. The chaplaincy is still in its formative stage, and we are witnessing here the emergence of a new social role in which the ideological clash between church and state is assuming what is, for the United States, a new form. The role of the military chaplain also offers an interesting subject for the student of personality. The instrument used in this study was not designed to reveal the individual personality characteristics of the subjects. Nevertheless, the replies to some of the items in the interview schedule suggest the existence of basic personality differences between those clergymen who choose the military chaplaincy as a career and those who do not. The hypothesis that a career in the military chaplaincy appeals more strongly to those possessing the characteristics of the "authoritarian" personality than to other types would be in order here. The student of institutional history and of the processes of social change should also find much in the study of the role of the military chaplain. The history of military chaplaincy, as an institution, covers several centuries, but its origin can be dated, and the various steps in its development can be located in time and space.

22   RACIAL AND MORAL CRISIS:
THE ROLE OF LITTLE ROCK MINISTERS

Ernest Q. Campbell and Thomas F. Pettigrew

INTRODUCTION   The role of the minister in the processes of desegregation and integration has come under increased
scrutiny since 1954. One of the early investigations of the inherent conflicts within the ministerial role is described in this study
by Ernest Campbell and Thomas Pettigrew. Using a sample of
twenty-nine clergymen in Little Rock, Arkansas, the authors identify five segregationist, sixteen inactive integrationist, and eight
active integrationist ministers. An estimated seventy-five percent
of all members in each of their congregations supported the segregationist viewpoint.

Is the religious institution to be a peaceful club or an institution with a mission? Is the role of the minister to be prophetic or
priestly? The lack of ministerial leadership in times of social conflict stems in large part from the control—sometimes heavy-handed
—the congregation exerts over the definition of acceptable ministerial roles. At Little Rock the clergy tended to rationalize their
lack of participation in the desegregation process by defining their
role in a priestly sense (see Burchard, Article 21). Rather than
criticize current injustice, uphold judicial decisions, or take bold
leadership toward the amelioration of the problem, the ministry
generally attempted to maintain a common middle ground in order
to serve as a bridge between those who sought change and those
who maintained the *status quo*. Ministerial attitudes tended to emphasize conciliation rather than leadership. Even today, the major-

Reprinted from the *American Journal of Sociology,* Volume 64 (March, 1959), pp.
509-516, by permission of the University of Chicago Press.

ERNEST Q. CAMPBELL is Professor and Chairman of the Department of Sociology at
Vanderbilt University. THOMAS F. PETTIGREW is Associate Professor of Social Psychology at Harvard University.

ity of Caucasian Protestant, Catholic, or Jewish clergy refrain from active involvement in social issues (see Pope, Article 2, for discussion of Negro ministerial involvement). Because an effective ministry is popularly judged in terms of congregational size, income, morale, and acceptance of the minister, the clergy has generally remained indifferent to social action. Through inaction clergymen have reinforced each other in the acceptance of the *status quo*. Under congregational forms of church polity (church organization) the minister is singly responsible for his actions (see Introduction to Part III). Little support or control is exerted by the regional or national church body. On the other hand, under the episcopal system, as exemplified in the Roman Catholic church, control of the clergy is maintained by directives from immediate superiors. If regional or national leadership supports participation in social action movements, the priest is protected by the strength and authority of the institution. More often than not, however, the Catholic hierarchy has condemned rather than supported those who participate. Jewish concern for social amelioration is high because the Jewish group in itself is a religious minority in America and has maintained a continuing emphasis upon social justice.

THIS PAPER ANALYZES the conduct of the ministers in established denominations in Little Rock, Arkansas, during the crisis over the admission of Negro students to the Central High School in the fall of 1957. How do ministers behave in racial crisis, caught between integrationist and segregationist forces?[1]

One might expect that Little Rock's clergymen would favor school integration. All the major national Protestant bodies have adopted forceful declarations commending the Supreme Court's desegregation decision of 1954 and urging their members to comply with it. And southern pastors have voted in favor of these statements at their church conferences—and sometimes have even issued similar pronouncements to their own congregations.[2] But the southern man of God faces serious congregational opposition if he attempts to express his integrationist beliefs publicly in the local community. The vast

[1] This study was supported by a grant from the Laboratory of Social Relations, Harvard University. The authors wish to express their gratitude to Professor Samuel A. Stouffer for his suggestions. Two brief popular accounts of aspects of this study have appeared previously: "Men of God in Racial Crisis," Christian Century, LXXV (June 4, 1958), pp. 113-65, and "Vignettes from Little Rock," Christianity and Crisis, XVIII (September 29, 1958), pp. 118-36.
[2] For example, local ministerial groups issued such statements in New Orleans, Louisiana; Richmond, Virginia; Dallas and Houston, Texas; and Atlanta, Macon, and Columbus, Georgia. For a review of national church statements see "Protestantism Speaks on Justice and Integration," Christian Century, LXXV (February 5, 1958), pp. 164-66.

majority of southern whites—even those living in the Middle South—are definitely against racial desegregation.[3]

The purpose of this study is to determine how the ministers of established denominations in Little Rock behaved in the conflict. In analyzing their behavior, we treat self-expectations as an independent variable. This is contrary to the usual course, in which the actor is important analytically only because he is caught between contradictory *external* expectations. The standard model of role conflict treats ego as forced to decide between the incompatible norms of groups that can impose sanctions for nonconformity. This model—which is essentially what Lazarsfeld means by cross-pressures—skirts the issue of whether ego imposes expectations on itself and punishes deviations. Pressure and sanction are external to the actor. Hence the typical model tends to be ahistorical in the sense that a finite number of cross-pressuring groups are used to predict the actor's behavior. It is assumed that the actor cannot have developed from periods of prior socialization any normative expectations for his behavior which would have an independent existence.[4] This additional variable—the actor's expectations of himself—is especially meaningful in the analysis.

Though it is a city of approximately 125,000, Little Rock has much of the atmosphere and easy communication of a small town. It is located in almost the geometric center of the state, and physically and culturally it borders on both the Deep South—like delta country to the east and south and the Mountain South—like hill country to the west and north. Thus Little Rock is not a city of the Deep South. Its public transportation had been successfully integrated in 1956, and its voters, as late as March, 1957, had elected two men to the school board who supported the board's plan for token integration of Central High School. And yet Little Rock is a southern city, with southern traditions of race relations. These patterns became of worldwide interest after Governor Faubus called out the National Guard to prevent desegregation and thereby set off the most publicized and the most critical chain of events in the integration process to date.

[3] A 1956 National Opinion Research Center poll indicated that only one in every seven white southerners approves school integration (H. H. Hyman and P. B. Sheatsley, "Attitudes toward Desegregation," *Scientific American*, CXCV December, 1956, 35-39). A 1956 survey by the American Institute of Public Opinion showed that in the Middle South—including Arkansas—only one in five whites approved of school integration (M. M. Tumin, *Segregation and Desegregation*, New York Anti-Defamation League of B'nai B'rith, 1957, p. 109).

[4] By showing that the actor may have a predisposition toward either a particularistic or a universalistic "solution" to role conflicts in instances where the particularistic universalistic dimension is relevant, Stouffer and Toby link the study of personality to that of role obligations in a way rarely done (Samuel A. Stouffer and Jackson Toby, "Role Conflict and Personality," *American Journal of Sociology*, LVI March, 1951, 395-406). This study, however, treats the personal predisposition as a determinant of conflict resolution rather than a factor in conflict development. Much the same is true of Gross's analysis (Neal Gross, Ward S. Mason, and Alexander McEachern, *Explorations in Role Analysis: Studies of the School Superintendency Role* (New York: Wiley, 1958), esp. chaps. xv, xvi, and xvii).

Only two ministers devoted their sermons to the impending change on the Sunday before the fateful opening of school in September, 1957. Both warmly approved of the step and hoped for its success. Other ministers alluded to it in prayer or comment. It was commonly believed that a majority of the leading denominations' clergy favored the school board's "gradual" plan. This impression seemed confirmed when immediately after Governor Faubus had surrounded Central High with troops fifteen of the city's most prominent ministers issued a protest in, according to the local *Arkansas Gazette,* "the strongest language permissible to men of God."

When Negro students appeared at the high school for the first time, they were escorted by four white Protestant ministers and a number of prominent Negro leaders. Two of the four whites are local clergymen, one being the president of the biracial ministerial association, the other, president of the local Human Relations Council. Many of the more influential ministers of the city had been asked the night before to join this escort. Some demurred; others said they would try to come. Only two appeared.

On September 23, the day of the rioting near Central High School, several leaders of the ministerial association personally urged immediate counter-action on the mayor and the chief of police. Later, support was solicited from selected ministers in the state to issue a declaration of Christian principle, but dissension over the statement prevented its publication. Indeed, *no* systematic attempts were made by the clergy to appeal to the conscience of the community. Such statements as individual ministers did express were usually—though not always—appeals for "law and order" rather than a Christian defense of the principle of desegregation.

Several weeks after the rioting, plans for a community-wide prayer service began to develop. Care was taken to present this service in as neutral terms as possible. Compromise and reconciliation were stressed: never was it described as organized prayers for integration. And endorsements came from both sides of the controversy—from President Eisenhower and from Governor Faubus. As one of the sponsors put it: "Good Christians can honestly disagree on the question of segregation or integration. But we can all join together in prayers for guidance, that peace may return to our city." The services in the cooperating churches were held on Columbus Day, October 12. All the leading churches participated, with only the working-class sects conspicuously missing. The services varied widely from informal prayers to elaborate programs, and attendances varied widely, too, and totaled perhaps six thousand.

These "prayers for peace" may best be viewed as a ritualistic termination of any attempts by the clergy to direct the course of events in the racial crisis. The prayers had met the national demand for ministerial action and the ministers' own need to act; and they had completed the whole unpleasant business. Despite sporadic efforts by a small number to undertake more effective steps, the ministers lapsed into a general silence that continued throughout the school year.

We began our work in Little Rock in the week after the peace prayers. Following a series of background interviews and a careful analysis of ministerial action as recorded in the press, twenty-nine detailed interviews with ministers were held.[5] Twenty-seven of them are Protestants and two are Jewish; the Roman Catholics did not cooperate.

This sample was not selected randomly; the so-called "snowball technique" was used in order to include the most influential church leaders. This involves asking each interviewee to name the members of the Little Rock clergy that he considers to be "the most influential." The first interview was made with an announced leader of the peace prayers, and interviewing was continued with all the men mentioned as influential until no new names were suggested. We added a number of ministers who were not named but who had taken strongly liberal positions during the crisis. Thus our sample is most heavily weighted with the pastors of the larger churches with the greatest prestige and the pastors of smaller churches who had assumed active roles in the conflict. These two groups, we anticipated, would have to contend with the greatest amount of incompatibility in role.

Most of the interviews were held in the church offices. Rapport, which was generally excellent, was partly secured by the authors' identification with southern educational institutions. A detailed summary, as nearly as possible a verbatim account, was placed on Audograph recording equipment shortly after the completion of each interview. Information in three broad areas was sought, and to this end a series of open-ended questions was developed. A series of questions was aimed at determining whether the respondent was a segregationist or an integrationist. A segregationist here is defined as one who prefers racial barriers as presently constituted; an integrationist is one to whom the removal of legal and artificial barriers to racial contact is morally preferable to the present system.[6]

Each interviewee was asked to give a complete account of what he had done and said in both his parish and in the community at large regarding the racial crisis. If he had not been active or vocal, we probed him for the reason and to learn if he had felt guilty over his failure to state the moral imperatives.

A final set of questions dealt with the pastor's perception of his congregation's reaction to whatever stand he had taken. If pressure had been applied on him by his parishioners, we probed him to learn exactly what pressure had been used and how.

THE SEGREGATIONIST.   Only five of the twenty-nine clergymen we interviewed were segregationists by our definition. None was avidly so, and, unlike

[5] Thirteen additional interviews were held with the sect leaders of an openly pro-segregation prayer service. None of these were members of the ministerial association or were in personal contact with any ministers of the established denominations. A detailed report on them will be published.
[6] Using the interview, three judges, the two authors and a graduate assistant, independently rated each respondent as either a segregationist or an integrationist. Agreement between the three raters was complete for twenty-seven of the twenty-nine cases.

segregationist ministers of the sects, none depended on "chapter-and-verse Scripture" to defend his stand. All men in their late fifties or sixties, they did not think that the crisis was a religious matter. One of them was a supervising administrator in a denominational hierarchy. Although all five were affiliated with prominent denominations, they were not among the leaders of the local ministerial body.

These five men have not been publicly active in defending segregation.[7] Each was opposed to violence, and none showed evidence of internal discomfort or conflict. All five co-operated with the neutrally toned prayers for peace. As one of them commented, "You certainly can't go wrong by praying. Praying can't hurt you on anything."

THE INACTIVE INTEGRATIONIST.   Inactive integrationists had done enough —or believed they had done enough—to acquaint their congregations with their sympathy with racial tolerance and integration, but during the crucial weeks of the crisis they were generally silent. These, representing as they do all major denominations, varied considerably as to age and size of church served. Included among them were virtually all the ministers of high prestige, many of whom had signed the protest against Governor Faubus at the start of the crisis and later were advocates of the peace prayer services. Some had spoken out in favor of "law and order" and in criticism of violence. They had not, however, defended the continued attendance of the Negro students in the high school, and they had not challenged their members to defend educational desegregation as a Christian obligation. They were publicly viewed as integrationists only because they had supported "law and order" and had not defended segregation.

Altogether, the inactive integrationists comprise sixteen out of the twenty-nine of our sample. Because it was not a random sample, we cannot draw inferences regarding the division of the total ministerial community or of ministers of established denominations into integrationist and segregationist camps. However, since the sample underrepresents the uninfluential minister who had not been in the public eye during the crisis, we may conclude that a large majority of Little Rock's men of God did not encourage their members to define the issue as religious nor did they initiate actions or participate in programs aimed at integration.

THE ACTIVE INTEGRATIONIST.   Eight of our respondents can be designated as active integrationists because they continued to defend integration in principle and to insist that support of racial integration is nothing less than a Christian imperative. They were, on the whole, young men who have headed their small churches for only a few years. Most were disturbed that the churches of the city were segregated; some have urged their churches to admit Negroes.

[7] Again, this is in contrast to the sect segregationists. One sect minister is president and another is the chaplain of the local Citizens' Council.

Most of the active integrationists had serious difficulty with their members because of their activities, evidence of which was lowered Sunday-morning attendance, requests for transfer, diminished giving, personal snubs and insults, and rumors of sentiment for their dismissal. One had concluded that his usefulness to his congregation had ended and accordingly had requested to be transferred. By the end of 1958, several others had been removed from their pulpits.

One thing all twenty-nine of the sample had in common was a segregationist congregation.[8] Without exception, they believed that the majority of their members were strong opponents of racial integration. The highest estimate given by any integrationist of the proportion of his congregation which supported his views was 40 percent; the median estimate for segregation was 75 percent. Only three interviewees thought that a majority of their members would "accept" a strong public defense of integration by their minister.

Personal integrity, alone, would lead the liberal Little Rock minister to defend integration and condemn those who support segregation. However, the minister is obligated to consider the expectations of his church membership, especially inasmuch as the members' reactions bear upon his own effectiveness.

When an individual is responsible to a public, we distinguish three systems as relevant to his behavior: the self-reference system (SRS), the professional reference system (PRS), and the membership reference system (MRS). The SRS consists of the actor's demands, expectations, and images regarding himself. It may be thought of as what the actor would do in the absence of sanctions from external sources. We have already seen that typically the SRS would support racial integration.[9] The PRS consists of several sources mutually related to his occupational role yet independent of his congregation: national and regional church bodies, the local ecclesiastical hierarchy, if any, the local ministerial association, personal contacts and friendships with fellow ministers, and, probably, an image of "my church." Finally, the MRS consists simply of the minister's congregation. We have already seen that it favored segregation or at least ministerial neutrality.

The net effect of three reference systems seems to favor the cause of integration. Were they equal in strength, and were there no contrary forces internal to any of them, this conclusion is obvious. The minister would then feel committed to support the official national policy of his denomination; his knowledge that fellow ministers were similarly committed would support him, and the local hierarchy would encourage him to make this decision and reas-

[8] Our study of a modest sample of church members bore out the ministers' estimates of predominantly prosegregation sentiment in their congregations.
[9] Although groups make demands, impose sanctions, and significantly affect the actors' self-expectations and self-sanctions, nevertheless, we treat the self-reference system as an independent variable in role conflict. This system seems especially significant where personal action is contrary to the pressure of known and significant groups.

sure him should his congregation threaten disaffection. These external influences would reinforce his own values, resulting in forthright action in stating
and urging the Christian imperatives. However, internal inconsistencies in the
PRS and the SRS restrain what on first examination appears to be an influence toward the defense of integration.

THE PROFESSIONAL REFERENCE SYSTEM.   Two overriding characteristics
of the PRS minimize its liberalizing influence. First, most of its components
cannot or do not impose sanctions for nonconformity to their expectations.
Second, those parts of the PRS that can impose sanctions also impose other
demands on the minister, inconsistent with the defense of racial integration
before members who, in large part, believe in racial separation and whose beliefs are profoundly emotional.

THE INABILITY TO IMPOSE SANCTIONS.   The national and regional associations that serve as the official "voice of the church" are not organized to
confer effective rewards or punishments on individual ministers. Especially is
this true in the case of failure to espouse national racial policy or to act decisively in the presence of racial tension. This is even more true of the local
ministerial association; it does not presume to censure or praise its members.
Conversely, the local church hierarchy is an immediate source of sanctions. It
has the responsibility of recommending or assigning parishes, and of assisting
the pastor in expanding the program of his church.

The probability and the nature of sanctions from fellow ministers among
whom one has personal contacts and friends are somewhat more difficult to
specify. However, it does not appear likely that he is subject to sanctions if he
does not conform to their expectations by liberal behavior on racial matters.
Should he indorse and actively support segregationist and violent elements,
this would be another matter. If he is silent or guarded, however, it is not
likely to subject him to sanction. The active integrationists in Little Rock expressed disappointment at the inaction of their associates while at the same
time suggesting possible mitigating circumstances. There is no evidence that
personal or professional ties had been damaged.

Among the various components of the PRS, then, only the local eccle-
siastica, which does not exist for some, and, to a considerably lesser extent,
fellow ministers, are conceivable sources influencing the minister's decision to
be silent, restrained, or forthright.

CONFLICTING EXPECTATIONS AND MITIGATED PRESSURES.   The role of the
minister as community reformer is not as institutionalized (i.e., it does not
have as significant a built-in system of rewards and punishments) as are certain other roles associated with the ministry. The minister is responsible for
the overall conduct of the affairs of the church and is judged successful or unsuccessful according to how they prosper. He must encourage cooperative
endeavor, reconciling differences, and bring people together. Vigor and high

morale of the membership are reflected in increased financial support and a
growing membership, and his fellow ministers and his church superiors are
keenly sensitive to these evidences of his effectiveness. His goal, elusive
though it may be, is maximum support from all members of an ever growing
congregation.

The church hierarchy keeps records. It hears reports and rumors. It does
not like to see divided congregations, alienated ministers, reduced membership, or decreased contributions. Responsible as it is for the destiny of the
denomination in a given territory, it compares its changing fortunes with those
of rival churches. In assigning ministers to parishes, it rewards some with
prominent pulpits and punishes others with posts of low prestige or little
promise. However exalted the moral virtue the minister expounds, the hierarchy does not wish him to damn his listeners to hell—unless somehow he gets
them back in time to attend service next Sunday. Promotions for him are determined far less by the number of times he defends unpopular causes, however virtuous their merit, than by the state of the physical plant and the state
of the coffer.

Now it is especially commendable if the minister can defend the cause
and state the imperative with such tact or imprint that cleavages are not
opened or loyalties alienated. If, however, the moral imperative and church
cohesion are mutually incompatible, there is little doubt that the church superiors favor the latter. One administrator told two of his ministers, "It's o.k.
to be liberal, boys; just don't stick your neck out." Indeed, ecclesiastical officials advised younger ministers, systematically, to "go slow," reminding them
of the possibility of permanent damage to the church through rash action.

Under these circumstances pressure from the national church to take an
advanced position on racial matters loses much of its force. The minister is
rewarded *only* if his efforts do not endanger the membership of the church:
"Don't lose your congregation." Similarly, the prospect of an unfavorable response from his congregation protects him from the (possibly liberal) church
hierarchy; he need only point to what happened to Pastor X, who did not heed
the rumblings in his congregation. The higher officials, themselves keenly
aware of local values and customs, will understand. And his fellow ministers,
too, are, after all, in the same boat. They give him sympathy, not censure, if
he says, "My hands are tied." An informal rationale develops that reassures
the pastor: "These things take time," "You can't change people overnight,"
"You can't talk to people when they won't listen." There is strong sympathy
for the forthright pastor who is in real trouble, but he is looked on as an object
lesson. Thus the ministers reinforce each other in inaction, despite their common antipathy to segregation.

THE SELF-REFERENCE SYSTEM. We still must reckon with the demands
the minister imposes upon himself. It is obvious that the actor has the power
of self-sanction, through guilt. A threatening sense of unworthiness, of inade-

quacy in God's sight, cannot be taken lightly. Similarly, to grant one's self the biblical commendation "Well done" is a significant reward. We have said that the self is an influence favoring action in support of desegregation. Can the inactive integrationist, then, either avoid or control the sense of guilt?

Our data are not entirely appropriate to the question. Nevertheless, four circumstances—all of which permit of generalization to other cases—appear at least partially to prevent the sense of guilt. These include major characteristics of the ministerial role, several ministerial values and "working propositions," certain techniques for communicating without explicit commitment, and the gratifying reactions of extreme opposition forces.

THE ROLE STRUCTURE. The church, as an institutional structure, sets criteria by which the minister may assess his management of the religious enterprise; it does *not* offer criteria by which to evaluate his stand on controversial issues.[10] This encourages, even compels, the minister to base his self-image, hence his sense of worth or unworth, on his success in managing his church. Thus, if church members do not share his goals, three types of institutionalized responsibilities restrain him in reform.

In the first place, the minister is required to be a cohesive force, to "maintain a fellowship in peace, harmony, and Christian love," rather than to promote dissension. Thus some ministers prayed during the Columbus Day services that members "carry no opinion to the point of disrupting the Christian fellowship."

Second, he is expected to show a progressive increase in the membership of his church. Pro-integration activity, lacking mass support, is likely to drive members to other churches.

Finally, his task is to encourage maximum annual giving and to plan the improvement and expansion of the plant. It is hardly surprising that several inactive integrationists who were engaged in vital fund-raising campaigns shrank from action that might endanger their success.

WORKING PROPOSITIONS. The minister makes certain assumptions about his work that reduce the likelihood of guilt when he does not defend moral convictions that his members reject. He is, first, a devotee of education, by which he means the gradual growth and development of spiritual assets—in contrast to his counterpart of an earlier period, who was more likely to believe in sudden change through conversion. He also believes that communication with the sinner must be preserved at all costs ("You can't teach those you can't reach") and for long enough to effect gradual change in attitude and behavior. A crisis, when feelings run high, is not the time to risk alienating those one wishes to change. For example, Pastor X acted decisively but, in so doing, damaged or lost his pastorate: "Look at him; he can't do any good now."

[10] Blizzard does not find a "community reformer" or "social critic" role in the ministry (see Samuel W. Blizzard, "The Minister's Dilemma," *Christian Century,* LXXIII April 25, 1956, 508-10).

COMMUNICATION TECHNIQUES. The minister may avoid committing himself unequivocally.[11] Some use the "every man a priest" technique, for example, the stating of his own opinion while expressing tolerance for contradictory ones and reminding his listeners that their access to God's truth is equal with his. Others use the "deeper issues" approach; generalities such as the brotherhood of man, brotherly love, humility, and universal justice are discussed without specific reference to the race issue, in the hope that the listener may make the association himself. Still another course is to remind listeners that "God is watching," that the question of race has religious significance and therefore they should "act like Christians." There is also the method of deriding the avowed segregationists without supporting their opposites. The "exaggerated southerner" technique, which may be supplementary to any of the others, involves a heavy southern drawl and, where possible, reference to an aristocratic line of planter descent.

These techniques do not demand belief in integration as a Christian imperative. Further, except for the "every man a priest" technique, they do not commit the speaker to integrationist goals as religious values; the listener may make applications as he chooses. The speaker, on the other hand, can assure himself that the connections are there to be made; he supplies, as it were, a do-it-yourself moral kit.

REACTION OF THE OPPOSITION. The ministerial body in Little Rock, except for pastors to dissident fundamentalist sects, is defined by agitated segregationists as a bunch of "race-mixers" and "nigger-lovers." For example, the charge was made that the peace prayers were intended to "further integration under a hypocritical veneer of prayer" and that the sect pastors sponsored prayers for segregation "to show that not all of the city's ministers believe in mixing the races." Indeed, ministers of major denominations were charged with having "race on the mind" so that they were straying from, even rejecting, the bibilical standard to further their un-Christian goals.

The effect of opposition by segregation extremists was to convince certain inactive integrationists that indeed they *had* been courageous and forthright. The minister, having actually appropriated the opposition's evaluation of his behavior, reversing its affective tone found the reassurance he needed that his personal convictions had been adequately and forcefully expressed.

Were the force of the membership reference system not what it is, the professional reference system and the self-reference system would supply support to integration that was not limited to "law and order" appeals and the denunciation of violence. However, since "Don't lose your congregation" is itself a strong professional and personal demand, the force of the PRS is neutralized, and the pressure from the SRS becomes confused and conflicting. In-

[11] For a full description and illustration of such techniques as used in Little Rock see our *Christians in Racial Crisis: A Study of Little Rock's Ministers* (Washington, D.C.: Public Affairs Press, 1959).

action is a typical response to conflicting pressures within both the internal and the external system.

It is not surprising, then, that most Little Rock ministers have been far less active and vocal in the racial crisis than the policies of their national church bodies and their sense of identification with them, as well as their own value systems, would lead one to expect. Rather, what is surprising is that a small number continued to express vigorously the moral imperative as they saw it, in the face of congregational disaffection, threatened reprisal, and the lukewarm support or quiet discouragement of their superiors and peers.

23 THE ROLES OF THE RURAL PARISH MINISTER, THE PROTESTANT SEMINARIES, AND THE SCIENCES OF SOCIAL BEHAVIOR

Samuel W. Blizzard

INTRODUCTION   Social change has greatly affected the nature of the rural ministry. Because Roman Catholics and Jews are concentrated in urban areas, the problem remains largely Protestant. Although structural community change has not been as great in the rural as in the urban community, disturbance of old ways is real and implications vast for rural-centered churches.

The unconsolidated rural parish is generally a small, rather poor parish. Because it does not have the wealth necessary to hire an able, vigorous and experienced minister, it tends to rely on new seminary graduates with minimal experience and low salary requirements or men retired or near retirement, who desire a less strenuous workload. If neither are available, the congregation may turn to an unordained, self-made "minister" or a part-time ordained clergyman. The small size of the rural parish militates against the raising of rural ministerial standards. Where urban congregations average more than three hundred persons, the number in open country and rural areas ranges from one hundred to one hundred and fifty persons per congregation. With continued out-migration, many are unable to sustain even this size.

The future of the rural church rests with congregational consolidation. Rural people, however, are loath to give up the family church or the cemetery which often sits beside the church building. Yet, the family rural church is a thing of the past. Those churches which cannot adapt to the changing situation will soon

Abridged and reprinted from the December 1955 issue of *Religious Education* by permission of the publisher, The Religious Education Association, 545 West 111th Street, New York, New York 10025.

SAMUEL BLIZZARD is Professor of Christianity and Society at Princeton Theological Seminary.

be on the road to decline or extinction. In the years between 1930 and 1945 some 20,000 churches closed their doors as the rural population moved to urban areas. If the predicted 90% of the American population comes to live in urban areas in the next century, even more rural congregations will close or relocate to nearby towns. The shift to the town, however, alters the effectiveness of the rural group to exercise intimate control over its membership. The relocated rural church soon begins to take on secondary rather than primary relations. Even the theological conceptions and sermonic illustrations begin to change from items characteristic of the open country to objects produced in the industrial and commercial setting of the town and city (see Shippey, Article 14).

Although the demands upon the rural ministry have changed, rural ministerial training has not changed significantly. Only limited work is being done to prepare students for the ministry to understand their communities or their roles. Most seminaries depend upon previous undergraduate training for such knowledge and skills. Rural ministers need to understand that many of the role tensions they face are not of their creation but are rooted in general social change. The former task of the minister to preach the gospel and administer the sacraments has continued but new community leadership duties have arisen. Samuel Blizzard of Princeton Theological Seminary suggests that a new type of man is needed in the rural church. The change taking place within society demands a clergy competent to relate successfully to the parishioners and the complex community. The minister of the rural church needs to possess greater resilience, capacity, and skill in dealing with current problems than have the clergy of the past age.

RECENT DEVELOPMENTS in American culture highlight the increasing complexity of community life in the United States. The whole fabric and social structure of our society is being rewoven, and new patterns of life are being established. Clergymen being trained in Protestant seminaries in the current decade walk out to face a different world than did those of a previous generation. Therefore, the parish minister must reexamine the way he functions, the roles he plays, and the methods he uses to make the theology of the church meaningful in terms of the problems and aspirations of the people he serves.

Many rural clergymen have adjusted their ways of ministering so that the gospel is meaningful in mid-century American rural life. Other ministers go right on doing what rural clergymen have always done, what they used to do before agriculture became a commercial endeavor rather than a subsistence enterprise. Some rural ministers conceive their work in the same way now that their predecessors in the profession did before hybrid vigor in crops and animals and mechanization became an accepted part of farming.

I.   American rural culture, as it changes, is depending more and more on professional leadership for community service and agencies. Since the turn of the century a new group of professionals has become important in the rural community. Half a century ago farmers got advice about crops and livestock from their neighbors. As disease problems threatened the farm enterprise and as management and marketing became more important in the agricultural economy, the county agent has increasingly become an important source of information and an advisor on farm problems and production methods. The home demonstration worker helps with food, nutrition and clothing problems now, whereas advice was formerly available mostly from relatives and neighbors or the local seamstress. The extension specialist from the agricultural college supplements the work of the local county professionals. Field men now play an important role in the way that cooperatives serve rural people. Paid employees who are highly trained in agriculture represent the interests of farmers through lobbying for legislation and witnessing at market hearings. Conservationists, foresters, and other new professional leaders in American rural life could be cited.

II.   The increasing complexity of American rural culture has also resulted in a change in the expectancies that rural people have of the minister. In the past in the culture of the agrarian areas of America, the roles of the clergyman have been generalized rather than specific, relatively unstructured, and informal.

The typical Protestant clergyman in the rural areas is serving more than one congregation. The demands of the rural religious public and the needs of parishioners in several churches are varied. Where there are several churches in a rural parish the definition of the minister may differ from community to community. One church may be dominated by the tradesmen and others by farmers or miners. Each will have an image of the minister that is different enough to require the minister to be sensitive to this variation. Even with these differences each church in a multiple charge will likely expect the minister to be a generalist, rather than to play many specialized roles. This will magnify the ambiguity of the minister's situation because his self-image may differ from the expected roles he finds in the church, or he may be ready to respond to one church more than another.

In urban areas, however, the roles a minister is expected to play are specialized, are more formalized, and are more highly structured by supporting institutional means and norms. In the rural areas specificity of role is likely to occur only where there is some type of collegiate ministry, or where a parochial school is related to the congregation. The minister, regardless of how specialized the expectations of the congregation, must still understand that people expect him to be their religious leader. His basic function as a minister of the gospel remains even though the roles he plays may be highly specialized.

More and more the role definitions of ministers in the metropolitan, industrial culture has permeated the rural areas. As the rural areas are influenced by urbanization forces, there is a tendency for other roles to be formalized. This is particularly apparent in the larger parish plan. The acceptance of a diversified ministry depends to a large degree on the willingness of parishioners to accept the specialized roles played by several ministers.

III.   The role expectancies that parishioners have of the rural minister show only one side of the picture. The other side is the self-image that the minister has. He also holds a definition of the roles he expects to play. The research being reported was designed for a clearer understanding of the minister's self-picture.

The instrument used to secure the self-image information consisted of thirteen legal-sized pages of questions. Most of the questions were of the open-end permissive type. The emphasis was on qualitative documentary data. About one-tenth of the questions sought to identify sociological data about the minister, including denomination, size of church, and staff, age, year ordained and marital status. The questionnaire was developed in a series of non-directive interviews with practicing parish ministers. Several forms of the instrument were pretested with the help of men in the pastoral ministry.

The rural panel was selected as representative of ministers in the American countryside by the Secretaries of the Rural Church in Boards of Missions in twenty Protestant denominations cooperating with the National Council of Churches. There were 516 ministers nominated for cooperation in this panel. Two-thirds (or 344) furnished information on how they saw themselves, how they functioned as Protestant parish clergymen, and how they evaluated their theological education.

The rural panel was invited to participate in the project through a letter from the denominational secretary who selected each nominee. The questionnaire was mailed to the potential informant from the research project office. Accompanying the instrument was a letter explaining the project, a set of instructions, and a stamped self-addressed return envelope.

IV.   The social characteristics of the rural panel informants show that as regards age they range from 20 to 74 years. The modal group was between 35 and 39 years of age. They are family men with 80 percent having two or more children.

These men represent the whole gamut of experience in the rural parish ministry. They are ministering to churches in every geographic region in the United States. Slightly more than half serve two or more rural churches. Almost all of these men are the only clergymen in the parish. Half of them have no lay professional workers (religious educators, musicians, etc.) helping them who are remuneratively employed. Less than ten percent have one or more full-time lay professional staff members. Eight out of nine do their own stenographic work. Most of the churches have only part-time maintenance and janitorial workers. In other words, nine out of ten of these ministers are the only paid workers in these churches. The average number of church members to which each ministers, is slightly less than 200. Two-thirds of the parishes have less than 200 in the Sunday School. The most typical local parish budget is between $5,000 and $7,500. The typical benevolence (or non-local) budget is less than $2,000.

The ministers represent a variety of educational backgrounds. A few (15 percent) have no college degree and fewer still have a Ph.D. In all, 85 percent have undergraduate degrees, principally the B.A. About 20 percent have college vocational majors in education, agriculture, engineering, and the like. Incidentally, five per cent have Bachelors of Science in Agriculture. Sixteen percent majored in social science, and seven percent in science, but the largest group (44 percent) majored in the humanities (including history).

Seven out of nine of these rural men graduated from a seminary. More than 80 seminaries are represented in the rural panel. Seventy-three percent went to seminaries accredited by the American Association of Theological Schools. Two-thirds did all their B.D. work at one seminary. Three quarters of them majored in the traditional seminary disciplines (Bible, church history, and theology), and one quarter in practical theology. They represent a cross section of rural ministers who are theologically trained in America.

V.   The informants in the rural panel were asked to list the essential types of work which make up their job as a minister. They rated these in order of importance. Rural ministers tend to think more frequently than do urban ministers that their most important functions are personal religious living and participation in the total mission of the church through evangelism. Among the specialized roles, some phase of preaching was thought to be most important by nearly half (47 percent) of the clergymen. The pastoral role was rated second, but it was mentioned only one-third as frequently as preaching. The priestly (or liturgical) role was mentioned about half as often as being a pastor. The administrative, organizational and teaching roles were rated as most important very infrequently. Taking a total look at the six major role images in terms of importance, as seen by the minister, the organizational and administrative roles were thought to be least important. The preaching and pastoral roles were thought to be most important. The priestly and teaching roles were in the middle ranges.

Parish minister informants were also asked about their sense of being effective and their feeling of enjoyment in performing the six roles. The effective-enjoyment evaluation pattern was related to the sense of importance attached to the roles. The preaching and pastoral roles rated as most important were also thought to be most effectively done and most enjoyed. However, the priestly and administrative roles were seen as least enjoyable and as being least effectively carried out. Teaching and organization work were in between the others in effectiveness and enjoyment.

The parish minister who is faced with a multiplicity of formal roles which he is expected to play may, as some do, follow the policy of catch-as-catch-can, or he may schedule time for each demand for his services. Regardless of how he rations his time, it is a bothersome and bewildering situation to be constantly switching from one role to another. Confusion may easily arise.

VI.   An examination of the implications of this research for the seminary begins with the pre-theological studies in an undergraduate college. These studies are the academic foundation on which seminary training is built. Traditionally the humanities have received priority. Nineteen out of twenty rural ministers agree that languages, literature, philosophy and history are valuable in preparation for the parish ministry. A like number would speak of the value of the pretheological preparation in the social sciences. The sciences (chemistry, biology, and mathematics) are felt to be less valuable than the humanites and the social sciences since only three out of four ministers rated these studies as valuable in their ministry. In short, practicing rural ministers strongly affirm the value of the humanities and the social sciences as preparation for parish work. It is significant that the social sciences as preparation for parish work are equated by practicing ministers with the humanities.

The 344 rural ministers were asked to rate these pretheological studies as to the adequacy of the training. They reported that their training in the humanities was most adequate and their social science training was least adequate. More than half felt that the background training in the social sciences which they received in college was insufficient. The value that they attach to social science as a part of pretheological studies would seem to indicate the need for more adequate offerings and requirements in sociology, psychology and anthropology.

It is sometimes advocated that ministers who anticipate work with special groups should be trained for a better understanding through undergraduate study in a college of agriculture, education, or engineering. The evaluation that the rural ministers give of this proposal is not decisive. Slightly more than half of those whose training was in a specific vocational college would recommend it to others for its value in preparation for the ministry. Many felt the value of an agricultural, business, or other vocational major had been overrated.

How do these rural ministers evaluate their seminary training? Since the minister is oriented as a person who is a believer, scholar, and practitioner, a convenient and meaningful way to report their evaluation of their seminary training is to focus in turn on each of these orientations.

Some ministers felt that the seminary could have prepared them to be a better minister through a more constructive and purposive program centered in the student's person. There is a concern for the seminary student's spiritual life and his evangelical zeal. For example, every eighth minister felt the devotional life of the seminary community was less helpful than it should be. Closely related to this need is that of more training in evangelism. Every eighth minister was concerned about his seminary training in relation to his sense of mission, and his ability to bring others to Christ.

There is also a concern that students be given counsel in the emotional resilience that the ministry will require of them. Seven percent of the ministers felt that seminaries should give greater emphasis to aiding the student in the development of maturity in his emotional life.

Rural minister practitioners stress the function of clergymen's personality and of his understanding of people in making the Gospel effective in the parish. "Ministers succeed or fail as local ministers," according to one minister whose church is typical of those served by men in the rural panel, "not on their ability to preach, nor on their knowledge of history; not on their Biblical understanding, nor any of the scholarly matters, but on their ability to effectively communicate a Christian concern for people. This is more a matter of personality than a matter of training."

Other rural ministers would advise seminary professors to "teach the student to reach people where they are rather than to superimpose a plan for the church as they find it." Or, "young clergymen need to know that they minister to people, not churches. They must have an understanding that the people are to be led rather than ordered about."

Training of the minister as a scholar in religion centers on the content disciplines. These rural ministers were asked to evaluate their seminary training in the traditional disciplines (Bible and biblical literature, church history, and theology) and in the non-traditional disciplines (communicative arts—speech, writing, etc.—or the sciences of social behavior). On the basis of a felt need for more or additional training their reactions to the traditional content studies in the seminary were analyzed. The need for more church history was mentioned least, and their felt need for more biblical studies was mentioned by every fourth rural ministerial informant. Frequently, this need was associated with its value in sermon preparation and preaching. In this connection, only one person in six felt the need for more training in the communicative arts (speech, writing, etc.).

Of the five content fields the need for additional substantive training was mentioned from least needed to most needed in the following order: historical (7 percent); theological (12 percent); communicative (17 percent); biblical (24 percent); behavioral (41 percent). Among the content areas, the greatest felt need was for further training in the sciences of social behavior. Two out of every five rural ministers thought that their ministry would be more effective if they had more sociology, psychology and anthropology *in the seminary*.

Rural ministers are concerned about relating seminary studies to the needs of students as prospective practitioners in the parish. This is expressed in four ways. *First*, they are concerned about the ability of all seminary professors to teach in terms of the parish minister's situation. One-third of these rural informants felt that there should be a greater emphasis on the minister as a practitioner of religion. This is related to all areas of content teaching. It is *not* a request for more courses in "practical theology." It is related to a desire that professors have a more appreciative understanding of the minister as both scholar and practitioner.

Rural clergymen feel (as one informant from the wheat area puts it) that "we need in today's minister a combination of scholar, thinker and man who is in touch with things as they are, who is motivated by an all-consuming love for people because they are God's redeemed." It is the integration of the scholastic and the practical that is desired.

Rural ministers have an intense desire that theological training be oriented to the life of the practitioner in the parish and they are critical of the seminaries when they fail to provide instruction within the context of the local parish.

Second, they are concerned that the sciences of social behavior be taught by competent scholars who can integrate their social science understandings with their theology and their ability to function in the every-day-world parish. This is the problem of the rural minister; he needs to be better prepared to be an effective actor in the human situation. The solution of the problem through seminary teaching is a task that is less easily accomplished. The application of social science knowledge to the ideological orientation and the practical situation in the parish requires imagination and ingenuity. To teach sociology or psychology in a liberal arts college is a much different assignment than teaching these subjects in a theological seminary. For the liberal arts student to know the types of disturbed persons is one thing, but for the minister to function in relation to a Sunday School teacher who has emotional problems is another matter. Explaining the table of organization in a bureaucracy to a college senior is one teaching problem, but explaining it to a minister when it involves board secretaries, benevolence budget quotas, and missionary promotion in the local church is a different teaching problem. The college student is not an actor in the bureaucratic organization. The minister is! His effectiveness as a clergyman is involved. What denominational board secretaries think of his cooperation colors the situation. It is not an abstract academic matter. The benevolence giving of a local church becomes a matter of record. Decisions regarding a future call to another parish may be influenced by whether or not the minister and his church met or did not meet a benevolence quota. These are dynamic questions involving real people and real situations.

Third, the training needs that are related to specific areas of practice in the parish vary with the role that is being played. The preacher, teacher, and liturgist roles have traditionally been more clearly defined and formalized. The roles of administrator, organizer and counselor are increasingly being more clearly defined and formalized. Among the practitioner roles, seminary teaching designed to prepare parish ministers to fulfill the role of counselor (and/or caller) is most frequently felt to be inadequate. Every parish minister expressed a need for more adequate training in counseling and parish calling (particularly on the sick, and disturbed, and those anticipating marriage). Almost as many (42 percent) felt that the seminary had not trained them adequately as administrators and/or organizers. Inadequate training in the traditional roles was mentioned much less frequently: teacher (20 percent), preacher (16 percent), and liturgist (14 percent). By comparison, a felt need for more training in the nontraditional roles (counselor and/or caller, administrator, organizer) was mentioned two to three times more often than in the case of the traditional roles of preacher, teacher, and liturgist.

In the administration of a local parish there are problems the solution of which requires something more than a thorough knowledge of church polity, helpful as this is. More than one clergyman has stumbled on "the silent six"— the power group in the church. Insights that the behavioral sciences have given us about power groups may not solve the problem in a local church, but knowledge about the functioning of these structures will help him understand and adjust to the "silent six."

Fourth, the place of supervised experience in developing the practitioner's point of view was also stressed. To be specific, one-third of those whose opinions we are reporting felt that seminary students should have more supervised field work and experience in church work outside of the seminary. Included in this group are those who favor a summer internship (with adequate supervision and interpretation) in industry and agriculture or clinical training in a hospital. Some felt that need for developing the practitioner's orientation could best be done through an intern year in addition to an intern summer.

VII.   The rural minister has been portrayed as a spiritually committed, theologically oriented practitioner of religion. Does a response on his part to the changed rural life in America mean that he may need to have a newer understanding of and appreciation for his theology? A thoughtful answer would require that it be recognized that the farmer's understanding of science has changed and that science has changed the way he farms. Certainly the apologetic for Christianity will differ today from that which was adequate before science became so integral a part of the agricultural way of life. It will also be recognized that producing for surplus and selling on a nation-wide (or world-wide) market for cash (or credit) raises different ethical issues than were raised when farmers raised crops largely for their own consumption. Face to face bartering with the local general store keeper is a different process from contracting with a chain of canning factories or selling for export through an agent one has never met. The rural minister will wish to examine the relevance of his theology and the ethical implications of it with care if he visualizes it as speaking to the spiritual needs of a mid-twentieth century rural America with pertinence and power.

The minister who has a parish in rural America in this decade must have a sophisticated knowledge of theology. He will be expected to know the Bible with an intimacy that includes an acquaintance with the most obscure biblical personage. He will be expected to know church history so that he can explain why Lutherans are Lutheran, or Methodists are Methodists. He will *also* be expected to know what mechanization is doing to change rural life in America.

However, these matters of knowledge are not ends in themselves. If they are, the minister may be living in a world of theological or sociological fantasy. Theological and sociological knowledge must be related to an end—a dynamic parish situation, a community of believers. The rural minister is a practitioner as well as a scholar of religion. The future rural minister should be prepared to play the roles of the practitioner and live in a world of real people and groups. This is not to discount the thoroughness of his scholarly preparation. Rather it is to underline the importance of combining the scholar and the practitioner for an effective rural ministry. The minister will want to be prepared to live as an expert in the world of people as well as the world of ideas. In short, the rural ministry is a profession to be practiced, and the practice of it requires a lot of faith, a lot of knowledge, and a lot of role skills in a wide variety of fields.

C. THE LAITY

24 CHURCH AND THE LAITY AMONG
PROTESTANTS

Paul M. Harrison

INTRODUCTION   The future of American religion rests
significantly with its laymen. Although the clergy historically have
dominated the religious institution, the secularization of society
has reduced the clerics' monopoly. Religious groups vary, however,
in their attitude toward the degree of lay participation in religion.
The sect group is generally a lay religion. Often arising as a protest to the ecclesiastical control found in the established church,
the sect reasserts the prime role of the layman. In the denomination and ecclesia (*see* Introduction, Article 11), on the other
hand, the distinction between lay and clergy is pronounced. The
distinction is viewed within most Protestant denominations as a
differentiation of roles due to past training and the amount of time
spent in daily religious activity.

The form of church organization (*see* Introduction to Part
III) affects the definition of the role and status of the clergy. The
congregational control in Judaism is reflected in the role of the
rabbi, a teacher of the synagogue who is looked upon with respect
but without supernatural power. The congregational polity of the
United Church of Christ, for example, makes the minister a member of the congregation worthy of respect because of his training and
current leadership responsibility. His equality within the group,
however, causes laymen to address him as "Mr." The Presbyterian
organization of the Presbyterian Church leads members to look at
the ministry as set apart, but yet as one of the congregational
group. The episcopal government of the Roman Catholic Church

Abridged and reprinted from *The Annals*, Volume 332 (November, 1960), pp. 37-49,
with the permission of the author and editors.

PAUL M. HARRISON is Associate Professor of Religious Studies at Pennsylvania State
University.

causes members to perceive the priest as possessing charismatic power; the laity stands below the priesthood in power and importance within the church.

The disestablishment of religion and the recognition of pluralism have seemingly led to a decline of religious power in America. Religious influence upon political and economic functions of the society has diminished. While the social influence of religion remains, it is being challenged by a syncretistic (union of conflicting beliefs) form of national morality. The power of religion is coming to rest more and more with the layman who is committed to his faith and its ideals. Whatever religious influence is exerted emanates from committed persons who have gained positions of power and trust rather than by religious institutions directly. The voice of the clergy has been ineffective in comparison to the early period of our nation when church and state relations were close (see Introduction to Article 6). And yet, paradoxically, religious ideals are becoming national policy as in the case of civil rights and at a time when ministers decry the weakening of American moral fibre and the flight of Americans from God!

These shifts in American society are not without their complications. Conflicting value systems have caused value ambiguity (see Glock, Article 7, and Hammond, Article 9). Legal and judicial decisions which have prohibited the sectarian training of the young in public schools have placed a heavier burden upon the family for religious education, a responsibility which many claim is not being met (see Thomas, Article 17).

Paul M. Harrison argues that Protestant lay activity has been held back by the clerical bureaucracy. Because there has been no clear-cut definition of the role of the laity, laymen have little sense of mission or concept of purpose. Because the role of the layman has never been clearly defined, laymen are susceptible to pressures from the clergy. Yet because the laity is more involved in the total culture, the role of the ministry is compromised through lay pressures. The future of the Protestant churches rests, therefore, on the reevaluation and definition of ministerial and lay roles necessary in this century of change.

EVENTS IN THE CURRENT century have disturbed the confidence of Christians. The advance of the Communist and nationalist ideologies, the heroic but retarded response of the churches to fascist barbarities, the collapse of evangelistic work in China, and the difficulties of missionary enterprise in Indonesia, Africa, and India have all had an effect upon the outlook of the leaders of the church. More immediately, the denominations in America are frantically attempting to keep pace with unheralded revolutions in urban, suburban, and rural society. In the age of the affluent society, pitchmen who hawk their wares on late and early television shows stand on the highest rungs of the nation's prestige ladder while the ministers who most effectively compete with them adopt their techniques and subconsciously pervert the meaning of the central symbols of the faith. Samuel Miller, Dean of Harvard Divinity School, notes that the Sermon on the Mount has been distorted to read: Blessed are the prosperous; blessed are those with fulness of spirit and aggressiveness; blessed are the cheerful, the optimistic, and those who think positively.[1] The meek, the humble, the poor, and the peacemakers are unfit companions in a land where ownership and virtue are one.

A SECULAR MINISTRY.   It is critical alterations like these which have been responsible for a renewal of interest in what churchmen call the ministry of the laity. The role of the professional clergyman is changing. Many of them realize that if they rigidly maintain their traditional patterns of action they cannot cope with the evolving situations of the revolutionary world.

Recent developments in this country, dramatized by such experimental projects as the East Harlem Protestant Parish, the Judson Memorial Church in Greenwich Village, and the Christian Faith and Life Community in Austin, Texas, emphasize "the development of an effective secular ministry in contemporary society."[2] Recognizing that a secularized church in a technological culture is not amenable to the customary practices of the ministry and that the pervasive image of revivalistic evangelism has placed the professional clergyman at a disadvantage, the leaders of these experiments are engaged in developing what they hope will result in a transformation of the layman's role. But these isolated events represent the exception to the lay situation in Protestantism. Less dramatic procedures portray the life of the ordinary churchman in the local congregations.

THE SCOPE OF THE SUBJECT.   There are so many Protestant laymen in so many churches doing and believing so many different things that almost any generalization can immediately be controverted by mutually contradictory facts. American Protestants report approximately sixty million laymen in 280,000 churches.[3] Among these people there is the dignified elder of St. John's Episcopal Church in New York City as well as the recent convert to the Two-Seed-in-the-Spirit Predestinarian Baptists of rural Kentucky.

Sociologists have discovered that one fruitful method of analyzing social phenomena is to develop a typology of the problem to be investigated. Thus in the sociology of religion typological distinctions have been made between

[1] Samuel H. Miller, "The Practice of Religion in a Technological Culture," in a lecture given at the American Baptist Convention, Rochester, N.Y., June 1960.
[2] *See* Ross W. Sanderson, *The Church Serves the Changing City* (New York: Harper & Row, 1955), chapter 8.
[3] *Yearbook of American Churches for 1959* (New York: National Council of the Churches of Christ in the U.S.A., 1960), p. 267.

churches, denominations, sects, and cults.[4] American laymen can be classified according to these four institutional types and generalizations can be made about each. The scope of the issue can be illustrated by developing other categories of laymen. Liston Pope, for example, has subdivided laymen into several types and subtypes on the basis of social class, occupation, education, and political preference.[5] Other classifications can be developed such as age and sex; residence—rural, urban, suburban; degree of church participation—dormant, marginal, modal, and nuclear; and intensity of belief.[6]

In order, however, to restrict the compass of this paper, attention will be paid exclusively to generalization about laymen in the major Protestant denominations in America and typological categories will be avoided for lack of space. Three topics will be considered: laymen in relation to religious organization, to the ministry, and to the secular community.

LAYMEN AND RELIGIOUS ORGANIZATION.   According to Roman Catholic theologians the "holy priesthood" refers in a general way, as in Protestantism, to the whole church, but it refers more specifically to the priestly hierarchy. The dogma of the Catholic Church places the hierarchy in a position which is ontologically prior to the existence of the laymen.[7] In the Protestant situation in America only a comparatively small number of churches, largely confined to the Lutheran and Episcopal traditions, are willing to abide by this hierarchical principle. The Reformation was grounded first of all in the doctrine of the absolute sovereignty of God and the finitude of all things under God—including priest and church. Secondarily, the Reformers emphasized the doctrine of justification by faith and the priesthood of all believers. Protestants have not been consistent in their support and understanding of these difficult doctrinal foundations. They admit that the believer cannot see God and often fails to confess his sovereignty, the sinner cannot fully experience justification, and the layman can clearly distinguish himself—and frequently prefers to disassociate himself—from the clergy.

Perhaps because of this situation the doctrine of the priesthood of all believers has never been efficacious on Protestantism.[8] At the lay experiment in Austin they are "perceiving the subtle clericalism in the Protestant Church and uncovering the meaning of the term 'laity.' They are insisting that the

[4] See Liston Pope, *Millhands and Preachers* (New Haven: Yale University Press, 1942), pp. 117-140.
[5] Liston Pope, "Religion and Class Structure," *The Annals of the American Academy of Political and Social Science,* Volume 256, No. 2 (March 1948) and Frederick A. Shippey, "Religio-Socio-Economic Characteristics of Urban Church Officers" (Unpublished doctoral dissertation, Northwestern University, 1947), pp. 52-93.
[6] Joseph H. Fichter, S.J., *Social Relations in the Urban Parish* (Chicago: University of Chicago Press, 1954); Yoshio Fukuyama, "Using Belief to Define Orientations to Religion," paper presented at a meeting of The Society for the Scientific Study of Religion, New Haven, 1959.
[7] Hendrik Kraemer, *A Theology of the Laity* (Philadelphia: The Westminster Press, 1958), pp. 78-79.
[8] *Ibid.,* p. 63.

primary ministry in the Church is that of laymen in the world." The fact that many Protestant leaders admit there is a critical need for a theology of the laity is indicative of some dissatisfaction with the work of the churches. The lay developments in this country and Europe represent an effort to distinguish between Christian ecclesiastical vocations and Christian secular vocations, between the valid ministry of the clergy and the equally legitimate ministry of the laymen. Among the majority of ministers there appears no sympathy for the lay movements except when they represent an effort to assist the institutional ministry.

THE ORGANIZATIONAL DILEMMA.   The Reformation tradition, and its reaffirmation by the neo-orthodox movement, places contemporary Protestantism in a paradoxical dilemma which has an important effect upon the life of every churchman. The doctrine of the finitude of all things under God explicitly includes the finitude of the visible church. Therefore, the church in history can never legitimately become an end in itself. But on the other hand, if the missionary and evangelistic obligations of the church are taken seriously the churches must develop efficient organizational forms which lead to the displacement of the original goals due to the requirements of bureaucratic procedures. The results are paradoxical since the values and goals which the organization was created to preserve and achieve tend to be uprooted by the goals and values of organizational self-perpetuation. Peter Selznick describes this process in terms of organizational imperatives. The bureaucracy creates needs of its own which must be met before the group can attend to the goals for which it was established.[9] These organizational imperatives impinge upon all the activities of laymen in the institutional church.

ORGANIZATIONAL LITERATURE.   Each of the self-perpetuating denominational bureaucracies of Protestantism includes an agency for lay activity. The author was graciously assisted by the executives of several of these groups when they sent a ten-inch stack of pamphlets and charts to augment the writing of this paper. The primary theme of this literature is an appeal to laymen to witness to the call of the gospel through support of the local churches and cooperation with the program of the denominations. For example, the intention of a pocket-size card distributed by the Southern Baptist laymen's organization can be summed up in the following phrases: "loyalty to Christ, to the church, and to the pastor as leader of all its work; cooperation with every agency and organization of the church and denomination; evangelism; increased circulation of denominational publications; tithes; advance in church budgets; patronage of denomination institutions."[10]

[9] Philip Selznick, *TVA and the Grass Roots* (Berkeley: University of California Press, 1953), p. 256. Also Robert Lee, "The Organizational Dilemma in American Protestantism," Sixteenth Conference on Science, Philosophy and Religion in Their Relation to the Democratic Way of Life, August 1960.
[10] "Aims and Objectives of the Brotherhood" (Memphis, Tenn.: Baptist Brotherhood Commission, Southern Baptist Convention).

For almost four centuries Protestants have indulged themselves with critical remarks on the subject of the intricacies of the Roman Catholic hierarchy. The Catholic Church is indeed a unique phenomenon in the realm of religious organization. However, the major Protestant denominations have kept pace with the organizational revolution which accompanies our industrial development. The organizational chart of one relatively minor subagency of the Missouri Synod Lutherans—the Lutheran Laymen's League—resembles closely the bureaucratic plan of Standard Oil of New Jersey.[11] There are no exceptions to this phenomenon among the large Protestant denominations.

LAY ATTITUDES TOWARD THE CHURCH.   It is not surprising that "the laity perceives the church as an organization," and that "they perceive the minister as the local functionary of that organization." The contributions the laymen are asked to make "are essentially aimed at maintaining the denomination as an organizational entity."[12] In the words of one layman, "the only time the minister calls is when he wants me to do a job. When I'm sick the assistant minister calls." The clergyman knows that his professional future depends upon his ability to fulfill the organization imperatives of the denomination, but the opinion of many laymen is expressed by the words, "I belong to St. Brick's, but they don't pay much attention to me until they want me to help with the Everymember Canvass."[13] But this is not necessarily the prevailing opinion among laymen. Whyte discovered that in the Protestant churches of suburbia the need to belong to a group was of key importance. The organizational methods that people learn in their secular pursuits are eagerly transferred to the sphere of the local church.[14] In relationship to their laymen the Protestant churches in America are engaged primarily in "picking up the pieces" and maintaining the equilibrium of individuals and social groups. There is a prevailing and increasing emphasis upon the development of personal and group counseling techniques, and the sermons on Sunday extol the virtues of togetherness, fraternal love for the brethren, harmony in group relations, a healthy family life, and protective concern for those in the community who are less fortunately endowed with the talents and material advantages of this life.

The interests of laymen, as well as the nature of the organizational imperatives of a local congregation, are revealed by an analysis of the kinds of jobs which laymen accept or reject. In a city church of 500 members in which there were 475 tasks for laymen, Frederick Shippey distributed the tasks among the eighteen basic categories. He found that 103 tasks, 22 percent,

11 "Official Manual, Lutheran Laymen's League" (St. Louis, Mo.: Lutheran Laymen's League), p. 1.
12 Thomas Bennett, "Discussion of Sam Blizzard's Paper entitled 'The Layman's Understanding of the Ministry,'" Conference on Motivation for the Ministry (Louisville, Ky.: Southern Baptist Seminary, 1959), p. 78.
13 John L. Casteel, "Laymen, Church, and Seminary," Journal of the Christian Faith and Life Community, Austin, Texas, Volume 6, Number 8, p. 1.
14 William H. Whyte, Jr., The Organization Man (New York: Simon and Schuster, 1956), Chapter 27.

were unclaimed by the lay people. The tasks which were fully appropriated were in the following categories: committee work, financial matters, property and buildings, missionary promotion, religious literature, and record keeping. Job categories which attracted the lowest number of participants were as follows: visitation of constituency, group work, office work, and entertainment.[15]

Protestant laymen willingly and even eagerly participate in the organizational process. Their occasional complaints and their constant efforts to avoid the less exciting and routine tasks only proves that they are not yet angels. In their work with laymen, denominational officials and local ministers may succumb to institutional pressures, they may be motivated by self-interest more often than the Christian idealist would prefer, and they may lack imagination or even the strength of their convictions. Nevertheless, for the most part laymen appear satisfied with the church as it is.

LAYMEN AND MINISTERS.   The polymorphic role of the Protestant clergy in contemporary America does not place these men in an enviable social situation. The lay membership of these voluntary religious associations look to their ministers for leadership in maintaining, at the same time, the material solvency and the spiritual integrity of their institutions. The minister must be an organizational director of the highest caliber, but because of the requirements of his religious vocation he must avoid any taint of bureaucratic officiousness. He must, nonetheless, be an efficient bureaucratic official.

Essentially the plan is this: A congregation selects a minister who serves as "chief of staff" of the church government. The church is then organized into various departments, each department allotted a certain task in the church's work. The congregation selects from its ranks the men and women who are to head these departments. These department heads form a kind of "cabinet" to assist the minister in the overall management of the church. Finally the minister and his "cabinet" appoint churchmen to various department committees.[16]

Charles Page emphasizes the relationship of antipathy which exists in every bureaucracy between the professional expert and the clients. These attitudes are not officially sanctioned by the policies of the bureaucracy, in fact, proclamations which emphasize the element of service to the clients are constantly made.[17] Antipathy occurs also in the churches where the laymen are being educated by the minister for they are the constant recipients of his specialized training, in pulpit, committee meeting, and classroom.

Although this characterization of the relationship which exists between clergy and laity can be overdrawn it corresponds to the ambivalence laymen

[15] Frederick A. Shippey, *Church Work in the City* (New York: Abingden, 1952), p. 181.
[16] Marx Rutherford, *The Christian Layman and His Church* (St. Louis: Bethany Press, 1958), pp. 27-8.
[17] Charles Page, "Bureaucracy in the Liberal Church," *Review of Religion*, Volume 14, Number 3 (July 1951), p. 140.

feel toward their participation in the work of the church. They love it and hate it. The church is critical of them and fills them with guilt, but it comforts them in their need; the church demands everything from them that they most dearly cherish but at the same time they confess that it promises them eternal redemption. So the Protestant laymen have come to terms with their clergymen and with their own ambivalence. They realize that under the pressures of the modern organizational environment the minister has necessarily become the pastoral director of an institution which differs in no significantly visible way from other institutions to which the layman claims membership. They believe that in an invisible way, in a manner which is not entirely explicable, the authority of God still resides in the church and its ministry despite the cultural adjustments which are inevitable.

The Protestant minister is respected and obeyed in his role as pastoral director insofar as he demonstrates a capacity for executive leadership and insofar as he is able to combine this with a spiritual authority derived from the Bible, from the traditional doctrines of the church, and from the dynamic of his own personality. As a source of authority, especially in Protestantism, the power of the minister's personality must never be underestimated.[18]

THE POWER OF THE LAYMEN.   Laymen exercise a tremendous power in the Protestant church, not because they possess an authority which is theologically legitimated by such doctrines as the priesthood of all believers, but because the doctrine of the church in the major portion of Protestantism is inadequately defined and the relationship between clergy and laymen has never been explicitly and fully developed. The authority of the clergyman prior to the Reformation resided in the traditional doctrines of the church which substantiated the official authority of the priestly hierarchy. Priestly authority further resided in the authority of the Scriptures, and the Scriptures were in turn interpreted by the hierarchy of the church. The Reformers rejected this procedure because they believed it was a circular validation of power. But in Protestantism the problem of authority has never been so rationally solved. There exists a pluralism of authority, so that even within a single denomination there can be found vast differences of opinion as to the legitimate locus of authority. The possible authorities are: the Bible, the creeds, the local minister, the whole group of the ministry and the agreement they reach, the national denominational council, the state or local council, the local church, and the individuals within the church. In recent years some American denominations have been seriously wracked by debate on the issue of authority.

Without a traditional and official source for the legitimation of his authority, the Protestant minister has been forced to insert into the vacuum left

---

[18] Kenneth Underwood, *Protestant and Catholic* (Boston: Beacon Press, 1957), pp. 97-122; Paul M. Harrison, *Authority and Power in the Free Church Tradition* (Princeton: Princeton University Press, 1959) chapters 4-5.

by the displacement of historical dogma the power of his own personality and the persuasiveness of his intellectual skill. This places an inordinate burden upon the local clergyman and upon his integrity as an individual divested of the comfort and support of his professional brethren. In times of social crisis the Protestant minister who opposes the dominant laymen of the community usually stands alone and is eventually forced to conform to the popular prejudices of the community.

MIDDLE CLASS VALUES.   Laymen willingly follow the leadership of the clergy in ecclesiastical affairs but distrust or ignore their opinions on issues of crucial secular significance. The authority of the Protestant minister in relation to the laymen has been critically tested in the Southern racial crisis. Most ministers who have been firm in their convictions and bold in stating them from the pulpit have been relieved of their posts. This situation has been summarized: when lay parishioners hold divergent views on an issue, the ministry will be equivocal in its position; when the laymen are partisan on an issue the ministers will be equally committed to the lay position.[19] Waldo Beach observes that even though the Episcopal Church "is officially inclusive, its witness has been stifled by culturally conditioned laymen.[20]

According to the denominational literature for laymen the churches must maintain a constructive relationship with the secular community. This literature, however, is more often directed toward the middle-class virtues than toward the transformation of existing political and economic structures which may be the source of social injustices.

The majority of Protestant laymen see through the glass darkly when they seek solutions for social problems. They dwell in a middle-class ghetto and remain so effectively isolated from the rest of the world that they readily accept the myth that they alone possess true virtue and protect all significant value. A bank president participating in a small church discussion group asked, "Why shouldn't the Board of Trustees be made up of prominent community leaders? They're the ones who are most aware of what's going on and can help the church do the things that are best for the community."[21] Contemporary American Protestantism often substitutes television for the golden harps, tail fins for angelic wings, the three day week end for heavenly rest, and the psychoanalyst's couch for the suffering of the cross.[22]

---

[19] Charles Y. Glock and Benjamin B. Ringer, "Church Polity and the Attitudes of Ministers and Parishioners on Social Issues," *American Sociological Review*, Volume 21, Number 2 (April 1956), pp. 148-56.
[20] Waldo Beach, "The Southern Churches and the Race Question," *Christianity and Crisis*, Volume 18, Number 3 (March 3, 1958), p. 18.
[21] Howard W. Meyers, "A Study of the Effects of Environment Upon the Attitudes and Actions of the Members of Two Churches" (Unpublished doctoral dissertation, Yale University, 1959), p. 249.
[22] See H. Richard Niebuhr, *The Kingdom of God in America* (New York: Harper & Row, 1959), p. 196.

LAYMEN AND THE WORLD.   Efforts are being made to relate the churches in new ways to the problems of the secular community. Laymen are in a unique position for they are related to the secular environment in ways which can rarely be achieved by the professional clergy. An effort is being made to discover ways in which laymen can carry the church into the world without compromising Christian theological and ethical ideals and without removing the laymen from participation in the vocation of their choice. The enormity of the difficulties is apparent to everyone. Few laymen are theologically trained for the task. The Sunday school clichés are useless, the advertising techniques of the religious organizations are believed to be self-defeating, the ancient symbolic phrases of the evangelistic crusades stimulate repugnance more often than they arouse nostalgia, but the greatest problem is the specific relevance of Christian doctrines to secular vocations. Having rejected the monastic ideal as well as distinctions of sanctity between clergy and laymen, Protestants are faced with the problem of discovering the meaning of the doctrine of the priesthood of all believers within the contemporary situation. This involves first of all the necessity of understanding the role of the professional clergy and the function of the institutional church. Those who are on the forefront of the lay movement believe that no longer can the laity be treated as assistants to pastors who are maintaining the institutional programs of the church.

It is not the duty of the laity to help the pastor to carry out his pastoral work: it is the pastor's duty to equip the laity to carry out their work in the world. We must not "missionize" the world into the church; but the church in its mission must go out into the world. If the life of the older and younger churches is examined from this point of view, a great deal of the activity of the church and of its missions will be exposed as wasted effort and church-narcissism.[23]

This raises another problem, for how can the Protestant minister whose basis of authority is already extremely tenuous engage in a serious conversation with the laity in order to discover the legitimate authority of the layman as a Christian missionary to the world? The vested interest of the clergymen militates against the efforts of the advocates of a lay priesthood.

The minister distrusts the laymen, not only because they threaten his authority, but because they conform so easily to the pressures and prejudices of the secular environment. It is the trustee more often than the minister who benefits from the profits of economic exploitation, and it is the deacon, seldom the minister, who is chairman of the White Citizens Council.

But if the preacher is rarely involved in these activities, it is equally true that he seldom engages in an extended, serious, and equal conversation with a layman to discover the full meaning of the emotional impact that confronts a man who refuses to participate in the anti-Semitic, anti-Negro, or antilabor

[23] Hans-Ruedi Weber, "The Ministry of the Laity in the Missionary Outreach of the Church," *The Student World*, Volume 49, Number 3 (Third Quarter, 1956), p. 224.

charades of his business colleagues. The import and significance of the daily pressures experienced by the laymen would be incomprehensible to the minister who has never once passed the portals of an executive office or a labor hall.

The leaders of the new lay movement believe that the "secular clergy" of Protestantism have much to teach the professional ministers if they are willing to fully associate and communicate with the layman in the midst of his weekly enterprise and become a participating witness to the amenities of the layman's secular career. It is this kind of technique which is used most effectively by ministers of the inner city slum parishes. Before they speak—certainly before they preach—to the Negro or Puerto Rican outcast they join him in his caste society. They may attend a movie with the gang at four in the morning, stand with them while they make the decision to go on a rumble, or sit with them while they try to come out of a heroin spin.

A young Protestant layman who practices law in East Harlem and who lives on the notorious block of East 100th Street between First and Second Avenues wrote a moving account of his experience which can be used to summarize the intention of the contemporary laymen's movement. He concludes that to be a Christian is to possess the extraordinary freedom to share the burdens of the "common, ambiguous, transient, perishing existence of men even to the point of actually taking the place of another man whether he be powerful or weak, in health or in sickness, clothed or naked . . . fed or hungry, at liberty or in prison, young or old, white or colored, rich or poor."[24]

[24] William Stringfellow, "Christian Poverty and the Practice of the Law," *Harvard Law School Bulletin,* Volume 10, Number 4 (June, 1959).

25 CHURCH AND THE LAITY AMONG CATHOLICS

John J. Kane

INTRODUCTION   The position of the layman within the Roman Catholic Church is ambiguous. Although the layman historically has been a religious equal to the priest, functionally he has occupied a position of secondary influence within the Roman Catholic Church. The comparison among Protestant, Jewish, and Roman Catholic (*see* Harrison, Article 24, and Sklare, Article 26) attitudes toward the laity indicates the low status of the Roman Catholic layman. The laity is the lowest rank in the organizational structure of the Catholic Church. Based upon episcopal church polity (*see* Introduction to Part III), Roman Catholicism vests the priesthood and its derivative hierarchy with theological and organizational power. Although unordained monks, other brothers, and nuns possess no clerical rank, they are considered above the level of the common layman because of their apparent dedication in the faith.

Since World War II, Roman Catholic laymen have been demanding increased voice within the ranks of their church. The growing anticlericalism of France, Italy, and Latin America has forced Roman Catholicism to reconsider the general position and role of the laity for coming generations. The exact definition of the role of the laity remains unclear, although the recent Vatican Council has suggested that laymen must be given greater voice within the workings of the church. However, the role of the laymen will probably remain advisory rather than legislative. The very nature of church organization suggests this limitation. At

Abridged and reprinted from *The Annals,* Volume 332 (November, 1960), pp. 50-60, with the permission of the author and editors.

JOHN J. KANE is Professor and Head of the Department of Sociology of Notre Dame University.

least it is certain that the role of the Roman Catholic layman will not be defined in terms similar to Protestant or Jewish practices. However, Joseph J. Kane, of the University of Notre Dame, apologetically suggests that the strength of the church centers around the involvement of its laity. Already steps have been taken in America toward a revised participation of the layman in new roles formerly closed to him.

THE ROMAN CATHOLIC considers his church a divinely instituted organization founded by Jesus Christ, the Second Person of the Trinity, true Man and true God, in which and through which he can work out his eternal salvation. At the beginning of life, unless he is a convert, he is inducted into the Church via the sacrament of Baptism and at the end of life he is prepared for eternity through Holy Viaticum and Extreme Unction. As a youth he is prepared for and receives the sacraments of Penance, that is, confession in which he tells his sins to a duly authorized priest, repents of them, and firmly resolves to sin no more in order to receive absolution; and Holy Eucharist, the reception of the Body and Blood of Christ. Shortly thereafter he is confirmed in his faith sacramentally, and later may be married in the sacrament of Matrimony, or if a male raised to priesthood through the sacrament of Holy Orders. Some Catholics, of course, never receive either Matrimony or Holy Orders. Thus the Church through an outward sign instituted by Christ to give Grace provides for the most important rites of passage in most human lives—birth, marriage and death.

The central fact of Catholicism is the sacrifice of the Mass which Catholics except for a serious reason, must attend on every Sunday and on holy days of obligation. There is also an annual obligation of receiving Penance and Holy Eucharist during Easter time, a period extending from the first Sunday of Lent until Trinity Sunday. Every Catholic parent must instruct his children in the faith. If possible, such instruction is supplemented by a child's attendance at Catholic schools or Sunday schools. There is a hard core of beliefs which Catholics must accept. They must also accept the moral obligations set forth in the ten commandments and the commandments of the Church.

This is not to say that every individual Catholic, even adult Catholics, is fully aware of all teachings of the Church on such matters. Neither would it be accurate to claim that all Catholics rigidly adhere to all obligations of the Church. Some fail through ignorance, some through human frailty. Others lose their faith and leave the Church. Contrary to a belief popular in Catholic circles, some embrace another religion.

On January 1, 1959, there were 39,505,475 Catholics in the continental United States including Hawaii, Alaska, and the personnel of armed forces and various overseas services. The world Catholic population is estimated at

527,643,000.[1] Unlike some Protestant denominations, the Catholic Church counts membership from the moment of baptism, thus including infants and children. In 1926 Protestants constituted 27 percent of the total population of continental United States; Roman Catholics, 16 percent. By 1958 Protestants made up 35.5 percent of this population, Catholics 22.8 percent. The rate of growth was almost identical for both, Protestants having a slight edge.[2]

PRESTIGE OF THE CHURCH. Sociological surveys of actual religious practice, such as the percentage of Catholics who usually hear Mass on Sunday, reveal that only about 48 percent attend Sunday Mass in Germany. In large European cities the percentage is even lower—27 percent in Munich and 26 percent in Nancy. The practice of Catholicism in some Latin-American countries, beset by a dearth of clergy, is poor. In some large American dioceses the number of Catholics reported by pastors on the basis of baptisms, with due allowances for deaths, immigrants, in-migrants and out-migrants, is almost 60 percent below the number that could be expected from such calculations. Similar estimates made on a national scale show the number of Catholics to be about ten million less than should be expected. Studies of regular attendance at Sunday Mass in some United States' dioceses reveal that they average between 30 percent and 46 percent.[3]

The number of invalid marriages, that is, those contracted outside the Church, in which one or both parties are Catholics is unknown. About three out of every ten valid Catholic marriages, in the United States, is a mixed religious marriage.[4] Investigations show that such marriages are a source of leakage from Roman Catholicism. Despite Church regulations that Catholic children shall be educated in Catholic schools, in the United States only about 60 percent of Catholic children in these age brackets do attend Catholic elementary or Catholic high schools. On the college level, only about one third of Catholic students are enrolled in Catholic colleges or universities. This is due only in part to the lack of adequate facilities. Vocations to the priesthood, the brotherhood, and the sisterhood have not kept pace with the demand, and the ratio of laymen to priests has become larger.

SANCTIONS. Sanctions exist within the Roman Catholic Church for the violation of the law of God or church regulations. Sins may be forgiven

[1] *The National Catholic Almanac* (Paterson, N.J.: St. Anthony's Guild, 1960), p. 354.
[2] *Christian Century*, Volume 16, p. 1045. In a population survey made in March 1957 sponsored by the United States Bureau of Census of 35,000 households in 330 sample areas across the nation those indicating religious preference 14 years of age or over, Protestants made up 66.2 percent, Catholics 27.7 percent. Dorothy Good, "Questions on Religion in the U.S. Census," *Population Index*, Volume 25 (Princeton: Office of Population Research, 1959), pp. 3-16.
[3] John G. Milhaven, "Sociological Soundings of U.S. Catholicism," *America*, Volume 93, Number 5, pp. 124-25.
[4] John L. Thomas, "Are They Marrying Their Own?" *Catholic World*, Volume 174, p. 125.

by the priest in the sacrament of Penance under the conditions noted earlier. Catholics who enter into marriage before a civil magistrate in some dioceses or a non-Catholic clergyman anywhere are excommunicated. The marriage is invalid. It should be noted, however, that this does not apply to the marriage of non-Catholics before civil or non-Catholic religious authorities. Such a marriage is considered valid, and in the event of divorce, a Catholic may not marry either of the divorced persons during the lifetime of the other partner. Strictly speaking, Catholic parents may be excommunicated if they fail to send their children to Catholic schools. In actual practice there are two reasons why this is rarely, perhaps never, carried out in the United States. First, Catholic schools are unavailable in certain parts of the country. Second, in very many cases it would be impossible for Catholic institutions to accommodate all Catholic students, particularly on the college and university levels. Excommunication is a very serious penalty in that it denies access to the sacraments. If the individual repents and satisfactorily alters his or her way of life, excommunication can be lifted. Severe sanctions exist for the priest who enters into marriage.

STRUCTURE OF CATHOLICISM.   The Roman Catholic Church is hierarchical in structure. At the apex is the Pope, the Bishop of Rome, whom Catholics believe is in direct succession to St. Peter. Immediately below him are the bishops of the world and under them are the duly ordained priests. Lowest in rank are the laity. Cardinals are members of the Sacred College of Cardinals who advise and assist the Pope in the government of the Church. There are three ranks, cardinal deacon, cardinal priest, and cardinal bishop. Except that a cardinal bishop must be a bishop these designations bear no relationship to the individual's rank in Holy Orders. Formerly, a primate was a bishop without the rank of patriarch who had jurisdiction over all metropolitans and bishops of a given area or country. He was himself subject only to the Holy See, that is, the Pope. This position is no longer recognized in canon law but the title is retained by some archbishops and, in certain cases, it provides a position of precedence outside of the local hierarchy.

A patriarch is a bishop who has the highest rank after the Pope in the hierarchy of jurisdiction. Today there are seven patriarchs: the Patriarch of the West, the Pope; the Coptic Patriarch of Alexandria, the Melkite, Syrian, and Maronite Patriarchs of Antioch, the Armenian Patriarch of Cilicia, and the Chaldean Patriarch of Babylon. While the power and importance of patriarchs, other than the Patriarch of the West, have declined greatly since the schism of the East, they are still independent of any authority except that of the Pope and his delegates. With the exception of the Coptic Patriarch, appointed by the Holy See, patriarchs are elected by their bishops and their election is confirmed by the Pope.[5]

From the third century onward it is necessary to distinguish another

[5] *A Catholic Dictionary* (New York: Macmillan, 1949), pp. 74, 371, 401.

category of the faithful: unordained monks and other religious brothers and nuns. In the strict canonical sense these are not clerics and have no hierarchical rank.[6] In actual practice, however, monks and nuns are not considered lay persons. Canon law recognizes their precedence over the laity in the first paragraph of Canon 491.[7] Unordained brothers, sisters, and monks take vows of poverty, chastity, and obedience, wear a prescribed type of dress known as a habit, and follow a religious rule. They may be engaged in the education of youth, in nursing, or in social work, or they may be engaged exclusively in contemplation, like the Carmelite nuns. Secular institutes have more recently been founded. These are composed of men or women who practice the evangelical counsels and take vows without losing their lay status.[8]

ROLES OF PRIESTS.   A priest is a sacred minister empowered through Holy Orders to celebrate Mass, administer the sacraments, to preach, and to bless. Priests may be divided into two major categories, the regular and the secular clergy. The regular clergy are members of religious orders or congregations and follow a religious role under a superior. They also take vows of poverty, chastity, and obedience. The secular clergy are immediately under their bishops, take vows of chastity, a vow of obedience to the bishop, but no vow of poverty. On January 1, 1959, there was a total of 52,689 priests in the United States. Of these, 31,961 were secular clergy, 20,728 were regular clergy.[9] While the roles of the regular and the secular clergy generally show some variations, there is a tremendous overlap. Most secular clergy are priests in parishes or occupy administrative offices within the respective dioceses. Regular clergy are more likely to staff high schools and colleges, to preach missions within their own country, or to go to foreign missions. But some of the regular clergy also staff parishes and some of the secular clergy teach in high schools and colleges.

A parish is a definite territorial area in which there is a church, a congregation, and a pastor who has the care of souls. In larger parishes the pastor may have one, two, or as many as four or five assistant priests or curates. But parishes reveal great variations by reason of size, the structure of the congregations and the geographical area in which they are located. These factors modify the roles of the parish priest.

While racial and ethnic parishes are now becoming a largely historical phenomenon, some still exist. They were established to care for the needs of the immigrants; the church was staffed by priests of the same national origin as the parishioners; sermons were delivered and confessions heard in this tongue and sometimes this language was taught in the parochial schools. They

[6] Yves M. J. Congar, O.P., *Lay People in the Church,* translated by Donald Attwater (London: Bloomsbury Publishing Co., Ltd., 1957), pp. 3-8.
[7] Msgr. Gerald Philips, *The Role of the Laity in the Church,* translated by John R. Gilbert and James W. Moudry (Chicago: Fides Publishing Association, 1955), p. 10.
[8] Ibid., p. 10.
[9] *The National Catholic Almanac, op. cit.,* p. 435.

probably slowed acculturation to American ways, but they also provided a cushion against a too rapid Americanization which could result in the "marginal personality."

The racial parish still exists and is apt to be so identified by some persons even after it has become integrated. In many sections of the United States, Negro Catholics may make a choice of the parish they will attend. They may become members of the parish within whose boundaries they live or, if they prefer, they may become members of a Negro parish if one exists in their city.

The social structure of most parish congregations is mixed, that is, it contains members of different social classes. But since most parishes have definite territorial boundaries, there is a distinct possibility that one social class may tend to predominate.

The roles of priests are also influenced by the part of the country in which the parish is located. The high status accorded to Catholic priests in Boston even by persons who are not Catholics can be attained only with difficulty in certain sections of the South where Catholics are sparse. The possibility of Catholic influence in community leadership in such areas depends very largely upon the personality of the priest, his unwillingness to mingle with non-Catholics, and to join with the community in civic activities.

THE LAITY.   The status and role of the laity in the Church are in a state of flux. This can be readily illustrated by two widely circulated anecdotes. Cardinal Aidan Gasquet tells of an inquirer who asked a priest, "What is the position of the layman in the Church?" The priest replied, "To kneel before the altar and to sit beneath the pulpit." The cardinal then added that the layman also had to put his hand into his pocket. Financial support of the Church is certainly an important function of the layman, and it is so stated in the commandments of the Church. But it is not his sole function. Another story is told of Pope Pius X who asked some cardinals what was the greatest need of the Church in contemporary times. One cardinal replied that more priests were needed, another that more churches were needed, another more schools. Finally the Pope interrupted them to say that what was most needed was a dedicated laity.

In Jewish and early Christian tradition the word laity referred to a sacred people and there is no distinction between lay people and clerics in the vocabulary of the New Testament. The first use of the word layman as opposed to priest occurs in a Roman document, a letter to the community at Corinth written by Clement of Alexandria.[10] Between the end of the eleventh century and beginning of the thirteenth century, Father Yves M. J. Congar believes, deep changes occurred in the clerical-lay relationship, and these changes have persisted until the present time. In 1092, confirming the foundations of the Canons of Raitenbach, Pope Urban II said, "From the beginning the Church

10 Congar, op. cit., pp. 1-2.

has offered two kinds of life to her children: one to help the insufficiency of the weak, another to perfect the goodness of the strong."[11] The implication seems to be that the lay state is a concession to human weakness. The dictionary of Catholic theology does not mention the word layman, and of 2,414 canons in the Code of Canon Law, only forty-four are devoted to the chapter on the laity, "De Laicis."[12]

A number of historical circumstances have contributed to the lower status of the laity in Catholicism. It was monks and priests who preserved the intellectual heritage during the barbarian invasions. During some periods of Western history, literacy itself was almost the exclusive prerogative of the cleric, and the right to the "benefit of clergy," a provision in civil law, was determined by ability to read.

The history of the Catholic Church in the United States is still haunted by the ghosts of trusteeism, a controversy which occupied the American Church from 1815 to the end of the Civil War. The first Catholics in the original thirteen colonies built churches and then sought priests to staff them. They administered the temporal matters, selected their pastors, determined their salaries, and eventually in the 1820's tried to nominate the Bishop of Philadelphia. Rome, in a most temperate letter, refused this request. Two factions were formed at St. Mary's Church in Philadelphia. Violence occurred at their meeting and militia had to be summoned to put down the riot. Trusteeism was not confined to Philadelphia, and it proved an embarrassing, humiliating experience for the young American Church. While trusteeism no longer exists, the fear it engendered of entrusting to the laity their rightful share of work in the Church still persists.[13]

Historically the American Catholic laity, with the exception of English Catholics who arrived prior to the Revolution, were usually of the laboring class, illiterate or poorly educated, as incapable as they were unwilling to assume their proper leadership. Out of sheer necessity priests spoke as authorities in areas rather far removed from ecclesiastical matters. To some extent they still do and this is at least in part due to a lack of lay initiative.

CLERICAL-LAY RELATIONSHIPS.   Three extreme attitudes in clerical-lay relationships are clericalism, anticlericalism, and laicism, none of which is presently found in the United States, although they are not absent in Europe and in Latin America. Clericalism occurs when the clergy unduly extends ecclesiastical authority and influence beyond its rightful sphere.[14] Anticlericalism opposes the Church's rightful concern about social, economic, and political affairs, even when these affect the religious welfare of its members, as in the case of Communist political activity. Laicism is the opposite of

[11] *Ibid.*, p. 9.
[12] Philips, *op. cit.*, p. 10.
[13] Rt. Reverend Monsignor Carl J. Ryan, "Ghosts of Trusteeism," *Homiletic and Pastoral Review*, Volume 57, p. 705.
[14] *A Catholic Dictionary*, *op. cit.*, p. 101.

clericalism; it is the undue extension of secular authority and influence into
ecclesiastical matters. So far as the Roman Catholic Church is concerned,
laicism is of less importance than anticlericalism today. The proper spheres
of church and lay authority are more easily defined theoretically than practically. Those who would attack the Church readily cry "clericalism," while
some churchmen, such as the one cited above, who consider it to be the
function of the laity to kneel before the altar and to sit beneath the pulpit,
may prematurely shout "anticlericalism."

Some Protestant spokesmen have noted what they consider the inferior
position of the laity in the Church and point particularly to the lay teacher's
position in Catholic educational institutions.[15] Certainly in the past the lower
status of the laity has been obvious. It has by no means disappeared although
at times it has been exaggerated by statements of disgruntled laymen who
project experiences at the hands of an excessively authoritarian pastor or
priest onto the entire clergy. Catholic laymen today have considerably more
formal education than in the past and many of them wish to have a more
active part in the apostolate.

Two milestones since 1930 clearly indicate the changing status of clerical-
lay relationships. One is the call to Catholic Action by the popes and bishops,
the other is the development of the Liturgical Movement. Catholic Action
under the ecclesiastical authority of bishops attempts to replace the priest by
laymen insofar as this is canonically possible. It is essential today because it is
impossible or unfeasible for priests to do the necessary work of evangelization
and teaching in some places where these are most needed.[16] The Liturgical
Movement generally means a more active participation by the laity in the
Church services, particularly the Mass. The Missa Recitata in which the congregation makes the responses to the priest at Mass and recites aloud certain
parts of the Mass, oddly enough, has been resisted by some lay people. Other
laymen, however, press vigorously for Mass to be said and sacraments to be
administered in the vernacular.[17] Neither Catholic Action nor the Liturgical
Movement should be considered something new; they are, rather, revivals of
past practices.

The increased birth rate following World War II and the consequent
demand for more Catholic schools and teachers to staff them mean an increasing use of lay persons as teachers and professors. The lay teacher has ceased
to be, as he was once considered, a necessary evil. Today he is a desperately
needed asset and in the future without his services the Catholic education
cannot continue even at its present level and certainly cannot be expanded
to meet future needs.

[15] Martin E. Marty, "Dialogue Within the Catholic Church," *American Catholicism, A
Protestant-Jewish View,* edited by Philip Scharber (N.Y.: Sheed, 1959), p. 23.
[16] Michael De La Bedoyere, *The Layman in the Church* (Chicago, Regnery, 1955).
[17] [The use of the vernacular Mass was recently approved by the Vatican Council.—*Editor.*]

THE FUTURE OF THE ROMAN CATHOLIC CHURCH.   The future of Roman Catholicism behind the Iron and Bamboo Curtains is uncertain. Thoroughly accurate information cannot be obtained, but, from what is known, its future seems precarious. But it should be recalled that such a situation is scarcely novel and that the Church has survived crises from her beginning. The words of her divine Founder that He will be with her till the end of time and that the gates of hell shall not prevail against her are a major source of reassurance. In some parts of Europe and Latin America the practice of the faith is less fervent than could be desired, particularly among the working classes. In other sections of the world—among which the United States is included—the Church is thriving. More active participation by the American laity and the development of various movements cited seem to indicate a fervor and vigor for the future that may exceed that of the past. On the purely sociological level, the truly great asset of the Roman Catholic Church is her ability to adapt to changing times without altering the repository of faith and morals. That such adaptations will have to be made is obvious; that they will be made seems certain.

26 CHURCH AND THE LAITY AMONG JEWS

Marshall Sklare

INTRODUCTION   Judaism in America is divided into
three main groups which are determined in large part by distinctions in practices and customs, in usage of the Hebrew language,
and in degree of religious acculturation to the new environment.
Orthodox Judaism remains the most conservative; *Reformed Judaism* has become the most liberal. *Conservative Judaism* bridges the
gap between Orthodox and Reformed. Orthodox Judaism is characterized by a close adherence to Jewish scriptures, writings, and
commentaries. The role of the rabbi remains central and authoritative in the interpretation of Hebrew writings. Reformed Judaism,
the result of an attempt by nineteenth century Jews in Germany
and the United States to relate to the modern social environment,
emphasizes the usage of the vernacular in place of Hebrew as the
language of prayer and study, and the elimination of many dietary
laws and religious practices which set the group apart as a distinct
religious minority. Although the rabbi retains the teaching role
within Reformed Judaism, his authority is not comparable to that
of the Orthodox rabbi. Conservative Judaism generally acknowledges many of the traditions of Orthodox Judaism, but places less
emphasis upon the literal interpretation of scripture, offering
thereby a third alternative to a *literal* Orthodox and a *liberal* Reform religious expression.

Lay control has remained a significant characteristic of all
forms of Judaism. Reformed, Conservative, and Orthodox Judaism
express a congregational polity and organizational form. Although

Abridged and reprinted from *The Annals,* Volume 332 (November, 1960), pp. 60-70,
with the permission of the author and editors.

MARSHALL SKLARE is Professor of Sociology at the Wurzweiler School of Social Work,
Yeshiva University.

Judaism is an ethnic church for all born Jews who have not become converts of another religion, the role of women within the congregation has been limited. Their role varies from full participation allowed in the Reformed church to the limited participation granted in Orthodox Judaism. The role of women has been increasing through the activities of the sisterhoods, a religious auxiliary.

Jewish tradition has not led to a clear differentiation of lay and clergy roles. The layman may serve as his own clergyman in some home religious observances. The family religious responsibility, basic to Judaism, may serve to supplant the strength of the larger congregation, accounting in part for the limited temple or synagogue attendance at times other than the High Holy Days. Although the rabbi and cantor express specialized religious roles within Judaism, they are viewed more as laymen than as members of a formal clergy. Because Jewish religion overlaps with membership in the Jewish community, all Jews have equal claim to membership in the Jewish church. The role of the rabbi remains essentially that of scholar and leader, although he may assume other secondary roles (see Blizzard, Article 20). However, the rabbi is only one among many learned men within the congregation and is set aside only by his full-time professionalism. The status distance existing between the layman and the rabbi is primarily a distance based upon professional training, personal prestige and occupational commitment. And yet, all branches of Judaism expect the rabbi as well as the layman to observe identical religious behavioral standards. All males are expected to perform the same religious exercises necessary to reach full manhood in the faith. The ideal of Jewish religious life is best summarized in the words of the prophet Micah: "What does the Lord require of you but to do justice, and to love kindness, and to walk humbly with your God?"

SEVERAL CHARACTERISTICS of the Jewish religion in terms of church and laity require analysis in order to establish a framework for a discussion of the contemporary American synagogue. Of prime importance is the ethnic stress of the Jewish religion, resulting in the fact that Judaism represents a type of ethnic church. Membership in the Jewish religion overlaps with membership in the Jewish community. The fact of birth entitles the individual to membership in the religious community. Furthermore, the definition of Jewish religious law—he is Jewish whose mother is Jewish—is reinforced by both Jewish and Gentile public opinion. In the United States only a small segment of ultra-Reform Jews and a group of Jewish converts to Christianity have seriously suggested splitting the atom of ethnicity-religion in Judaism.

The results of this articulation of religion and ethnicity include the fact that there can be no strong division in Judaism such as exists in other religions between the "saved" and the "damned," between those who have "confessed" and those who have not done so, between those who have accepted the "truth" and those who live in error. All Jews may claim equal membership in the Jewish "church."

Nevertheless, several important distinctions are encountered in Judaism. One is the distinction between the learned and the ignorant. The students of the vast corpus of Jewish religious law are to be distinguished from those who remain in ignorance of all but its most simple stipulations and to whom its intricacies will remain unknown. The other distinction is between the pious and the nonobservant, between those who carry out ritualistic and moralistic requirements and those who neglect them.

The contrast between the learned and the ignorant has been obscured on the contemporary scene. The rise in secular learning, the changing character of Jewish scholarship, and the impact of non-Jewish religious traditions have severely attenuated this long standing distinction. The division between the observant and the nonobservant continues, though not in accordance with the rigid categories of yesterday. The contemporary distinction is generally between degrees of observance rather than between those whose observance is perfect and those whose observance is only partial.

To the Jewish layman the present-day rubrics of Orthodox, Conservative, and Reform are not always designations indicating denominational affiliation. Rather they may measure the degree of observance of the commandments—*mitzvoth*—of the Jewish sacred system. The individual may continue to observe *kashruth*—the laws relating to food—in the home but neglect them on the outside. Consequently he may no longer describe himself as an Orthodox Jew but rather as a Conservative Jew. Another comes to neglect *kashruth* both outside as well as inside the home; he no longer describes himself as a Conservative Jew but rather he feels that he is a Reform Jew.

While all three groups—Reform, Conservative, and Orthodox—are in the midst of elaborating an institutional structure which appears to be denominational in character, the articulation of religion and ethnicity in Judaism limits the impact of such elaborations. The fundamental distinction continues to be between Jews and Gentiles rather than between the three wings of American Judaism.

LAITY AND CLERGY.   It has been emphasized that the ethnic stress in Judaism results in both believer and nonbeliever holding equal membership in the Jewish church. We may now explore the distinction between laity and clergy. As elaborated in Judaism this distinction contrasts sharply with the dichotomy which is characteristic of many other religions. According to Jewish tradition, identical behavior is expected of the layman and the rabbi. Spiritual exercises and religious observances are equally incumbent upon all males. Furthermore, the areas where rabbinical intervention is required are few in number. All *rites de passage* can be celebrated, all holidays observed, all religious services held, all *mitzvoth* performed without rabbinical supervision. The traditional agenda of the rabbi does not include serving as a priest—a conductor of public worship; a preacher; a cleric—an official empowered by the state to perform certain ceremonies; a rector—an administrator of a religious institution or parish; or a pastor. No "call" is ordinarily heard by the fledgling rabbi.

The rabbinical office derives from a distinction suggested earlier, the gulf between the learned and the ignorant. All scholars are entitled to respect; the greatest masters of Jewish learning are qualified to serve as conservators and interpreters of the tradition. More exactly, the rabbinical degree entitles the holder to serve as the head of an academy of Jewish learning and as the president of a tribunal. He is thus a teacher and an adjudicator; he possesses a doctor of laws degree and a license to teach. Since the cultivation of learning is incumbent upon all, it is expected that some of the scholarly will pursue learning as an avocation and hence will not exercise rabbinical prerogatives. In contemporary Orthodox schools of higher learning—*yeshivoth*—it is still not assumed that all advanced students are aspirants for the office of rabbi. Reform and Conservative schools, however, are largely seminaries, that is, training institutions for religious professionals.

These changes serve as clues to the departure from traditional norms and hence to a growing distinctiveness between the functions of the layman and the rabbi. The addition of pastoral, priestly, clerical, and several other roles serves to transform the rabbi into a clergyman and the nonprofessional into a layman. The distinctiveness of the roles is hardened not only by general societal trends toward specialization but also by the sharp limitations of Jewish knowledge evidenced by lay persons; such limitations preclude their sharing in functions formerly reserved for nonprofessionals.

The institutionalization of differences in religious obligations between laity and clergy has not yet been achieved. Nevertheless in practice a wide distance between the level of religious observance of the rabbi and that of the layman is evident. This occurs in Reform, Conservatism, and Orthodoxy. In all three the difference in level of observance of *mitzvoth* between clergyman and layman tends to be substantial. There is a tendency to accept the difference as an appropriate one and to castigate as insincere the rabbi who is only as observant as the layman.

CONGREGATIONAL AFFILIATION. While membership in the household of Israel and in its religion is a hereditary right and obligation, membership in a congregation is an act of conscious affiliation. Such membership is characteristic of American Jewish life; in the European lands from which the ancestors of most American Jews came the individual did not affiliate with a congregation in the sense customary in the United States.

The typical American Jewish congregation is formed by local residents who join together to hold religious services and to establish a school for their children. They raise the funds necessary to build an edifice and to hire a professional staff. Generally the synagogue is organized in the form of a corporate body which holds periodic membership meetings at which the affairs of the institution are discussed, officers and board members elected, and contractual obligations with the rabbi and other professionals reviewed.

Membership in the congregation is open to all. There is generally no test of the applicant's religious attitudes or of the intensity of his religious observance. In many Reform or Conservative congregations the applicant is commonly sponsored by a member of the congregation or by one of the professional staff. Individuals who are financially irresponsible or who have an abhorrent moral reputation may thus be screened. There are a few Orthodox congregations which inquire into the applicant's level of observance; they restrict their roster to those whose behavior is in conformity with certain selected religious norms.

Motivations for affiliation are extremely varied, but the desire to give a Jewish education to one's children plays a leading role. Jewish religious schools are increasingly becoming institutions sponsored by individual congregations rather than independent entities. This is particularly the case in suburban areas. Some congregations make membership mandatory for enrollment while others adjust their tuition fees to provide a financial incentive for membership.

The desire to attend religious services on the High Holidays—*Roth Hashana* and *Yom Kippur*—is another leading motivation for congregational affiliation. Daily services, Sabbath services, and festival services are open to all, but on the High Holidays tickets are distributed only to members. In some instances tickets are sold to the public and members are afforded a reduction in fee. Most High Holiday services are conducted by congregations.

The desire of a considerable segment of the Jewish population for elementary Jewish education and for seats at High Holiday services, when combined with present institutional arrangements, assures many congregations of a sizeable membership roster and long-term fiscal stability. However, those who are motivated solely by the desire to have their children confirmed—*Bar Mitzvah, Bas Mitzvah,* or Confirmation—are poor prospects for long-term membership. They delay joining until the child is of elementary school age and may resign soon after the performance of the ceremony.

Membership dues provide the bulk of the income of most Reform and Conservative congregations. Where the practice is to allow each family two seats for the High Holidays, dues may average about $175 per year. New or expanding congregations will add building assessments. School fees may be additional.

Some Orthodox congregations are large institutions organized along the same lines as Reform and Conservative synagogues. Others place no emphasis on developing a membership roster; they derive the major portion of their income from High Holiday seats, from the auctioning and sale of synagogue honors, from individual solicitations, and from periodic appeals to worshipers. There are also instances of Orthodox synagogues which are not organized as corporate bodies. One example is the prayer houses of Chassidic groups. Here we encounter an instance in the Jewish community of sectarian rather than denominational behavior, for the adherent becomes a follower of a dynastic religious leader endowed with charismatic qualities rather than a voting member of a corporate body. The followers of the Chassidic leader, *rebbe,* elect no officers or board. The *rebbe,* and those designated by him, constitute the leadership.

CONGREGATIONAL PROGRAMS.   The traditional program of the synagogue was confined largely to religious worship and the use of its quarters for groups devoted to the study of various sacred texts. One important departure from this program, the development of elementary Jewish schools, has already been noted. Previously, *melamdim,* elementary-level teachers, formed their own schools, conducting classes in their place of residence or sometimes giving instruction in the homes of pupils. This system was still in use in immigrant areas; however, the *talmud torah,* or communal school, soon became popular. This was followed by the congregational school, presently the regnant form of elementary Jewish education.

The provision for religious services remains an important area of congregational functioning. Their frequency, duration, and character vary markedly, according to whether the congregation is Reform, Conservative, or Orthodox. There is also some variation within each of the three groups. Orthodox congregations generally hold services three times each day. (The daily prayers, however, can be recited at home as well as at synagogue.) Reform congregations, on the other hand, generally hold services only on the Sabbath.

Levels of attendance differ widely, but in most cases it is only on the High Holidays that the majority of the congregation attends any one service. Then the crowds strain the facilities and attendance is high regardless of the day of the week on which the Holidays fall. While a core of faithful daily or weekly worshipers is commonly encountered in all three groups, the typical member attends only a handful of services during the year in addition to those held on the High Holidays. The ten-man quorum necessary for holding a public service is present in most Orthodox and in many Conservative congregations daily.

Sisterhoods are found in all medium- and large-sized Reform and Conservative congregations, and in some Orthodox congregations. The prosperity of the sisterhood is indicative of the increasing importance of women in the functioning of American Jewish congregations. Women did not take part in the study circles of the traditional synagogue, and while they could attend the religious services they came as auditors rather than as full participants. At contemporary Reform religious services, however, the proportion of women is frequently higher than men and their participation in the service is extensive. The trend in Conservative congregations is more attenuated but still very noticeable. The election of women to congregational boards is now commonplace. It came about initially because of the importance of the sisterhood in the total program of the synagogue. Women sometimes serve as officers in Reform congregations.

The men's club is less successful than the sisterhood, but is nonetheless an important organization in Reform and Conservative congregations. Programs are less elaborate and frequently less serious in content than those of the sisterhood. Fund-raising is more casual.

While all adult females are invited to join the sisterhood and all adult males the men's club, several age-graded and specialized clubs are found in the well-organized congregation.[1] One of the most successful is the "couples club" composed of younger married persons. Another is the parent-teacher organization. Some congregations have "golden-age clubs" meeting on their premises, and some have organizations or hold entertainments for younger unmarried adults.

Programs of youth activity are sponsored in most Conservative and Reform congregations. Since only a small proportion of young people continue their Jewish education during the high school years, such groups serve as the only tie with the institution. Parents value the organizations for the recreational opportunities which they afford as well as for their indirect influence in discouraging dating across ethnic-religious lines.

A recent development is the growth of summer camping for children and youth. Camping previously was in private hands or under the sponsorship of secular Jewish organizations. During the past decade both the Reform and Conservative movements have developed a network of camps throughout the nation. Much less vigorous has been the development of adult retreats.

The recreational programs of individual congregations vary widely. Some, particularly in the East, maintain swimming pools and gymnasiums. Models for such developments were the settlement houses and the Jewish centers founded at the turn of the century in immigrant neighborhoods or in areas of second settlement. Many congregations now sponsor day camps during the summer months and nursery school programs during the school year.

ADULT STUDY.   The final aspect of the congregational program which requires review is the traditional one of serving as a center for the study by adults of Jewish sacred texts. This type of activity has been continued in many Orthodox synagogues although in attenuated form. For several decades many Reform and Conservative groups shifted their educational emphasis to public forums featuring nationally known speakers on general topics of current interest.

[1] See Arnold Jacob Wolf, "Experimental Synagogue in Suburbia," *Reconstructionist*, Volume 26, Number 7 (May 13, 1960), pp. 15-19.

In recent years such forums geared to attracting the widest possible audiences have been de-emphasized and in many institutions such courses dealing with textual study have sometimes been reinstituted in modernized versions. Current study programs are more likely to include Hebrew language courses, instruction in how to conduct various ceremonies in the home, instruction in the ritual of the synagogue, survey courses of various periods of Jewish history, and courses which deal with contemporary Jewish problems. While guest speakers are utilized, their topics are more closely geared to Jewish concerns. It is generally conceded that adult study is a frontier area with activity lagging behind the interest manifested in the congregation's recreational and associational program.

PHILANTHROPY. In the traditional synagogue funds were raised or donated for a wide variety of philanthropic purposes. With the growth of Jewish federations and welfare funds in the early decades of the century, fund-raising for local, national, and international Jewish needs became centralized; the larger fund-raising organizations made little use of the synagogue for their campaigns. Such organizations did not wish to limit their solicitation to synagogue members. They found, furthermore, that even affiliated persons gave in modest amounts when approached through the synagogue. One important reason for this result was that the focus of the activity of the individual was becoming more occupational than congregational. In a community of independent businessmen and free professionals, many of whom had close interpersonal contacts or a thorough knowledge of each other's affairs, an occupationally based campaign was feasible. This type of solicitation has been highly effective and is still the fundamental mode of organization for large campaigns.

There is, however, a trend toward returning to the older tradition of the utilization of the synagogue as an avenue for fund-raising efforts. The rise in synagogue affiliation makes a larger public available than formerly through congregational channels. The development of varied congregational programs has given the average member a stronger tie with the institution. The ability of the synagogue to evoke sizeable contributions for its own purposes and for "denominational" bodies has given the institution new stature in the eyes of fund-raising executives. All of this has resulted in greater utilization of the synagogue for solicitation for general Jewish causes. Congregations in the larger communities are asked to sponsor fund-raising dinners and commonly do so for selected campaigns. While a sizeable proportion of the largest donations announced at such dinners do not represent "plus giving," the donor having already been contacted through the trade division of the campaign, some additional money is raised through these affairs.

At the dinners for local, national, or international Jewish needs the sights are high. Most congregations also sponsor a variety of funds established for the receipt of small donations. These are given to mark a variety of occasions—

a birth or a birthday, an engagement or a marriage, the recovery from an illness, the death of a relative or a friend.

THE IMPACT OF THE SYNAGOGUE.   Because there are no studies which provide data on the changes which take place as a result of joining a congregation, it is difficult to give a valid account of the impact of the synagogue upon its membership. And because the impetus for joining is frequently the desire to provide a Jewish education for one's children with the attendant willingness to modify the Jewish atmosphere of the home to conform somewhat more closely with that of the religious school, it would be difficult to trace any changes which occur in the life pattern solely to the results of congregational affiliation.

Given Judaism's ethnic church character and the fact that all Jews are equal members in the household of Israel, were there even less secularism in the Jewish community than obtains at present we would expect few dramatic instances of religious transformation which motivate or follow upon congregational affiliation and involvement. Instances where a type of conversion experience has taken place are occasionally described in the press, but these generally have little connection with belonging to a congregation. The usual correlate of synagogue affiliation—even for the more seriously involved person —is the shift of the individual to a network of new interpersonal associations, to give him a somewhat richer insight into spiritual problems and Jewish values, and to confront him more directly with the problem of his observance of *mitzvoth.* Whatever changes in life pattern occur can frequently be traced not so much to a conventional conversion experience but to cooptation into the leadership and committee structure of the congregation with consequent exposure to and emulation of those who follow a pattern of life which is richer in Jewish content.

The operation of the modern congregation demands a variety of professional specialists. The newest is the executive director, an official who specializes in the administrative, fiscal, promotional, and building-maintenance problems of the congregation. But even with the addition of this manager the structure of the synagogue provides a variety of positions for the congregation member. Whether or not actual power is in the process of shifting from volunteer to professional, the tradition of lay control is well established. The table of organization calls for a sizeable number of committees, with some turnover in their personnel inevitable. Opportunities for workers thus are numerous. And there exists the possibility that the individuals will assimilate some of the ideal norms of the institution in whose behalf they labor. This process, however, occurs only in a limited number of cases. The available research points to the existence of a wide disparity between the norms preached from the pulpit and those established in creed and code, and the actual beliefs and pattern of life of the laity.

In Orthodoxy the model of required observance is clear but the model is less clear in Reform and Conservatism. The desire for a code of normative beliefs and practices has been articulated in the Reform movement. It has been claimed that unless religious standards are unambiguous and certain essentials required of every Reform Jew, the impact of the movement will necessarily be limited. Those who have had reservations about the promulgation of a code of normative beliefs and practices have questioned whether the very concept of a code, and any implication of sanctions, is not antagonistic to the central ideals of Reform Judaism. The diversity of practice among Reform Jews has prompted critics to ask whether a code might not multiply strife and defection rather than increase normative adherence. The critics have prevailed and "guides" rather than "codes" have been promulgated. The guides have been issued by individual rabbis rather than by authoritative Reform bodies.

The approach of the Conservative movement has been similar to that of the Reform. Although standards are less ambiguous, no substantial attempt has been made either to promulgate a code, to interfere with the freedom of the individual, or to penalize the nonconformist. One approach of the Conservative movement has been to stress standards of congregational rather than individual practice. Thus no inquiry is made into the observance of *kashruth* by synagogue members but the "Standards for Synagogue Practice" of the United Synagogue states that:

> Recognizing *kashruth* as another basic tenet of Judaism, congregations will take all steps necessary to insure proper observance of *kashruth* at all functions on the premises of the synagogue and at functions away from the synagogue which are held under their auspices.

Another approach of the Conservative movement has been to inaugurate campaigns aimed at increasing adherence to particular religious observances rather than calling for a generalized reawakening to all religious norms. Program materials and congregational aids are generally issued, but results have not been objectively measured. The most notable campaign has concerned observance of the Sabbath, a crucial aspect of the Jewish sacred system and one where the distance between religious norms and the life pattern of the laity has been exceedingly wide. The campaign publicity not only stressed the man-God relationship but also emphasized the social utility of Sabbath observance for, in this case, its contribution to improved mental health.

CONCLUDING REMARKS.   The successful institutional adaptation of the synagogue has been made on a variety of levels. The role of the rabbi has been redefined—new roles have been added and the older ones of judge and teacher have either lapsed or been reformulated. The synagogue member has become a layman. Modest demands are made upon him for religious observance and manifold opportunities are provided for participation in synagogue affairs. Religious education and recreation for the young are stressed as well as attractive leisure-time activities for the mature. The modern synagogue is conducted in a way which is in accord with the advancing class and status level of the Jewish community. Increasingly less emphasis is given to adherence to a deviant culture in addition to loyalty to religion. To the individual the existence and prosperity of the neighborhood congregation point to the promise of Jewish survival at a time when the acculturation process is sufficiently advanced to make it difficult to take such survival for granted.

The institutional growth of the synagogue movement since World War II has been exceedingly impressive. There has been some growth also in the Jewish community center movement. The centers are almost exclusively devoted to providing for the leisure-time activities of members of the Jewish community. They have group workers rather than rabbis for leaders, and they offer little systematic instruction in formal Jewish culture to the young. Although the center movement has expanded, the synagogue movement has expanded far more rapidly and seems to be more appealing within the Jewish community.

The prosperity of the synagogue is also impressive when congregational gains are compared with those made by Jewish organizations. Some associations—Zionist groups, for example—have declined. Other mass organizations, like the B'nai B'rith, have maintained their membership or made small gains. But the rate of growth even of the successful agencies does not compare with the gains made by Reform, Conservatism, and, to a lesser extent, Orthodoxy.

There is, then, a strong predilection among members of the Jewish group for synagogue affiliation in spite of considerable secularization and of consequent wide departures in attitudes and life patterns from religious norms. Such a predilection presents a challenge of considerable proportions for a religious institution: its very success may serve to mask its failure. Furthermore, the expansion of synagogues in contrast to the rate of growth of Jewish ethnic associations presents the synagogue with ever more grave responsibilities for determining the future character of Jewish life in America.

PART V

RELIGION AS A SOCIAL PROCESS

INTRODUCTION

A NY DISCUSSION of the function of religion as a social process assumes an answer to the question of whether religion initiates change or is itself changed by outside forces and influences. The two positions are not mutually exclusive, however, since both processes may be at work simultaneously. In the last two centuries this argument has been heated within both religious theology and sociological thought. Theology assumes that God is the cause and source of goodness. In this sense religion is viewed as an independent variable. Evil exists in the rejection of God, and, thereby, of goodness. The Judeo-Christian belief maintains that the Fall of Adam into sin in the Garden is illustrative of the current condition of men. Born in sin, men must repent and return to God. Although the means of return may vary (see Introduction, Article 30), God initiates the action in which men concur.

Social theorists, on the other hand, are unconcerned about the supernatural origin of causation. Because their focus is upon the measurable aspects of human behavior (see Introduction, Part I), they argue that life is composed of logical or illogical ideas and resultant actions. Although the idea of God may possess specific consequences to human behavior patterns, the action is carried out by men rather than through a supernatural intervention of the divine in daily history. The works of Karl Marx, Max Weber, and Richard Tawney argue this theoretical dilemma. Karl Marx believed that religion is used by the bourgeoisie to control the proletariat. Religion is the dependent variable, reliant upon economic factors for definition of purpose and survival. Rather than being the initiator of change, religion is the sanction which serves to institutionalize injustice. As long as religion is able to convince men that world suffering will be overcome in the life to come, those who define religion will maintain the power to manipulate the masses.

Max Weber challenged Marx's analysis in *The Protestant Ethic and the Spirit of Capitalism*. Rejecting the idea that religion is simply a dependent variable, Weber argued that the growth of capitalism was not possible without the rise of Protestantism and its ensuing new definitions of theology and religiosity (see Vernon, Article 4). Basing his argument upon the differential

283

participation of Roman Catholics and Protestants in the development of the capitalist system, Weber concludes that several aspects of Protestantism, especially the concepts of calling and asceticism, were instrumental in capitalism's growth. Underlying Weber's thesis is the idea that religion is an independent variable capable of initiating change within society. Richard Tawney presented a compromise alternative to the two views in stipulating that religion both acts to produce change and yet is acted upon by other forces in a society, serving both as a dependent and independent variable. Current evidence (see Glock, Article 7) supports this viewpoint. Modifying the economic determinist position of Marx and the historical analysis of Weber, Tawney maintained that religion is a product of culture and yet creates culture (see Introduction, Part II).

Because religion is practiced within a social context, it is subject to the same processes which operate socially for any group or institution. Religious groups generally begin as small bodies, potentially progressing from sect to denominational status (see Johnson, Article 11). As they grow in size, they become institutionalized. On the other hand, size may be influential in creating group factions and divisions. The separation (differentiation) of one group from the main body may result over issues of church mergers, membership requirements, or doctrinal and language changes (see Douglass, Article 13, and Shippey, Article 14).

In Part Five, four articles partially illustrate the function of Religion as a Social Process. Thomas O'Dea discusses the challenges of institutionalization to the religious group. Because the supernatural must be expressed in concrete forms, faith must be resolved in the form of practice. Allen and Mary Spitzer investigate the changes occurring when Roman Catholic belief is superimposed upon the native cult of the Montana Blackfeet. The accompanying changes and tensions result in a syncretistic religious expression which is both native and Roman Catholic. James Coleman discusses the functions of social conflict in society, tracing their origin to the organization of society and the nature of religion. Because of its inherent character, religious conflict will continue to exist in spite of efforts at unity and cooperation. Oliver Graebner studies the response of Missouri Synod Lutheran pastors to the assassination of President Kennedy, a Roman Catholic. Historically suspicious of Roman Catholicism, member ministers show a wide variety of responses at a time of national mourning.

27 FIVE DILEMMAS IN THE INSTITUTIONALIZATION OF RELIGION

Thomas F. O'Dea

INTRODUCTION   In the process of *institutionalization*
groups progress from simple and informal associations to more complex and formal structures (*see* Introduction, Part III). The
growth of a sect to a denomination illustrates the process (*see*
Johnson, Article 11). Religious institutionalization is essentially
the attempt to develop that degree of religious permanence necessary to guarantee the continuity of the group and its beliefs. The
institutionalized religious group becomes increasingly formal, organized, influential within society, inclusive, authoritarian, distant
from original beliefs, and ecumenical.

The process of institutionalization, as suggested by Charles
Cooley, involves four basic and potentially overlapping stages of
development. During the period of *incipient organization,* persons
who will compose the later formal group are in a sympathetic state
of noncommitment. Gripped by some concern, feeling, or fear
which has not been satisfied, potential members coalesce into an
informally structured group for self-protection and mutual support.
As the group formally organizes, it begins to seek the stage of *efficiency,* in which the values of the group are more explicitly defined and realized. The early rudimentary organization is replaced
by a more formal structure. The tension and concern which
marked the period of incipient organization diminishes. The group
begins to make adjustments to survive over the long run. The stage
of *formalism* results when organizational structures, leadership
roles, religious ritual and belief, and ecclesiastical purpose are
rigidly defined and supported by a bureaucratic organization which

Abridged and reprinted from the *Journal for the Scientific Study of Religion,* Volume 1
(October, 1961), pp. 30-39, with the permission of the author and editors.

THOMAS F. O'DEA is Professor of Religion at Columbia University.

interprets the essentials of faith and belief to the layman. *Disorganization,* however, may result when the institution begins to disintegrate, losing its sense of purpose, organization, and even membership.

Institutionalization is not without its limitations. Thomas F. O'Dea, suggests that five dilemmas—mixed motivation, symbolism, administration, delimitation, and power—exist within the growth of the institution which are both its present source of strength and future source of disorganization. Because religion is supraempirical and yet expressed in practical forms, these dilemmas are characteristic of organized religion.

ALTHOUGH MUCH FRUITFUL research has been done in the sociology of religion the explicit formulation of an adequate conceptual scheme for observation and interpretation of data still leaves much work to be done. American thinking in this field in recent years has largely been in terms of what may be called a "functional" frame of reference. While helpful in the study of many aspects of religious life, the functional approach does not focus attention squarely upon the problems of the sociology of religion as such. Rather it raises two questions, important in their own right. First of all it concerns itself with what religion does for and to society, seeing religious institutions as one set of institutions among others, and interesting itself in the contribution of religious institutions and religious ideas to the maintenance of the ongoing equilibrium of the social system. In a more psychological, but still basically functional frame of reference, it also asks what is the contribution of religion to the preservation and achievement of adequate adaptation and stability for the individual personality.

The first question is not, of course, the sociology of religion in any but a peripheral sense. It is rather the sociology of total social systems, particularly concerned with the contribution of one institutional complex, in this case the religious, to the functioning of society. The second, while directing our understanding to important problems involving religion and stratification, religion and social disorganization, religion and social change, and the general area of problems involved in selfhood and identity, does not aim its sights squarely upon religious phenomena in their own right.

The functional approach sees the importance of religion in that religion gives answers to questions that arise at the point of ultimacy, at those points in human experience that go beyond the everyday attitude toward life with its penultimate norms and goals. The study of religion is an important part of the study of human society because men are cognitively capable of going to the "limit-situation," of proceeding through and transcending the conventional answers to the problem of meaning and of raising fundamental existential questions in terms of their human relevance. Such "breaking points" of routine experience often appear in the context of experienced uncertainty, of adversity and suffering, and in the frustrating but inevitable experience of the limitations of human finitude.[1]

Moreover, the ultimate tends to be apprehended in a special modality all its own. In terms of Durkheim and Otto, man experiences the "sacred" or "holy" as an irreducible category of existence that is drastically other than the ordinary prosaic workaday world.[2] From a functional point of view religion is important because it sustains life precisely at these breaking points. From the religious point of view, however, these breaking points are important precisely because they are the occasions of the experience out of which religion arises. Talcott Parsons years ago emphasized the importance in sociological study of taking the point of view of the participators in the social action studied.[3] Since religious institutions arise out of this experience of ultimacy and the sacred, the sociology of religion must begin with considerable empathy precisely at this point.

From the unusual religious experiences of unusual people the founded religions emerge, translating and transforming the insights of founders into institutional structures. Thus there arise the formed and formulated entities of belief-systems, systems of ritual and liturgy, and organization.[4] It is important therefore especially in the study of the founded religions to begin with a phenomenological analysis of the religious experience as such, for out of it emerge the chief dimensions of religious institutions as well as their chief functional problems. Here man is seen neither in terms of the Cartesian "I think, therefore I am" which was the model of 17th century thinking, nor of the "I do, therefore I am," of 19th century thought. Rather he is recognized as a being who is not a dichotomous compartmentalization of "adaptive" and "expressive" needs but one capable of and exhibiting holistic response and commitment to what he experiences as impinging upon his consciousness. It is indeed because man is primarily a responding animal and because his responses in interaction with those of his fellows become crystallized into stabilized expectations and allegiances, that contemporary sociology has proved its greater adequacy for the study of human action over the rationalistic conceptions of the past century. Yet modern sociological theory often reads as though it had not in fact superseded those older partial views of man.

Religion is first of all a response and a response is to something experienced. The religious response is a response to the ultimate and the sacred which are grasped as relevant to human life and its fundamental significance.

---

[1] See Talcott Parsons, "The Theoretical Development of the Sociology of Religion," Essays in sociological theory (New York: Free Press, 1959) pp. 194-211.
[2] Emile Durkheim, The Elementary Forms of Religious Life, translated by J. W. Swain (New York: Free Press, 1954), and Rudolf Otto, The Idea of the Holy, translated by J. W. Harvey (London: Oxford University Press, 1923).
[3] Talcott Parsons, The Structure of Social Action (New York: Free Press, 1949), passim.
[4] Joachim Wach, Sociology of Religion (Chicago: University of Chicago Press, 1944), chapter II.

While the religious response is indeed peripheral and residual to the day-to-day life of men and the penultimate ends of that life and related to them only as their ultimate ontological underpinning, it is central to the religious life. It is its constitutive element and out of it proceeds the process of the elaboration and standardization of religious institutions. Since such institutionalization involves the symbolic and organizational embodiment of the experience of the ultimate in less-than-ultimate forms and the concomitant embodiment of the sacred in profane structures, it involves in its very core a basic antinomy that gives rise to severe functional problems for the religious institution. In fact this profound heterogeneity at the center of religious institutionalization constitutes a severe and unavoidable dilemma from which problems arise for religious movements and institutions that recur again and again and can never be finally solved. Moreover, since the religious experience is spontaneous and creative and since institutionalization means precisely reducing these unpredictable elements to established and routine forms, the dilemma is one of great significance for the religious movement.

This view which concentrates upon religious phenomena makes possible an "internal functionalism" of religious institutions themselves since it concentrates attention upon the peculiarly religious problems or more precisely the specific problems of religious institutions qua *religious* institutions.

An institutional complex may be viewed as the concrete embodiment of a cultural theme in the ongoing life of a society, as the "reduction" of a set of attitudes and orientations to the expected and regularized behavior of men. These institutionalized expectations include definitions of statuses and roles, goals, and prescribed and permitted means, and they articulate with the culture of the society and with the personality structures that the socialization processes have produced in a given society.[5]

It is the great virtue of social institutions from the point of view of the functioning of social systems that they provide stability in a world of inconstancy. Yet the achievement of the necessary stability involves a price. It involves a certain loss of spontaneity and creativity, although these are often found operating in some measure within the expectations of institutional patterns.

The founded religions display this fundamental antinomy in their histories. They begin in "charismatic moments" and proceed in a direction of relative "routinization." This development necessary to give objective form to the religious movement and insure its continuity may in Weber's terms proceed either in a traditional or a rational-legal direction.[6] Such routinization is an unavoidable social process, and as such represents for religious institutions a many-sided and complex paradox. . . .

[5] *See* Talcott Parsons, *The Social System* (New York: Free Press, 1951).
[6] Max Weber, *The Theory of Social and Economic Organization*, translated by Talcott Parsons and A. M. Henderson (New York: Oxford University Press, 1947) pp. 363ff. Also, Max Weber, *Essays in Sociology*, translated by Hans Gerth and C. Wright Mills (New York: Oxford University Press, 1946), pp. 53, 54, 262ff., 297, 420.

In bringing together two radically heterogeneous elements, ultimacy and concrete social institutions, the sacred and the profane, this necessary institutionalization involves a fundamental tension in which five functional dilemmas take their origin.

In other words, religion both needs most and suffers most from institutionalization. The subtle, the unusual, the charismatic, the supraempirical must be given expression in tangible, ordinary, and empirical social forms. Let us now examine the five dilemmas which express this fundamental antinomy inherent in the relation of religion to normal social processes.

THE DILEMMA OF MIXED MOTIVATION. In the preinstitutionalized stage of a religious movement, the classical type of which is the circle of disciples gathered about a charismatic leader, the motivation of the followers is characterized by single-mindedness. The religious movement does satisfy complex needs for its adherents, but it focuses their satisfaction upon its values and their embodiment in the charismatic leader. The charismatic call receives a wholehearted response. With the emergence of a stable institutional matrix, there arises a structure of offices—of statuses and roles—capable of eliciting another kind of motivation, involving needs for prestige, expression of teaching and leadership abilities, drives for power, aesthetic needs, and the quite prosaic wish for the security of a respectable position in the professional structure of the society.

It is precisely because of its ability to mobilize self-interested as well as disinterested motivation behind institutionalized patterns that institutionalization contributes stability to human life. Yet if this mobilization of diverse motives is its great strength, it is paradoxically also its great weakness. It may in fact become the Achilles' heel of social institutions. The criteria of selection and promotion within the institutional structure must of necessity reflect the functional needs of the social organization and emphasize performance and therefore will not distinguish very finely between the two types of motivation involved. Thus it may develop that the self-interested motivation will come to prevail. There will then result a slow transformation of the original institutional aims, in many cases amounting to their corruption. When the institution so transformed is suddenly confronted by threat or crisis, the transformed motivation and outlook may reveal itself as impotence. Careerism that is only formally concerned with institutional goals, bureaucratic rigorism of a type that sacrifices institutional goals to the defense or pursuit of vested interests,[7] and official timidity and lethargy are some evidences of the transformation.

Such developments give rise to movements of protest and reform, ever recurring phenomena in the history of the founded religions. The Cluniac reform of the Middle Ages offers a striking example as does the Protestant Reformation of the 16th century.

[7] Robert K. Merton, *Social Theory and Social Structure* (New York: Free Press, 1957), especially "Social Structure and Anomie," pp. 131-160.

This dilemma of mixed motivation is found not only among those who occupy important positions in the religious organization. It is also characteristic of changes in the composition of the membership with the passing of the charismatic movement and the founding generation. The passing of the founding generation means that the religious body now contains people who have not had the original conversion experience.

THE SYMBOLIC DILEMMA: Objectification Versus Alienation.   Man's response to the holy finds expression not only in community but also in acts of worship. Worship is the fundamental religious response but in order to survive its charismatic moment worship must become stabilized in established forms and procedures.[8] Thus ritual develops, presenting to the participant an objectified symbolic order of attitude and response to which he is to conform his own interior disposition. Worship becomes something not immediately derivative of individual needs, but rather an objective reality imposing its own patterns upon the participants.

Such objectification is an obvious prerequisite for common and continuous worship, for without it prayer would be individual and ephemeral. The symbolic elements of worship are not simply expressions of individual response, but have an autonomy enabling them to pattern individual response. Yet here too the element of dilemma appears. The process of objectification, which makes it possible for cult to be a genuine social and communal activity, can proceed so far that symbolic and ritual elements become cut off from the subjective experience of the participants. A system of religious liturgy may come to lose its resonance with the interior dispositions of the members of the religious body. In such a case the forms of worship become alienated from personal religiosity, and whereas previously cult had evoked and patterned response and molded personal religiosity after its own image,[9] now such an overextension of objectification leads to routinization. Liturgy then becomes a set of counters without symbolic impact upon the worshippers. It may of course retain its element of sacredness through the very fact of its obscurity and mystery, a situation conducive to the development of a semimagical or magical attitude.

What we have indicated with respect to cult could also be traced out with respect to graphical and musical expression as well. Here too, overextension of the objectification of symbols can turn them into counters, themes can degenerate into clichés, and at times symbols may become simply objectively manipulatable "things" to be used for achieving ends. In the last case religion becomes semimagic. Parallels can be made with verbal symbolism where the statements of important religious insights in words suffers routinization and

---

[8] See Louis Duchesne, *Christian Worship: Its Origin and Evolution* (New York: Gorham, 1904).

[9] See Dietrich von Hildebrand, *Liturgy and Personality* (New York: Longmans, 1943).

a consequent alienation from interior religiosity and deep understanding occurs. Profound statements then become merely facile formulae.

The alienation of symbolism is one of the most important religious developments and its possibility and likelihood derives from the fact that the religious symbol is in itself an antinomy—an expression *par excellence* of the dilemma of institutionalizing religion.[10] To symbolize the transcendent is to take the inevitable risk of losing the contact with it. To embody the sacred in a vehicle is to run the risk of its secularization. Yet if religious life is to be shared and transmitted down the generations the attempt must be made.

THE DILEMMA OF ADMINISTRATIVE ORDER: Elaboration Versus Effectiveness. Max Weber showed that charismatic leadership soon undergoes a process of routinization into a traditional or rational-legal structure made up of a chief and an administrative staff. There is an elaboration and standardization of procedures and the emergence of statuses and roles within a complex of offices. One important aspect is the development in many cases of a distinction between the office and its incumbent, which has become characteristic of the bureaucratic structures of the modern world. The Catholic Church has been the chief prototype in this evolution of the concept of office in European society.

It is characteristic of bureaucratic structure to elaborate new offices and new networks of communication and command in the face of new problems. Precedents are established which lead to the precipitation of new rules and procedures. One result may indeed be that the structure tends to complicate itself. This state of affairs evolves in order to cope with new situations and new problems effectively. Yet such self-complication can overextend itself and produce an unwieldy organization with blocks and breakdowns in communication, overlapping of spheres of competence, and ambiguous definitions of authority and related functions. In short, developments to meet functional needs can become dysfunctional in later situations.

This dilemma of the necessity of developing a system of administrative order versus the danger of its overelaboration must be seen in relation to the first dilemma—that of mixed motivation. For the involvement of secondary motivation in bureaucratic vested interests complicates this third dilemma considerably. Genuine organizational reform becomes threatening to the status, security and self-validation of the encumbents of office. The failure of many attempts at religious and ecclesiastical reform in the 14th and 15th centuries is significantly related to this third dilemma and its combination with the first.

Certainly such self-complication of procedures and offices is one of the elements involved in Arnold J. Toynbee's observation that an elite seldom solves two major problems challenging its leadership, for successful solution of the first transforms and incapacitates it for meeting the second.

[10] *See* Mircea Eliade, *Comparative Patterns of Religion* (New York: Sneed, 1958).

THE DILEMMA OF DELIMITATION: Concrete Definition Versus Substitution of Letter For Spirit.   In order to affect the lives of men, the import of a religious message must be translated into terms that have relevance with respect to the prosaic course of everyday life. This translation is first of all a process of concretization. It involves the application of the religious insight to the small and prosaic events of ordinary life as lived by quite ordinary people. In that process the religious ideas and ideals themselves may come to appear to be of limited prosaic significance. Concretization may result in finitizing the religious message itself. For example, ethical insights are translated into a set of rules. Since rules, however elaborate, cannot make explicit all that is implied in the original ethical epiphany, the process of evolving a set of rules becomes a process of delimiting the import of the original message. Translation becomes a betraying transformation. Moreover, the more elaborate the rules become in the attempt to meet real complexities and render a profound and many-sided ethic tangible and concrete, the greater the chance of transforming the original insight into a complicated set of legalistic formulae and the development of legalistic rigorism. Then, as St. Paul put it, the letter killeth but the spirit giveth life.

Yet the fact is that the ethical insight must be given some institutionalized concretization or it will remain forever beyond the grasp of the ordinary man. The high call of the ethical message may well, however, be reduced to petty conformity to rules in the process. Brahmanic developments of ritual piety, Pharisaic rituals in late classical Judaism and legalism in Catholicism offer three examples. This fourth dilemma may be compounded with the third and the over elaboration of administrative machinery be accompanied by a deadening legalism. It may also become compounded with the second and the delimitation of the religious and ethical message may contribute to and be affected by the loss of interior resonance of the verbal and other symbols involved.

THE DILEMMA OF POWER: Conversion Versus Coercion.   The religious experience exercises a call. In Otto's words, its content "shows itself as something uniquely attractive and *fascinating*."[11] Moreover, the propagation of the religious message in Christianity has involved an invitation to interior change. This interior "turning" or "conversion" is the classical beginning of the religious life for the individual. With institutionalization of the religious movement, such a conversion may be replaced by the socialization of the young so that a slow process of education and training substitutes for the more dramatic conversion experience. Yet even in this case, the slower socialization in many instances serves as a propadeutic for conversion. Christians, both Catholic and Protestant, agree that the act of acceptance must be voluntary, involving such interior turning.

However, as religion becomes institutionalized it becomes a repository of

[11] Rudolf Otto, *op. cit.*, p. 31.

many of the values from which much of the life of the society derives its legitimation. Thus the preservance of religious beliefs and even the maintenance of the religious organization can come to be intertwined with societal problems of public order and political loyalty. This tends to become the case whether or not there is a legal separation of church and state.

In addition, since religion is dependent upon interior disposition and since that disposition is subject to numerous unexpected shocks and is always weak among those merely nominally religious, there is always the subtle temptation for religious leaders to avail themselves of the close relation between religion and cultural values in order to reinforce the position of religion itself. A society may find itself unable to tolerate religious dissent, since such dissent is seen as threatening the consensus upon which social solidarity rests. Religious leaders may be tempted to utilize the agencies of a society so disposed to reinforce the position of their own organization.

While such an interpenetration of religious adherence and political loyalty may strengthen the position of religion in the society, it may also weaken it in important respects. It may antagonize members of the religious body who are political oppositionists, and it may antagonize political oppositionists who otherwise might have remained religiously neutral. Second, it may produce an apparent religiosity beneath which lurks a devastating cynicism. History offers many examples of such a coalescing of religious and political interests. Punitive use of the secular arm, the later confessional states in both Catholic and Protestant countries with their "union of throne and altar," and the real though unofficial identification of Protestantism with American nationalism and even nationality in the 19th century offer some cases.

A genuine dilemma is involved. Religion cannot but relate itself to the other institutions of society since religious values must be worked out to have some relation to the other values of a particular cultural complex. Since religion is concerned with ultimate values which legitimate other values and institutions, a relation with established authority and power structures is unavoidable. Such partial identification of basic values in religion and culture tends to strengthen both religious conformity and political loyalty. Yet with the progressive differentiation of society, the confusion of the two soon tends to be detrimental to both. It weakens the bonds of the religious community by weakening voluntary adherence and thereby diluting the religious ethos and substituting external pressures for inner conviction. It weakens the general society by narrowing the possibility of consensus among the population by insisting on a far greater area of value agreement than would in fact be necessary to the continued life of society. Yet some relation between the functionally necessary values in a society and the ultimate sanction of religion is necessary and it necessarily involves a relation between religious institutions and power and authority structures.

These five dilemmas represent five sides of the central dilemma involved in the institutionalization of religion, a dilemma which involves transforming the religious experience to render it continuously available to the mass of men and to provide for it a stable institutionalized context. The nature of the religious experience tends to be in conflict with the requisites and characteristics of the institutionalization process and the resultant social institutions. From this incompatibility there derive the special problems of the functioning of religious institutions delineated in this paper. Some of these antinomies have their analogues in other social institutions. Yet there is reason to suspect that because of the unique character of the religious experience, its elements of incompatibility with institutionalization are more exaggerated than is the case with other areas of human activity. Yet *mutatis mutandis* these dilemmas are applicable to other institutions as well.

28 RELIGIOUS REORGANIZATION AMONG THE MONTANA BLACKFEET

Allen Spitzer   Mary L. Spitzer

INTRODUCTION   In his textbook on *The Sociology of Religion* Thomas Hoult suggests that "most institutionalized aspects of human life, including religion, are basically specialized expressions of underlying cultural norms and social relationships." Therefore, he argues that in a less complex society, indigenous and acculturated institutions tend to be mutually compatible. Because society is marked by a "strain toward consistency," constant pressure to uniformity results. The strain toward religious and cultural consistency, and its results, are under examination in this article by Allen and Mary Spitzer. Note the manner in which past and present religious forms and practices differ among the Montana Blackfeet. Notice the syncretism (combination of different forms and practices) in religion which results as a second religious expression is merged with the first. The Roman Catholic Church has been most successful historically in adapting the faith to the religious expression of a subcultural group. Stressing the essentials, but allowing for differences in nonessentials, Roman Catholicism has productively gained converts from non-Christian religions.

The process by which group members change religious self-identifications has been best described by Glenn Vernon. Becoming *dissatisfied with the older identification,* or at least feeling it to be out of date, the individual begins to *associate with members of other religious groups.* Among the Montana Blackfeet, both Roman Catholic and Protestant groups are represented. New religious ideas, beliefs, practices, and physical symbols are introduced

Abridged and reprinted from *The Review of Religious Research,* Volume 2, Number 1, Copyrighted 1960, by the Religious Research Association, Inc.

ALLEN SPITZER is Professor of Anthropology at St. Louis University. MARY SPITZER is currently associated with Catholic Charities of St. Louis.

to the person. *New religious definitions become increasingly acceptable,* although full acceptance of new teaching may not result. As conversion continues, doubts are replaced with the certainty that the new way is the right way, although personal insecurity may lead the person to maintain dual religious observances. In the case of the Montana Blackfeet duality of religious expression is most common among the aged. As the *new self-definitions are accepted,* the individual learns to identify fully with the new group. At this point the new convert will often show greater zeal in the faith than his fellow members in the attempt to prove his allegiance to his new peers. As the *new group accepts the new convert,* contacts with the old group may be terminated and full integration of the convert into the group accomplished. At this stage religious assimilation becomes a reality.

WHEN ONE RELIGIOUS STRUCTURE is superimposed upon another and older religious structure, a reorganization of religious expression occurs. There is a tendency for the symbols of earlier beliefs to grow through the overlay of new concepts, resulting in a syncretic fusion of what are regarded to be the absolutes in both systems, which may or may not be in conflict.

When a religion is thus superimposed upon an already existing cultural system, the recipient will make that religion play a vital role in terms of his indigenous value system, although this occurs in a process of social and cultural change.

STATEMENT OF THEORY AND HYPOTHESIS. The authors' work along these lines was indicated in the culturally Catholic village of Tepoztlan in southern Mexico, and in the Peninsula of Yucatan. Arbitrarily assuming the religious culture to be Catholic, a typology in the form of a continuum was distinguished, in which this structure was analyzed in terms of formal, nominal, cultural, and folk Catholicism. These studies were made in areas where the Spanish influence came into contact with either the Aztec or the Mayan culture at the time of the Conquest.

Pursuing the same typology, a study was then made of an American Indian tribe—the Montana Blackfeet—which is estimated to be 88 percent Catholic, where there is some Protestant influence at present, and where the original impact of Christianity developed under circumstances which were different from those which obtained in Latin America.

Three generations ago, the Southern Piegan, to whom we shall refer in this paper by their legal title, the Montana Blackfeet, began embracing Christianity as a result of their contact with Jesuit missioners. Old Ignace Lamoose, an elderly Iroquois, who had learned of Christianity at the Jesuit Mission of

Caughnawaga, near Montreal, migrated with a small group of Indians westward from the St. Lawrence Valley and settled, prior to 1830, among the Flathead Indians, who were neighbors of the Blackfeet. At his encouragement, the Flatheads sponsored delegations to the Jesuit headquarters in St. Louis in 1835, 1837, and 1839, to ask for a missionary. Among the reasons why the Blackfeet wanted Christianity was the belief that this new religion contained medicine which would give the tribe power over neighboring enemies.

In checking statistics from a variety of sources, it was reckoned that some 88 percent of the Blackfeet adhere to Catholicism, and that the remaining 12 percent belong to one of the several Protestant denominations found on the reservation. There are some tribal members who are sophisticated, practicing Catholics, and these are designated as formal Catholics. Large numbers of tribal members are what we term nominal Catholics and surely do not in general practice fully the proscriptions of their faith.

There are, to be sure, a number of Catholic practices which significantly resemble religious ceremonies of the Indians' forefathers, such as the ritual consumption of the sacred buffalo tongue during the Sun Dance, and a form of public confession which preceded this act. To a formal Catholic, these are but interesting similarities which are not to be taken seriously. There are others, particularly among the less acculturated Blackfeet, who cling to Indian religious concepts and ceremonies while thinking of themselves as being Catholic, and in some sense fulfilling certain obligations of formal Catholicism. These Indians we designate as folk Catholics. Folk Catholicism is a reality among the Blackfeet. In this paper we shall endeavor to illustrate some of these folk aspects within the Catholic framework.

DESCRIPTION OF THE PARISHES AS NATURAL AREAS.   The Blackfeet Indian Reservation in the northwestern part of Montana is an area of roughly rectangular shape comprising over a million and a half acres located along the eastern slope of the Rocky Mountains and reaching to the Canadian border. The Great Northern Railroad, which bisects the reservation from east to west, is the line which divides this region into two quadrangular areas which constitute the two parishes. The center of the numerically larger parish is in the town of Browning, which is also the site of the Federal Government Agency. This parish maintains missions where Mass is said regularly in recently constructed chapels which are strategically situated.

The other parish is centered in Heart Butte, a largely fullblood community about thirty-two miles south of Browning. Mission stations are maintained at three points within a radius of about fifteen miles from Heart Butte, including the communities of Mad-Plume, Swims-Under, and the Holy Family Mission. Both parishes are under the direction of the Bishop of Helena. The pastor in Browning is a Canadian diocesan priest, invited over five years ago to serve in this community. The pastor at Heart Butte is a Jesuit priest, whose services were continued by a special arrangement with the diocese after the

Holy Family Mission was officially closed by the Jesuit Order in 1940. He has been with the Blackfeet continuously for over twenty-five years. According to the official estimates of the pastor, the Browning parish numbers about 2,800 Indians and 700 whites. These all dwell north of the railroad.

Large numbers of Indians who may be considered nominal Catholics are accustomed from early missionary times to attendance at Mass only on the great feasts of Christmas and Easter. The older Indians are considered by their peers to be practicing Catholics if they attend Mass at these times only, since this was a part of their experience at a time when there were no priests to say Mass regularly on Sundays and on other holy days.

Some thirty-two miles south of Browning, in the small fullblood hamlet of Heart Butte, is St. Anne's Church, which is the center of the other parish on the reservation. One hundred thirteen families live in the vicinity, although the total number of Indians living in the parish is estimated at between 1,500 and 1,600 of whom about 99 percent are baptized Catholics. According to the pastor, about 40 percent of this number are "practicing" Catholics.

The population for the two parishes, as estimated by the pastors, is 4,400. In 1958, the official estimate of the total number of Indians living on the reservation was 4,957, according to the government agent. In addition to these people, some 2,437 Blackfeet live away from the reservation, making a total of 7,394 Indians officially recognized as members of the tribe.

REORGANIZATION OF RELIGIOUS VALUES.   Early Blackfeet religious beliefs are similar to those of other Plains Indians but have their distinctive characteristics. Napi, the Old Man, was believed to be the creator of the world and all living things. After making the world and all the animals, he made himself a wife, who helped him design people. After teaching them all that they needed to know so as to be able to survive, he climbed a high mountain and disappeared. Although Napi is regarded with respect, he is also considered as something of a scamp, and many stories about his antics are still repeated with great merriment. Belief in the existence of supernatural powers was seriously held by the Blackfeet, who regarded these powers as residing on land, in the skies, and in the waters. Assistance in any important undertaking was sought from supernatural forces, as well as protection from enemies and other harmful or evil influences. Land spirits were believed to be resident in such animals and birds of the area as buffalo, bear, and eagles. The most potent sky spirits were thunder and sun, while otter and beaver represented the underwater spirits. Appeals were made to the powers of the sky, earth, and water to "have pity" on the supplicant, and to give him "some of its power."

A person seeking supernatural power usually withdrew to a quiet place, away from human activity, and spent several days and nights in prayer and fasting, during which time repeated appeals were made to the Sun, the Above People, Napi, the Earth People, and the Underwater People. The supplicant would eventually have a dream in which some animal or bird appeared and talked with him, telling him what to do in order to receive and maintain the desired power. Sacred objects were shown to him, which he was to find or make, and which would then comprise his personal medicine bundle. The objects were regarded as symbols of the power, but if the bundle were lost or captured by an enemy, he who originally had received the power could remake the bundle and continue to exercise it throughout his life unless he relinquished it through formal transfer to another. A complex ritual, preceded by purification rites, and including ceremonial painting of the face and body, with dances and songs, was necessary for the transference of such a bundle.

The Blackfeet believed in the survival of the soul after death, in an existence similar to earthly life. Although they were invisible to the living, the dead were thought to communicate with them.

Before their contact with the "blackrobes," the Blackfeet had not differentiated religion from the rest of their society; hence theirs was a sacred society. As contact with the white man developed, and the acculturation process evolved, there remained this persistence to retain the remnants of the sacred society as exemplified in the fusion of Indian and Catholic religious ideas.

Questions formulated in the minds of the investigators were shaped to distinguish among these variations which appeared to be on the continuum from formal to folk Catholicism. They were put to the informants according to their understanding, but may be briefly stated here in general terms. (1) About how many Blackfeet would you say fully practice the Catholic faith? (2) How many Indians do you think have a strong belief in the Catholic faith but do not practice it? (3) Do you think that some Indians do not really believe in the Catholic faith or try to practice it but see Catholicism as something good or beneficial, socially and culturally? (4) Do you think that there are Indians who combine some Catholic practices with the ancient religious practices of the Blackfeet prior to contact with Christianity? Responses to these inquiries threw light on the position of religion in the societal structure.

In the sacred society, religion is a part of the whole of life and is not compartmentalized. This was the form of society which existed among the Blackfeet prior to their contact with the white man and his religion. On the reservation today, however, religion is compartmentalized, and the form of the society is now secular. The old Indian religion had features which have managed to survive, and these are still acceptable because they stem from an all-inclusive conception of religion. In formal Catholicism, as in the lives of those defined as saints, this might likewise be true. Inside of Catholicism, which thinks of itself as the "true" religion, there is differentiation, but, because Catholicism is universal in its avowed conception, it can and does include borrowings from the all-inclusive concept of the sacred society. Thus, while folk Catholicism contains some seemingly "pagan" elements, it is a part of Catholicism by the nature of that religion. This is true in the anthropological sense, although there are degrees of sophistication in a theological sense.

The Blackfeet mentality does not dichotomize between two religions, since, if his society were sacred and his concept of religion were not compartmentalized, he would not identify the old religion as a separate thing but rather assume it to be part of his culture organization. Also, his Indian religion and his Catholicism may be studied under the typology of cultural Catholicism since there is an element of cultural retention in the preservation of his Indian ways. If he fuses the old Indian practices with Christianity, or if he has Catholic practices which are indigenous to his group, this would be folk Catholicism.

One illustration of the fusion of Catholic and Indian religious ideas was seen in the experience of an elderly full blood who had never been baptized. He became ill, suffered from visions (which were most likely hallucinations), and decided that he was being harassed by the Devil. He sent for a Catholic priest, who visited him and said some prayers with him. The ill man then asked to be baptized and received into the Catholic Church. After a period of instruction, his request was granted, and he attended Mass faithfully upon his recovery. When he saw children receive their First Communion, he was impressed, and requested instruction for the reception of this Sacrament. His entire life as a full blood had been devoted to Indian values, but surely his attraction for the new religion involved the cultural acceptance of that religion as part of his Indian and reservation life and experience.

Another example of such dualism was seen in the case of an aging and ailing full blood who has had considerable prestige as a representative of the ancient culture and tradition. When the pastor came to call, he found a large group of visitors. He offered the ill man a rosary, whereupon the patient produced one from his pocket, indicating that he always carried it with him. Others present were impressed and accepted rosaries when the priest offered them. It was later learned that, after the pastor's departure, the full blood led the entire group in the recitation of the rosary. The pastor commented that the Indians like to pretend that they are pagan. We would interpret the situation as a need to remain loyal to Indian ways.

In the matter of the Christian attitude toward sex, it would seem that Indian attitudes prevail. There is some difficulty in adjusting to the Christian mores. One notes considerable sexual laxity, and the prevailing norm is not entirely that endorsed by Christianity.

It is still the case that some values of Christianity and some Indian values come into conflict. Some of the Indian prayers are considered to be acceptable within the framework of Christian worship, but certain religious practices as later to be described in connection with the Sun Dance are not all Christian in content. A devout Catholic mother will not object to the ceremonial naming of her children according to Indian tradition, so that an infant baptized Catherine later receives the name Bird's Nest in a ceremony for which she is prepared by having her face painted in a certain manner. It is required that this ceremony take place out-of-doors, and a ritual including Indian prayers is followed. Here the religious connotation of the ceremony has given way to social significance. No one feels that there is any conflict between the Indian and Christian practices.

Another aspect of current reorganization may be seen in the increased attendance at church when something is to be given away. On Ash Wednesday, for example, when ashes are distributed and on Palm Sunday when palms are given to each worshipper, there are significantly large congregations. In Indian times, the idea of receiving something had supernatural importance, associated with the objects of the medicine bundle.

Many Blackfeet are "death-bed" Christians, sending for the priest and making their peace with God and the church at the end of their lives. Some simply do not practice their Catholicism although they maintain a cordial social relationship with the priest and value him as a member of the community who cares for the welfare of the Indian. A few who are only nominally Catholic can be expected to "come around later," says one pastor.

One of our informants gave an amusing illustration of the reorganization of religious values. She recalls her childhood experiences of attending an annual Indian encampment, during which there was the Sun Dance. Her mother, who was a full blood, took her into the sweat lodge, where their faces were painted by the man in charge of the ceremony. Throughout the week they and their friends and playmates followed the ritual faithfully. A few years later, after her mother had become Catholic, she remembers quarreling with her playmates and ending with the taunt, "Your mother still prays to the sun, and my mother prays to the true God."

DOCTRINAL ELEMENTS.   As indicated earlier, the idea of an obligation to attend Mass on Sunday is not strong with the older Indians even though they consider themselves to be practicing Catholics. They are attracted more to what the Church describes as sacramentals rather than to the Sacraments. Such spiritual aids as holy water, blessed candles, and the like play a stronger part in their lives than, let us say, going to confession or receiving Holy Communion. We think that this is an indication of the way in which Catholicism is something of an overlay on Indian religious practices, which emphasize medicine bundles and other paraphernalia. The older Indians are hard to instruct. Instruction attempts to produce an understanding of the fine points of doctrine and overt practices, such as the reception of the Sacraments.

There are some marriages among baptized Catholics which are not witnessed by the priest. Such unions keep those partners from receiving the Sacraments.

The practice of prayer is an important element in the Blackfeet concept of religion. Interviews with several informants emphasized that the Blackfeet originally prayed not merely to the sun but to the creator or power beyond the sun. Blackfeet prayers were translated for us on numerous occasions, indicating that the opening words were addressed to that power. For example, Juniper

Old Person, an elderly full blood known as a practicing Catholic, explained to us that when the "blackrobes" presented the doctrine of the Trinity, they sought to show that God the Father is this power beyond the sun. The second person of the Trinity is represented by the sun itself as proceeding from that power. The word Christ was seldom used, and there seemed to be no clear picture of the Incarnation or the concept of the Holy Spirit. Another mature full blood, Mrs. Mary Grounds, a practicing Catholic, possesses a medicine bundle. She obtained this during World War II to assure the safe return of one of her sons. We inquired if we might see the contents of the bundle but were told that it could be opened only with proper ceremony and for a valid reason. Although her position may appear to be inconsistent, she sees no conflict between her adherence to Christianity and holding the medicine bundle to be sacred.

Many of the full bloods still take a walk at sunset and say their prayers in the Blackfeet language. They see no conflict at all in the fusion of Catholic with Indian prayers. It is only the acculturated mixed bloods who have a clear conception of what is formal in Christianity and what remains Indian in content.

In Heart Butte the priest handed out a litany of prayers to Mary, Queen of the Sun, which seems to be a way of coping with a Blackfeet concept in Christian terms.

THE SUN DANCE.   The ceremonial pattern of the Blackfeet medicine bundle appears to have been woven into the tribal Sun Dance, which, by the time the "blackrobes" came among them, was the major religious festival, observed annually during a midsummer encampment. The leading role was that of the medicine woman, who might be any woman of the tribe who had lived a virtuous life, being at all times faithful to her husband. At some time during the previous year, in a moment of crisis, such an exemplary woman vowed to the sun that, if her petition were granted, she would in return make the personal sacrifice of being medicine woman at the Sun Dance. This was a public ceremony in which the entire tribe usually participated in varying ways, such as in construction of the medicine lodge, the performance of special dances, and the partaking of the sacred buffalo tongues. Fasting, prayer, and purification took place prior to the Dance. In the erection of the medicine lodge, a rudimentary form of the cross was used prior to the Indians' contact with the "blackrobes." The Blackfeet medicine woman and her helpers, both men and women, were known for their good lives and their purity.

It cannot be said that the Blackfeet no longer want the Sun Dance. There is, however, the substitution of a kind of pan-Indian festivity called Indian Days, entirely social, in which anyone may participate. This compromise seeks to preserve the social values of the Sun Dance without its religious implications.

MEDICINE AND RELIGION. Closely related to the religious beliefs of the Blackfeet are those involving medical practices. The two concepts are so intertwined that attempts at medical cure originate in religious practices. While a child is being given medical care in a modern government hospital, his elderly full blood relatives may come together for a Holy Smoke Ceremony. In this ritual, which usually lasts throughout the night at the home of one who owns a medicine bundle, both men and women participate. Here there are ritual singing, prayer, ceremonial smoking, and the making of an offering for the cure of the ill one. There is little doubt that the Blackfeet believe in the efficacy of this ceremony. The authors feel that it is religious and that it also brings out a basic concept found in many religions. For example, proof of more than one miraculous cure is associated with the canonization of a saint.

It may also be pointed out that the Blackfeet depend upon their knowledge of local roots and herbs for medicinal purposes, as do most other Indian tribes. The Indians claim that many white people living on the reservation have faith in these Indian medicines. It is well known that many drugs currently used had their origins in the wisdom of the medicine men of various Indian tribes.

The primitive relationship between religion and medicine is still a part of Blackfeet life. However, one might distinguish between medical superstition and religious superstition. Each might be mistaken for the other among the older Blackfeet today.

SUMMARY AND CONCLUSION. To summarize the foregoing observations, it may be said that the people of Browning have some problems which are similar to those found in the Heart Butte parish. There is more religious mobility, however, in the Browning area. From a theological point of view, it seems that the Blackfeet as a group have not as yet achieved a mature Catholicism. There is a range from deep faith, through superficial allegiance, to a combination of sacred and folk elements, some Indian, some Catholic, which forms an institution inclusive within the Catholic framework. Some representatives of the Church maintain that the old religion is just a facade. This is usually argued on the basis of the widespread Catholic heritage and the fact that, when an older Indian is ill or dying, he will send for the priest. We see this, however, not so much as a facade as, rather, an expression of a need, partly social, and in some ways reminiscent of the pan-Indianism of this day, not to cut loose from the old ways, the Indian ways, in short, the culture of the past. It would appear that, despite the activity of formal Catholicism, the need for the past and the resurrection of Indian practices from time to time have deeper roots than the concept of a facade would indicate.

The difficulties for the tribe are numerous. There is heavy drinking among the Blackfeet, perhaps no worse than in prohibition and bootleg days, but surely more public and possibly involving more young people. There is little church activity in terms of leisure time and recreational opportunities. Many Indians marry outside the Church, and many have had their marriages (if successful) subsequently blessed by the Church, since, worldly-wise, they often wish to see if their marriages will work. There may be a correlation between excessive drinking and civil marriage. There are certainly many conflicts.

A rounded picture indicates that the tribe is in the midst of a process of religious reorganization. The older full bloods, although nominally Catholic, have strong leanings toward the Indian ways of the past, which are religious and sacred and yet in the current situation may have a strong social character. The Catholicism to which a majority of the Blackfeet adhere is something of an overlay, set on top of the Indian religion, making strides through similarities, although historically having proven to be malleable insofar as doctrinal exposition is concerned. Protestant denominations have attracted a number of the Indians, but there seems to be some movement back and forth between the two Christian ideologies. From the viewpoint of Christian leaders, the Blackfeet are considered to be a largely Catholic tribe, although this has one set of implications from the viewpoint of apologetics and another from that of anthropological definition.

There is some official rejection by the pastors regarding the participation in the Sun Dance, but the sentiment for the tradition has not disappeared.

Religious reorganization involves stress as well as change. The strides made by the Montana Blackfeet are in no small measure the result of the competent leadership provided by the Christian churches, together with the innate capacities and genuineness of the people themselves.

29 SOCIAL CLEAVAGE AND RELIGIOUS CONFLICT

James S. Coleman

INTRODUCTION   Although religious groups tend to progress from simple and informal groupings to more formal and complex structures (*see* O'Dea, Article 28), the larger structures may in turn separate into a series of smaller groups. *Differentiation* results as conflicting values and social changes produce social adjustments to new situations. The emergence of Reformed Judaism as an attempt to Americanize Orthodox and Conservative Judaism illustrates this process. Whereas Protestantism has had a tendency throughout history to separate into sects based upon new or forgotten emphases within religious faith and tradition, Roman Catholicism has been more successful in maintaining a unity of diverse religious groups (orders, schools of theology, nationalities). The emergence of Methodism from the structure of the Church of England was due in part to the middle and upper class orientation of the Anglican Church. The development of Christian Science from Protestantism centered in the reemphasis upon healing by faith. The current "glossolalia" movement (speaking in tongues) has been the attempt to recapture the faith of the Christian Pentecost.

Some time ago H. Richard Niebuhr observed that many of the religious denominations in America had resulted from earlier socioreligious conflicts which had been transported to the United States by immigrants. The results of these conflicts still stand. Although Vatican Council II has set a new theme in Protestant-Roman Catholic relations, the suspicions engendered by centuries of social cleavage and distrust have been hard to put to rest. The

Abridged and reprinted from the *Journal of Social Issues*, Volume 12 (1956), pp. 44-56, with the permission of the author and editors.

JAMES S. COLEMAN is Professor of Social Relations at Johns Hopkins University.

modern ecumenical movement (move toward unity and religious cooperation without organic union), however, has sought to replace religious conflict with positive interdenominational religious cooperation. The threat of modern atheism and nonsupernatural scientific humanism has forced religious groups to seek some type of religious accommodation (see Hammond, Article 9).

The ecumenical movement of the twentieth century has attempted to reverse eighteenth and nineteenth century trends towards religious differentiation through the development of such agencies as the National Council of Churches of Christ in the United States of America (NCC) and the World Council of Churches (WCC), federations of autonomous religious organizations. Developing from experimental efforts in Protestant missionary cooperation in the early 1900's, the attempts at accommodation have exerted a greater effect than originally anticipated. The continuing national and international dialogue among Roman Catholic, Jewish, Episcopalian, Lutheran, Congregational Christian, Methodist and other American churches has left its mark upon the current century. On the other hand, fundamentalist groups have countered by establishing the American or International Council of Churches (ACC or ICC) and other competing conservative associations.

The persistence of antireligious ideologies has motivated religious cooperation, and, potentially, also the combination of smaller religious groupings into larger organizations. Whether these efforts will result in new denominational unions remains to be seen (see Glock and Stark, Article 49).

R ELIGIOUS CONFLICT CAN mean many things, and it is important at the outset to be clear just which of these meanings is under discussion. For one, there is conflict *between established religious groups,* such as may exist in a community controversy centered around two local churches. There is conflict *within* a religious group, which sometimes leads to the breaking off of a new sect from the main body. The number of Christian sects all stemming from a single source attests to the frequency of such conflict. And there is conflict *between religious groups and secular society.*

Keeping in mind that because of these and other variations religious conflict is no simple and unitary social phenomenon, it is the purpose of this paper to point out (a) some of the sources of social conflict which seem inherent in the organization of society; and (b) some of the sources peculiar to religious conflict which seem inherent in the nature of religion.

SOURCES OF SOCIAL CONFLICT

CONSENSUS AND CLEAVAGE IN SOCIETY. First of all, it is important to recognize that cleavage between groups is in many respects only the obverse of consensus within groups. When people feel strong identification with a particular group, whether it is national, religious, ethnic, or another, they are necessarily setting themselves off from persons not in the group.

Given that men do identify themselves with groups, given that there is high consensus within such groups, then cleavage is simply the other side of the coin. The analysis of social controversy, then, is not so much an analysis of *why* there is cleavage between groups, but a study of *which* groups are the foci of consensus and cleavage.[1]

Thus the interesting question becomes this one: What are the different consequences of the lines of cleavage in society running one way rather than another? What are the consequences, for example, of having the primary psychological attachments being to national groups rather than religious groups? Or to local communities rather than a national community? Or to race rather than social class?

In some simple cases these differing consequences are obvious. If the waves of immigrants to this country in the 19th century had not come with an initial and remarkably strong identification as "Americans," they could hardly have been assimilated. Much has been made of the evils of the melting pot concept of assimilation because of the debilitation of culture; and third-generation Americans often look with nostalgia at the cultural values their first- and second-generation parents have so eagerly shed. Yet if their parents had not shed these values, and had failed to make being "American" a major group identification, this country might have been little more than a battle-ground for different ethnic groups.

A second example makes even clearer the effect of configurations of attachment. Suppose that social class overrode race as a boundary between groups in the United States, as it does in some European countries. Then since class carries no ineradicable distinguishing marks as does race, a man could move from stratum to stratum in an anonymous society like ours. It would be impossible to classify a man irrevocably, as a Negro is classified by his skin color, and thus impossible to deny him the potentiality of society's highest rewards.

More generally, the consequences stem from this one question: When a crucial choice exists, when the issues are clear, then how are men going to line up: Which attachments are going to come to the fore and delineate the lines of cleavage? A man has many roles, and the crucial question is which of them dominates in a situation where they lead to different paths of action. The one underlying reason why interreligious conflict has been so important through the ages is that religious attachments have been among the most powerful men can feel. Only insofar as religion comes to play a lesser role in

[1] *See* Bernard Berelson, Paul F. Lazarsfeld, and William McPhee, *Voting* (Chicago: University of Chicago Press, 1954), for a discussion of areas of consensus and cleavage in politics, and the relation of political parties to lines of cleavage. *See also* James S. Coleman, *Community Conflict* (New York: Free Press, 1957), for a discussion of lines of cleavage in community controversies.

men's lives can the potential for religious conflict become weaker. This does not mean, of course, that the level of conflict between religious groups is fixed and invariant whenever the importance of religion in men's lives is fixed. Many other factors play a part; but insofar as religion is important to men, it constitutes the *potential* battle lines along which men may divide when conditions are right.

LINES OF CLEAVAGE AND LEVELS OF CONFLICT.   Perhaps the most important variable having to do with the location of lines of social cleavage is the level at which these lines crosscut society. By this I mean that major lines of cleavage may come *within* individuals or *between* individuals. If the lines of cleavage come within the individual, this is tantamount to saying that numerous roles are important to him, and that he will feel cross-pressure when faced with an issue—such as, for example, the issue of released time from public schools for religious instruction. The cross-pressured man is the man whose attachments lead him in both directions at once: to side with his religious beliefs, and to side with his attachments to secular public education.

The question is, what makes for or against cross-pressures? What brings the lines of cleavage within individuals or keeps them between individuals? The answer is simple: cross-pressures are absent when the major meaningful kinds of classification in society coincide. When such important lines of potential cleavage as ethnicity and religion and social status coincide, then there are few cross-pressures.

One of the reasons that Jews have been a major focal point of conflict is that there have seldom been cross-cutting lines of cleavage which tied various segments of them to other persons in society. Partly out of choice, partly out of necessity created by persecution, they have constituted not only a religious group, but a cultural group, an ethnic group, a particular economic stratum of society, and a group closely knit by associational bonds.

Group conflicts are at their strongest, are most likely to develop and least easily dissipated, when no conflict is felt within the person. This is one reason that conflicts between religious groups, as conflicts between national groups, have often been of considerable intensity. Members of a religious group feel little cross-pressure when faced with a conflict between their religious group and another. In contrast, conflicts between a religious group and the secular society comprised primarily of the same persons have been less strong. And least intense, in terms of the actual tactics of combat, has been the conflict within a religious group like the Catholic Church, resulting in the splitting off of fragmentary groups. It is only after a splinter group has irrevocably cut the bonds, so that such internal cross-pressures no longer exist, that these conflicts reach the intensity of interreligious conflicts.

When men are cross-pressured, they characteristically take one of several alternatives: they withdraw from the controversy, they delay taking sides, they attempt to keep others to whom they are attached out of the conflict, they maintain a low intensity of feeling toward either side.[2] But one response is to

[2] *See* Berelson, Lazarsfeld, and McPhee, *op. cit.*, chapter 13.

take one side or the other. When this occurs, as it does initially when the conflict is between men who feel no cross-pressures, then a whole new set of responses occur. Men attempt to influence others who are uncommitted, they break off attachments which are inconsistent with their position, they change from mere disagreement with the other side to direct antagonism toward it, they invent new and diverse issues with which to gain new adherents and reinforce their position. This set of responses closely corresponds to the well-known "runaway" or "explosive" nature of conflict.[3] When such responses exist among large numbers of people, that is, when large numbers of people are not at all cross-pressured, then the conflict takes on this explosive character, and can no longer be contained.

LINES OF CLEAVAGE AND THE SIZE OF MINORITY GROUPS. One area about which little is known is the effect of the *size* of a minority group on inter-group conflict. Yet there are certain regularities which await research. In the South today, one of the few generalizations arising from segregation controversies is the relation between proportion of Negroes and resistance to desegregation. The more Negroes, the more resistance by whites.

The history of religious restrictions in civil law in this country is also suggestive concerning the effects of minority size. When the colonies were religiously homogeneous without any organized minority in the earliest days, religious restrictions in civil laws were great, and religious conflict took the form of persecution. Yet from the early 19th century until the early 20th century, as religious diversity increased with immigration and mobility within the country, these restrictions were broken down.

However, since 1913, and despite some Supreme Court decisions, there has been a growth of local and state laws compelling Bible reading in the classroom, released time for religious instruction, and similar measures reaffiliating religious and secular education. The reason for this is obscure, but one possibility is this: minority religions, particularly the Catholic Church, which once opposed an affiliation of religion and education because this threatened their existence, have now become well-established and powerful enough so that, rather than being threatened by such an affiliation, they are aided by it. Thus the very minority religious groups which once opposed such measures now support them, merely as a consequence of a shift in size and security.

INTRINSIC SOURCES OF RELIGIOUS CONFLICT

THE PRIVATE NATURE OF RELIGIOUS EXPERIENCE. Much has been made by social scientists of the organized, institutional character of religion. But religious experience is also a mystical, private thing, a relation between a man and his God. Sometimes, as in Protestantism, this individual, private nature of religion is carried to the extreme. Yet Catholicism and Judaism, even with all their institutional aspects, have nearly as important a private meditative

[3] *See* Coleman, *op. cit.*, for a discussion of these responses in community controversy.

character as well. One consequence of this "communication with God" is that every man who so indulges is in communication with a different "person outside society," a person he has in part shaped with his own thoughts. That is, whenever a mystic or a monk or a devout believer engages in meditation and interpretation of the scripture, he can create a new creed. This possibility poses a constant threat of cleavage within a religious group. In an organized doctrinal religion, like Catholicism, this threat comes mainly from individual *interpretation* of the doctrine; in sects, it comes mainly from individual *communication* with the deity. But in both cases, the threat to religious unity arises from religion's private and personal character.

THE POWER AND STATUS FUNCTIONS OF RELIGIOUS LEADERSHIP.   Another source of cleavage within religious groups arises from the other half of religion's double nature as a private experience and a social institution. As a recognized organization in society, a religious group provides status and power for its leaders. Men feel the "call" to become a preacher, priest, or rabbi for a multitude of reasons; not the least of them is the status this leadership confers.

Here as elsewhere is apparent the curious combination of private and public, individual and social, which constitutes organized religion: it is much more appealing to an ambitious leader to strike out on his own, gathering his flock around him to nurture a new belief; yet a religious belief depends for survival on social acceptance and respect, which a new sect may never win. A religion ridiculed by everyone is no religion at all; and unless a group of followers reaches a "critical size" so that its members can effectively reassure one another in the face of ridicule, the infant sect cannot survive. The emphasis in religious creeds on adhering to the one true belief, and the sanctions applied to those who break away from the organization which purports to uphold this belief, are a strong deterrent to religious deviation. But even with such deterrents built into all religious creeds, there remains the attractiveness for an ambitious leader of leading his people in really new directions.

RELIGION AS A SOURCE OF ALTERNATIVE VALUES.   A further basis for religious conflict—this time conflict between religious and secular society, or between different religions—is perhaps even more fundamental, for it derives from the function which religion has always performed for poor, oppressed, or unhappy people. It was Karl Marx who pointed out that religion acted as an opiate of the masses to divert them from pure class consciousness and from their struggle for a classless society. This is simply another way of saying that religion serves a peculiar and important function for the oppressed and the poor in society: it provides them with a hope and belief that sometime, somewhere, there will be a different set of values by which status is derived, a set of values which will make them the "chosen people" or those who "inherit the earth."

It is easy to see the necessity for some such belief if a depressed person is to maintain his self-esteem, if in fact he is to maintain his personal equilibrium and continue to function in society. It is equally easy to see that the comfort provided by such beliefs may act as the "opiate" of which Marx spoke, for this very comfort lessens tensions which could otherwise be channeled into activity against economic oppression. But what is not so evident is the fact that this fundamental function of religion sets the stage for religious cleavage which may carry over into more general social conflict.

When religion tells the oppressed and burdened that *they* are the chosen people, or that *they* are among the select few who will pass through the gates of heaven, religion thereby gives them a release from the values of a society which locates them so low in the eyes of themselves and others. A belief in religion thus acts just as does a deviant political ideology in freeing men from the value constraints imposed by society. If they were forced to hold these accepted social values and no others, a psychological equilibrium would hardly be possible for the poor and oppressed. Religious values, in helping maintain such an equilibrium, also provide the possibility of cleavage, division, and ultimately conflict.

One of the most important derivatives of religion's "alternative-value" function is the establishment of strong ingroup feelings. Particularly if the group is small, such feelings are necessary if the group members are to maintain their alternative values in a hostile or indifferent environment; but in turn such feelings are further generated by these values, which emphasize the goodness of one's fellow-members. Each religious sect is, in a sense, a mutual admiration society.

Feelings of group identity of course help set the stage for conflict, as discussed earlier, for they establish a "we" and "they," and bring about an investment of the ego in the group. This ego-investment, in turn, means that all the defenses and needs of the ego are expanded to encompass the whole group. Whether a man is a Jehovah's Witness, a Jew, a Catholic, or a Presbyterian, a slight or insult to his religious group is a personal one, to be reacted to as a personal insult. It is obvious, then, that such group identification, derived in part from the alternative values which religion provides, creates a basis for conflict between religions or between a religious group and secular society.

THE GENESIS OF CLEAVAGE BY ASSOCIATION AND DISSOCIATION. One fundamental social process which plays an important role in conflict between religious groups is the genesis of disagreement through dissociation. Catholics associate with Catholics, Jews with Jews, and Protestants with Protestants. Now given that this is true, numerous consequences follow. The process through which dissociation leads to disagreement is one of the most important. Sociopsychological mechanisms come into play to create suspicion, hostility, and fear within each group that is socially isolated from another.

GENERATIONAL TRANSMISSION. Another source of religious conflict, obvious though it may be, is nevertheless distinct from those that have gone before. It is due to the fact that religion is usually a family matter, transmitted from generation to generation as part of a general cultural heritage. Thus religious differences are built into children at an early age, either as direct transmission of values, or indirectly through their effect on child-rearing practices. Such differences have a double effect in creating diversity paralleling religion: they provide different sets of *values* from a very early age; but even more fundamentally, they create different *personalities*. A Baptist mother, a Catholic mother, and a Jewish mother bring up their children quite differently. It could almost be predicted that these children would fail to understand each other as adults, when their personality structures as well as their values differ.

Parochial schools of course reinforce these potentialities for cleavage, for they maintain an environment for the child which shapes his whole perception of the world. An excellent indication of how these differences arise is provided by passages from three textbooks used in a small Dutch community in a Catholic school, a Calvinist school, and a Dutch Reform school:[4]

Catholic	Calvinist	Dutch Reform
Philip II was a religious sovereign. To him the Catholic cause was beyond anything else. In those days, apostasy was generally considered as a crime and had to be punished. Very many sovereigns did not bother about it too much. But Philip did. He was not too popular in the Netherlands. He was a proud Spaniard, and did not feel quite at home in the Netherlands.	Philip did not like the Dutchmen and the Dutchmen did not like him. He was a typical Spaniard: proud, ambitious, unfriendly, and a merciless persecutor of heretics. People understood quite well why the Spanish soldiers received orders to stay here. It was to wipe out heresy from the country, to rob the Dutchmen of their freedom, in the long run.	Philip II was by far not such a clever sovereign as his father. He was a typical Spaniard, and had nothing in common with the Dutchmen. He could not even understand their language. The purpose of his rule was as follows: the extirpation of the reformed religion in the Netherlands. Everybody had to become a Catholic!
The tensions and agitations in the country increased. Everywhere hedge-sermons were held; the preachers often used inflammatory words to incite rebellion.	These calm people who came to sing here in the fields and pray and listen to the old man who speaks to them from the Bible? These women and children? Oh no, this all seems to be so calm and weak. From these people there comes obviously no force, no redemption for the poor, suppressed country.	Suddenly a grave incident took place. In Flanders, the Calvinists revolted. They broke into the Catholic churches and smashed the statues and paintings to pieces, destroyed the altars and windows and stole what they could. There was naturally much scum among these bands. This riot, known as "iconoclasm" spread to Holland and Zeeland. There was a great tumult, throughout the country.

These passages treat the same historical events; yet they perceive these events in three quite different ways. With such differences "built into" children from the very beginning, the seeds of religious cleavage are well sown. It is no wonder that such cleavages regenerate themselves with each new generation.

SUMMARY

The major argument of the present paper has been this: the potential for social conflict exists by the very way in which people identify themselves with

[4] I. Gradourek, *A Dutch Community* (Leiden: Stenfert Kroese, 1956), pp. 545-7.

groups, forming lines of consensus and cleavage in society; but beyond this, the potential for religious conflict exists by virtue of the very functions which religion performs for people. For both these reasons, insofar as religion fulfills the same functions for people as it has in the past, it will be attended by intergroup diversity, conflict, and cleavage.

The sources of general social conflict examined were:

(a) Cleavage between groups exists in society as the simple obverse of consensus within groups. This means that the question for analysis is not *why* is there cleavage, but *what* are the lines of potential cleavage in society, and what are the consequences of one configuration rather than another.

(b) One important variation in patterns of consensus and cleavage is the degree to which lines of potential conflict are lodged *within* individuals rather than *between* individuals. If they are within, this creates internal cross-pressures, and as a consequence a set of responses which dampen and dissipate controversy. If they are between individuals, this creates a set of responses which amplify controversy and provide an explosive potential.

(c) The size of minority groups has an important effect on the potentialities for controversy in a number of ways. Both majority- and minority-group members act differently when the minority is not permanent, and a small one; but perhaps more important, an organization acts differently when it is secure and potentially dominant than when it is in a rigid and one-sided majority.

These factors affecting social conflict are supplemented by some attributes peculiar to religion, which create a potential for religious conflict:

(a) A major source of cleavage within religious groups is the private, personal nature of religion. Since any man can communicate with his own God or interpret the scriptures anew, a diverse array of beliefs can spring up, inhibited only by the fact that religious belief needs the company of at least a few if it is to survive.

(b) A second source of cleavage within religious groups, closely tied to the first, is the status and power rewards available to a leader by successfully establishing a new cult or sect. Given the private revelations which constitute the basis of religion, an ambitious leader has the possibility of breaking away and has much to gain from a successful break with the parent church (though, to be sure, much to lose if he fails).

(c) Religion's function of providing an *alternative set of values* creates a potential for conflict between religion and secular society. These values elevate in one's own eyes his religious group above its social position. Thus like a political ideology they provide the ferment for conflict by releasing members from the dominant values in society and providing an alternative set of values, and a group identity to go with them.

(d) Closely related to feelings of group identity is a pattern of *association*. Both induced by feelings of identity, and acting in turn to reinforce these feelings, the ingroup associations of religion determine lines of social interaction to a degree surpassed only by a few other groupings, such as race. Lack of association with other groups generates the familiar feelings of distrust, fear, and hostility between groups, and these are the stepping-stones to social conflict.

(e) A final source of religious diversity, cleavage, and conflict is the generational transmission of religious values and of personality derivative from these values. Thus the cultural heritage which is so much a part of us from early childhood has a high religious component.

30 PASTOR AND PEOPLE AT KENNEDY'S CASKET

Oliver E. Graebner

INTRODUCTION   As Bronislaw Malinowski and Emile
Durkheim have theorized, religious awareness to many of the faithful begins and ends in the recognition of the supernatural. Most
religions rest upon the belief that some form of future life will
reward those who uphold the tenets of religious faith, however
described and practiced. On the other hand, those who reject
supernatural dictates will be punished. Although such groups as
Reformed Judaism and Ethical Culture possess a minimal eschatology (study of life after death), most Christian theology is based
upon the recognition of the life to come. Eschatology offers the
hope for a new life free from the fallacies and weaknesses of the
old. The hope of future life is based upon the belief that righteousness will prevail in heaven, even if unfulfilled on earth.

Attitudes toward life after death are closely related to religious
attitudes toward the present world. If the religious group views the
world as a *place of justice,* and therefore basically good, concern
for eschatology may be secondary or nonexistent. Rational humanism, grounded in the belief that present action determines
whether justice or injustice will prevail, shows little concern with
the question of life after death. On the other hand, if the world is
interpreted as *essentially evil but subject to potential salvation,* the
concern for righteous living on earth and future rewards after
death are both held to be paramount. Most Christian groups,
Protestant and Roman Catholic, hold this view of the world and
the future of man. If the world is defined as a *place of evil and
suffering* as a third alternative, life in the world to come takes on
special meaning. Only through entrance into the world beyond

Abridged and reprinted from the *Review of Religious Research,* Volume 6, Number 2,
Copyright 1965, by the Religious Research Association, Inc.

OLIVER GRAEBNER is Professor of Psychology at Valparaiso University.

death can men be free of the injustice of the current life. Such an interpretation of the world is most commonly found in Hindu and Buddhist thought.

Generally, religion seeks to save men from sin. Although most religions agree that men can be saved, they differ in their delineation of the processes which will lead to salvation. Men may overcome world suffering, evil, and injustice through either *religious activity, religious faith,* or *right knowledge,* singly or in combination. When *religious activity* serves as the path to salvation, sacramental observances and acts of piety possess special importance. Where *religious faith* is the determinant, devotion and total commitment to the object of faith become central. If *right knowledge* is the key, mystical concern or, conversely, scientific truth, become foundational elements for religious salvation.

The Missouri Synod, one of the three largest and the most conservative branch of Lutheranism in America, defines the world as being *essentially evil but subject to salvation.* Members have been encouraged to seek salvation through *religious faith* in Jesus Christ. Although theologically conservative throughout its history, in recent decades the Missouri Synod has taken increasing recognition of the ecumenical movement (*see* Coleman, Article 29). Possessed by a historical distrust of Roman Catholicism, differential responses to the death of President John F. Kennedy could be anticipated. Through a content analysis of the special and weekly sermons preached by Missouri pastors, Oliver Graebner has succeeded in capturing the wide diversity of responses within one American religious group in the days following the assassination of the first Roman Catholic President in the United States. Even at a time of national mourning and shock the effects of social and religious cleavage left their mark.

WHAT WAS THE EFFECT of Kennedy's death upon the local religious leader, upon priest and pastor and rabbi, and upon their people? How did the churches respond in this emergency? What kinds of things did clergymen preach about, what were their sermon themes?

Burchard (1964)[1] reports in his study of 1244 staff members of a State university during the week following the funeral of President Kennedy that 95 percent reported that they had seen a memorial religious service on television, whereas 39 percent actually attended a "religious memorial service" at a local church or synagogue; 69 percent of the faculty had done so. In the National Opinion Research Survey (1964)[2] of the Kennedy weekend, the

[1] Waldo Burchard, "Reactions to the Assassination of President Kennedy—A Preliminary Report (1)," Unpublished paper, Northern Illinois University, DeKalb, Illinois, 1964.
[2] Paul B. Sheatsley and Jacob J. Feldman, "The Assassination of President Kennedy— A Preliminary Report on Public Reactions and Behavior," National Opinion Research Center, University of Chicago, February, 1964.

data indicate no marked change in church attendance following the death and burial of the President and the Gallup averages of 50 percent attending church on any given Sunday was probably maintained during the November 22-24th period, and during the Sundays to follow.

The present chapter presents the findings of a nationwide survey which purported to investigate what happened in Lutheran congregations during the weekend of the death and burial of President Kennedy. Due to the exigencies of the situation, the study was limited to one segment of the Lutheran Church, the Missouri Synod, which numbers 2,500,000 members, with approximately 4,400 active clergymen.

How, for instance, would a group of clergymen, trained in the Lutheran tradition, respond to the murder of a national figure, their President, who was Catholic and who was identified with leadership in the Democratic party? What kind of sermons would be preached and what would be done to recognize this great national tragedy? Would the general atmosphere of ecumenicity be reflected in any way?

THE LUTHERAN STUDY. During the week following the burial of John F. Kennedy a two-page questionnaire was mailed to 230 pastors of the Lutheran Church-Missouri Synod, distributed across the United States, Alaska and Hawaii, representing large and small congregations, in big cities, in medium and small, with and without parish schools, young as well as old congregations, and to a number of chaplains. *"What happened in Lutheran congregations during the weekend of the death and burial of President Kennedy?"*—was the title of the questionnaire, which included questions such as: "What were the sermon topics? How do you feel about the total weekend and its impact upon your people?"

The answers came in quickly from 25 of the most populated states in the Union. The composite picture is one of active involvement by the majority of pastors and congregations in a national tragedy; of deep concern for understanding the religious significance of a crisis; of bewilderment among some pastors and many people by the sudden tragedy; but also, a picture of cultural aloofness, of parochial isolation, of "Jeremiac dooming" on the part of a small number of clergymen.

To what extent has the Lutheran Church-Missouri Synod truly become a part of the American scene, become identified with life in these United States? After decades of struggle to become a distinctive church in America, to work through her own problems of theological position, of gaining recognition for work in certain spheres of religious activity, of overcoming the barriers of a foreign tongue, how did the Lutheran church meet crisis situations occasioned by the sudden death of other national leaders, such as Harding and Roosevelt?

As we reread the editorials upon the death of Harding and Roosevelt and then of Kennedy, there seems to be a progression over the past 40 years in which a church moves from standing *alongside* the culture in which the church is living and moving to a position *inside* the culture; the Church not so much standing in judgment and making pronouncements about the world about her, as being concerned with the problems which grow out of man's selfish nature.

Is there in the present survey of pastors the country-over a further indication of a growing social consciousness in the Missouri Synod?

THE SAMPLE.   One hundred and sixty-one questionnaires were returned (3.6 percent of the total active Missouri Synod clergy in the U.S.), which constituted 70 percent of the total number mailed out, for which the following tables give a distribution along several categories. These tables give survey data compared with data from the 1962 Statistical Yearbook,[3] the Lutheran Church-Missouri Synod.

TABLE 30-1
The sample of respondents.

142	Pastor of Congregations
12	Chaplains
161	Total = 3.6% of the Total Active Mo. Synod Pastors in the U. S.

TABLE 30-2
Survey responses by regions.

East Coast States	Mid- west States	Plains States	West Coast, Alaska Hawaii
20%	36%	30%	13%

It may be seen from the tables that the sample was geographically widespread, was typical in percentage of churches which have schools, and had a distribution in terms of size of church membership roughly equating that of

TABLE 30-3
Respondents having parish schools.

	Yes	No
Number	49	101
Percent	32	67
Percentage of total schools in Missouri Synod = 3.6%		

TABLE 30-4
Age of respondents' congregations.

	No.	Percent
Under 15 yrs.	32	21
Over 15 yrs.	117	78

the Missouri Synod generally, except that there was a somewhat larger proportion of returns from ministers of larger congregations and from urban centers.

[3] *Statistical Yearbook,* The Lutheran Church—Missouri Synod, St. Louis, Missouri, 1962.

TABLE 30-5   Responses categorized by locale.

	Big City	Average City	Suburb	Small City	Rural
1963 Survey Responses	18.5%	25%	17%	34%	5%

1963 Survey Responses	Total urban 60.5%		Total rural 39%
Mo. Synod 1962 Membership Locale	Total urban 59%		Total rural 41%

TABLE 30-6   Membership of congregations.

Members	1-199	200-499	500-999	Over 1,000
Mo. Synod 1962 Data	51%	33 %	12%	4%
1963 Survey Respondents	21	43.5	27	8

CHANGES IN SERVICES.   Three-fourths of the pastors reported that they had made changes in the time or in the number of the kinds of services held during the "Kennedy weekend"; one-fourth that no changes had been made. Changes usually involved a devotional service on Friday evening of the Assassination Day; one-half the respondents introduced a memorial service on Monday (morning, afternoon or evening). About 10 percent held a special service on Saturday. A small number held special services on Friday, Sunday, and Monday—they went "all-out" in recognizing and meshing-in with the occasion.

LEADING FROM BEHIND?   When it is recalled how citizens the country over reacted in "stunned disbelief" over the violent death of the President, how empty the highways and great travel routes were during that weekend, how the radio and television networks recorded, reviewed and restated the sequence of events to a wearisome close on Monday night and how families remained at home, cancelling meetings and social gatherings, it is remarkable that any community, even in more remote rural settings, would have passed through this time without providing special services other than and in addition to the regular Sunday service. It was the one-fourth who stated that no-change-had-been-made who most frequently also reported little else as happening in their parishes that weekend. Were these men out of touch with their people? Did each merely sit before his TV set and follow the great march of the "C's," as one pastor suggested, (Commander-in-Chief, laid in a casket, carried by cadets, rested upon a catafalque, borne upon a caisson to the capitol, thence to the cathedral for religious ceremonies conducted by Cardinal Cushing of the Roman Catholic Church and finally laid to rest in Arlington Cemetery)? Did they give a sermon as usual on Sunday morning, a prayer for the President's family and for the nation and that was all?

SPONTANEOUS ACTIVITY.   *"Was there any spontaneous activity among your people, such as coming to church without announcement of service, or prayer groups in homes?"* Approximately one-half reported "many telephone calls; a few people came to my study or to the church." Many pastors seemed puzzled by the question.

The next question refers to the same general matter of concern, *"Was there any special or unusual religious involvement or activity among your members?"* Answers to these two questions usually reflected increased church attendance during that weekend and on Thanksgiving Day, but little else. In contrast, twelve chaplains (in the sample), most of whom serve college communities, reported an immediate and extended response on the part of men and women on their campuses, such as they had never seen before. Perhaps the case at Valparaiso University is somewhat unique; nonetheless, within 40 minutes of the news of Kennedy's death the chapel was crowded with 3,000 students, faculty, and citizens from the community. This was repeated at the Memorial service Friday evening and on Monday. Similar spontaneous responses marked the occasion in Lutheran Chapels at universities in Michigan, Illinois and California.

COLLEGE VS. COMMUNITY RESPONSE.   Two avenues of thought suggest themselves. Were perhaps the "spontaneous activity" and "special religious involvement" by people in regular community life channeled via the family and the radio and television media at home so as to preclude other religious involvement? Or, did the rush of students to the chapels on their campuses represent for them perhaps a genuine concern for spiritual meaning and help, or primarily a shelter in the storm, a place to go, away from home, in a national crisis? From the descriptions given by chaplains it would appear to have been considerably more than the latter. It is suggestive that the religious center on a college campus has potentially great significance in the lives of students who live there; that many young people are quick to react to a crisis which has strong religious, moral and spiritual significance. The depth of this interest and concern, the duration of it, etc.—these are open questions.

BENEFITS OF JFK BURIAL.   *"Do you think that the strong religious flavor surrounding President Kennedy's death and burial was beneficial to the Roman Catholic Church?"* The following from a pastor in Iowa sums up the opinion of many:

> I don't think Cardinal Cushing acquainted himself creditably. There was not much comfort given to the family in the service. Ninety-two nations represented at the funeral, but little evidence of Christ in the funeral ceremony, except at the grave the witness came, "I am the resurrection and the life. . . ."

From a review of many questionnaires it would appear that while in general there was admiration for Kennedy as a man, as the President, as a Christian father, there was little feeling of consonance with the Roman ritual. While many commented upon the exemplary bearing and conduct of Mrs. Kennedy and members of the family as models of Christian fortitude in time of great grief, some of the spirit of suspicion or criticism of Catholicism crept through, in a few returns.

One of the noteworthy findings of the study is the restrained tone in sermons and church bulletins and in comments written upon the questionnaires by Mo. Synod clergymen. A few warned "against the Pope and his representative in Washington," but these were a mere handful (2 percent). Ninety percent of the respondents had voted for Nixon in the last election, ten percent for Kennedy, yet the language of sermons and bulletins was restrained, respectful, sympathetic, and in about 20 percent of the cases, frankly admiring and bordering upon eulogy. The recognition of Kennedy's concern for the rights, the dignity, the future of fellow human beings was perhaps the most repeated theme.

SERMON TOPICS. While there was a total of 142 clergymen participating in the survey, a total of 123 sermon themes was reported, which are categorized under the following headings by topics:

NO.	GOD
13	The Judge
12	The forgiving and reconciling God
24	The Creator-Preserver of the Universe who is and always will be
12	The Savior who seeks sinners reaches down to man
61	subtotal 50%

	KENNEDY
8	The Man
10	The President
8	The Significance of Kennedy's Death for the United States
6	The Significance of Kennedy's Death for Christians generally, and specifically, for the Lutheran Church
6	National Sorrow
38	subtotal 30%

	MAN
10	The Guilt of man (general)
4	The Guilt of man (entire U.S. and the world)
10	The Guilt of man (the Church)
24	subtotal 20%
123	Total

CONTENT ANALYSIS OF SERMONS.   Twenty-seven sermons were received by the investigator, along with church bulletins and questionnaires, sermons which had been preached during the Kennedy weekend. Some of these sermons were delivered in special memorial services, others at the regular time of worship. All were connected with and related to the death of the President.

Twenty-one of the sermons had as one of the major themes either President Kennedy or the significance of his death. In twenty-five of the sermons the preacher sought to reassure his people by themes which stressed the forgiving and reconciling God, or, God, the creator-preserver of the universe.

Fourteen of the sermons specifically pointed out the significance of Kennedy's death—eight, the significance for the United States, and six, the significance for Christians and the Lutheran Church. Fifteen sermons spoke of the guilt of man but without expressions of condemnation. Instead they stressed the realization of responsibility, dependency upon God and hope for the future.

Only two of the twenty-seven sermons were dedicated to preaching "hell and damnation" upon the evils of the world, and these emanated from preachers living in small towns. Many of the sermons dealt with the problem of evil in the life of man but most of them sought to get at the source of the evil and to make religion relevant.

A total of fifty-two references were made to President Kennedy as a fellow Christian, distributed in slightly over one-half the twenty-seven sermons under review. He was referred to as a Catholic in six of the sermons and all of these were made with a favorable connotation.

Lutheran pastors are trained to base their homiletics upon some portion of or quotation from the Bible, to preach upon a Scriptural text, no matter what the occasion might be. In the exigencies of the Kennedy weekend many of the aforementioned pastors were moved to disregard the principle of textual exegesis and homiletics and instead spoke directly upon the topic at hand— the death of the President. This phenomenon is further highlighted by the fact that many memorial worship services were announced and conducted, not as services "upon the occasion of the death of the President," but simply,

IN MEMORIAM

JOHN F. KENNEDY

While much space was used in the sermons to describe the life of the President and his contributions to the world, with frequent references also to his family life, pastors suggested that their congregations take a definite part in supporting men like the President and his proposals for the government of our United States; that support be given in offering of prayers and in "political action."

Summarizing the analysis of sermons delivered by Lutheran ministers in their respective parishes on the Kennedy weekend, one-half of the sermons sought to relate God, the Judge, the forgiving and reconciling one, the creator and preserver, to the awesome events of that fateful time. Thirty percent were devoted to Kennedy the Man, the President, and to the significance of his death for church and state. A third group of topics which was elaborated upon in twenty percent of the sermons, regarded the problem of Guilt—the guilt of man in general relative to the murder of the President, or the guilt of the church and professing members of the church.

WORD COUNT. A further analysis of the sermons was made to determine the amount of space which was set aside for each of the five following subjects:

1. Placing the guilt on someone.
2. Concern with the problem of evil in the life of man.
3. Preaching "hell and damnation" upon the evils of the world.
4. The sovereignty of God who brings good out of evil and runs the world.
5. National mourning, Kennedy tribute, Christian mourning.

A word count was made for each of the five subjects, which resulted in the following graph, showing the average of the number of words spent on each of the subjects in the 27 sermons.

TABLE 30-7   Proportion of Word Count of twenty-seven sermons, by subject matter.

(1) Placing the guilt on someone	3%	—
(2) Concern with the problem of evil in the life of man	28%	————————————
(3) Preaching 'hell and damnation' upon the evils of the world	8%	———
(4) The sovereignty of God who brings good out of evil and runs the world	26%	———————————
(5) National mourning, Kennedy tribute, Christian mourning	35%	—————————————
	0 10% 20% 30% 40%	

It is apparent that the least amount of time and energy was spent in placing the guilt on someone (3 percent), or in preaching "hell and damnation" upon the evils of the world (8 percent). The remainder of the sermon content dealt with the problem of evil in the life of man, or with a reminder of the sovereignty of God, or with a tribute to the President on a day of national mourning.

It would seem reasonably safe to state that if these are typical sermons, they signify a rather decided shift by Lutheran pastors from a former position of nonentanglement with the national or political scene. The acculturation process of the church seems to have continued in its identification with the national concerns of people in the United States. Lutheran pastors and people wanted to be "counted in" at the casket of President Kennedy.

NORC SURVEY.   The National Opinion Research Center[4] reported that 75 percent of their respondents offered special prayers for the President and for his family. Only 50 percent of the sample had attended church during that weekend (while the national average of church-going is 46 percent). The strength of religious belief, after the Kennedy weekend, remained very nearly the same. *What lessons were gained from the Kennedy death?* Respondents in the writer's survey did not call for "greater toughness," about one-fourth said the chief lesson was a call for less hatred, and more national unity. *What good do you see coming from it?* One-half felt that it produced "no good"; about 18 percent, less intolerance.

The Lutheran clergy responses reflect a higher church attendance than the NORC sample reported. The call for "less hatred" and "more national unity" was echoed as a side-effect among Lutheran people as well. The low estimate of "good coming from the event," as reported by NORC, is perhaps reflected by the Lutheran clergy estimates which ranged from "no lasting effect," to, "it had a tremendous impact for good."

SUMMARY.   In summary, these observations seem pertinent:

1. President Kennedy, the first Catholic president, was referred to by many Lutheran preachers, in sermons and prayers, "brother in Christ," "a princely president," "Thy servant, John," "Thou hast redeemed him," "a prince and a great man has fallen in Israel," a Christian man who made no attempt to hide it," "Marked by the sign of the cross," "dedicated to righteousness." There seems to be evidence that well over one-half of the 5,000 churches in the Missouri Synod held memorial services in which Kennedy was honored by name, many with printed programs and orders of service, entitled, "Memorial Service for J. F. Kennedy" (not, "memorial service on the occasion of the death of," or, "for the President and the Nation"—but, *for the man!*)

2. "We were brought closer together as *American Christians*" summarizes the view of about one-third the respondents. There was evidence of a growing social consciousness, of the duty of the church to its communion and to its community. "We must carry forward the work begun by Kennedy for humanity." However, those who had already been practising this sort of activity were typically the ones who also in the national emergency went about doing it. Others were too overwhelmed or unprepared to rise to the occasion.

3. There is apparently a very conservative group, located it seems principally in rural and small town communities, who viewed this event rather distantly, did not become involved in it, and pontificated rather laboriously about

4 Sheatsley and Feldman, *op. cit.*, 1964.

evil in general. Perhaps it is understandable why several of them should have written on their otherwise blank question sheet, "What do you expect to find out by this survey?"

4. More than one-half the respondents felt that there was little or no beneficial effect of the entire Kennedy weekend upon Christianity in general, or upon the local Lutheran Church in their community. Only about 10 per cent were uncertain about its effect. The majority of clergymen who answered this portion of the questionnaire seemed to feel quite certain about the negative or negligible value of the entire event, from the long-range point of view. This would seem to raise some questions about the accuracy of these observations, and possibly also, whether clergymen in general are given to making quick judgments, often beyond their knowledge.

5. "It was tragedy beyond party lines." Although many churches were described as "strongholds of Republicanism," response to the tragedy was deeply personal, and reflected a sense of great loss. Kennedy had apparently won his way through to the admiration and support of even many staunch Lutherans, and of many Lutheran Republicans.

6. There were a few pockets of American life which did not respond to the stunned disbelief, the casket and caisson—e.g., in Wisconsin the deer season opened that weekend and "churches were empty as usual that Sunday," Kennedy or no Kennedy. Racetracks and nightclubs took notice but not the doughty hunters of the deer.

PART VI

RELIGION, STRATIFICATION,

AND MINORITY LIFE

INTRODUCTION

RELIGIOUS GROUPS are steadily confronted by the need to maintain the future membership of their youth (*see* Elkind, Article 16, and Thomas, Article 17) and to secure new converts. But attempts to reach the general population often fall on deaf ears. Failure to attract the masses is due in part to the image which the masses possess of a specific church. In almost every country some religious denomination or group holds a position of privilege over others. Even in the United States, where the establishment of religion is prohibited by the Constitution, several religious groups (Episcopal, Congregational, and Unitarian) are unofficially established by social custom. In spite of religious attempts at universalism, church membership is nonetheless largely a symbol of class membership. Although Roman Catholicism has maintained a theological universalism, congregations and dioceses often reflect clear class distinctions. Theoretically, Roman Catholic theology possesses a unity, and yet careful students of the faith have noted variations of interpretation variously favorable to one class or another. St. Francis appealed to the lower classes. The Jansenists and Jesuits reached out for the intellectuals and upper classes. Cardinal Newman had little effect upon the workingman of France, even though he was able to excite the imagination of student-scholars of England.

The three branches of Judaism, too, illustrate class differences. In America Orthodox Judaism attracts the lower class. Conservative Judaism remains the expression of middle-class Jews; and Reformed Jews come primarily from the upper class.

Although the Protestant is supposedly free to join the denomination of his choice, his choices are, in fact, determined largely by his social class. An upper class Episcopalian is generally unlikely to become a member of the Southern Baptist Church, except through marriage, and that very rarely. The common tendency of the Episcopal husband and the Methodist wife to "compromise" on Presbyterian Church membership involves both religious and class factors. Class foci go back to religious origins. Moral Rearmament began with an obscure Lutheran minister who spoke to the middle and new upper classes. Unitarianism developed as an attempt of intellectuals to flee the bonds of Puritan conservativism. Christian Science, founded by Mary Baker Eddy, remains a middle class movement due in part to its original appeal and unique theological position. The lower class Black Muslim movement remains the handiwork of Negroes discontented with the middle class orientations of modern Protestantism. Yet class is not the whole story either. Variations of class appeal are due to differences of personal intelligence, educational opportunity, variety of life styles, cultural and language differences, ecological factors, racial characteristics, and group outlook toward the world (see Graebner, Article 30).

Minority status also affects the practice of religion. Generally, ethnic minorities are identified by cultural differences, while racial minorities are differentiated by physical characteristics. Within minority groups, factors of stratification and interaction are apparent. The fact that Negroes are bound together by race does not obscure class distinctions within their minority group; middle and upper class Negroes attend their own churches or those of existing white denominations (see Pope, Article 2, and Alland, Article 8). Although Jews may be found in all levels of social class, their predominant middle class orientation has caused Conservative Judaism to maintain a sustained growth.

As people with diverse cultural and racial backgrounds interact, various social alternatives are possible. Through *assimilation,* peoples of diverse backgrounds and beliefs may be fused together to form a common culture or social unity. The fusion may involve an unequal sharing of cultural traits by both members, although it may result in the development of a third cultural alternative. In *amalgamation* a biological union of two distinct races or racial subgroups is accomplished. *Segregation* may minimize interaction through the separation of one group from the other. Voluntary religion segregation is quite common among groups antagonistic to modern materialism. Enforced segregation of American Indians on reservations in past generations illustrates the opposing pole.

Conflict often marks religious groups vying for power, purity of theological interpretation, or access to greater membership. The history of Greek Orthodox and Roman Catholic church relations have involved all three. Historic conflict between Protestants and Roman Catholics, or Protestants and brother Protestants, has centered on theological and political issues. On the other hand, *pluralism* has become part of the American way of life. Allowing for the different cultural and religious backgrounds of the people, peaceful and harmonious living takes precedence over conflict. Recent Supreme Court decisions on prayer and Bible reading in the public schools have institutionalized religious pluralism as an essential ingredient in the concept of American democracy.

Five articles provide the focal point for the discussion of Religion, Stratification, and Minority Life. Albert Mayer and Harry Sharp suggest that religion may foster cultural factors which may be instrumental in determining economic success. William Kephart analyzes American funerals and concludes that class variations account in large part for the differences in behavior toward death. J. Oscar Lee evaluates the practice of religion among ethnic and racial minorities and concludes that minority churches developed to serve the religious and social needs of the group. Henry Clark studies attitudes toward the open housing covenant and concludes that religious leadership leaves much to be desired in social action situations. Harold L. Sheppard illustrates that minorities share the process of prejudice and discrimination, although they too may be victims of prejudices of the majority.

31 RELIGIOUS PREFERENCE AND WORLDLY SUCCESS

Albert J. Mayer   Harry Sharp

INTRODUCTION   In spite of their equalitarian ideals,
American religious groups are subject to influences of social stratification. Although Protestants generally expound the priesthood of
all believers, most Protestant churches are led by their more successful middle or upper class members (*see* Douglass, Article 13).
Because American religion is dependent upon voluntary financial
and social participation for survival, men of wealth come quickly
to leadership positions. Only in Roman Catholicism is the equalitarian ideal seemingly realized in the form of open class religious
universalism. But even here the type of congregation is determined
by the social ecology of the parish. Even here the actual control of
the religious group rests with the prestigeous priesthood.

Sects tend to appeal to persons who have been unsuccessful
in life, while denominations tend to undergird the successes of
middle and upper class persons (*see* Johnson, Article 11). The
composition of congregational membership partially determines
the type, style, and content of religious preaching. Norman Vincent Peale soothes the worries of the insecure middle class. Billy
Graham answers the emotional revivalistic needs of the lower and
new middle class. Oral Roberts reaches those who feel rejected,
partially successful, or physically handicapped. Cardinal McIntyre
responds to the segregationist desires of many "respectable" Los
Angeles Roman Catholics. Although priests and pastors deny they
mirror any stratifying influence, their sermons reflect their training, outlook, and social class. The conservative posture of the

Abridged and reprinted from the *American Sociological Review*, Volume 27 (April,
1962) pp. 218-227 with the permission of the authors and editors.

ALBERT J. MAYER is Professor of Sociology at Wayne State University. HARRY SHARP
is Professor of Sociology and Director of the Wisconsin Survey Research Laboratory of
the University of Wisconsin.

clergy is due to their role as sanctifiers of the existing social system (*see* Glock, Article 7) and their own vested interest in maintaining their high status.

Religion cannot escape the effect of stratification; and stratification cannot avoid the influence of religion. Sociological research reveals that the upper class is more likely to be composed of white Protestants rather than Roman Catholics or Protestants of other races. Members of the lower class are more likely to be found in sect groups or Baptist and Roman Catholic denominations, although every denomination has a proportion of lower and upper class membership. Evidence shows that lower class sects tend to express a greater sense of emotionalism, while upper class denominations move to express a more liturgical worship pattern. Storefront churches normally concentrate in inner city areas of greatest social change and personal anomie (normlessness). Most religious groups tend to be differentiated (separated) by race. The most segregated congregations are most likely to be found in suburban rather than in inner city areas.

Sociology suggests the idea that no society can ever become fully classless. Wherever men define others as superior or inferior, some form of stratification will exist. Wherever men receive different salaries, occupy more responsible positions, or possess variable levels of education, stratification cannot be avoided. Because religious organization is likely to follow the general lines of community development, persons of similar religious interest and stratification are likely to compose the church.

Albert Mayer and Harry Sharp, using data gathered in the University of Michigan's Detroit Study of 1954-59, find support for Max Weber's thesis that religious preference is correlated with the individual's success in daily life (*see* Introduction, Part V). Religion plays an essential role in controlling, limiting, and guiding economic behavior. In the study of *The Religious Factor* Gerhard Lenski found corresponding support, although numerous racial and urban variables received greater consideration (*see* Winter, Article 5).

———

To what extent does the theory of the Protestant ethic apply to the population of a modern American metropolitan community? Previous research has pointed out some of the significant social and economic differences that exist among the major religious groupings in the United States.[1] In this paper we are concerned primarily with the specific relationship

[1] See, e.g., Liston Pope, "Religion and the Class Structure," *Annals of the American Academy of Political and Social Science*, 256 (March, 1948), pp. 54-91; David Goldberg and Harry Sharp, "Some Characteristics of Detroit Area Jewish and Non-Jewish Adults," in Marshall Sklare, editor, *The Jews: Social Patterns of an American Group* (New York: Free Press, 1957), pp. 107-18.

between religious preference and worldly success. Dependence on the writings of Weber, Sombart, and Tawney is obvious.[2] We fully appreciate the disservice paid to these scholars when their theories are applied directly to a mature industrial community. Nonetheless, the "Weberian controversy," as Lenski calls it,[3] is an important concern of many social scientists who basically are interested in understanding contemporary western society.

An inquiry into the meaning of religion to different denomination groups and the strength of religious expression, valuable as this would be, is beyond the scope of the present paper. Rather, we are here accepting only the denominational label with which an individual associates himself, and investigating the hypothesis that differing religious preferences are associated with varying degrees of worldly success.

This hypothesis is founded on the assumption of a basic distinction in the life orientations which are held by Catholics as compared with Protestants. The powerfully reinforced and traditional Roman Catholic Church tends to orient its members toward the hereafter; successful performance in the market place and the acquisition of the symbols of economic achievement are of relatively little importance as an indication of the Catholic's status after death. On the other hand, adherents of Protestantism are assumed to be highly concerned with worldly success and the attainment of material possession, status, and the prestige that is associated with upward social mobility. These things often are viewed as indications that salvation is assured, or at least is more probable.

To the degree that religious orientations toward life are reflected in behavior, this theory would lead us to expect Protestants to excel Catholics in the race for worldly success. Protestantism in contemporary America, however, is hardly a homogeneous religious faith. We expect variations among the major Protestant denominations both with respect to adherence to the Protestant ethic and to economic achievement.

Members of the Jewish faith and adherents of the Eastern Orthodox Church do not fit into the theory as summarized above. According to Sombart, the Jews played a prominent supportive role in the rise of capitalism.[4] On this basis, we would hypothesize that the Jewish group should bear a greater resemblance to Protestants rather than to Catholics, were all religious groups measured by a scale of economic achievement. The comparative standing on an achievement scale of the adherents of Eastern Orthodoxy was not predicted at the start of the research.

Religion does not exist as an independent attribute of the individual, but is closely bound to important cultural variables such as urbanism, ethnicity,

---

[2] Max Weber, *The Protestant Ethic and the Spirit of Capitalism,* translated by Talcott Parsons (New York: Scribner, 1930); Werner Sombart, *The Jews and Modern Capitalism,* translated by M. Epstein (London: G. Allen, 1913); R. H. Tawney, *Religion and the Rise of Capitalism* (New York: Harcourt, Brace & World, 1926).
[3] Gerhard Lenski, *The Religious Factor* (New York: Doubleday, 1961), p. 6.
[4] Sombart, *op. cit.*

nativity, and experience in a specific community. Thus, in an investigation of the type proposed here, the question must be answered: Is it the religion itself, operating through a network of values stemming from one's religious faith, that produces varying degrees of economic success? Or are other factors, correlated with but not "caused by" a given religious preference, instrumental in the degree of success achieved by a given religious group?

THE DATA.   The data employed in this research were collected by The University of Michigan's Detroit Area Study. Each year since 1952 the Detroit Area Study has conducted a survey of the metropolitan Detroit community.[5] The present discussion focuses on data obtained from 1954 through 1959. The objectives of these surveys required a sample of the adult population of greater Detroit that would be representative, within known confidence limits, of all non-institutionalized adults in the community.

For this research, strict probability samples were constructed which allowed the assignment of specific addresses at which interviews were to be obtained. No substitutions of any kind were permitted. Certain information was obtained about every adult who lived in the sampled dwelling units. Although the specific topics covered by each annual survey varied, demographic and socioeconomic data were collected in a uniform manner. In this paper, the six surveys taken between 1954 and 1959 were combined and analyzed as though they constituted a single operation. By doing so, we are able to work with a maximum N of over 9,000 adults.

Adults in the sample were classified by religious preference on the basis of their answers to these questions:

> Do you have a religious preference?
> (If Yes) Are you Protestant, Catholic, Jewish, or somthing else?
> (If Protestant) What specific denomination is that?

For purposes of analysis, the total sample was grouped into twelve denominational categories: Catholic, Jewish, Eastern Orthodox, Episcopalian, Lutheran, Calvinist, Methodist, Baptist, Small Neofundamentalist Protestant Sects, Nondenominational Protestant, Semi-Christian Churches, and No Religious Preference.

ANALYSIS PROCEDURE.   From one perspective, life in a modern community may be viewed as a hotly contested foot race in which families vie with one another in the hope of material reward. The rewards are rather well defined in western society; they include such achievements as economic success, collection of worldly assets, and the status to be derived from the attainment of these culturally approved goals.

Through the use of a number of indices, all of which repeatedly have

[5] See Harry Sharp, "Graduate Training Through the Detroit Area Study," *American Sociological Review,* 25 (February, 1961), pp. 110-4.

been shown to be highly interconnected, we have measured the relative success of the major religious denominations in this race.

Each of the variables measured by the indices used here can be categorized as *achieved* or *ascribed,* following the conceptualization developed by Linton.[6] The relative position of a given religious group on an *achieved* variable index may be regarded as the result of the efforts of the individuals comprising that group. Correspondingly, the position of a given group on the *ascribed* variable index is here regarded as an "accident of birth"; ascribed status is given to the individual when he is born or while he is still a dependent minor.

Continuing with the analogy to a foot race, a system of "handicapping" has been devised which at least partially removes the effect of ascribed factors on worldly success. The handicapping consists of weighting the ascribed variables in such a way that no group has an unfair advantage at the start of the contest. Thus, the relationship of religion to achievement can be more clearly seen.

ASCRIBED FACTORS. Ascribed background factors were analyzed through the use of three continua: rural-urban background, foreign-native background, and extent of experience in metropolitan Detroit. Each major religious group in the Detroit area was ranked with respect to these factors. In this ranking, one polar extreme would be a religious group all of whose members had no rural experience, were born in this country of fathers who were also native-born, and had spent their entire adult lives in greater Detroit. The advantages for this hypothetical group are maximal since its members would have had the greatest opportunity to acquire property, education, and maximum familiarity with the cultural setting in which they now live. The opposite extreme would consist of a group of all of whose members had a rural background, are of foreign birth, and have had a relatively short residence in greater Detroit. For this hypothetical denomination, familiarity with the ways and customs of a modern metropolis, and hence opportunities for success, would be at a minimum; their ascribed advantage would therefore be minimal.

Each of these ascribed background factors was further redefined. Rural-urban experience was measured in three ways: (1) percentage of each group having no farm experience (the higher the proportion without farm experience, the greater the presumed familiarity with an urban way of life); (2) percentage of each group born in cities of 50,000 or more persons; and (3) percentage of each group born outside the rural South. An additional handicap was given for rural southern United States birth under the assumption that cultural differences between the North and the South constitute a substantial disadvantage for those residents of metropolitan Detroit who were born in the southern United States.

[6] Ralph Linton, *The Study of Man* (New York: Appleton-Century-Crofts, 1936), Chapter 8.

Three indices, each with a somewhat different connotation, were used in measuring the effect of foreign background: (1) percentage of each group whose fathers were born in the United States; (2) percentage of each group whose fathers were of Northwestern European derivation (this measure attempts to "correct" for ethnically based differences in social status by assigning a higher handicap to persons of non-Northwest European stock); and (3) percentage of the members of each group who themselves are native-born Americans or were born in Canada.

It was also assumed that adults who have spent all or a major share of their lives in greater Detroit have an economic advantage over more recent arrivals in the community. Two indices were built for this ascribed factor: (1) the proportion of a given group's adherents who are native Detroiters; and (2) the percentage of each group's members who came to the Detroit area before the age of fifteen. Together, these indices measure specific experience in this particular cultural environment.

Table 31-1 presents the data for the ascribed factors. White and Negro Detroiters are considered separately in this table; given the social significance of race in American society, it would be completely unrealistic to do otherwise.

Although the figures in Table 31-1 reveal some striking relationships, full comprehension of these data is difficult without further summarizing. Therefore, in Table 31-2 each index of the three ascribed factors was analyzed in terms of quartiles. Of the twelve religious preferences in the white population, the three ranking highest on each ascribed characteristic were given the weight of four, the next three highest were given the weight of three, and so forth. The four religious categories in the Negro population were handled in a comparable manner on the relevant variables, with the obvious exception that only one preference was in each quartile of the index.

For whites, the foreign and rural background categories each consisted of three indices. The third factor (Specific Detroit Background) consisted of two indices. Specific Detroit Background was given a weight equivalent to each of the first two factors by increasing it 50 percent. As a result, each of the three ascribed variables had a possible maximum weight of twelve (4 x 3, or 6 x 2). The grand total maximum weight for the ascribed factors in the white population would therefore be 12 x 3, or thirty-six.

For Negro Detroiters, quartile rankings on Specific Detroit Background were also increased by 50 percent. Since foreign background was not a variable for Negroes, the grand total weight for this population group was 12 x 2, or twenty-four.

In the white population, Lutherans (with a value of 28.8) are in the most advantageous position with respect to the ascribed factors, followed by a cluster of three groups: Jews (27.0), Episcopalians (26.7), and Calvinists (26.5). Detroiters of the Eastern Orthodox faith possess the least advantage (12.3) with the members of the small sects (16.0) and the Baptists (18.0) also at a comparative disadvantage.

TABLE 31-1 Ascribed factors, by religious group and race.

| | Ascribed Factors | | | | | | | | |
| Religious Group and Race | Rural Background | | | Foreign Background | | | Specific Detroit Background | | Number of Cases[a] |
	% with No Farm Background	% Born in Cities of 50,000+	% Not Born in Rural South	% with Native Born Fathers	% with Fathers of N-W European Stock	% Born in U.S. or Canada	% Born in Detroit Area	% in Detroit Before Age 15	
White									
Catholic	77	54	99	36	46	81	45	68	3,307
Episcopalian	84	44	100	46	95	82	32	42	289
Lutheran	74	53	99	52	84	90	42	55	778
Calvinist	75	46	98	59	90	90	33	46	723
Methodist	64	34	92	69	92	95	24	36	750
Baptist	44	24	72	80	96	97	17	29	727
Small sects	49	26	85	68	87	93	21	33	232
No denomination	60	35	70	68	91	92	12	42	194
Semi-Christian	64	50	92	63	89	96	26	39	96
Jewish	90	63	100	4	10	70	42	58	234
Eastern Orthodox	61	33	99	3	8	42	19	33	169
No preference	74	44	94	49	64	85	39	54	239
Negro									
Catholic	76	50	89	..	..	..	23	41	75
Methodist	62	39	73	..	..	..	12	26	316
Baptist	43	23	68	..	..	..	7	20	938
Other	60	36	72	..	..	..	18	32	164

a The *N*'s given here are applicable to all following tables.

TABLE 31-2   Quartile ranking and total weights of ascribed factors, by religious group and race.

| | Quartile Ranking on Ascribed Factors | | | | | | | | |
| Religious Group and Race | Rural Background | | | Foreign Background | | | Specific Detroit Background[a] | | Grand Total All Ascribed Factors |
	% with No Farm Background	% Born in Cities of 50,000+	% Not Born in Rural South	% with Native Born Fathers	% with Fathers of N-W European Stock	% Born in U.S. or Canada	% Born in Detroit Area	% in Detroit Before Age 15	
White									
Catholic	4	4	3.3	1	1	1	6	6	26.3
Episcopalian	4	2.5	4	4	2	2	4.5	3.8	26.7
Lutheran	3	4	3.3	2	2	2.5	6	6	28.8
Calvinist	3	3	3	3	3	2.5	4.5	4.5	26.5
Methodist	2	2	2	3	4	4	3	3	24.0
Baptist	1	1	1	4	4	4	1.5	1.5	18.0
Small sects	1	1	1	2	3.5	3	3	1.5	16.0
No denomination	1	2	1	3	3.5	3	1.5	3.7	18.7
Semi-Christian	2	3	2	3	3	4	3	3	23.0
Jewish	4	4	4	1	1	1	6	6	27.0
Eastern Orthodox	2	1	3.3	1	1	1	1.5	1.5	12.3
No preference	3	2.5	2	2	2	2	4.5	4.5	22.5
Negro									
Catholic	4	4	4	...	...	...	6	6	24.0
Methodist	3	3	3	...	...	...	3	3	15.0
Baptist	1	1	1	...	...	...	1.5	1.5	6.0
Other	2	2	2	...	...	...	4.5	4.5	15.0

a Quartile weights for Specific Detroit Background inflated by 50 percent to equalize weights between background factors.

The rankings on the ascribed variables are generally in accord with pre-conception. Detroit area Lutherans, Jews, Episcopalians, and Calvinists are highly urban, and, as a group, have a very large proportion of native-born Detroiters. The Jewish advantage is tempered, however, by the greater proportion of foreign-born among Jews as compared to other religious preferences. The Eastern Orthodox are economically handicapped, not only because a majority of these persons are foreign-born, but also because of their limited urban background before coming to Detroit and the comparatively late age at which they arrived in this community. The Baptists, although largely of native birth, are among the lowest of the religious groups in urban background and specific Detroit experience.

Among Negro Detroiters, the Baptist faith is by far the most common denomination. Negro Baptists also are in the least advantageous position with respect to the possession of those ascribed characteristics which, we have assumed, lead most readily to economic achievement. Negro Catholics (a minority within a minority, to be sure) are a comparatively urban group and therefore rank at the top of each of the indices of ascribed factors.

In following the above procedure, we obviously have assumed that one unit of urban experience, one unit of specific Detroit experience, and one unit of foreign birth can be considered as equivalent. This assumption was necessary as a result of summing these different measures to produce a unique index value.

ACHIEVED FACTORS.   Five indices were used in measuring the social and economic achievements of the major religious groups in greater Detroit: (1) relative ranking on family income, given as the percentage of each group earning $2,000 or more *above* the median Detroit area family income for a given year; (2) percentage of self-employed in each group; (3) percentage of the members of each group who are in high status white-collar occupations (professionals, managers, proprietors, or officials); (4) median school year completed; and (5) percentage of persons of each religious preference who are members of three or more formal social groups.[7] These five indices, then, attempt to measure worldly success. They are shown in Table 31-3.

The quartile grouping described above for the ascribed factors was applied in a comparable manner to the achieved factors. For both whites and Negroes, the total maximum weight that any religious group might have on the achieved factors would be twenty (4 x 5). The results of these operations may be seen in Table 31-4.

With respect to the white population, Jews (with a rating of 20.0) show the greatest achievement as we have measured it. They are followed by Episcopalians (17.7), Calvinists (16.7) and the semi-Christian group (16.0). The

[7] For example *see:* Morris Axelrod, "Urban Structure and Social Participation," *American Sociological Review*, 21 (February, 1956), pp. 13-18.

other end of the scale represents low achievement. Here are found Baptists (5.0), and Catholics and small Protestant sects (both with a rating of 8.0).

TABLE 31-3   Achieved factors, by religious group and race.

Religious Group and Race	Achieved Factors				
	% $2,000 and Above Median Income	% Self-Employed	% in High Status Occupations	Median School Year Completed	% in Three or More Formal Groups
White					
Catholic	27	7	19	10.0	14
Episcopalian	35	9	42	12.5	42
Lutheran	30	6	28	12.2	17
Calvinist	35	11	37	12.5	21
Methodist	32	8	27	12.3	23
Baptist	21	6	15	9.8	8
Small sects	16	11	17	9.5	9
No denomination	29	11	26	12.0	17
Semi-Christian	24	15	39	12.4	19
Jewish	42	41	62	12.5	45
Eastern Orthodox	35	15	13	9.3	8
No preference	23	9	28	10.0	7
Negro					
Catholic	6	4	7	10.0	8
Methodist	7	5	6	9.8	12
Baptist	8	3	3	9.1	7
Other	12	10	15	9.8	10

Among Negroes, the greatest achievement is shown by adults who are categorized as "Other" in Table 31-4. They score 17.5 on our measure. Negro Methodists rank second on achievement (13.5), and are followed closely by Negro Catholics (12.0). Negro Baptists are a rather distant fourth with a rating of 7.0.

In general, the achievement rankings shown here are consistent with the findings of previous research, both on a national basis[8] and for individual communities.[9] Episcopalians, Calvinists, and Unitarians are usually ranked high on economic status. Also, Jews generally are a relatively high economic status group in metropolitan centers other than New York City.[10] Moreover,

[8] Pope, *op. cit.*
[9] August B. Hollingshead, *Elmtown's Youth* (New York: Wiley, 1949), pp. 107-8; Lloyd W. Warner, Marcia Meeker, and Kenneth Eells, *Social Class in America* (Chicago: Science Research, 1949), pp. 52-6.
[10] S. Joseph Fauman, "Occupational Selection Among Detroit Jews," in Sklare, *op. cit.*, pp. 119-37; Nathan Glazer, "The American Jew and the Attainment of Middle Class Rank," in Sklare, *op. cit.*, pp. 138-46; Goldberg and Sharp, *op. cit.*

the very low status of Baptists and small Protestant sects is not surprising, although the relatively low ranking of Detroit area Catholics is not consistently
reported by other studies.

TABLE 31-4   Quartile ranking and total weights of achieved factors, by
religious group and race.

			Quartile Ranking on Achieved Factors			
Religious Group and Race	% $2,000 and Above Median Income	% Self-Employed	% in High Status Occu-pations	Median School Year Completed	% in Three or More Formal Groups	Grand Total All Achieved Factors
White						
Catholic	2	1	1	2	2	8.0
Episcopalian	3.7	2	4	4	4	17.7
Lutheran	3	1	3	3	2.5	12.5
Calvinist	3.7	3	3	4	3	16.7
Methodist	3	2	2	3	4	14.0
Baptist	1	1	1	1	1	5.0
Small sects	1	3	1	1	2	8.0
No denomination	2	3	2	2	2.5	11.5
Semi-Christian	2	4	4	3	3	16.0
Jewish	4	4	4	4	4	20.0
Eastern Orthodox	3.7	4	2	1	1	11.7
No preference	1	2	3	2	1	9.0
Negro						
Catholic	1	2	3	4	2	12.0
Methodist	2	3	2	2.5	4	13.5
Baptist	3	1	1	1	1	7.0
Other	4	4	4	2.5	3	17.5

RELATIONSHIP OF ASCRIBED TO ACHIEVED FACTORS.   To
evaluate the contribution of ascribed background factors to variations in socioeconomic status, the ascription handicap was subtracted from a *weighted*
achievement rating for each religious group. Weighting of the achievement
measure was necessary to convert this variable to the same scale as the ascribed
rating. The total achievement rating for each white denomination was
weighted by nine-fifths; for Negro religious groups, the weight was six-fifths.
It should be noted that this process in no way changes the relative weights,
but simply facilitates comparison between achieved and ascribed factors. The
results of this procedure are shown in Table 31-5.

Returning once more to the analogy of a foot race, we are now in a position to judge the results of this contest. To review, in investigating the relationships between religious preference and worldly success in metropolitan
Detroit, we endeavored to place all denominations on an "equal footing" with

TABLE 31-5   Total inflated weights of achieved factors less total weights of ascribed factors, by religious group and race.

Religious Group and Race	Total of Factors		
	Achieved Factors[a]	Ascribed Factors	Achieved Less Ascribed
White			
Catholic	14.4	26.3	− 11.9
Episcopalian	31.9	26.7	+ 5.2
Lutheran	22.5	28.8	− 6.3
Calvinist	30.0	26.5	+ 3.5
Methodist	25.2	24.0	+ 1.2
Baptist	9.0	18.0	− 9.0
Small sects	14.4	16.0	− 1.6
No denomination	20.7	18.7	+ 2.0
Semi-Christian	28.8	23.0	+ 5.8
Jewish	36.0	27.0	+ 9.0
Eastern Orthodox	21.0	12.3	+ 8.7
No preference	16.2	22.5	− 6.3
Negro			
Catholic	14.4	24.0	− 9.6
Methodist	16.2	15.0	+ 1.2
Baptist	8.4	6.0	+ 2.4
Other	21.0	15.0	+ 6.0

a Totals inflated by 1.8 for whites and by 1.2 for Negroes to equalize weights between ascribed and achieved factors.

respect to those background factors which are conducive to high economic achievement in an urban environment. Actual achievement was then measured against the potential for this performance. The final ranking of the religious groups, taking the starting handicaps into consideration, is as follows:

White: Jewish
        Eastern Orthodox
        Semi-Christian
        Episcopalian
        Calvinist
        Protestant, no denomination
        Methodist
        Small sects
        No preference, Lutheran (tie)
        Baptist
        Catholic

Negro: Other than the below
        Baptist
        Methodist
        Catholic

For many religious groups, the handicapping produced a final ranking which was comparable to that based on achievement alone. However, several interesting exceptions may be seen. The most significant change in rank occurred in the Eastern Orthodox group which, when its handicap was applied, jumped high on the scale. The Baptists also rose one notch on the scale, thereby surpassing Catholics among both whites and Negroes.

A striking picture emerges from these data. Members of the Jewish, Greek Orthodox, and semi-Christian faiths appear to have made the greatest achievements, given the system followed here. Behind these three groups are the several major Protestant denominations, with Baptists ranking below those white Detroiters who have no religious preference. For both whites and Negroes, the Catholics have had the least economic success as measured by our index.

Although these indices are crude and the resultant quantification somewhat specious, the major findings are not easily dismissed. We believe that no amount of statistical manipulation, even if more precise or elegant than that employed here, would appreciably change the broad outline of these rankings. To summarize our findings as they apply to white residents of greater Detroit: (1) Jews, followed closely by Episcopalians and Calvinists, have achieved the greatest worldly success. In the middle range are the remaining Protestant groups, with Baptists falling toward the end of the economic scale. Catholics have achieved the least. (2) If an ascription "handicap" is considered, the Eastern Orthodox group, closely followed by adherents of the semi-Christian faiths, join the Jewish group at the top of the scale. An additional conclusion is that Catholicism is related to economic achievement among Negroes much as it is among whites.

INTERPRETATION.   Previous research, in general, has failed to reach agreement as to the nature of the relationship between religious preference and economic achievement. Several investigations have discovered a comparative absence of Catholics among the economic and social élite of America.[11] Low Catholic achievement motivation has also been pointed out.[12] On the other hand, a number of researchers have found little evidence for the proposition that the Protestant ethic hypothesis is descriptive of the relationship between religious preference and worldly success in contemporary urban society.[13]

[11] *See* Neil Jack Weller, "Religion and Social Mobility in Industrial Society," Unpublished Doctoral Dissertation, Department of Sociology, The University of Michigan, 1960, and Lenski, *op. cit.*
[12] *See* Fred L. Strodtbeck, "Family Interaction, Values, and Achievement," in Sklare, *op. cit.*, pp. 147-65; Lenski, *op. cit.*; Gerald Gurin, Joseph Veroff, and Sheila Feld, *Americans View Their Mental Health* (New York: Basic Books, Inc., 1960), p. 244.
[13] Raymond W. Mack, Raymond J. Murphy, and Seymour Yellin, "The Protestant Ethic, Level of Aspiration, and Social Mobility: An Empirical Test," *American Sociological Review*, 21 (June, 1956), pp. 295-300; Seymour Martin Lipset and Reinbard Bendix, *Social Mobility in Industrial Society* (Berkeley: University of California Press,

The results of the present study may be interpreted as supporting the Weberian approach in part, while presenting some important modifications. Religious preferences appear to have meaningful consequences for economic success, quite apart from other background factors associated with religion. It would seem, therefore, that religion continues to play an essential role in controlling, limiting, and guiding economic behavior. As Weber proposed, most Protestant denominations far exceed the Catholics in economic standing. The various Protestant denominations are ranked in a general order which further supports the Weberian thesis. As Sombart proposed, moreover, the Jews seem to be the most successful and worldly oriented. Thus, where it has been hypothesized that a general ordering would appear, it has appeared.

Not all religious preferences, however, fall into a neat, predictable rank order. This finding leads to a further interpretation in which religion per se is of lesser importance in guiding economic achievement in contemporary society than are other cultural factors associated with the religion. As part of their cultural heritage, members of particular religious groups may have certain occupational roles. The Eastern Orthodox in Detroit, for example, are primarily Syrians, Lebanese, and Greeks—traditionally traders, shopkeepers, merchants, and entrepreneurs. Granting that originally their religion strengthened, abetted, and possibly even forced them into these pursuits, their total cultural environment presently is consistent with entry into these occupations.

Much the same case can be made for Jews. Although three or four generations ago the Jewish religious link to worldly success was probably direct, the contemporary teachings of this religion may not be nearly as crucial as are other cultural characteristics which foster success and achievement patterns. Thus, the presence of intervening variables may alter the original linkage between religion and worldly success.

Future phases of this study will turn to an investigation of intervening variables such as residential segregation, family solidarity, and specific occupational inheritances. It is also planned further to refine our measurement of religious affiliation by introducing such factors as church attendance and church membership. The significance of the present study will be greatly enhanced if it is found, for example, that active Catholics are less successful than inactive Catholics; and conversely, that active Calvinists are more successful than inactive Calvinists.

1959), pp. 51-2. An evaluation of these and similar studies is found in Weller, *op. cit.*, pp. 30-4.

32 STATUS AFTER DEATH

William M. Kephart

INTRODUCTION   The influence of social status upon
religious practice is most clearly indicated in a 1955 study of Roman Catholic saints who were cannonized during twenty centuries
of Christian history. Of the 2,494 saints examined by Katherine
and Charles George, only 122 (5 percent) had been members of
the lower class. On the other hand, the upper and middle classes
constituted 1,950 (78 percent) and 422 (17 percent) respectively.
The general discrepancy of status is most apparent when compared with the predominant lower-class composition of the Roman
Catholic Church membership throughout history. In nearly 2,000
years of Christianity an estimated five percent of the total population have been classified as upper class. Ten to fifteen percent
compose the middle class, while the remaining eighty to eighty-five
percent comprise the lower-class population.

 William Kephart discusses the many variables which affect
funeral decisions. Although his discussion is economically dated,
Kephart suggests that class variations take precedence over religious attitudes in the final determination of the funeral process. In
the last few decades church funerals have diminished in number
in favor of the seclusion of the funeral home. Status competition
among funeral directors has caused them to offer special services
to the family, often unheard of in the church. In one funeral
home, for example, the director takes great pride in the electrically-
operated doors which shield the open coffin from the view of
mourners following the funeral rite and allow the family a last
opportunity to kiss the corpse farewell.

Abridged and reprinted from the *American Sociological Review*, Volume 15 (October,
1950), pp. 635-643 with the permission of the author and editors.

WILLIAM KEPHART is Professor of Sociology at the University of Pennsylvania.

The solemn funeral of a midwesterner following the public viewing of the body the night before, and the Negro wake and procession from the New Orleans cemetery to the jazz strains of "When the saints come marchin' in" reflect differences in personal status as much as religious perspective. The mourners of the successful middle-class midwesterner may pay less attention to the requisites of faith and ignore the theological meaning of the funeral in order to fulfill the prestige demands of his social life. On the other hand, the mourners of the lower-class Negro in Louisiana may turn joyously to death as the opportunity to equalize the injustice of the world through the rewards of heaven (see Graebner, Article 30).

Jessica Mitford has been a most vehement critic of the American way of death. Writing in a volume by the same title, she suggests that the affluent society has ushered in the rise of an affluent undertaking establishment. Comfort, durability, beauty, and craftsmanship, signs of quality and prestige, now find expression in the elegance of the funeral. Following the leadership of the advertising agencies, status consciousness has taken death out of its human and spiritual perspective. The funeral has become an ornate status symbol replete with maximum luxury. Emphasis upon the "memory picture" and "grief therapy" has resulted in the attempt to recapture youth in death. Even the editor has found that the greatest complement one can pay a funeral director is to say of the corpse, "My, he looks so natural!"

BEHAVIORAL DIFFERENCES as a reflection of social class have been reported for a variety of cultural phenomena. The purpose of this paper is to present findings which suggest that observable differences in class behavior exist "after death"; that is, with reference to funeral and burial customs and in practices associated with bereavement.

HISTORICAL ASPECTS

The existence of class distinctions after death is not new. Funeral and burial customs in our society are, in good part, outgrowths of Christian practices many of which, in turn, were borrowed from the so-called "pagan peoples." Such borrowings would include closing the eyes and mouth of the deceased, embalming, correct position of the limbs, anointing the body, clothing the body, holding a "wake," extended mourning, etc., and Rush points out that many of the "pagans," recognizing class differences among the living, assumed that these differences prevailed after death.[1]

Of the development and transformation of funeral and burial customs

[1] Alfred Rush, *Death and Burial in Christian Antiquity* (Washington, D.C.: Catholic Press, 1941), pp. 2-4.

from Christian antiquity to modern times, no historical account exists which sheds any sustained light on possible class differentials. Fragmentary evidence suggests that such differentials have always existed in Western culture, but the derivation and nature of such patterns are, for the most part, unknown. Available historical accounts indicate that lavishness of funeral is directly correlated with social class, and incidental bits of information can be gleaned from works dealing with funeral customs.

MINISTERING TO THE DEAD AS A BUSINESS

Ministering to the dead is big business in the United States. There are about 25,000 funeral directors and some 520 casket manufacturers currently in business,[2] and the number of cemeteries has been estimated at about 40,-000.[3] (In the Philadelphia area—the site of the present study—there are in excess of 500 funeral directors and 100 cemeteries.)

There are several national periodicals which deal with the disposition of the deceased, and which contain advertisements for everything from the latest embalming chemicals to multi-thousand dollar hearses, as well as routine assortments of caskets and memorials. Caskets can be purchased today for as high as $15,000, and mausoleums sometimes run well over the $100,000 mark, although in both cases the market is small and no attempt is made to "push" such items.

Funeral directors, as a group, are rather conscious of their position. They prefer the name "funeral director" to "undertaker" or "mortician," and their periodicals stress the undesirability of the latter terms. Another aim of the funeral director is to be considered, occupationally, as "a professional man, on the same level as a doctor or lawyer."[4] To this end the academic requirements for funeral directors have been raised in recent years, the present requisites being (a) high school graduation, (b) a course at a mortuary college, (c) an apprenticeship, and (d) state examination. There are twenty-four mortuary colleges in the United States, two of which are affiliated with major universities.

With respect to the amount of money spent on funerals, the Department of Commerce estimated that in the year 1942 the American people spent $560,900,000 for this purpose. In the same year tuition for all schools, colleges, and universities was estimated at $578,300,000, and payments by patients to all hospitals and sanitaria amounted to $513,100,000. The foregoing estimate for the cost of death does not include expenditures for flowers, estimated (prewar) at $60,000,000.[5] Although it is difficult to gauge the accuracy of such estimates, it seems probable, when rising prices are considered, that the American people pay more than $700,000,000 yearly as the price of death.

[2] *Business Week,* September, 1943, p. 38.
[3] *New Republic,* April 21, 1947, p. 28.
[4] See *An Analysis of Attitudes Towards Funeral Directors,* The National Funeral Directors Association, 1948.
[5] See *Harper's,* December, 1945, p. 500, and *Forum,* September, 1939, p. 130.

REPORTED CLASS DIFFERENCES

METHODOLOGY. The bulk of the information in the present study was obtained through personal interviews with the managers of the following types of businesses in the Philadelphia area: (a) funeral parlors, (b) cemeteries, (c) monument makers, (d) flower shops, (e) mourning shops, with most of the data being derived from the first two sources. Letters explaining the nature of the study were sent to forty funeral directors and fifteen cemetery managers. Two of the former and two of the latter refused to grant interviews, hence the problem of the nonrespondent was minimal.

The establishments were chosen on the basis of geographical location and economic level. With respect to the latter, for example, the funeral parlors visited ranged from one of the world's largest funeral establishments (handling thousands of funerals a year) to ramshackle neighborhood parlors where funerals occur at the rate of less than one a month. It was necessary also to consider religious and nationality factors in the sample, since many local establishments deal preponderantly with specific minority groups such as Jews, Italians, Irish, etc. Although not part of the sample, several Negro funeral directors were interviewed, and some of the results will be mentioned briefly.

Since the writer had had no previous experience in the matter, it was necessary to hold four trial interviews for the purpose of establishing the field of inquiry and framing the questions which might unearth possible class differences. From these trial interviews a schedule was drawn up with questions relating to the following categories: (a) place of funeral, (b) cost of funeral, (c) caskets, (d) cremation, (e) elapsed time between death and burial, (f) viewing the body, (g) flowers, (h) emotionality, (i) mourning and mourning clothes, (j) the funeral and funeral procession, (k) cemeteries.

LIMITATIONS OF THE STUDY. (a) Verifiability. The information contained in our study is subject to the limitations of the personal interview method. Although rapport was apparently established with the bulk of the respondents, it is the writer's opinion that one of the principal functions of the interview method is to provide behavioral *cues* that can either be verified or refuted by evidence of a more empirical nature.

(b) Geographical differences. Class patterns of behavior described in this paper apply only to the Philadelphia area. Behavior patterns after death are probably a function of geographical area as well as of class, religion, race, and nationality, and the extent to which such behavior is influenced by locale must await studies made in different sections of the United States, both urban and rural.

(c) Religious and nationality differences. The problem of religious and nationality differences as interrelated with class differences presents a special problem. The Italians, for example, have a unique set of culturally prescribed behavior patterns following the death of a friend or relative. To many "Americans," however, Italians and other minority groups represent the "lower classes," other criteria to the contrary notwithstanding.

(d) Definition of class. For the purposes of this study the definition of "class" presented the most serious difficulty. There are few businesses today in which the manager knows enough of the customer's background to identify accurately the social class to which the person belongs. To some extent this applies to the funeral director and cemetery manager. However, the managers of the larger establishments are, in most cases, able to make a fair estimate of the class to which the family belongs *when class is defined in terms of economic level*. In the case of the neighborhood funeral parlors, the manager often knows the family background and, of course, it is part of his business to know something of the economic position of the family. It became apparent, then, that the most suitable definition to work with was one in terms of economic status.

(e) Nondefinitive middle class. Respondents had no difficulty identifying behavior patterns of the "well-to-do" and the "poorer classes," but gradations in the middle economic bracket proved to be too vague for eliciting reliable answers.

The writer's conclusion was that in the field under study the middle class—unlike the two extremity classes—has few *distinctive* behavior patterns, but rather falls in the middle with respect to *frequency or degree of a behavioral index*. For example, cremation is almost entirely an upper class phenomenon; it is seldom found in the lower classes, and in some lower class groups is never found. What can be said about the middle class? Simply that cremation is more frequent than among the lower classes, but not nearly so frequent as in the upper economic brackets.

(f) The Social Register. The writer was fortunate in obtaining considerable information with respect to after-death procedures of members of the Philadelphia Social Register. This group will be referred to as "registerites," and as will be seen, their behavior as an upper status group differs in many respects from that of the upper economic classes.

PLACE OF FUNERAL. The large majority of funerals in Philadelphia start from a funeral parlor. Estimates received from cemetery managers and funeral directors ranged from eighty-five to ninety-five percent. None of the persons interviewed would commit himself as to whether preference for a funeral parlor was operative on a class basis. From opinions received, this matter does not reflect class differences but apparently is a function of the age structure, the older and more "conservative" people sometimes preferring a home funeral following the death of a spouse.

Whether nationality, religious, or racial differences with respect to place of funeral exist is not clear in the light of our limited sample, although estimates made by Negro funeral directors regarding the percentage of Negro funerals starting from the funeral home were among the highest estimates received.

COST OF FUNERAL. It comes as no surprise to learn that the upper classes spend the most for funerals and the lower classes spend the least. However, this is not the whole story, and is, in fact, somewhat misleading, for *proportionately* both the lower and middle classes spend more in relation to their income than do the upper class. It is not uncommon for a lower class family to spend their entire savings of four or five hundred dollars on a funeral, or, if there is a $500 or $1,000 life insurance policy, to use a good share of it to defray funeral expenses. The bulk of lower class and perhaps the majority of middle class families take out life insurance on the supposition that it is to be used as "funeral insurance."

There has been a marked tendency in recent years for the upper classes to curtail the amount of money on funerals, although for some minority groups such as the Italians this generalization would not apply.

CREMATION. As has been mentioned, cremation is largely an upper class phenomenon. It was the unanimous opinion of respondents that the proportion of cremations in the Philadelphia area is increasing yearly, although most of the increase has been among the upper classes. At one midcity funeral home records showed that cremations there have increased from 7 percent to 17 percent in the last ten years. This particular establishment caters largely to upper class clientele, hence the percent increase is not representative of the Philadelphia area as a whole. From other estimates received, however, this figure seems to be a valid index of the increase in cremations among the upper classes.

For funeral directors who deal largely with upper class whites, and for all non-Catholic and non-Negro cemeteries, the trend toward cremation presents a serious problem financially, since cremation urns are comparatively inexpensive, the price range being in the vicinity of $25 to $150. The increase in the number of such cases, of course, means that "upper class" funeral directors can no longer rely on upper class clientele to sustain their business. Today—for most funeral directors—the aim is to get as many funerals as possible, regardless of class levels.

For cemeteries, too, cremation presents a problem. The normal four- or six-grave lot holds eight or twelve bodies, so long as they are interred in caskets. (Unless the graves are, in cemetery language, "dug deep" to permit three layers of caskets. Some cemeteries place the maximum "deep digging" at two layers.) However, with the increase in cremation, an almost unlimited number of urns can be placed in a small lot, with a corresponding decrease in the sale of new lots. Many of the urns are placed in niches, whose cost, again, is cheaper than a burial lot; this practice, moreover, eliminates much of the payment for flowers, memorials, upkeep of the lot, etc.

ELAPSED TIME BETWEEN DEATH AND BURIAL. In the Philadelphia area, position on the class scale is inversely correlated with elapsed time between death and burial, when allowances are made for religious and nationality differences. (Jews and Italians, for example, have prescribed customs which nullify the foregoing generalization as applied to these two groups.) For the upper class the average elapsed time is from two to three days; for the lower class the average is slightly over four days, with the middle class, again, falling in between these two figures. The shortest elapsed time between death and burial takes place among the registerites, the average reported time being about two days. Occasionally, however, the entire procedure for a registerite is completed within twenty-four hours.

Why a time differential of this kind should exist among the classes can only be conjectured. The respondents themselves differed as to the explanation. Some of the interviewees believed "the lower classes are more superstitious"; others felt that the "lower classes are slower to react"; others pointed out that in the case of the upper classes, friends and relatives of the deceased who live at distant points have the facilities for quick transportation to the funeral, whereas in the lower classes there is more of a time lag. In the writer's opinion the explanation seems to be partially related to the fact that the occurrence of death in a lower class family has a much more disorganizing effect than in the case of an upper class family. The average lower-class family, for example, seldom makes arrangements for burial lots or memorials prior to death; in fact, such a family at the time of death often lacks appropriate funeral clothes, either for the deceased or for the bereaved, hence they must be purchased. In short, the lower class family waits until after a death occurs to make most of the necessary arrangements, and, of course, this entails considerable time.

VIEWING THE BODY. While most Philadelphia families follow the custom of having a viewing of the body, the viewing in all classes has become restricted to one day or one night, customarily the night before the funeral. Again, exceptions to the foregoing statement occur in the case of nationality groups such as the Poles and Italians, where the viewing lasts for three days.

The growing tendency among the upper classes is to eliminate altogether the more or less "public viewing" which characterizes most lower and middle class families. Interviewees estimated that between fifty and seventy-five percent of the upper class families restrict the viewing to members of the immediate family and close friends. In the case of the registerites this figure was reported to be about ninety percent. Interestingly, an estimated two or three percent of the upper class families have no viewing whatsoever, the casket remaining closed even to the immediate family. Among the registerites this figure was estimated at ten percent.

FLOWERS. There are no reported class differences in kinds of flowers used at funerals and in cemeteries. Cemetery managers, funeral directors, and florists agreed that species of flowers are determined by availability of supply and season of the year, and are not dependent on class preferences.

However, what is a function of class level is the arrangement of the flowers. Baskets and sprays are characteristic of the upper classes. Not uncommon among the lower classes are upright wreaths, pillows of flowers, and "bleeding hearts," and occasionally used are set pieces such as "gates ajar," "clocks" (showing the time of death), ribboned wreathes with such phrases as "beloved father," etc.

Funerals in which the family makes the request that no flowers be sent (or in which the request is made to send money to a specified charity) are increasing in number, but as yet the increase is largely in the upper classes. A reported ten to twenty percent of upper class families are so characterized.

EMOTIONALITY. With respect to emotionality, or control of emotions, interviewees were emphatic in their statements that the lower classes had the least control of their emotions following a bereavement. There is relatively little show of emotion among the upper classes, and in the case of the register-ite funerals and burials respondents reported that "weeping was simply not done."

The popular notion that certain minority groups are exceedingly emotional in their mourning is true; at least, all respondents stated that such was the case, and nearly all named the Jews, Italians, and Poles. And yet emotionality is apparently a function of class position *within* these groups. Italian funeral directors stated that upper class Italians were much more restrained in their mourning, and the same situation was reported for the Jews and Poles.

MOURNING AND MOURNING CLOTHES. In all classes extended periods of mourning and the wearing of mourning clothes are disappearing phenomena. Even in the case of various nationality minorities, the European custom of wearing mourning clothes for long periods following the death of a spouse is rapidly disappearing. Arm bands have largely vanished in all classes and in all groups, as has the custom of placing a crepe on the door following a death in the family.

Neighborhood funeral directors who deal primarily with lower class clientele report that a custom that is still practiced by a very small minority of lower class families is the shuttering of the windows and the stopping of the clock to show the hour of death. This practice was never reported for an upper class household, although interviewees admitted that such a custom could exist without their knowledge.

THE FUNERAL AND FUNERAL PROCESSION. The relationship between size of funeral (number of persons in attendance) and social class is not clear, since the number of friends, relatives, and acquaintances who attend a funeral depends on a variety of factors many of which are independent of the class level involved. However, when an upper class funeral leaves the funeral parlor, the majority of those attending do not proceed to the cemetery. The upper class funeral procession is marked by the hearse and a very few limousines or passenger cars. Among the lower classes, on the other hand, practically every one who attends the funeral proceeds to the cemetery, hence—with individual exceptions—the twenty- and thirty-car funeral processions that are seen tend to be indicative of lower class funerals.

Nationality differences change the general picture. Italians, for example, customarily have large funerals and large funeral processions; in fact, within this group, size of funeral and length of funeral procession seems to vary directly with social class.

In both neighborhood and well-to-do funeral parlors it was reported that in the case of the lower class funerals much interest is shown in the appearance of the body. People attending center around the casket and comments are made regarding the appearance of the body. To some extent this is true of the middle class. But among the upper classes, even when the casket is open, respondents report that the majority of those attending show little interest in the body; many never go near the casket.

CEMETERIES.   In a general way it is true that just as there are funeral directors who cater predominantly to upper, middle, and lower class strata respectively, there are also upper, middle, and lower class cemeteries. However, in the Philadelphia vicinity this threefold classification has only limited significance. Today most cemetery managers try to deal with all classes, so long as they are white and Protestant. With the exception of the registerites—who have somewhat exclusive final resting places—class distinctions are to be found within rather than among cemeteries.

Traditionally, class distinctions within the cemetery were based on size of lot and size of memorial or mausoleum. Historically the rich man's grave was marked by a large memorial or mausoleum, the poor man's by a small head or footstone, or perhaps by the absence of a stone.

Today the upper class family is much more likely to buy a moderate-sized lot with a moderate-sized, conservative memorial, free of elaboration and epigram. While the mean size of the lot, and the mean size and price of the memorial in lower class families is doubtless smaller, the tremendous disparity among the classes seems to be disappearing. At the present time economic class differences are more likely to be found in connection with the location of the lot, which in turn hinges on such factors as who is buried nearby, whether the lot is on "high ground," and general accessibility to the particular area. All in all, the ecology of a Philadelphia cemetery shows the same kind of class distinctions—though less marked—that exist in the spatial hierarchy of the city itself.

POTTER'S FIELD.   A pressing fear among many lower class families is the vision of a burial in potter's field. Such families, it was reported, will go to almost any length to avoid this kind of burial. Individuals interred at potter's field are stripped of all the symbols which classify them as human beings. They are buried without flowers, without clothes, without graves, and without names. Burials take place in long rows of trenches, with a number on a wooden paddle marking each body. If the body is not claimed in a certain length of time, it is dug up and burned in the adjoining crematory. Since about 90 percent of the bodies are never claimed, cremation is necessary in order to make room for the new bodies, which arrive at a rate of between fifteen and twenty-five a month. Before the idea of cremation became popular, it was necessary to keep moving potter's field, and a check with the Pennsylvania Historical Society revealed that at present there are nine extinct fields within the city limits.

REGISTERITE CEMETERIES. At the other extreme, registerites in the Philadelphia area customarily are buried in registerite cemeteries, which are usually located in the churchyards of upper class Episcopal churches. Where the registerite is a non-Episcopal the foregoing statement does not apply, although such cases are in the minority. Historically in Philadelphia churchyard burials of this kind have always been the normal procedure in the event of registerite death. With the passing of time, however, these churchyard cemeteries have become filled because of limited space. Several of these "filled" cemeteries still exist in the city—the church still functions even though there are no further burials. In all cases these cemeteries are marked by their simplicity: the tombstones are small and unelaborate. Some of the famous Philadelphia names—signers of the Declaration of Independence and the Constitution, for example—can be seen on simple stone tablets.

As these cemeteries were filled, and as the registerites moved to the Philadelphia "main line," they followed the same historical burial pattern. Present registerite cemeteries are all characterized by the same theme: simplicity and uniformity. There are no "choice locations," the lots are uniform in size and price, and the memorials, while not identical, are generally similar with respect to size and style.

CONCLUSIONS

When class is defined in terms of economic level, and when the locale is restricted to the Philadelphia area, class differentials have been reported in many of the behavior patterns associated with bereavement, funerals, and burials. Most marked are the differences between the upper and lower classes, these differences being both of kind and degree. Distinctive middle class patterns fail to emerge, reported differences being almost wholly a matter of degree.

Coexisting with class differences there are characteristic religious and nationality differences, although at the present stage of our study the indication is that class differences exist within these groups.

Within the upper "social" class—members of the Philadelphia Social Register—differential patterns were reported which are recognizably different from the upper economic class.

In terms of the class stratification as herein defined, differentials have been reported for the following specific categories: Relative cost of funeral, frequency of cremation, elapsed time between death and burial, viewing the body, flower arrangements and the elimination of flowers, emotionality, funeral customs, ecology within the cemetery.

Funeral and burial customs reputedly vary according to geographical location, and probably vary according to size and kind of city. The extent to which these and other factors were operative in the above study can be tested by further studies in other localities.

33 RELIGION AMONG ETHNIC AND RACIAL MINORITIES

J. Oscar Lee

INTRODUCTION   Majority and minority status depend
in large part upon factors of race, religion, and nationality.
Although a Roman Catholic is a member of the majority Caucasian race, he is a member of a religious minority in America. An
American Protestant of German heritage is a member of the Caucasian race but is also a member of a religious majority. The Japanese American, a member of the Mongoloid race, shares in either
minority Buddhism or majority Christianity. Although the Negro
shares in a majority Protestant denomination (for example, Methodism), his color makes him a member of a racial minority. Where
Irish are predominant, non-Roman Catholics may be minorities.
But where Mormons dominate, the Irish in turn may occupy the
minority position.

The actual definition of minority status is dependent in large
part upon the visibility of the person or group. Without characteristics which identify the member or group as dissimilar from
the majority, the majority would not be able to designate a specific group as objects for prejudice. Skin color, type of clothing,
etiquette procedures, and vocabulary serve to indicate variations
from majority characteristics. The present trend is toward the
gradual amalgamation (intermarriage) of ethnic minorities (nationality groups less clearly differentiated) and the agonizingly
slow assimilation of racial minorities.

Louis Wirth claims that minorities may be categorized in one
of four types. The *pluralistic minority* recognizes group differences

J. Oscar Lee is Secretary of Program Services, Division of Christian Life and Mission
of the National Council of Churches of Christ in the United States of America.

Abridged and reprinted from *The Annals*, Volume 332 (November, 1960), pp. 112-125
with the permission of the author and editors.

and accepts a form of peaceful coexistence. Will Herberg (*see* Herberg, Articles 43 and 46) claims that American religion is primarily a form of pluralism based upon the tacit acceptance of minority religious groups by the majority and vice versa. Whereas in the past nationality differences determined personal identity, modern religious membership is now most important. Both the majority (Protestants) and the minority (Roman Catholics and Jews) have accepted a pluralistic outlook. Although adhering to a limited number of characteristic cultural patterns, each group participates in society and expresses tolerance of dissimilar viewpoints. The *assimilationist minority* may seek absorption into the dominant group through intermixture with divergent racial and ethnic strains. Although assimilation may simply result in a composite culture in which past cultural characteristics of the group are dispersed to form a new broader culture, assimilation may be hastened through amalgamation (intermarriage). The formation of Reformed Judaism resulted from the attempt of American Jews to adjust to the new cultural environment. The *secessionist minority,* on the other hand, tends to withdraw from participation with majority groups. Rejecting both cultural pluralism and group assimilation, they seek a stage of religious self-determination and group purity. Fundamentalists seek adherence to the absolute interpretation of religion most often identified with the past. Seeking to remain free of liberal religious groups, they will often express antagonism to the established culture (*see* Ahlstrom, Article 1).

A *militant minority* attempts to reverse existing majority-minority statuses. Rather than accepting equality, the militant minority attempts to secure conditions in which the group may prevail over those which formerly dominated it. Religious minorities have been known to become most coercive once they have established themselves as local majorities. Early Jewish Zionism reflects the aggressive attitude of the militant minority. The Black Muslim movement represents both a secessionist outlook and an organizational militancy. Using Muslim faith as a religious vehicle, it attempts to gain political goals which will result in minority territorial sovereignty.

J. Oscar Lee, Secretary of Program Services, Division of Christian Life and Mission of the National Council of Churches, observes that racial and ethnic minority churches have developed to serve the religious and social needs of their minority constituents (*see* Douglass, Article 13). Although churches serving Europeans have been rapidly integrated, non-European Negro, Puerto Rican, Spanish-speaking, American Indian, Chinese American, and Japanese American churches have remained differentiated at least partly because of community segregational patterns. However, the movement toward desegregation, equal opportunity, urbanization, and ecological and status mobility is exerting pressures upon the original institutions, which may result in a slow demise of the fully segregated church. Because the Negro is marked by ready visibility, the integration of Negro denominations will probably progress at a minimal rate (see Pope, Article 2).

O NE CANNOT DEAL with religion among ethnic and racial minorities without seeing it in the context of the churches' concern about race relations. The churches have been especially preoccupied with this problem in the past twenty years. This interest has included: an examination of the pattern of racial segregation in American society; a determination of the religious and ethical implications of racial segregation; and movement to eliminate racial segregation from the life and work of the churches. One result of this process is that an increasing number of Christians agree that racial segregation must be rejected since it is a violation of the spirit and the teaching of the Christian gospel.

The problems of ethnic and racial minority groups are a concern of most of the churches in the nation. Mobility and urbanization, however, and other socioeconomic changes which have affected the lives of people belonging to these ethnic and racial minority groups have special meaning for the churches of which they are members. The changes in goals, functions, and programs which many of the churches have faced in the past twenty years are not only in response to demands for adjustments to new ways of life, but also may be indicative of changes in attitudes about the role of religion in meeting the needs of persons and groups.

THE NEGRO CHURCHES.   The largest nonwhite minority group in the United States is the Negro-American group. In 1950, the United States Census indicated that there were 15,482,000 nonwhites in the United States and that Negroes constituted more than 95 percent of this group. Negroes are mainly found in separate Negro denominations. These denominations are the National Baptist Convention, United States of America, Incorporated; the National Baptist Convention of America; the African Methodist Episcopal Church; the African Methodist Episcopal Zion Church, and the Christian Methodist Episcopal Church. While accurate membership figures for these denominations are not available, it is estimated that the five Negro denominations have approximately ten million members.[1] Comparisons of this estimate with estimates made in previous years would seem to indicate that these denominations are growing in membership. There are approximately 600,000 Negro members in the predominantly white Protestant denominations of which about 366,000 are in the Methodist Church.[2] According to the Na-

---

[1] Yearbook of the American Churches, 1960 (New York: The National Council of Churches, 1960), pp. 253, 257.
[2] "Proceedings of the General Conference of the Methodist Church, 1960," Daily Christian Advocate, Vol. 1, No. 3 (April 29, 1960), p. 105.

tional Catholic Almanac for 1960, there were, as of January 1959, about 595,-155 Roman Catholic Negroes in the United States. This is an increase of 20,-000 over the preceding year.[3]

These figures point to the central place that the churches have occupied and continue to occupy in the life of the Negro community. In a very real sense, it is the Negro's own institution in that it is organized, led, developed, owned, and controlled by Negroes.

CENTER OF OPPORTUNITY.   Blocked as the Negro is by the pattern of racial segregation from full participation in the total life of the community, the Negro church affords him the opportunity for full participation in an organized group.

The Negro churches are not only composed of the masses of the people, but the churches are also an important medium through which these masses shape and express their aspirations. Moreover, the Negro minister has the historic role of leader in the community. In the days after slavery, he was the principal if not only leader in many communities. He still has direct contact with the masses of the people who are members of his congregation and who look to him for counsel and guidance on many problems.

MOBILITY AND URBANIZATION.   The movement of Negroes to urban areas first gained momentum during World War I and continued in the period between 1920 and 1930. In the depression years there was very little movement. During World War II it gained considerably greater momentum. According to data published by the United States Bureau of the Census in 1900, 77 percent of the Negro population lived in rural areas and 23 percent in urban areas. By 1950 this has changed radically; 37 percent lived in rural areas and 63 percent in urban areas. Also, much of this movement has been from the southern to the northern, midwestern, and western areas of the country. Indicative of this trend is the fact that the Negro population in the thirty largest cities of the North, Midwest, and West more than doubled in the decade 1940 to 1950. This trend appears to have continued in the decade 1950 to 1960.

In the movement from rural areas to urban areas, Negroes encounter a different group of social problems. Major problems are racial discrimination in housing and the slum conditions in city areas where most Negroes are forced to live. These are often accompanied by poor housing, poor schools, and poor community facilities and services. Another set of problems revolve around unemployment and underemployment.

SOCIAL RELEVANCE.   There appears to be substantial agreement among many Negroes that in addition to worship and religious education the church should be active in promoting the social advancement of the race. There is an expectation among an increasing number of Negroes that the churches should be active in the improvement of the community, cooperate with community

[3] *National Catholic Almanac, 1960* (Garden City, N.Y.: Doubleday, 1960), p. 473.

welfare and civic organizations, and engage in social action to correct injustice, particularly in race relations. Possibly the classic example of the realization of this expectation is the Montgomery, Alabama bus boycott which was led by ministers with the full and active support of their churches. This movement drew the admiration and support of Negroes nationally. These expectations have affected the programs of many churches which are including such activities as education in social and community problems, recreation, social service, and social action. Changes in the status of Negroes as well as the social problems which they confront in urban areas are factors in stimulating these expectations and this development.

CONTRAST OF OLD AND NEW.   This is not to imply that the religious beliefs which are traditional in the Negro church have disappeared. There are still a substantial number of Negro church members who hold to religious concepts which emphasize personal salvation, pietistic individual living, and a better life after death. Also, there are many people who find escape in emotional expression. However, despite this, the emphasis on social concern and action may mean that such factors as the pressure of urban problems, increased education, and a better understanding of methods of group action are effective in changing the traditional attitudes of Negroes about the role of religion.

STORE-FRONT CHURCHES.   Emotional expression as a factor in the religious experience of the Negro raises the question of store-front churches and the movements of "personal saviors." Dissatisfaction about emotional expressions works two ways, and it is at least one index to class stratification in the churches. There are those people, usually members of the growing Negro middle class, who resent emotional expression in the church. Some of these people become members of churches with more restrained services. These churches usually emphasize a rational and action-oriented approach to religion under the leadership of a well-trained minister. At the other end of the spectrum are those who are dissatisfied with the restraint on emotional expression or who feel that the church does not provide the warmth of fellowship or who may have a doctrinal difference. These people withdraw to organize a church of their own. Many of these groups start as store-front churches.

Leadership appears to be a key factor in the destiny of these churches. Some are started for no other reason than that a person with some leadership capabilities decides to organize a church. The ministers of many of these churches have practical leadership capabilities but little academic or professional training. Some of these churches have a short span of existence because they are led by people who aim to exploit the members; others are quite permanent and still others grow into larger, established congregations. The people, usually of limited educational background and opportunity, who are members of these churches seem to find security by participating in a small group which emphasizes what is called the "old time religion." Some of these store-front churches may be affiliated with one of the five Negro denominational groups mentioned above, but the large group of them are identified as Holiness Pentecostal, Faith Healing, or Spiritualist.

PERSONAL SAVIORS.   Many of the movements of the "personal saviors" are national in scope. Some of the better known examples are the United House of Prayer for All People, the Father Divine Peace Movement, and, more lately, the movement of Mr. Elijah Mohammad which calls itself "Muslim." It is difficult to summarize these movements because they vary greatly in purpose, organization, content of belief, and practices. While there are no reliable figures, it is apparent that the vast majority of Negroes do not belong to them.

CHURCHES OF ETHNIC GROUPS.   The great immigration from European countries prior to World War I made its impact upon the churches. The immigrants brought the religion of their home countries with them. In these immigrant churches the language of the homeland was spoken and some of the customs as well as traditions were maintained. As the children of these immigrant families grew older, they wished to be thought of as Americans; they spoke English and exhibited little desire to master the language of their parents. This made it necessary for the churches to hold some services in English. In effect, the churches became bilingual, but even this was temporary. The stoppage of the tide of European immigration, the depletion of the first generation by death, and the opposition of the second and third generations to the use of a foreign language have produced a gradual disappearance of the bilingual feature in many of these churches. In some cases these churches have had to close because the second and third generations have moved to other neighborhoods. In the cases in which these churches have made successful transitions, they have had to forego their preoccupation with European customs, traditions, and language in order to serve the current needs of their congregations. It is the judgment of many competent observers that when such a church fails to do this, its future is not promising.

This is only a part of the story of ethnic groups in the United States. Puerto Ricans, Spanish-speaking people of the Southwest, American Indians, Chinese Americans and Japanese Americans have churches with distinctive characteristics.

SPANISH-SPEAKING PEOPLE.   The Spanish-speaking population in the United States is a large one. This brief statement will deal with two groups, the Puerto Rican and the Spanish-speaking people of the Southwest. The latter group is defined to include naturalized immigrants from Mexico, native-born persons with parents or grandparents born in Mexico, alien Mexicans in the United States either on a temporary or permanent basis and Spanish Colonials largely concentrated in New Mexico and southern Colorado.[4]

[4] Bureau of Research and Survey, *Spanish-Speaking Americans* (Unpublished manuscript by Blair, Lively, and Trimble; New York: National Council of Churches, 1959), p. 14.

The Migration Division of the Department of Labor of the Commonwealth of Puerto Rico estimated that the population of Puerto Rico as of July 1, 1958 was 2,317,000 and that as of December 31, 1958 there were 849,000 Puerto Ricans living on the mainland of which 77 percent were living in New York City.[5] The 1950 United States Census reported that there were 2,448,-977 white persons of Spanish surname in five Southwestern states and persons in other states born in Mexico or with one or more parents born in Mexico. Of this number 1,998,415 were native born and 450,562 were Mexican born. It is also reported that 1,519,812 of the Spanish surname population in 5 Southwestern states or 66 percent were urban dwellers. The five Southwestern states are Arizona, California, Colorado, New Mexico, and Texas.

There are substantial differences between the Puerto Rican population and the Spanish-speaking population of the Southwest. For instance, one of these differences is that Puerto Ricans are citizens of the United States and movement within the country constitutes migration. On the other hand, the people of Mexican origin are immigrants from another country. There are some similarities. Many of the people of Mexican origin came from an agrarian society and some of the Puerto Ricans came from a similar type of society. Both groups came from societies in which the characteristics of Spanish culture and the traditions of the Roman Catholic Church are predominant. The majority of both groups have settled in urban areas. They speak Spanish and those who have not mastered English experience difficulty in communication. Both groups experience a lack of full acceptance in American society because of their ethnic background. Even though some people of Puerto Rican and Mexican background, because of education and skill, have gained a degree of acceptance, these groups are victimized by socioeconomic disabilities.

These factors are reflected in the churches. The Spanish-speaking people of the Southwest come from a Catholic background. Catholicism was taken for granted in Mexico. There was little knowledge that other religious forms existed, and this was true of Protestantism, also. Religion was deeply interwoven into the life of the community.

MEXICANS. Mexican Americans in the United States are attracted to Protestant churches, but the total number is small. Some attend English-language Protestant churches. It is reported, however, that few local Protestant churches in the border areas exhibit active interest in attracting Mexican Americans. The fear of not being accepted as well as difficulties of language may deter many Mexican Americans from joining these churches. Also, there are churches which serve Mexican Americans. A study of eighty-one Mexican churches in 1959 indicated that fifty-one claim less than one hundred members each. Sixty-three of these churches reported under one hundred in average attendance. Twenty-five of the churches reported using some English in the services and fifty-three used no English. The denominational distribution of these churches was as follows: Disciples—three; United Presbyterian,

[5] *Ibid.*, p. 49.

United States of America—twenty-one; Methodist—twenty-two; Congregational—three; American Luthern—six; Church of God—two; Episcopal—five; American Baptist—nineteen.[6]

PUERTO RICANS. The fact that Puerto Rico is predominantly Roman Catholic in religious background is well known. It is reported that probably 80 percent of the island population would say they were Catholic if pressed with the question of religious orientation. However, most recent observers note that perhaps 20 percent or less actually practice the public and obvious manifestations of the Roman Catholic faith.[7] It is estimated that at least 10 percent of the population of the island could be characterized as Protestant. Protestantism has been on the island for about fifty years. Protestant denominations are working in 522 areas of service on the island; 413 of these areas are identified as rural.[8]

Puerto Ricans bring their religious traditions to the mainland with them, but some observers believe that a larger proportion of Puerto Ricans in New York City than on the island do not have an active relationship with the Roman Catholic Church.[9] However, many Roman Catholic parishes serve the religious and social needs of Puerto Ricans.

The few English-language Protestant churches that do serve Puerto Ricans offer activities designed to integrate them into the congregation, such as released time religious classes, Scout troops, athletic leagues, forums, and other types of leisure-time and recreational activities. Some churches conduct worship services in Spanish at various times and a few churches have Spanish-speaking staff members.

Some information was gathered about 169 non-Roman Catholic Spanish-speaking churches in New York City in 1953. Ninety-two of the 169 churches were identified as Pentecostal; thirty-eight were conducted by Protestant denominations; thirty-four were independent; and five were connected with New York City Mission Society. Ninety-six of the 169 churches which returned completed questionnaires reported 9,965 church members of which 8,239 were said to be active. The average total number of members per church was about 103 and the total average attendance at the main Sunday Worship Service was about 102. Seventy-one of the ninety-six churches reported memberships of less than one hundred each and forty of the seventy-one had memberships under fifty. It should be pointed out that three of these churches had more than three hundred members and three others had more than five hun-

[6] Bureau of Research and Survey, *Missionary Opportunity Among Spanish-Americans, Report on Local Church Questionnaires* (Mimeographed; New York: National Council of Churches, September 1959), pp. 1, 6, 9.
[7] *Midcentury Pioneers and Protestants: A Survey Report of the Puerto Rican Migration to the U. S. Mainland* and, in particular, *A Study of the Protestant Expression Among Puerto Ricans in New York City* (Mimeographed; New York: Protestant Council of the City of New York, March 1954), p. 3.
[8] *Ibid.*, p. 2.
[9] *Ibid.*, p. 10.

dred members. However, seventy-nine of these churches are completely self-supporting and forty-five have full-time pastors. The number of these churches appears to be growing. Seventy-one of the ninety-six churches were organized between 1940 and the first six months of 1953.[10] Most of these churches are small, but they are self-reliant and active institutions.

AMERICAN INDIANS. Both Roman Catholic and Protestant churches have conducted missionary activities among American Indians for a long period of time. In 1951, thirty-six Protestant denominations were doing mission work among these people. While there are no reliable statistics, it is estimated that there are between 65,000 and 70,000 Protestants and about 95,000 Roman Catholics among American Indians.

Of the 400,000 persons counted as Indians in the United States about 300,000 live on or near reservations. The movement of Indians to urban centers has become pronounced since World War II. This movement flows into cities such as Minneapolis, Minnesota, Rapid City, South Dakota, Chicago, Illinois, Salt Lake City, Utah, and Los Angeles, California. Migration to urban centers confronts Indians who have lived in rural areas with the problems which are connected with adjustment to urban life.

The churches, both Roman Catholic and Protestant in many cities, have recognized the need to help American Indians adjust to and become a part of church and community life in urban centers. The result is that they have established programs to work with other interested community agencies to accomplish this.

CHINESE. The United States Census of 1950 reported 117,629 Chinese in the United States. The estimated total for 1958 is 135,000.

The Protestant home missionary movement started work among Chinese about 1853. The Roman Catholics started work in San Francisco about 1900. San Francisco today is the largest center of Catholic activities among Chinese.

A study of sixty-two Protestant Chinese Churches in 1952 shows some of the characteristics of these churches.[11] Forty-three are denominational, five are interdenominational, and fourteen are independent. Twelve are self-supporting groups; twenty-six receive some aid from denominational mission boards; fifteen depend entirely upon, or receive the major part of their support from mission boards; and seven are small groups with limited programs. The average Chinese Church has 155 members with the range running from less than fifty members to over one thousand. The average budget is about $5,260.

INTEGRATION IN THE CHURCHES. The previous discussion has considered the churches among racial and ethnic minorities. In a sense, this is testimony to the fact that these groups are separated in varying degrees from

10 Ibid., pp. 10-22.
11 Horace R. Cayton and Anne O. Lively, The Chinese in the United States and the Chinese Christian Churches (New York: Bureau of Research and Survey, The National Council of Churches, April 1955), pp. 48-68.

the main body of the churches. The concern about the elimination of segregation from religious institutions has been mentioned. The positive goal is the inclusion of persons in the congregation and the activities of the church or church-related institution on the basis of religious commitment without regard to race or ethnic origin. The churches are taking positive steps in this direction.

The Roman Catholic Church has been clear and forthright in its policy that racial segregation is contrary to the teachings of the Church. On this basis it has moved forthrightly to eliminate it from the local parishes, parochial schools and church organizations where it exists.

The National Council of Churches and most of the major Protestant denominations have adopted statements either renouncing the practice of segregation in the churches or affirming a ministry which is inclusive of all people regardless of race or ethnic origin who desire to participate in a particular church or church-related institution.

These statements have provided the basis for the achievement of integration of national and regional church organizations. Significant integration has taken place in councils of churches. Racial minorities are integrated in the organization of the National Council of Churches. This is true also in state and city councils of churches, even in states where segregation is enforced by law. Several of the predominantly white denominations have moved to eliminate racial segregation from their national and regional organizations. Several are currently grappling with the problem. The Negro denominations face the problem of integrating white people into their organizations. A number of denominations with predominantly white membership are carrying on various types of programs aimed at the elimination of segregation in local churches and church-related institutions.

The local church has presented a difficult problem, but even here there is movement. While there are no reliable figures on the total number of Protestant churches which have members of more than one race, recent studies by denominations indicate they are increasing in number. While the figures of the denominational studies are not comparable, they would seem to indicate that possibly 10 percent of the Protestant churches have members of more than one race and that most of these churches are located in urban communities where people of two or more races live together. To be sure, the percentage is small, but it involves hundreds of churches, and it is significant because movement among Protestant churches appears to be in the direction of integration.

CONCLUSION.   It seems clear that a major function of the churches of ethnic and racial minorities is to serve the religious and social needs of their people. This function is shaped and reinforced by ethnic and racial discrimination, which is a dominant factor influencing every aspect of the lives of people belonging to these minority groups. Their aspirations are an influential factor in shaping the goals toward which these churches work. The church programs are determined to a large extent by the problems and needs which confront ethnic and racial minority peoples. These churches are dynamic in that they are affected by social changes such as mobility and urbanization as well as the increasing and imperative demand for full participation in community life on the basis of ability without regard to ethnic or racial background. There is evidence that this in turn has affected the expectations of people about the role or roles of the churches in meeting the needs of people who face the necessity of adjusting to these changes.

The very existence of churches which serve people belonging to a particular ethnic or racial minority group is, in a sense, a testimony to the pervasiveness of racial segregation in our society. It is clear that segregation based on ethnic or racial background is a major problem confronting the churches. At the same time, many people in the churches recognize that this is a basic contradiction of Christian principles and teaching. In recognition of this, there is a movement to eliminate segregation and to achieve inclusive practices in all areas of church life. While the churches face the responsibility of taking increasing initiative in accomplishing this, it must be recognized that desegregation and integration of the churches is related to desegregation and integration of the total community. For instance, many churches find that racial segregation in housing makes it extremely difficult, if not impossible, to achieve integration in fact in the churches. Therefore, the churches face the challenge to work for the elimination of segregation from every aspect of American society.

34 CHURCHMEN AND RESIDENTIAL DESEGREGATION

Henry Clark

INTRODUCTION   The problem of race is national. Whether North or South, East or West, the issue touches the heart of religious faith and causes reaction among religious leadership and membership (*see* Campbell and Pettigrew, Article 22). Although the nature of the problem differs in such diverse settings as a Negro urban ghetto of a northern city and a rural textile community of a southern state, religious persons typically manifest racial prejudice.

Prejudice patterns are reinforced, of course, by conditions quite apart from religious institutions themselves—income, housing, degree and type of mobility which has occurred—all affect religious ideas and participation. Minority exclusion from the better suburban and urban residential housing, for example, has been due in large part to the economically exclusive character of housing developments. Where costs are high, minority members find difficulty in raising necessary down-payments. Where real estate salesmen and local banks refuse showings or to extend loans on property in interracial areas, minority members are virtually forced to live in ghettoes. Where minority visibility is most clear (*see* Lee, Article 33), segregation in housing is apt to be most intense. Minority members themselves do not desire to live in an area of tension. Although there are occasional interracial "pioneers," the masses of minority members prefer to remain secure in the subsociety of their "own kind." Meanwhile the general attitude regard-

Abridged and reprinted from *The Review of Religious Research*, Volume 5, Number 3, Copyrighted 1964 by the Religious Research Association, Inc. Also drawn from *The Church and Residential Desegregation* (New Haven: College and University Press, 1965).

HENRY CLARK is Assistant Professor of Church and Community at Union Theological Seminary.

ing housing matters is typified by the recent repeal of fair housing legislation in California (the Rumford Act) under the pretext that each person should have the right to sell to whomever he desires. In practice this decision results in the maintenance of racial and ethnic segregation.

Residential segregation contributes to segregation in schools, community associations, and employment as well as in churches. School boundaries have often been drawn to minimize the number of integrated schools. Although the neighborhood school concept has been the cornerstone of American education, in practice it has resulted in educational segregation. Likewise churches serving a local segregated area remain themselves segregated (see Lee, Article 33). Even in areas where majority and minority members meet, the number of persons willing to share in an integrated religious institution have been few (see Pope, Article 2). Minority community associations have often been organized to provide social outlets for minority members who are barred from participating in the local country club or fraternal organization.

Because minority members have proverbially been the last hired and the first fired, their employment remains unstable. Limited by education, social training and forms of discrimination, the minority member generally finds little market for his unskilled ability. Although the Jews have risen above these limitations, Negroes, Spanish-speaking persons, and American Indians, remain the victims of discriminatory patterns. Japanese Americans and Chinese Americans possess greater mobility, although they encounter prejudice in more subtle ways.

PUBLIC AWARENESS OF the problem of racial injustice has attained unprecedented heights during recent years, and most major religious bodies have attempted to heighten that awareness and channel it into social action designed to help overcome the problem. One of the types of community action most often undertaken in Northern cities, frequently under the sponsorship of local religious leaders, is the "open housing covenant" (OHC) campaign. In contrast to the racially restrictive covenant—which was declared legally unenforceable by a 1948 Supreme Court decision, but which is still being signed and observed by homeowners unaware of the Court's action—the OHC affirms the signer's willingness to live beside, rent, or sell to any responsible person without regard to race, creed or national origin. The purpose of an OHC campaign is to demonstrate that a large number of the citizens in a given community are in favor of nondiscriminatory practices in the sale and rental of housing, and thus to encourage realtors and private citizens to make transactions on a nondiscriminatory basis.

The findings reported in this essay arise from the study of an OHC campaign conducted under religious auspices in a Northern city of about 35,000 inhabitants which we shall call *Newfield*. Data were gathered in tape recorded interviews of approximately one-hour to one-hour-and-a-half duration with twenty-eight clergymen of the city, and in a questionnaire responded to by 225 laymen. Most of the items on the interview schedule for clergymen were open-ended questions designed to provide information regarding the respondent's definition of the situation in which the OHC appeal was launched, his attitudes toward the OHC as a device for dealing with the problem, and his approach in presenting the OHC to his parishioners. Most of the items on the questionnaire for laymen were "Yes/No" or multiple choice questions intended to furnish information regarding lay attitudes toward the OHC, church sponsorship of the covenant, and factors affecting one's decision to support it or not to support it.

RESPONSES FROM CLERGYMEN. There were substantial reasons for supposing that clerical support for the open housing covenant in Newfield would be virtually unanimous and quite vigorous. Roman Catholic priests had the backing of their diocesan bishop, Negro Protestant ministers had an obvious stake in any community effort to overcome racial discrimination, and none of the white Protestant clergymen had openly voiced strong reservations about, much less genuine opposition to, the covenant campaign when it was proposed in the Clergy Fellowship's meeting.

Virtually all of the clergymen contacted during the course of this study had a fairly liberal attitude about race relations in general. There were no objections to integration as a desirable goal in the most important areas of public life and few objections to it as a desirable possibility in private life. Only one of the men who disapproved of interracial marriage did so on grounds that "mixing the races" was contrary to the will of God, and none showed the kind of negative emotional reaction to the very question which would have been characteristic of some clergymen in any section of the country and of a great many ministers in the South. Only three of the clergymen opposed civil rights legislation; only four disapproved of the NAACP as a necessary instrument for the achievement of racial justice. Fifteen endorsed boycotts as a legitimate tactic. Other civil rights organizations and tactics did not receive majority approval or disapproval, but there were thirteen who favored sit-ins and twelve who approved of freedom rides.

Several questions probed into the attitudes of Newfield clergymen concerning the relationship between Christian faith and social concern. There was almost no compartmentalization evident in their verbal affirmations of the essential link between belief and action, and they unanimously approved of official church pronouncements on vital public issues. With few exceptions, all of the white ministers were sophisticated enough not to expect any semimagical guidance from prayer or from the Bible.

Despite their insistence that the church should speak out on public issues, however, most of the clergymen were very poorly informed on the subject of public affairs in general and race relations in particular. They relied on denominational publications, daily newspapers or the popular news magazines (such as *Time* or *Newsweek*) for their knowledge of these subjects. A Negro pastor reported that the major Negro weekly newspapers were unavailable in Newfield, and the only nonnewspaper source mentioned by any of the Negro clergymen was *Jet*. The denominational publications most often mentioned were the "family-type" periodicals rather than the more analytical journals, and only three ministers reported regular reading of nondenominational publications such as *The Christian Century, Christianity and Crisis, Worldview*, etc. Only one man kept up with any of the semipopular public affairs magazines that offer reasonably good coverage of racial news, and only two men demonstrated familiarity with social science literature in this field. Most of the ministers had no recollection of ever hearing about the Congress of Racial Equality (CORE) or the Southern Christian Leadership Conference (SCLC), even though they had all heard of the Reverend Martin Luther King. All of the men reflected a knowledge of the NAACP, but almost without exception they prefaced their remarks on it by saying something to the effect that "I don't know very much about it, you understand, but . . ." and their approval of it was nearly always qualified.

There was a discrepancy, too, between the clergymen's assertion of the absolutely necessary link between Christian faith and social action, on the one hand, and, on the other, the low priority they assigned to the minister's role of community leader. All other ministerial roles were considered more important in terms of what the clergyman actually did with his time, what he enjoyed doing, what he felt his parishioners expected of him, and what he thought a minister ought ideally to do. Ministers thought that parishioners also were of the opinion that they should spend a relatively small amount of time in community activities. This pattern of thought was reflected in the fact that the role of "organizer" was actually given very little time.

Indifference to the church's role in community organization is also reflected in the almost total absence of lines of communication between Newfield clergymen of different faiths and races. Catholic priests and Protestant ministers barely knew each other, and there were no informal friendships between men of different religious persuasions to lubricate the machinery of interfaith cooperation when the need arose. Negro pastors were theoretically members of the Protestant Clergy Fellowship of Newfield, and they attended its meetings occasionally. But their participation in this group was marginal in the extreme, partly because of the 10:00 a.m. weekday meeting time (which excluded the Negro preachers, all of whom had eight-hour-per-day, five-days-per-week jobs) and partly because of an atmosphere in which some of the Negro clergymen felt unwelcome.

In light of these findings about the lack of informed social awareness and communication among Newfield clergymen, it is hardly surprising that the open housing covenant campaign did not call forth the whole-hearted support of every minister and priest in the community. Interviews with twenty-eight clergymen revealed that three clearly opposed the OHC, fifteen who professed approval did nothing (or virtually nothing) to support it, and eight who made more than a half-hearted gesture in support of the covenant were ineffective in obtaining signatures.

Three of the fifteen clergymen who must be classified as "half-hearted" actually made no effort to present the OHC to their parishioners. One of these ministers declared that the governing body of his church had refused to allow presentation; another failed to act because he felt the OHC approach was inadequate as a means of combating discrimination in housing; the third indicated in the interview that he was going to present the covenant "later on that winter," but he never did so. The remainder of the half-hearted limited their support of the OHC to placing the covenant cards in the vestibule of the church "for any who were interested," pulpit announcements of the availability of the cards, or token recommendations of support were unaccompanied by any follow-up action. Very few signed covenant cards were obtained in these churches: for example, one Roman Catholic parish with a membership of more than one thousand families turned in no signed covenants, another parish with more than two thousand families turned in only three, and the three Negro churches obtained signatures from only a handful of their parishioners.

The reasons for failure on the part of the clergymen who were more than half-hearted in their support of the OHC, yet nevertheless ineffectual, deserve closer examination. Five of the eight men in this category were "sermonizers": they participated in the common pulpit emphasis on behalf of the covenant which was asked of all Protestant ministers, but there was little or no follow-up action after the sermon had been delivered. None of these pastors succeeded in obtaining signatures from as much as ten percent of their congregation.

In the two churches where a large percentage of the membership supported the OHC—one hundred forty-one signatures from a membership of three hundred ninety in one case, one hundred twenty-six from a membership of six hundred in the other—several factors not operative in less successful churches were evident. A vigorous sermon urging support of the OHC was followed by personal efforts on the part of the minister to confront individual members and groups of parishioners with their moral responsibility concerning the covenant. One pastor always carried some covenant cards in his coat pocket, and he made it a habit to offer one for immediate signature whenever he encountered a parishioner who had not yet returned a signed card. (When one parishioner demurred on the grounds that "some of the leading people in our church are not supporting this thing," the pastor asked him to name one such person—and when the reluctant parishioner discovered that each of the three persons he named had in fact signed the covenant after all, he agreed to add his name to the list!) In both of these successful parishes the church's social action committee played an active role in distributing covenant cards and soliciting signatures. Parishioners heard favorable mention of the OHC in repeated pulpit announcements, in articles in parish publications, in meetings of various groups in the church, and in personal conversation with the pastor and a variety of laymen. It is also noteworthy that in each of the successful churches, covenant cards were distributed *and collected* as a part of the worship service where the sermon focused on the problem of discrimination in housing and the OHC as a means of attacking it.

VIEWS OF LAYMEN. The findings regarding lay opinions are based on a return of two hundred twenty-five questionnaires from a mailing of 1100 copies of the instrument to a random sample of members in four parishes. One hundred fifty-seven questionnaires were returned by signers of the OHC; sixty-eight by nonsupporters (fifty-seven from nonsigners and eleven from persons who were unaware of the OHC until they heard of it in the letter accompanying the questionnaire).

The principal findings regarding lay opinion are as follows: (1) "Multitudinist" channels of communication[1] are not altogether worthless, for one third of the signers responding heard of the OHC through a parish publication and one-fourth heard of it through the newspaper. But multitudinist channels are not sufficient: results in Newfield confirm the experience of other communities where OHC campaigns have been held, revealing that face-to-face presentation of the covenant elicits more signatures than reliance on impersonal modes of presentation.

(2) Repeated confrontation with the OHC is also essential in obtaining signatures. Forty-three percent of the nonsupporters were not opposed to the OHC upon first hearing of it, and one-third were *favorably* disposed initially. If this large proportion of nonsupporters had been urged repeatedly by church representatives to sign the covenant, a large number of them might have done so.

(3) Among the factors influencing signers, the moral authority of their pastor is still a potent consideration: forty-two percent declared that utterances of their clergyman were important in their decision, and one-third asserted that they were influenced by a sermon or some other pulpit pronouncement made by the minister. The influence of the pastor was mentioned with significantly greater frequency by blue collar workers and persons of relatively low educational attainment. The ambiguity of contact with Negroes is confirmed by the fact that this influence was cited by some nonsupporters, but the probable liberalizing value of equal-status contact is suggested by the fact that this factor was mentioned twice as often by signers. The influence of family, neighbors and associates other than neighbors was relatively slight on both signers and nonsupporters.

[1] Martin E. Marty, *The New Shape of American Religion* (New York: Harper and Row, 1958), pp. 134ff.

(4) Reasons for not signing the OHC were significantly indefinite. Concern over property values was cited by only eighteen percent of the nonsigners, and fear of racial intermarriage was admitted by only one-eighth of the nonsupporters. That fifteen percent of the nonsupporters stressed anxiety about use of their names or final disposition of the OHC cards suggests that a fuller explanation of the covenant appeal might result in more signatures from the hesitant. That one-third gave no reason for not signing the OHC indicates an uncertainty of mind which could perhaps be overcome by a persuasive supporter of the covenant.

(5) A large majority of the respondents acknowledge the reality of the problems which the open housing covenant was intended to help solve and they grant that the churches have a responsibility to help solve them. Only four percent of the signers were hesitant about endorsing church sponsorship of the covenant, but twenty-seven percent of the nonsupporters had doubts about the propriety of religious sponsorship and nineteen percent flatly opposed it. The figures on willingness to endorse the preaching of sermons on the open housing covenant are almost identical; 92 percent of the signers favor sermons on the issue, but only 56 percent of the nonsupporters do so. Among signers as well as nonsupporters, acknowledgement of the inferiority of existing housing for Negroes was far from unanimous, much less so than acknowledgement of discrimination against Negro homeseekers. Only about three-fourths of the signers and five-eighths of the nonsupporters acquiesced to the proposition that "A majority of Negro families in Newfield live in housing that is inadequate," whereas nine-tenths of the signers and five-sixths of the nonsupporters admitted the reality of housing discrimination. Only three nonsupporters (4 percent) denied this: only eight (12 percent) claimed to have no opinion on this question. It is clear, then, that although they were comparatively unwilling to grant that the churches of the community had a legitimate interest in sponsoring the OHC, even nonsupporters were compelled to concede the existence of the housing problem for Negroes.

(6) When asked to name the methods of overcoming racial discrimination which they endorsed or opposed, both signers and nonsupporters showed a striking preference for educational methods over all other methods. Nine-tenths of the signers and one-half of the nonsupporters approved "education of white people so that they become more favorable to integrated neighborhoods and apartments"; seven-tenths of the former and three-fourths of the latter endorsed "education of Negroes to have higher standards." Civil rights legislation was approved by only thirty-eight percent of the signers and ten percent of the nonsupporters: it was explicitly rejected by eight percent of the former and by twenty-seven percent of the latter. Nonviolent direct action received the endorsement of less than ten percent of both groups of respondents, and it was actively opposed by thirty percent of the signers and forty-one percent of the nonsupporters.

INTERPRETATION AND EVALUATION. The two great developments in Christian social action in this country during the present century are the two movements usually known as the "Social Gospel" and "Christian Realism." The former represented a recognition on the part of the Church of her responsibility to "Christianize the social order"; *i.e.*, to improve conditions in society as well as to redeem individuals from sin in their personal lives. The latter represented a more temperate assessment of the possibilities and impossibilities of social reform on the basis of second thoughts about the nature of man and the structures of society. The social gospel was a mighty surge forward in the church's pilgrimage toward moral wisdom; Christian realism, although it included highly significant advances in moral wisdom, was even more important as a forward thrust along the path to technical wisdom. Our analysis of the OHC campaign in Newfield offers much food for thought concerning the degree to which the lessons embodied in these two movements have in fact been learned by rank-and-file church members and lower echelon church leaders.

The churchmen of Newfield seem to have a relatively well developed sense of the need for the church to be aware of social problems and active in combating them. The pattern of response on this point is more encouraging in Newfield than was the pattern discerned in several other studies. Pope and Underwood discovered that clergymen in North Carolina in the thirties and those in Massachusetts in the forties had very little concern for social issues, and in Underwood's findings the rejection of housing as a proper concern of the church was explicit among Roman Catholic priests.[2] The percentage of laymen favoring sermons on the OHC in Newfield is considerably higher than the percentages favoring church stands on public issues reported by Lenski and by Glock and Ringer.[3]

But there are many indications that the lessons of the social gospel have been learned only in a superficial way, and the lessons of Christian Realism hardly at all. One cannot help but conclude from an analysis of the Newfield findings that there is a crippling discrepancy between affirmation of the church's responsibility and performance of it.

One discerns, first of all, certain defects in the definition of the situation. Despite approval of civil rights legislation by most of the clergymen and by about one-third of the laymen, the strong preference for educational methods of overcoming racial discrimination and the suspicion of militant organizations and tactics reflected in the interviews and questionnaires indicate a serious lack of both moral and technical wisdom. Preference for remedial measures

[2] Liston Pope, *Millhands and Preachers* (New Haven: Yale University Press, 1942), pp. 162-186; and Kenneth W. Underwood, *Protestant and Catholic* (Boston: Beacon Press, 1957), pp. 307-308.
[3] Gerhard Lenski, *The Religious Factor* (Garden City: Doubleday, 1961), p. 24; and Charles Glock and Benjamin Ringer, "The Political Role of the Church as Defined by its Parishioners," *Public Opinion Quarterly* (Winter 1954-55), pp. 337-347.

aimed at changing the minds and hearts of men so that they will be "ready" for changed behavior patterns suggests that love of *order* rather than *justice* is still falsely regarded as the preeminent norm in social ethics. It also suggests that prejudice rather than prejudiced behavior is still falsely regarded as the most pressing dimension of the problem of racial injustice. Adequate theological wisdom would have made Newfield churchmen aware that the injustice of residential discrimination is a problem of the utmost urgency, one which demands prompt, comprehensive remedial action. Adequate technical wisdom would have made them aware that "changing attitudes first" is a very uncertain way of changing behavior, whereas changing behavior directly is both possible and often the best way of effecting changed attitudes.[4]

It is particularly noteworthy that few clergymen perceived the problem of residential exclusion as a crucial matter *for the church*. The integrity of the Christian Church is at stake every time it is confronted with an important social problem concerning which ameliorative action needs to be taken, for every such challenge to which the Christian community fails to respond is an indication that the gospel of Jesus Christ has not been comprehended in its fullness. Despite the admirable lack of compartmentalization that characterized their understanding of the relationship between Christian faith and social action, most of the Newfield pastors appeared to view engagement with the housing problem as an optional matter.

In defense of these pastors it might be said that nonparticipation in the OHC program does not necessarily indicate hardness of heart toward Negroes nor dullness of spirit in regard to the church's mission in society. Nonparticipation might simply be the result of a calculated decision that, in one's fulfillment of his vocation as a pastor, other items of concern were more important. That is why the question asked about criteria for making ethical decisions was of such significance.

Defining the situation so as to make the OHC an optional matter for churchmen, yet doing so without clearly articulated or valid criteria for declaring it to be of only secondary importance, may have latent functionality for the church as an institution. Complacent assurance that "the really important always finds a place in the program of the church," reluctance to "promote" social action (based on the assumption that it should "grow as a fruit of faith" and not be "forced"), and concern for "a well-balanced program of church activities" are certainly more likely to attract members and keep them happy than a ministry which emphasizes ultimate rather than institutional ends of the church. But that which may be described as functional in regard to a congregation's satisfaction with the personality, the style, or the "reasonableness" of the pastor may be dysfunctional from a normative standpoint.

The equivocal definition given to the situation by Newfield clergymen led to errors of omission as well as errors of commission in their presentation

[4] Earl Raab and Seymour Martin Lipset, *Prejudice and Society* (New York: Anti-Defamation League of B'nai B'rith, 1959).

of the OHC to parishioners. In the half-heartedness of many ministers, the perhaps fervent but limited zeal of the sermonizers and the total absence of follow-up action following the OHC campaign we see evidence of the same tendency deplored by Kenneth Underwood in his study of Paper City: an inclination on the part of clergymen to be content with "spontaneous, spasmodic 'one shot' crusades on a variety of unrelated issues."[5] In the inordinate emphasis upon "the freedom of each parishioner to make up his own mind about this thing" and in the failure of most pastors to make a stronger appeal to the spiritual authority of denominational pronouncements on racial justice we see hints of the individualism endemic to American culture and the pseudo-transformationism typical of popular religion.[6] In the willingness of most clergymen to endorse the NAACP and civil rights legislation we see an indication that Christian Realism has at least partially taken root in centers of theological education—but in the opposition of Newfield churchmen to militant organizations and tactics we read insufficient appreciation of the necessity of the use of power in seeking political objectives. (Only two men, for example, evaluated the freedom rides in terms of the *results* obtained—the ICC ruling against segregated waiting rooms and restaurants, encouragement of local Negroes, etc.—rather than in terms of the motivation of freedom riders.) In some sermons we find counter-suggestion cues and use of the "deeper issues" approach, faulty communication techniques which vitiate the impact of the ostensibly prophetic words of the minister.[7] We find, in short, far too many signs that the portrait of American religious life given by many critics—that of introverted "organization churches" where bad faith is ratified, that of a tri-faith religious establishment whose social function is its irrelevancy[8]—is disturbingly accurate.

[5] Underwood, *op. cit.*, p. 314.
[6] Will Herberg, *Protestant-Catholic-Jew* (Garden City: Doubleday Anchor Books, 1960), pp. 116-117; and Louise Schneider and Sanford M. Dornbusch, *Popular Religion* (Chicago: University of Chicago Press, 1958), pp. 96-101.
[7] Schneider and Dornbusch, *op. cit.*, pp. 106-111, and Ernest Campbell and Thomas F. Pettigrew, *Christians in Racial Crisis* (Washington: Public Affairs Press, 1959), p. 103.
[8] In this connection, see especially Gibson Winter, *The Suburban Captivity of the Churches* (New York: Macmillan Paperbacks, 1962); Peter Berger, *The Noise of Solemn Assemblies*, and *The Precarious Vision* (Garden City: Doubleday and Company, 1961); and Arthur J. Vidich and Joseph Bensman, *Small Town in Mass Society* (Princeton: Princeton University Press, 1958).

35 THE NEGRO MERCHANT: A STUDY
OF NEGRO ANTI-SEMITISM

Harold L. Sheppard

INTRODUCTION   Tensions between majority and minority groups are common to our society. Few persons, however,
realize that prejudice and discrimination are also common among
minorities. Harold L. Sheppard of the W. E. Upjohn Institute discusses Negro anti-Semitism. Spanish-speaking peoples meanwhile
look down on the Negro. American Indians disparage the attention
given to Negro civil rights efforts. Japanese Americans are dis-
counted by the Mexican Americans.

Bernard Kramer suggests that prejudice involves cognitive,
emotional, and action levels. The *cognitive level* refers to the recognition of the minority as a minority. At this stage the minority
member is depicted as a "sly" Jew, "lazy" Mexican, "oversexed"
Negro, or "illiterate" Chinese as the need may be. The *emotional
level* involves the feelings which grip the person as he recognizes
"inappropriate" behavior by a minority member. The Negro using
a white washroom could provoke a high emotional response in a
southern rural town. A Jewish woman showing displeasure with
the sales clerk may provoke emotional responses within a nearby
shopper. Emotional responses may, however, take a variety of
forms: sympathy, disgust, fear, contempt, love, hate, or pity. The
action level alludes to the tendencies to action which the majority
expresses against the minority. Where *tendencies* to action become
overt action, *discrimination* is the result.

The Negro merchant in the study of Sheppard illustrates the
cognitive, emotional, and *tendency to action* phases of prejudice

HAROLD L. SHEPPARD is a member of the staff of the W. E. Upjohn Institute for
Employment Research.

Abridged and reprinted from the *American Journal of Sociology,* Volume 53, pp. 96-99,
by permission of The University of Chicago Press.

formation. A limited form of overt action and discrimination is also illustrated. The Jewish merchant becomes the scapegoat for a minority unable to attack the majority white businessmen without personal repercussions. Because of the ethnic character of the white merchants, antagonism centers upon the Jewish merchant. The attempt to "buy Negro" is characteristic of a secessionist minority (*see* Lee, Article 33).

I N 1944 AND THE first part of 1945, the writer was engaged in research concerning alleged anti-Semitic sentiments among Negroes in Chicago. If any anti-Semitism of an organized nature did exist, it seemed likely, on the basis of preliminary investigation, that it would appear in the relationship between the Negro and white merchants of the Chicago Negro community.

Of particular interest was the presence of two businessmen's associations in the Negro business district. Since a neighborhood generally has but one such association representing its merchants, the existence of two in the Black Belt indicated conflicting interests. One association was composed entirely of Negroes, the other, of both whites and Negroes. Research into the backgrounds of the two organizations and of their attitudes toward each other serves as a means of gaining an adequate understanding of some significant phases of Negro anti-Semitism.

This research necessitated the relating of the associations' origins, purposes, and activities to certain social movements within the Negro community, especially (1) the rise of a Negro business spirit and (2) the growth of "Negro business chauvinism."

The emergence of a business spirit among Negroes is significant, being (*a*) the appearance of a "business ethic" among a people just two generations away from slavery, (*b*) the seeds of what was later to develop into "race consciousness" among Negroes, (*c*) an emphasis upon the degree to which Negroes might improve their status without outside assistance. This optimism (*c*) minimized or ignored certain factors which eventually disillusioned the adherents of the Negro business spirit, e.g., a limited market, the low buying power of the Negro masses (who quite often depend on the "easy credit" offered by white merchants), white competition, and the vicissitudes of the larger economic system. The depression of the 1930's marks the beginning of disillusionment. As Frazier remarks,

> . . . suddenly, the purchasing power and the savings of the masses began to melt . . . and the hothouse growth of Negro business behind the walls of segregation shrivelled and died, often swallowing up the savings of the black masses. . . . In their disillusionment some of the . . . professional men . . . formed a class to study Marx. But *disillusionment did not breed radicalism among a very large group. It appears*

that more often they turned to racial chauvinism as a way of realizing their dreams.[1]

"Negro business chauvinism" thus developed among large numbers of previously hopeful and exuberant petty entrepreneurs.

Slogans, such as "Spend Your Money Where You Can Work," and "Patronize Your Own," soon became part of Negro business chauvinism. The pertinent features of this ideology are (1) the bid to the Negro community for patronage on the grounds of racial loyalty and (2) intense antagonism toward white businessmen, who are pictured as the chief obstacle to Negro economic independence and social betterment—an antagonism which often takes the form of anti-Semitism.

In the early 1920's, one could find frequent allusions to the Jewish merchant as the model for Negro businessmen to follow.[2] However, during the years of heightened unemployment and economic deprivation among Chicago's Negroes—laborer and entrepreneur alike—there developed demands for more concrete solutions of the economic problems of Negro consumers and businessmen. Such allusions no longer were the rule; instead such publications as the now defunct *Dynamite* made their appearance, with verbal attacks against the community's Jewish merchants.

At the same time, a group of Negro businessmen formed what will be called here the "All-Negro Businessmen's Association," with the slogans "Patronize Your Own" and "Sustain Negro Enterprise." Unlike the ordinary businessmen's association, it seeks the support of the consumer through its emphasis on the self-assumed role of race-protector. The association's president, at the time of the writer's research, defended this policy, declaring: "This situation boils down to the law of nature known as the struggle of the survival of the fittest. And our slogans, our program, are a weapon in that struggle. . . . The Jews' weapons are reputation, business contacts, control of the best districts, and a good training in business. The Negro doesn't have those weapons and if he's going to survive and get ahead, then he's got to insist that his people patronize his store, and not the Jew's. After all, the Jew can open up a store outside of the Black Belt, but can the Negro?"[3]

To the small, struggling Negro merchant faced with the superior competition of the white merchants, there is no alternative to the policy of appealing to racial solidarity in bidding for Negro patronage. While nearly half of the business establishments in "Bronzeville" are owned and operated by Negroes, a survey before the war revealed that they received only about 10 percent of all the money spent by Negroes within the community. There is no

[1] E. F. Frazier, "Some Effects of Depression on the Negro in Northern Cities," *Science and Society*, II (1938), 496ff. (Italics mine).
[2] For example, *see* the *Whip*, March 19, 1921. This Negro newspaper is no longer in existence.
[3] Interview.

reason to believe that this percentage has changed much in recent years.[4] This is the condition which underlies the development and activities of the All-Negro Businessmen's Association in Chicago. Although by no means enjoying the active membership of even a majority of Bronzeville's business people, this group may be said to voice the aspirations, protests, and bitterness of a large part of the community's Negro business people.

It would be a mistake to infer that no other elements in the area have agitated against the white merchant and for greater Negro economic independence. A weekly magazine, ostensibly written for the high-school age group, but nevertheless reaching the general Negro public through the corner newsstands, frequently carried editorials attacking the Jewish merchants. In response to the expressed concern of certain Jewish civil-rights organizations, the editor of the magazine wrote the following editorial in the spring of 1944:

LOVE THY NEIGHBOR

Jewish leaders pleading for tolerance and an abatement of anti-Semitism among Negroes should look at the score! Such apparent hatred as may be held by Negroes against Jews is a direct out-growth of abuses practiced by the children of Israel on their black brethren. While calling upon the world to sow good will toward the Jew, these people do nothing themselves to restrain the greed of Jewish merchants, realtors and money-lenders. Here in Bronzeville an organization of Jewish business men arbitrarily holds down competition. No Colored merchant is permitted to operate a competing establishment in a good location except under conditions which make bankruptcy inevitable. . . . .

Let the Jewish church and civic leaders who ask our help in the world fight on Jews, bring the social criminals of their race to task. Stop overcharges, let down residential barriers and elevate business ethics. Day-to-day fair play will drive our hate away.

The formation of the Biracial Business Association, with a membership (in spring, 1945) 80 percent white, nearly all of whom were Jewish, followed in the wake of the race riots in Detroit and Harlem—riots in which considerable damage was done to the white-owned stores in the Negro areas.[5] The group has attempted to give itself the appearance of a spontaneous "grass-roots" organization—organized for the same reasons for which any other businessmen's association is formed. While it is generally understood that the main objective of a typical business association is business *promotion*, it would not be exaggerating, in the writer's opinion, to state the main objective of this organization to be business *protection*.

[4] Cf. "Negro Business: Fact and Myth," in Horace Cayton and St. Clair Drake, *Black Metropolis* (New York: Harcourt, Brace & World, 1945).

[5] For example, see Harold Orlansky, *The Harlem Riot: A Study in Mass Frustration* (New York: Social Analysis, 1943). Donald C. Marsh, of Wayne University, at one time engaged in a comparable study, has published a brochure on the subject.

It appears that the white merchants realized that any action on their part would probably be resented and branded as "patronizing" by certain vocal groups within the Negro community. Therefore, they selected a few prominent Negroes to become part of the association. In an effort to show the community that such Negro businessmen were fully represented in the organization, the group placed a disproportionate number of them in leading positions. In mid-1945, although Negroes made up 20 percent of the total membership, they constituted 42 percent of the association's officers and directors.

The membership of the All-Negro Association, when compared to the Negro membership of the biracial one, included a higher proportion of businessmen who owned enterprises which generally compete with white-owned businesses. Such a distribution is to be expected in the light of the conflict between the Negro and the white merchants of the community.

The members of the All-Negro Association view the other organization as an example of the organized effort of the white merchants to weaken the movement for a successful Negro business class by "appeasing" Negro merchants and by "pacifying" the Negro public into accepting whites as the natural group which should engage in business activities in Bronzeville. The editor of the weekly magazine quoted above also registered his reaction to the formation of the Biracial Association, in the following editorial:

> These Israelites have formed all sorts of organizations here in this area in the past decade of years, with a few of our sons of Ham blended in for ornamentation. . . . With the majority of Bronzeville's Jewish merchants living in . . . "Master Race" communities and a goodly number of them "restrictive covenant signers," the writer is prone to believe that the newly formed Jewish-Negro organization is just another one of these "front cliques" [sic] with an ulterior motive. The President himself has already been labelled as a typical Negro hater as a result of his relentless fight to dominate or break up small Negro merchants in the district. . . .
>
> The fact of the matter is that we are not anxious for any typical Jewish merchant to dominate a hundred-per-cent Negro district where in the past, they have milked a million dollars a day from us and then labelled us "ignoramuses." . . . We have had enough of his dictates over our economic activities and we are tired of him taking all the good credit of the district such as war bond sales . . . and crediting the Negro with racketeering . . . and banditry.

Chicago's Negro society is undergoing a change, which is inevitably accompanied by a disruption of the traditional relationship that existed between Negroes and the dominant group. Out of this has emerged a conflict between two minority groups, each possessing an image of the other, derived in large part from participation in the broader, non-Jewish and non-Negro society and from the experiences indigenous to the particular situation in Bronzeville.

The study reported in the present paper substantiates the view that intergroup tensions arise when part or all of the members of one group develop a new conception of themselves contrary to a conception that more or less sanctioned an older type of relationship between that group and another. The All-Negro Association represents an organized attempt to develop and sustain among Negroes a new image of themselves as aspiring entrepreneurs, "self-made" businessmen, and not as laborers dependent upon the patronizing sentiments of the dominant group. In the round of daily activities of Bronzeville's inhabitants there exists a large number of white merchants identified as Jews —members of a group which has traditionally served as a hated and feared "scapegoat" of many social movements. In this case the social movement is centered around the rise of a Negro business class.

In the writer's opinion any attempts to explain anti-Semitism among Negroes must go beyond partial—if not superficial—suggestions, such as "Fascist propaganda," or too general, question-begging ones, such as "frustration-aggression." Research of a far more fruitful nature will result from a concentration on the movements and ideologies accompanying changes in the class structure within Negro society.

PART VII

RELIGION AND OTHER
INSTITUTIONAL CONTEXTS

INTRODUCTION

THE RELATIONSHIPS BETWEEN religion and other major institutions (such as family, education, government, and business) vary according to the nature of the society and its overall values. In totalitarian societies the religious institution becomes the chief sanctifier of totalitarian action. In democratic societies, the role of religion may be limited through stress upon separation of church and state and upon individual salvation (*see* Ahlstrom, Article 1; Petersen, Article 6; and Fuchs, Article 37). In a totalitarian society the educational system may be merged with the religious institution to support the basic character and goal of the state. On the other hand, the educational system and religious institutions in the democratic state may remain largely free of national political influence. In American society the largely separate cultures of church, education, business and government have resulted in the emergence of conflicting value systems which have severely undermined former patterns of cultural unity.

American concepts of culture and family organization, principles of government, approaches to education, attitudes toward welfare, theories of penology, and concepts of economic enterprise have, however, been heavily influenced by religion. The influence of organized religion is felt in every family, whether atheist or church participant, if for no other reason than the assumption in our society that everyone has a "church home," "a pastor," or at least a "religious preference." The church-related family more positively provides the early cultural setting in which social as well as religious values are taught as foundations for daily life.

Religious bodies themselves, however, rarely combine to present a united institutional voice in political or economic matters. Sects (at odds with the world) and churches (deeply committed to existing social life) will often take opposing positions regarding social programs (*see* Johnson, Article 11, and Young, Article 12). Whether the church should even engage in political activity at all is a question debated with great heat. Interestingly, families deeply committed to religious doctrine are more likely to demand the exclusion of political matters from the pulpit than are those persons for whom religious ideology is less vital. The control of church life by persons of middle and upper class (*see* Introduction to Part VI, and Mayer and Sharp, Article 31) has resulted in a conservative institutional posture regarding political and economic matters. Less successful persons in the lower class usually vote for programs offering greater social security, while at the same time offering the greatest adherence to otherworldly fundamentalist sects.

Religion in these institutional contexts is the subject of Part VII. In the first of this series of seven articles Gerhard Lenski traces the effect of religion upon secular institutions. Surprising to some, Lenski finds that religion is a major determinant of social attitudes and activity. Religious influences in voting behavior are analyzed by Lawrence Fuchs in the second article dealing with the American Jewish vote in presidential elections. Because Jews are highly concerned with social justice, they tend to vote for political leaders who show consideration for minority views. Eduard Heimann discusses the Christian foundation of the social sciences and notes a lingering problem of education, one of norms versus facts. Although Western society is shaped by past religious beliefs which have been institutionalized, science seeks facts based upon empirical research (*see* Introduction to Part I, and Yinger, Article 3).

Reginald Stackhouse discusses the potential alliance between religion and science as he traces the effect of Darwin's *Origin of Species*. The emergence of science in the late eighteen hundreds resulted in the rise of the Neoorthodox movement which sought to blend a social liberalism with a conventional theological system (*see* Ahlstrom, Article 1). R. B. Dierenfield measures the effect of religious belief and practice in public education. In spite of the separation of church and state, Dierenfield finds that religious influence in public schools is largely determined by the policies and practices of the local school board, and so commitment to religious ideals varies from community to community as well as from region to region within the United States. In his second article Gerhard Lenski reviews the many social variables which religion influences. Although many aspects of social life may be affected, the religious influence is especially evident in family life. Glenn Vernon concludes the section with a discussion of data distortion regarding interfaith marriages. Vernon suggests that the divorce rate of religiously mixed marriages is generally not as high as one is led to expect from incomplete data analysis.

36 RELIGION'S IMPACT ON SECULAR INSTITUTIONS

Gerhard Lenski

INTRODUCTION   Whether men are superficially attracted to religious participation or are deeply committed to religious precepts and doctrines remains an unanswered question in modern religion. Because those arguing the point often attempt to equate past religious expectations with current religious functions, no comparable base for evaluation can be established. Whereas Hammond (Article 9) argues that religion no longer informs culture through the singular establishment of value systems, Herberg (Article 46) stresses the idea that religion has become so institutionalized that personal identification in our mass society is still related to one's recognition of his Protestant, Catholic, or Jewish heritage. Although the postwar religious revival remains suspect to some, religious faith, whether superficial or not, has had consequences far beyond those which it deliberately attracts. To equate the totality of religious meaning with church attendance and other auxiliary activity is to segment religion and society into tangential spheres of influence. The rapid growth of knowledge through discovery and invention has meanwhile led thinking men to question the "eternal" assumptions of religious doctrines. The rational emphasis of modern education has caused men to review the socioreligious cleavages of the Great Schism and the Reformation in a new light.

Those who look for the demise of religious influence in a secular society will find little support in the article by sociologist Gerhard Lenski. In an article published before his major work in

Abridged and reprinted from *The Review of Religious Research*, Volume 4, Number 1, Copyrighted 1962 by the Religious Research Association, Inc.

GERHARD LENSKI is Professor of Sociology at the University of North Carolina (Chapel Hill).

American religion, *The Religious Factor*, Lenski finds religion to be a factor comparable to social class in its influence on secular society. The confusion surrounding religious influence has evolved in part from the general failure to distinguish among the cultic (rites, rituals), dogmatic (doctrines, theology), and social applications of religion. Far too often, religious critics have correlated a cultic or dogmatic decline with a total religious decline. On the other hand, current evidence suggests that while emphasis upon the cultic and dogmatic has diminished, the social influence of religion has increased. The social implications of religion, too, need to be differentiated. Lenski's description of three levels of morality (personal, social or group, and sectarian) suggest the complexity of the question. The rise of a religious subculture which includes both sacred and secular elements has become the new way of life. Those who argue that an increase in church participation suggests a religious revival, while a parallel secularization of society implies that God is dead, remain superficial analysts of the American religious scene. The correct appraisal of the situation lies somewhere in between these two extremes. But closer to which?

D URING THE LAST decade the subject of religion has received considerable attention both in popular and scholarly circles. Much of this has been devoted to the recent religious revival and its causes. Little attention has been devoted to the consequences of religious belief and practice in the everyday lives of the masses of men. Yet from both the sociological and religious standpoints, these could be of crucial importance.

Such interest as there has been in this latter problem stems chiefly from the work of Max Weber half a century ago. In his many writings on the sociology of religion, Weber set forth the thesis that each of the major religions of the world has developed its own distinctive orientation toward all aspects of social life, and, furthermore, he asserted, these differences have had profound consequences for the development of human societies.

Not all social scientists have shared Weber's views, by any means. On the contrary, if we may judge from the literature, most modern social scientists regard religion as a matter of minor importance, at least in contemporary society. Frequently the subject of religion is ignored entirely in their analyses of major social institutions, and when it is mentioned, it usually receives no more than passing comment.

Several years ago it was my good fortune to obtain the resources necessary to explore the relevance of Weber's thesis for a portion of contemporary American society. At that time I was named principal investigator for the Detroit Area Study for the academic year 1957-58. Each year a different problem is studied, depending upon the interests of the principal investigator. In my year I chose to study the impact of religion on three crucially important areas of life in our society: politics, economics, and family life.

The opportunity provided by the Detroit Area Study to investigate this subject was unique for two reasons. In the first place, it provided an opportunity to study the impact of religion in the context of a modern metropolis. In the second place, the Detroit Area Study provided me with a unique opportunity to follow up on one of the really important insights of Weber.

Weber was largely unconcerned with these rather obvious, deliberate, and calculated efforts to influence secular institutions in which most religious groups occasionally indulge. Rather, he was concerned with the fact that all religious groups are *continuously* shaping and molding the personalities of their adherents who then, as private individuals, staff the economic, political, educational, and other institutional systems of society. This he felt to be the far more influential process by which religious groups influence secular life.

Since the Detroit Area Study provided a means of studying the lives of a cross-section of the residents of a modern metropolis, it provided an ideal facility for my purposes.

IS RELIGION A MAJOR FACTOR? With this by way of background, let me turn now to some of my findings. For those who regard religion as a factor of minor importance in the life of our society, there will be many startling findings. However, none will be more startling than the basic conclusion to which I ultimately came as a result of my study. This was the conclusion that religion is a factor *comparable to social class* in its influence on the behavior of individuals and hence on the life of society as a whole.

It is safe to say that there is no other factor which sociologists have found to have greater influence than class. The class position of individuals influences everything from the political party for which they vote to the types of recreation in which they engage. In short, it is regarded as a factor of major importance both because of the *range* of behavior influenced by it, and because of the *magnitude* of the influence exercised.

My data indicate that religion is a factor of comparable importance in *both* respects. It influences an equally wide range of behavior, and the magnitude of the influence exercised is comparable.

At one point in my analysis I divided the white Christians in my sample into four categories: (1) middle-class white Protestants, (2) working-class white Protestants, (3) middle-class white Catholics, and (4) working-class white Catholics. These four categories were then compared with respect to thirty-five different matters pertaining to politics, economics, and family life. Taking all thirty-five items together, the differences between religious groups with class level held constant were slightly greater on the average than the differences between classes with religion held constant.

This does not mean that there are not some areas of behavior which are more strongly influenced by class than by religion. However, for each such area, there was another for which the reverse proved true. In short, far from being a factor of minor importance in the most highly urbanized segments of our population, these data indicate that religion is a factor of major importance —equal, in fact, to social class.

POLITICS AND THE THREE RELIGIONS.   To become more specific, let me cite the case of party preference. Prior to my study, a number of other studies had shown that there are differences in party preference linked with socioreligious group membership. White Protestants (everywhere except in the South) have always been found to be the strongest supporters of the Republican Party. Catholics, Jews, and Negro Protestants have just as consistently been found to lean toward the Democratic Party.

For a time is was argued that these differences were merely reflections of differences in the class composition of the several groups. However, the work of Lazarsfeld and his colleagues at Columbia proved decisively that, even when comparisons between Protestants and Catholics were limited to persons similar in class position, substantial political differences remained.

The skeptics then retreated to the argument that these differences were due to nineteenth-century patterns of immigration. After the Civil War, the white Protestants of the North came to control the Republican Party, and hence newer immigrant groups were driven into the Democratic Party in order to find a vehicle for political action. Since party preference, like religious preference, tends to be handed down within families from one generation to the next, present-day Jews and Catholics tend to be Democrats, since they are the children and grandchildren of the immigrants who came after the Civil War. By contrast, white Protestants tend to be Republicans, since they are the descendants of the earlier immigrants.

In an effort to test this very plausible hypothesis, I inquired into the party preferences of the fathers of the Detroiters whom I interviewed. I was interested to see whether it could be shown that, when the political preference of the *fathers* of Catholics and Protestants was held constant, religion would still make a difference. I found that clearly it does. For example, among the sons and daughters of *Republican* fathers who were interviewed, only 13 percent of those who were white Protestants had become Democrats, compared with 44 percent of those who were Catholics. Similar differences were found both among the children of Democratic fathers and among the children of fathers with no political preference. From this it seemed clear that the current differences in party preference between Catholics and white Protestants represent something more than a lingering heritage of the nineteenth century.

In the political area differences were not limited merely to party preference. Significant differences were found in many other areas of political life as well. For example, I found significant differences in the interpretation of the Bill of Rights as it applies to the area of freedom of speech. White Protestants and Jews were somewhat more likely than Catholics to put a liberal construction on the Bill of Rights and see it as protecting the rights of Communists, Fascists, and atheists to express their points of view. These differences were especially marked among *middle*-class members of these groups, a fact of great significance since most government officials, both elected and appointed, are persons recruited from the middle class. It is also noteworthy that differences were much more marked when comparisons were limited to those who were regular participants in the worship services of their respective groups. All of these differences were found when comparisons were limited to persons of similar class level.

ECONOMIC BEHAVIOR AMONG THE FAITHS.   A second major area I explored was that of *economic* behavior. Here I found, as have others previously, that there are significant differences in the degree to which members of the several groups have gotten ahead in our competitive economic system. Jews were the most successful, both in terms of income and in terms of the percentage in business or professional occupations. White Protestants ranked second, white Catholics third, and Negro Protestants last.

Here again, these differences have been explained away on the grounds that they reflect the influence of factors other than religion. Often it is argued that the relative lack of success of Catholics and Negro Protestants is a function of their late arrival in the urban centers of the North. Coming as immigrants long after many of the white Protestant families had established themselves, they were obliged to take the least desirable positions. Hence, present-day Catholics and Negro Protestants are more often manual workers with limited incomes than are white Protestants, simply because their fathers were not able to give them the same advantages as the sons and daughters of most white Protestants.

Again this is a very plausible argument, particularly if you do not examine it too closely. However, critical examination of this argument should lead one to ask why the Jews have fared so well. While they are not as recent migrants to the urban North as the Negro Protestants, they are generally more recent immigrants than the Catholics. Hence, one would expect them to rank behind the Catholics, when in fact they rank ahead of even the white Protestants.

When the argument is subjected to an empirical test, still further weaknesses become apparent. For one thing, my own research and that of one of my former students indicate that, when you compare white Catholics and Protestants whose fathers were in comparable occupations, the sons of white Protestant fathers have fared better than the sons of Catholic fathers. For example, if you compare the Catholic and Protestant sons of unskilled or semiskilled manual workers, the Protestants are more likely to have risen to the ranks of business or professional men, Catholics are more likely to have dropped into the ranks of the semiskilled and unskilled. Differences were most evident at the upper-middle-class level.

The explanation for these differences proved to be rather complex. It is not simply a matter that Protestants and Jews have more ambition or drive than Catholics or that they value material success more. So far as my evidence indicates, differences in these respects are not great. Rather, a series of other, less obvious, factors seems responsible.

In view of the limitations of space, I shall attempt to describe only two of the lines of analysis which proved profitable in my study of this problem. One of the questions which I asked all of the men we interviewed was whether they would quit their work if suddenly they were to become financially independent. Regardless of how they answered, I then asked them to explain why they felt as they did.

The answers to these questions proved extremely interesting. Basically, responses fell into three major categories. First, some men told us that they would never quit work if they could avoid it since they enjoyed it so much. Some of these men said life would hardly be worth living if they were not able to work. A second category of men told my interviewers that they would quit work immediately if they were able to do so: they worked only because they had to for financial reasons. Finally, some men expressed an ambivalent attitude toward work.

When the several religious groups were compared, it was found that, among whites, Jews were the most likely to have a positive attitude toward work, while Catholics were the least likely. But what proved even more important, those Protestants and Jews in responsible positions were the members of their groups who were most likely to have a positive attitude toward work, while among Catholics those in responsible positions were the most likely to have a negative attitude. Among Catholics, those in menial occupations were more likely to have positive attitudes toward work than those in responsible positions. This was surprising.

The significance of this finding became clearer when I analyzed the responses to a further question. Each person interviewed was asked which of the following was most important for a child to learn to prepare him for life: (1) to obey, (2) to be well liked, (3) to think for himself, (4) to work hard, or (5) to help others when they need help. They were then asked which they thought was next most important, and so on until they had ranked all five.

The most important differences involved the relative ranking of the first and third items—those involving obedience and intellectual independence. To begin with, there were marked differences between the several *classes* in their ranking of these two items. The higher the class position of individuals, the more likely they were to regard it as important for the child to learn to think for himself. The lower the class position, the more likely they were to regard it as important for the child to learn to obey.

Equally important, however, was the finding that beliefs on this subject are strongly linked with religious preference, even when comparisons are limited to persons in the same class. White Protestants and Jews are a good bit more likely than Catholics to rate intellectual independence ahead of obedience.

On the basis of all we know about the more responsible positions in our society today, it is extremely important for a person to be able to think for himself. This is especially true in the rapidly expanding fields of science. The person who can only obey and follow instructions will not advance far. *Creativity* is the quality most in demand, and creativity presumes a capacity for autonomous thought. What is true in science is also true to nearly the same degree in the free professions such as law, medicine, and architecture. Even in the middle and upper levels of management, far more is required than mere obedience to orders. Initiative and imagination are qualities still sought and valued, William Whyte notwithstanding.

Yet these are qualities which Catholics apparently bring to the job world somewhat less often than either white Protestants or Jews. This, I believe, explains in part why Catholics are less likely to rise to the more responsible positions in our economy, and why also, when they do, they are less happy in them.

Repeated studies have shown that Catholics are far less likely to enter careers in science than Protestants and Jews, and Catholic institutions to higher education produce only a small fraction of the number of scientists produced by non-Catholic institutions even when numbers of graduates are held constant. Catholic leaders are aware of these studies and in recent years have taken certain steps to remedy the situation. However, my findings suggest that the differences between Catholics and non-Catholics in this area cannot be entirely eliminated merely by administrative reforms in Catholic colleges. Rather, the root of the problem seems to lie in fundamental differences in basic values which separate Catholics and non-Catholics and which are internalized in individuals early in life.

DIFFERENCES IN FAMILY LIFE.   In my attempts to understand why Catholics were less successful in competition for the better jobs in our society, I was inevitably led into an examination of the area of *family life,* following up a clue provided by Max Weber. In one of his later writings on the interrelations between religion and economics—a comparison of Puritanism and Confucianism—Weber developed the thesis that one of the reasons Puritanism gave rise to the spirit of capitalism was because it succeeded in "smashing the fetters of the sib," or the extended family system. He argued that Puritanism replaced the community of blood with the community of faith. It placed the ties of faith ahead of the ties of kinship. Thus it was possible for new patterns of social relations to emerge—patterns in which the ties of kinship were wholly ignored.

In seeking to follow up on this thesis, I inquired into the place of the kin group in the lives of those whom I interviewed. It quickly became apparent that the kin group is more important to Catholics and Jews than to Protestants. Catholics and Jews visit their relatives more often, and see less of neighbors and co-workers in the off-the-job relations. Furthermore, they are less likely to migrate and thus break their ties with kith and kin. Finally, they are less likely to become divorced.

More interesting than this was the relationship between church attendance and these indices of kin-group loyalty and involvement. Not too surprisingly, I found that the more faithful Catholics are in their attendance at Mass, the stronger is their tie with the kin group. By contrast, among Protestants just the reverse proved true. The more faithful Protestants were in their attendance at worship services, the weaker were their ties with their kin group. In short, my data led me to the conclusion that church and family stand in a rather different relationship among Protestants than among Catholics. Whereas these two important institutional systems appear to be mutually reinforcing agencies in the lives of Catholics, there is evidence that they conflict with one another to some degree in the lives of Protestants.

This is not to say that the Protestant churches criticize or demean family life—far from it. However, it does appear that Protestant churches with their intensive programs of organizational activities throughout the week compete with the kin group for the time, energies, and loyalties of men.

It is my conclusion that to the degree that the Protestant churches weaken the hold of the kin group on the individual—especially the extended kin group—to that degree they aid their members in rising in the job world. Success in the job world increasingly presupposes a willingness on the part of the individual to migrate and leave family and friends.

INFLUENCE OF PAROCHIAL SCHOOL EDUCATION. One of the less surprising findings was that those Catholics who have received all or most of their education in Catholic institutions are more faithful in their observance of Catholic norms than those who received all or most of their education in non-Catholic institutions. For example, 86 percent of the former claimed to attend Mass at least once a week compared with 71 percent of the latter. How much of this difference is attributable to the influence of Catholic schools and how much to the influence of parents is difficult to say, but there is probably some residue of school influence operative here.

I found that, the further one moves from the more visible, outward aspects of religious practice to the more inward and private, the smaller the differences between the two groups became. For example, whereas there was a difference of 15 percentage points between the two groups with respect to attendance at Mass, there was only an 8-point difference in frequency of daily prayer. In view of the secondary character of social relationships in a school setting, this difference is not too surprising, but I suspect it is important.

One of the great fears of non-Catholics concerning the Catholic school system is that it fosters intolerance and prejudice toward non-Catholics. On logical grounds there is good reason for expecting this, since ethnocentric attitudes frequently flourish where there is an absence of primary type relations. However, despite the reasonableness of the logic, I could find no evidence that exposure to the Catholic educational system produces intolerance toward Protestants, Jews, or Negroes as individuals. At least it had no influence which could be detected when the adult graduates of these schools were compared with Catholics who had attended non-Catholic institutions.

However, while attendance at Catholic schools did not seem to foster intolerance of non-Catholic *individuals*, it did appear to produce intolerance of non-Catholic religious *groups*. This was especially evident when I analyzed the responses of Catholics to the question of whether ministers of other faiths should be permitted to preach publicly (as on the radio) things contrary to Catholic teaching. Fifty-five percent of the Catholics who had received all or most of their education in non-Catholic schools felt that ministers of other faiths should be permitted to do this, but only 31 percent of those who had received all or most of their education in Catholic institutions shared this view.

On a more encouraging note, the Catholic school system seems to stimulate an appreciation of the democratic process. Or at least, this is suggested by the fact that those who have attended Catholic schools are more likely to vote than those who attended non-Catholic schools.

Not only does attendance at Catholic schools stimulate voting—it also has an impact on party preference. It creates converts to the Republican Party. The basis for my statement is this: Among these Catholics who received all or most of their education in non-Catholic institutions, there were just as many Democrats with Republican fathers as there were Republicans with Democratic fathers. In other words, there was no net shift among these Catholics. However, among those who had attended *Catholic* schools, only 11 percent had fathers who were Republicans, but 27 percent of the children were. In other words, there was a net shift of 16 percentage points, or a net gain of one child out of six for the Republican Party. No wonder President Kennedy opposed federal aid for parochial schools!

Another important difference linked with attendance at Catholic institutions was the attitude which men developed toward work. This difference was especially evident among the middle-class Catholics whom we interviewed. Only 6 percent of those with all or most of their education in Catholic institutions expressed a positive attitude toward work. By contrast, 28 percent of the middle-class Catholic men with a non-Catholic education expressed such an attitude. I also found that, among middle-class Catholics, attendance at Catholic institutions was linked with a greater appreciation of the value of obedience and less appreciation of the value of intellectual autonomy. Finally, I found that ties with the kin group were stronger among those who had received most of their education in Catholic institutions than among those who had attended non-Catholic institutions. In short, the Catholic school system seems to foster this interesting and important cultural syndrome which simul-

taneously results in strong familial ties on the one hand and limited enthusiasm for the job world and relative lack of success in it on the other.

THREE MORALITIES CONSIDERED.   By now I suspect that some
may be thinking, "This is all well and good to show that religion is a factor
influencing the outcome of elections, the production of scientists, and similar
matters, but this is not what really concerns us. We are concerned with religion as a regenerative force in society. We are chiefly concerned with whether
the various religious groups are influential in this respect."

This is surely a legitimate and proper interest of clergymen—and of social
scientists as well. However, I would insist that we cannot ignore the fact that
religion has consequences other than those which it deliberately seeks to produce or those which are socially beneficial. More than that, the clergy bear
some responsibility for the former. Religious leaders and religious groups cannot claim credit for the good which results from their efforts if they are not
prepared to answer for other consequences as well. Yet it is my impression
that, by and large, this is precisely what is usually done.

As a sociologist it seems to me to be the height of folly to pretend that
religious groups are not in part, at least, human institutions and reflect human
nature in all of its varied aspects. Thus religious groups are not merely vehicles for the expression of divine grace, they are also vehicles for the expression of human ambition, avarice, and folly.

In the course of the interview, two of the questions asked dealt with what
might be designated *personal morality.* First, we asked whether our respondents would return change at a supermarket if they received a bit more than
was due them. Second, we asked whether they would pay the fine if ticketed
for parking overtime in a strange city. If they said, "Yes," to this question, we
then asked whether they would pay if they were in a hurry and knew that
they would never be caught if they ignored the ticket.

On the question concerning the supermarket, Catholic and Negro Protestant churchgoers were somewhat more likely to say they would return the
change than marginal members of the same groups. Among white Protestants
there was no difference associated with church attendance. On the question
concerning the parking ticket, Negro and White Protestant churchgoers were
more likely than nonchurchgoers to say they would pay the fine regardless.
Here there was no difference among Catholics. However, among whites, both
Catholics and Protestants, the differences between churchgoers and nonchurchgoers were so small that it is difficult to say that involvement in these
churches has any great effect on personal morality. Only in the case of the
Negro Protestants was the difference great enough to assume any real social
significance.

I also explored the area of what might be designated as *social* or *group*
morality. By this I mean the attitudes of individuals with regard to the moral

standards of the groups to which they belong—especially the community and nation. For example, I asked Detroiters whether they believed that our country should spend money abroad even when it could not be justified in the interest of national defense. In all of the groups, churchgoers were more likely than nonchurchgoers to take the humanitarian position and advocate foreign aid even if it could not be justified on the grounds of national defense. Similarly, churchgoers were more likely than nonchurchgoers to favor racially integrated schools. I was especially interested to find that this was true even among the Southern-born white Protestants, who are rather numerous in Detroit. However, except in the case of these Southern-born Protestants, differences were not large in any of the groups.

I also explored a third area which, for lack of a better term, I have designated as *sectarian morality*. By this I refer to those moral standards, both personal and social, which some one religious group supports in the face of the opposition of most other groups. For example, many Protestant denominations have long been opposed to drinking and gambling and have sought to discourage their members from engaging in these practices but have found no support for this from Catholics or Jews. Similarly, Catholic teaching with regard to birth control might be designated as sectarian morality, since almost all Protestant and Jewish groups have conflicting views.

This is the one area in which the churches clearly make a powerful impact on their adherents. Differences between churchgoers and nonchurchgoers on questions dealing with these matters are extremely large. For example, 70 percent of the active Catholics expressed the belief that the practice of birth control by married couples is always or usually wrong from the moral standpoint. By contrast, only 25 percent of the Catholics who did not attend Mass regularly shared this view. Or, in the case of white Protestants, 70 percent of the regular churchgoers believed gambling is always or usually wrong from the moral standpoint, but only 45 percent of the marginal members shared this view.

There is, of course, an obvious logic to the practices of the churches as revealed by these findings. Each church feels it can leave the problem of reinforcing the basic moral standards of society to other agencies since, after all, it has no monopoly on such things as the belief in the rightness of honesty and social justice. However, since only one's own group is aware of the rightness of certain sectarian moral standards, these are the ones which must be supported by all available resources. Thus, while striving to be a regenerative force in society, the churches often come to be divisive agencies concerned far more with sectarian morality than with the more basic problems of personal and social moralities. In this connection, it is interesting to speculate whether the pressures of intergroup competition and conflict have not led American religious groups to stress certain aspects of their message out of all proportion to their true importance.

TRUE NATURE OF RELIGIOUS GROUPS.   These findings which I have sketched in so briefly raise almost as many questions as they answer. For one thing, if religion has as important an influence on secular institutions as I indicated earlier, why is it that the experts have so frequently underestimated it? Furthermore, how is it possible that religious groups have as much, or more, influence on job careers, voting behavior, and similar matters than they have on basic individual and social morality? The answers to both of these questions are, in my opinion, tied together.

Far too often religious groups have been equated in our minds with the churches. In other words, far too often they have been thought of as merely one more type of specialized, formal association—the counter-part of the corporation, the labor union, the Kiwanis Club, or the P.T.A.—except, of course, that the religious group is thought to be far less influential than most since it brings its members together for only an hour a week and even then attracts only a minority of the population.

This view corresponds with certain obvious facts but ignores others. It is the truth, but not the whole truth. The crucial fact which it ignores is that religious groups are basically endogamous—their members normally marry within the group. As a result, interaction among the members of a family also normally involves interaction among members of the same religious group, with all that this implies.

This is not to say that Catholic families, for example, are *merely* subunits of the Catholic church, any more than we would say that American families are merely subunits of American society. However, just as American families function as subunits of our society, reinforcing by rewards and punishments those societal norms which they adopt for their own, so too, religiously homogeneous families serve as subunits of religious groups, reinforcing their norms. In this connection it should be noted that the special interdecennial population survey of the Bureau of the Census in 1957 revealed that more than 93 percent of the American families are religiously homogeneous.

What is true of the great majority of American families is also true of a very large number of other primary groups. They, too, are often religiously homogeneous, and, when this is true, they also tend to function as subunits of religious groups.

As a consequence, most individuals are exposed to the influences of their religious group every day of the week and in a variety of social relationships—especially those they cherish most. Not only are they exposed to the influences of the religious group on Sunday morning or Friday evening—they are also exposed to these influences in most of the more intimate social relationships in which they are involved. On the basis of all we know about the socialization of the individual and the process by which the personality of the individual is shaped and molded, this is largely accomplished through just such relationships as these.

Because of this, it is a serious mistake to equate the religious group with the churches or synagogues. The churches and synagogues are only a part of the social system constituting any major religious group. Religious movements normally give rise to *communities* of persons united by ties of kinship and friendship as well as to the associations formally established for specifically religious purposes. Too often we ignore or overlook the communal aspects of religious groups and thus are led to underestimate their power and influence.

This brings me to a second major point. Though the interest of religious associations are often somewhat limited and circumscribed, the interests of religious communities typically encompass all phases of human life. Religious communities are vitally concerned with such mundane matters as politics and economics, even though the religious associations with which they are linked may have but limited interest in such matters. What is more, they are often concerned about these matters in basically selfish terms. In a pluralistic society such as our own, religious communities easily become embroiled in a not very attractive competition for political power, social status, and the other rewards society has to offer.

As a consequence, each of the major religious groups tends to develop a rather complex subculture. These subcultures include secular as well as sacred elements. Far too often we make the mistake of thinking that religious groups are only concerned with theological doctrines, ritual practices, and matters of church government. Nothing could be further from the truth. The subcultural heritage of modern Judaism contains countless elements of a strictly secular nature. The same is true of the subcultural heritage of contemporary Protestantism and Catholicism.

Once these facts are recognized, we can more easily understand why it is that scholars have so often underestimated the influence of religion in contemporary society. Once these facts are recognized, we can also more easily understand why religious groups often have so much more influence on partisan politics and other mundane matters than on matters of basic morality. These things cease to be such a mystery once we grasp the complexity of the network of social relationships which constitutes the typical religious group, and once we grasp the corresponding complexity of the cultural heritage which these groups preserve and develop.

37 AMERICAN JEWS AND THE PRESIDENTIAL VOTE

Lawrence H. Fuchs

INTRODUCTION   The principle of separation of church and state is an official tenet of American political philosophy (*see* Petersen, Article 6). Although they may be legally separated, the deeper social relationship between the two cannot be terminated (*see* Lenski, Article 36). Religious groups look to the state for protection of their rights as a religious community. Officially, the state remains the protector of all groups at the expense of no single group. Rather than operate a state church, the state maintains an objective neutrality in religious matters. Religious groups, however, do not maintain the same objectivity. All groups work to achieve group-defined ends, whether through the use of lobbyists, public opinion, or favorable legislation supported by legislators elected with the help of some religious group (*see* Hammond, Article 9).

Religious influence in social decisions is apparent in Jewish voting patterns in presidential elections. Lawrence Fuchs of Brandeis University traces the shifts of voting statistics and Jewish resistance to class influences at the polls. Because the Jewish concern for social justice is a religious tenet as well as a practical concern of a minority group, Jews tend to support officeholders who are sensitive to minority problems.

Of all religious groups in America, the Jews are probably the most secularized. As Lenski notes (*see* Article 36), religious influence is still strong. Although the temple and synagogue remain centers of Jewish cultic (rites, rituals) and dogmatic (theology,

Abridged and reprinted from *The American Political Science Review*, Volume 49 (June 1955), pp. 385-401, with the permission of the author and editors.

LAWRENCE FUCHS is Professor of American Civilization and Politics at Brandeis University.

doctrine) expression, daily ethical practices have come to possess greater importance. The pragmatic quality of Judaism has replaced allegiance to doctrine or overemphasis upon cultic observance. The crowds of worshippers attending the High Holy Days are not present during the normal Sabbath celebration. Group secularization has caused Jews to remain consistent supporters of the complete separation of church and state (see Petersen, Article 6).

A more recent study (1960) of Jewish voting patterns in Baltimore by Edgar Litt concludes that when differences of socioeconomic status are constant, Jews normally present a stronger vote for Democratic candidates than white Protestants of northern European extraction. Socioeconomic status makes less difference among Jewish than among Gentile voting patterns. Although the Jewish vote for the Democratic Party has declined from the level established during the New Deal, it remains at a higher level than that of Gentiles. The Jewish preference for president is directly related to the candidate's recognition of minority concerns, a consideration which is also noted by Fuchs.

THE PURPOSE OF this article is threefold: first, to trace briefly the shifts in Jewish vote preference in recent decades through the use of aggregate election statistics; second, to probe the significant motivations of Jewish voters in 1952, primarily by analyzing the results of a sample survey conducted after the 1952 election in the city of Boston; and third, to suggest some of the basic reasons for Jewish resistance to class influences at the polls.

Between the election of William McKinley in 1896 and the beginning of the World War in 1914, more than two million Jewish immigrants came to the United States. Most of them were refugees from the anti-Semitism and poverty of Eastern Europe. They crowded into the tenements in the slums of New York and, to a lesser extent, those of Boston, Chicago, and Philadelphia. A large majority became laborers and peddlers or worked as cutters and tailors in the needle-trades.

While to an extraordinary number of these Russian and Polish Jews the parties of the radical left (particularly the Socialists) provided the only political answers,[1] the majority chose between the major parties. Of these politically orthodox Jews, more voted for Republicans than Democrats in every presidential election from 1900 to 1928, with the possible exceptions of 1900 and 1916.

Republicans were preferred for a wide variety of reasons. Among the most important were hostility towards the Irish; gratitude to the philo-Semitic

---

[1] See Morris Hillquit, Loose Leaves from a Busy Life (New York: Macmillan, 1934); Harry Rogoff, An East Side Epic: The Life and Work of Meyer London (New York: Vanguard, 1930); Louis Waldman, Labor Lawyer (New York: Dutton, 1944).

Theodore Roosevelt and William Howard Taft; and advice from established coreligionists.

The radical shift from Republican allegiance in the 1920's to the current predominantly Democratic loyalties of American Jews is dramatically expressed in the party enrollment figures for Ward 14 in the city of Boston, a consistently heavy Jewish area from 1924 until this day. In 1928, 78 percent of the enrolled voters there were Republicans. By 1952, only 14 percent of the enrolled electors in Ward 14 called themselves Republican.

American Jews have spurned Republican candidates in every presidential election since 1936. In 1936, Ward 24 in Chicago was probably the most Jewish ward in the nation. There Roosevelt received 96 percent of the vote. Elsewhere Jews were not as solidly Democratic. Four years later, Jewish wards in Boston and assembly districts in New York showed an appreciable increase in Democratic strength. Over 90 percent of the Jews in New York County's 17th Assembly District cast ballots for F.D.R. In 1944, Jewish Democratic strength increased still further. In Boston's Jewish Ward 14, more than 95 percent of the Jewish votes cast went to Roosevelt.

The results of national sample surveys conducted by the American Institute of Public Opinion and by the National Opinion Research Center show that more than 90 out of every 100 Jews voted Democratic in 1940 and 1944.

The results of these surveys also revealed that American Jews had considerably improved their relative economic position since the twenties. By 1944, they were among the best paid and best educated of all denominational groups. On occupational prestige scales the Jews were consistently rated higher than the most Republican denominational groups—the Congregationalists, Presbyterians, and Episcopalians.[2]

Jewish Democratic strength diminished in 1948, but the combined Truman-Wallace vote was almost as high in Jewish wards and assembly districts as it had been for F.D.R. in 1944. The Wallace vote was essentially Democratic. In Ward 14 the Progressive candidate received over 12 percent of the vote. In the heavily Jewish Bronx 7th Assembly District he won 27 percent of the vote. In the not-quite-as-Jewish Bronx 2nd Assembly District he received 21 percent. The combined Truman-Wallace vote in both districts reached almost 90 percent. In Hartford, Wallace ran strong only in predominantly Jewish Wards 4 and 12. In Los Angeles all five precincts which Wallace carried comprised Jewish neighborhoods. Even in suburban Brookline, Massachusetts over nine percent of the votes in its most Jewish precinct were counted for Wallace.

Although 1948 was a year when most Democrats could be sharply separated from Republicans by status characteristics, Jewish voters could not be so

[2] See Wesley and Beverly Allinsmith, "Religious Affiliation and Politico-Economic Attitude," *Public Opinion Quarterly*, Vol. 12 (Fall, 1948), pp. 377-89; and Liston Pope, "Religion and Class Structure," *The Annals of the American Academy of Political and Social Science*, Vol. 256 (March, 1948), pp. 84-92.

simply divided. The most radical candidate, Wallace, won the votes of many well educated upper-middle class Jews who had heretofore voted for Franklin Roosevelt, but the Republicans gained very little over 1944.

In 1952 all segments of Truman-Wallace strength except Negroes shifted somewhat to Eisenhower.[3] But analysis of aggregate returns from Jewish areas and the results of national surveys show that the Jewish defection was slight indeed.[4] In Jewish Assembly Districts in New York City, in Boston's Ward 14, in Hartford's Wards 2 and 4, in Cleveland's Ward 27, in Pittsburgh's Ward 14, and in Cincinnati's Ward 13, Stevenson appears to have matched or increased the Truman percentage of the *two-party* vote.

It was primarily in the suburbs that inroads were made on the Jewish Democratic vote—in such places as Westchester, New York; Newton, Massachusetts; and West Hartford, Connecticut.

RESULTS OF A POST-ELECTION SURVEY IN BOSTON'S MOST JEWISH WARD

In the big cities the Jews were loyal to the Democratic party; according to the results of a "quasi-random" sample survey[5] of eligible voters conducted in Ward 14 in the city of Boston following the 1952 election, differences in Stevenson strength in the urban Jewish population cannot be accounted for by differences in income, occupational, or educational levels.

The total number of Jews in any national sample is invariably too small to permit the subdivision of the sample into meaningful subgroups. Thus a quasi-random or "systematic" sample of 351 names was drawn from the 1952 Boston police list for Ward 14. Of these, 276 were finally interviewed.

The main purpose of the survey was to discover what the salient motivations of Jewish voters were in 1952. Questions were designed to produce responses which could be scaled by indices for socioeconomic status, political liberalism, and ethno-religious involvement. Other census-type questions were asked on age, sex, education, nationality background, and other matters. One question called for an explanation of the vote. All questions were pretested on Brandeis University students; some were also pretested in a pilot mail questionnaire sent to the parents of students.

Nearly 84 percent of the voters in the sample were Jewish. Of the 37 voting non-Jews, 28 were Catholic (nearly all Irish). The Jews in the sample lived in better homes, held better jobs, and made more money than the Christians; nonetheless, the Israelites gave Stevenson 70 percent of their vote while their Gentile neighbors voted only 46 percent Democratic.

[3] See Angus Campbell, Gerald Curin, and Warren E. Miller, *The Voter Decides* (New York: Harper & Row, 1954), pp. 70-3; Louis Harris, *Is There a Republican Majority?* (New York: Harper & Row, 1954), p. 161.
[4] Harris, *op. cit.*, pp. 160-3.
[5] Mildred Parten, *Surveys, Polls, and Samples: Practical Procedures* (New York: Harper & Row, 1950), pp. 266-7.

TABLE 37-1   Democratic vote of Jews and Gentiles in Boston's Ward 14
                  by occupational-income status.

Occupational-Income Group	Jews		Gentiles[a]	
	Number	Voted Democratic %	Number	Voted Democratic %
Low SES	36	64	15	60
Middle SES	101	66.3	12	41.7
High SES	53	72	10	30

a The distribution of Gentiles is like that found in the Roper national survey for three income groups of Irish descent: upper income 15%, lower-middle income 45%, and low income 75% Democratic. See Harris, op. cit., p. 222.

SOCIOECONOMIC STATUS AND THE JEWISH VOTE.   A total SES score was computed by combining income and occupational prestige scores, giving a double weight to occupation. Non-Jews in the sample, as in all national surveys, displayed much greater Republican strength in the high SES groups than they did in the low groups. However, differences in Stevenson strength among Jews in Boston cannot be accounted for by differences in socioeconomic status.

EDUCATION AND THE JEWISH VOTE.   There was a slight tendency for better-educated Jews to prefer Eisenhower in 1952, but the pattern is hardly

TABLE 37-2   Democratic vote of Jews and Gentiles in Boston's Ward 14
                  by educational groups.

Educational Group	Jews[a]		Gentiles	
	Number	Voted Democrat %	Number	Voted Democrat %
Some elementary school or less	39	79.5	1	100
Elementary school graduate	21	71.5	4	75
Some high school	24	73.9	9	66.6
High school graduate	62	64.4	9	33.3
High school plus vocational or business school	15	53.4	4	0
Some college	14	64.3	5	20
College graduate	22	68.3	5	60

a There appears to be a slight inverse correlation between SES and education among Jews because so many successful Jewish businessmen have little or no formal education, while some of the college graduates are young men and women not yet established in whatever they do.

significant. In fact, the percentage of Jewish college graduates in Ward 14 voting for Stevenson was almost as high as that for all Jews in the sample. The results for Gentile voters support the accepted view that Republican choice is associated with high education among non-Jews.

AGE AND THE JEWISH VOTE. The results of surveys in which a breakdown of ethno-religious groups by age is made reveal that when any group —Irish Catholics, Italians, Negroes—shift from their expected political predisposition, it is the younger voters who swing the most. Since the Jews did

TABLE 37-3   Democratic vote of Jews and Gentiles in Boston's Ward 14 by age groups.

Age Group	Jews		Gentiles	
	Number	Voted Democratic %	Number	Voted Democratic %
21-34	53	70	12	25
34-54	86	63	20	50
54 plus	54	76	5	80

not shift their loyalties appreciably in 1952, there was little difference in the Democratic vote among age groups in Ward 14, while the pronounced defection of Irish Catholic voters to Eisenhower was most noticeable among the younger voters.

Thus, in Ward 14 the presidential choice of non-Jews in 1952 was oriented along class lines. High education, high SES, and youth all disposed Gentiles favorably toward Eisenhower. On the other hand, Jewish voters for Stevenson could not be distinguished from the Eisenhower electors by any of the usual separators. It is not clear from the demography of the Jewish vote in Ward 14 just what it was that made one in every four Jewish voters choose the General while the large majority preferred the Governor.

ETHNO-RELIGIOUS INVOLVEMENT AND THE JEWISH VOTE. Questions were designed to test the depth of Jewish involvement felt by the respondents. Separate questions were used to measure the depth of cultural, religious, and social Jewishness. When added together, the scores of all three yielded a total ethno-religious involvement score which could be scaled.

It was recognized that voters might have commitments to Judaism which ran deep but which were psychological or intellectual and could not be measured by the EI scale. For that reason all Jewish respondents were also asked to pick three statements from a list (made originally by respondents in the pilot survey in answer to an open-end question) which best expressed what their religion meant to them.

Results show that Stevenson voters scored slightly higher EI scores on the cultural and social Judaism tests, while Eisenhower voters scored slightly higher on the religious Judaism scale. The overall means of each group were quite close, only one-tenth of a point separating them on a five-point scale.

From the results given in Table IV, it is not likely that differences in the vote could be attributed to differences in ethno-religious involvement, at least as measured by these scales. Moreover, Eisenhower and Stevenson voters chose approximately the same kinds of statements in about the same distribution to express best what their religion meant to them.

As with the results from the SES, EI, education, and age questions, the breakdown of the Jewish vote by nationality background and generations offered no clue to explain continued Jewish Democratic strength in the face of the Eisenhower landslide. Nor do any of the results reported so far suggest

TABLE 37-4   Democratic vote of Jews in Boston's Ward 14 by ethnic-involvement groups.

Ethnic-Involvement Group	Number	Voted Democratic %
High EI	13	46.2
High-medium EI	47	72.4
Medium EI	72	69.5
Low-medium EI	43	60.5
Low EI	20	80.1

what it was that prompted a minority of the Jewish voters to vote for Eisenhower.

THE JEWISH RESPONSE TO STEVENSON.   What did the Jews perceive in Stevenson and the Democratic party in 1952 that made them so preponderantly Democratic, almost without regard to socioeconomic and religious characteristics?

It was hoped that the answer to that question would be forthcoming in the replies to three questions placed in the interview schedule. One question was designed to test the political liberalism of respondents. This particular test was aimed at discovering the basic attitudes of respondents toward the use of power. Because of this and because the liberalism index was also used for purposes not discussed in this paper, the criteria for defining liberalism on which the question was based were: (1) a disposition to share power with out-groups, and (2) a disposition to respect those who are different.

It may be said that these criteria actually define political altruism and not liberalism at all as it is commonly understood. Whether the question yields an altruism index or a liberalism index is not crucial. The results show that there was considerable difference in the Jewish and Gentile response to the question in Ward 14. After the answers were scaled, respondents were divided into six categories ranging from "very strong liberals" to "very strong illiberals." While 40 percent of the Jews qualified as liberals or altruists, only 26 percent of the Gentiles did so.

The results were not surprising in the light of reports on other liberalism-conservatism or egalitarian-authoritarian tests.[6] No matter what criteria have been used to define liberalism and conservatism, Jews invariably have been rated overwhelmingly more liberal than Christians.

Did Jews perceive liberalism in Stevenson and the Democratic party? All Stevenson voters were asked to pick three statements from a list (all statements were originally made by respondents in answer to an open-end question in a pilot survey) which best expressed why they preferred Stevenson. They were also asked to choose two statements from another list which best expressed what they liked least about Eisenhower.

The results are instructive. To a much greater extent than the Christians the Jews in the sample emphasized the personal qualifications and liberalism of Stevenson and/or the Democratic party. Christians tended to stress the fact that the Democrats and/or Stevenson favored their own economic group while Eisenhower and the Republicans did not.

The results from these questions do not prove that it was the political liberalism of the Jews which kept them Democratic in 1952, but this evidence, taken together with the findings of Mr. Louis Harris of the Elmo Roper organization, at least suggests that the Jews did tend to think of Stevenson as the more "liberal" candidate and the Democratic party as the more "liberal" party.[7]

LIBERALISM AND THE STEVENSON-EISENHOWER CHOICE. If, as suggested, it was the "liberalism" of the Jews which oriented them toward a Democratic choice, it might be supposed that those Jews who were least liberal were the Eisenhower voters. Although it is true that a higher proportion of liberal or politically altruistic Jews voted for Stevenson than voted for him in the moderate or illiberal groups, the total number of liberals is quite small, and the differences between groups are not large.

It is entirely possible that the overwhelming disposition of the Jews to vote Democratic in recent decades is a function of their liberalism, but it is also possible that Jewish votes for Eisenhower were something other than a manifestation of illiberalism. Literally dozens of Jewish voters indicated in their replies to open-end questions that they thought Eisenhower was a liberal himself.

---

[6] Gordon W. Allport, "The Composition of Political Attitudes," *American Journal of Sociology*, Vol. 25 (Sept., 1939), pp. 220-38; *also* Allinsmith, *op. cit.*, pp. 379-80, and Ernest Haveman and Patricia West, *They Went to College* (New York: Harcourt, Brace & World, 1952).

[7] Harris, *op. cit.*, pp. 161-3.

TABLE 37-5   Democratic vote of Jews and Gentiles in Boston's Ward 14 by liberalism groups.

Liberalism Group	Jews		Gentiles	
	Number	Voted Democrat %	Number	Voted Democrat %
Liberals (Altruists)	25	87.5	4	50
Moderates	124	67	24	. 52.3
Illiberals	43	64.5	9	38.5

INTERPRETATION

PRIMARY GROUP INFLUENCES AND THE JEWISH EISENHOWER VOTE.   For a satisfactory explanation of the slight Jewish Democratic defection in 1952, it would be well to start with the proposition that a certain proportion of Jews were bound to be affected by the factors which caused an Eisenhower landslide in the nation at large. But which Jews were influenced and which Jews were not? It was not necessarily the rich Jews, or the well educated Jews, or the third generation Jews, or the less ethnically involved Jews, or the young Jews who showed disproportionate Republican strength in 1952.

Such evidence as is available strongly suggests that the Republican vote went up among those Jews who had the most frequent and extensive contact with non-Jews in primary groups.

Three sets of data tend to support this hypothesis: first, the difference in the Stevenson vote between the men and the women in Ward 14; second, the results of election surveys in predominantly Jewish colleges; third, the election results from Jewish suburban areas compared with those for metropolitan centers.

JEWISH MEN AND WOMEN VOTERS IN THE 1952 ELECTION.   Although the Survey Research Center reported[8] that males and females in the nation as a whole voted for Eisenhower in about the same proportion, the results of the survey in Ward 14 show that 83.3 percent of the Jewish women voters preferred Stevenson as compared with only 59.4 percent of the men, while there was no difference in the Stevenson vote between Gentile males and females. To be sure, the results of national surveys in the past have shown Jewish women to be somewhat more Democratic than Jewish men,[9] but the percentage difference between them was three or four and not 24.

[8] Campbell, Gurin and Miller, op. cit., p. 70. The Roper organization found that women were generally more attracted to Eisenhower than men. Harris, op. cit., chapter 7.
[9] Robert T. Bower, "Voting Behavior of American Ethnic Groups" (New York: Bureau of Applied Social Research, Columbia University, September, 1944), and Samuel J.

Keeping in mind the possibility of sampling and reporting bias, the results still appear to defy explanation until consideration is given to the importance of primary group contacts in the formulation of electoral decision.

It is now well established that face-to-face contacts are of major importance in the shaping of vote choice.[10] And there is evidence from the results of the Ward 14 survey to suggest that differences in the male-female vote can be largely explained by the fact that Jewish women in Ward 14 have little contact with primary groups which include non-Jews, while their husbands, fathers, and brothers are thrust into such groups quite often.

Most of the women rarely leave the Ward itself. Their contacts are almost exclusively neighborhood and family contacts, nearly all of which are Jewish.

In 1952 the Jewish group held fast to its Democratic moorings while the nation, for many reasons, swung to Eisenhower. While Jewish men were exposed to the opinions of non-Jewish friends at the work bench, of customers in the store, or of clients in the office, Jewish women were insulated from those cross-pressures to a considerable extent.

But, it will be asked, were not those pressures to which men were subjected filtered to most wives through their husbands? Yes, but they were diluted.

JEWISH COLLEGE COMMUNITIES AND THE 1952 ELECTION. At least suggestive of the importance of immediate group contacts for the Jewish vote in 1952 are the results of polls taken at Yeshiva College and Brandeis University. At Yeshiva, a school which is 100 percent Jewish, Eisenhower received a mere four percent of the vote. Brandeis is a nonsectarian Jewish-sponsored school. Probably as much as 10 percent of the student body there is not Jewish. In the Brandeis poll Stevenson received 88 percent of the vote.

The Jewish Brandeis students represent a cross-section of American Jewry —religious, irreligious, urban, small town, suburban, poor, well-to-do. Yet the Brandeis vote for Stevenson, including the vote of the non-Jewish students, was 14 percent higher than that reported for the national Jewish population by survey organizations and 10 percent higher than that reported for the sample of 59 of their own parents and relatives questioned in a pilot survey.

Jewish students came to Brandeis and Yeshiva with strong Democratic leanings. Finding their own opinions almost unanimously reinforced in student face-to-face groups, there were few defections. At home their parents were exposed to more frequent contacts with non-Jews in Republican-oriented groups.

SUBURBAN JEWRY AND THE 1952 ELECTION. It has already been shown that returns from Jewish wards and assembly districts in the large cities re-

---

Korchin, "Psychological Variables in the Behavior of Voting," unpublished dissertation (Harvard University, 1946).
[10] See Campbell, Gurin, and Miller, op. cit., p. 207, and Paul Lazarsfeld, Bernard Berelson, and Hazel Gaudet, The People's Choice (New York: Duell, Sloan & Pearce, 1948), chapter 16.

vealed little Democratic loss from 1948. It is reasonable to conclude that what Democratic losses there were (national surveys show some overall loss) occurred among those Jews who are dispersed in Gentile areas or who live in the suburbs. The votes of the former group cannot be reported, since, as in San Francisco, they are buried in the aggregate returns for non-Jewish wards. But simple arithmetic suggests that defections took place in just such cases.

Moreover, the returns from suburban Jewish areas support the hypothesis of the importance of primary group contacts for Jewish voting choice in 1952. Reports from Westchester and Long Island in New York, and from Brookline and Newton, near Boston, indicate that Jews in the suburbs were primarily responsible for the Jewish defections which did take place.

Although Jews may cluster together in tree-lined neighborhoods and country clubs in the suburbs, they are exposed to much greater contact with Gentiles in primary groups than are the Jews of Ward 14 or the Bronx. Jewish families in the suburbs participate in community affairs. Both men and women meet their non-Jewish neighbors in primary groups. They discover a common interest in the tax rate or the problems of the high school. Their interest in the local Synagogue may be more lively than it ever was back in Brooklyn, but their associations are no longer so preponderantly Jewish.

In 1944, suburban Jewry was hardly less Democratic than coreligionists in the city, because Jewish group involvement in the outcome of the election was so high. Even in Precinct 8 in suburban Brookline, F.D.R. received 79 percent of the vote. In 1952 the vote there slipped to 52 percent of the total. Brookline is a bedroom area for Boston. Its voters were subjected to cross-pressures in primary groups which even many of the well-to-do in Dorchester and Mattapan (Ward 14) did not experience, and in 1952 those pressures were strongest in the suburbs where the Eisenhower plurality was the greatest.

THE DEMOCRATS AND THE JEWS.   More important than the reasons for Democratic defection in 1952 are the causes of persistent Democratic attachment over the last three decades. In order to understand the fidelity of Jewish voters to the Democrats in 1948 and 1952, it is necessary to go back to Franklin Roosevelt and the almost solid Jewish vote for Roosevelt in his last three contests.

Roosevelt had the overwhelming support of Jews in his quest for a "New Deal" and his efforts at intervention in behalf of the Allies against the Fascists and Nazis. As interventionists the Jews were "internationalists," in the political parlance of the 1930's, and as New Dealers they were "liberals." The internationalism and liberalism of Roosevelt were both congenial to the interests of the Jews.

JEWISH INTERNATIONALISM.   During the late 1930's there was no stronger interventionist group in the United States than the Jews. The survival of world Jewry itself made such a course mandatory in the 1930's and 1940's. Roosevelt, of course, had begun in 1935 a series of private and public protests against anti-Semitism in Germany and was the political leader of the interventionist forces in the country. Jews could not help but be drawn to the one man who could lead Americans to a more active role in European affairs.

Recent studies show that Jewish support for internationalism persisted long after the defeat of Hitler. Survey results for 1948 and 1952 reveal that Jews support, much more strongly than Gentiles, the United Nations, Point Four, aid to Europe, liberal immigration policies, and world government plans. According to one survey of college graduates in 1948, almost twice the proportion of Jews as Catholics and Protestants were classified as internationalists, i.e., displayed stronger enthusiasm for the United Nations, liberal immigration, lower tariffs, helping other nations, and the reconciliation of international conflict.

Did Jews think that internationalism would be best served by the election of Truman or Wallace rather than Dewey in 1948? Presumably the answer is yes, otherwise it would be impossible to explain the extraordinary Jewish vote for Wallace. The Progressive candidate based much of his campaign on the failure of Truman to carry on the internationalism of Roosevelt (negotiation with Russia) while the Republicans, when they debated foreign policy at all, chided Truman for being too internationalist.

What of 1952? Did Jewish internationalism manifest itself then? In the Ward 14 sample, a much higher proportion of Jews than Gentiles supported the United Nations and the extension of aid to Africa and Asia. Elmo Roper found that Jews were much more for the United Nations and world government plans than non-Jews.[11] According to Louis Harris, one of the chief attachments of Jews to Adlai Stevenson was the compatibility of the Jewish and the Democratic positions on foreign policy.

JEWISH LIBERALISM. Other than foreign policy issues, the questions which have divided Americans in recent years have dealt with the distribution of economic power, Negro rights, and freedom of the mind. On each of these questions the Jews have taken what in everyday parlance has been called the "liberal" position. In each case Jewish opinions have been closer to the position of the Democratic candidates for President than to the one held by their Republican adversaries.

The results of surveys show that Jews have been strong supporters of the "New Deal" and the "Fair Deal." In 1932 and 1936 such views made economic sense to the Jews themselves. Like other Americans of recent immigrant stock, they felt the cruel blows of the depression and were no doubt grateful to Roosevelt for his efforts to lessen the effect of those blows. However, even though the Jews began to climb the economic class ladder in the late 1930's and 1940's, they persisted in their adherence to "New Deal" and "Fair Deal" ideas.

[11] Elmo Roper, "American Attitudes on International Organization," *Public Opinion Quarterly*, Volume 7, (Winter, 1953), p. 410.

According to the results of American Institute of Public Opinion surveys in 1944, the Jews were the only high economic status group to look with favor on governmental guarantees against economic insecurity. The results show that 53.8 percent of the Jewish business and professional men were for such government guarantees, as compared to an average of about 20 percent for non-Jews in these same occupations.

Other survey evidence showed that, even though there were proportionately fewer Jewish manual laborers than in any other religious denomination, a higher proportion of Jews than of any other group wanted to give more power and influence to working people. While 58.8 percent of the Jews wanted to give more power to working people, only 31.1 percent of the Congregationalists, 37.1 percent of the Presbyterians, and 34.7 percent of the Episcopalians —the other high occupational status groups—agreed.[12]

In 1948 Jewish college graduates were less hostile to socialism and government planning than non-Jewish college graduates. Sixty-six percent of the Jews were indexed as pro-New-Deal compared to 39 percent of the Catholics and 34 percent of the Protestants, in one study.[13]

In the survey of Ward 14, respondents were asked one question on the role of the national government in aiding economically underprivileged groups. Proportionately three times as many Jews as Gentiles were in strong agreement with such action.

The results of all studies show American Jews to be economic "liberals," in the sense of looking with approval upon the growth of governmental and labor power in economic affairs—even though they themselves are a favored economic group. Such economic views were crucial in the shaping of Jewish vote choice in the 1932 and 1936 elections. They were unimportant in 1940 and 1944, when Jewish interest in interventionism-internationalism was sufficient to unite them behind Roosevelt. In 1948 and 1952 the economic liberalism of the Jews again played a contributing role in sustaining their Democratic attachment.

On the issues of civil rights (in particular, Negro rights) and civil liberties (freedom of the mind) Jews have tended strongly to favor what is usually called the "liberal" position. The Jews were solid in their backing of President Truman in his quest for a Federal FEPC. Samuel Lubell reported that no white group was stronger in 1948 for FEPC measures than the Jews.[14] Again in 1952, the results of surveys on Negro rights questions showed that Jews were zealous in their quest for legislation protecting those rights. And in 1952, as in 1948, Jews thought that the Democrats could do much more about accomplishing such legislation than the Republicans.[15]

What is here labeled the "freedom of the mind" issue is really made up

[12] Allinsmith, op. cit., p. 379.
[13] Haverman and West, op. cit., pp. 98-9.
[14] Samuel Lubell, The Future of American Politics (New York: Harper & Row, 1952), pp. 96-7.
[15] Harris, op. cit., p. 162.

of a number of different issues, including communism in government, the rights and wrongs of congressional investigating committees, the Federal security program, and the use of high position to make reckless and unsubstantiated charges. According to 1952 surveys on these issues, the opinions of Jews were at variance with those of the rest of the population. Gallup and Roper public opinion polls found the Jews more hostile to McCarthy, less disturbed by charges of Democratic tolerance of communism in government, and more zealous in defending nonconformity than Catholics and Protestants. While these issues played little or no part in the 1948 campaign, the Jewish view of them no doubt fortified their Democratic leanings in 1952, and perhaps even played a vital role in bolstering Democratic loyalties.

Economic hardship may have made the Jews Democrats in 1932 and 1936; concern for the fate of coreligionists abroad may have made them Democrats in 1940 and 1944. But by 1948 and 1952 Jews were perched high on the economic status ladder, and the Nazis had been beaten, yet they continued to be "liberals" on economic issues, on civil rights, and on civil liberties. They continued to be internationalists in matters of foreign policy. And they continued to vote for Democratic candidates for President.

SOURCES OF JEWISH INTERNATIONALISM AND LIBERALISM. It must be clear that Jewish support for internationalism and liberal government is no transitory thing. Both are deeply rooted in the history and character of the Jewish people. It is no surprise that Jews support internationalist policies. They have been dispersed over the face of the globe for over 2,000 years, never long in one homeland and often in contact with coreligionists abroad. Jewish culture, language, folklore, and religion are truly international. Moreover, the experience of the last three decades has convinced American Jews that their own security lies in international guarantees (United Nations world government, genocide convention, international bill of human rights) and in the playing of a strong international role by the United States, whose beneficence in international affairs in behalf of Jews has been well demonstrated.

There are two primary sources of Jewish political liberalism. One is the basic insecurity of the group. The other lies in Jewish group values. Of the first, it may be said that Jews are engaged in a continuing quest for security even in free and pluralistic America. No matter how high they are placed on socioeconomic scales, Jews are considered by non-Jews to be an out-group, and more often than not an undesirable one.[16] There are few Jews who do not feel this in their bones. And there are few indeed who do not sense that the security of the Jewish group depends in great measure upon the largess of liberal government. Those who had doubts of this had them smashed for our time by the forces of anti-Semitism unleashed by Adolph Hitler and now so strong in Soviet Russia. Thus, while American Jews may be members of high income

16 See Muzafer Sherif and Carolyn W. Sherif, Groups in Harmony and Tension (New York: Harper & Row, 1953), pp. 78-9.

and occupational status groups, there are other reference groups in which their involvement, even when vicarious, runs deeper—those of the underprivileged and oppressed.

The second primary source of Jewish liberalism, probably less obvious and less understood than group insecurity, is in the ethno-religious values of the Jewish group. According to a vast impressionistic literature and growing systematic study of Jewish culture, those elements of culture most valued by Jews (including American Jews) are: Learning (*Torah*), Charity (*Zedakeh*) and, for want of a better word or phrase, Nonasceticism.

In probably no other American subculture is so high a value placed upon learning and intellectuality, or upon the helping of the poor by the rich and the weak by the strong, or upon living a good life upon earth in full use of one's body.

American Jews are practically unaffected by the bleak influence of Calvinism or by the harsh political implications of Social Darwinism. Nor are the American Jews as yet more than touched by the American pragmatic tradition disparaging learning for its own "impractical" sake.

These Jewish values have had special relevance to some of the major issues and candidates of our time. *Zedakeh,* which is the word for charity used in the Old Testament and the Talmud, and which is one of the few Hebrew words carried over into the Yiddish idiom, actually means "righteousness" or "justice"—"social justice" would be more accurate. Even though most American Jews may be unfamiliar with the word itself, the concept of *Zedakeh* is still highly prized in Jewish community life. To give is still a *mitzvah* (blessing). Within the framework of the Jewish cultural tradition, wealth, learning, and other tangible possessions are channeled from the strong to the weak and from the rich to the poor *as a matter of right*. It is easy to see the relevance of *Zedakeh* to politics, for both deal with the distribution of power. *Zedakeh,* as well as Jewish insecurity, would help promote Jewish sympathy for the Negro, and help induce a favorable attitude toward progressive taxation, Roosevelt's war on economic royalism, social security, and most of the programs which constituted the New Deal. It would also explain the favorable attitude of Jewish business and professional men toward an extension of power to labor, as long as they thought of laborers as being relatively weak or underprivileged. It would also explain the results of the liberalism or altruism test given to the voters of Ward 14 in 1953, the much greater willingness of the Jewish voters to be taxed to aid the less fortunate in Kentucky, or even in Africa and Asia. *Zedakeh* would also help explain why the results of referenda studied by the writer show that Jewish wards and precincts are more favorable to such things as pensions for the aged, raising the minimum wage, and aiding the disabled than are non-Jewish voters.

The Jewish reverence for learning has also played a role in making the Jews political liberals in recent decades. It has influenced the Jewish response to individual candidates as well as to specific issues. The positive Jewish response to Wilson and to Stevenson was in part a function of Jewish respect for learning. Twenty-two and one half percent of the reasons given by Jewish Stevenson voters in Ward 14 for preferring the Governor concerned his personality and intelligence, compared to only 13.8 percent of the reasons given by non-Jewish Stevenson voters. It was partly the Jewish love of learning that assured their positive response to the Roosevelt brain trust. The idea of professors in government did not seem incongruous to them, as it did to many Gentiles. For centuries Jews have been taught that the most learned men ought to run the affairs of the community. They were not repulsed by the notion of planning in government as were many of their fellow Americans. Charity (welfare) requires planning. That is a Jewish tradition. If the state is to take an active role in assuring the welfare of its citizens, it ought to put its best brains to work to plan how this will be done.

The respect of Jews for learning has also helped to make them fierce defenders of intellectual independence in connection with civil liberties issues. While almost 12 percent of the Jewish voters in the Ward 14 sample were in strong agreement that even Nazis and Communists ought to have free speech, not a single Gentile respondent was in agreement with that position. To be sure, the insecurity of the Jews prompts their anxiety about civil liberties, but the value which Jews place on knowledge plays a role as well.

The influence of Jewish nonasceticism on the political behavior of American Jews has been subtle, but probably no less important than the influence of *Zedakeh* and *Torah*. On such questions as the liquor or birth control issue it is easy to see how the nonasceticism or this-worldliness of the Jews influenced their position. But how has the nonasceticism of the Jews helped to make them political liberals as that term has been used in recent decades? The answer is that by Jewish emphasis on this-worldliness and the enjoyment of life here and now, Jews have been made more receptive to plans for a better life, for reconstructing society, for remaking man's environment, for socialism, and for millennialism.

Zedakeh, Torah, and this-worldliness have, along with the insecurity of the group, all promoted political liberalism among Jews in our time. Their liberalism and internationalism have favorably disposed them to a Democratic choice in recent presidential elections and largely explain the resistance of Jews to class politics.

38 CHRISTIAN FOUNDATIONS OF THE SOCIAL SCIENCES

Eduard Heimann

INTRODUCTION   The educational process is vital to the continuity of religion. No religious group may long continue to exist without either socializing its children to religious ideals or converting new membership to doctrinal positions (*see* Elkind, Article 16). Because religious behavior is learned behavior, socialization success determines the future strength and purpose of the group.

The rise of formal educational systems can largely be traced back to religious socialization attempts. From the early Jewish synagogue to the later Christian university, educational and religious concern have been intertwined. Although the separation of church and state has resulted in the subordination of religion as an academic discipline on many state campuses, private and parochial schools give religion varying degrees of primacy. Religious implications in drama, art, values, ethics, and literature cannot be avoided whether in a private, parochial or state setting.

The modern expression of natural and social science has developed out of the theological-philosophical speculation of the Renaissance period. Believing that truth can only be reached through empirical and logical processes, modern science has rejected concepts of supernatural intervention which early theologians believed marked the progress of history. The changing nature of human reality has led to a deepened sense of cultural relativity in which absolute ideals have been replaced by relative values. Traditional religious convictions founded upon faith have been challenged by

Abridged and reprinted from *Social Research*, Volume 26 (October, 1959), pp. 325-346, with the permission of the author and editors.

EDUARD HEIMANN is Emer. Professor of Social Sciences at the University of Hamburg and Honorary Professor of Christian Social Ethics at the University of Bonn.

modern social postulates built upon research (*see* Stackhouse, Article 39). Eduard Heimann, formerly of the Universities of Hamburg and Bonn, observes that the problem existing between philosophy-religion and social science is one of *norms* versus *facts*. To Heimann, the tendency to separate social science from the life of faith can only lead to calamity. To science, life may be a collection of facts, but facts are meaningless, he says, unless interpreted in the context of norms. Heimann argues that Christian doctrine and culture must assimilate the heresies of Marx, Nietzsche, and Freud if they are to include all truth within their confines.

T HE MODERN NOTION of the science of society and of its subject matter derives from Greek philosophy, despite the formidable distance between the Greek quest for wisdom and the modern doctrine of technical knowledge and control. What the two have in common is an appeal to man's mind and a trust in it. Thus Socrates was at pains to open to the common people the way from their daily experiences to the sanctuary of wisdom, for the blessing of insight into harmonious nature—that is, reason—behind and above life instils virtue into the soul and thus enables people to live together in peaceful organization. Indeed, according to the aristocratic Plato, it is only the few really wise who are able to rise from the cave of human existence into the pure ether of eternal essences. In any case, neither the Greek doctrine of wisdom nor the modern doctrine of science is aware of any other primacy than man's mind; in this sense both are of humanist-rationalist sentiment. It is fully logical that Plato drew from his premise the conclusion that the philosophers should be kings because their superior wisdom strongly incorporates the state-forming and state-preserving virtues. And likewise the modern social scientists say that their science imparts the competence necessary for correctly guiding society.

Nevertheless the conflict between the two is bound to make itself felt. A doctrine of wisdom is naturally a doctrine of norms; science, however, is defined as a doctrine of facts. It is true that the bridge between the two is easy to find: the norms that the state, for example, must comply with in order to function correctly can be developed only from knowledge of the state, and further back, of the people to be organized by that state. Yet the difference between the doctrine of norms and that of facts cannot be overemphasized. The doctrine of norms plainly says that compliance with the norms is the condition for the structure to exist; the doctrine of facts takes the structure as given and extant, and describes it. Or in a different turn of thought, the doctrine of wisdom is, by very definition, less optimistic than the doctrine of facts: to the former the task is to secure the existence of the structure, while to the latter the task is analysis of the given structure and, on that basis, control of the processes within the structure, with a view to influencing and modifying them at will.

It could be objected that those factors that make the existence possible—the subject matter of the doctrine of wisdom—must appear in the inventory of the facts analyzed by science in the given structure. But this is precisely the reproof to the conventional doctrine of facts. That doctrine, beginning only after the basic question of existence has been solved, takes the conditionally secure existence as simply given. The spiritual decay or even the physical death of societies is all too familiar to the historian but unknown to the modern social scientist in his work. He treats the developed society as if it were immortal as long as people propagate. Society is regarded as a piece of human nature, because it is rational for man to live in society, and reason is a piece of human nature. Nature is eternal, at least from the point of view of social science, and hence society is eternal too.

THE RATIONAL INTEREST AS FUNDAMENTAL CONCEPT.
To see the problem is a great achievement but is not tantamount to solving it. What is rationalism's solution?

Rational judgment teaches man the value of living in society. This is, properly speaking, a doctrine of norms. We know that man does not always and not only live judiciously, and that he hurts himself if his passions gain the better of him: judgment ought to curb passion. The judiciousness, the rationality of man, is the principle, and it leads him into society because he lives infinitely better in association, with division of functions and exchange of goods and services, than otherwise. Exactly this was taught by Plato and Aristotle. And, more or less elaborated, it also is the starting point from which the modern social sciences rush to their favorite problems, those of particular processes.

There are, however, two opposite attitudes of socialized man, both of which serve his rational interest in his welfare, each in its own way: cooperation and rivalry, the one in order to increase the common output, and the other in order to increase our own share in the common output. The two are opposite even though rivalry, in the special form of competition, appears as a particular form of cooperation, under the guidance of an "invisible hand" that functions "behind the backs of the agents." If society is defined as cooperation through division of functions, its rationality is beyond doubt. But if rivalry and competition be added, the situation becomes ambiguous.

Rivalry is the decisive problem of our analysis, because it is the rational impediment to allegedly rational solidarity in society. This is implied in the rational premise of the entire theory, which ultimately says that since people are led into society by insight into the conditions of their private welfare, society is a means for private ends. Hence an antisocial attitude will be chosen as the rational means if it best serves the private welfare. This does not even contradict the proposition that rationality demands life in society: one can behave in an antisocial manner only in society.

Frequently it is attempted to make a long-range, short-range distinction between the rational interest in the durable existence of society and the interest in exploitation and other irregularities: the former is seen as prevailing eventually and as holding down the short-run interests to the position of short-sighted irrationalities. According to this view, injustice cannot endure, because the oppressed rise for the battle of justice, and hence the prudent man will prefer right to wrong in his own rational, that is, long-range interest.

But his advantage in physical or intellectual or military or financial or other power, which enables him to exploit the weaker people, also enables him to perfect the exploitation durably and systematically by physically holding down and morally degrading the defeated. While it is true that such a policy is not always successful, it is successful often enough to appear as the real rational interest of the strong. In world history injustice is all too often victorious and encourages imitation by such people and groups of people as feel themselves strong enough. Wherever we may look in a hypothetical world of the pure rational interest, solidarity is only one, and not the strongest, of its possibilities. Rational interest leads into conflict, and the actual durability of society must rest on a deeper and firmer ground.

In our own days the rational conflict, professing as it does the principle of rationalist humanism, has split the world of white mankind into two opposing camps, which are armed for mutual destruction and are paradoxically held back only by mutual fear. It is easily seen that the West-East conflict is only a newly developed form of the age-old rational conflict, and that it equally does not permit of logical settlement by subsumption under a higher logical principle. The East is taught by its dialectical self-understanding to regard itself as the higher stage of the West's pattern of life. The latter was first in exploring the rational possibilities of life in all directions, under a maximum of individual liberty and at a corespondingly high cost in waste and friction; now the East can sift the results and organize and develop them in systematic unity. The propelling force, here too, is the rational quest of welfare. The collective interest, more specifically the proletarian class interest, arises explicitly from the rational conflict of private interests: it is the sum of the private interests of the economically weak and drives to the destruction of the adversary, but it preserves the class solidarity beyond the situation of conflict because there is now, after the elimination of the adversary, complete rational homogeneity. This is the doctrine.

The new thing in this collective stage of the rational interest is the reversal of the means-end relationship. The rational conflict arose from the rational interest in increasing one's own share in the total revenue at the expense of the other shares, within a social order that accords the liberty to assert such aspirations. The dialectically transformed, summed-up private interest of the victorious collective claims the right to crush opposing interests or opposing interpretations of the (never unequivocal) collective interest, for the sake of ideological and social homogeneity. The collective, the sum of the homogeneous private interests, is the supreme end or the supreme authority that determines the end, and the members are means in the service of the end and can and must be rejected if this appears expedient.

Within a rationalist system the relationship between the person and the community can be understood only in the categories of means and end; only one of the two can be the end, and the other is then nothing but means and is subject to considerations of expediency without any dignity of its own. But the decision on which of the two shall be the end and which the means is purely dogmatic. In purely rational logic supremacy is accorded to the rational individual, while in dialectical logic it is accorded to the homogeneous collective as the sum of the rational homogeneous individuals; one solution is as logical and as arbitrary as the other. And if the two hostile solutions claim to organize the two halves of the modern rational world, this world is split dogmatically. The doctrine that rationality constitutes the society of rational people ends, with paradoxical but compelling logic, in the split of society. What it does constitute is a logically insoluble conflict. This is the self-refutation of rationalist social science.

RELIGION AS THE FUNDAMENTAL CONCEPT.   The struggle for shares in the society of rational individuals, the struggle against deviations in the society of the rational collective, and the struggle between the two versions of the rationalist principle in a world that has now shrunk to technical unity ensue from the presumption of rationality. If society is relatively durable, it must have a deeper foundation, a foundation able to bear the conflict; or in other terms, the conflict must be overarched by a higher principle, since society does exist.

Society is constituted by religion. As regards the so-called primitive societies of our time the primacy of religion is probably recognized by all anthropologists, particularly those who see a primitive trait in the predominance of religion. The center of the controversy is the question whether the highly developed societies, too, rest on religion, or whether they can replace that "erroneous science" by the more solid authentic science. William Graham Sumner, from whom we have the designation, was fully aware of the disciplining, moral, ennobling effects of religion. A hundred years before, Robespierre, the dictator of anti-Christian Enlightenment, was so fully aware of those effects that he tried to establish, after the cult of the goddess Reason, a religion of the "Supreme Being," and for it confiscated Notre-Dame de Paris. It is just as characteristic and as grotesque that Auguste Comte, the founder of positivism, wanted to stabilize its universal empire by a "Positivist Church" (leaning on the Catholic Church at that), for he and the French sociologists following him regarded as the true object of religious worship, in however mythical disguise, society itself, which imparts poise, purpose, and dignity to man by integrating him into a greater whole. National Socialist and Communist youth confirmations, organized to compete with Christian confirmation, are all too well known today. Respectable people have maintained in all seriousness that America's real religion is democracy. The fact that society rests not on scientific rationality but on religion is familiar enough to all these deniers of religion to press them toward attempts to found counter-religions.

But that achievement is not so simple as a rationalist or positivist may imagine. And in any case the secularized, science-proud society in West and East does not live on any of the atheist religions but on its own age-old religious tradition, even where this tradition has long been divested of any official function. While the rational principle proves to be ambiguous, aiming at cooperation on the one hand and at rivalry on the other, religion provides society with the requirements of durable existence: it unites people by their common belief in overarching powers, and it disciplines people by the teachings in social ethics that are derived from the supreme religious propositions. If social ethics is to outweigh the centrifugal effects of rationality, it must be and remain anchored in religion.

But this last proposition requires substantiation. If nothing has been bequeathed to us by the atheist religions, all of which come down to the self-worship of society, our humanists must resort to the postulate of autonomous morals independent of religion. These must be inborn in the human mind, and in this sense ideal. Truth, oneness, justice—man cannot think without believing in the truth; he cannot correctly act without believing in justice; and there must be only one truth and one justice if he is to think and act correctly. No historical revelation need be resorted to if the natural structure of the human mind contains everything that is required, even if many millennia are needed for unfolding the full power and effectiveness of that structure.

No humanist and rationalist understands what history is. Because he denies God and trusts only human reason, he believes he has cut off the religious tradition. But in doing this not even his head is successful, far less his person. Not even his head succeeds in doing it: since he finds the traditional content in his mind he interprets it as the natural content of his natural reason, but it is the content of the tradition he rejects, a tradition that has formed the minds of his forefathers for over a thousand years and whose categories—save the one word God—are so familiar to him that he takes them for his nature. He thinks he does not need religion because he has morality; he does not see that he has morality only because his forefathers had religion.

If it is true that morality is the fruit of religion, morality may survive religion for one or two generations, but must then follow it. Humanism is often a moving, but always a tragic phenomenon. It lives on what it fights against; it destroys the mysterious foundations of its own spiritual life and of the hoped-for rational society.

CHRISTIAN FOUNDATIONS. With these reflections we have at last entered the framework of our own tradition, the Christian tradition. Western society—however many of its present members may deny it—is a Christian society, in the sense that the forms of thought and life that are employed by its members are decisively shaped by the interpretation of the Christian message, and are thereby distinguished from those of all other societies. This is not the place to try even the most sketchy survey of the sociologically relevant parts of the doctrine. I want to stress only certain points that are relevant to this inquiry into the method of the social sciences.

PERSON AND COMMUNITY. The first point is the primacy of love, which the Great Commandment derives directly from the love of God, not properly as a commandment—for the commandment of love is, strictly speaking, a contradiction in itself—but as a description of the creative power. Love, of course, was not created or even discovered by Christianity—any more than virtue was. In a certain sense all classical philosophy is a doctrine of virtue, and the power of love was familiar to the classical philosophers.

The Christian principle of love is not a means of self-realization, because it cannot be willed: love is the end of the self-seeking individual and the beginning of personal life. Through the principle of love as a creative power, the fatal cleavage in the present world, the cleavage between individualism and collectivism, is overcome. In the real world there is neither the individual nor the corresponding collective. The self-enclosed individual, greedy for his "self-realization," is incomplete and unredeemed. He is made complete and is redeemed from himself by love, which pulls him out of himself and makes him forget himself. Hence person and community coincide,[1] they arise *uno actu* from the creative power of love, of which there are infinitely many kinds and hues. A collective—a sum of unconnected self-seeking individuals—exists as little as the individual; rather, they both arise only from the withering of something alive, and once more *uno actu*. Community, however, is community of persons, one axis with two poles of equal dignity.

What binds people to one another and into community is thus more profound and higher than the rational interest, the fundamental concept of the social sciences. Interest does not bind, it calculates, and the calculation may recommend a new policy in each new situation. A society of human beings cannot live that way; it rests on lasting bonds, not on the varying results of varying calculation. The durable existence of society logically precedes the conflict of interests in society. The binding power is called love, not in the sense of romantic enthusiasm between teen-agers or enamored young people (although this may very well lead into love), but in the sense of confirming, understanding, living with the other, of standing up for and trusting each other, of bearing with each other and seeking for reconciliation and harmony in the unavoidable small and big conflicts between the tempers and the varying claims of incessantly changing persons.

---

[1] The distinction, introduced by F. Tönnies and very influential in Germany, between "community" (*Gemeinschaft*) and "society" (*Gesellschaft*) is not practicable for present purposes. Entirely in line with nineteenth-century tradition, Tönnies opposed a romantic past of organic community to the sane, clear present of society resting on deliberate construction. The distinction is not valid here.

It is also the contrast between Christian personalism and Oriental mysticism—and this leads to a second point. In all Biblical teachings, culminating in the doctrine of incarnation, spirit is embedded in nature. Idealists like Plato, who believe in spirit purified of earthly stuff, lament that the conditioning of spirit by nature degrades spirit; in truth it ennobles nature, because it penetrates it with spirit. Biblical realism is always aware that the life of spirit on this earth depends on natural conditions, although it is not at all determined thereby, as the materialists hold. To study the natural and historical-social conditions and limitations of spiritual life has thus been a task of religious dignity for the Christian universities since their founding in the eleventh and twelfth centuries.

Particularly in the great Oriental religions, salvation by love means something quite different, because the understanding of man is different. The Oriental solution extinguishes the suffering of individuation by extinguishing the individual; the Christian solution develops the individual to the person, because love here is love between persons, who give themselves to each other freely and freely receive each other. Freedom and justice can be tasks of religious dignity only in a world educated by Christianity; only here is life on this earth affirmed rather than depreciated, as in the Orient. All genuine problems of our life can thus be developed from the Christian doctrine, and the false and insoluble ones—individualism versus collectivism—follow from a decay of understanding, whereby the religious dimension wastes away and the material basis of life is absolutized. Hence the yearning of many Western intellectuals today for Oriental absorption.

HISTORY. The overvaluation of earthly life through the loss of spiritual orientation is systematized in the modern social sciences. As was emphasized above, their reference to classical philosophy is devious, because they water down the strictly normative concept of reason to make it the methodological premise of their analyses of facts. But they are closer to the Greeks than to the Bible, in that they regard as worthy of and in need of scientific explanation only what is constant, not what changes, unless it be a constant change, as between the phases of the business cycle in economics. Also, it is necessary to interpret the concept of the "constant" liberally enough to include development, in so far as it results from a given constellation through rearrangement of the data; on this basis hypothetical tendencies of development can be derived, a procedure in which one tries to select the data and their hypothetical change in as realistic a way as possible.

Nevertheless, the verdict stands that in focusing on the rationally intelligible we fail to find access to that dimension of social reality which transcends the rational. Even in seeking access to change we remain in the framework of the given, the known. In principle, nothing new can happen, only variations of the same theme, for the types of behavior are known, the motives from which they flow have been accurately analyzed. Human beings do not act, they react, and hence they are controllable. The motives pass through the human beings but are not particular to them. This is the image of man behind the search of the social sciences for "regularities" in social life.

This image of man contradicts the nature of history, which is not a mere unfolding of the already known, but an unpredictable creative renewal in the midst of unresolved misery and insoluble tragedy. In spite of everything, there are in history freedom and hope. But society has, beyond that, a spiritual dimension in which the natural, social, and political material is consciously shaped and reshaped. History is not only suffered, it is also made. A science that programmatically denies this, is inconsistent with its basic concepts, may and does teach us many useful things of second and third importance, but fails in its principal task: to give us understanding of the nature and limits of human freedom. Creative freedom in history explodes the freedomless image of human society which is presupposed in scientific manageability. If the latter be willed, freedom must be excluded, not only from the scientific image but also from the reality to be formed in this image. The learned specialists may be enthusiasts of freedom outside their work, but in their work they more or less unconsciously serve the enemies of freedom.

Freedom, though not included in their formative concepts, is not incompatible with them. Logically there is no obstacle to including among the causal forces passing through man a force of different nature and efficacy, which we may call freedom or core or decision. Its peculiarity lies in the fact that, contrary to the causal forces, it is not always active; for shorter or longer periods it abandons the field, and thus permits the rise of regularities, but in times of distress and peril it pulls itself together and, by its unforeseen contribution, deflects the causal forces from their regular effect and creates something new. Such a formal concept of liberty is logically possible. It is also realistic, for it recognizes that man's freedom is always surrounded on all sides and squeezed by necessities of many kinds: it is not the creative power of God.

What do we thereby achieve? Scripture promises us "the glorious freedom of the children of God" (Romans 8:21), which in the historical context of the Epistle to the Romans is freedom from the moral and ritual law of the Pharisees and scribes, but means something comparable, of course, in any other historical situation. Our scribes have built the rational law of scientific rules as a protection against the mysterious, incalculable, danger-fraught freedom of man, which they count among the "irrationalities." But their law is precisely what splits the nation and the nations; it is not life but death—and is death perhaps not among the regularities of natural reason? In the Bible (John 3:3, 6, 8) we are promised "rebirth of the spirit"; the greatest Christian statesman of recent times, Abraham Lincoln, in his funeral address for the dead of both sides on the battlefield of Gettysburg, calls for a "new birth of freedom under God." This is no moral injunction. Rebirth is not in our power; only with God is nothing impossible. But rebirth is not a merely emotional or edifying experience either; it is a transformation, occurring over and over in the great crises of personal and historical life.

To be sure, this happens only in the great crises; divine grace in the midst of our sins is not to be had at a cheaper price than a deep shock. It is a fact in individual life as in history that as long as things seem to work smoothly we have no use for renewal, that is, for becoming new and different. But it is a fact too that all regularities drive toward an ending, because life is motion; what was formerly the adequate and fair attitude turns false and unfair—becomes wrong precisely because it was right. At that point man is faced with the decision of his life. He can continue the earlier way, because it was right, and pursue it to the bitter end. But he can also set a new beginning, a new form of the common life with new aspirations and customs, which are to be fair to the newly growing forces. This is a rise to a higher plane, because a new vision of justice for the concrete case has been gained, and a new power of love, tested in overcoming the self, fills the new form. Likewise in the life of society, the moment comes when the newly swelling forces threaten to explode the accustomed form of the cohesion. In such a time of distress a new power of love may abandon the familiar form, seize a new vision of justice, and erect a new structure thereupon. This event in history is called reform; the true conservative is a reformer.

The word reform is of religious origin, of course, and the event is of religious nature because in it the regularities or laws of the natural process are broken through and the formidable venture of a new beginning is inaugurated.

The victor on the battlefield of Gettysburg asked for a new birth of freedom, as the old form had perished in the terrible catastrophe of the civil war; he was assassinated soon afterward, and the work remained unfinished. More far-reaching is the reconstruction that the entire Western world has accomplished as "social reform," proceeding step by step in the course of the last hundred years, under the constant menace of a proletarian explosion, until that menace was exorcised and the Marxist revolution was pushed off from the industrial countries of its program to the preindustrial countries. Was Marxism wrong? It was right, so right that its bitter criticism of capitalist injustices in the midst of the productive achievement of capitalism was accepted by the countries of capitalism. Also it was wrong, as wrong as the capitalist theory, for each, faithful to scientific procedure, logically elongated its structural principles until the two proved irreconcilable and nothing remained but catastrophe. To take hostile criticism to heart is the sign of renewal, and its beginning. The new birth of freedom is no scientific rule; it is the venture of faith out of deep distress, and it is the historical reality that matters.

There is no dialectical law of history under which a logically insoluble contrast must find its fruitful resolution on a higher plane, with both contending parties coming into their own and being reconciled with each other. Repentant insight into one's own wrongness, which turns hate-inspired criticism into an opportunity for renewal, is no law; it transcends the law under which we started and are driving toward the end. And much less can we attribute the character of law to the divine grace without which freedom cannot be born anew and the vision of justice cannot become real. The technical

material for the new structure is contributed by us, but that in it which is
spirit, creation, life, descends from grace, as does the repentance that draws the
power of renewal from the distress. The new birth of freedom is not law, and
ruin is always possible in history.

But over and over again, from crisis to crisis, the Western world has renewed itself in the course of the centuries. This is its history, nay, that makes
history of what would otherwise be a blind sequence of events, as in nature.
History has meaning and direction; its measure, its goal beyond itself, is promised to us and hidden before us as the kingdom of God. In this sense history
is Christian history. That is why the social sciences miss the great decisions
and problems and confine themselves to what is accessible to their technical
logic. And—still more important—that is why the non-Christian peoples have
no history: no meaning capable of interpretation is contained in the events
that happen to them. Only the world educated by Christianity knows the mystery of reform.

I have attempted here to emphasize that dimension of social life which
the social sciences exclude by their formative concepts. God, spirit, and liberty
in history exist in reality but not in the social sciences. Thus the latter, if they
would be realistic, must be capable of integration into a Christian theory of
life and history. Hence this programmatic attempt to uncover Christian foundations of the social sciences.

But this program has still another aspect: revalidation of the Christian
doctrine in the sphere of society. What is called creation on this earth, the
putting up of meaning and justice in concrete forms where nothing of the
like had been there earlier, is not accessible to explanation by a theory of rational processes; much less can it be foreseen and controlled. In the Christian
doctrine, however, it becomes intelligible, and the world becomes wide and
open. The Christian doctrine establishes room for hope.

The displacement and splitting off of the social sciences from the structure of faith, which began in the Renaissance and has been completed in our
days, is a terrible calamity, for which the churches were originally to blame because they did not offer room. Now the social sciences have developed outside
the churches, and in the process have unavoidably assumed many heretical-
utopian traits. The catastrophes of our time reduce confidence in the moral
power of man to absurdity, and confirm the Christian view of the several
dimensions of human and historical existence. But the revalidation of the
Christian doctrine must never neglect or repress the truths that the human
mind has discovered without the churches, and often against their resistance.

The greatest thinkers of the past generations were heretics; no Christian
thinker of that time is a match for Marx, Nietzsche, or Freud. Marx teaches
that this is a world of injustice. Is this an un-Christian proposition? It is a
profoundly Christian proposition, even though Marx, the heretic, drew from
it conclusions that short-circuited it. Freud teaches that man's soul is split,

and that the unconscious violates the conscious will. And is this an un-Christian proposition? It is found in the letter to the Romans, where indeed what is missing in Freud is found too. Today, in wrestling with Marx, Nietzsche, and Freud, the Christian doctrine has at last become wide and high enough again to offer room to all truth. By assimilating the heretics the Christian doctrine revalidates itself. It justifies the heretics by assimilating and re-Christianizing them, and it towers above them because it knows what the heretics do not know.

39 DARWIN AND A CENTURY OF CONFLICT

Reginald Stackhouse

INTRODUCTION   The problem of norms versus facts,
suggested by Eduard Heimann (*see* Article 39), is the central
issue in the antagonism which has existed historically between
science and religion (*see* Vernon, Article 4). Although the early
forms and intensity of the argument have somewhat abated, the
issue remains in the form of the fundamentalist-modernist controversy within religion (*see* Ahlstrom, Article 1). The rapid rise
of science following the investigations of Charles Darwin and the
publication of his *Origin of Species* issued a major challenge
to traditional theology in the last half of the nineteenth century.
The natural sciences offered new facts about the age of the earth
and the evolution of life. Psychology and sociology suggested that
human motivation and behavior was more than a matter of simple
will or personal choice. Anthropology presented a new understanding of the relativity of religious belief and practice by studying
primitive societies. Within theology itself Biblical "higher criticism" challenged many of the accepted facts of scriptural interpretation. To combat these new heresies, defenders of the faith came
to battle with zeal. The culmination of this argument resulted in
the famous Tennessee "monkey trial" of John Scopes in 1925.
    The issue was evolution, and yet the issue was *more than* evo-
lution. The argument was one of strict religious orthodoxy against
religious interpretations based upon or at least tempered by empirical knowledge. The question was and still is one of norms
versus facts. Should religious orthodoxy determine the direction of
knowledge or should rational science determine belief? Should

REGINALD STACKHOUSE is a member of the faculty of Wycliffe College (Toronto).

theological doctrines determine educational policy or should education be based upon principles of free investigation? Although the antievolutionists won the trial, Scopes being convicted and later freed on a technicality, they were pictured as ignorant bigots. The attempt to prevent the teaching of evolutionary theories by law quickly collapsed, although statutes against teaching evolution still remain in a few states. Even today, periodic attempts are made by fundamentalist religious groups to purge the local educational system of "heretical" evolutionist doctrines. The recent attempt to censor high school biology textbooks in Texas is an example of this latent attitude. Most denominations have accepted the influence of scientific discovery within their theology, but the struggle still continues. No longer is the argument between science and religion but rather between *fundamentalists* (truth based upon revealed norms) and *modernists* (truth based upon empirical facts) (*see* Ahlstrom, Article 1, and Ford, Article 10). The vast population of America, however, belongs to neither of these extremes. Instead, they variously include norms (often derived from beliefs) and facts (based upon evidence) in their conceptions of religion. Most major denominations now proclaim a theology which allows for both the historicity of faith *and* the discoveries of science. Reginald Stackhouse suggests that no book of science will ever again possess the impact upon religion as did Darwin's *Origin of Species*.

WHEN CHARLES DARWIN published his *Origin of Species* in 1859, two consequences surprised him. One was immediate: the entire first edition of the book sold on the day of publication. The second and long-range consequence of his mildly written treatise was a bitter doctrinal controversy of such magnitude that it split churches into hostile factions, led to papal encyclicals, transformed halls of learning into arenas of conflict, prompted acts of state legislatures, and still today influences the dogmas of religious groups.

BOOK OF THE CENTURY.   No book has had more influence on the religious outlook of the past hundred years. More than any book before or since, it caused people to question traditional biblical interpretations.

In his book, Darwin presented evidence which he claimed showed that the various species of life in the world today had not been here in those shapes from the beginning but had evolved from simpler forms. This idea was called evolution. It was not a new idea. Indeed, hundreds of years before Christ, Anaximander had advocated a theory of evolution, and over the ages it won the support of many philosophers, among them, incidentally, Darwin's grandfather, Erasmus Darwin. But Charles Darwin was the first to back the theory with strong scientific evidence.

Darwin had been collecting the evidence ever since, twenty-eight years before, he had sailed the South Seas as official naturalist on H.M.S. "Beagle." During that voyage he became conscious that the large variety of species and their peculiar distribution throughout the world pointed to evolution as the answer to the question, How did all these kinds of animals get here? His observations then and later studies of insect life on his country estate gave him the factual data to support the theory. He concluded that the species now in existence not only had evolved from lower beings but had developed by a process of "natural selection," by which Darwin meant that the species which survive over the ages are those that are able to meet the demands of their environment, while all the others perish. In other words, the species existing today are here not by design but simply by survival of the fittest.

The effect of Darwin's careful and persuasive argument on the British public was electric. Most people then believed that this creation had been accomplished in six days some 4,000 years before Christ, and the idea that all species had developed into their present form over perhaps millions of years seemed to challenge the very first principles of Christianity. When the public discovered that this theory applied to man too, the battle was joined. A large section of the British people were not prepared to accept the claim that they, the descendants of the Saxons and Normans, were also the descendants of apes. The fight was on.

Perhaps Darwin was aware of the possibility of these repercussions, for he concluded his book not with a denial of a divine creator but with this tribute: "There is grandeur in this [evolutionary] view of life with its several powers having been originally breathed by the Creator into a few forms or into one; and that, while this planet has been circling on according to the fixed law of gravity, from so simple a beginning endless forms, most beautiful and most wonderful, have been, and are being, evolved." That was not enough to appease the defenders of the faith, however, and within months a showdown came between those who stood with Darwin and those who stood with Genesis or rather with their understanding of Genesis.

WILBERFORCE VS. HUXLEY.   The showdown occurred at a meeting of the British Association in June 1860, when the validity of Darwin's claim was challenged by Samuel Wilberforce, bishop of Oxford. Primed by Sir Richard Owen, a critic of Darwin and one of the leading biologists of the time, the bishop set about to refute this theory which had attracted such interest. With the eloquence and wit that led some to call him "Soapy Sam," he not only defended the traditional account of creation but also lampooned the theory of evolution in the hope that the public would not believe in something it laughed at. In this spirit, he ended his address by asking if the advocates of evolution were descended from monkeys through their grandfathers or through their grandmothers. Up rose the man who was to become the staunch-est champion of evolution in the years of controversy that followed, Thomas Huxley. A scientist and a professor, Huxley replied on behalf of the Darwin-ists (Darwin being absent because of illness) that he would rather be the de-scendant of a monkey than be connected with a man who used great gifts to obscure the truth.

That exchange was the beginning of what became not only the religious battle of the century but a war which fought some of its fiercest engagements in the next century and which is still going on as a kind of "spiritual cold war." From the outset, the conflict has followed much the same lines as the debate between Wilberforce and Huxley. On one side have appeared cham-pions of religion arguing against evolution not so much with scientific reasons as with appeals to the Bible, and deriding the advocates of evolution as in-fidels. The other side has been dominated by the scientists who have treated Darwin's hypothesis as an absolutely proved fact and have regarded all critics as narrow-minded bigots. For a century no Christian communion has been free from this debate, and just as both sides retired on that Sunday in Oxford in 1860 without either achieving a clear victory, so both sides are still send-ing doctrinal salvos at each other.

PAPAL ENCYCLICAL. The most vigorous battles of this war have been fought within and among the Protestant denominations, but the Roman Catholic Church has not been wholly free from the conflict. In fact, one of the major issues in that church for almost thirty years was a controversy which stemmed indirectly from the debate over evolution. Darwin's book not only changed the public's thinking about biology but led many people to study many aspects of life in a new way. They began to apply the scientific method to everything and to interpret everything according to evolution. For example, some were moved to study the Scriptures in what seemed to them a scientific fashion and also to regard doctrines as having evolved over the gen-erations rather than as having been revealed directly from heaven. Among these were a number of Roman Catholic theologians. Eventually their views were silenced in the Roman church, but not before Pope Leo XIII had issued a special encyclical, and his successor had required all clergy and professors to take an oath renouncing what the Vatican called "modernism."

Lacking anything comparable to the Vatican with its absolute authority, the Protestant churches proved a far bloodier battlefield, especially in the United States. The first American reaction was vehement rejection. Slowly but steadily, however, Darwin's viewpoint attracted converts, and in the nineties, according to the church historian James H. Nichols, "the educated leadership of the Protestant ministry ceased to oppose evolution." While this may have been so of the "educated leadership," it certainly was not true of the "unedu-cated leadership" and the rank and file. Heresy trials were held in many denominations, and intense struggles took place.

As the years went on there was a hardening of opinion on both sides, and especially on the part of the traditionalists. At the time of World War I the debate which had started in 1860 was still going strong. Both sides were strongly entrenched. The champions of Darwin's views were derisively called "modernists," the opponents, "fundamentalists." The issues between them involved more than the acceptance or rejection of evolution, but that was the basic cause of their division. In the 1930's this doctrinal war reached its Armageddon in two major battles. The first was the attempt to compel the outstanding preacher of the time, Harry Emerson Fosdick, to submit to a form of loyalty oath which would require him to be a fundamentalist. He refused, left the Presbyterian pulpit which he occupied in New York, and became pastor of the great Riverside Church on condition that this church grant him a free pulpit.

This was a turning point in the struggle in the United States, for until then much of the official strength of the churches had remained in fundamentalist hands. But the fundamentalists' failure to harness Fosdick to their bandwagon resulted in the transference of power in the major Protestant denominations to the exponents of liberal religion. Within a few years fundamentalist influence significantly waned, although schisms occurred among the Presbyterians and other groups.

THE SCOPES TRIAL.   The second struggle, and by far the more publicized, was the great battle of Dayton, Tennessee. "Modernism" had failed to make much advance in the southern states, where the Southern Baptist Convention was the major religious body. Here was the fundamentalists' stronghold. Their influence was such that they were able to secure in four states—Texas, Tennessee, Arkansas and Mississippi—the enactment of laws prohibiting the teaching of the evolutionary theory in schools. These laws were called "monkey bills" because evolution was popularly linked with the idea that man was descended from monkeys.

John Scopes, a high school teacher in the Cumberland village of Dayton, Tennessee, was accused of violating this law and was arraigned in court. His trial attracted nationwide attention and became a *cause célèbre* when the names of the opposing counsel were announced. The attorney for the prosecution was William Jennings Bryan, three times unsuccessful candidate for the presidency. Out of politics, Byran had found a new outlet for his crusading spirit in the cause of fundamentalism and was a leader of the movement to ban the theory of evolution from the schools. The attorney for the defense was Clarence Darrow, the most eminent criminal lawyer of his day, a self-confessed agnostic who delighted in giving lectures on his religious views.

The real interest of the trial was not in the guilt or innocence of Scopes but in the debate between these two rhetorical giants over evolution. The debate was joined in a dramatic way. Darrow called Bryan to the stand as an expert on the Bible. The hero of the fundamentalists consented readily to this procedure, but it proved his undoing. He was quickly shown to be as ignorant of the scientific basis of the theory of evolution as Wilberforce had been in 1860, and when he stepped down it was as a beaten man. Scopes was found guilty, but this verdict was reversed by the supreme court of the state. Thus, the moral victory clearly went against the fundamentalists.

THE LIBERAL VICTORY.   The debate was joined on many fronts as the controversy divided churches and colleges. By the thirties, it appeared that the liberals had defeated their opponents and that the long running fight was over. Irving Stone, the biographer of Darrow, wrote of his hero's success at Dayton, "This dealt a death blow to Fundamentalism." In a sermon Dr. Fosdick proclaimed: "The triumph of Modernism is complete." Certainly there was much evidence to support that conclusion as clergy of modernist views became the leaders of churches and colleges. Church people came to interpret the Bible less literally and to appreciate ministers who could show them how they could be Christians while at the same time accepting the findings of science. Ironically, many ministers became known more for what they did not than for what they did believe.

Yet the last had not been heard from fundamentalism. It still swayed several major denominations like the Southern Baptist and some varieties of Lutheranism, and was the only brand of religion known to hundreds of sects. Since World War II, these churches and sects have grown steadily.

No doubt the long struggle between fundamentalism and some sort of modernism would have developed had there been no Darwin, through the impact of other scientific advances on religious thinking. But it was Darwin's theory that gave the great impetus to this conflict and has remained its focal point. Today the division is still with us. It is not the direct confrontation that it once was, for the two sides seem to have settled into a form of peaceful coexistence, each carrying on its own life without reference to the other. How long this armed truce will last is not clear.

Charles Darwin's name is being honored this year [1959] because he lifted a theory out of the area of philosophical speculation and secured it on the foundation of scientific data. But his name should also be noted for his unwitting contribution to one of the great doctrinal disputes of modern times. Surely there is nothing in the history of belief and thought to equal this—a century of religious conflict because of a theory of science. In the future, there will be books to equal *The Origin of Species* in scientific importance, but it is unlikely that there will ever again be a book of science that will have as far-reaching an impact on religion.

40 THE EXTENT OF RELIGIOUS INFLUENCE IN AMERICAN PUBLIC SCHOOLS

R. B. Dierenfield

INTRODUCTION   The current ambiguity of relationship between church and state (*see* Petersen, Article 6) finds clear expression in the conflict concerning prayer and Bible reading in the public schools. In the *Engle v. Vitale* decision of 1962 the United States Supreme Court rejected a 22-word nondenominational prayer recited by students at the direction of the New York Board of Regents. Although the students were taught merely to pray "Almighty God, we acknowledge dependence upon Thee, and we beg thy blessing upon us, our parents, our teachers, and our country," the Court maintained that under the Constitution's provisions separating church and state formal prayer is not a function of the public school.

In the 1963 decisions involving the *Murray v. Board of School Commissioners of Baltimore City* and *The School District of Abingdon Township v. E. L. Schemp* et al., the definition became more explicit. In the first instance Mrs. Murray objected to the Baltimore requirement that teachers in the public schools without comment should read "a chapter in the Holy Bible and/or the use of the Lord's Prayer," as stipulated by the Commissioners. In the Schemp case Unitarian parents read and discussed the Bible at home with their children. Rather than have their children leave the school room during the religious exercises, they brought suit to invalidate the practice. The Supreme Court ruling, when issued on June 17, declared that "in the relationship between man and religion, the State is firmly committed to a position of neutrality."

Abridged and reprinted from the May-June 1961 issue of *Religious Education* by permission of the publisher, The Religious Education Association, 545 West 111th Street, New York, New York, 10025.

R. B. DIERENFIELD is Associate Professor of Education at Macalester College (St. Paul).

Although this decision has not been a popular one, the pluralistic nature of American society (see Herberg, Article 46), effected this judgment. In essence, the Supreme Court decided that the majority has no right to use the machinery of government to exercise its beliefs at the expense of the minority. It argued that "one's right . . . to freedom of worship . . . and other fundamental rights may not be submitted to vote; they depend upon the outcome of no elections."

Because religious socialization is no longer legally allowed in the public schools, religious groups have made several attempts to provide some form of religious education. One early attempt was made by providing ministerial *instruction at a public school* during school hours; a practice later terminated by court decision inasmuch as the school had no responsibility to gather children for religious denominations. A second alternative, called *released time,* allowed the youths to travel during one or more periods per week to a nearby church for religious instruction. Under the third alternative, *dismissed time,* the student was dismissed from his classes early in the day in order to finish his study at a local church. In recent years a new concept has been growing in usage. Under *shared time* students spend part of their day in a parochial or private school, studying subjects related to religious or denominational teachings, and complete the remainder of the day in public schools where nonreligious subjects may be taught. *Shared time* has developed as a compromise solution to the overcrowded condition of parochial schools and the public refusal to grant state aid to nonpublic educational systems.

Although such agencies as the Supreme Court render national decisions affecting educational policy, public education remains in the hands of local officials who tend to reflect the attitudes of the local subculture. Where religious pluralism is most obvious, separation of religion and education is most evident. Dierenfield compares regional differences towards ethical and religious teaching in the public schools. Although his investigation was completed before the 1962 and 1963 decisions, his data suggests that religious influence will remain in public schools in spite of U. S. Supreme Court decisions to the contrary.

FOR OVER ONE HUNDRED and fifty years public school educators in America have been faced with the problem of what religious influence to allow in their schools. The issue looms as large and appears as complex today as it did during the past century and a half. Some groups exert pressure in favor of a greater amount of religious influence in curricular and extracurricular activities while other factions object to anything involving such emphasis. The teacher and administrator, already caught between these conflicting viewpoints, must also reconcile their own convictions with local practice and state laws on the subject.

A real understanding of the situation should include the knowledge of what is presently going on in American public schools regarding the handling of various religious influences. A helpful contribution in studying the issues would be to determine how the public schools in the United States are now dealing with religious influences in their curricular and extracurricular activities.

With this as his goal the writer constructed and mailed out to school superintendents a questionnaire designed to obtain this information. A sample of 4,000 communities was selected using proportional stratified, and random sampling procedures. The country was divided into four areas: the East, South, Midwest, and West. In addition five population categories were set up: 500-2500; 2500-5,000; 5,000-25,000; 25,000-100,000; and over 100,000. The number of usable questionnaires which were returned is listed below together with the totals.

Section	Questionnaires Sent	Number Returned	Percentage
Midwest	1,180	874	74.06%
West	519	297	54.21%
East	1,140	621	54.29%
South	1,161	391	33.67%
Total	4,000	2,183	54.57%

Although a return of 54.57 percent does not justify statistical inference it is sufficient to furnish a general picture of the policies and practices in a large number of varied educational operations.

RELIGION AND THE CURRICULUM.   In attempting to analyze the current situation regarding this problem, one of the most important areas to investigate is the curriculum. For the purposes of this consideration, the curriculum will be thought of as consisting of the course content and patterns of courses which combine to make up the formal academic offerings of any school.

QUESTION: Do the aims and objectives of your school system include the teaching of moral values? (Moral values would include such qualities as honesty, courage, loyalty, responsibility, etc.)
United States as a Whole
    RESULTS: 99.44% Yes
                    .56% No

QUESTION: Do the aims and objectives of your school system include the teaching of spiritual values? (Spiritual values would include such qualities as love, faith, reverence for a Supreme Being, etc.)

United States as a Whole
    RESULTS: 78.71% Yes
                21.29% No

By Sections of the Country

West	*Midwest*	*South*	*East*
68.86% Yes	77.21% Yes	94.32% Yes	75.39% Yes
31.14% No	22.78% No	5.68% No	24.61% No

QUESTION: Does your school system provide materials to classroom teachers to help in teaching moral values?

United States as a Whole
    RESULTS: 77.51% Yes
                22.49% No

QUESTION: Does your school system provide materials to classroom teachers to help in teaching spiritual values?

United States as a Whole
    RESULTS: 46.34% Yes
                53.65% No

By Sections of the Country

West	*Midwest*	*South*	*East*
38.19% Yes	48.06% Yes	63.58% Yes	37.41% Yes
61.81% No	51.94% No	36.42% No	62.58% No

QUESTION: Does your school system provide materials to classroom teachers to help in teaching *about* religion?

United States as a Whole
    RESULTS: 76.06% Yes
                23.94% No

QUESTION: Are there regular classes in the Bible in the schools of your system?

United States as a Whole
    RESULTS: 4.51% Yes
                95.48% No

By Sections of the Country

West	*Midwest*	*South*	*East*
8.57% Yes	4.14% Yes	9.00% Yes	1.32% Yes
91.43% No	95.86% No	91.00% No	98.68% No

It seems evident from the figures cited above that religious influence cannot be ignored as a factor in the public school curriculum. Spiritual values are listed as aims in a majority of school systems. In many communities teachers are provided with materials to assist in the instruction of these values. Results of the survey also indicate that organized units on the part religion has played in shaping our culture and society are seldom found in elementary schools. In secondary schools such units are found most often in World History (51.53% Yes) and in high school literature courses (32.02% Yes).

Instruction in the Bible is provided in only a small proportion of the public school systems. Religious emphasis appears centered around general spiritual values and religion as a cultural and historical influence.

RELIGION AND NONCURRICULAR ACTIVITIES. In classifying the activities described in this section it should be remembered that "noncurricular" activities refer to programs and practices provided by the school in addition to formal coursework. Their importance in the total impact of the school on students cannot be overlooked.

QUESTION: Are Gideon Bibles distributed in your school system?
United States as a Whole
RESULTS: 42.74% Yes
57.26% No

By Sections of the Country

West	Midwest	South	East
39.66% Yes	50.35% Yes	54.77% Yes	26.24% Yes
60.34% No	49.65% No	45.23% No	73.76% No

By Size of Community

500-2500	2500-5000	5000-25,000	25,000-100,000	Over 100,000
50.29% Yes	47.95% Yes	39.76% Yes	31.46% Yes	32.00% Yes
49.71% No	52.05% No	60.24% No	68.54% No	68.00% No

QUESTION: Are Baccalaureate services conducted in connection with high school graduation?
United States as a Whole
RESULTS: 86.84% Yes
13.16% No

By Sections of the Country

West	Midwest	South	East
92.16% Yes	93.69% Yes	96.00% Yes	68.13% Yes
7.84% No	6.31% No	4.00% No	31.87% No

By Size of Community

500-2500	2500-5000	5000-25,000	25,000-100,000	Over 100,000
92.52% Yes	89.21% Yes	83.89% Yes	76.92% Yes	64.71% Yes
7.48% No	10.79% No	16.11% No	23.08% No	35.29% No

QUESTION: Are homeroom devotional services held in the schools of your system?

United States as a Whole

RESULTS: 33.16% Yes (all schools in the system)
17.06% Yes (some schools in the system)
49.76% No

By Sections of the Country

West	Midwest	South	East
2.41% Yes (all)	6.40% Yes (all)	60.53% Yes (all)	68.33% Yes (all)
6.21% Yes (some)	19.55% Yes (some)	28.16% Yes (some)	11.83% Yes (some)
91.38% No	74.05% No	11.32% No	19.83% No

QUESTION: Is there any type of regular chapel exercise held in the schools of your system?

United States as a Whole

RESULTS: 22.07% Yes
77.93% No

By Sections of the Country

West	Midwest	South	East
1.35% Yes	14.69% Yes	70.86% Yes	12.62% Yes
98.65% No	85.31% No	29.14% No	87.38% No

QUESTION: Is Bible reading conducted in the schools of your system?

United States as a Whole

RESULTS: 41.74% Yes
58.26% No

By Sections of the Country

West	Midwest	South	East
11.03% Yes	18.26% Yes	76.84% Yes	67.56% Yes
88.97% No	81.74% No	23.16% No	32.44% No

QUESTION: Are religious holidays observed by any kind of activities in the schools of your system?

United States as a Whole

RESULTS:

	Yes
Christmas	87.92%
Hannukah	5.39%
Easter	57.82%
Passover	2.17%
Thanksgiving	76.75%
Other	.48%

The results of the survey regarding noncurricular religious influence in American public schools point to wide variations in practice. Sectional differences over the country are particularly pronounced in this respect. Public schools in the southern states give greater emphasis to this type of influence than do their counterparts in other sections of the country. The vast majority of American schools support Baccalaureate exercises and celebrate Christmas and Thanksgiving with school activities. The amount and nature of other noncurricular religious influence in the public schools, however, seems dependent in large measure on the area of the country.

THE PUBLIC SCHOOLS AND RELIGIOUS GROUPS.   The relationship of public education and sectarian religious bodies has long been subject to dispute. At the present time controversy is flaring over several aspects of this relationship. For this reason a number of questions were asked touching on this area and the answers provide an indication of the present situation.

QUESTION: Does your school system cooperate in a program of released time instruction?

United States as a Whole
    RESULTS: 29.66% Yes
              70.43% No

By Sections of the Country

West	*Midwest*	*South*	*East*
29.32% Yes	27.39% Yes	10.74% Yes	44.46% Yes
70.68% No	72.61% No	89.26% No	55.54% No

QUESTION: Does your school system provide bus transportation for students attending parochial schools?

United States as a Whole
    RESULTS: 19.86% Yes
              80.14% No

By Sections of the Country

West	*Midwest*	*South*	*East*
11.39% Yes	16.79% Yes	3.59% Yes	37.96% Yes
88.61% No	83.21% No	96.41% No	62.04% No

QUESTION: In your school system are any public school classes held in church buildings?

United States as a Whole
    RESULTS: 7.76% Yes
             92.24% No

QUESTION: Are there any members of religious orders teaching in the public schools of your system?

United States as a Whole
>   RESULTS: 5.76% Yes
>   94.24% No

The results listed above indicate a moderate relationship between public schools and sectarian religious groups. Nearly one school system in three allows for released time religious instruction. An interesting sidelight shows that one system in eight which has a released time program holds these classes in school buildings. Transportation of students to sectarian religious schools by public school buses is provided in nearly one system in five as a national average although sectional figures differ greatly. The use of church buildings for public school classrooms and the employment of members of religious orders as public school teachers appears to be quite uncommon.

THE SCHOOL ADMINISTRATOR AND RELIGION IN THE PUBLIC SCHOOLS. Since the school superintendent is the most important single person in regard to policy making in a school system, it is useful to know his reaction to some issues bearing on religious influence in the public education.

QUESTION: What is your opinion regarding the celebration of religious holidays by school activities?

United States as a Whole
>   RESULTS: 14.46% Not proper
>   61.96% Can be done if care is used
>   23.58% School has the right to do this

Sample Comments:
>   "The education of the whole child requires holiday observances."
>   "It is not proper unless all are celebrated and this causes many disruptions in the school program."
>   "Such observations can help teach basic understandings and appreciations of various beliefs."
>   "This is not the duty of the schools."

QUESTION: Do you favor the distribution of Gideon Bibles in the public schools?

United States as a Whole
>   RESULTS: 54.80% Yes
>   45.20% No

By Sections of the Country

West	Midwest	South	East
49.44% Yes	56.56% Yes	82.30% Yes	38.41% Yes
50.56% No	43.44% No	17.70% No	61.59% No

By Size of Community

500-2500	2500-5000	5000-25,000	25,000-100,000	Over 100,000
60.85% Yes	64.48% Yes	48.84% Yes	43.40% Yes	35.55% Yes
39.15% No	35.52% No	51.16% No	56.60% No	64.45% No

Sample Comments:

"I am not in favor as it opens the door for distribution of any religious materials."

"It can't do harm and might do much good."

"Bibles can be obtained by other means."

"I would appreciate some now for distribution to classes."

QUESTION: Do you favor baccalaureate services in connection with high school graduation?

United States as a Whole

RESULTS: 89.26% Yes

            10.74% No

By Sections of the Country

West	Midwest	South	East
93.71% Yes	92.66% Yes	97.33% Yes	76.84% Yes
6.03% No	7.34% No	2.67% No	23.16% No

Sample Comments:

"All occasions to impart spiritual truths should be utilized."

"Not necessary—carry over from church operation of schools."

"Practiced so long that discontinuance would be protested."

QUESTION: Do you believe your school system is dealing in an adequate way with religion?

United States as a Whole

RESULTS: 77.47% Yes

            22.53% No

Sample Comments:

"We are not a church or a home—there is not enough time for school-work."

"I believe courses in religion can and should be offered to all those who wish to elect them."

"Only the Lord knows."

The views of the school superintendents can be summarized as follows: They look with reservation on released time programs, the majority feeling they have some value but twice as many oppose them as favor them. They view with caution the celebration of religious holidays by school activities believing care must be exercised in any such enterprise. A small majority approve of the distribution of Gideon Bibles in public schools. They are solidly in favor of baccalaureate services as a part of high school graduation. They are satisfied, for the most part, with the way their systems are handling religion.

GENERAL SUMMARY OF RESULTS.   A detailed review of the material presented in this article would be repetitious and would serve no useful purpose. The figures themselves tell most of the story. It might be worth while, however, to point out some conclusions which seem evident on the basis of the results obtained.

1. A close similarity exists among school systems in the methods employed to handle some aspects of religious influence. The amount of difference in dealing with several of the practices surveyed was small not only among sections of the country but in regard to the size of the community as well.

2. On the other hand there are a number of practices involving religious influence in which marked variations are common. Greater differences are found among the four areas of the country than among the five population categories.

3. Religious influence appears to play a larger part in the schools of the South than in the other sections. While this is not universally true, it is so pronounced that the conclusion is inescapable.

4. Many of the practices which are employed by school systems to deal with religious influence might be called into question in the light of legal decisions on the subject.

5. The American public school cannot be charged with being a Godless institution. Religious influence does exist in the schools in varying kinds and amounts, depending on the section of the country and size of community.

41 SOCIAL CORRELATES OF RELIGIOUS INTEREST

Gerhard Lenski

INTRODUCTION No discussion of the influence of religion within the larger institutional context can be complete without consideration of the family (*see* Elkind, Article 16, and Thomas, Article 17). Religious attitudes permeate personal and group attitudes concerning mating patterns, style of family life, authority patterns, member relationships, sexual attitudes, and family size. In order to preserve membership, youth are encouraged to marry within the faith (*see* Vernon, Article 42).

Although religious pluralism has resulted in lessened religious influence in marriage matters, religious influence remains substantial. Differences in family life style are very evident in the Mennonite and Amana communities. Set apart by different patterns of dress (Mennonite) or communal relationships (Amana), members exist within the broader society while remaining primary members of the specific religious group. Male authority patterns are often derived from religious sanction. Attitudes toward sex, birth control and family size may have a religious basis. If sex is simply for procreation, the moral responsibility to have children is emphasized. Where personal enjoyment is the aim, contraception becomes a matter of personal convenience. Family size is then likely to decline.

Although people usually join churches as individuals, functional membership in the religious group is normally by family units. Whenever family unity is impaired through divorce, desertion, or death, the church also suffers. Churches which serve an

Abridged and reprinted from the *American Sociological Review*, Volume 18 (October 1953), pp. 533-544, with the permission of the author and editors.

GERHARD LENSKI is Professor of Sociology at the University of North Carolina (Chapel Hill).

overrepresentative group of single men or women and families with only one parent face lessened financial support and suffer from unbalanced religious programming. Religion attempts to cultivate family goals and establish norms upon which the family is expected to act. Because the family serves as the socialization agency for the broader society (*see* Elkind, Article 16, and Thomas, Article 17), religious groups attempt to instill their perspectives within the family group (*see* Introduction to Part IV).

Lenski discusses the effect of religion upon such sociological variables as sex, parenthood, mobility, occupation, wealth, income, and education. The relationship of marriage to religion comes under close scrutiny. Although the original data was derived from a 1941 study, the student should note the procedures followed in this scientific research (*see* Introduction to Winter, Article 5). How accurate the specific findings may be for the present generation and for places other than Indianapolis even at that time, or for that sizable group of the population excluded because of the selective criteria used, are matters for individual evaluation.

IN MODERN INDUSTRIAL societies it is clearly evident that individual interest in religion varies tremendously—from fanatical zeal at the one extreme to utter and complete indifference at the other. Yet despite the growing interest of sociologists and social psychologists in religious phenomena, the relationship of these variations to such key sociological variables as sex, parenthood, occupation, wealth, income, education, vertical mobility, denominational affiliation, and so forth is still not clearly understood. While much has been written concerning these relationships, the empirical foundation on which these writings rest is extremely limited in most cases.

SOURCE OF THE DATA

The data on which this report is based were gathered by the Committee on the Social and Psychological Factors Affecting Fertility, sponsored by the Milbank Memorial Fund. In 1941 this committee conducted a household survey of the white population of Indianapolis. Short schedules were completed for the white occupants of 102,499 dwelling units.

Shortly thereafter, an intensive follow-up study was made of a highly restricted sample of the population. In addition to the previous limitation on race, certain further restrictions were imposed on the sample. These were as follows:

1. Household must include a married couple.
2. Both husband and wife must be native born.
3. Both must have spent most of their married life in cities.
4. The couple must have been married in 1927, 1928, or 1929.

5. The wife must have been under thirty, and the husband under forty years of age, at the time of marriage.
6. Both husband and wife must be Protestant.
7. Both must have completed the eighth grade.
8. The marriage must be unbroken at the time of the interview, and neither spouse previously married.

On the basis of information obtained in the earlier survey, it was found that 2,589 families met all of these requirements. The data on which this present report is based were obtained in the intensive follow-up interviews with 860, or 33.2 percent, of these families.

The key question in the interviews, so far as the present study is concerned, was the query, "How much have you been interested in religion since marriage?" This question was asked in *separate* interviews of both husband and wife. All responses were coded in one of the following categories: (1) very much; (2) much; (3) some; (4) little; and (5) very little.

Of the 860 sample couples, 92 were childless. Both husbands and wives among these childless couples were asked not only how interested in religion they had been since marriage, but also the additional question, "How frequently have you attended church or Sunday School during your married life?" The relationship between the responses to this behavioral question and the responses to the attitudinal question on degree of interest in religion is presented in Table 41-1 below.

From an inspection of this table it may be seen that a very close relationship exists between the attitudinal and the behavioral variables. More than 70 percent of those who rarely attended church or Sunday School reported "little" interest in religion. Similarly, more than 70 percent of those who frequently attended church or Sunday School reported "much" interest in religion. A majority of those who reported irregular attendance responded that they had "some" interest in religion.

TABLE 41-1   Degree of interest in religion since marriage, by reported frequency of church or Sunday School attendance since marriage, in percentages.

Reported Frequency of Attendance	N	Interest in Religion			
		Little	Some	Much	Total
Very seldom	46	71.7	28.3	0.0	100.0
Seldom or sometimes	102	31.4	54.9	13.7	100.0
Often or regularly	36	2.8	25.0	72.2	100.0

Chi-square = 90.9; d.f. = 4; P less than .001; C = .575. Maximum possible C value for this table is .767.

In view of this close relationship it would seem that the response to the query into degree of interest in religion since marriage may be regarded as a reasonably reliable measure of the individual's interest in the *organized* religious activities of the community. More than that, it may be regarded as a reasonably reliable index of the individual's *participation* in such activities.

FINDINGS

SEX. Among the sociological variables related to religious interest and activity, none has been more widely recognized in American society than the sex variable. As may be seen in Table 41-2 below, the data gathered in Indianapolis provide further evidence in support of the hypothesis of greater interest among women. Sixty percent more women than men expressed "much" interest in religion since marriage.

This variation in religious interest along sex lines has been more often observed than analyzed. The traditional explanation that "women are by nature more religious than men" is hardly satisfactory from the sociological point of view. Yet sociologists have failed to provide a more satisfactory explanation.

TABLE 41-2   Degree of interest in religion since marriage, by sex, in percentages.

Sex	N	Interest in Religion				Summary Score
		Little	Some	Much	Total	
Male	860	33.5	42.6	24.0	100.1	90.5
Female	860	19.8	41.8	38.4	100.0	118.6

Chi-square = 60.2; d.f. = 2; *P* less than .001.

From the sociological point of view, this difference in religious interest would seem to be directly related to the very different social environments in which the average husband and the average wife in American society live, and the variations in the demands made on the individual in those differing environments. The average husband spends the major part of his waking hours in the highly competitive job world. The average wife, by contrast, spends the major part of her waking hours in the relatively protected, noncompetitive world of family activities.

These very different environments tend to produce quite different, though not incompatible, personality types. Successful adjustment in the job world not uncommonly requires the development of personality traits and behavior patterns which conflict with basic Christian ethics. Successful adjustment in the family relationship, which is of relatively greater importance for the wife, places a premium on the development by the wife of just those personality traits and behavior patterns stressed by the churches (i.e., altruistic attitudes and actions).

PARENTHOOD.   A second variable investigated was that of parenthood. On the basis of previous research, there seemed little indication that a significant difference in religious interest among Protestants might be found when childless couples were compared with those with children. Since, however, the pattern of married life is so profoundly altered in many ways by the arrival of children, it seemed that the relationship of this factor to degree of religious interest should be examined.

As an inspection of Table 41-3 indicates, a highly significant difference was found between the degree of religious interest expressed by couples with children and those without. Half again as many of the couples with children reported "much" interest in religion as compared with the childless couples.

TABLE 41-3   Degree of interest in religion since marriage, by composition of family unit, in percentages.

| Composition of Family Unit | N | Interest in Religion | | | | Summary Score |
		Little	Some	Much	Total	
No living children	184	35.9	42.4	21.7	100.0	85.8
One or more children	1,536	25.5	42.1	32.3	99.9	106.8

Chi-square $= 12.0$; d.f. $= 2$; P less than .003.

To the present writer it seems not unreasonable to regard both factors (parenthood and religious interest) as causal under certain conditions. Since the Protestant churches generally share with the Catholic church the view that parenthood should be the natural consequence of marriage (though Protestants usually reject the Catholic view that there must be no "artificially" established limit to family size), devout Protestants would probably have greater difficulty in rationalizing a childless marriage than would those whose ties with the church were more tenuous. In this sense, religious interest may function as the independent variable, and parenthood as the dependent variable.

Casual observation has suggested to the writer, however, that once children arrive there is often a quickening of religious interest on the part of the new parents. This frequently develops when the problem of transmitting the cultural heritage to the children is faced. Under such conditions religious interest may function as the dependent variable and parenthood as the independent variable.

OCCUPATION.   A third major variable investigated was that of the occupational role of the family head. Despite the recognized importance of this
variable as an influencing factor in the behavior of family members generally,
only a beginning has been made in the task of determining how variations in
the occupational role of the family head are related to variations in the religious behavior and attitudes of family members.

Stratification-oriented studies of American communities have indicated
that individual Protestant congregations tend to be class-typed, and that the
occupational role of the family head plays an important part in determining
the particular congregation with which a family unites.[1] However, with respect to the present problem of whether interest in religion in general (as
opposed to interest in a specific congregation or denomination) varies with
differences in the occupational role of the family head, the evidence is unclear.

TABLE 41-4   Degree of interest in religion since marriage, by longest
              occupation of husband, in percentages.

| Longest Occupation | N | Interest in Religion | | | | Summary Score |
		Little	Some	Much	Total	
Professional	168	29.3	32.9	37.8	100.0	108.5
Managerial[a]	222	33.3	33.3	33.3	99.9	100.0
Clerical-sales	406	26.4	45.1	28.6	100.1	102.2
Skilled	358	22.1	44.4	33.5	100.0	111.4
Semiskilled	466	25.3	46.6	28.1	100.0	102.8
Unskilled[b]	88	30.7	35.2	34.1	100.0	103.4
Others and N.A.	12	33.3	50.0	16.7	100.0	83.3

a Managers, proprietors, and officials.
b Laborers and service workers.
Chi-square = 10.2; d.f. = 10; P more than .4.

FINANCIAL STATUS.   If variations in religious interest are related to differentiation in the secular structure of society, a relationship between the financial status of families and their interest in religion might be expected in a
society such as our own in which economic considerations are so important.
Most previous research in the area suggests that this is the case, although the
nature of the relationship has not been made clear.[2]

[1] For example see Walter Goldschmidt, "Class Denominationalism in Rural California
Churches," American Journal of Sociology, 49, pp. 348-55; Liston Pope, Millhands and
Preachers (New Haven: Yale University Press, 1942); A. B. Hollingshead, Elmtown's
Youth (New York: Wiley, 1949); Louis Bultena, "Church Membership and Church
Attendance in Madison, Wisconsin," American Sociological Review, 14.
[2] See Hadley Cantril, "Educational and Economic Composition of Religious Groups:
An Analysis of Poll Data," American Journal of Sociology, 48, pp. 574-9; Bultena, op.
cit.; Hollingshead, op. cit.; Anonymous, "How Important Religion is to Americans,"
Catholic Digest, 17 (February, 1953).

In the present study, data were obtained both on the net worth of the sample families and on their income. Analysis of the relationship of each of these variables to religious interest indicated that the greatest interest was to be found among the families in the middle economic range. The relationship between net worth and religious interest was so ill-defined, however, that the chi-square test indicated that the null hypothesis could not safely be eliminated ($P > .08$).

The relationship between average annual income and religious interest was somewhat more pronounced. From an inspection of Table 41-5 it may be seen that those families which had enjoyed an average annual income of between $1,200 and $2,999 expressed "much" interest in religion more frequently than did those with either larger or smaller incomes. The chi-square test indicated that the difference in religious interest between the $1,200-2,999 category and the $3,000 and more category was significant at the one percent level, while the difference between the $1,200-2,999 category and the under $1,200 category was significant at the two percent level.

TABLE 41-5   Degree of interest in religion since marriage, by average annual income, in percentages.

Average Annual Income	N	Little	Some	Much	Total	Summary Score
$3,000 or more	136	38.2	35.3	26.5	100.0	89.3
$2,400-$2,999	128	22.8	39.4	37.8	100.0	115.0
$2,000-$2,399	194	27.3	38.6	34.0	99.9	106.7
$1,800-$1,999	154	26.0	42.2	31.8	100.0	105.8
$1,600-$1,799	166	19.3	48.2	32.5	100.0	113.2
$1,400-$1,599	284	27.1	40.1	32.7	99.9	105.6
$1,200-$1,399	290	22.1	45.2	32.8	100.1	110.7
$1,000-$1,199	210	30.5	44.8	24.8	100.1	94.3
Less than $1,000	156	29.5	43.0	27.6	100.1	98.1
Not ascertained	2	0.0	100.0	0.0	100.0	100.0

Chi-square = 28.1; d.f. = 16; P less than .05.

The tentative conclusion to which the present study points is that the middle class (when defined in purely financial terms) exhibits greater interest in religion than either the upper or lower classes. If, however, this generalization is sound, two important qualifications must be added. First, the middle class when defined in these terms is a most inclusive category. More than 70 percent of the sample families were included in the group which had an average annual income of between $1,200 and $2,999. Second, the difference in the degree of religious interest between the middle category and the upper and lower categories, while statistically significant, is not great. For example, in the middle income category only 33.3 percent of the respondents expressed "much" interest in religion, while in the higher and lower income categories 26.5 percent and 26.0 percent, respectively, indicated just as great an interest.

EDUCATION. Another major variable associated with many behavioral and attitudinal differences in American society is the degree of formal education obtained by the adult members of the family unit. With respect to the relationship between extent of formal education and degree of religious interest, three plausible hypotheses suggest themselves. All have some support in previous empirical research.

First, as a derivative of the "middle class conformity hypothesis" it might be predicted that the greatest degree of religious interest would be found in the middle educational groups. Hollingshead found evidence to support this hypothesis in Elmtown, as did West in Plainville.[3]

A second hypothesis which suggests itself is that the degree of interest in religion varies *inversely* with the degree of formal education. This hypothesis would be consistent with the doctrine of logical posivitism and the viewpoint of the evolutionists that religious beliefs are a survival from man's more primitive past, and thus destined to disappear with increasing knowledge of the nature of the world in which man lives. This hypothesis would seem to be supported by the recent survey conducted by the *Catholic Digest*.[4]

A third hypothesis which must be considered is the hypothesis that interest in religion varies *directly* with the degree of formal education. This hypothesis may be derived from the more general finding of recent research which indicates that participation in formal voluntary associations tends to vary directly with status. Participation is presumably not unrelated to interest. This hypothesis has been supported in studies of church membership by Cantril and Bultena.[5]

TABLE 41-6   Degree of interest in religion since marriage, by educational level attained, in percentages.

Highest Educational Level Attained	N	Interest in Religion				Summary Score
		Little	Some	Much	Total	
College	320	28.8	40.3	30.9	100.0	102.1
High school	1,035	25.5	44.3	30.1	99.9	104.6
Grammar school	364	28.0	37.6	34.4	100.0	106.4

Chi-square = 6.9; d.f. = 4; *P* more than .1.

3 Hollingshead, *op. cit.*, Chapter 5; James West, *Plainville, U.S.A.* (New York: Columbia University Press, 1945), p. 130.
4 *Catholic Digest, op. cit.*
5 Cantril, *op. cit.*, Bultena, *op. cit.*

Data gathered in Indianapolis fail to provide support for either hypothesis one or three. They tend to support hypothesis two, but as may be seen from an inspection of Table 41-6, the differences in religious interest by educational level are so slight that the null hypothesis cannot be rejected.

TABLE 41-7　　Degree of interest in religion since marriage, by success in completing high school or college, in percentages.

Educational Success	N	Interest in Religion				Summary Score
		Little	Some	Much	Total	
Graduates	614	24.9	39.9	35.2	100.0	110.3
Nongraduates	733	28.0	45.4	26.6	100.0	98.6

Chi-square = 16.2; d.f. = 2; P less than .001.

While no significant relationship was found to exist between *general* educational level attained and degree of religious interest, a *year-by-year* breakdown of the educational data revealed a significant relationship between religious interest and success or failure in completing a given unit of education. College graduates expressed greater interest in religion than did those who had attended but failed to graduate. The same was true of high school graduates and nongraduates. Those who had completed grammar school expressed greater interest than did those who had gone on, but had failed to graduate from high school.

Although this relationship is statistically significant, it is not easily explained. One possible hypothesis which occurs to the writer is that successful completion of a given unit of education is related to the degree of an individual's integration into the life of the community. Those who are more fully integrated would be expected to participate more fully in voluntary corporate activities, both religious and secular, and through participation develop greater interest. Such persons would also be expected to achieve the educational goals appropriate to their status level with greater frequency than those less thoroughly integrated. The latter might be expected to fail more often in their efforts to achieve this goal, since lack of integration would contribute to a lack of awareness of the norm or of the importance attached to it, and also to a relative imperviousness to informal community sanctions supporting the norm. This interpretation, however, is highly speculative.

VERTICAL MOBILITY. While the relationship between the static aspects of the status system (as indicated by the data on occupational status, net worth, income, and education) and religious interest are not pronounced, the Indianapolis data pointed to a marked relationship between intragenerational income mobility and religious interest.

As may be seen from an inspection of Table 41-8, the degree of religious interest tended to vary *inversely* with degree of upward-mobility. Those who had enjoyed the greatest income gain since marriage expressed the least interest in religion, while those who had suffered an income loss during this period indicated the greatest degree of interest.

Here again, it is less difficult to demonstrate the existence of a relationship than to account for it. Marx's thesis that religion is an opiate might seem relevant here, since those who have been the "failures" with reference to income express a greater interest in religion than do the "successes." But would Marx predict this? Upper classes have a control intent in religion. Such a view, however, presents some difficulties when an attempt is made to reconcile it with the previous finding of greater interest among those who successfully completed a given unit of education than among those who failed to achieve this important life goal.

TABLE 41-8   Degree of interest in religion since marriage, by intra-generational income mobility since marriage, in percentages.

Mobility Status	N	Interest in Religion				Summary Score
		Little	Some	Much	Total	
Maximum income gain	172	38.6	36.8	24.6	100.0	86.0
Medium income gain	436	30.0	41.3	28.7	100.0	98.7
Small income gain	774	24.4	44.3	31.3	100.0	106.9
Stable income	192	22.9	41.1	35.9	99.9	113.0
Small income loss	92	18.5	38.0	43.5	100.0	125.0
Maximum income loss	46	19.4	45.7	34.8	99.9	115.4

Chi-square $= 29.1$; d.f. $= 10$; P less than .002.

Possibly a more plausible explanation might be achieved through an analysis of the requirements which are generally necessary for economic advancement in contemporary American society, and the relationship of those requirements to the requirements of active church membership. Economic advancement generally demands long hours devoted to the job, which would result in a conflict with the role of active church member. Also, if the work of Sutherland and others on white collar crime and its frequency is at all valid, it would seem that success in the job would not uncommonly depend upon the individual's willingness to violate legal codes and Christian ethics. Thus, as a result of such role-conflicts, the would-be successful individual is often forced to break his ties with one or the other of the conflicting groups. Whether the break is with the business group or with the church, the result is the same—a significant inverse relationship between economic advancement and religious interest. A "role-conflict" hypothesis of this sort would be consistent not only with the vertical mobility data, but also with the evidence indicating greater interest in religion among women than among men.

RURAL VS. URBAN ORIGINS. Past research has revealed an inverse relationship between community size and religious interest and activity.[6] It has not been made clear, however, whether these differences have a lasting effect on those raised in different environments, or whether migrants to the cities from rural areas adopt the dominant urban cultural patterns after migration.

As may be seen from an inspection of Table 41-9, the data gathered in the present study fail to provide a clear answer to this question. Those who were raised on farms expressed somewhat greater interest in religion than did those not raised on farms. The indifference, however, is not statistically significant. The findings suggest that influences of the urban environment on rural migrants may be stronger than influences of the farm background. In view of the absence of adequate controls, however, this conclusion is most tentative.

DENOMINATIONAL PREFERENCE. The final major variable to be considered is that of denominational preference. Variations in the degree of religious interest among the adherents of the three major faiths is widely recognized. Catholics are generally credited with being the most zealous in their religious interest, while Jews are thought to exhibit the greatest degree of indifference. Limited research in this area has suggested that some important differences may also exist *within* the Protestant group.[7]

TABLE 41-9 Degree of interest in religion since marriage, by farm vs. nonfarm background, in percentages.

| Background | N | Interest in Religion | | | | Summary Score |
		Little	Some	Much	Total	
Farm	358	23.8	40.8	35.5	100.1	111.7
Nonfarm	1,362	27.4	42.5	30.1	100.0	102.7

Chi-square $= 3.4$; d.f. $= 2$; P more than .1.

This was the case in Indianapolis, as the data in Table 41-10 indicate. Those who recorded a preference for the Pentecostal bodies ranked highest in interest, followed by the Lutherans, the Evangelical and Reformed and the Christian Scientists. At the other extreme, the Episcopalians, Quakers, and United Brethren expressed the least interest in religion.

On first inspection, the status variable seems to afford a satisfactory ex-

[6] For example see William F. Ogburn and Clark Tibbitts, "The Family and Its Functions," *Recent Social Trends* (New York: McGraw-Hill, 1938), p. 661 ff; Frederick A. Bushee, "The Church in a Small City," *American Journal of Sociology*, 57, pp. 181-2.
[7] See Bultena, *op. cit.* or *Catholic Digest, op. cit.*

planation for the variation in religious interest by denomination. Obviously the Pentecostal groups recruit the vast majority of their members from the lower strata of society, while the Episcopal church has been noted for its singular attraction for the socially elite. This suggests that denominational variations in religious interest are simply a function of the social status of the members of the group.

Unfortunately, however, when the analysis is carried beyond the extreme cases, this relationship is no longer apparent. For example, the Lutherans and the Christian Scientists, who ranked well ahead of the Methodists and United Brethren in religious interest, also enjoy a higher social status in Indianapolis, if that may be judged by such status-related variables as income, education, net worth, occupation of husband, and rental value of home.

TABLE 41-10   Degree of interest in religion since marriage, by denominational preference, in percentages.

Denominational Preference	N	Interest in Religion				Summary Score
		Little	Some	Much	Total	
Pentecostal	26	7.7	7.7	84.6	100.0	176.9
Lutheran	85	20.0	25.9	54.1	100.0	134.1
Evangelical and Reformed	55	16.4	38.2	45.4	100.0	129.0
Christian Scientist	53	18.9	35.8	45.3	100.0	126.4
Nazarene	25	20.0	36.0	44.0	100.0	124.0
Baptist	188	19.1	50.5	30.3	99.9	111.2
Disciples of Christ	296	20.6	48.0	31.4	100.0	110.8
Presbyterian	149	28.2	40.9	30.9	100.0	102.7
Unitarian, etc.[a]	17	17.6	64.7	17.6	99.9	100.0
Methodist	451	27.1	46.6	26.4	100.1	99.3
United Brethren	36	30.6	41.7	27.8	100.1	97.2
Quaker	17	35.3	41.2	23.5	100.0	88.2
Episcopalian	21	47.6	33.3	19.0	99.9	71.4
Miscellaneous	66	19.7	25.8	54.5	100.0	134.8
No preference	115	53.0	37.4	9.6	100.0	56.6
Not ascertained	119	42.0	37.0	21.0	100.0	79.0

a Includes Congregationalists and Universalists. Chi-square = 146.3; d.f. = 26; P less than .001.

A second factor which may account for a part of this variation is the stress, or lack of it, placed on theological considerations in the several denominations. All of the five leading denominations are ones in which theological considerations are strongly stressed (though in varying fashion).

A third factor which may contribute to systematic variations in religious interest along denominational lines is the varying importance attached to the religious education of the young. This factor, while undoubtedly related to the previously mentioned factor of theological emphasis, deserves separate mention since it is probably to some degree an independent variable. Certain denominations, particularly those of continental European background, have laid much greater stress on the religious training of the young than is characteristic of denominations of British or American origin.

Finally, the peculiar ethnic character of certain denominations, particularly those of continental European background, has probably been a factor also. Many persons with Lutheran, Evangelical, or Reformed membership in Europe came to this country, but did not affiliate with these groups after arrival. Membership in these denominations tended to be selective on the basis of either ethnic loyalty or religious loyalty or both. Those immigrants or their children who lacked either or both of these loyalties tended to drift out of these denominations and very often into other, "more American," denominations. Thus, the element which remained in these groups tended to include an unusually high proportion of intensely interested individuals. This selective factor may very well have produced consequences which will endure for an extended period of time.

TABLE 41-11   Degree of interest in religion since marriage, by degree of religious homogeneity in family unit, in percentages.

		Interest in Religion				Summary Score
Type of Marriage	N	Little	Some	Much	Total	
Mixed marriage	302	33.1	41.7	25.2	100.0	92.1
Unmixed marriage	1,146	20.8	43.9	35.2	99.9	114.4

Chi-square = 23.2; d.f. = 2; P less than .001.

MIXED MARRIAGES.   The great importance of denominational ties was further indicated by an analysis of the degree of religious interest expressed by those who were married to spouses with similar denominational ties at the time of the interview, as contrasted with those then married to spouses with differing ties. As may be seen in Table 41-11, the proportion of persons expressing "much" interest in religion was significantly greater among those whose spouses shared their denominational preference, than among those married to partners with differing ties.

These findings are also of interest since they emphasize the importance of the family unit as a factor influencing religious interest. The reinforcing tendencies which result from religious unity within the family seem to be of great importance. Conversely, the absence of such mutual reinforcement frequently seems to be associated with a relative lack of interest in religion. The data on mixed marriages together with those on childlessness suggest the great importance of the family unit as a factor influencing religious attitudes and behavior, and the need for further research in the area.

42   INTERFAITH MARRIAGES

Glenn Vernon

INTRODUCTION   Most religious groups express some
degree of concern for those members marrying outside the faith.
Although opposition varies in intensity, group concern stems from
the implied rejection of the faith and the potential loss of membership (*see* Lenski, Article 41). If the religious group perceives
itself to be the "true church," it is likely to prohibit as much contact with persons of other religious traditions as is possible. Because
marriage is a contract between two consenting individuals, isolation
of group members from others of differing faith and sex lessens the
potentiality of interfaith (religiously mixed) marriages. Although
Protestants vary in their acceptance of interfaith marriages, they
are generally more tolerant than Jews or Roman Catholics. However, the endogamous goal (to marry within one's group) remains
the stated aim of all religious groups. All groups attempt to avoid
split religious families in which one of the members refuses to participate or is a member of a conflicting religious group.

   The number of religiously mixed marriages varies from group
to group. Fewer than 10 percent of American Jews are estimated
to marry outside the Jewish faith; where such marriages do occur,
the Jewish male is more likely to marry outside the faith than is the
female. Roman Catholic interfaith marriage rates vary with location, population, educational background, and social class. About
30 percent of all Roman Catholics marry outside their church in an
approved manner (with the permission of the priest, which previ-

Abridged and reprinted from the July-August 1960 issue of *Religious Education* by
permission of the publisher, The Religious Education Association, 545 West 111th
Street, New York, New York 10025.

GLENN VERNON is Head of the Department and Professor of Sociology and Anthropology at the University of Maine.

ously involved the signing of a prenuptial agreement). Another 10-20 percent ignore the desires of the church to contract their own marriages in a nonapproved manner. Approximately 40–50 percent of all Roman Catholic marriages involve persons who are not Catholic. In America generally, nearly one of every four marriages is a religiously mixed marriage involving a Protestant, Jew or Roman Catholic with a partner of a second faith. Because inter-Protestant marriages are so common, Protestants are treated as a collective group.

For years the American public has been told that interfaith marriages result in higher divorce rates. Although this is technically true, Glenn Vernon suggests that a study of *marriage success* indicates greater interfaith marriage stability than is popularly assumed. Although religiously mixed marriages are not without their pitfalls, the high disintegration assumed by clergy and marriage counselors is open to serious question. The theoretical and methodological approach of the investigator here as everywhere else affects the processes of data collection and interpretation (*see* Vernon, Article 4). An investigation of *successful interfaith marriages* contradicts the extreme interpretations when *failure rates* alone are compared.

THE RELIGIOUSLY MIXED marriage excites the interest of a large number of people today. The social scientist, particularly the sociologist and the psychologist, share this interest—especially those who have concerned themselves with the so-called problem areas of human behavior. Of all those mentioned, the social scientist plays a somewhat unique role, in that he attempts to see the situation through scientific eyes. He attempts to see the data objectively.

This interest has led to the gathering of facts and figures by the social scientist so that he would not have to rely upon guesswork, hunches, or preconceived conclusions. Since religion is involved in the interfaith marriage issue, there is a possibility that the human tendency for the individual to see what he wants to see may be exaggerated, thus making accurate statistics very necessary.

We are fortunate that some limited statistics are available. This article is concerned with the influence which some of these statistics may have upon our students and the reading public. More specifically, the concern is with the manner in which they have traditionally been presented, at least as evidenced in the current text books in the area. This concern also extends to the reflection which this presentation makes upon our profession, in that we profess to be impartial, objective scientists.

The statistics to which I refer are those which compare the divorce rate of religiously homogeneous and religiously heterogeneous marriages. When the sociologist considers this area, the figures most often quoted are those from the Landis study done in Michigan.[1] The Weeks study[2] and the Bell study[3] are also frequently used. Let us look at the traditional presentation of the results of the Landis study.

PERCENT DIVORCED

Both Catholic	4.4
Both Jewish	5.2
Both Protestant	6.0
Mixed, Catholic-Protestant	14.1
Both none	17.9

The main emphasis of this chart is that once we begin to cross religious lines in marriage, the likelihood of divorce increases tremendously—about two to three times, in fact. Speaking in terms of percentages, it suggests that the chances for divorce increase from 200 to 300 percent in an interfaith marriage as compared to a one-faith marriage. From this, although the figures do not actually say it, it is easy for the student or the reader to leave with the impression that interfaith marriages are almost doomed to failure from the beginning —after all, a difference as high as 200 to 300 percent is a big one.

One wonders whether the effect upon the student would be any different if the reverse set of figures were presented—the percent of couples staying together. In this case the figures would be as follows.

PERCENT ENDURING

Both Catholic	95.6
Both Jewish	94.8
Both Protestant	94.0
Mixed, Catholic-Protestant	85.9
Both none	82.1

It would seem that quite a different impression would be left with the reader from an analysis of this set of figures. In the first place, all of the figures are high ones—well above 75 percent, so that even though he may not remember any exact figures, he is left with the impression that the great majority of marriages do endure, including interfaith marriages. There is a differential rate of success to be sure, but in this case, the difference is not from 200 to 300 percent, but rather the difference is around 10 percent.

The differential impression is also suggested by bar graphs illustrating the two sets of figures. Let us look at Figure 42-1 which Duvall and Hill[4] present in their text.

[1] J. T. Landis, "Marriages of Mixed and Non-Mixed Religious Faiths," *American Sociological Review*, 14 (1949), p. 403.
[2] W. Ashley Weeks, "Differential Divorce Rates by Occupation," *Social Forces*, 21 (1943), p. 336.
[3] Howard M. Bell, *Youth Tell Their Story* (Washington, D.C.: American Council on Education, 1938), p. 21.
[4] Evelyn Millis Duvall and Reuben Hill, *When You Marry*, rev. ed. (Boston: Heath, 1953), p. 391.

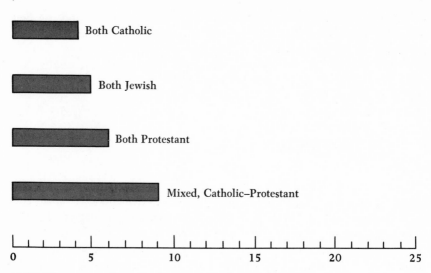

FIGURE 42-1   Percent of marriages ending in divorce.

Again the differences are very evident and very marked—some lines being almost three times as long as the others. However, when the bars show the percent of couples staying together, as in Figure 42-2, the picture is again quite different.

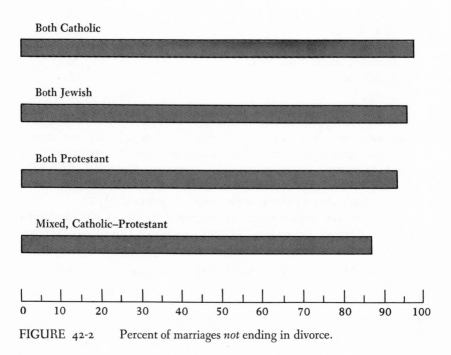

FIGURE 42-2   Percent of marriages *not* ending in divorce.

It is suggested that the second sort of presentation would have quite a different effect upon the student or reader than the first. No solid proof of this is available, so this is advanced merely as a hypothesis which would justify further investigation. Suggestive evidence, however, has been found in the classroom experiences of the author. In the "Family" class, which is composed mainly of seniors, in which specific attention is called to the facts which have just been outlined here, there have always been, in the past, some students who miss the following question:

> "Using divorce as our measure of failure, the chances are greater that an interfaith marriage will fail than that it will succeed."

This possibly reflects previous convictions which the class presentation was unable to shake, but these convictions, probably, stem in part at least, from being exposed to the traditional set of figures, or to individuals who have thus been exposed.

The whole difficulty is emphasized in a recent book written by a religionist[5] who states that in the ministry he has been called upon to do a good deal of counseling, and also states that he has yet "to deal with a problem or discern a solution which was not at root religious." His statement suggests that we might expect his biases to show through, but nonetheless, his writing illustrates the point being made. In discussing interfaith marriages, he states:

> Suppose you wanted to fly the Atlantic and asked the agent: "Is it a safe trip?" and he answered, "Oh, yes, every once in a while a plane gets through," I doubt if you would book passage. What you would want to know—if you still had the courage to pursue the matter further —is "What are the chances?" What is important to a young couple contemplating the matter is not that this or that couple seem to have worked it out all right, but rather, what by and large is the success of mixed marriages? Fortunately this is a question we are able to answer—in a rough and ready way to be sure, because the answer is in terms of divorce and separation—which is only a partial reflection of the scope of unhappiness and dissatisfaction which it suggests.
>
> From what is called the "Maryland Study" we learn about the religious connections of the parents of twelve thousand young people and whether their parents were living together or not. . . . The figures show that where both parents were Protestant . . . 6.8 percent of the parents were separated. . . . Where both parents were Roman Catholic 6.4 percent of the parents were separated. In the case of mixed marriages 15.2 percent represented broken homes. . . . In short, there was in the case of mixed marriages 2¼ times as much separation and divorce as in the families where there was religious homogeneity.

The author starts his discussion by suggesting that what we really want to know is how many "get through," and indicates that he has some rough

5 James A. Pike, *If You Marry Outside Your Faith* (New York: Harper & Row, 1954), pp. 26-7.

answers. However, he does not present them, but reverses his field, and presents figures as to how many did not get through, thus permitting him the telling point that the difference was about 2¼ times greater that the interfaith marriage would fail, rather than about 10 percent less that an interfaith marriage would get through.

It would seem possible that our concentration upon the one set of figures with the 200 to 300 percent difference may have contributed to religious scapegoating as far as religiously mixed marriages are concerned not only on the part of the parents and friends, but on the part of the individual participants in such marriages. Thus, we may unintentionally be creating additional hazards for the interfaith marriage.

It is certainly not the intent of this article to minimize the problems which frequently accompany a religiously mixed marriage, but neither does it seem proper to over-emphasize potential difficulties, and thus help make these predictions somewhat self-fulfilling. It would seem that we have an obligation to our students and readers to point up the chances for such marriages staying together as well as the chances for breaking up. It is further suggested that the fact that the reverse statistics are implicit in either presentation does not relieve us of this obligation. If the text or the professor emphasizes but one set, the chances are good that this is the emphasis which will be retained by the student or reader.

This article should not be construed as an endorsement of interfaith marriages. Neither is it an indictment of such marriages. The scientist is not concerned with either of these approaches. The question is being raised as to whether intentionally or unintentionally our biases are showing in the set of statistics which we seem to consistently select for presentation to our readers and students.

PART VIII

RELIGION IN THE MIDST OF

MODERN CHANGE

INTRODUCTION

SOCIAL CHANGE, as we have already seen in several readings, has had many effects upon religious institutions. Ministers are faced with great role conflicts; clergymen move more often than did their predecessors; families are less integrated into the congregation; worship intensity and frequency has declined; religious mobility has become almost a way of life; denominational affiliations have diminished. The need for creative leadership within the church has led to the enlistment of laymen in activities formerly assigned to the clergy. There are those who feel that the future of religion in America rests strictly with the degree of lay participation.

Some religious groups have adjusted to social change more rapidly than have others. *Churches* have met social change more effectively than *sects* (*see* Johnson, Article 11). And yet not all *churches* have been successful in adjusting to change, as witnessed by the decline of membership and attendance in the inner city areas throughout the nation (*see* Shippey, Article 14). In Cleveland, for example, one can travel down Euclid Avenue, a central street flowing to the east, and trace the steady physical decline of churches as the several communities have changed their composition. Many of these buildings are now inhabited by small sects that serve the lower class people whom the wealthier congregations avoid.

Various groups and activities compete with religious groups for member time, attention, and commitment. And yet, theologically, religion claims to be more than "just another" community association. In many instances, however, the religious institution is not convincing about the special reasons for its existence. Martin Marty, in *The New Shape of American Religion*, critically argues that "particularity is challenged by a blurry, generalizing religion; distinctive witness is confronted by amiable syncretism; theological content is often replaced by sentiments about religion. The process of erosion has been long and gradual and its full effect has only recently become noticeable." And yet, others like Charles Glock (Article 7) and Will Herberg (Article 43), do not support the dire pessimism reflected in Marty's viewpoint. The true condition of American religion probably rests somewhere between these two views (*see* Glock, Article 49).

Because religion is a social institution, it is subject to social forces that affect all institutions. Religious institutions cannot avoid the consequences of member's and clergymen's mobility, the aftereffects of war, demographic change, minority problems, personal deviance, social disorganization, or cultural lag. Religious institutions are very much the victims of personality conflicts, role tensions, group competition, definitions of success, quantitative evaluations, and leadership concepts. But the problem remains: How to be *of* the world and be *above* the world? Possibly to attempt both is to try to grasp both horns of the dilemma. Has the church been influenced by urbanization, commercialism, industrialization, totalitarianism, and secularism to such an extent that it has become merely a *reflection* of modern mass American life? Has religion lost its social initiative? Has it lost its *raison d'être*? In its attempt to *influence* society, the religious institution has come to *reflect society* (*see* O'Dea, Article 27). In its attempt to gain the broadest popular power to achieve goals, religious groups have often accepted conflicting ideals in their own and their member's value systems. For example, the practical need for national security has led to a justification of protective war (known also as a "just" war), a concept essentially at odds with the higher motivation of love for fellowman. Even now there are those who view capitalism as the epitome of religious faith and reject current welfare developments as "unchristian." The future potential of religion rests with its ability to provide an integrated network of values, something science cannot do, which may serve to integrate personality and society. On a functional level the concept of the American Way of Life, described by Herberg (*see* Articles 43 and 46), offers such a unifying potential. Many religionists, however, reject this concept as a "watered-down version" of explicit religious teaching and theology, as cologne is a mere fragrance of perfume.

In the first article, Will Herberg argues that America is at once the most secular and yet the most religious nation in the world. Americans have institutionalized religion in a form he calls the American Way of Life, an ideal expressed in three accommodating groups of Protestant, Catholic, and Jew. Then Yinger discusses the function of sects and cults (*see* Johnson, Article 11, and Young, Article 12) among the disprivileged. Arguing that religion is part of a complex interacting system, Yinger interprets the rise of sects and cults against the backdrop of social change. In his second article in this section Yinger discusses the conflicts between affluence and religion. Because the hope for future rewards can be met within American society now, religious groups are facing an adjustment caused by increased wealth and the general social affluence of their constituents.

Will Herberg in his second article notes that the United States has been transformed from a Protestant to a three-religion country. As a result "religious belonging has become a mode of defining one's religious identity." Religious beliefs have become assimilated to the ideas and values of the American Way. Benson Y. Landis evaluates the current numerical state of religion in

America. Noting the limited reliability of religious statistics (see Petersen, Article 6), Landis suggests that they offer poor data for measurement of religious vitality or decline. Richard D. Lambert discusses the trends in religion since World War II. The rise of popular piety has been accompanied by other movements toward revisionist theology. New attempts at religious unity have been supported by the increased importance of the layman (see Harrison, Article 24; Kane, Article 25; and Sklare, Article 26). Charles Glock and Rodney Stark suggest, however, that Protestantism is far more diverse than generally expected. Differences in theology cause Protestants and Roman Catholics to be differentiated into five generic theological camps which limit potential Protestant unity.

43 RELIGION IN A SECULARIZED SOCIETY: THE NEW SHAPE OF RELIGION IN AMERICA

Will Herberg

INTRODUCTION   The concepts of *sacred* and *secular* have both been by-products of man's attempt to understand his environment. Historically, men have designated that which is set apart from common life as sacred, or as related to supernatural sources. Emile Durkheim noted in his *Elementary Forms of the Religious Life* that from the earliest times men have recognized two domains of existing phenomena: the *sacred* and the *profane* (essentially, the secular). In essence, they represent the difference between the *ideal* (sacred) and the *real* (secular or profane). The concepts of profane and sacred have permeated all levels of human life, including symbols and rites, economic policy, theological definition, and even types of government. The theory of the Divine Right of Kings, for example, attributed a sacred character to a monarchical system. Concepts of the priesthood (*see* Kane, Article 25) even now assume an inherent holiness within the consecrated priest which is supposedly lacking in the common layman. The Judeo-Christian concern for human life is a derivative of the belief in the sacred nature of humanity, a creation of God. In general, that which is profane is common, relates to this world, and is secular. Whereas the secular is transient, the idea of the sacred includes a sense of timelessness.

Harvey Cox, in *The Secular City*, takes great pains to distinguish between *secularization*, the historical process by which society and culture pass from singular religious control to a broader, total institutional influence, and *secularism*, a form of coercive ideology which operates much as a religion, especially within a

Abridged and reprinted from *The Review of Religious Research*, Volume 3, Number 4, Copyrighted 1962, by the Religious Research Association, Inc.

WILL HERBERG is Graduate Professor at Drew University.

totalitarian framework. Secularization takes place as religious values are institutionalized within the former nonsacred system. Cox suggests that the origin of secularization rests in the Judeo-Christian religious tradition. "The *disenchantment of nature* begins with the Creation; the *desacralization of politics* with the Exodus; and the *deconsecration of values* with the Sinai Covenant, especially with its prohibition of idols." *Secularization* has developed as a natural consequence of Biblical faith (*see* Hammond, Article 9, and Lenski, Article 36). *Secularism* has emerged as a naturalistic attempt to avoid traditional religion.

Will Herberg reviews the importance of religion in contemporary American culture at a time when society is secularistic and pluralistic (*see* Ahlstrom, Article 1, and Winter, Article 5). In this article he suggests that the ideas of religion and secularism are open to several alternative variations and interpretations. As an antireligious drive, secularism has made little impact upon America, although philosophers, theologians, and social scientists often fear a downgrading of conventional religion at the expense of so-called nonreligious activity. The concept of the American Way of Life, while identified with *secularization,* has provided a common basis for resolution of the sacred and secular problem. The fact of our age is that secularization has *invaded* religion, but religion has *also confronted* the world. The American Way of Life testifies to this event (*see* Herberg, Article 46). No longer will the separation of the sacred and the secular assume the same proportions as it has in the past (*see* Heimann, Article 38).

I T HAS BECOME a platitude, though it remains a paradox, that America is at once the most secular and the most religious of nations. The statement which I thus take for my text suggests that religion is playing a very important role in contemporary American society, but at the same time that this society and its culture are, in some important sense, secularistic. Our problem is to scrutinize these two assertions, and should we find them measurably the case, to try to understand the relation between them.

SOME DEFINITIONS AND CLARIFICATIONS.   But before we approach our main task, we should have some preliminary notion of what we mean when we use such terms as "religion" and "secularism."

RELIGION.   The term "religion," it seems to me, is susceptible to three different usages. (1) In the first place, "religion" is properly used for the system of attitudes, beliefs, feelings, standards, and practices that, in the particular society, generally receive the name of religion. For our purposes, we will designate religion in this usage as "conventional religion." We can speak of Christianity, Protestantism, Lutheranism, Judaism, Islam, Buddhism, Roman

Catholicism, and the like as examples of conventional religion. (2) In the second place, "religion" may be taken to signify that system of attitudes, beliefs, feelings, standards, and practices that actually *does in fact* provide the society with an ultimate context of meaning and value in terms of which social life is integrated and social activities are validated. This I will call the "operative religion" of a society. It may or it may not be the same as the conventional religion. German *Rassen*—or *Volksgemeinschaft* and the American Way of Life are two very different examples of operative religion in this sense. (3) In the third place, "religion" may be understood existentially as the structure of one's being oriented to one's ultimate concern, as (to use Robert Calhoun's celebrated phrase) "man's life insofar as it is defined by his supreme loyalty and devotion."

SECULARISM. Let us see if we can find some stable spots of intelligibility in the confusing flux of meaning. (1) In the first place, "secular" may simply mean interests and activities that are outside the realm of sacral—that is, outside the realm of institutionalized activities associated with religion in the first sense, with conventional religion. In this usage, we speak of business, law, teaching, or warfare, for example, as secular affairs, over against the "spiritual" or cultic activities of religion. (2) But, in the second place, "secularism" may also be used to express the conviction that these nonsacral interests and activities are independent and autonomous, coexisting side by side with religion, but in no sense subordinated to it, not even "spiritually." This seems to be a view widely prevalent in modern Western culture. (3) Finally, "secularism" may be used as a total philosophy of life, insisting on the extrusion of religion from the realm of reality, meaning, and value, and the organization of life and thought on a religion-denying premise. The odd thing that secularism in this antireligious sense itself becomes something very like religion in the third, or existential, usage listed above. The circle is thereby closed.

Now, it should be clear that the religion from which secularism in these senses sees itself as distinct, independent, or opposed is conventional religion; I doubt very much if secularism can be given any meaning at all over against religion in the second or third acceptations of the term. Indeed, secularism often finds in the operative religion of society, never understood as religion, of course, its point of vantage against the conventional religions it opposes; and in its own affirmations and denials it frequently becomes, in fact, the existential religion of its proponents.

RELIGION IN PRESENT-DAY AMERICA. For mid-twentieth century America, religion in the sense of conventional religion refers predominantly, of course, to the so-called "three great faiths," Protestantism, Catholicism, and Judaism; sometimes, the major Protestant denominations are also implied; and on occasion, too, such groups outside the tri-faith orbit as Islam or Buddhism. There is little practical difficulty in clarifying our reference on this level.

As to existential faith, religion in the third sense, it is only partly and very inadequately open to sociological scrutiny, especially macroanalysis. We will only infrequently make reference to it, and then only for special purposes.

This leaves us with religion in the second sense, religion in the sense of the operative religion of our society. Sociologists and anthropologists are virtually unanimous in the conviction that religion is one of the primary functional prerequisites of society. "Every functioning society," Professor Robin M. Williams has said, "has, to an important degree, a common religion. The possession of a common set of ideas, rituals, and symbols can supply an overarching sense of unity even in a society otherwise riddled with conflicts."[1] Without some such "common religion," no society could long survive. But this "common religion," let us hasten to add, need not be what is conventionally understood as religion—in other words, it need not be the conventional religion of society.

What is the "common religion" in which American society, as a "functioning society," finds its unity and cohesiveness? What for the mid-twentieth century American is really the unifying context of meaning and value beyond the confusion and fragmentariness of everyday life? I do not think any one would be temerarious enough to suggest that it is any one of the conventional religions, no matter how large and influential it might be. Clearly, it is not Protestantism, Catholicism, or Judaism, with their varying "sets of ideas, rituals, and symbols," that supplies the American people with their "overarching sense of unity"; in a religiously pluralistic society such as ours, this would obviously be impossible, if indeed it would be possible in any society in the modern Western world. I think it is plain, and my whole discussion will tend to document it, that the "common religion" of Americans today, in the sense of the operative religion of our culture, is the entity generally known as *The American Way of Life*. It is the American Way of Life—sometimes called just *American democracy*—that provides us with the "common set of ideas, rituals, and symbols" by which we integrate our social life. Of course, we do not ordinarily speak of the American Way of Life as religion, though we have coined the quasi-religious phrase, "the moral and spiritual values of democracy"; yet whatever we may call it, or indeed whether we have any special way of designating it or not, the American Way does in fact constitute the operative religion of Americans, both undergirding and overarching our society.

There are societies in which the conventional religion and the operative religion are the same; perhaps the Greek polis before the age of the sophists and philosophers would be an example. In such societies, there is really no problem of secularism, because secularism, in any but the harmless first sense, could not arise. In fact, secularism as a problem might be said to appear only when conventional religion and operative religion no longer coincide, but rather begin to diverge, and perhaps even to conflict. We may indeed define

[1] Robin M. Williams, Jr., *American Society: A Sociological Interpretation* (New York: Knopf, 1951), p. 312.

a *secularized* culture as a culture in which the conventional religion is no longer the operative religion in the sociological sense but has been replaced, in that function, by another "set of ideas, rituals, and symbols." This is obviously the situation we have in this country today, and it is in this sense that we can speak of American society today as in an advanced state of secularization.

Note that I prefer the words "secularized" and "secularization," for if a society is secularistic in the strong senses of the term, it is always because it has undergone secularization; no society is, so to speak, secularistic to start with. What later becomes the conventional religion as over against the operative religion was, at an earlier time, itself the operative religion of the society and only gradually, through a complex cultural development, was forced to give way. Most, if not all, societies we know are already more or less secularized, but the fact that there are various phases and forms of secularization is sufficient to indicate that a degenerative—or, by another reading, a progressive —process has been underway from an integrated sacral society to whatever stage of secularization has been reached.

It is with secularism in the second sense that we are primarily concerned, since secularism in the first sense—the mere distinction between cultic and noncultic interests and activities—in itself constitutes no great problem; and secularism in the third sense—an antireligious drive for the comprehension of all life on an explicitly religion-denying basis—does not possess, and indeed has never possessed, much strength in this country, except among small groups of intellectual *esprits forts*. But secularism in the second sense—the immanent claim to total autonomy over religion (which here means conventional religion) on the part of the so-called nonreligious interests and activities—is very widespread in this country and has been recognized as a problem by many philosophers, theologians, and social scientists.

THE NEW ROLE OF RELIGION IN AMERICAN LIFE.   The American Way of Life allows religion—I mean conventional religion, in which sense I will now use the term—a high and honored place in its scheme of things. This high estimate of religion was, with some fluctuations, characteristic of our culture through the nineteenth and into the twentieth century; and foreign observers—Tocqueville, for example—were quick to note it.

If one were required to elaborate in more detail the place conventional religion enjoys in the scheme of things defined by the American Way, I think it would be fair to assert that the American Way involves acquiescence in the following beliefs:

1. The belief in God. Indeed, over 95 percent of Americans affirm this belief, and regard it as essential for every good American.
2. The belief that religion is a "very good thing," both for the individual and the nation. All Americans, it is felt, ought to support the "religion of their choice," and of course they ought to have a choice.

3. The belief that being a Protestant, being a Catholic, and being a Jew are the three variant ways of being religious in the American Way. Other religions are also generally recognized as "good," but not "good" for Americans. Protestantism, Catholicism, and Judaism are the "three great faiths," the three American religions.

These three articles, I think, constitute the American creed as to religion. Americans, of course, believe, or think they believe, many other things religious; but, by and large, though with some notable exceptions, they do not hold these other beliefs with the same unquestioning conviction, with the same incapacity to understand or tolerate disbelief, that they do the three articles I have listed. Robin Williams has very aptly pointed to the criterion. "Men," he says, "are always likely to be intolerant of their central ultimate values."[2] Judging by this standard, we can, I think, conclude: (1) that the "central ultimate values" of Americans are defined in and through the American Way of Life; and (2) that the three essential articles of religion in the American creed are belief in God, belief in religion, and belief in the three-faith system. To question any of these three fundamentals is, in effect, to reveal oneself as "un-American" and is so felt even by those few who harbor dissident views.

In brief, it is my thesis, first presented some six years ago in my study of religion in America, that whereas it is the American Way that operates as America's "common religion" it is the function—though, of course, by no means the *only* function—of conventional religion in the tri-faith system to establish the context of belonging in terms of which Americans now increasingly tend to define their identity within the totality of American life. I am in the fortunate position of being able to summarize my position in the percipient account given by Professor Gerhard Lenski in his recent noteworthy volume, *The Religious Factor*. Let me quote.

> The traditional view of urbanism as it affects religion has recently been questioned by several writers. Most notable among these is Will Herberg. In his provocative essay, *Protestant-Catholic-Jew*, Herberg asserts that urban conditions of life promote what we shall here call *communal*-type religion, as contrasted with *associational*-type religion. According to the classical theories of urbanism, religion in the modern metropolis becomes a highly specialized aspect of life. The church itself becomes a formal association, and ceases to be a nucleus around which a variety of social relationships is organized, as in the typical agrarian community. Herberg suggests, however, that the very impersonality of so much of modern life creates in individuals a need for a communal-type relationship, broader than the immediate family, but narrower than the total society.
>
> Earlier in American history, ethnic groups served such a function, and individuals were able to enjoy this sense of communal identification and participation as members of the German, Polish, Italian, or other

[2] *Ibid.*, p. 320n.

ethnic colonies established in this country. Today, such groups have largely disintegrated, but many of the needs they served continue to be felt. In this situation, Herberg argues, Americans are turning increasingly to their religious groups, especially the three major faiths, for the satisfaction of their need for communal identification and belongingness. In short, the specialization and compartmentalization inherent in the urban way of life drive men to transform their religious groups from narrow, specialized associational-type groups into groups which are communal in character.[3]

Such is Lenski's summary of my thesis, a better summary than I could give myself. Now let us turn to Lenski's conclusions drawn from the Detroit area study.

Among the possible trends cited above, one deserves special comment, both because of its far-reaching implications, and because many of these implications have received so little attention from the general public. This is the possible trend toward increased socioreligious group communalism. As we noted in Chapter 2, communalism along socioreligious group lines seems to have been gaining in strength in recent years, and promises to continue to gain in the foreseeable future.

This development is one which has been greatly hastened by the rapid decline of the older ethnic subcommunities in recent years. . . . Until about a generation ago, the American population was sharply divided into a rather large number of relatively small ethnic subcommunities. . . . These groups, however, were unable to preserve their organizational integrity in the face of powerful and pervasive pressures to Americanization. . . . The successor to the ethnic subcommunity is the socioreligious subcommunity.[4]

"The successor to the ethnic subcommunity is the socio-religious subcommunity": This seems to me to describe with precision one very important aspect of the functionality of conventional religion and religious belonging in present-day America. To put it in a somewhat oversimplified, but not altogether inaccurate way: being a Protestant, being a Catholic, being a Jew, are rapidly becoming three variant ways of being an American, of defining one's identity within the totality of American life. This, I think, helps account for the extraordinarily high place granted to conventional religion in the American scheme of things, as well as for the near-unanimity of religious identification in America today. Conventional religion has acquired a high functionality within the "common religion" of the American Way.

SECULARISM AND RELIGION IN PRESENT-DAY AMERICA.
Let us now return to the problem of secularism. If we think of secularism as

---

[3] Gerhard Lenski, *The Religious Factor: A Sociological Study of Religion's Impact on Politics, Economics, and Family Life* (Garden City, N.Y.: Doubleday, 1961), pp. 10-11.
[4] *Ibid.*, pp. 326-7.

the autonomous organization of the life of society upon a nonreligious base and within a nonreligious system of meaning and value, without necessarily denying religion a place, and perhaps even a very honored place, in the scheme of things, we can, I suggest, understand secularization as the increasing separation of the operative religion of the culture from its conventional religion. Divergence between operative religion and conventional religion: that is substantially what secularization implies. Sometimes this divergence means opposition and conflict, but it need not; and in this country today, it does not. Operative religion and conventional religion are quite different in present-day America, but there is no hostility between them: the operative religion—the American Way—often expresses its meanings, standards and values in the traditional vocabulary of conventional religion; while the conventional religions —Protestantism, Catholicism, and Judaism—see themselves as functioning within the operative religion, serving its purposes and implementing its values.

Secularization, even in its benign form, means the subversion of the normative relation between religion and culture. Instead of the culture standing under the judgment of the God to whom religion witnesses, religion (that is, conventional religion) tends to understand itself as an expression of, and a utility for, the culture.

It is this kind of benevolent coexistence, amounting, in effect, to a kind of syncretism on both sides, that accounts for much of the paradox of contemporary American religion—the paradox of the religiousness of a society in an advanced state of secularization. Secularism and religion in this country today are not enemies, not even opponents; on the contrary, each one, in a way, has come to serve the other, and it is often very hard to tell them apart.

On the one side, religion has invaded secularism, so that being religious has become a primary value of the secular system known as the American Way. The junior high school girl in a suburban New Jersey town, who, in a composition on her best friend, rebuked her severely, saying, "Martha is not the least bit patriotic; she doesn't even go to church!", and former President Eisenhower, who could not imagine how it was possible *not* to be religious, since "democracy (could not) exist without a religious base," and we "believe in democracy,"[5] were both merely testifying to the common conviction of the American people that believing in God, being religious, and going to church are (and I am borrowing a phrase from former President Eisenhower) "basic expressions of Americanism." Our secularism, advanced and pervasive though it be, is emphatically a *pro*religious secularism.

On the other side, secularism has invaded religion (I mean conventional religion), so that "democracy," or the American Way, has become the real context of validation for large and influential numbers of the adherents of the conventional religions. If our secularism has become pervasively proreligious, our religion has become pervasively secularistic. The challenge of secularism

[5] *The New York Times,* May 4, 1948.

has now become a matter *within* religion, rather than an issue between religion and a hostile force outside.

One more illustration that may help to focus the question, as well as bring us back to what I have said about the new role of religion in American life. Sunday school enrollment is growing fairly rapidly in this country today, largely, of course, among Protestants, and yet, as almost every one acquainted with the situation has noted, the very same parents who enroll their children in the Sunday schools know little, and care less, about what goes on in these Sunday schools—the children might just as well be cutting out paper dolls, which is very often what they do! Now why should parents be so concerned about sending their children to Sunday school and yet be so unconcerned about what goes on in the schools? May it not be that the primary function of having children enrolled in Sunday school actually has very little to do with the program of education or instruction? "Through its institutions," Oscar Handlin notes, describing the role of religion in the mid-twentieth century America, "the church supplied a place where children came to learn who they were."[6] Sending children to Sunday school, I suggest, has become the appropriate way of answering the child's anxious question: "But, Mummy, what *am* I?" The Sunday school, the church, tells the child who and what he is by locating him in the socioreligious subcommunity where he belongs; he is thus given a name, a place, an identity.

Conventional religion in America has come to serve a function largely dissociated from its traditional belief-content. Indeed, it may even be said, with some exaggeration, that conventional religion today serves its function better the more vacuous and empty of content it is, for religious content, if taken seriously, may well interfere with the social function of religion as a way of American identification. At any rate, the two—religion as religious identification and belonging, and religion as religious belief—have little essential connection in present-day America. That is why we have been witnessing an upsurge of religiousness side by side with an advancing secularization of our culture. That is why the paradox of America being at once the most religious and the most secularistic of nations—the paradox of religionless religion—need not perplex us unduly; it is very much what we might expect under contemporary American conditions.

POINTS OF RESISTANCE AND COUNTER-CURRENTS.   The drift toward secularized religion in this country is a sweeping and pervasive one, but it would be a gross mistake to ignore certain points of resistance and certain counter-currents that are making themselves felt in contemporary America. These, I think, may largely be grouped under four headings.

First, there are the sects. The sects, because they find themselves on the margin of American society, and see themselves as "outsiders," refuse to fit

[6] Oscar Handlin, *The American People in the Twentieth Century* (Cambridge: Harvard University Press, 1954), p. 222.

into the three-faith scheme of American religion and certainly do not under-stand their sectarian belonging as the definition of their American identity. For the sect, the secularizing separation of operative religion from conventional religion has only barely begun, and the typical sectarian believer is very much concerned about the belief-content of his religion. Some sectarian leaders are aware of the general drift of American religion and are warning their follow-ers against it, with what success we shall have occasion to see. In any case, the sect groups do constitute the most obvious, if not the most important, point of resistance to the sweep of secularistic religion.

A significant second group is composed of the churches with a strong credal or confessional tradition, some of which resemble the stabilized sect. Mormons, Missouri Synod Lutherans, and the like may be taken as examples. The heavy specific gravity of creed and confession tends to impede dissolution in the American system of religion-in-general, as Martin Marty calls it, and members of these churches tend to be intolerant about more than merely non-belief in God or disrespect for religion. Yet credal and confessional systems are not forever resistive, and they have a curious way of becoming detached and preserved in a fossilized state, without much real influence on the actual pat-terns of religious behavior. For the time being, however, it seems clear that these credal and confessional churches, along with some of the larger stabilized sects, form another noteworthy point of resistance.

Third, along with the credal and confessional churches should go the older ethnic churches, consisting of incompletely assimilated immigrants. Like the sects, the immigrant churches—and they still constitute a considerable fac-tor in the religious life of this country—feel their marginality, and therefore their being different. It should be remembered that, as Sidney Mead has pointed out, the characteristic syncretism between conventional religion and the operative religion of the American Way emerged first within American Protestantism in the second half of the nineteenth century; in those days, Catholicism and Judaism, not yet being American, were not yet caught up in the process. As they became American, however, and entered to make up the present three-faith system within the past three or four decades, they became "Protestantized" in this, as in so many other ways. Many immigrant churches, however, still remain unabsorbed and therefore are, in a way, a "hold-out" against the sweeping Americanization of religion.

The fourth group I should like to mention really constitutes more of a counter-current than a mere point of resistance; this is made up of the theo-logically interested, theologically concerned, theologically oriented people, in the churches or out. With the notable revival of theology and religious phi-losophy as intellectual disciplines in the past generation, and with the deep-ening of serious religious interest among the younger people on the college campuses and in the suburban communities, this fourth group is by no means as insignificant in number as one might think. Whatever its size, it is the source of most of the serious criticism American religion has been subjected to in recent years. The critique of American religion has become the preoccupation of the theologians, and of the neo-orthodox theologians at that, rather than of secularist opponents of religion, as was the case in an earlier age. The theologically oriented person generally feels an acute distaste for the secularistic erosion of religion and possesses a standpoint from which the secularizing tendency can be detected and exposed. Generally, too, the theologically oriented person is an intellectual and shares the intellectual's dislike for the homogenizing mass culture of which American secularized religion is but an aspect. The criticism of popular religion thus becomes a vanguard cultural activity and is sometimes carried on by persons whose connection with the world of faith is tenuous indeed, for whom this kind of criticism really serves as an indirect way of criticizing religion itself, the only way practicable in contemporary America. There is thus a curious common front established between the theologian and the crypto-unbeliever against what both regard as the shoddy and superficial religiosity of popular religion. Together, they constitute a not inconsiderable force on the higher cultural levels.

Yet, not unexpectedly, the final formulation of the secularized syncretism that characterizes American religion comes from the very same group. The integration of the conventional religions into the superordinate structure of the American Way has been explicitly urged and recommended by religious leaders of many affiliations. I call attention to the writings of Ira Eisenstein, Eugene Kohn, and Mordecai Kaplan; to Conrad Moehlman's warm description of "democracy" as the "religion of the American majority";[7] and to J. Paul Williams' recommendation that "democracy" be recognized as America's religion, and that governmental agencies, including the public schools, be required to "teach the democratic ideal as religion."[8] But the classic formulation of the benevolent syncretism that constitutes America's secularized religion comes from the pen of a distinguished philosopher, Horace M. Kallen, a thinker very friendly to religion, though himself religiously unaffiliated. In a celebrated article, significantly entitled "Democracy's True Religion," Dr. Kallen laid out the matter with admirable lucidity and breadth of mind.

> For the communicants of the democratic faith [he said], it [democracy] is the religion of and for religions. [It is] the religion of religions; all may freely come together in it.[9]

It is precisely this generous all-comprehensiveness of "democracy," of the American Way, as superreligion, ready to grant a place and a function under its aegis to the conventional religions, if only they will behave "democratically," and give up their exclusiveness and intolerance, that constitutes the real

---

[7] Conrad Moehlman, *School and Church: The American Way* (New York: Harper & Row, 1944), pp. IX, X.

[8] J. Paul Williams, *What Americans Believe and How They Worship* (New York: Harper & Row, 1952), pp. 71, 78, 368, 374.

[9] H. M. Kallen, "Democracy's True Religion," *Saturday Review of Literature*, July 28, 1951.

shape of secularized religion in mid-twentieth century America. And it is precisely this generous all-comprehensiveness of "democracy," of the American Way, as superreligion that arouses grave misgivings among theologically concerned believers, who take their belief seriously and cannot easily be persuaded to dissolve it in the generalized religiosity of the American Way.

44 RELIGION AND SOCIAL CHANGE: FUNCTIONS AND DYSFUNCTIONS OF SECTS AND CULTS AMONG THE DISPRIVILEGED

J. Milton Yinger

INTRODUCTION   The effect of social change upon religion is apparent in the rise of religious sects. Although inclusive of many types (*see* Young, Article 12), sects generally reflect a conservative-puritanical morality and serve as gathering points for the socially disinherited lower class, although in some instances sects may be oriented to the more successful classes (*see* Yinger, Article 45). While sects are rather reactionary to modern life, they tend to modify their views as they succeed and grow in size (*see* Johnson, Article 11). Although small in size, their participation and financial contribution rates often put institutionalized religious groups to shame. Because sects call for the purification and maintenance of faith in the midst of change (*see* Graebner, Article 30), they tend to remain on the periphery of the social and religious community. In effect, the sect provides its own community in which the members find acceptance and personal meaning. Characterized by small primary groups, the sect offers a highly integrated life for those who adhere to the austerity of the group.
Tithing (giving 10 percent of one's earnings to the church) becomes a testimony of faith. The future life offers the hope for overcoming the injustice and evil of the world. Although the sect usually cannot afford the luxury of the full-time minister, the semi-professional clergyman who serves the sect is able to stimulate the group to a spontaneous dependence upon the Holy Spirit who frees them from the limitations of the day (*see* Alland, Article 8, and Young, Article 12). The social expression of one's faith often results in personal confession and testimony to the group. The

Abridged and reprinted from *The Review of Religious Research*, Volume 4, Number 2, Copyrighted 1963, by the Religious Research Association, Inc.

J. MILTON YINGER is Professor of Sociology at Oberlin College.

need to relate favorably to the future life with God results in an extensive program of public worship throughout the week.

Some years ago Russell Dynes found that supporters of sects are more likely to be found among persons of lower socioeconomic groups. They tend to accept greater emotionalism, evangelistic concern, and nonliturgical worship patterns. Because they are highly integrated within the group, sect members participate in community organizations at a lower rate than those who are members of an established denomination. Close personal friends are more likely to come from the membership of the sect, suggesting the tendency toward self-reinforcement existing within the group. Sect members derive greater social satisfaction from church activity than do members of organized churches.

J. Milton Yinger theorizes that sect development may best be understood as a fundamental response of the social group to the changing environment. A wide variety of sect responses, ranging from personal demoralization to full-scale group assimilation, are alternatives open to the group. The exact nature of the sect response depends in large part upon the special need of its members. Sects, however, bridge the gap between individual need and social situations. Although they may be at odds with the world, Yinger argues that sects actually serve to reorient the individual to the society.

THE COMPLICATED TASK of studying the subtle and intricate ways in which religion is related to society is made somewhat easier if we direct our attention to times of rapid social change. Because the forces producing change almost invariably affect the parts of a social system at different rates, and to different degrees, the mutual adjustment of parts that is relatively characteristic of stable periods in the life of a society is disturbed. Change may begin with technology, with increase of population, with economic improvement or decline, with growth of contact with other societies, with the pronouncements of a prophet, or in other ways. If the force of change is strong, strain is felt throughout the system.

Religion is part of a complex interacting system. On some particular issue and from the perspective of a given point in time, religious developments may best be understood as responses to fundamental changes in their social environment. The new religious forces then "feed back into" the system from which they came, influencing the course of its development. On another issue, viewed again from a given point in time, religious change may be the dynamic factor. The influences thus set in motion become, in turn, conditioning and constraining forces that affect the religion which released them.

BRIDGING FUNCTION OF SECT AND CULT. Among the most interesting of the religious developments in the modern world have been the sects and cults that have appeared among groups caught in conditions of severe disprivilege. Frequently these are racial or cultural minorities who have been overrun by a militarily and industrially more advanced society or a more powerful segment of their own society. Prerequisites to their traditional way of life are destroyed: belief in the efficacy of the old ways declines; values and desires are taken over from the powerful intruding force; and yet full acceptance of the new way—including its religion—is neither possible nor permitted.

Responses to these conditions of "cultural shock" range from personal demoralization to traditional reaffirmation, to aggression against the invading culture, to acculturation and assimilation. Our primary interest is in religious movements that arise in such contexts.

How would the individuals and groups in question respond to the dramatic changes in the world around them if the religious movement in question were not available?

To answer this question, it is well to remember that there are certain facts in the situation which are scarcely subject to change by the disprivileged group. Any individual or social development must be carried on in the context of these facts. Whether one is dealing with tribal societies among the Melanesian Islands, with American Indians, or with peasant Negroes suddenly transferred to an industrial, urban world, these things are true:

The old way of life has been brought under severe pressure and can no longer be maintained. Traditional religious beliefs and practices, embedded as they were in the old order, lose their appeal. A new style of life, including a new religion, is needed; yet the religion of the conqueror, though often strongly urged by missionary activity, is not fully meaningful and adequate. It is embedded in the whole social system of the dominant group—a system only partly experienced and understood by the conquered or minority groups.

The traditional separation of individuals and tribes imposes serious problems in the new context. Formerly separate, and even antagonistic, groups now find themselves caught up in a common situation. Unifying themes are needed.

Personal demoralization, in the several meanings of that phrase, has become more common. Perhaps two aspects are most critical: a growing gap between what individuals hope for in life and what they expect weakens motivation; and, in the more literal meaning of the term *demoralization*, the breakdown of the old order has left many individuals without a coherent value system.

Religious innovations are not inevitable under these conditions, but the strains which the conditions impose add new dimensions to the age-old problems of salvation. Among the many ways of struggling with the new situation, religious movements occupy a prominent place.

It is the thesis of this paper that religious cults and sects—even those that seem most bizarre and carry most seriously the threats of conflict—have at least the potentiality of helping to carry their members over into a new life. In situations that demand rapid change, including drastic reorganization of personality, religious movements can serve a bridging function.

CULTURAL CONFUSION AND THE MILLENIAL DREAM.   For over three-quarters of a century the islands of Melanesia have been swept by millenarian movements that demonstrate how sensitively religion registers the currents of change. Instability in the European-dominated economy has created hardship for many of the islanders and undermined their confidence in rational planning to satisfy their needs. A great demand for labor in the mines and plantations has drawn large numbers out of their tribal societies for years at a time. Harsh recruitment methods, dreary barracks life, low pay when set beside the new-found wants, forceful domination by the white men, and bitterness at the deterioration of their own cultures have created powerful anti-white hostility. Contrasts between the values of the white plantation overseers and the teachings of the missionaries added confusion. In such a situation, the natives could not go back—the white men had not only disrupted their societies, but had given them new wants and new values—nor could they go ahead, for their pay was minimal, their opportunities few, and their command of the white men's ways entirely marginal.

> The stage was truly set . . . for the development of independent native movements, and for the casting of social and economic aspirations in religious form. . . . The hysterical phenomena found in most of the cults . . . are the product of the ambivalent attitudes and feelings of men torn between hatred of the white people who had destroyed the old way of life and who now dominated them by force, and the desire to obtain for themselves the possessions of these very whites.[1]

Early religious responses to such a situation tended to be nativistic and revivalistic.[2] The old order, it is affirmed, will be reestablished and the invader driven from the land. In 1877 and the years following in Fiji, for example, a self-proclaimed prophet declared that the order of things would soon be reversed, ancestors would return to the island, and independence would be restored. The white men would be driven into the sea.

In the decades that followed, cults in many parts of Melanesia developed along similar lines. In many of them the theme of "stolen cargo" became prominent. From the point of view of the natives, as Worsley tells us, the white men received their vast supplies of goods by steamer or plane from unknown lands. They did not manufacture them, and they merely sent back scraps of paper. It was not difficult for the natives to believe that the goods were made by their own ancestors and stolen from them by the whites, who had control over some secret. The secret was obviously not work. Prophets appeared to re-

---

[1] Peter Worsley, *The Trumpet Shall Sound: A Study of "Cargo" Cults in Melanesia* (London: MacGibbon and Kee, 1957), p. 44.
[2] *See* Anthony Wallace, "Revitalization Movements," *American Anthropologist*, Vol. 58 (April, 1956), pp. 264-79.

veal the way to secure the cargoes and to reestablish native supremacy. The Cargo cults often have led to tension, if not to open conflict with white overlords; they encouraged persons to neglect their gardens and other economic activities. On the other side, however, these cults contributed to the breaking down of village and tribal barriers that prevented effective joint action to deal with their new and shared fate. During a difficult period of transition they helped to prevent serious social disorganization by supporting belief in the ancestors and reduced personal disorganization by maintaining hope.

Although there are significant differences, much of the description of the Cargo cults can be applied to the Ghost Dance among some American Indians. We find again a background of cultural confusion, white domination, economic instability, and inability to carry out the traditional ways. Many prophets appeared in this setting, calling for a revival and describing the beliefs, group patterns, and dances necessary for salvation. As Lesser describes it with reference to the Pawnee in 1890:

> Into this situation of cultural decay and gradual darkness, the Ghost Dance doctrine shown like a bright light. Indian ways were not gone, never to be recovered. Indian ways were coming back. Those who had lived before in the "golden age" were still carrying on old ceremonies, old dances, old performances, and old games in the beyond. They were coming back; they were bringing the old ways and the buffalo. Dance, dance, dance. The white man would be destroyed by a great wind.[3]

Such religious attacks on the dominant society are not limited to conquered peoples. If, within a society, a group lacks an independent and successful past which can serve as the focus of the millenial dream, they can affirm that they are the true defenders of a tradition shared with their oppressors, who have fallen into sinful ways; they alone are "Jehovah's Witnesses." Such proletarian movements, in the sense that Toynbee, Cohn, and others have used this term, are in a society, but not of it. They are scarcely less critical of the existing institutions than a conquered tribe. This world, they declare, is full of sin and it is doomed. From all the ages, 144,000 are destined to rule with Jesus; but others who accept the Witnesses will live forever and enjoy a heaven without sin and trouble.[4] "The poor are going to become rich, the downtrodden are to be raised above the mighty, the sick and frail are to be made whole, the aging and the old are to become young again!"[5] Thus the Jehovah's Witnesses also attack the rich and powerful, although there is no race theme involved, as did the members of the Fiji Tuka Cult and the Indian Ghost Dance; and they attack the society by downgrading its institutions and refusing to accord it final loyalty.

[3] Alexander Lesser, "Cultural Significance of the Ghost Dance," *American Anthropologist* (January-March, 1933), pp. 108-115.
[4] Werner Cohn, "Jehovah's Witnesses as a Proletarian Movement," *The American Scholar*, Vol. 24 (Summer, 1955), pp. 281-98.
[5] Royston Pike, *Jehovah's Witnesses* (New York: Philosophical Library, 1954), p. 136.

Continuing to overlook the important differences, let me describe still another interesting religious movement in such a way as to emphasize its similarities with those just commented on. The Black Muslims, like the Jehovah's Witnesses, are in but not of American society. Like the Indian and Melanesian cults, they emphasize a race theme. Like them all, they point to the past, but always in a way that shows their great concern for the present and the future. For past glories, one might have expected American Negroes to renew a sense of identity with African Negro societies, as the Ras Tafari cult in Jamaica has done, for example. But this would keep alive the very Negro identity that the Black Muslim movement seeks to destroy. Hence the themes, "We are the lost nation of Islam; our salvation rests on the rediscovery of this tradition." All science is the product of the discoveries of twenty-four original black scientists, thousands of years ago. By redefining one's racial identity, by repudiating the white man's religion and attacking him as a knave, the 100,000 or more members of this movement seek for salvation from their soul-crushing lives. Most of the members are recent migrants into large cities, where their old accommodative patterns of life have been destroyed, their aspirations raised, their sense of power enhanced. Yet the painful facts of disprivilege and discrimination remain. It is in this context that the young, mostly male, mostly lower-class, often functionally illiterate Negroes join the Black Muslims. In Eric Lincoln's words:

> The true believer who becomes a Muslim casts off at last his old self and takes on a new identity. He changes his name, his religion, his homeland, his "natural" language, his moral and cultural values, his very purpose in living. He is no longer a Negro, so long despised by the white man that he has come almost to despise himself. Now he is a Black Man—divine, ruler of the universe, different only in degree from Allah Himself. He is no longer discontent and baffled, harried by social obloquy and a gnawing sense of personal inadequacy. Now he is a Muslim, bearing in himself the power of the Black Nation and its glorious destiny. His new life is not an easy one: it demands unquestioning faith, unrelenting self-mastery, unremitting hatred.[6]

SECT AND CULT IN TRANSITION. Such religious movements, or religiopolitical movements, in a minority or suppressed group are usually impermanent. Whatever they may do to maintain or restore self-respect and to achieve group solidarity (that is, however much they may be functional for the minority), they are seldom regarded with favor by the dominant groups. Insofar as they mount an attack on the society or deny the validity of its basic values and institutions, they are scarcely functional for that society. Even in societies where freedom of religion is the rule, there is little tolerance for those efforts to win salvation that involve direct attack on the social order, including

[6] C. Eric Lincoln, *The Black Muslims in America* (Boston: Beacon Press, 1961), pp. 108-109.

the dominant religious organizations. Almost universally, the response of those in power is suppression, the jailing of leaders, the curtailment of activities. Through the years, many of the leaders of the Cargo cults in Melanesia have been jailed and the movements suppressed. The Ghost Dance was smashed militarily at the Battle of Wounded Knee. Hundreds of Jehovah's Witnesses have been jailed in the United States because their search for salvation involves a sharp disagreement with dominant institutions. Although there has as yet been little suppression of the Black Muslims—their attack having been almost entirely verbal—they are kept under close scrutiny.

By the nature of their relationship to society, then, the "attack" type of sect or cult is fairly short-lived. It is often true, however, that the conditions from which unstable attacking sects and cults developed do not remain the same. Because of the influence of the religion itself on the members and because of changes in the surrounding society, more stable religious forms tend to appear. Although empirically there is often a mixture of types of response, two basic varieties of religious groups tend to follow a vigorous protest movement: If hope for restoration of an earlier culture and independence fades, the way is paved for a more accommodative religious movement. If, on the other hand, there is a growth in hope, if there is status improvement—perhaps as a result, in part, of the influence of the religious group itself on its members— the transition is likely to be toward a religious orientation close to that of the dominant members of the society; that is, the familiar sect-to-church transition takes place. Further search for greater income and power is carried on by more distinctly economic and political means.

There is no clear pattern of evolutionary stages in this sequence of events. Dramatic social changes and culture contacts may continually create the context for the emergence of new protest movements, as the history of Christianity so vividly shows.

Among American Indians, religious movements have occupied an important place in the search for adjustment to the new world created by the coming of the white man. Military and symbolic efforts to reestablish Indian supremacy were doomed to failure. In several different settings they have been followed by religious movements that emphasized personal salvation, social reform, and peaceful acceptance of the white man, not Indian restoration and hostility to the newcomer. These religious movements have helped to shape the new values and the new personalities needed for life in a society where the old Indian ways were clearly gone (for better or worse). They have served, to use the concept introduced above, a "bridging function." Military defeat came first of all to the Indians in the Northeastern section of the United States, and in this area appeared the first prophets calling for peace, reform, intertribal harmony, and personal morality—often in terms of an interesting Christian-Indian blend.

The religion of Handsome Lake sought to validate a new personality and a new social order. His fellow chieftains were reactionary (in the purely

descriptive meaning of the term—they wanted to re-establish Indian supremacy); but in that direction lay only destruction. His Great Message movement
emerged from the contemporary scene. It was supported—as religious movements must be among Indians, as in so many other societies—by revelation. As
in so many situations, it took a religious movement to supplant a religious
movement, or more accurately, a social system buttressed by religion.

Did the Great Message of Handsome Lake succeed? The answer depends,
of course, on one's definition of success. If one means, Did it allow the continuation of Indian societies in their drastically altered environment, thus
rescuing them from total destruction, and did it give to individuals a new
dignity and self-respect in the context of vast cultural confusion, suffering, and
demoralization? the answer is yes. It served and serves these functions reasonably well.[7]

If one means by success the relatively graceful destruction of Indian societies and the absorption of individuals into the dominant society, the Great
Message of Handsome Lake has failed. But such a test would be to stretch the
meaning of functionalism severely and perhaps to distort it with an ethnocentric bias.

A century after these events among the Iroquois, a similar sequence of
Indian movements developed among the Plains tribes. I have commented
briefly on the Ghost Dance as a religiopolitical effort to recapture the land
from the white settler and to reestablish Indian power. When it was defeated,
there emerged among many of the same tribes the Peyote Cult, a peaceful,
accommodative movement whose most obvious feature is the search for peace
by consumption of the peyote button (a form of cactus) with its narcotic
effects. This religious movement has also served a number of functions for
tribes and individuals: the playing down of intertribal conflicts, union of
Christian and Indian elements, elimination of organized hostility toward the
white man—which in its earlier forms was leading only to destruction—and the
recovery of a system of values. In Spindler's terms, "Identification with Peyote
literally saves the self and gives it sanctions and directives for an integration of
conflicting cultural patterns."[8]

Granted the conditions facing the Indian tribes involved, Peyote permitted a viable adjustment of their cultures and a manageable situation for
them as individuals, while allowing them to continue to be Indians. The alternatives are to fight (either militarily, or in such religious terms as the Ghost
Dance), to give up in the face of culture shock, or to assimilate to the ways of
the white man (if he would permit it).

Many religious protest movements take a different line of development

[7] See Fred Voget, "The American Indian in Transition: Reformation and Status Innovations," American Journal of Sociology, Volume LXII (January, 1957); also Merle
Deardorff, The Religion of Handsome Lake, Smithsonian Institution, Bureau of American Ethnology, Bulletin 149, 1951.
[8] George Spindler, "Personality and Peyotism in Menomini Indian Acculturation," Psychiatry, Vol. 15 (1952), p. 155.

from that of passive accommodation. In terms somewhat overly sharp, one can say: If the protesting group is a subordinate segment of a society rather than a conquered society (e.g., lower-class city dwellers in the United States rather than an Indian tribe), and if, partly because of this fact, they draw their religious protest from the same religious tradition accepted by the dominant group (in contrast to the syncretist movements so characteristic of African Negroes, Melanesian Islanders, and American Indians, for example), then the protest movement will tend to move in the direction of assimilation rather than accommodation. Conflicts with the established order will be abated; the group may become a church.

This is not, of course, a foregone conclusion. Results as various as Methodism and Quakerism (which I will call a denomination or class church and an established sect, respectively) can occur. A central problem in the sociology of religion is the specification of the conditions under which one or the other of these patterns of development will take place. As a merest hint, one might propose the hypothesis that the depth of the original alienation from society represented by the religious protest will strongly affect the course of its development. Quakerism, heir of the radical attacks on English society in the seventeenth century, represented severe alienation. Winstanley's call for political and economic revolution was transposed, although not entirely, into a call for religious "revolution."

As a general principle, those sects develop into churches which from the beginning have emphasized problems of individual anxiety and guilt, with the implication that these lead to social ills. Those that have emphasized social evils first, with the implication that they are the source of individual anxiety and sin, tend to develop into established sects.

Many groups are difficult to classify according to this principle. The Jehovah's Witnesses, for example, seem nearer to seventeenth-century Quakers than to eighteenth-century Methodists, but there are aspects of both. We should also qualify or refine this principle in two ways: It may often be that a religious organization will move from sect to church (from sharp conflict with major social institutions to acceptance of them), but that individual members will not. Bureaucratic processes of accommodation may take place on the organizational level which do not touch the lives of the individual members. They drop out, often to search for another movement which properly represents or helps them to struggle with their sense of alienation from society. On the other hand, an unintended consequence of the teachings, even of the most radically protesting sect, may be to establish values and personality tendencies that lead to success in society, and thus to the likelihood that its norms and institutions will be more fully accepted.[9]

RESPONSES OF A DISPRIVILEGED MINORITY.   The analysis of a sectarian religious movement is strengthened by seeing it not only in the larger

[9] See Benton Johnson, "A Critical Appraisal of the Church-Sect Typology," American Sociological Review, Vol. 22 (February, 1957), pp. 88-92.

secular context but also in comparison with or contrast to other modes of response among the members of the group being studied. The contemporary Black Muslim movement, for example, is more adequately interpreted if we study it in connection with other religious and secular processes among American Negroes. Even a quick glance at the headlines tells us that Negroes respond to their disprivileged status in America today in vastly different ways, ranging from well-disciplined "freedom rides" to utter demoralization. It is difficult to impose a system of classification on the wide variety of activities, but let me attempt to do so by ranging them along two variables: hope and discipline. On the basis of these two variables, one could describe four possible types of religious activity or of functional alternatives to religious activity. There could be movements which expressed neither hope nor discipline, others that expressed hope but not discipline, discipline but not hope, and both hope and discipline.

One can place various contemporary protests among American Negroes in each of the four type positions created by these two variables. This is an obvious oversimplification, but if used with care the procedure may help to clarify the concept of functional alternatives. The accompanying chart shows the logical possibilities and notes groups that approximate them.

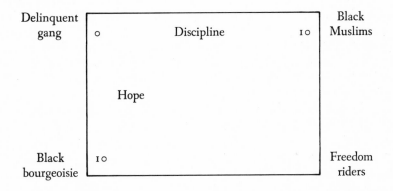

I would like to inquire whether, viewed in this context, two religious movements that seem to be extreme forms of protest do not take on a different appearance. It is possible that, granted the facts of American life today, they represent considerably more constructive developments than alternative roads to salvation.

Delinquent gangs are by no means a monopoly of Negroes, of course, nor even of the disprivileged, but they represent one of the efforts of some boys and young men to struggle with the sense of powerlessness, low status, and frustration. In *Millhands and Preachers*, Liston Pope described the way in which the small sects of the mill workers substituted religious status for social status—the last shall be first. As Albert Cohen has observed, a gang, with its own system of norms and values, can also be seen as an effort to find salvation from a crushing life. From one point of view the values and activities of the gang declare, "If we can't find some sense of dignity and cannot struggle with our most serious problems by means demanded by the dominant community, we will support or create a group whose standards we can meet." The standards of a gang may be not only different from, but in some ways exactly the reversal of, those of the "respectable" community—a drastic contraculture.[10]

In a perceptive account of Negro responses to their status in New Orleans, Rohrer and Edmonson describe the gang, one of their five types of "subcultures," in terms that clearly mark it as a religious substitute. The very grounds of self-respect are lacking for most lower-class Negro men. In the female-dominated families they have no way to learn what it is to be a man. The churches of the community are fatally identified in their minds with white domination and effeminacy. If salvation is not to be found in church, community, or family, it will have to be fashioned *ad hoc*, in terms of the conditions they face.[11]

Granted the conditions that exist—the crushing burden of prejudice and discrimination, the ignorance and poverty that follow in their wake, the unstable, female-dominated family (a heritage of slavery and the discriminations that followed it)—and one can readily see the gang as a "necessary institution," as Rohrer and Edmonson put it. Unhappy as are many of its consequences, by generally accepted standards, it may actually serve to curtail a more abysmal deterioration and alienation. That is about all that can be said for it, however. As a religious substitute it hardly ranks high. For that reason, we should be particularly interested in a slightly more orthodox religious movement that springs from the same vastly difficult conditions. The Black Muslims also draw most of their members from lower-class Negro males, some of them with criminal records, all of them struggling for a sense of dignity in an environment that gives them little help. They emphasize virility and toughness as the gang does. Without such an emphasis they could scarcely appeal to the same kinds of persons. If the hatred they express, the threats of violence, the demands for one fifth of the country, and the extravagant interpretations of history seem both absurd and dangerous, we might be wise to ask what the alternatives are. Should we expect Negroes who have escaped the isolation of the plantation and discovered with their own eyes and ears the promises of a democratic and wealthy society to continue to accept unalloyed otherworldliness? Should we expect them to accept, enthusiastically, Christian churches which are fully implicated in segregation and discrimination? If it is granted that those choices seem unlikely, at least for many, perhaps we should ask whether we prefer the gang pattern, or alcoholism, or drug addiction, or utter demoralization? These may be the only real alternatives to the Black Muslims, or similar movements, for many persons.

[10] J. Milton Yinger, "Contraculture and Subculture," *American Sociological Review*, Vol. 35 (October, 1960), pp. 625-35.
[11] John H. Rohrer and Munro S. Edmonson, (eds.), *The Eighth Generation: Cultures and Personalities of New Orleans Negroes* (New York: Harper & Row, 1960), p. 160.

What I am suggesting is that if you strengthen the gang—or the kinds of persons attracted to the gang—with dreams and discipline, but little hope, you get the Black Muslims. Arm them with hope as well, and you may get the freedom riders. But one finds few freedom riders among the functionally illiterate and deeply frustrated residents of our slums. For them, it is already a long religious step from the gang to the Black Muslims. In the group they are learning to plan, to sacrifice, to share and commune with others. These changes can serve as a bridge to fuller participation in the larger society, despite the explicit attack on that society. Through the Muslim symbolism, the selection of a new name, a new homeland, and a new group identity, deeply frustrated and self-hating persons see some hope of salvation.

We should be careful not to exaggerate the extent to which Muslims break away from the dominant values and even the dominant religious themes to which many of them have been trained. Although the sect explicitly repudiates Christianity—"the white man's religion"—its appeal draws much from the Christian doctrine of rebirth. The ideology is not "otherworldly" in the usual sense, but for all of its castigation of Christianity—and of Negroes who accept it—the symbolism of the Black Muslims is not so far from that expressed by "my home is over Jordan" as it appears at first glance.

From the perspective of the sociology of religion, the Black Muslim movement is the kind of religious protest one would expect in an uprooted, disprivileged group, made suddenly aware both of the American dream and of the forces preventing them from sharing it. Add to this the exciting rise to independence of the African states and the relative indifference of Christian churches to discrimination, and the development of such a vigorous religious protest is readily understood.[12]

But we have said that an attacking sect is soon constrained by the society which it attacks, or it is changed by its own inner development, or both. I think it can be confidently foreseen that the Black Muslim movement will become more accommodative, devaluing the worldly success which it now emphasizes or calling for quiet reform; or it will shift over to culturally more acceptable modes of protest—political and economic; or it will die out. Those members who find life less humiliating and filled with more promise will not want to continue to identify with a group that attacks society too vehemently. Thus the almost certain transformation of the Black Muslims does not mean the end of vigorous and even violent protest movements, often of a religious nature, among American Negroes.

Perhaps this development can be illustrated by a brief reference to the "black bourgeoisie," described so critically by Frazier. These are the middle- and upper-class Negroes who have hope, at least for individual economic and occupational success, but few of the disciplines necessary to take part in a religious or secular movement that struggles with their deeper problems. They

[12] E. U. Essien-Udom, *Black Nationalism: A Search for Identity in America* (Chicago: University of Chicago Press, 1962), pp. 14-15.

still feel isolated, despite their relative economic success, from the society of which they are a part. The discrepancy between their economic standing and their social status is especially galling. They are too sophisticated to accept the extreme otherworldliness of most Negro sects or the "this-worldly escapism" of the Muslims. They are too alienated from the white world, which refuses to accept them even after they have won some of the measures of success, to embrace its religious perspectives. And their accomplishments, having been won for the most part on an individualistic basis, give them no sense of a shared fate from which a group protest might arise. They illustrate a paradox often found in religious matters: they are too well off to believe that they can afford a really demanding religion. The black bourgeoisie, however, are receptive only to an easy religious substitute. Their search for salvation takes the form of a relentless pursuit of recreation and pleasure. Much of this activity centers around poker, which has become much more than a game or a way of winning money.

> In fact, poker is more than a form of recreation; it is the one absorbing interest of Negro "society." . . . The role of poker as a "religious" force in the lives of the black bourgeoisie can not be discounted.[13]

Even in so brief a commentary as this, we cannot disregard another religious movement among Negroes which is significantly different from the secular and religious responses to disprivilege we have discussed so far. Beginning, perhaps, with the "race churches" of the 1930's—those churches in the Northern cities that began to join the protest movement among Negroes—on to the Montgomery Improvement Association (organized at first to obtain the desegregation of the buses in Montgomery, Alabama, but growing to larger purposes), to the sit-in movement, and, most recently, to the freedom riders, there has been a succession of protests that are close to classic Christian sectarianism. Some of these developments are carried forward by groups not explicitly religious in organization, and are doubtless supported by some persons who interpret their actions in nonreligious terms. But there is little doubt that religious influences have been important. In terms of the four types which we described above, the sit-in and freedom-rider style of protest is characteristic of persons who have both the discipline necessary to plan and to suffer and the hope that they can struggle with their deepest problems without escaping or denying the society around them. They believe that the search for salvation need not involve a sharp attack on society and its dominant religion, but only on practices and institutions that are considered to be distortions of the society's basic values.

Who, in a disprivileged minority, will act on the basis of such a belief? I would stress here the subtle interaction of a religious tradition and a social environment. A religious tradition that has encouraged passive adaptation, but has seeds of criticism within it, becomes something new in the minds of those

[13] E. Franklin Frazier, *Black Bourgeoisie* (New York: Free Press, 1957), pp. 211-2.

who are aware of the changes in American society in the last generation, have come in contact with or heard about white persons religiously motivated to eliminate racial discrimination, have begun to climb the educational and occupational ladders, and are encouraged, by religious leaders sensitive to these developments, to reformulate their interpretations of life. In this context, we are not surprised to find a protesting sectarian movement similar to many others that have preceded it in Christendom.

FUTURE PROSPECTS. What can we expect in the future? Will continued alienation from self and society support the growth of religious substitutes, from gangs to poker? Will we see a succession of movements akin in sociological meaning, if not in symbolism, to the Black Muslims? Or will we see a growth in the disciplined protests of the freedom riders, developing perhaps into an established sect, if our formula for this transformation, given above, is correct? The answer to these questions lies, of course, not only in the balance of the functions and dysfunctions of these various movements for the individuals involved and for society. It lies also in the course of development of American society. If we want more gangs or more Black Muslims, we certainly know how to create them; the procedure lies before us in the record of the last several decades. We also can see how to stimulate the growth of the somewhat mores traditional Christian sectarian protests. The one thing we cannot do is to eliminate all of these movements, for they represent the range of endeavor among disprivileged persons to wring some dignity and meaning from life.

45 RELIGION AND SOCIETY: PROBLEMS OF INTEGRATION AND PLURALISM AMONG THE PRIVILEGED

J. Milton Yinger

INTRODUCTION   Although many sects attract persons from the lower socioeconomic classes (*see* Yinger, Article 44), others appeal to a middle class clientele. Personal insecurity coupled with employment dependency, increased wealth, extensive leisure, and bureaucratized life in a mass society profoundly affect these people. The search for the Gospel of the Rich and the Newly-Arrived has led many to religions which justify wealth and alleviate anxiety. Rejecting the world before the world potentially rejects them, these anomic (rootless, normless) people search for new understandings in intellectual, meditative, and contemplative movements. Others find security in the appeal to Old Testament absolutes. Those who claim membership in the Cults and Sects of Reassurance find solutions within their ideological systems. Whether they remain unorganized cultic followers of Norman Vincent Peale and Bishop Fulton Sheen or formal members of such movements as Moral Rearmament, Unity, I Am, or Psychiana, those in need find some comforting patterned answer within the group. Depending upon a high degree of personal and group interaction for the discovery of truth, the seeker finds his hope in the group religious consciousness. Religion thus becomes a creation of its adherents. The typical member is alienated from conventional formal religion, although he remains religiously motivated to search for the truth in protest-type movements.

Two categories of *established sects* (*see* Johnson, Article 11), the Judaistic and the Gnostic, gain the attention of Horton Davies. Each appeals to a substantial middle class group. The Judaistic

Abridged and reprinted from *The Review of Religious Research*, Volume 4, Number 3, Copyrighted 1963, by the Religious Research Association, Inc.

J. MILTON YINGER is Professor of Sociology at Oberlin College.

sects have developed in the attempt to formalize the dynamic of Christianity in legalistic terms. Seventh-Day Adventism, Jehovah's Witness, Mormonism, and British-Israel (belief that the British Commonwealth and the United States are descendants of the ten lost tribes of Israel) are attempts to formalize the teachings of the Old Testament in modern vehicles. Seventh-Day Adventism returns the concept of the sabbath to prominence. Jehovah's Witness looks for the return of the justice of God in the Millenium (the 1000 year reign of Christ). Mormonism reiterates patriarchal ethics and an apocalyptic (prophetic) vision. British-Israel relegates God to the level of an Anglo-Saxon tribal deity.

The Gnostic sects are eclectic, seeking to find common denominators of human experience which may become the foundation of world religious unity. Theosophy, Spiritism, and Christian Science, generally composed of former Christians, appeal to intellectuals and offer instant immortality. Viewing the world as illusory, members offer little interest in social change. Meditation is the prescribed means of salvation. Theosophists seek unifying concepts of reality. Spiritists affirm the doctrine of the Resurrection and the belief in the Communion of Saints. Christian Scientists offer the power of faith as a solution to the sickness of humanity.

The problem of affluence and its effects upon modern religion is analyzed by J. Milton Yinger. Extended life expectancy has changed the focus of religious concern from interpretations of the meaning of death to ideas regarding the meaning of wealth. No longer is religion primarily shaped by concepts pertaining to famine, disease, and death in America, but instead by wealth, leisure, and general social affluence. In the quest for human unity men continue to remain religiously separate.

FOR THE FIRST TIME in human history there are societies within which poverty—a shortage of basic goods and services—is no longer a central fact. Patterns of distribution leave some persons, perhaps even many persons, in poverty in the new affluent societies; but a larger number find themselves in relative comfort. Concomitant changes include the reduction of illness and the lengthening of life, a great increase in mobility, growth of leisure time, increased education, and the extension of contact across group lines. At the same time, many persons in these societies are concerned about loneliness in a sea of acquaintances, meaninglessness in a world of colliding values, self-alienation in a context of contradictory role requirements, and persistently awkward and tense interpersonal and intergroup relations. Illness and premature death, basic subsistence, lack of a position of minimum dignity—primordial problems that still loom large for most of mankind and for the disprivileged in the wealthy societies—are pushed into the background of experience.

Some of the "ultimate questions" with which men struggle religiously spring from the universal human condition—man's finite quality, his capacity for self-centeredness, the tension between his ability to envisage "the fair city" and his inability to travel very far toward it. But closely related to these questions are others that relate to particular societies and particular conditions. And to those who struggle with these latter questions, they seem no less ultimate, no less religious, than those which are universal to man.

Think for a moment how changes in the population facts have affected the context of religion in the last two centuries. Life expectancy at birth in mid-eighteenth century was twenty-five years. In France, for example, Jean Fourastié reminds us, 430 to 440 out of 1,000 lived to marriage age. Half of the marriages reached their fifteenth anniversary. At fourteen years of age, the average child experienced the death of a parent. He was one of five children only half of whom lived to see their fifteenth birthday. Later, as the father of five children, he saw two or three die before his own death, at age 52. He had survived two or three famines, long periods of serious food shortage, and several epidemics that cut down large numbers of persons in his community. "In former times death was in the midst of life as the cemetery is in the middle of the village. Since then, death, poverty, and suffering are retreating."[1]

It is important to remember how recently this situation has changed. For persons in the technologically advanced societies, there has been a revolutionary transformation. Life expectancy at birth is 70 years, not 25. The average person is 42, not 14, when his first parent dies. Where formerly both parents were dead when the youngest child of a family reached maturity, it is now true that the normal couple lives fifteen years after the marriage of their youngest child.

I use these data only to say: the context within which religion is shaped has been suddenly transformed in the affluent societies. If, with Reinhold Niebuhr, we define religion as "a citadel of hope built on the edge of despair," we must note that the despair springs from a somewhat different series of tragedies and frustrations from those that have characterized human experience from the beginning, including, of course, the period when the major religious traditions were shaped.

RELIGIOUS INTEREST AMONG THE PRIVILEGED.   Against the background of change briefly sketched above, let us discuss two religious trends among the privileged members of modern societies with special reference to the United States. Many interpreters have spoken of the growing interest in religion in the very context of apparent secularization. More recently there has been increasing discussion of religious separatism in the very context of ecumenicity. Not surprisingly, both of these trends have been interpreted as paradoxes. It is not always clear, however, which of the various meanings of

[1] Jean Fourastié, "Three Comments on the Near Future of Mankind," *Diogenes* (Winter, 1960), pp. 1-16.

the word paradox is intended. Perhaps most frequently the religious developments are believed to be paradoxical in the sense of a phenomenon with contradictory qualities. But underneath this common meaning of the word, a second connotation often appears: Contemporary religious developments are paradoxical because they are unexpected, difficult to explain, and contrary to received opinion.

The paradox in the first sense—the existence of contradictory trends—already has been carefully examined by many persons. I shall only ask: Are the trends as contradictory as they appear? With respect to the second paradoxical quality of current religious events, we shall study somewhat more carefully this question: Are they actually surprising and contrary to what we might expect from knowledge of social trends and theories of the relationship of religion and society?

Most observers believe that in the last twenty-five years there has been a strong increase in religious activity and interest. I will not ask whether or not the changes "really" represent religious developments, for the asking of such a question usually implies a substantive definition of religion that is too narrow for our purposes. (Only particular beliefs and practices—usually highly traditional ones—are defined as religious. One can then explain away all other developments—happily or unhappily—as merely pseudoreligious.) Briefly, church membership seems to be up from about half of the population over 12 years of age in 1940 to nearly 65 percent today. For the last several years, new congregations have been formed in the United States at the rate of 10,000 per year; in 1960 nearly one billion dollars were spent on the construction of religious facilities.[2] Berger in *The Noise of Solemn Assemblies,* has recently argued that religion has become so deeply embedded in American society that we have to think in terms of an establishment, in a nontechnical sense of the word. And Lenski found, contrary to widely held views concerning the influence of the city and of "Americanization," that the most urbanized and most Americanized segments of the Detroit area population were the strongest supporters of the churches for most groups.[3]

Despite such evidences of growing support for churches and strengthened interest in religious questions, American society is often described as highly secularized. It is not entirely clear, however, what secularization means. There is some tendency to make it synonymous with a decline in orthodoxy or a reduction in the acceptance of traditional beliefs. In such a definition secularization becomes synonymous with religious change. Herberg, in his influential study notes that over four-fifths of adult Americans accept the Bible as the revealed word of God, yet seldom read it and know little of its content.

[2] Truman Douglass, "Ecological Changes and the Church," *Annals of the American Academy of Political and Social Science* (November, 1960), p. 81.
[3] Gerhard Lenski, *The Religious Factor* (Garden City, N.Y.: Doubleday, 1961), pp. 39-50. For a contrary view, emphasizing the continuity of religious influence in the United States, see Seymour Lipset, "Religion in America: What Religious Revival?" *Columbia University Forum* (Winter, 1959).

. . . the religion which actually prevails among Americans today has lost much of its authentic Christian (or Jewish) content. Even when they are thinking, feeling, or acting religiously, their thinking, feeling, and acting do not bear an unequivocal relation to the faiths they profess. Americans think, feel, and act in terms quite obviously secularist at the very time that they exhibit every sign of a widespread religious revival.[4]

In this statement, Professor Herberg implies a standard definition of the concept of secularization—the separation of religious motives, feelings, and decisions from other aspects of life; but he also suggests another meaning—persons acting religiously in a way that does not express directly the faith they profess. These two processes are not the same; and I believe it is a mistake to use the same term with reference to them. It is one thing to have many of life's decisions carried out without reference to religion—the usual dictionary meaning of secularization. It is another thing to redefine one's religion while disguising or obscuring the process by holding, somewhat superficially, to many of the symbols of the earlier religious system. Religious change is usually a latent process, carried on beneath symbols of nonchange. Only if one defines religion statically—the received beliefs and practices are religious, departures from them are not—is it meaningful to think of religious change as secularization. Herberg does not define religion statically. His double meaning of the term secularization derives, I believe, from the fact that he is unhappy about the religious trends—the decline of "authentic Christian (or Jewish) content," and the rise of humanistic and nationalistic themes. He is not quite ready to call the current developments religion; yet his analysis leads him to the conclusion that they are. He resolved the dilemma by using the word "secularization" in two ways, referring on the one hand to religious movements that lack "authenticity" and on the other to the application of nonreligious standards to life.

Peter Berger shows the same dual meaning for the concept of secularization in his interesting book, *The Noise of Solemn Assemblies*. Religious motives, he suggests, are segregated within the religious institution in contemporary America; they are thought to be of little relevance to other aspects of life. Despite the current attention to religion, it scarcely affects the course of the revolutionary developments of the day—urbanization, the transformation of the sexual ethic, business and political processes. Professor Berger then proceeds, however, to describe the ways religion in America today supports American institutions and values. The churches aid the search for "social adjustment" (the pressures to submerge one's own views, to be a "regular guy," to avoid the "dark side of life"). Religion has become so closely related to our political institutions and processes that Berger believes, as we have noted, that

[4] Will Herberg, *Protestant-Catholic-Jew* (Garden City, N.Y.: Doubleday, 1955), p. 15. Herberg has somewhat changed and developed his conceptions of Secularism in his paper, "Religion in a Secularized Society," *Review of Religious Research* (Spring, 1962), pp. 145-58.

we should speak in terms of an establishment—not, of course, in the legal or technical sense, but in the sense of strong mutual involvement of our religious beliefs with our political processes and institutions.

Perhaps Berger's thesis can be summed up in his phrase that religion affirms "the O.K. World." It supports the dominant values and institutions of society.

IS CHURCHLIKE BEHAVIOR IRRELEVANT?   I wonder if it is not a mistake to think of such "churchlike" behavior as irrelevant? It is highly relevant to the process of supporting the basic institutions and values of the society. What Berger, Herberg, and others are saying is that the church has too little relevance for the "prophetic task" of reforming the world. America is highly "secular," in their view, because there is so little tension between the prevailing religious institutions and the secular order. This is the ancient prophetic cry that the church has lost its vision; it has been conquered by society and is useful for little more than sanctifying the social order with its weaknesses and injustices. I do not object to this value declaration in the least—indeed I share a great deal of the view that there ought to be substantial tension between religion and society and nation. Such a view ought not to be used, however, to obscure our analysis of the fact that the churches of those who are comfortable in a society are almost always well accommodated to that society. This is not secularization. It is instead one of the most persistent functions of religion—whether we applaud or lament the fact. Those of us who share sectarian religious tendencies—who want religion to stand in constructive tension with society—need to keep our values fully in view when we speak of secularization. It would not be at all easy to demonstrate that Christianity in 1900 or 1850 or 1800 was more "universal," less bound by class and nation in America than it is today. The church, as contrasted with the sect, works within the structure of the established social order. What is often called secularization today is the inevitable adjustment of the church to dramatic changes in the world within which it works.

Religious research and analysis would be better served by distinguishing clearly between secularization and religious change. If we do so, we will observe, I believe, that American society is not highly secularized. The religious "boom" of the last quarter of a century is not a superficial phenomenon that hides much stronger tendencies toward religious decline. It is just as "authentic," just as "genuine" a religious development as a revival of more traditional beliefs would be. What we are witnessing is the development of new religious forms. The life conditions of the middle and upper classes in our urban societies, so dramatically different from anything mankind has ever before experienced, are having significant religious consequences. The changes are being obscured by the continuity of symbols; they are, quite understandably, opposed by most religious professionals—with the result that much of the new religion is developing at the hands of laymen—but the changes continue nevertheless.

To say that the increasing identity with churches alongside the growth of non-traditional symbols and forms is a religious movement, not secularization, is not to say that one applauds the course of events. I am simply recording the fact that American religious perspectives are changing as society changes. This is precisely what we would expect, among the privileged as well as the disprivileged, from sociological theory of "the church." The alternative to the development of a "cultural religion," as it is often called—a religion that supports and interacts fairly harmoniously with the values and institutions of the society—is not the triumph of some prophetic message, bringing full justice to society. The alternative is some quasi-religion that attempts to perform the function of lending legitimacy to the values of the society. It is well to remember that such a substitute, an openly nationalistic movement, for example, would develop largely in separation from the sectarian dimension of religion that helps to prevent such thorough sanctification of the *status quo* that the dynamic adjustments vital to a changing society are blocked.

If one defines religion statically—in terms of a system of beliefs and practices that emerged at a given time and subject thereafter to no *essential* revision—religious change is nearly identical with secularization. It represents the falling away from the great tradition. If one thinks of religion, however, as an ongoing search, subject to changed forms and revised myths, then lack of orthodoxy does not mean the weakening of religion. It can be a sign of strength.

In short, the increase in religious activity and interest in the very context of supposed "secularization" is paradoxical only to the sectarian, not to the analyst. It is an indication of an expected *churchlike* response to dramatic changes in the conditions of life among the middle and upper classes in a prosperous society. The changes have been fundamental and rapid, as social changes go. One would expect a reviewed and new religious movement to develop in an effort to struggle with the new aspects of the problems of group cohesion and individual salvation.

As stated above, the permanent problems of the human condition remain, so that the new are heaped upon the old, creating a complex religious situation. The catastrophic wars of the last few generations, the vast cruelties of totalitarian governments, the incredible threats of future war make it apparent to even the most insensitive of us that man has won no salvation from premature death, injustice, and the capacity for hostility. These developments also support the religious revival, but less strongly among the laymen in the United States than among religious professionals. Theologians, made sensitive to these tragedies by their heritage, have seen in them a confirmation of their orthodox views. This same heritage has made them less sensitive to the new crises of affluence, mobility, and anomie. If the new religious boom seems shallow in intellectual content, poor in symbolism, and lacking in universality it may be largely because the religious leaders who might overcome these weaknesses are not at home in the urban world and ill equipped by their traditional views to grapple with many of the contemporary religious issues.

THE PARADOX OF ECUMENICAL TRENDS.   Many observers of the American scene speak of another paradox. There are strong pressures toward cultural unity, expressing themselves religiously in the form of denominational mergers, interdenominational councils and cooperation, and other ecumenical activities. At the same time there remain at least three distinctive religious structures which support many separate influences. There is a tendency for Protestants, Catholics, and Jews to live in separate neighborhoods, to belong to separate associations of various kinds, and to insist strongly on intrafaith marriage.

We shall ask if both of these at least partially conflicting things are true. If so, are they paradoxical not only in the sense of a phenomenon with contradictory qualities, but also in the sense of being contrary to what one would expect on the basis of accepted ideas concerning the relationship of religion and society?

THE SOCIAL SOURCES OF CHURCH UNITY.   Lee has summarized in a very helpful manner the wide variety of ways in which the movement toward church unity is expressing itself in the United States. It is taking place in the context of such unifying secular developments as these: the reduction of differences between country and city, the decline of sectionalism, racial desegregation, the compressing of our stratification pyramid, the lessening of the sense of ethnic differences with the sharp reduction of immigration, and the growth of a more completely shared culture as a result of the national communication networks and mobility. Reversing Richard Niebuhr's thesis that sectional, ethnic, class, and racial differences were among the important "social sources of denominationalism," Lee argues that these unifying trends in American society are social sources of ecumenicalism. The variety of ways in which church unity is being expressed is wide: The National Council of Churches, mergers of denominations, local community churches, coordination of activities on college campuses, the use of common literature, and the development of a "common-core Protestantism" are among the most important expressions of unity.

It is readily apparent that the trend toward unity encompasses little outside Protestantism. Even within Protestantism, Lee notes that there are some tendencies toward heightened denominationalism, a continuing separate group of sects, a vigorously anti-unity fundamentalist movement, and the largely separate Southern Baptist Convention. Much of the resistance to ecumenicalism found in these forces can be explained by the continued operation of secular influences that divide on the basis of class, race, and region.

The same explanation—continuing secular differences—is less helpful, however, in explaining the separation of Catholics, Protestants, and Jews, among whom only small evidences of cooperation are found. Secular differences of class, occupation, educational level, and the like have declined. There is no reason, in principle, to expect the social pressures toward unity and ecumenicity to stop at the point where the deeper lines of cleavage have run—the

lines between Protestants, Catholics, and Jews. To be sure, one would expect
more and longer-lasting forces toward secular similarity and unity to be needed
to bridge these deeper and historically more significant lines of cleavage. The
direction of change, however, should be the same if secular differences among
the major religious groups are declining. Most evidence suggests that the social
sources of religious divisions are declining; yet separation remains, in the judgment of many persons, as sharp as ever.[5]

PERSISTENT RELIGIOUS PLURALISM.   To return to the question
of interaction across religious lines in the United States, we must observe that
most students of the situation believe that the distinctiveness of the three subcommunities has scarcely been modified. Among many others, Kennedy, Herberg, and most recently Lenski have emphasized the extent to which Protestants, Catholics, and Jews remain separate in American society despite the
sharp reduction of differences among them on many secular grounds. Ethnic,
class, and regional differences *within* these three groups have been reduced;
barrier to interaction, cooperation, and intermarriage between Irish Catholic
and Italian Catholic, German Jew and Russian Jew, English Protestant and
Swedish Protestant have been reduced. But the three major groups remain
distinctive. In Kennedy's well-known phrase, America has developed not a
single, but a triple melting-pot.[6] The degree of separation is nowhere nearly
as great as that shown by the "columns" of Catholic, Protestant, and humanist in the Netherlands, where separation by residence, education, and work
situation is the rule.[7] Nor does the United States look like Austria, where the
division into Socialist, Nationalist, and Christian-Social Conservative *Lager*
(Alfred Diamont—*Austrian Catholic and the First Republic*) has sharply split
the society for decades. Yet there are clear evidences of separation in the
United States. Lenski wisely notes that we must distinguish the associational
(church membership) aspects of religious groups from the communal aspects
(family, friends, and neighborhood interaction). One may remain strong
while the other declines. Thus Jews have weak associational but strong communal ties with one another. Catholics have strong associational ties, indicated by regular church attendance and widespread acceptance of Catholic
doctrines. Their communal ties are of medium strength. The family is a strong
religious unit, but there is some intermarriage, and Catholics have many non-
Catholic friends. Although neighborhoods are not religiously homogeneous,
there is a strong tendency toward religious clustering in the city and its sub-

[5] *See* James S. Coleman, "Social Cleavage and Religious Conflict," *Journal of Social Issues,* XIII, No. 3 (1956), pp. 47-8.
[6] Ruby Jo Kennedy, "Single or Triple Melting Pot? Intermarriage Trends in New
Haven, 1870-1940," *American Journal of Sociology* (Jan., 1944), pp. 331-9; and "Single
or Triple Melting Pot? Intermarriage in New Haven, 1870-1950," *American Journal of
Sociology* (July, 1952), pp. 56-9.
[7] David Moberg, "Social Differentiation in the Netherlands," *Social Forces* (May, 1961),
pp. 333-7.

urbs. Protestants demonstrate medium strength of both associational and communal ties. Although he recognizes the various tendencies, Lenski summarizes the situation by referring to "our current drift toward a 'compartmentalized society.' "[8]

Although such data seem to challenge the principle of the social sources of church unity (secular differences between Protestants, Catholics, and Jews having been reduced), they may instead simply point to the offsetting influence of other principles. In a mobile and rapidly changing world, we cling rather tightly to our religious subcommunity as one of the few points of stability. Even in less perilous times men hold tenaciously to their religious identity; for one does not lightly revise the way he has learned to deal with his ultimate problems. The strength of religious organizations supports these forces. It is clear, for example, that some aspects of the influence of the Roman Catholic Church are "antiacculturative," as Spiro puts it. Through the parochial school and by other separating procedures, the Church isolates its children from some elements of the dominant culture; it organizes their lives around a somewhat different set of sacred symbols.[9] On the basis of his data from the Detroit area, Lenski holds that the distinctiveness of the Catholic subculture is not being reduced by the shift from immigrant to "old American" nor by status improvement. Middle class Catholics of a third or earlier generation are in some ways more deeply involved in the partially separate community than are lower class first or second generation Catholics.

SOCIAL SOURCES OF RELIGIOUS PLURALISM.   There need to be made, however, two modifications of this description of America's distinct religious groups. In the first place, such differences as exist are still to be explained, to an important degree, not as existing in spite of drastic reduction of secular differences but because of the continuation of significant secular differences. If Richard Niebuhr were to revise his classic study, first published in 1929, he would find no shortage of material to document "the social sources of denominationalism." There are still regional, class, rural-urban, occupational, educational, and ethnic differences among the major religious groups. Prejudice still produces group cohesion. The arrival of large numbers of Catholics and Jews at the third generation in America is not the end of a process of change, but the beginning of a new situation in which memories of one's grandparents mingle with contemporary experiences.

In a highly mobile and changing society, indicators of social status are capricious and unreliable, a fact that encourages some persons to cling tightly to such indicators as are available. This tendency creates one of the strongest obstacles to racial desegregation of neighborhoods, because residential area and house have to substitute for the family connection that marks status in a

[8] Lenski, *op. cit.*, chap. 2 and pp. 326-30.
[9] M. E. Spiro, "The Acculturation of American Ethnic Groups," *American Anthropologist* (Dec., 1955), pp. 1240-52.

stable society. The same influence creates barriers to unity among churches on the local level. One's church in the United States is an important, although not infallible, status indicator. Lee observes that mergers are usually between churches that draw from the same class range; and Underwood (*Protestant and Catholic*) found that Catholic churches in "Paper City" were more class segregated than the Protestant churches. On the national level, interdenominational and interfaith cooperation is strongly affected by the class system, lending support to Berger's statement: "Not only is this 'interfaith' solidarity functional in maintaining the social system as it now exists, but it also has an ideological function as well—namely, it serves to obscure the reality of class segregation. Having participated in the rhetorics of tolerance and mutual good will, one may now harbor the illusion that the social divisions of the society have been superseded by religious solidarity."[10]

In the second place, there is something of a tendency among some writers to exaggerate the extent of separation among the three major religious groups. I will discuss this with reference to one question, interfaith marriage, which can well be considered the most sensitive index of the extent of separation across religious lines. The data, as is well known, are inadequate; but there has been sufficient improvement in the last few years that we can speak with a little confidence. Earlier studies of interfaith marriages tended to emphasize how infrequently it occurred and sometimes to project a trend into the future without any specification of the conditions that inhibit or promote intermarriage. Hollingshead, for example, in his study of a sample of all marriages performed in New Haven in 1948 found that 25.6 percent of Protestants, 6.2 percent of Catholics, and 2.9 percent of Jews had married outside their religious group. He then observes: "From the viewpoint of assimilation, marriages across religious lines are crucial if the triple melting-pot is to become a single melting-pot. But as Kennedy's and our data show, we are going to have three pots boiling merrily side by side with little fusion between them for an indefinite period."[11] It is difficult to see how he arrived at this prediction with data in hand. What would be required to make such a prediction meaningful is a careful specification of previous rates and a study of trends in those social forces believed to be related to the extent of intermarriage.

Kennedy's study, cited by Hollingshead, recorded an increase in religious intermarriage in New Haven, between 1870 and 1940, from five to sixteen percent among Catholics, from one to twenty percent among Protestants, and from zero to six percent among Jews. Although Hollingshead found that the rates for Catholics and Jews were lower in 1948 than in 1940, in her study of the 1950 records, Kennedy found intermarriage rates of 30 percent, 27 percent, and 4 percent for Protestants, Catholics and Jews. These data certainly

---

[10] Peter Berger, *The Noise of Solemn Assemblies* (Garden City, N.Y.: Doubleday, 1961), p. 90.
[11] A. B. Hollingshead, "Cultural Factors in the Selection of Marriage Mates," *American Sociological Review* (Oct., 1950), p. 624.

do not support the statement that there will be little fusion for an indefinite period. We need to ask: What is the effect of the proportion of persons of a given religious group in a society or a community on its rate of interfaith marriage? What happens when economic, educational, and occupational differences among religious groups are reduced? How is the intensity of identification with a particular church, or the degree of orthodoxy of belief, involved? How does prejudice affect the rate of intermarriage? If the intermarriage rate goes up or down, does this mean a change in personal inclination or the recommendations of religious leaders, or does it reflect a change in the extent of housing segregation based on religion, so that more or fewer young persons of different religious training meet?

Keeping such questions in mind, we can begin to hazard a guess about the extent to which religion today enters into marriage decisions and the likelihood that it will tomorrow. The special United States Census study of religion in 1957 found that 21.6 percent of marriages involving Catholics were religiously mixed, as were 8.6 percent of those involving Protestants and 7.2 percent of those involving Jews.[12] Simply to take these figures without examination is probably to underestimate the extent of interfaith marriage. Even if religion played no part whatsoever in marriage choice, approximately 70 percent of Protestant, 25 percent of Catholic, and 4 percent of Jewish marriages would be intrafaith. For the country as a whole, this means about 55 percent of all marriages would be intrafaith and 45 percent interfaith if the religious beliefs of partners were a matter of pure chance. The 1957 census sample found that approximately 12 percent of the marriages were in fact across religious lines at the time of the census. In other words, over a quarter of the "possible" interfaith marriages occurred.

These data, in fact, probably seriously underestimate the intermarriage rate since they do not take into account the effects of change of religion by one or both partners after marriage. If information from one community is a guide, it is important to distinguish between interfaith marriage at the time of the wedding and later. Lenski reports that for the Detroit area sample, 32 percent of the white Protestants and Catholics had married outside their religious group. Only 15 percent, however, indicated that at the time of the interview their marriage partner was of a different faith. Conversion of one partner to the religion of the other was thus common, although we have no knowledge of the strength of the new church identity. We are greatly in need of study of the religious and other consequences of such intrafamily conversion.

There is another reason why the census figures may tend to exaggerate the extent to which religion enters into marriage decisions: they are based on national data that disregard regional, class, educational, and racial differences which affect the results. Tabulate Negro Protestants and white Protestants

[12] United States Bureau of the Census, "Religion Reported by the Civilian Population of the United States: March, 1957," *Current Population Reports,* Series P-20, No. 79, 1958.

separately, and the interfaith marriage rate of the white Protestants is seen to be significantly higher than the total Protestant rate. Negro Protestants doubtless have a low rate of religious exogamy, although I know of no data on this question, because there are relatively few colored persons in other religious groups. Assuming that most persons from the South marry persons from the South, we get a high rate of intrafaith marriage regardless of any influence of religious motives, because of the relative religious homogeneity of the region.

In his study of midtown Manhattan, based on an area-probability sample, Heiss found that 21.4 percent of Catholics were intermarried, 33.9 percent of Protestants, and 18.4 percent of Jews.[13] Although one cannot generalize to other areas from these data, they may indicate what takes place when the three religious groups live in quite close proximity. Among these three groups, 25 percent were intermarried. On sheer chance grounds—that is, if no religious factors were involved—59 percent would have intermarried. To put this in other terms, out of one hundred interfaith marriages that might have occurred, forty-two did occur, and this despite the possible inhibiting effects of differences in race, class, age and sex distribution, and specific neighborhood.

Regarding Jewish exogamy, which is generally the lowest among the three major religious bodies in the United States, Rosenthal reports percentages, for various years from 1953 to 1959, of 11.5 in Washington, 31 in Iowa, 17.2 in San Francisco, and 20 and 37 for two counties in the San Francisco area.[14] These data may give further support to the hypothesis that members of a group are more likely to intermarry, other things being equal, when they make up a small proportion of a community rather than a large proportion.

In the absence of good comparative data for the United States which could indicate changes through time, information from Canada is of value. Between 1927 and 1957, rates of religious exogamy doubled, from 5.8 percent to 11.5 percent. The percentage increase among Protestants was from 5.0 to 11.6, for Catholics from 7.2 to 11.5, and for Jews from 3.0 to 6.8. Intermarriage rates are lowest for a group where it makes up a large proportion of the population of a province. The reduction of association between ethnic group, class, and religion is doubtless involved in the increased rate.[15] Since the Canadian rate in 1957 is almost identical with the rate of interfaith marriage found in the special census in the United States in 1957, it is tempting to assume that the pattern of change since 1927 has been about the same; but the societies are sufficiently different to make that only a guess.

In my judgment the rate of interfaith marriage is higher than is usually noted and the forces that seem to increase it are growing stronger. But the more important question relates to its various consequences. Here our informa-

[13] Jerold Heiss, "Premarital Characteristics of the Religiously Intermarried in an Urban Area," *American Sociological Review* (Feb., 1960), pp. 47-55.
[14] Erich Rosenthal, "Acculturation Without Assimilation? The Jewish Community in Chicago, Illinois," *American Journal of Sociology* (Nov., 1960), pp. 275-88.
[15] David Heer, "The Trend of Interfaith Marriages in Canada: 1922-1957," *American Sociological Review* (April, 1962), pp. 245-50.

tion is even less good. In the many studies of marital success and happiness, for example, there is a tendency to compare the religiously intermarried with the intramarried without attention to other possible differences between them. To say that interfaith marriages have a higher rate of divorce is not to indicate what the causes are. The appropriate question is: Would these same people have had greater success had they married within their religious group? We cannot know this, but we can try to compare them with otherwise equivalent persons who have married within their religious group. Only when two groups similar in class, educational level, urbanness, degree of religious fervor and other personality measures are compared can any observed differences in marital happiness or success be related to religious endogamy or exogamy. Lacking such controlled comparisons, we are left an open field for the operation of value judgments in the research process. I do not imply by this that religious difference is unimportant in marriage. There are grounds for expecting it to be associated with some problems. But research that fails to eliminate the influence of other factors cannot explore the question adequately.

The possible consequences of interfaith marriage for religion are equally important. It is the marginal member of a religious group, not the strongly identified member, who is most likely to intermarry. This may swell the ranks of the unchurched, if casual member marries casual member, with neither interested in taking the lead. It may, however, lead to new religious identities, if the partners move together into new interests. Or it may lead to the conversion of the less concerned partner to the faith of the more concerned. This too, can have a chain of consequences as a group acquires as adults numbers of persons brought up in a different religious tradition. It is not impossible that a broader ecumenicalism than we now can see might be given some reenforcement in a context of extensive interfaith marriage. Or new religious developments, springing from a society where older identities were being obscured might be promoted. These are only speculations on my part offered in the hope that they may help us to avoid the overly easy interpretations of the consequences of interfaith marriage.

And thus I can come back to the theme of this section—the paradox of ecumenicity in the context of continuing religious separation. Both tendencies can certainly be found in the United States today. This makes analysis difficult; but study of social trends and social pressures by the methods of the sociology of religion makes both trends comprehensible. In this sense, there is no paradox.

DYSFUNCTIONS OF RELIGIOUS PLURALISM. Is the continuing separation of American religious subcommunities—to the degree that this exists —a good thing? Is pluralism the best arrangement for a complex society? Are signs of the weakening of the internal cohesion of the traditional groups, intermarriage particularly, unhappy indicators of a loss of strength and fervor? For the most part, those who take a liberal view of American society support religious pluralism. Distinctive religious traditions, all free to develop in their own ways, are essential to the religious quest and to a democratic society. To the individual they represent freedom and yet a significant tie to his own heritage. To the society they represent the kind of competing points of view that help to maintain flexibility, because there is no official religion to give undue sanctity to our imperfect human institutions. The liberal view would only add that the separate religious groups should not be thoroughly separate communities, distinctive in occupation, class, region, and ethnic origin, as well as religion, because such piling-up of differences leads to serious conflict. It is best when the members of each religious group are dispersed through the geographical, class, and occupational systems.

There is some conservative challenge to this view. Some Catholics believe that a genuinely healthy society and full individual salvation are possible only when all men have returned to the one true church. Most Catholics who take this view have learned patience in the American scene, indicating a kind of qualified acceptance of pluralism. Some Protestants look upon Catholics and Jews as at least slightly un-American and wonder why they are so recalcitrant in becoming Methodists or Baptists or Presbyterians.

Now I am much closer to the liberal than to the conservative view. I am not, however, entirely happy with pluralism as it is usually described and would like to comment on some of its possible dysfunctions. In a period of such dramatic change as man is now experiencing, the need for new ideas and new actions—including religious ideas and actions—is enormous. Most of us are religiously lazy. We take part in the search for new political forms, new economic ideas, new ways to build our cities, new technological processes, but our conceptions of religion are static. This distinction should not be drawn too sharply, of course. One need only mention the continuing use of the ideas of Thomas Jefferson and Adam Smith to indicate how difficult it is to sort out the universal from the local and temporary in government and economics as well as in religion. These giants are complex mixtures of the contemporary and the outmoded in economic and political affairs. The tendency to use them as fully adequate guides today demonstrates that it is not only religion that needs to be "demythologized," to use the current term.

But our concern here is with religion, and I think one can argue that emphasis on distinctive pluralistic traditions implies a measure of religious stagnation and isolation. The best way to justify continued separation is to point to different origins, histories, and traditions. To some degree, American religious groups are like our Indian tribes: they lose their liberals to the "secular" world, because the emphasis on preservation of distinctiveness is inherently backward-looking. The churches "boom" in this day of upsetting change and continual crisis; but the messages they preach are tuned to an earlier time, so the people are "secularized"—indifferent and unbelieving and religiously ill-informed—even while they participate in the "boom."

Viewing this situation, I certainly would not want to take an antipluralist position, to argue in favor of some one religious orthodoxy. A unified church would all the more surely be conservative and static; and in view of the great heterogeneity of people in a large society, no one religious view is able to reach all the people.

CONTEMPORARY VS. HISTORICAL PLURALISM.   Is there any way out of this dilemma? A possible road is suggested by introducing the concept of "contemporary pluralism," in contrast to the more familiar "historical pluralism." The latter might be briefly defined in these terms: Preservation of ties to the religious community (and ethnic group—for some of the same questions arise in this area) of one's parents is good; respect its traditions; a free society must encourage this in the name of tolerance, flexibility, and individual freedom. There is more than a little nostalgia and sentimentality connected with this idea. These qualities are often heightened by those professionally identified with a group, whose preservation as a distinctive entity is necessary for their professional existence. They are also heightened by persons working in the field of inter-group relations and other liberal-minded individuals who, again with generous motives, support and encourage group-identity as a way of developing mutual respect and tolerance.

Historical pluralism may be crucial and valuable in one period and not in another. At a time when the development of pride and self-confidence and feelings of identity to something smaller than the baffling, complex, total society are important, historical pluralism may contribute to religious growth and a strong relationship between religion and society. But to continue to promote religious and ethnic separation in a new context, when the tie to the earlier situation has been broken, may be unwise. Perhaps the necessary pluralism today is not a process whereby each of us binds his children to the ancestral religious groups, while teaching them to respect the rights of others who are different. Perhaps we need to open up interaction and choice among several contemporary efforts to struggle with the human condition, each a hybrid, each a product of religious contact and growth.

This point is made somewhat more easily with respect to ethnic groups and perhaps I can clarify my argument by a brief reference to this related question. In Hawaii, for example, many people say: Won't it be a shame when there are no longer distinctive Chinese, Japanese, native Hawaiian, and other communities and subcultures? For myself I doubt that the decline of distinctive subcommunities is unfortunate. A dynamic view of life and society sees this decline as inevitable. Contemporary life cannot be carried on by the preservation of styles, however dignified and intrinsically important in their points of origin, in vastly different contexts. What would be unfortunate would be the loss of contributions from each of the now declining communities to the new heterogeneous and varied culture of modern society. Choice and variety for the individual and flexibility for our systems of belief and action are perhaps a higher ideal than choice and variety among traditional groups.

We cannot cling to the culturally and religiously integrated patterns of the past. If we think we are doing so, we hide the loss of their vitality and the emergence of competing systems of value (nationalism as a religion, for example). The inherent rigidity of historical pluralism obscures the new problems faced by men today, for which we need vital contemporary religious thought and action.

There is less pressure on privileged people to revise their received religions than on the underprivileged. They are more likely to support a religious revival than a reformation. This means that if great new issues arise, as a result of dramatic changes in the life of man, the churches of the privileged are not well equipped to deal with them. Subterranean religious movements develop; quasi-religions appear. Perhaps careful study of this fact can help, in some small measure, to make it less probable.

46 RELIGION IN A SECULARIZED SOCIETY: SOME ASPECTS OF AMERICA'S THREE-RELIGION PLURALISM

Will Herberg

INTRODUCTION   America faces the paradox of increased religious participation on one hand and heightened secularization on the other (*see* Herberg, Article 43). No longer do
Americans read the Bible to the same extent as their forebearers,
although the Bible continues on the best-seller list. Seminaries
have been forced to revise curricula, recognizing that even students entering the ministry possess limited knowledge of Biblical
content. "Church shopping" has replaced denominational loyalty
with loyalty to the pleasing ministerial personality. The oft-quoted
statistics that 95 percent of all Americans believe in God, 60–75
percent believe in the life to come after death, and 66 percent annually read some portion of the Bible testify to the general nature
of American religiosity (*see* Vernon, Article 4). The King James
Version has given way to other Biblical versions which suggest
some potential variations from traditional beliefs (for example, the
belief in the Virgin Birth). The inner-directed personality (the
person who acts upon internalized values) has been challenged
by the other-directed organization in which the group determines
the values (*see* Seidler and Ravitz, Article 18). The sabbath, formerly a day of rest, has become the day of general recreation and
professional athletics. Social welfare responsibility has been transferred from the church to the state. Religious participation in education has been further reduced by the Supreme Court decision
that recitation of group prayer *under state sponsorship* now constitutes a violation of the Constitution.

Various changes have ushered in a new American religious

Abridged and reprinted from *The Review of Religious Research*, Volume 4, Number 1,
Copyrighted 1962, by the Religious Research Association, Inc.

WILL HERBERG is Graduate Professor of the Faculty of Drew University.

understanding. Although known as a Christian nation, America is only Christian in the sense that it adheres to a predominant Christian formal belief system which the state either upholds or ignores as conditions demand. *Selected* religious values are accepted as social values. Arguing that religion is a personal matter, many Americans have accepted a secondary religious system fostered by the group which largely ignores explicit religious training, tradition, and heritage. While dogmatic religion has faced a decline, religious influence has to a degree become institutionalized in the state (*see* Introduction to Part VIII). The denominational supporter has increasingly become a marginal man in the American system.

One result of the religious revival and ensuing secularization (*see* Yinger, Article 45) has been the tendency of Americans to seek social identity through loose identification with a generalized religious community. Religion is equated with democracy in this framework. Denominational variations are minimized at the expense of tripartite religious unity. Ethnic subcommunities have given way to religious subcommunities. Dogmatism has yielded to social tolerance. Religious norms no longer fully inform modern culture (*see* Hammond, Article 9, and Lenski, Article 36). The concept of American religion, formed within the Protestant tradition, encompasses and yet minimizes distinctive religious traditions in the name of national unity. There are those who question whether this religion any longer is religion, or whether it is a mere prop of the existing state.

THE BASIC FACT defining the contemporary religious situation in this country is the transformation of America, in the course of the past generation, from a Protestant nation into a three-religion country. It is necessary to examine somewhat more closely the nature of this transformation, and its concomitant circumstances.

Writing just about thirty years ago, André Siegfried described Protestantism as America's "national religion," and he was largely right, despite the ban on religious establishment in the Constitution. Normally, to be born an American meant to be a Protestant; this was the religious identification that, in the American mind, quite naturally went along with being an American. Non-Protestants felt the force of this conviction almost as strongly as did the Protestants; the Catholic and the Jew experienced their non-Protestant religion as a problem, perhaps even as an obstacle, to their becoming full-fledged Americans; it was the mark of their foreignness. In a very real sense, Protestantism constituted America's "established church."

This is no longer the case. Today, to be born an American is no longer taken to mean that one is necessarily a Protestant; Protestantism is no longer the obvious and natural religious identification of the American. Today, the evidence seems to indicate, America has become a three-religion country; the normal religious implication of being an American today is that one is either a Protestant, a Catholic, or a Jew. As I have already suggested, these three are felt, by and large, to be three alternative forms of being religious in the American way; they are the three "religions of democracy," the "three great faiths" of America. Today, unlike fifty years ago, not only Protestants, but increasingly Catholics and Jews as well, feel themselves to be Americans not apart from it, or in spite of, their religion, but in and through it, because of it. If America today possesses a "church" in the Troeltschean sense—that is, a form of religious belonging which is felt to be involved in one's belonging to the national community—it is the tripartite religious system of Protestant-Catholic-Jew.

SECULARIZATION AND RELIGIOUS GROUP TYPES. The sociology of secularization has been widely discussed, and many attempts made, since Troeltsch, to relate degree of secularization with organizational type. Professor Harold W. Pfautz has suggested a series of five organizational forms, in order of increasing secularization, as follows: the cult, the sect, the institutionalized sect, the church, and the denomination. Understanding by secularization the widening gap between conventional religion and operational religion, there is much to be said for this series of organizational types. I think, however, that the present-day American situation suggests certain qualifications and elaborations.

The cult, to begin with, seems to exhibit the lowest degree of secularization possible in modern society. For the member of the cult fellowship, there is a minimum distinction between conventional religion, operative religion, and existential religion, though it may be noted that in this country cult members are sometimes members of established denominations as well. The cult is not so much at war with the world and its ways as outside of them.

Cults suffer a high degree of mortality. If a cult survives, it becomes a sect, and undergoes the familiar sociological changes in size, leadership, associational structure, and the like. The sect follower has already advanced on the road to secularization, but it is hard to say how far since the sect too is not very stable. Sooner or later, it either disappears, or else develops into something quite different: in Europe, it generally became a church; in this country, however, the line of development has been toward the denomination, which in America, has come to mean something quite distinctive. A variant is the institutionalized, or "established," sect.

In the strict Troeltschean sense of the term, this country has not had a church since colonial times. Denominationalism became the established religious pattern in the wake of the great revival movements; and in denominationalism we have a further and very advanced stage of secularization. For denominationalism, in its very nature, requires a thoroughgoing separation between conventional religion and operative religion, and this is the mark of secularization.

The denomination, as we know it in this county, is a settled, stable religious body, very like a church in many ways, except that it sees itself as one of a large aggregate of similar bodies, each recognizing the proper status of the others in legitimate coexistence. The denomination in America is not at all the "nonconformist sect" that it is in Europe; or rather, it is the "nonconformist sect" become central and normative. It differs from the church in the European acceptation of the term in that it would never dream of claiming to be the national ecclesiastical institution; it differs from the sect in that it is socially established, thoroughly institutionalized, and nuclear to the society in which it is found. So firmly entrenched is the denominational idea in the mind of the American that even American Catholics have come to think in such terms; theologically, the Catholic Church, of course, continues to regard itself as the one true church, but in their actual social attitudes American Catholics, hardly less than American Protestants or American Jews, tend to think of their church as a kind of denomination existing side by side with other denominations in a pluralistic harmony that is felt to be somehow of the texture of American life.

Obviously, the denominational system implies the emergence of a "common religion" distinct from the conventional religion of the denominations, for without such a "common religion" the society in which the denominations find their place in mutual legitimation would hardly be able to hold together. Denominational pluralism, on the American plan, means thoroughgoing secularization. The movement from sect to denomination is a movement of rapid secularization. Economic prosperity and cultural advance appear to exert a double effect: on the one side, they impel better advantaged members of the sect to leave the sect and join a recognized denomination; on the other side, they tend to raise the entire sect in the sociocultural scale on the way to denominational status.

The first movement is difficult to document since it is composed of millions of unrecorded personal or family decisions; yet every observer is well aware that it is going on. As to the second movement—the elevation of the entire sect to denominational status—the evidence is easily at hand. Such great denominations as the Baptists and Methodists in this country came out of sects; and somewhat later, the Campbellites, against their own intention, gave rise to the Disciples of Christ. Because it emerged so late, the Disciples became only a small denomination by American standards; the field had already been well charted out by the others.

Exactly the same process is taking place before our very eyes today. The Nazarenes, over a large part of the country, are indistinguishable from small Protestant denominational churches. The Assemblies of God have their liberal arts colleges and graduate schools of religion; their men's associations, their women's councils, and their Sunday schools; their publicity, promotion, and public relations agencies, including an international radio program. But the most astonishing illustration is provided by the Jehovah's Witnesses. The Jehovah's Witnesses would certainly seem to constitute the model sect group: a "disinherited," "outsider" group, militant, growing, arrayed against the culture and its values, promoting a typically sectarian ideology. Yet in a recent issue of a Witnesses journal, there appeared an article on "How to Dress Well." In this article, the Witnesses are told that neatness is the first requirement, that they should never wear a patterned sports jacket, with patterned slacks, that shoes and socks should complement, not clash with, clothes, and other such bits of esoteric wisdom. This article, I think, is of immense significance. It shows several things: it shows that large numbers of Witnesses are now able and eager to dress well, but simply do not know how since they come from strata of society where such things are not learned at the mother's knee; it shows also that the Jehovah's Witnesses leadership is very much concerned that they learn what they want to know, and in general that Witnesses learn to fit into lower-middle-class suburbia and be accepted by it. Obviously, the sectarian "outsider" stance is beginning to give way, some of the values of the culture at least are being accepted, and others will be at an accelerating rate. Jehovah's Witnesses do not yet constitute a denomination, not even in the sense in which the Nazarenes or the Assemblies of God do; but the Witnesses are on their way, and the way is the way of growing secularization.

This way leads from the cult, to the sect, to the denomination. With the denomination, secularization reaches its most advanced stage. But, in the American system, denominations have their groupings within a scheme of mutually legitimated coexistence: specifically, they group themselves into the three great socioreligious subcommunities known as the "three great faiths." We can thus carry the series further: *cult-sect-denomination-socioreligious community.* Despite denominational rivalries at top administrative levels, American Protestants and American Jews—Catholics do not enter the picture here since their "denominational" lines are within the one church—American Protestants and American Jews, especially the younger people, are becoming less denominational-minded, tending to identify themselves as Protestants or Jews rather than by denominational labels, choosing where they can "united" or "community" churches, or converting existing churches along such "non-denominational," "ecumenical" lines. This process—in which denominations are increasingly being articulated within the religious community—seems to be already well under way.

Now I want to get back to the trifaith system. What I should like to suggest is that, whereas America does not have a church in the Troeltschean sense as an organized institution, America does possess an overall religious entity that corresponds to the Troeltschean church, and that is the trifaith system of Protestant-Catholic-Jew. This is the kind of religious belonging that today, normally and naturally, goes along with being an American; it is, in a real sense, the nation on its religious side.

If there is any truth to this view at all, it would seem that there is still a further stage of secularization beyond the religious community. The series can now be completed: *cult-sect-denomination-socioreligious community-trifaith system*. Beyond this, secularization cannot go. In the trifaith system, conventional religion and operative religion have been almost completely separated and almost completely syncretized.

THREE-RELIGION PLURALISM AND RELIGIOUS GROUP TENSIONS.   The transformation of America from a Protestant nation into a three-religion country has also exerted a far-reaching influence upon the patterns of religious group tension in this country.

It is my contention that the transformation of America from a Protestant nation into a three-religion country, along with the concomitant upward movement of the Catholic population in the sociocultural scale in the course of the past generation, has had a double effect: in the short run, it has tended to exacerbate and sharpen Protestant-Catholic tensions; in the long run, however, I think, the very same process will tend to alleviate these tensions and mitigate their sharpness. And this duality of operation is closely connected with significant generational differences in outlook and attitude.

It is not difficult to see why the processes we are considering should make for a certain exacerbation of tensions. Protestants in this country are now faced with the prospect of the loss of accustomed status. The mass of the older Protestants have had their attitudes formed in an America that understood itself as a Protestant nation; the country, in a very real sense, was theirs, belonged to them, was their home. Now, within one generation, their own generation, the country has, almost literally, been taken away from them, to be parcelled out among the "three major faiths": what was once their own home they are now being compelled to share with two interloper groups. No wonder they feel dispossessed; no wonder they feel threatened. There was a time, not so long ago, when the middle-class Protestant in this country hardly came across a Catholic in those community institutions and organizations that really counted. Today, the Protestant, wherever he turns in community life, confronts Catholics on every side; no wonder he is convinced that Catholics have multiplied enormously and are taking over the country, whatever the statistics may say. Once, too, the general American institutions were simply Protestant institutions. Protestants did not need any separate organizations of their own, because the general community organizations and institutions were Protestant and obviously theirs. Jews and Catholics, on the other hand, and incidentally Negroes too had begun their very existence in American life as minority groups, requiring special institutions, organizations, and agencies to represent and protect them, and these institutions, organizations, and agencies they rapidly built up. Today, Protestants, in most parts of the country, can no longer take the general community institutions for granted as theirs; but (aside from the Negro group) they have not managed to develop any significant institutions of their own, or at least did not get to developing these till very late. As a consequence, they frequently find themselves at a great disadvantage and are very resentful at the "separatism" of the Catholics and Jews, whose institutions they denounce as "divisive" and "un-American."

Where the older Protestants are faced with the grave threat of loss of accustomed status, American Catholics, on their side, are exceedingly anxious over their newly acquired status in American society; they are status-anxious. They feel that their recently achieved status as Americans, and as good middle-class Americans, is not being adequately acknowledged by the older masters of American society, the Protestants; and they therefore tend to be belligerent and resentful. They are suspicious and touchy, easily tempted to self-assertiveness and to gross overcompensation. But, above all, they feel hampered and closed in, denied their proper recognition; they see themselves ever anew threatened with exclusion and segregation. They therefore tend to develop what the editor of the *Christian Century*, to match the "Protestant paranoia," has called "Catholic claustrophobia."

Aside from these quasi-clinical designations, it is not difficult to see why, in this transition period from a Protestant to a three-religion country, there should be a certain exacerbation of Protestant-Catholic tensions, and of Protestant-Jewish tensions, too, in those places where Jews have made a sudden appearance in significant numbers in an older Protestant community. But, by the same token, there is every reason to expect an alleviation of tensions in the longer run.

We already have sufficient evidence to suggest that there are significant generational differences in attitudes that relate to religious group tensions. Younger Protestants tend to take a very different view, and to respond very differently, from the older members of their group; and this is true, though not so markedly, for the younger Catholics as well. It is well known, for example, that on the so-called "Jack Kennedy" question, which the Gallup organization has been asking for the past twenty years—I mean the question: "If your party nominated a generally well-qualified man for the presidency this year, and he happened to be a Catholic, would you vote for him?"—the younger voters have uniformly taken a far less anti-Catholic attitude; and this attitude they have tended to retain as they have grown older, so that there is a marked long-range trend in the same direction. Whereas in 1940, 31 percent of the respondents answered "no"—they would *not* vote for a Catholic, even though he was a well-qualified man and a member of their party—by 1956, the proportion had fallen to 22 percent. In that year (1956), the "no" vote was 31 percent for respondents 50 years of age and over, 17 percent for those between 30 and 49, and only 14 percent for those between 21 and 29. This pattern is borne out by every other available bit of information, including community studies.

Again, it is not difficult to see why this should be so. The younger Protestants have not had their attitudes formed in an America that was a Protestant nation, but rather in an America that was emerging as a three-religion country; consequently, they do not feel particularly dispossessed, threatened, or overwhelmed. On the contrary, to them Catholicism is a legitimate part of American religion, one of the "three great faiths," while Catholics are just good, middle-class Americans, an integral part of the American people. The response one gets from these younger Protestants—I am thinking of a community survey of a New England town not yet published, a town once entirely Protestant, now about half Catholic—the response one gets from these younger Protestants is something sociologists ought readily to understand. It runs something like this: "What's all the excitement about? So they *are* Catholics! But they're our kind of people, and after all, we're all Americans, aren't we?"

As Catholics become more obviously "our kind of people," and equally Americans with the rest of us, as American opinion becomes more and more defined by the generation that has grown up in a three-religion country, the group tensions that now disturb us will tend to allay. This would appear to be a safe prognostication.

It seems worth noting, I think, that this analysis of Protestant-Catholic tensions proceeds without any reference to the social and religious issues that are alleged to divide the two communities. This is not because I regard these issues to be of no importance; on the contrary, I think they are issues of great importance, which deserve careful consideration on their own account. But I do not believe that they are so much the source of the tension as the expression of it. They become issues precisely because they arise in an already established context of tension and become vehicles of this tension and antagonism. Moreover, even though they have become issues in Protestant-Catholic conflict, they are not usually questions on which Protestants are aligned all on one side, and Catholics all on the other; on the contrary, on every one of these questions there are differences and divisions within both communities, with sizable minorities in each group crossing the lines.

However that may be, it will be observed that the better relations emerging between Protestants and Catholics are grounded in the "common religion" of American belonging—"After all, we're all Americans!"—and its predominance over the conventional religions of the three groups, not in opposition but in comprehension. In other words, the promising alleviation of religious group tensions would appear to be due to the advancing secularization of American life and religion. However we may feel about secularism, this should be noted and appreciated. It is the advanced state of secularization in the three-religion pluralism of contemporary America that is the decisive factor in the emergence of better religious group relations in this country.

Yet there is another side to the story, which may not be ignored. If, for the great mass of Americans, the new tolerance is a by-product of the emerging solidarity of the secularized "common religion," for a small group of theologically concerned people, something very like it comes from the opposite direction. Of recent years, we know, there has been a rapprochement, in America as in Europe, between theologically concerned Protestants and Catholics, even between theologically concerned Christians and Jews, precisely as a consequence of their theological concern. It is not the "common religion" of the American Way that binds them; it is rather their common Christian, their common Biblical, faith and understanding. Indeed, suspicion of the American Way as a substitute-religion serving Americans as their ultimate context of meaning and value is a common premise. Whereas, for the great mass of Americans, the operative formula is "After all, we're all Americans," for the theological elite, it would run something like, "After all, we're all Christians, standing on the same Bible," or where Jews are included, "After all, we acknowledge the same God and recognize in Abraham our common father in the faith." The two attitudes are often confused under the vague rubrics of "tolerance," "unity," and "ecumenicity"; but they are very, very different and ought to be carefully distinguished.

The intergroup situation in this country at the present time is thus a very complicated one. There is a significant sweep toward better understanding as a result of extensive secularization at one end, and of a theologically oriented reaction against secularization at the other. In between are masses of Americans caught in the grip of the transition from the old America to the new, from the Protestant nation to the three-religion country, and driven to fear, hostility, and a kind of defensive aggressiveness as a result. For completeness, we ought to mention small groups of anti-religious secularists and self-styled "liberals" who find in anti-Catholicism a more viable, and even more respectable, form of antireligion. As Peter Viereck has well pointed out: "Catholic-baiting is often the anti-Semitism of the liberals." But these elements are dwindling, and the prospect is definitely for a steady improvement of intergroup relations among the religious communities. And largely this is the result of increasing secularization, either directly, or indirectly by way of reaction.

THREE EMERGING GENERALIZATIONS.   How shall we evaluate the sweeping secularization of American life and religion? No theological assessment will here be attempted. But there are certain things that will occur to every serious observer of American religion who has reflected on recent developments.

Secularization, which has been advancing at an increasing pace in Western society ever since the high middle ages, has taken a special and characteristic form in the United States, reflecting the special and characteristic pattern of acculturation of the many diverse groups of immigrants who have come to make up the American people. First, the emergence of the well-known system of multidenominational pluralism; then, the recasting of American society in terms of the socioreligious community, in which the denominations are typically grouped: these are the two major phases of the structural development of American religion since the early nineteenth century. Each of these phases marks a further stage of secularization.

The restructuring of American society along the line indicated has transformed America from the Protestant nation it has been since its beginning into a new kind of socioreligious entity—a three-religion country, in which social identification takes place by way of religious belonging. This transformation has obviously had far-reaching consequences, which are by no means all of one piece.

1. Religious belonging has become a mode of defining one's American identity. In this way, the two great non-Protestant religions—Catholicism and Judaism—have acquired American status and been granted a place in the three-religion system. Catholics, Jews, Lutherans, and others, who remember how formidable an obstacle to the preservation and communication of their faith the taint of foreignness once was, will not be altogether ungrateful for what has happened. And all Americans may be thankful for the new spirit of freedom and tolerance in religious life that the emergence of the tripartite system of the three great "religions of democracy" has engendered; it makes increasingly difficult the sinister fusion of religious prejudice with racist or nationalist chauvinism. But these gains have come out of a thoroughgoing secularization of religion, in which conventional religion—Protestant, Catholic, and Jewish—has been integrated into the "common religion" of the American Way and made to serve a nonreligious function. As a result, American religiousness has been growing increasingly vacuous—a religiousness of belonging, without religious commitment, religious concern, or religious passion. To many religiously concerned people, this seems a very high price to pay.

2. Religious belief today tends to be assimilated to the ideas and values of the American Way. The conventional religions—Protestantism, Catholicism, and Judaism—are typically understood as variant expressions of the "Common faith" which all Americans share by virtue of their participation in the American Way of Life. Consequently, religion enjoys a high place in the American scheme of things, higher today, perhaps, than at any time in the past century. But it is a religion thoroughly secularized and homogenized, a religion-in-general that is little more than a civic religion of democracy, the religionization of the American Way. Here, too, the price may be a very high one to pay.

3. Religious group relations in this country, despite a certain exacerbation for the moment, seem headed for a very considerable improvement in the foreseeable future. Every American will welcome this prospect, and will welcome it without qualification. But again, it is coming largely, though not entirely, as the consequence of a secularizing evacuation of conventional religion. The price here, too, is a heavy one.

It is not my purpose to draw any balance sheet. All I have attempted to do is to call attention to certain aspects of the secularization of religion in contemporary America that may help illumine the paradox with which we began our discussion, the paradox that America is at once the most religious and the most secularistic of nations. I hope it is now possible for us to see in what way this paradox is true, and what this paradox has come to mean for the social and religious life of America.

47 TRENDS IN CHURCH MEMBERSHIP IN THE UNITED STATES

Benson Y. Landis

INTRODUCTION   Religious groups have continued to grow in membership ever since 1776. Much of the increase has been due to immigration, but the growth has also been enhanced by conversion of native sons. Although accurate statistics documenting this growth are unavailable, estimated church membership in the 1780's numbers less than ten percent of the population. Sixty to seventy percent of the population now claim membership in some church of their choice, although an even higher percentage assert some religious identity or church "preference." Part of the numerical increase is due to relaxed membership requirements, changes in membership definitions (such as children being counted as members by some groups), and generally inaccurate statistical reporting.

General statistical information shows that Protestants are underrepresented in the Northeast and overrepresented in the South. Jews and Catholics, on the other hand, show strength in the Northeast. Jews comprise a religious plurality in New York City. Catholics claim a majority in New England, New Jersey, Illinois, Louisiana, Michigan, New Mexico, Arizona, Montana, and California. Baptists constitute a majority in Georgia, South Carolina, Mississippi, Tennessee, and Alabama, while also maintaining strong influence in most other southern states. Mormons hold the majority in Utah and Idaho. Lutherans dominate in Minnesota, North Dakota, and South Dakota, while Methodists are predominant in Ohio and Delaware. Not too surprisingly, most

Abridged and reprinted from *The Annals*, Volume 332 (November, 1960), pp. 1-9, with the permission of the author and editors.

BENSON Y. LANDIS is Editor of Research Publications for the National Council of Churches of Christ in the United States of America.

Jews and nearly seventy-five percent of the Roman Catholics live
in metropolitan areas. Over fifty percent of the Protestants reside
in nonurban areas (in small towns or the open country).

Measurement of religious *influence* is always hard to deduce
from the analysis of membership statistics. Because no accurate
figures are readily available for analysis, exact information concerning the modern religious revival is largely nonexistent (*see*
Petersen, Article 6). However, data concerning American religious
groups indicate that more than ninety percent of all church members are found within eighteen established denominations of more
than 1,000,000 members. It is still true, in any case, that quantitative data cannot reproduce information concerning religious vitality. Those who attack the superficiality of American religion and
charge that preoccupation with mere membership statistics may
be deceptive may also fail to appreciate the effect that more than
314,000 churches, synagogues, and temples may have. Although
American social life may revolve around the semireligious concepts
of the American Way of Life (*see* Herberg, Article 46), local religious institutions often possess greater vitality and integrating
power for individual members than normally assumed by critics of
modern religious groups.

A T NO TIME in American history have more people or a greater proportion
of the people been affiliated with religious bodies. Statistics supplied
by the current *Yearbook of American Churches* reveal that 109,557,741
persons, or 63 percent of the total population of the United States, are affiliated in 251 religious bodies. The *Yearbook* is a reference work compiled and
published annually by the National Council of Churches, New York. Its reports indicate membership totals mainly for 1958 or for a twelve-month period
ending in 1958. Statistics were gathered from the forty-nine states and the
District of Columbia.

REPORTS FROM ALL FAITHS.   Reports come from all faiths and are
sent to the *Yearbook* by the statisticians of the religious bodies. With the exception of the Church of Christ, Scientist, all the religious bodies in the
United States appoint persons to gather figures from their local congregations
or parishes. The Church of Christ, Scientist, reports that it has a rule forbid-
ding the compilation of its church membership as well as the reporting of such
figures for publication. It does report the number of branches throughout the
world, 3,200, a figure published in the *Yearbook of American Churches* for
1960.

The *Yearbook* reports "the latest information" that is available from the
headquarters of the religious bodies. Many denominations, however, do not
publish figures annually. The information published in 1960 includes figures

for probably more than half of the local parishes or congregations for the year 1958. A few of the reports are for the year 1936. Others are for recent years prior to 1958. These exceptions notwithstanding, the data officially reported to the *Yearbook* does account for all but a relatively small percentage of the persons claimed as members by the religious bodies.

WHAT IS A RELIGIOUS BODY? The religious bodies for which the *Yearbook* has reported figures during recent years are virtually the same as those listed in the *Census of Religious Bodies*, 1936. Although the term religious body, or denomination, has never been strictly defined, the *Yearbook* lists those bodies which have been generally accepted through the years as separate denominations. These are characterized by more than one local unit, by a program broader than that of a local church, by a denominational literature, and by some method of ordaining or licensing clergy or leaders. There are many informal fellowships or associations that are more or less religiously oriented which are not regarded as denominations. These are not listed. The *Yearbook* also does not list groups commonly regarded in the United States as cults. And a few very small sects are omitted because documentary information is impossible to obtain.

The number of local churches reported by the 251 religious bodies was 309,449. This number refers to local organizations. It does not take into account buildings or houses of worship. The number of local church buildings has not been compiled in recent years. In the *Census of Religious Bodies*, for 1906, 1916, 1926, and 1936, the number of local churches which reported buildings of their own consistently was about 90 percent of the total number of churches. According to annual estimates made by the United States Department of Commerce, there has been a marked rise in expenditures for new religious buildings since World War II: from $251,000,000 in 1948 to $935,-000,000 in 1959.

MEMBERS PER LOCAL CHURCH INCREASING. The average membership of the local church has been increasing for all religious bodies. Since 1926, the number of members per local church has increased about 50 percent: from 235 in 1926 to 354 in 1958.

Among the 251 religious bodies reporting statistics for 1958 there were 82 with memberships of 50,000 or more. These had over 98 percent of the total church membership. Thus there were 169 bodies with constituencies equal to only about 2 percent of the total membership.

Data on age groups, sex, occupations, and attendance are seldom recorded locally and are not reported nationally by the religious bodies. It is also not reported what proportion of the members counted contribute money to their churches, or in what ways members are involved in local church life.

STATISTICS NOT STANDARDIZED. Can comparisons be made between the latest information and earlier statistics? What can be said about trends? Between 1890 and 1958 there were thirty compilations of church membership. Five of these were made by the Bureau of the Census according to standardized methods. The other compilations were made by the *Christian Herald,* a periodical published in New York, and by the Federal Council of Churches and the National Council of Churches. The National Council has compiled the latest information annually since 1951.

The federal religious censuses were made by means of standard forms mailed to the pastors and clerks of local congregations. The figures were summarized by denominations and were distributed by states, counties, and cities. The *Census of Religious Bodies* for 1926 is generally regarded as the most adequate book on church statistics ever published in the United States. The 1936 statistics were much less satisfactory. The Bureau of the Census stated that the census for that year was "incomplete." It seems that about 20 percent of the local churches did not report to the Bureau even after a series of requests. The number of local churches recorded by the census was about 20 percent lower than the number reported that year to the *Christian Herald,* which had collected figures in various previous years. The 1946 *Census of Religious Bodies* was begun but never completed owing to the refusal of Congress to make an appropriation sufficient for the project. In 1956 no recommendation was made to Congress by the administration concerning the matter, and no member of Congress appears to have been sufficiently interested to raise a question about it, and no official of a religious body appeared before a congressional committee to request an appropriation for the purpose. Officials of religious bodies have occasionally made representations to the Bureau of the Census regarding the value of these projects.

As the censuses between 1906 and 1926 indicate, there has been a tendency on the part of some religious bodies to report on a more inclusive basis in the later as compared with the earlier years. Thus some of the alleged gains reflect in part changes in the method of reporting. It would appear, however, that there have been no major changes in the basis of reporting since the year 1926.

WHAT DEFINITIONS OF MEMBERSHIP?   Since the year 1926, the following seem to be the bases on which memberships are reported. The Eastern Orthodox Churches include all persons in the nationality or ethnic groups being served. The Jewish congregations regard as constituents all Jews in communities having congregations. The Roman Catholics count all baptized persons, including infants. Most Protestant bodies count only the persons who have attained full membership, and previous estimates have indicated that all but a small percentage of these are over thirteen years of age. The Lutheran bodies and the Protestant Episcopal Church, it should be noted, report all baptized persons rather than only those who have been confirmed and have attained full membership.

Another factor affecting membership statistics is the high mobility of the people during recent decades on local church records and record keeping. This is hardly documented at all. Church affiliation is a formal matter, and when people change their residences their local church affiliations are not automatically changed. Many persons moving from rural to urban areas have been commonly observed to retain their memberships in the rural churches for considerable periods. The same situation has recently been noted when people move from suburb to suburb, or from city to suburb. It may not be unusual, as a suburban minister recently remarked to the writer of this article, for a church to have 900 members on its rolls but not to have a mailing address for 200 of them.

Finally, about seventy religious bodies, including some that are large, have been reporting their memberships in round numbers which appear to be estimates.

SOME COMPARISONS.   Because of the nature and the limitations of the data, a discussion of trends must be done with recognition of the inadequate sources for strict and direct comparisons.

In general, religious affiliations reported have been increasing more rapidly than the population. For example, total church membership as officially reported in the *Yearbook of American Churches* for 1960 has been estimated to include 36 percent of the population in 1900 and 63 percent in 1958.

Considering only the statistics of the larger groups, and referring as bases to the federal religious censuses of 1906 and 1926, some comparisons can be made.

In 1906 there were 35,068,058 members of bodies of all faiths, of whom 14,210,755, almost 40 percent, were Roman Catholics. In 1958 there were recorded in the *Yearbook* 109,557,741 persons of all faiths. Of these, 39,509,-508, or 36 percent were Roman Catholics. Protestants in 1906 numbered 21,-040,835 persons, or almost 60 percent of the total of 35,068,058 persons as members of all faiths. In 1958 Protestant Churches reported 61,504,669 persons, or 56 percent of the total of 109,557,741 members of all faiths. In 1906 the number of persons neither Catholic nor Protestant was reported to be only about one half of 1 percent of the total. During the interval the marked gains were registered by the Eastern Orthodox, who reported only 129,606 constituents in 1906, and 2,545,318 in 1958. The Jews, who reported only heads of families in 1906—101,457 persons—reported 5,500,000 persons in 1958, an estimate of the number of all Jews of all ages in communities having Jewish congregations. Both Roman Catholics and Protestants reported smaller proportions of the total religious affiliations in 1958 than in 1906, both being less by approximately 4 percentage points.

Over a shorter period, 1926 to 1958, the following comparisons can be made. Protestants numbered 31,511,701 persons in 1926 and were 27 percent of the total population of the nation. In 1958 Protestants numbered 61,504,669 and were 35.5 percent of the population. Roman Catholics numbered 18,605,-

005 in 1926, 16 percent of the population; and 39,509,508, or 22.8 percent of the population, in 1958.

For the period since 1950, we find that the Roman Catholics numbered 27,766,141 in 1950, according to the *Official Catholic Directory*, and 39,509,-508 in 1958—a gain of over 42 percent. Protestants, according to reports in the *Yearbook of American Churches*, numbered 50,021,960 in 1950 and 61,504,-669 in 1958—a gain of 23 percent. Thus the gains of the Roman Catholics have been generally more rapid than those of the Protestants since the year 1950.

TRENDS IN GROWTH.   "The more conservative groups have had greater success in enlisting members than have the more liberal groups,"[1] observes Richard C. Wolf, Associate Professor of Church History in the Oberlin Graduate School of Theology. For seven years Professor Wolf studied changes in American religious life. The article compares the 1906 statistics of church membership which appeared in the *Census of Religious Bodies* with statistics of fifty years later as reported by the religious bodies themselves.

During these fifty years the estimated population increased almost 100 percent, while the officially reported church membership of all bodies in 1956 —100,162,529—represented a gain of about 190 percent over the 1906 figure of 35,068,058, which is the corrected figure published in the 1916 Census. In 1906, 186 denominations reported; in 1956, 258 reported.

The increases in membership in the large bodies and the large families of bodies have been pronounced. In 1956, eleven denominations and families of denominations, each with over 1,000,000 members, reported 92 percent of all Christians; in 1906 these eleven bodies and families of denominations had 90 percent of all Christians. There were sixteen Baptist denominations in 1906, and twenty-six in 1956; fifteen Methodist bodies in 1906, twenty-one in 1956; twenty-four Lutheran bodies in 1906; eighteen in 1956; four Eastern Churches in 1906, eighteen in 1956. Professor Wolf concludes that neither merger nor division seems to have a "definitive role in denominational growth." Nor does he find the growth explained by the type of organization or by the type of program. Considering the eleven large bodies and groups each with 1,000,000 or more members in 1956, and arranging them by rate of growth and by "theological mood," Professor Wolf finds that the more conservative bodies report by far the largest gains.

EXAMPLES CITED.   Some examples of denominational growth should be cited. In the fifty-year period, the Churches of Christ, the Latter-day Saints, the Lutherans, the Baptists, and the Roman Catholics reported gains much above those of the Presbyterians, Methodists, Disciples of Christ, and the Congregationalists.

[1] Richard C. Wolf, "Religious Trends in the United States," *Christianity Today,* April 27, 1959.

The Southern Baptists report a gain far in excess of the American Baptists, formerly the Northern Baptists. The Lutheran Church, Missouri Synod, reports a gain above that of the United Lutheran Church. The Presbyterian Church in the United States, often called the Southern Church, reports a gain in excess of that of the United Presbyterian Church in the United States of America.

Adventists, Brethren, and Mennonites give figures showing gains far above those of the Friends, Universalists, and Unitarians.

Roman Catholic gains are below all of the following: consistently conservative Lutheran bodies, the Latter-day Saints, the Baptist bodies generally, the Churches of Christ, the Mennonites, and the Adventist bodies.

Professor Wolf concludes in these words: "Admittedly such statistical study cannot say anything precise about the relative impacts which the various denominations have made upon the nation's religious life. Nevertheless the study has value in the degree to which it throws light on some trends which have marked the American religious community, especially the Christian segment of that community, in the first half of the twentieth century."

VARIOUS INTERPRETATIONS.   Two additional sources on religious affiliation should be noted: a church distribution study and a survey of a sample of the civilian population conducted by the Bureau of the Census. Data from 114 religious bodies for the year 1952 were published in a series of eighty bulletins entitled "Churches and Church Membership in the United States" by the National Council of Churches. These bulletins revealed a total membership of 74,125,462 persons in 182,856 local churches in the 114 religious bodies cooperating. Roman Catholic and Jewish figures were included along with figures for many large Protestant denominations. The large Negro Protestant bodies as well as many others, totaling 137 in number, were not studied because the figures were not obtainable for states, counties, and cities on a comparable basis. This study brought out significant differences between the metropolitan and the nonmetropolitan areas. Fifty-seven percent of the people of the nation lived in metropolitan areas, according to the 1950 Census of Population. In these areas were found 46 percent of the Protestants included in the study and 75 percent of the Roman Catholics and all but a small percentage of the Jews. Forty-three percent of the people lived in nonmetropolitan areas. These included 54 percent of the Protestants studied and 25 percent of the Roman Catholic membership. On a regional basis, comparing denominational strength with population distribution, the Protestants were strongest in the South and weakest in the northeast; the Catholics were strongest in the northeast and weakest in the South.

A RECENT SURVEY.   On February 2, 1958, the results of a voluntary inquiry appeared under the title *Religion Reported by the Civilian Population of the United States; March 1957.* Two out of every three persons fourteen years of age and over reported themselves as Protestants and one out of every four as Roman Catholic. More women than men were reported for the major religious groups. Ninety-six percent of the respondents reported a religion; 3 percent stated that they had no religion; and 1 percent made no report on religion. It was found that the more rural the community, the higher the proportion of Protestants; the more urban the community the higher the percentage of Roman Catholics. About 100,000 persons were included in the sample. Figures were stated to be not comparable with the reports of the religious bodies, because the latter included only formal affiliation, while the survey of the population asked simply about religion.

48 CURRENT TRENDS IN RELIGION:
A SUMMARY

Richard D. Lambert

INTRODUCTION   The wave of religious optimism sweeping America at the turn of the century has been superceded by a more realistic and moderate outlook. The missionary Student Volunteer Movement, for example, which sought to win the world for Christ in one generation, has been replaced by localized attempts to establish more modest grass-root religious commitments. Richard D. Lambert, sociologist, traces the new direction of religion. The declining support of intellectuals, emphasis upon bland piety, attempts at revisionist theology, decline of ministerial candidates, enhanced participation by the laity, adaptation of business methods to church financing, and institutional merger and unification are all products of the new order.

Attempts to meet social and institutional change have resulted in creative experiments and suggestive ideas. Protestants have recently cooperated in the formation of an Urban School in Chicago at which selected ministers spend several weeks in training among the people of the inner-city community. Realistic experience results when a minister-student takes the "plunge" and is set free in a poverty area with a limited amount of money and instructed to live incognito in the community for two or more days. Middle-class-oriented ministers find that such experiences shake their concepts of the traditional ministry. Moves toward the formation of cooperative inner city ministries have developed among Protestants as in the New York East Harlem Protestant Parish and the Cleveland Inner City Protestant Parish. Started as experimental ministries, these cooperative endeavors have served as experimental sta-

Abridged and reprinted from *The Annals*, Volume 332 (November 1960), pp. 146-156 with the permission of the author and editors.

RICHARD D. LAMBERT is Professor of Sociology at the University of Pennsylvania.

tions for the adjustment of rural-based Protestant religion to an urban setting.

One of the more interesting recent proposals, although similar to a proposal suggested by Washington Gladden in the late nineteenth century, is the formation of interdenominational, community or city-wide churches. Stephen Rose, a Presbyterian minister writing in *Renewal* magazine, suggests the abolition of traditional denominations in order to form regional cooperative ecumenical churches. In effect, Rose suggests the elimination of national ecclesiastical systems, replacing them with community-oriented religious institutions. Because denominations have become bureaucracies, the service work of the church has been hindered. Role conflicts could be eliminated by dividing ministerial candidates into three categories of pastors, teachers, and leaders of social reform. Although all would undergo seminary training, only the pastors would be ordained. The cooperative ministry, Rose argues, would renew the mission and outreach of Protestantism, replacing "routinized 'ecumenical' theology" with genuine ecumenical dialogue. In future generations, the Church would be known not as Methodist, Episcopal or Baptist, but instead as the "Church in Chicago, the Church in New York, the Church in Boston." Although it seems improbable that this form of ministry will readily develop, denominations already are forming similar team ministries among their constituents in major cities of the United States.

THE PURPOSE OF the present article is to present in capsule form the main arguments and viewpoints which emerge from the fuller treatments in the earlier articles.

First, how many people are involved in church activity in our country? Table 48-1 presents data from the decennial census on the number of people who return clergyman as their occupation. It also contains a set of comparisons of the number of church members and the total population per clergyman and the proportion that clergymen represent in the economically active section of the population.

TABLE 48-1   Clergyman in United States, 1910-1950.

Census Year	Number in Thousands	Church Members Per Clergyman	Total Population per Clergymen	Clergymen Per 1,000 Economically Active
1910	118	326	779	3.2
1920	127	380	832	3.0
1930	149	394	824	3.1
1940	141	457	934	2.7
1950	171	507	881	2.9

It will be noted that there was in 1950 one clergyman for every 507 church members and for every 881 persons in the population at large. The number of clergymen has not increased as fast as church membership, nor has it increased as fast as the general population or that portion of the population which is economically active. The increasing number of lay church members per clergyman is both a result of the increasing size of congregations concomitant with the urbanization of America and of the decline in recruitment for the ministry in the face of competition from other professions.

Table 48-2 contains the estimated changes in the number of people who are members of religious bodies for the same decennial census years.

TABLE 48-2   Total Membership in United States Religious Bodies, 1910-1950.

Census Year	Number in Thousands[a]	Percent Total Population Members	Percent Population Aged 13 and Over Members[b]
1910	38,497[c]	41.2	55.0
1920	45,251[c]	45.6	54.1
1930	58,754[c]	47.8	53.4
1940	64,502	48.9	50.7
1950	86,830	57.6	63.7

a Source: "Membership of Religious Bodies: 1890-1957," *Historical Statistics of the United States* (Washington, D.C.: United States Bureau of the Census, 1960), p. 228.
b Source: Michael Argyle, *Religious Behavior* (London: Routledge and Kegan Paul, 1958), p. 28.
c Estimated for these years by straight line interpolation between religious census years.

Landis, in his article for this issue, reports that there were 251 distinct religious bodies in 1958 with a total membership of 109,557,741 members equivalent to 63 percent of the population. It will be seen from column two that the percentage of the population of the United States which was claimed by the religious bodies as members had increased steadily since 1910. Religious figures are notoriously inaccurate as a result, at least in part, of the differences in the definition of church membership over time and among denominations. But one disturbing factor is removed from the calculations in column three. By restricting the comparison to those who are over thirteen years of age both among church members and in the population, we correct both for the aging of the United States population and for the varying practices in reporting children as members. We note from this comparison that church affiliation declined mildly from 1910 to 1940 and then took a spectacular jump after 1950 which gives every indication of continuing to the present time. The correction for age makes the mid-century religious revival even more spectacular.

AUTHENTICITY.   The fact of this revival has been amply documented and discussed. What is surprising is the almost unanimous suspicion with which it is greeted. Ahlstrom reflects the attitudes of the vast literature on the subject when he frowns upon the "pious utilitarianism," the peace of mind cults, the contentless faith in faith, the bland conformity in the upsurge of popular piety. But Ahlstrom describes another aspect of the revival which he considers more durable and more valid, namely, the increasing religious trend of the intelligentsia. This reverses the ecclesiastical malaise of the nineteen twenties and thirties when intellectuals tended to consider religion one of the least worthy forms of irrationality and to believe that man's relationship to the universe was a scientific, as distinct from a theological, problem. During the nineteen forties and fifties theologians have vigorously reentered as scientific specialization has tended to withdraw science from the broader stage. The two streams of popular piety and intellectual resurgence are antipathetic, an antagonism reflected in the almost uniform disdain which intellectuals among the clergy heap upon the instrumental, circumscribed piety which they observe as so characteristic of the American public today. This expression of clerical disapproval of popular religion is, in a way, the price paid by the clergy for freeing itself from the onus of the Scopes trial and the Babbitt image. More importantly, though, it reflects a conflict between the desire of our religious "middlemen" to attend to their relationship with God and the demands of the public that they attend to their relationships with their clientele.

THE CLERGY AND THE LAITY.   The relationship between the clergy and the laity is full of contradictions and imprecision. Differences in the sanctification of the clergy and the power of the clergy over the lives of the laity lie at the heart of the classic institutional contrasts among denominations and religions. Kane begins his article on "Church and Laity Among Catholics" by saying, "The Roman Catholic considers his Church a divinely instituted organization founded by Jesus Christ." Later he indicated that "A priest is a sacred minister empowered through Holy Orders to celebrate Mass, administer the sacraments, to preach, and to bless." Harrison points out in his article "Church and Laity Among Protestants" that "only a comparatively small number of churches, largely confined to the Lutheran and Episcopal traditions, are willing to abide by this hierarchical principle." And elsewhere, quoting from Charles Kean, he writes, "The priesthood of all believers refers to the priestly character of the Church as a whole from which individuals both clerical and lay derive a common priesthood." Sklare, in his article on "Church and Laity Among Jews," notes that "According to Jewish tradition identical behavior is expected of the layman and the rabbi. . . . The rabbinical office derives from a distinction—the gulf between the learned and the ignorant." In practice, however, the three great traditions are moving closer together. Among Catholics, while the priest remains the key figure in the parish, the role and status of the laity in religious affairs have been rapidly increasing. Among

Protestants, "Whenever the authority of the layman is raised, 'the finger of an exclusively priestly voice and authority is immediately raised also.'" Among the Jews there is "a growing distinctiveness between the functions of the layman and the rabbi. The addition of pastoral, priestly, clerical, and several other roles serves to transform the rabbi into a clergyman and the nonprofessional into a layman."

All three groups, then, have a new balance of power in clerical-lay relationships. This new balance is, in part, a result of the disappearance of the monopoly of education by the clergy. But, to a greater extent, it arises from what Harrison, quoting Philip Selznick, calls the "organizational imperatives" of religious life in America which are common to Catholics, Protestants, and Jews alike. The very size of the enterprise, the repetitiveness of the activities, the large number of functionaries involved at all levels of the religious endeavor impel religious organizations to take on a bureaucratic form, and the needs of this form of organization become primary ends in themselves, often taking precedence over the stated goals which the organization is dedicated to serve. This is a phenomenon by no means limited to religion, but its growth is made easier by the fact that the religious enterprise does not measure its success by objective standards. In business, monetary success provides a ready scoreboard by which organizational efficiency can be measured. There is no way in which a religious bureaucracy can measure in quantity or quality the piety it has generated among its followers. It is not surprising that several authors have remarked upon measures borrowed by churches from the field of business. Many churches have adopted the concrete measures of success such as the sumptuousness of the buildings as an indicator. And they count the number of their adherents in the manner of a Trendex rating. The numerology of membership, like its prototype, pays little attention to the attitudes among the audience so long as the audience is captured regularly.

FINANCIAL PROPORTIONS.   The magnitude of the endeavor contributes to the impression that religion is big business in America. For new church construction alone, Americans spend close to a billion dollars annually. To this sum must be added salaries and maintenance for the church physical plant, the cost of seminaries and other educational institutions and hospitals, funds for missionary projects, and the unaccounted ancillary enterprises such as the production of Bibles, vestments, periodicals and tracts, rosaries and religious medals, and the like. The sum becomes staggering. Leach reports that for a congregation of five hundred people the cost of real estate and architectural and landscaping fees alone will be at least four hundred thousand dollars. In addition to this there will be an annual operating budget ranging from twenty to fifty thousand dollars.

Unlike other institutions of comparable size, however, churches in America have few ways of guaranteeing a regular income. Their product, if such a term may be used, operates in the worst buyers market imaginable. Churches cannot enforce the payment of dues as a labor union can. They do not enjoy the coercion available to the state in its taxing power. Although tax exemption may lighten the costs to some extent, nothing is thereby added to income. The traditional way of financing the church—real estate ownership—today provides some income, but most churches in America are making payments on the mortgage rather than collecting rent. Since church income depends, then, upon voluntary contributions—which, at best, fluctuate widely—it is not surprising that religious institutions seek to employ all the pressures they can command to regularize and maximize their income. They must do so under an embarrassing ethic which treats monetary affairs as slightly defiling for spiritual preceptors. And they must be cautious lest too gross an assault on the clientele will defeat its purposes. As a result of the continual hunger for funds, local churches must devote a considerable portion of their energies to promotional activities. Consequently, as Harrison remarks, the church appears to many of its members to reach them only in financial drives. This impression is deepened by the increasing use of the professional fund raiser whose techniques have a depressing sameness whether he is speaking in the name of an American Legion post, a church, or a political party.

Two tendencies are noticeable in the pursuit of funds. One is, as Leach remarks, a "growing effort" to find some new scheme which can produce the money necessary without the tiring work of personal visitations." The second is the attempt to regularize the flow of income with annual budgets, prorated pledges, and weekly envelopes for all members styled along the lines of installment buying. In view of all this, the cost accountant can be seen to achieve the same dominance he is coming to enjoy in so many other areas of American life.

THE NEED TO EXPAND. The constant need of the local church for funds to carry on its present activities is at war with the built-in institutional imperative to expand both its membership and its functions. The competition over membership figures is notorious. To some extent the comparative figures reflect different conceptions of what makes a member. The Roman Catholic Church and some Episcopal and Lutheran bodies consider all baptized children as bona fide members whether they become active in church affairs as adults or not. Those religious bodies whose definition is primarily ethnic, such as the Jews and the Eastern Orthodox, enumerate all members of their ethnic or cultural group who reside in a community where there is a congregation. Most Protestant groups count only those who have, by their own volition and maturity, accepted full membership in the church. The attention given to the size of membership and to its constant expansion derives to some extent from the evangelical mission of the church. A correlative to that seems to be that the validity of the message and the effectiveness of the clergy somehow depend upon the number of adherents, particularly new adherents. There are some groups for which this is not true, particularly the ethnic churches, where proselytizing is at a minimum. Here the emphasis is upon drawing the ethnically-defined clientele into fuller participation and upon preventing its assimilation into other denominations. It is also true that some churches, particularly in suburban areas, are disturbed by the large numbers of uncommitted persons who fill the pews but remain outside the organizational reach of the church. The way Jewish temples have adapted themselves to this circumstance is interesting. They realize a part of their income through the sale of seats for the few annual rituals at which participation is almost compulsory.

All religious groups extend their organizational boundaries by encouraging the formation of satellite lay organizations which are church-based but primarily fraternal, educational, or recreational in their interests. The combination of these three interests with the doctrinal message is the most characteristic organizational form in American religion. The dilemma this poses for the church is mentioned by Harrison, who quotes Thomas Bennett. "The congregations become one more organizational activity. They make the same demands upon the behavior of people as do other organizations in society."

EDUCATION IN RELIGION.   The most important of these secondary organizations and the ones most closely related to the churches' principal purpose are the educational institutions. Hunt tells us that about 42 percent of the United States population between the ages of three and eleven is enrolled in Protestant Sunday Schools. About four million Catholics and 350,000 Protestants are enrolled in full-time, church-related elementary and secondary schools. Almost half the Jewish children of elementary school age receive instruction in Jewish schools. Some 80 percent receive "some Jewish schooling at some time during school age," usually for three or four years. The number of people of all denominations who receive some formal religious instruction attests to the demand for such services from the American public, but the proper relationship between religious and secular education has been a vexed one throughout American history. The question has been "settled" many times only to become unsettled again. The current resolution whereby religion is something to be added to a hard core secular education, whether by released time or an occasional school period or the ritual of morning prayer or any other device, is subject to constant negotiation. The infusion of religion throughout the curriculum is practiced only in the church-related schools and even there the insertion of religious doctrine into a subject like trigonometry is most difficult. No one argues for a return to the days when religious instruction was the sole function of organized educational institutions. Nor does anyone argue that churches do not have a right to utilize the organized educational process through which all of our young must pass for the propagation of religious ideas. The argument is over who shall pay the bill. The current debate wears the linguistic garb of an ideological dispute over the separation of church and state. Sometimes the relative primacy of the parent as against the state is drawn into the argument. Its essence, however, is graphically demonstrated by such an uncivil exchange as that between Cardinal Spellman and Mrs. Roosevelt over the provision of funds. We are back, then, in the area most essential to church survival. The California electorate recently defeated a threat to withdraw tax exemption from Catholic schools. There is constant Catholic pressure for support of such ancillary services as school buses, lunches, and medical care. These are cases in point which illustrate that behind the debate lies the fear that one side or the other will gain an advantage in the interdenominational wars for membership.

CHURCH JURISDICTION.   Where the jurisdiction of any set of social institutions overlaps with other social institutions, there is a jousting for supremacy. This may involve business and government, family and the educational system, or it may involve the church in relation to all of these. The least formal of the disputes is the sovereignty of the church over the family, and the denominations differ widely upon the extent to which family affairs are considered within their domain. The variation ranges from rather detailed family canon among the Catholics to celebration of minimal rites of passage and the provision for mediation in cases of family discord among some Protestant groups. The interlocking of education and religion has already been discussed. In the areas where religion and business impinge upon each other, church efforts have been generally confined to a rising tide of books and pamphlets aimed at raising the ethical level of business transactions.

Under the aegis of the social gospel, many of the clergy have felt impelled to promote policies which they interpret as the embodiment of the ethical principles in their religious code. This call carries the cloth into many a reformist battle where the immediate relevance of religious doctrines has not been altogether clear to the laity. Their ventures into secular policy can, for the most part, be identified with the liberal viewpoint. Racial equalitarianism remains almost the only surviving issue for liberalism today. As Lee points out, this, more than any other issue, tears at the cleric in numerous ways. The position of his denomination and his personal position as well frequently are at sharp variance with the sentiments of his congregation, which are strongly felt and anti-integration. The members of his congregation are armed with powerful sanctions. They may withhold financial support, boycott the church, or request a new pastor if he strays too far beyond the parochial culture of his parishioners. The churches are uneasy in the face of this issue. The uneasiness reflects not only genuine ambivalence among the clergy but also an awareness of the pressures which the laity can potentially use against the clergy. Generally, the effective limits to the adventures of the clergy in public policy are those cultural limitations which characterize the laity and those views from which the laity will not be parted. Few clergymen pursue a course beyond those limits. A surprisingly large portion of clergymen, in view of the limitations, have taken positions on integration which are far in advance of their congregations.

AREAS OF CONTROVERSY.   The most controversial institutional overlap of the churches with secular affairs is in the field of politics. As Ebersole points out, until recently the impact of religion on politics was primarily a matter of pressure brought to bear in specific issues about which the Protestant clergy felt strongly. The outstanding examples of such issues are prohibition and the abolition of slavery. Perhaps Washington felt more beleaguered in the heydays of the Women's Christian Temperance Union and the Anti-Saloon League, but many church groups retain well-staffed lobbies in the capital today with a view to exerting pressure over specific issues. In the nineteenth century, Catholicism was important as a primary target on the national political scene for the nativist parties such as the Know-Nothings and the American Protective Association. On the local scenes, the ethnic vote, much of it Catholic, contributed to the success and durability of the political machines in the metropolitan areas of the northeast and spawned a tradition of ethnic and religious distribution of appointive posts. Since the short-lived party of Bishop Hughes in 1841 which swung the balance between the Whigs and Democrats in New York, there has never been an avowedly Catholic party. Nonetheless, the expression "the church" in politics refers to the influence of the Catholic hierarchy upon the political opinions of their laity. This takes several forms in operation. The most conspicuous are the church pronouncements on legislation which the church considered directly related to dogma. The issues which generate the most conflict with other denominations concern the prohibition of information, particularly birth control information, and the censorship of entertainment considered immoral by an official of the church. As in the Holyoke incident of 1940 and the bitter political campaigns in Massachusetts of 1942 and 1948, these matters strike Protestants as unjust interferences by the church into politics and as a denial of civil liberties. Ironically, the Catholics in Massachusetts were working to prevent the repeal of a birth-control law, a law which had been passed in 1869 at the urging of the Protestant clergy. Catholicism has entered politics less directly in the second type of issue wherein the strength and interests of the church are involved. Such issues, in the main, relate to public support for Catholic education and vary in scope from local school board fights to the United States Congress where dispute was generated by the Barden Amendment to the Federal Aid to Education Bill (HR4643). A third type of issue concerns unofficial church support for a variety of political views such as opposition to right-to-work laws or support of strong anticommunist legislation. The church stand on these issues often is indistinguishable from the stand of a broad section of the general public. On such issues the church is at its least organized and is probably among the least effective of the interested political pressure groups.

All of the issues mentioned above come to focus in the current debates over the Catholic vote and the submission expected of Catholic office-holders to church discipline. Most politicians operate upon the assumption that Catholic voters will tend to choose a Catholic candidate over a non-Catholic candidate. The current drift of opinion seems to indicate that the Catholicism of a candidate is always significant for Protestants in the more fundamentalist bodies. It gains significance for others if there is an issue related to religion in the campaign. By and large, Catholicism does not currently seem to be an insurmountable handicap, and possibly, on balance, it could become an asset.

SURVIVAL. One of the most enduring generalizations about religion in general is that it is the most resistant to change of all institutions. It is for this reason that most major religious changes throughout history have come about through conquest or revolutionary upheaval. Significantly, though, Kane remarks that "The truly great asset of the Roman Catholic Church is her ability to adapt to changing times without altering the repository of faith and morals." We can be sure that the adherents of other denominations would claim as much for them. This juxtaposition of conservatism and flexibility shows up in the attempts of various churches to adapt to the rapidly changing culture and environment of America today. Among the most far-reaching changes is the decline in importance of such older centers of loyalty as geographic locale and ethnic affiliation which were the rocks upon which the churches were built in America. The rigid boundaries formed by these differences nurtured denominational separateness and provided the churches with clienteles already defined. The more recent great mobility of the American people and the blurring of ethnic lines has produced what Marty refers to as the loss of the diagrammatic effect or the spatial metaphor for defining community and communication. Marty suggests that the growth of sects is a "reaction against the erosion of spatial settings." The set provides the comfort of conservatism because its doctrines are immune to the evidence of the worldly setting. And it substitutes for "physical spatial contradistinction from other groups . . . various substitutes in psychological distinction and distance." The cult, Marty argues, does not seek separateness for it is internally bound by a sort of hierarchical togetherness in which the interpersonal relations are more important than the doctrine.

The majority of church groups have sought neither the answer of the sect nor of the cult. Rather, clinging to the old spatial orientations, they have fled the cities for the suburbs in pursuit of their clientele. They have tried to adjust to the cafeteria-like religious services and the denomination-blurring homogenization of the suburban church. Douglass notes the churches' embarrassment in having adjusted so easily. He observes guilt over their abandonment of the urban proletariat, now racially and ethnically separate. He sees the decline in the relevance and meaning of what he calls the "separated clans and tribes of the Christian family."

Only the urban-based churches of ethnic groups which feel themselves under assault retain the old tradition. Among the Jews, for instance, the vignette of our times is the chic, suburban, middle-class Jewish mother who tries to raise her children in a ritualistic tradition she earlier discarded in the name of intellectual enlightenment. The flourishing of the Hasidic community is a more extreme case. Lee, quoting Charles Johnson, points out that the Negro church has provided a substitute for political organization and has furnished a channel for social as well as religious expression. It has been the center for face to face relations, for communication, for recreation, and for physical as well as psychological escape from troubles. It has been welcomed by Negroes even in areas where physical separation in worship was not demanded. Other ethnic and racial groups such as the Puerto Ricans, Spanish-speaking peoples of the Southwest, American Indians, Chinese-Americans, and Japanese-Americans still retain in their church affiliation some of the functions which the immigrant churches of the great Atlantic migration performed.

For other groups, however, a man's ethnic affiliation is no longer so important a fact in his life. Time has blurred the old highly fragmented sectarian and denominational differences into the "triple melting pot," three great communities with religious labels reading Protestant, Catholic, and Jewish. It is one thing, however, to indicate the declining relevance of minor sectarian splits for the laity. It is another thing to demonstrate it for the clergy. Self-contained formal organizations resist vigorously all tampering with their boundaries, whether these organizations be the branches of the military service, companies, educational institutions, or churches.

The ecumenical movement, in an attempt to reunite the fragmented denominations in the face of strong institutional resistances, proposes as a solution a loose confederation which permits the retention of denominational sovereignty in internal affairs while supporting a uniform foreign policy. Barnes makes the point that advocates of this movement take great pains to reassure wary denominations that they will not be submerged in the overarching bureaucracy. The ecumenical drive has had some notable successes among Protestant groups, but it has made little progress in wooing Catholic support. It does not extend to the Jews.

The future of denominationalism is difficult to assess. We can be reasonably sure that a church will survive. At no time in history has there not been between men and their gods other men who spoke more intimately, more knowingly, and perhaps more effectively in the sacred discourse. From time to time a people has tried to sweep away these middlemen as they would sweep cobwebs from their eyes, but others always have taken the places. Today, the sweeping aside takes the form of secularization and homogenization in the churches themselves. As old doctrinal cleavages, so irrelevant in American thought today, fade in importance, it is probable that new doctrinal and procedural distinctions more suited to the current divisions within our society either will establish new denominations or will be quietly adopted by the old ones.

49 IS THERE AN AMERICAN PROTESTANTISM?

Charles Y. Glock   Rodney Stark

INTRODUCTION   Church historians identify the Twentieth Century as the Age of the Ecumenical Movement. Discussions toward intradenominational and inter-Protestant unity have
marked the past sixty-six years. The mergers of sixteen branches of
the Lutheran Church into three major groups, the union of the
Christian and Congregational Churches, and the recent Blake Proposal for the alliance of the Protestant Episcopal, United Church
of Christ, United Presbyterian (USA), Methodist, Disciples of
Christ, African Methodist Episcopal, and Evangelical United
Brethren Churches illustrate the movement toward "oneness." In
several instances the unity is organic; in others unity remains on
the simple level of interchurch dialogue and cooperation. The
impetus toward unity among Protestants has issued in a parallel
movement of cooperative unity within Roman Catholicism. Vatican Councils I and II and the historic meeting between Pope
Paul VI and Archbishop of Canterbury Ramsey (Church of England) continue this trend.

   In the preceding article Richard Lambert suggests the declining importance of doctrinal positions among American Protestants. Charles Y. Glock and Rodney Stark, research sociologists,
temper this optimism with data which indicates the continuing
theological diversity of American Protestantism. Because American Christianity is divided into five generic theological camps,
Glock and Stark reject the assumption of Will Herberg (*see* Arti-

Reprinted from *Transaction*, Vol. 3, No. 1 (November–December, 1965), pp. 8-13, 48-49
with the permission of the authors and editor.

CHARLES Y. GLOCK is Professor of Sociology and Director of the Survey Research Center
of the University of California (Berkeley). Rodney Stark is a Research Analyst with the
Center.

cle 46) and Robert Lee that Protestantism can be described as a single group possessing a common core of belief. Inasmuch as Protestantism is marked by the extreme of fundamentalism and modernism, Protestant unity is merely a statistical myth. Glock and Stark argue that the theological differences among Protestants are generally greater than between conservative Protestants and Roman Catholics.

D O YOU, PERSONALLY, believe in God? To this recurrent question on Gallup polls, 97 percent of Americans answer yes. Supported by such findings, commentators on contemporary American life are unanimous in asserting that all but an insignificant fraction of Americans believe in God.

Another prevalent judgment about religious life in this country is that all Americans are coming to believe pretty much in the same things. The primary feature of American religion today seems to be no longer its diversity—based on the existence of several hundred Christian bodies—but its unity of outlook. Furthermore, the recent series of denominational mergers has fostered rising hopes for a general ecumenicalism.

Will Herberg in his now famous book, *Protestant-Catholic-Jew*, speaks of the "common religion" of America; the differences between Protestant denominations he considers to be organizational and ethnic rather than theological, and far outweighed by the consensus of beliefs. Robert Lee, in the *Social Sources of Church Unity*, suggests that a "common core Protestantism" exists because our urban, mobile, national society has broken down old parochial religious boundaries.

The major arguments have shifted away from whether this convergence in American religion has taken place, to the question of whether it is a blessing or a curse. Some churchmen contend that the homogenization of belief portends a loss of religious concern and authenticity; some social scientists condemn it as another symptom of the moral corrosion of mass society and the "O.K. world" of suburban complacency. On the other hand churchmen and social scientists hail the sloughing off of old divisions as symbolic of a new era of brotherhood, in which all can unite in a common quest to ennoble the human spirit.

We believe this debate is much too premature. We mean to raise a much more basic question: Have such changes really taken place? Is there really a "common core" belief in American Protestantism? Do the 97 percent of Americans who believe in God believe in the *same* God?

Our extensive survey shows that there are still a great many basic differences of belief among Protestant denominations in America.

The notion that American religion has undergone doctrinal agreement rests on two main premises:

1.   That the old disputes (such as adult versus infant baptism) have lost their force and relevance; that nobody much believes in, or cares about, the idiosyncrasies that once rent Christendom.

2.   That the demise of these historic differences leaves Americans in general agreement, sharing in the essential core of Christian (and Judaic) teachings. That is, Americans now are in consensus on such bedrocks of faith as the existence of an all-powerful, personal God, the moral authority of the Ten Commandments, and the New Testament promise of salvation.

But systematic evidence supporting these premises has been extremely scanty. Important and sweeping assertions about American religion need more careful examination, and firmer evidence. So we shall draw upon empirical data from our study of Christian church members to see to what extent American religion really is homogeneous.

SUPERNATURALISM

As noted at the outset, American adults report a virtually unanimous belief in God. But what do they believe *about* God? And to what *degree* do they believe?

Table 49-1a demonstrates definitely that Americans are anything *but* unanimous in their beliefs about God; and that the distinctions are not only sharp between individuals, but between denominations as well.

Only 41 percent of the Congregationalists indicated unquestioning faith in a personal God (Table 49-1a). This rises to 60 percent of the Methodists, 63 percent of the Episcopalians, about 75 percent among the center denominations, and is virtually unanimous among Southern Baptists and members of the fundamentalist sects. Overall, 71 percent of the Protestants endorsed the orthodox position, as compared with 81 percent of the Roman Catholics.

The second line shows that most of those who rejected unquestioning faith did not hold a different image of God, but were uncertain in their belief. They conceived of a personal divinity, but had doubts about his existence. Denominational differences here too are marked: 34 percent of the Congregationalists doubted; but only 1 percent of the Southern Baptists.

The fourth question is especially interesting, for it indicates a different conception of God, rather than mere doubt. Again, contrasts are striking: 16 percent of the Congregationalists, 11 percent of the Methodists, 12 percent of the Episcopalians—and *none* of the Southern Baptists—substituted some kind of "higher power" for a personal God.

Two percent of the Congregationalists, Episcopalians, and Methodists were agnostics, and 1 percent of the Congregationalists said they did not believe in God at all.

If the first four lines are added, then 98 percent of both Protestants and Catholics may be said to believe to some extent in some kind of God. Superficially, this supports the Gallup figures. But the Gallup poll implication of uniformity and piety are entirely misleading.

TABLE 49-1   Some contrasting doctrinal beliefs among American Christians.

a. Belief in God   "Which of the following comes closest to what you believe about God?"

	Congregationalists	Methodists	Episcopalians	Disciples of Christ	Presbyterians	American Lutherans	American Baptists	Missouri Lutherans	Southern Baptists	Sects	Total Protestants	Catholics
"I know God really exists and I have no doubts about it."	41%	60%	63%	76%	75%	73%	78%	81%	99%	96%	71%	81%
"While I have doubts, I feel that I do believe in God."	34	22	19	20	16	19	18	17	1	2	17	13
"I find myself believing in God some of the time, but not at other times."	4	4	2	0	1	2	0	0	0	0	2	1
"I don't believe in a personal God, but I do believe in a higher power of some kind."	16	11	12	0	7	6	2	1	0	1	7	3
"I don't know whether there is a God and I don't believe there is any way to find out."	2	2	2	0	1	0	0	1	0	0	1	1
"I don't believe in God."	1	*	*	0	0	0	0	0	0	0	*	0
No answer	2	*	1	4	*	*	2	0	1	1	1	1
Number of respondents	(151)	(415)	(416)	(50)	(495)	(208)	(141)	(116)	(79)	(235)	(2326)	(545)

b. Belief in the Divinity of Jesus   "Which of the following statements comes closest to what you believe about Jesus?"

	Congregationalists	Methodists	Episcopalians	Disciples of Christ	Presbyterians	American Lutherans	American Baptists	Missouri Lutherans	Southern Baptists	Sects	Total Protestants	Catholics
"Jesus is the Divine Son of God and I have no doubts about it."	40%	54%	59%	74%	72%	74%	76%	93%	99%	97%	69%	86%
"While I have some doubts, I feel basically that Jesus is Divine."	28	22	25	14	19	18	16	5	0	2	17	8
"I feel that Jesus was a great man and very holy, but I don't feel Him to be the Son of God any more than all of us are children of God."	19	14	8	6	5	5	4	0	0	0	7	3
"I think Jesus was only a man, although an extraordinary one."	9	6	5	2	2	2	1	1	*	*	4	1
"Frankly, I'm not entirely sure there was such a person as Jesus."	1	1	1	0	1	0	0	0	0	0	1	0
Other and no answer	3	3	2	4	1	2	2	1	1	1	2	2

TABLE 49-1 continued.

	Congregationalists	Methodists	Episcopalians	Disciples of Christ	Presbyterians	American Lutherans	American Baptists	Missouri Lutherans	Southern Baptists	Sects	Total Protestants	Catholics
c. Additional Beliefs About Jesus												
"Jesus was born of a virgin."												
Completely true	21%	34%	39%	62%	57%	66%	69%	92%	99%	96%	57%	81%
"Jesus walked on water."												
Completely true	19	26	30	62	51	58	62	83	99	94	50	71
"Do you believe Jesus will actually return to the earth some day?"												
Definitely	13	21	24	36	43	54	57	75	94	89	44	47
Probably	8	12	13	10	11	12	11	8	4	2	10	10
Possibly	28	25	29	26	23	18	17	6	0	1	20	16
Probably not	23	22	17	12	12	6	6	4	1	2	13	11
Definitely not	25	17	11	6	8	7	5	1	1	3	10	12
No answer	3	3	6	10	3	3	4	6	0	3	4	4
d. Life Beyond Death and Belief in the Devil												
"There is a life beyond death"												
Completely true	36%	49%	53%	64%	69%	70%	72%	84%	97%	94%	65%	75%
Probably true	40	35	31	32	21	23	19	10	3	4	24	16
Probably not or definitely not true	21	13	13	0	7	5	7	4	0	2	9	5
"The Devil actually exists."												
Completely true	6	13	17	18	31	49	49	77	92	90	38	66
Probably true	13	15	16	34	17	20	17	9	5	5	15	14
Probably not or definitely not true	78	66	60	38	48	26	29	10	1	5	43	14
e. Sin												
"Man can not help doing evil."												
Completely true	21%	22%	30%	24%	35%	52%	36%	63%	62%	37%	34%	22%
Probably true	36	36	34	36	35	30	28	20	14	15	31	29
Probably not or definitely not true	39	38	31	38	25	15	27	13	22	42	30	43
"A child is born into the world already guilty of sin."												
Completely true	2	7	18	6	21	49	23	86	43	47	26	68
Probably true	2	4	7	2	7	12	9	4	3	3	6	10
Probably not or definitely not true	94	87	71	90	68	37	65	9	55	46	65	19

f. Requirements for Salvation: Faith

"Belief in Jesus Christ as Saviour."												
Absolutely necessary	38%	45%	47%	78%	66%	77%	78%	97%	97%	96%	65%	51%
"Holding the Bible to be God's truth."												
Absolutely necessary	23	39	32	58	52	64	58	80	61	89	52	38

g. Requirements for Salvation: Works

"Doing good for others"												
Absolutely necessary	58%	57%	54%	64%	48%	47%	45%	38%	29%	61%	52%	57%
"Loving thy neighbor"												
Absolutely necessary	59	57	60	76	55	51	52	51	41	74	58	65
"Tithing"												
Absolutely necessary	6	7	9	12	10	13	16	7	18	48	14	10

h. Barriers to Salvation: Improper Faith

"Being completely ignorant of Jesus as might be the case for people living in other countries."												
Definitely prevent salvation	3%	7%	3%	8%	11%	15%	17%	36%	41%	32%	14%	4%
Possibly prevent salvation	13	23	16	38	24	29	31	28	39	46	25	24
"Being of the Jewish religion."												
Definitely prevent salvation	1	3	3	8	7	16	7	31	25	23	10	1
Possibly prevent salvation	6	9	10	18	12	16	25	23	28	33	15	11
"Being of the Hindu religion."												
Definitely prevent salvation	1	5	4	10	14	20	14	40	32	37	15	2
Possibly prevent salvation	12	11	12	28	15	22	25	16	27	31	17	13

i. Barriers to Salvation: Improper Acts

"Drinking liquor."												
Definitely prevent salvation	2%	4%	2%	0%	2%	2%	9%	1%	15%	35%	8%	2%
"Practicing artificial birth control."												
Definitely prevent salvation	0	0	2	2	1	3	2	5	16	4	2	23
"Discriminating against other races."												
Definitely prevent salvation	27	25	27	34	22	20	17	22	16	29	25	24
"Being anti-Semitic."												
Definitely prevent salvation	23	23	26	30	20	15	13	22	10	26	21	20

Note: Asterisk denotes less than ½ of 1 percent.
Some columns fail to sum to 100% due to rounding error.
The number of respondents shown for each denomination in this table is the same for all other tables. Sects include the Assemblies of God, The Church of God, The Church of Christ, the Church of the Nazarene, The Foursquare Gospel Church and one Independent Tabernacle. American Lutherans include the Lutheran Church in America and the American Lutheran Church.

Gallup studies also report that American Christians are virtually unanimous in believing Jesus Christ to be the Divine Son of God. But this faith too needs to be qualified.

Table 49-1b shows important contrasts in belief in the divinity of Jesus. Denominational differences are virtually identical to those in the belief in God. Only 40 percent of Congregationalists had *no doubts* that "Jesus is the Divine Son of God." This rose abruptly to 99 percent of Southern Baptists. The total Protestant figure is 69 percent versus 86 percent for Catholics.

Examining some of the other orthodox beliefs about Christ (Table 49-1c) brought differences into even sharper focus. Only 57 percent of all Protestants believed it "completely true" that "Jesus was born of a virgin," compared to 81 percent of Catholics. But the differences between the purportedly "common core Protestants" was much more startling: only 21 percent of Congregationalists believed it, rising to a peak of 99 percent of Southern Baptists.

The Southern Baptists remain rockbound in their faith in Jesus for all questions. Was it "completely true" that "Jesus walked on water?" Here the firm believers in this miracle fell to a small minority of the large liberal denominations, and counted only half of all Protestants. Even the Catholics fell to 71 percent. But the Southern Baptists held at 99 percent.

THE SECOND COMING

Like the existence of God, the Saviorhood of Christ causes mixed reactions among American Christians. On the promise of the second coming of Christ ("Do you believe Jesus will actually return to the earth some day?") the differences between the Protestant denominations were far greater than that between Protestants as a whole and Catholics. A sizable majority of Congregationalists felt that Jesus would "definitely" or "probably" not return compared to only 2 percent of Southern Baptists. Only 13 percent of Congregationalists and 21 percent of Methodists thought he would "definitely" return—compared to 75 percent of Missouri Synod Lutherans and 92 percent of the unshakable Southern Baptists. Less than half of Protestants as a whole, as well as Catholics, thought the second coming "definite," and less than 60 percent thought it probable. Protestants can no longer sing, "Christ crucified, risen, coming again," with one voice, since less than half of total American Christendom really believes it true.

Table 49-1d deals with two basic religious beliefs about deity.

1. "There is a life beyond death." On this central tenet of Christianity only 36 percent of Congregationalists thought the statement "completely true," along with 49 percent of Methodists, and compared to 97 percent of Southern Baptists.

2. The controversial statement "The Devil actually exists" brought on a much wider spread of Protestant opinion. Only 6 percent of Congregationalists and 13 percent of Methodists consider Satan's existence certain, against 92

percent of Southern Baptists. Overall, 38 percent of Protestants and 66 percent of Roman Catholics were certain.

CONCEPTS OF SIN

Unlike the supernatural, sin is related directly to the nature of man. Acceptance of man as sinful by nature increases in the usual pattern (Table 49-1e), from the more liberal denominations on the left to the more conservative ones on the right; however, compared to differing beliefs in the supernatural, the spread is generally more even.

But on the acceptance of "original sin" ("A child is born into the world already guilty of sin"), there are some abrupt departures from the spectrum: those denominations with a liturgical or "high church" tradition are readily distinguishable by their willingness to accept this belief. Original sin cannot be absolved by personal efforts, but only through the church, especially those churches which emphasize ritual. Thus, the ritualistic Episcopalian church stands out sharply from the liberal group, and the American Lutherans from the other center groups. The strongly ritualistic Catholic church contrasts greatly with the Protestants in general, 68 percent to 26 percent.

It is clear that a general relationship exists between belief in original sin and theological conservatism, so that Lutherans are much more likely to hold this view than Episcopalians; yet the marks of the formal doctrine show up all across the table. Thus, on the left of the table the traces of old doctrinal differences on original sin may still be detected, while on the right these differences retain much of their old force.

SALVATION

What of the central concern and promise of all Christianity: salvation?

FAITH. Christians have long battled over the question of whether faith *and* works were necessary to be saved; but there has been no argument that faith at least was absolutely required. The central tenet of this required faith is belief in Jesus Christ as the divine son of God who died to redeem men from their sins. Some Christian traditions hold that more is necessary ("Faith without works is dead"); but all agree that there is no salvation outside of Christ.

However, we have seen that members of American denominations do not all believe Jesus divine. Therefore, it is not surprising to find them also disagreeing over whether belief in Christ is absolutely necessary for salvation.

In the liberal groups, only a minority consider faith in Christ "absolutely necessary." (Table 49-1f) Among the conservative and fundamentalist groups, however, there is almost complete consensus about the necessity of faith in Christ for salvation. Overall, 65 percent of Protestants and 51 percent of Roman Catholics gave this answer.

It seems likely that among all Protestant groups, persons who accept the promise of eternal salvation beyond the grave are also likely to feel that this eternal reward is contingent upon belief in Christ as savior.

All denominational groups are less likely to feel that one must hold "the Bible to be God's truth" in order to be saved. Overall, the pattern follows the now familiar increases from left to right, with one notable exception. The Southern Baptists had been most unanimous in their assertion of traditional Christian positions, yet they are not importantly different from the center on the importance of Bible literalism. This probably reflects the great emphasis they put on Christ as the primary source by which one attains grace.

WORKS.   Having become accustomed to increases from left to right in proportions of those holding faith necessary for salvation, it comes as a surprise to see these trends reverse in Table 49-1g.

Table 49-1g deals with the necessity of *works*. Those denominations weakest on the necessity of faith for salvation are the strongest on the necessity of "doing good for others." In fact, the proportions of people on the left who think doing good for others is required for salvation is higher than those of the same groups who think faith in Christ absolutely necessary. More people in the liberal churches believed in the absolute necessity of doing good than believed in life after death. On the other hand, the conservative groups do not give "good deeds" any special importance in the scheme for salvation.

We suggest that these responses on "doing good" by those who essentially reject the traditional notion of salvation represent their desire to ratify the ethical components of their religious outlook. Indeed, ethics are likely *the* central component of their religious beliefs.

Turning to the matter of tithing, it is clear that Christians in general are not inclined to connect this with salvation. Only 14 percent of the Protestants and 10 percent of the Roman Catholics thought tithing absolutely necessary.

To sum up: marked contrasts do exist among Christian denominations in their conceptions of what is required for salvation.

BARRIERS TO SALVATION

IMPROPER FAITH.   If faith in Christ is essential for salvation, what acts and beliefs are an absolute barrier to it? Looking at the data in Table 49-1h, those denominations strongest on requiring faith in Jesus for salvation are also strongest on rejecting salvation for non-Christians. However, in all denominations there were many who held faith in Christ to be absolutely necessary who were also unwilling to deny that persons *outside* the Christian faith could be saved. For example, only 14 percent of the Protestants and 4 percent of the Catholics said that "being completely ignorant of Jesus, as might be the case for people living in other countries," would definitely prevent salvation. Among Protestants, the proportion varied from a mere handful of Congregationalists, Methodists, Episcopalians and Disciples of Christ to 36 percent of the Missouri Lutherans, and 41 percent of the Southern Baptists. However, an additional and sizable group of Christians were somewhat inclined to accept this view. Twenty-five percent of the Protestants and 24 percent of the Roman Catholics thought ignorance in Jesus would "possibly prevent" salvation.

Jews, of course, are not "completely ignorant" of Jesus. Can they be saved? Relatively few thought it impossible for a Jew to be saved: only 10 percent of all Protestants and 1 percent of Catholics. Again, however, there were great contrasts among Protestant groups. One percent of the Congregationalists and 3 percent of the Methodists and Episcopalians took this position, while 31 percent of the Missouri Lutherans and 25 percent of the Southern Baptists saw no hope for Jews. A sizable group thought it "possible" that a Jew could not be saved, and taken together, more than half of the members of the more fundamentalist groups at least doubted the possibility of a Jew's salvation.

In summary, a substantial minority of American Christians consider persons in non-Christian religions as beyond the hope of salvation.

IMPROPER ACTS. American Christians no longer regard drinking as a certain road to damnation (Table 49-1i). Only 8 percent of Protestants and 2 percent of Catholics thought it was. Only among the Baptists and the followers of fundamentalist sects did more than a handful attach temperance to their scheme of salvation.

Virtually no Protestants (only 2 percent) thought the practice of artificial birth control would prevent salvation, but perhaps even more interesting and surprising, *less than a quarter of the Catholics held this view.* Whether or not Catholics approve of birth control, more than three-quarters of them are unwilling to agree it carries the supreme penalty of damnation.

The last two items in Table 49-1i, dealing with racial discrimination, seem especially interesting, and repeat the pattern of evaluation of good works. On virtually all other "barriers to salvation," the conservative and fundamentalist bodies have been most likely to see them as absolutely necessary. However, on questions of racial discrimination and anti-Semitism, the Southern Baptists are the *least* likely of all religious groups to see them as relevant to salvation. Thus, while 27 percent of the Southern Baptists thought cursing would definitely prevent salvation, only 10 percent of them viewed anti-Semites as disqualified from entrance into God's Kingdom, and only 16 percent saw racial discrimination as a definite barrier. On the other hand, while only 13 percent of the Congregationalists thought that taking the name of the Lord in vain would definitely prevent salvation, 27 percent thought that racial discrimination and 23 percent that anti-Semitism would be barriers. Perhaps an even more suggestive contrast appears when we consider that about half of the members of all denominations thought it necessary to "love thy neighbor."

To sum up the findings on salvation: Christian denominations in America differ greatly in their beliefs about what a man must do to be saved. While most denominations give primary importance to faith, the liberal Protestant groups are inclined to favor good works. Protestants in a ritualistic tradition and Roman Catholics place greater emphasis on the sacraments and other ritual acts than do those from low-church traditions.

UNITY AND REALITY

To return to the questions posed at the beginning of this article: Is religion in modern America accurately characterized as unified? Do such concepts as "common core Protestantism," and "common American religion" bear any important resemblance to reality?

We suggest that they do not. Differences in the religious outlooks of members of the various denominations are both vast and profound. On the basis of our data it seems obvious that American religion has indeed undergone extensive changes in recent decades, but it seems equally obvious that these changes have been greatly misperceived and misinterpreted.

Has American religion become increasingly secular? As noted, many commentators claim that the mystical and supernatural elements of traditional Christianity have been replaced by a demythologized (ethical rather than theological) religion.

In light of the data, important changes of this kind have indeed occurred to *some* American denominations. We have no comparable data on the past; but compelling historic grounds exist for assuming that the typical Episcopalian or Congregationalist in the mid-nineteenth century firmly believed such tenets as the Virgin Birth and the Biblical miracles. If true, obviously secularization has indeed taken place in these religious bodies, for only a minority of them adhere to these beliefs today. On the other hand, among the Southern Baptists and the various sects, commitment to traditional Christian theology has been virtually impervious to change. The fact that these more evangelical and traditionalist denominations have been growing at a faster rate than the mainline denominations suggests that two simultaneous and divergent trends have been taking place:

1. Many people have been staying with or turning to "old-time" Christianity.

2. Others have been, to some extent, changing their theological outlook away from the supernatural and miraculous toward a more naturalistic view.

These opposed trends seem to hold significant implications for the future.

THE NEW DENOMINATIONALISM

Historically, the schisms in Christianity were largely marked by subtle doctrinal distinctions, and disagreements on proper ritual or organization. All observers generally agree that these issues have lost much of their relevance and divisive potential in contemporary America. Our data confirm these judgments.

But the data also suggest that new and generally unnoticed splits have appeared in Christianity that may well hold greater potential for division than the old disputes.

Earlier disagreements were bitter; nevertheless they took place among men who usually shared belief in such basic components of Christian theology as the existence of a personal and sentient God, the Saviorhood of Christ, and the promise of life-everlasting.

But today, our data indicate, the fissures which map what might well be called the "New Denominationalism" fragment the very core of the Christian perspective. The new cleavages are not over such matters as how to properly worship God—but whether or not there is a God it makes any sense to worship; not whether the bread and wine of communion become the actual body and blood of Christ through transubstantiation, but whether Jesus was divine at all, or merely a man. These disagreements, it must be emphasized, are not only between Christians and secular society, but exist *within* the formal boundaries of the Christian churches themselves.

How, therefore, can we account for all the hope and talk about general ecumenicalism? For those groups close together to begin with, such a possibility may well exist. At least there seem no overwhelming theological barriers to merger. But how are we to interpret exploratory talks between Roman Catholics and Episcopalians, or between Methodists and Baptists? Do the participants in the ecumenical dream simply misperceive one another's theological position, or do they consider such matters unimportant? Perhaps both of these factors are operating; but there are also signs that church leaders are becoming more aware of the doctrinal chasms that separate them.

Apparently most general ecumenical rhetoric comes from the most secularized mainline denominations. Probably the theological changes in these bodies have been accompanied by a lessening of concern for theology itself. Therefore, they may not view theological barriers as especially significant. But it is not true that the conservative groups are similarly unconcerned about doctrine. A good illustration comes from the relations between the National Council of Churches and fundamentalist bodies. Fundamentalists continually and bitterly denounce the National Council; yet it retains its composure and continues to encourage these hostile groups to become members.

Note that those bodies least amenable to the idea of ecumenicity are those which have the greatest consensus in religious belief. Among Southern Baptists and the various sects, for example, from 90 to 99 percent take similar positions on major articles of faith.

In bodies most concerned about ecumenicity, however, such as the Congregationalists and Episcopalians, members tend to be spread across a wide range of views on theology. Looking at these apparent conflicts on doctrine, the question rises. How do the liberal bodies manage to remain united? Examination of the data suggests several reasons:

1.   Persons in the more liberal bodies place considerably less importance on religion and on their own church participation than do members of the more conservative bodies.

2.   Persons in the liberal bodies who do hold traditional beliefs have many friends in the congregation, while persons with more secularized outlooks report that most of their friends are outsiders.

3.   The sermons preached in these denominations tend to be topical and ethical rather than doctrinal, while confessions and other rituals retain traditional form and content.

Thus it seems possible that the orthodox minority could remain unaware that the majority do not share their beliefs because the people they know in the congregation, their friends, do share these beliefs. Meanwhile, the majority, not being linked into the congregation by friendship bonds, may remain largely unaware of the fundamentalist segment of the congregation.

These factors may largely prevent potential conflicts from coming into the open. There are recent signs, however—such as the rise of theologically conservative lay groups within the more liberal denominations and the current growth of "tongues speaking" groups—that strains are developing even in these bodies because of theological differences.

One further fact ought to be mentioned. The liberal bodies that have most transformed their doctrines generate the least participation and concern among their members. By a strikingly wide margin, proportionately fewer attend worship services, join church organizations, pray privately, or believe in the importance of religion in their daily lives. Even within these more secularized denominations, those members who retain an orthodox theological outlook are consistently the more active in the life of the church. Probably, therefore, if a denomination is going to adopt new theological forms, it may have to find new organizational and ritual forms as well, or run the risk of becoming less significant in the lives of men. Mission societies, the Ladies Aid, and other traditional church activities may be inappropriate and even distasteful to those who bring an ethical rather than a theological concern to the church, and who are perhaps more interested in social betterment than worldwide conversion. Such persons may also be more attracted to sermons raising moral questions about social problems than in messages of peace of mind in Christ. In any event, the churches are presently failing to obtain much participation from members with the most modernist religious views.

THE PROTESTANT SPECTRUM

At least four and probably five generic theological camps can be clearly identified among the American denominations. The first, the *Liberals*, comprises the Congregationalists, Methodists, and Episcopalians, and is characterized by having a majority of members who reject firm belief in central tenets of Christian orthodoxy. It is likely that the changes that have gone on in these bodies, since they are among the highest status and most visible Protestant groups, have largely produced the impressions that Protestantism in general has shifted toward a secular and modernized world-view.

The second group, the *Moderates*, is composed of the Disciples of Christ and the Presbyterians. This group is less secularized than the Liberals, but more so than the *Conservatives*, who are made up of the American Lutheran group and the American Baptists. The *Fundamentalists* include the Missouri Synod Lutherans, the Southern Baptists, and the host of small sects.

Because of historic differences with Protestantism, the Roman Catholics are perhaps properly left to form a fifth distinct group by themselves. But on most theological issues, both those presented here and many more, the Roman Catholics consistently resemble the Conservatives. Only on special Protestant-Catholic issues such as Papal infallibility (accepted by 66 percent of the Roman Catholics and only 2 percent of the Protestants) were the Catholics and the Conservatives in any extensive disagreement.

Merging the denominations to form these five major groups is the greatest degree of clustering that is statistically permissible. It seems very unlikely that ecumenical clustering could result in fewer.

Finally, the data seriously challenge the common practice of contrasting Protestants and Roman Catholics. Protestant-Catholic contrasts are often large enough to be notable (and often, too, remarkably small), but they seem inconsequential compared to differences found among the Protestant groups. The overall impression of American Protestantism produced when members of all denominations are treated as a single group (the "Total Protestant" column in the tables) at best bears resemblance to only a few actual Protestant denominations. Indeed, in some instances these "average Protestants" do not closely correspond to *any actual* denomination.

When we speak of "Protestants," therefore, we tend to spin statistical fiction. It seems unjustified to consider Protestantism as a unified religious point of view in the same sense as Roman Catholicism. Not that Roman Catholicism is monolithic either—clearly there are several theological strands interwoven in the Catholic church—but at least it constitutes an actual, organized body. Protestantism, on the other hand, includes many separate groups and the only possible grounds for treating them collectively would be if they shared a common religious vision. This is clearly not the case.

AUTHOR INDEX

Ahlstrom, Sydney, 4, 5-16, 58, 358, 387, 388, 430, 431, 471, 534
Alland, Alexander, Jr., 17, 71, 83-92, 137, 330, 482
Aquinas, Thomas, 14
Aristotle, 14, 420
Augustine, 8, 14
Aulen, Gustave, 8

Barth, Karl, 7, 8, 14
Barton, Bruce, 7
Becker, Howard, 123, 124
Bell, Howard M., 461
Bennett, Thomas, 537
Berdjaev, Nicolas, 8
Berger, Peter, 124, 499, 501, 506
Blanshard, Paul, 64
Blizzard, Samuel W., 180, 181, 212-217, 218, 240-249, 271
Bonhoeffer, Dietrich, 14, 16
Bossard, James, 202
Brunner, Emil, 8
Bultena, Louis, 453
Bultmann, Rudolf, 14, 16
Burchard, Waldo W., 180, 218-227, 228, 316
Burgess, Ernest, 159
Bushnell, Horace, 6, 9, 14

Calhoun, Robert, 472
Calvin, John, 8, 33
Campbell, Ernest Q., 181, 228-239, 368
Cantril, Hadley, 453
Clark, Henry, 138, 331, 368-377
Coleman, James S., 284, 305-314, 316

Cohen, Albert, 491
Cohn, Werner, 486
Comte, Auguste, 93, 422
Congar, Yves M. J., 266
Cooley, Charles, 202, 285
Cox, Harvey, 470, 471
Cranmer, Thomas, 13

Daniels, V. E., 83
Darwin, Charles, 388, 430, 431, 432, 433, 434, 435
Davies, Horton, 496
Dewey, John, 12
Diamont, Alfred, 504
Dierenfield, R. B., 388, 436-445
Douglass, H. Paul, 158, 159, 160
Douglass, Truman, 122, 147-156, 284, 332, 358, 540
Durkheim, Emile, 3, 27, 31, 59, 74, 287, 315, 470
Duvall, Evelyn Millis, 461
Dynes, Russell R., 105, 483

Ebersole, Luke, 539
Edmonson, Munro S., 492
Eisenstein, Ira, 480
Elkind, David, 180, 182-187, 189, 196, 204, 329, 418, 446, 447
Emerson, Ralph Waldo, 9

Fichter, Joseph, 101
Ford, Thomas R., 71, 103-118, 137, 431
Forsythe, Peter Taylor, 8
Fosdick, Harry Emerson, 434, 435

Fourastié, Jean, 498
Frazier, E. Franklin, 17, 379, 493
Freud, Sigmund, 419, 428, 429
Fuchs, Lawrence, 387, 388, 402-417

Gladden, Washington, 6, 7, 532
Glazer, Nathan, 10
Glock, Charles Y., 3, 18, 71, 72-82, 83, 94, 204, 251, 284, 306, 333, 375, 467, 469, 542-555
Gogarten, Friedrich, 8
Goldstein, Israel, 66, 67
Graebner, Oliver, 284, 315-325, 330, 347, 482
Graham, Billy, 10, 11, 45

Hammond, Phillip E., 71, 93-102, 204, 251, 305, 389, 402, 471, 514
Handlin, Oscar, 53
Harris, Louis, 409, 413
Harrison, Paul M., 181, 250-260, 261, 469, 534, 535, 536, 537
Hegel, Georg W. F., 14
Heidegger, Martin, 14
Heim, Karl, 8
Heimann, Eduard, 388, 418-429, 430, 471
Heiss, Jerold, 508
Herberg, Will, 3, 39, 46, 47, 48, 49, 52, 53, 54, 55, 56, 129, 358, 389, 437, 467, 468, 470-481, 499, 500, 501, 504, 513-522, 524, 542, 543
Hilgard, E. R., 90
Hill, Reuben, 461
Hollingshead, A. B., 506
Hooker, Richard, 14
Horton, Douglas, 7, 8
Hoyt, Homer, 159
Hunt, Rolfe Lanier, 537
Huxley, Thomas, 433

James, William, 12
Jefferson, Thomas, 510
Johnson, Benton, 17, 84, 121, 122, 123-135, 137, 148, 167, 284, 285, 332, 387, 467, 468, 482, 496
Johnson, Charles, 541
Jung, Carl, 207

Kallen, Horace M., 480
Kane, John J., 181, 261-269, 469, 470, 534, 540
Kaplan, Mordecai, 480
Kean, Charles, 534

Kennedy, Ruby Jo, 504, 506
Kephart, William, 331, 346-356
Kierkegaard, Soren, 8
Kincheloe, Samuel C., 160
King, Martin Luther, Jr., 15, 22
Kinsey, Alfred C., 59
Knudten, Richard D., 3-4, 71, 121-122, 179-181, 283-284, 329-331, 387-388, 467-469
Kohn, Eugene, 480
Kramer, Bernard, 378

LaFarge, John, 24
Lambert, Richard, 469, 531-541, 542
Landis, Benson Y., 468, 523-530, 533
Landis, J. T., 461
Lazarsfeld, Paul F., 230, 392
Lee, J. Oscar, 331, 357-367, 368, 369, 379, 503, 506, 538, 541
Lee, Robert, 543
Leibman, Joshua Loth, 9, 11
Leiffer, Murray H., 158, 159
Lenski, Gerhard, 3, 39, 46, 47, 48, 49, 50, 51, 52, 53, 54, 55, 56, 333, 334, 375, 388, 389-401, 402, 446-458, 459, 471, 475, 476, 499, 504, 505, 507, 514
Lincoln, C. Eric, 487
Linton, Ralph, 336
Litt, Edgar, 403
Long, Herman, 152
Lowrie, Walter, 7
Lubell, Samuel, 414
Luther, Martin, 8, 10, 14, 98

Malinowski, Bronislaw, 36, 315
Mann, Arthur, 11
Mannheim, Karl, 29
Marcel, Jean, 8
Maritain, Jacques, 8
Martin, D. A., 124
Marty, Martin, 11, 467, 479, 540
Marx, Karl, 59, 283, 284, 310, 311, 419, 428, 429, 455
Maurice, F. D., 14
May, Henry F., 32
Mayer, Albert J., 330, 332-345, 388
McCann, Richard, 180, 204-211
Mead, Sidney, 479
Mencken, H. L., 7
Merton, Robert, 28, 29
Miller, Samuel H., 252
Mitford, Jessica, 347
Moehlman, Conrad, 480
Murray, John Courtney, 11
Myrdal, Gunnar, 23

Nichols, James H., 433
Niebuhr, H. Richard, 7, 14, 124, 305, 503, 505
Niebuhr, Reinhold, 7, 14, 498
Nietzsche, Friedrick, 419, 428, 429
Nygren, Anders, 8

O'Dea, Thomas F., 284, 285-294, 305, 468
Odum, Howard W., 193
Otto, Rudolf, 287, 292
Owen, Richard, 432

Packard, Vance, 151
Page, Charles, 256
Parsons, Talcott, 138, 287
Pascal, Blaise, 8
Peale, Norman Vincent, 9, 11, 496
Petersen, William, 4, 27, 57-68, 387, 402, 403, 436, 469, 524
Pettigrew, Thomas F., 181, 228-239, 368
Pfautz, Harold W., 515
Pfeffer, Leo, 65, 66
Pike, James A., 64, 67
Plato, 14, 419, 420
Pope John XXIII, 15
Pope, Liston, 3, 4, 17-25, 152, 229, 253, 330, 359, 369, 375, 491

Rauschenbusch, Walter, 6, 7
Ravitz, Mel Jerome, 179, 180, 196-203, 513
Reisman, David, 197, 202, 203
Ringer, Benjamin, 375
Robespierre, 422
Rohrer, John H., 492
Roper, Elmo, 413
Rose, Stephen, 532
Rosenberg, Milton J., 10
Rosenthal, Erich, 508
Royce, Josiah, 12
Russell, Bertrand, 54

Sanderson, Ross W., 158
Schelling, F. W. J., 14
Schleiermacher, Friedrich, 14
Schweitzer Albert, 7
Sears, Charles H., 159, 160
Seidler, Murray, 179, 180, 196-203, 513
Selznick, Philip, 535
Sharp, Harry, 330, 332-345, 388
Sheen, Fulton J., 11, 496
Sheppard, Harold L., 331, 378-383

Shils, Edward, 138
Shippey, Frederick, 122, 157-166, 241, 255, 284, 467
Siegfried, André, 514
Simmel, Georg, 3, 27
Sklare, Marshall, 181, 261, 270-280, 469, 534
Smith, Adam, 510
Smith, Robertson, 27
Socrates, 419
Sombart, Werner, 334, 345
Spencer, Herbert, 6
Spindler, George, 489
Spiro, M. E., 505
Spitzer, Allen, 284, 295-304
Spitzer, Mary, 284, 295-304
Stackhouse, Reginald, 388, 419, 430-435
Stanley, Manfred, 122, 158, 167-176
Stark, Rodney, 306, 469, 542-555
Stone, Irving, 435
Sumner, William Graham, 6, 422
Sutherland, Edwin, 455
Swift, Arthur L., Jr., 160

Tawney, Richard, 283, 284, 334
Temple, William, 8
Thomas, John L., 180, 188-195, 196, 251, 329, 446, 447
Tillich, Paul, 7, 8, 14
Tocqueville, Alexis de, 100, 101, 102, 474
Toynbee, Arnold J., 291, 486
Troeltsch, Ernst, 3, 27, 123, 124, 125, 126, 129, 132, 515

Unamuno, Miquel de, 8
Underwood, Kenneth W., 375, 377, 506

Van Vleck, Joseph, Jr., 158, 159
Vernon, Glenn, 4, 39-45, 46, 283, 295, 388, 430, 446, 459-464, 513
Viereck, Peter, 521

Wach, Joachim, 3, 29, 31
Washington, Booker T., 20
Weber, Max, 3, 27, 29, 33, 46, 124, 126, 127, 132, 283, 284, 288, 291, 333, 334, 345, 390, 391, 395
Weeks, W. Ashley, 461
Wesley, John, 31
Whitehead, Alfred N., 12, 14
Whyte, William H., Jr., 255, 395
Wilberforce, Samuel, 432, 433, 435

Williams, J. Paul, 480
Williams, Robin M., Jr., 473, 475
Wilson, Bryan, 136
Winstanley, Gerrard, 490
Winter, Gibson, 3, 4, 39, 46-56, 58, 189, 333, 471
Wirth, Louis, 357
Wolf, Richard C., 528, 529

Worsley, Peter, 485

Yinger, J. Milton, 3, 4, 26-38, 58, 124, 137, 388, 468, 482-495, 496-512, 514
Young, Frank, 122, 136-146, 148, 387, 468, 482